REPUBLIC

HEILUNGKIANG

Harbin

Changchun

KIRIN

INNER MONGOLIA

Huhehot

Shenyang

LIAONING

Anshan

NORTH
KOREA

⊛ Peking

Tientsin

HOPEH

Taiyüan

SHANSI

NINGSIA

Yenan

Tsinan

SHANTUNG

Tsingtao

SOUTH
KOREA

Lanchow

Hwang Ho

River

JAPAN

SHENSI

Loyang

Chengchow

KIANGSU

Sian

HONAN

Hofeh

Nanking

Soochow

EAST

Shanghai

CHINA

Chengtu

Yangtze

River

HUPEH

ANHWEI

hungking

Wuhan

Hangchow

SEA

Nanchang

CHEKIANG

Changsha

KWEICHOW

HUNAN

KIANGSI

Kweiyang

Shaoshan

Foochow

FUKIEN

Taipeh

TAIWAN

KWEILIN

KWANGTUNG

Wuchow

Canton

KWANGSI

Nanning

Hong Kong

NORTH
VIETNAM

PACIFIC OCEAN

HAINAN

PHILIPPINE
ISLANDS

MAO AND CHINA

MAO AND CHINA

From Revolution to Revolution

STANLEY KARNOW

Introduction by John K. Fairbank

The Viking Press / New York

To the memory of my father

Copyright © 1972 by Stanley Karnow
All rights reserved
First published in 1972 by The Viking Press, Inc.
625 Madison Avenue, New York, N.Y. 10022
Published simultaneously in Canada by
The Macmillan Company of Canada Limited
SBN 670-45427-3
Library of Congress catalog card number: 77-187967
Printed in U.S.A.

Acknowledgment is made to Praeger Publishers, Inc., for
material quoted from Shanghai Journal by Neale Hunter.
Copyright © 1969 by Frederick A. Praeger, Inc.
Reprinted by permission.

INTRODUCTION

URING the years after 1965, while Americans were becoming
disenchanted with the bombing in Vietnam, the Chinese
people were going through a vast, confusing struggle known as the
Cultural Revolution. American firepower in Vietnam hit tele-
vision-watchers in the United States only visually, and sometimes
in their conscience. The far bigger revolution in China hit millions of people there much more closely. Where Vietnam was
mainly a scene of destruction, China saw a struggle not only
against bureaucratic evils but also for moral regeneration, for a
new unselfishness. While the Cultural Revolution wound up in
violence, it seemed to be mainly a crusade to change the personality of China's quarter of humankind. It was a bigger story
than Vietnam but so impenetrably confusing to outsiders that few
could grasp it. Now that Chinese and Americans are both trying
to make new beginnings at home and abroad in the 1970s, it is
essential that we understand what happened in China.

Stanley Karnow gives us the first comprehensive account of the
Cultural Revolution, a feat made possible only by his special
qualifications. First of all, as a journalist he long trained himself
not only to get at the human facts but also to interpret and
synthesize them. Journalists easily become historians, just as historians occasionally become journalists, because they are both

] v [

devoted to putting the picture together. They also try to write in intelligible English for the intelligent layman, avoiding the quagmire of definitions and frames of reference in which social scientists sometimes bog down. Mr. Karnow is able to tell us what happened in China without reference to "coefficients of growth" or the "political culture."

His objectivity concerning China is also aided by perspectives gained in Europe. Stanley Karnow came from New York City and was graduated from Harvard in 1947. During the next decade, while Cold War attitudes became dominant in American thinking, he was mainly in Paris, first as a student at the University, then at the Institut des Études Politiques, and then for seven years as the Paris correspondent for *Time*. In 1957 and 1958 he was back at Harvard as a Nieman Fellow in Journalism. Subsequently, after a year as bureau chief for *Time-Life* in North Africa, he went to Hong Kong and spent the next decade there as a China-watcher, first as special correspondent for *Time* and then for two years as Far East correspondent for the *Saturday Evening Post*. He joined the *Washington Post* in 1965. In this way, having lived in the French part of the world, he was inoculated against some of the ideological clichés of the Dulles era and also against the China specialist's fallacy of assuming all things Chinese are unique.

By the time he got to Hong Kong, facilities had accumulated there that made it the main base for studying contemporary China—files of the mainland press in original and in translation, a corps of specialists in the United States Consulate General and the official establishments of other countries, a skilled and lively press corps, refugee Chinese informants to talk to, European and Asian travelers passing through. Stanley Karnow was on the scene in Hong Kong early enough to appraise the disastrous aftermath of the Great Leap Forward of 1958 and watch the unfolding of the Sino-Soviet split after 1960. When the Cultural Revolution erupted in 1966, he was no doubt as mystified as anyone, but he had his feet more firmly on the ground than most, and in his reports for the *Washington Post* he began to sift out the significance of events, the aims of the protagonists, and the long-term trends underlying all the confusion.

Introduction

After the great upheaval had ground to a halt in 1969, he arranged to spend 1970 and 1971 as a research fellow at Harvard, where he completed most of this book. By this time the East Asian Research Center here had built up a staff of specialists who could be of use to a contemporary historian. Voluminous files of documentation were also available, mainly translated by the United States Consulate General in Hong Kong (an important service that deserves more public appreciation).

When he came to put the story together in 1970, Mr. Karnow's synthesis of startling events and the dramatic confrontations between Mao and his adversaries could be given color and impact by the denunciations and confessions which had come out during the Cultural Revolution and which revealed so many aspects of the intra-party struggle during the decade before 1965.

Mr. Karnow unifies his narrative by focusing on Chairman Mao, without whom there would have been no great upheaval. Mao is one of history's angriest men. His generation inherited a country that had long prided itself on its creation of a sophisticated ruling class that knew how to hold power by methods of indoctrination and bureaucratic government. But this ancient Chinese system by 1800 was already past its prime and in decay. By 1949, it was a real shambles. The failure of the old ruling-class system had occurred all across the board: the emperor's supremacy over foreign rulers, the Manchu military domination of China, the superiority of China's material technology, the intellectual and ethical majesty of classical Confucianism, the administrative capacity of the imperial government to meet its problems—all these collapsed. To be sure, it was a gradual process, like an avalanche in slow motion. The process had been mitigated by continual reform efforts during the last century, ever since the 1850s. But the reform efforts never caught up with China's crisis.

Mao Tse-tung was most aware of the holdovers from the traditional ruling class, most conscious of the great gulf in life styles between it and the common people. When Mao was a youth, the ordinary Chinese peasant could not expect to read, vote, get medical help, drive a car, travel, or complain successfully against extortion unless he resorted to violence. On the other hand, no member of the upper class would normally expect to move heavy objects, sweep the courtyard, carry in water, or otherwise use muscle power for a living. The two worlds of the ruling class and the common people were separate but actually symbiotic. Indeed, the old order lasted as long as it did because its upper-class values had permeated the society to the point where even the lowliest peasant would bind and deform a daughter's feet in the style that began at the court a thousand years ago. An ambitious commoner could aim only to get into the upper class.

Mao's greatness lies in the courage and skill with which he attacked the old ruling-class tradition, including its network of special privileges and personal deals among insiders. After coming to power in 1949, the Communist movement put through great changes. But the habits of two thousand years are not easy to overturn, and the old patterns re-emerged within the new Communist regime. How Mao attacked them is Mr. Karnow's story. Historians of the year 2072 will write about these years in China stressing, no doubt, more abstract considerations visible over the long term, but I doubt that anyone will write an account with greater vitality. By his careful use of the record, Stanley Karnow makes Mao and his antagonists speak out in the heat of their struggle as no one has done before.

JOHN K. FAIRBANK

East Asian Research Center
Harvard University
February 1972

PREFACE

T HIS is a book about a man in collision with a country. The man is Mao Tse-tung. The country is China.

With the establishment of a Communist regime in China in 1949, Mao and his comrades assumed nominal control over a people whose attitudes and conduct had been determined by codes of behavior dating back thousands of years. These codes, largely derived from the Confucian ethic, placed a premium on harmony with the family as the center of political and social relations. Thus traditional Chinese society was essentially cellular and fragmented, and, as such, unable to mobilize to meet the challenges of the mid-twentieth century. Mao's ambition was to destroy this ancient system, and to transfer the loyalties and dedication of the individual away from the clan to the nation. In so doing, he hoped to release the energies of the "masses" and channel them into the construction of a powerful China.

But as he struggled to promote his concepts during the years after 1949, Mao perceived that the Communist take-over of China was not the revolution he had envisioned. He gradually recognized that the realization of his dream was being thwarted by China's workers, peasants, soldiers, and intellectuals as well as by his own Communist Party colleagues, who either clung to old customs or favored conventional, bureaucratic paths toward modernization modeled on the experience of the Soviet Union. By late 1965, therefore, Mao was consumed by an obsessive urge to launch another revolution that would dramatically change China's political and social culture. That effort was the Great Proletarian Cultural Revolution. It was one of the most convulsive episodes of contemporary history.

The Cultural Revolution shattered the Chinese Communist Party apparatus, sweeping away many of Mao's oldest associates —foremost among them the nation's chief of state, Liu Shao-ch'i. But like all revolutions, it also devoured its most zealous proponents. Many among the millions of Red Guards and other radical activists unleashed by Mao in 1966 were afterward suppressed. The "close comrade-in-arms" designated by Mao to be his heir, Marshal Lin Piao, had been purged by the end of 1971 along with a host of other major figures who had risen to prominence during the period. By February 1972, when President Richard Nixon was received in Peking, the Cultural Revolution seemed to be a dim memory. And, in many ways, China appeared to resemble the China that Mao had desperately sought to alter. A new bureaucracy was emerging and, as before, the accent was on technocratic expertise rather than ideological purity. Yet the Cultural Revolution had instilled in the Chinese people an egalitarian spirit that was different from their rigid attitudes of the past. In that respect, Mao had succeeded to a certain extent in breaking down the age-old barriers that had separated the cities from the countryside, intellectuals from common folk, and the ruling elite from the citizenry. What remained, however, was for the Chinese leadership to devise and build new institutions. But until those institutions could be shaped, China was bound to face continuing instability.

This attempt to record the cataclysmic events that shook China during the Cultural Revolution grew out of my assignment as a correspondent in Hong Kong over a period of eleven years. The Cultural Revolution inspired an extraordinary eruption of newspapers, tracts, handbills, pamphlets, and wall posters, most of them published by Red Guards and other activists in Peking and throughout the Chinese provinces. Although their style was often florid and their accounts exaggerated, these documents constituted the first really free press to emerge in China under the Communists.

Preface

Thousands of these documents flowed into Hong Kong, providing detailed descriptions of skirmishes, texts of important speeches, official directives, and other invaluable information. Most of this material was compiled by the United States Consulate-General in Hong Kong in its daily *Survey of the China Mainland Press,* upon which I have relied heavily in the preparation of this book. Other primary sources included Peking's official New China News Agency and provincial Chinese radio broadcasts as monitored by the Foreign Broadcast Information Service of the United States Government and the British Broadcasting Corporation. I also depended for information on extensive interviews with refugees from China as well as with diplomats and journalists based in Peking—information I was able to confirm during a visit to the People's Republic of China in February 1972. Many of the accounts portrayed China as having been under great stress during the Cultural Revolution. Mao Tse-tung himself confirmed this when, on December 18, 1970, he told his trusted American biographer Edgar Snow: "When foreigners reported that China was in great chaos, they were not telling lies. It had been true. Fighting was going on."

The problem of analyzing information during the Cultural Revolution and its aftermath was crucial. Many journalistic, academic, and diplomatic colleagues and friends were most helpful in this respect. In particular, I wish to acknowledge the assistance of Anthony Ashworth, A. Doak Barnett, Gordon A. Bennett, John Gittings, William Gleysteen, Merle Goldman, Jean-Yves Gory, Charles Hill, Neale Hunter, Ellis Joffe, Donald W. Klein, Burton Levin, Sydney Liu, Ronald N. Montaperto, Harald Munthe-Kaas, Victor Nee, Charles Neuhauser, Nicholas Platt, C.V. Ranganathan, Thomas W. Robinson, Allen Romberg, Franz Schurmann, Benjamin I. Schwartz, Stein Seeberg, Richard Solomon, Ross Terrill, James C. Thomson, Jr., Ting Wang, William W. Wells, Allen S. Whiting, William Whitson, and Edward K. Wu.

Nancy Evans, who served as my assistant in Hong Kong, deserves special mention for her unstinting aid in researching this book. I am also grateful to Mrs. Elisabeth Sifton, my editor at The Viking Press, for her encouragement, cooperation, and comments.

I am in enormous debt to John K. Fairbank, director of the

East Asian Research Center at Harvard University, for providing me with financial support, intellectual guidance, and the inspiration to launch and complete this study. I wish to express my thanks as well to Ezra Vogel, deputy director of the East Asian Research Center, for his invaluable advice. This project could not have been undertaken without the help of the Institute of Politics of the John F. Kennedy School of Government at Harvard University. I am therefore indebted to Richard E. Neustadt, former director; Alvin J. Bronstein, former associate director; and the staff of the institute. I also wish to extend my thanks to Benjamin C. Bradlee, executive editor, and Philip Foisie, assistant managing editor of the *Washington Post*, for giving me the time and latitude to research and write this book.

Finally, I must express my gratitude to my wife, Annette, and to my children, Curtis, Catherine, and Michael, who displayed patience, understanding, and solicitude beyond the call of familial duty, and who have thus been true "comrades-in-arms" on the Long March of authorship.

Hong Kong   S. K.
Cambridge, Massachusetts
Washington, D.C.

CONTENTS

CONTENTS

PART FOUR

From Revolution to Reaction

PART FIVE

The Pendulum Swings

ILLUSTRATIONS

Following page 240

Mao in 1935 (*Sovfoto*)
Mao in Yenan in the late 1930s (*Sovfoto*)
Mao in Peking in early 1949 (*Wide World*)
Mao during the Cultural Revolution in 1966
Mao and his wife, Chiang Ch'ing (*Sovfoto*)
Lin Piao in the uniform of a marshal in the People's Liberation Army (*UPI*)
Premier Chou En-lai (*Wide World*)
Chinese Communist leaders in the summer of 1963 (*Eastfoto*)
Liu Shao-ch'i, former Chief of State (*Sovfoto*)
Marshal P'eng Teh-huai, former Minister of Defense (*Eastfoto*)
P'eng Chen, former Politburo member and ex-mayor of Peking (*Eastfoto*)
General Lo Jui-ch'ing
Chiang Ch'ing (*Eastfoto*)
Ch'en Po-ta, Mao's private secretary, later purged
K'ang Sheng, member of the Cultural Revolution Directorate (*Eastfoto*)
Yao Wen-yuan, a young Shanghai official (*Eastfoto*)
Chang Ch'un-ch'iao, another Shanghai official (*Eastfoto*)
The Peking leadership welcomes Red Guards to the capital in the late summer of 1966 (*Eastfoto*)
Chu Teh, venerated "Father of the Red Army" (*Eastfoto*)
The late Ch'en Yi, commander of the Third Field Army during the civil war
Liu Po-ch'eng, the famous "one-eyed dragon" (*Free Lance Photo Guild*)
Yeh Chien-ying, believed to have replaced Lin Piao as Defense Minister
Teng Hsiao-p'ing, former Secretary General of the Chinese Communist Party
T'ao Chu, formerly the leading Communist in south China (*Wide World*)
Hsieh Fu-chih, formerly Vice-Premier and Minister of Security (*Eastfoto*)
General Huang Yung-sheng, one-time Chief of General Staff (*Eastfoto*)
General Wu Fa-hsien, formerly commander of the Air Force (*Eastfoto*)
General Li Tso-peng, formerly chief political commissar of the Navy (*Eastfoto*)
Marshal Yeh Chien-ying and Huang Hua welcome Henry Kissinger

PART ONE

MAO AND
CHINA

Marxism can be translated into reality only through a national form. . . . The need, therefore, is to Sinicize Marxism.

— MAO TSE-TUNG, *1938*

CHAPTER 1

The Vision and the Challenge

Classes struggle, some classes triumph, others are eliminated. Such is history, such is the history of civilization for thousands of years.

— MAO TSE-TUNG, August 1949

NO CONTEMPORARY LEADER displayed such determination over so long a time in his struggle to achieve his goals as did Mao Tse-tung in his attempt to permeate China with his unique concept of communism. Nor has any modern statesman brought such profound and pervasive change to so many millions of people within so short a span of history. By the closing years of his life Mao's essential ambition had not been fulfilled, yet the magnitude of his effort was equal to the extravagance of his dream.

Beginning as an obscure peasant agitator, Mao fought nearly thirty years of protracted warfare in order to gain control of the most populous nation on earth. Once in power, his regime gave China greater political cohesion, social stability, economic promise, military muscle and international prestige than that vast, unwieldy land had known in centuries. But these accomplishments, in Mao's view, were not enough. After consolidating his authority, he attempted to set in motion a process of perpetual revolution that would purify the "soul" of the Chinese people, cleanse them of their individualistic and materialistic tendencies, and ultimately spawn a new species of "Communist man" capable of propelling China toward wealth and strength through self-sacrifice and dedication. Persuaded that his theories had universal validity, he believed that this spiritual

] 3 [

revolution would eventually inspire the entire world to imitate the Chinese model.

Thus Mao's ideology, with its stress on human perfectibility, was largely moralistic, missionary zeal cloaked in his own version of Marxist-Leninist language. His famous "little red book" of *Quotations*, which was designed to vitalize his followers, seemed to combine Confucian proverbs and Biblical axioms with homilies of the kind popularized by Benjamin ·Franklin and Samuel Smiles.[1] * His sermons, usually preached to small groups of activists, also emphasized his fundamentalism. Addressing a rump session of the Communist Party Central Committee in October 1966, for instance, Mao decried those who "strive only for personal fame and profit, power and position," and called for the cultivation of "men of the new morality . . . Communist men wholeheartedly and completely devoted to the people." They, rather than investment capital, modern technology, and advanced weapons, were to be the "determining factor" in the construction of the nation. "Men are central," he asserted. "To overlook men is to overlook the greatest productive force." [2]

Mao's persistent, obsessive drive to create this new human species repeatedly brought him into collision with the very attitudes he sought to transform. He was opposed by large numbers of Chinese intellectuals, who would not conform to his rigorous doctrines despite their initial sympathy with his practical programs. He was challenged by important figures among his early military supporters, whose later sophistication led them to question his premise that guerrilla techniques should take precedence over contemporary strategies of war. He was defied by economic specialists, who favored caution and rationality rather than his visionary mobilization schemes. He was rejected by a significant segment of the Chinese Communist Party apparatus, for whom government meant bureaucratic continuity rather than episodic upheavals. Even his cherished "masses," the poor peasants and workers, subtly subverted his efforts to harness them into China's primary source of energy—though, in the traditional style of Chinese genuflecting to ancient imperial edicts, they went through the ritual of celebrating the cult of his personality. This widespread resistance to his ideo-

* Numbered reference notes begin on page 519.

logical impulses finally prompted Mao to launch his last, most intensive campaign, the Great Proletarian Cultural Revolution. In February 1967, explaining his reasons for having instigated that traumatic upheaval, he said:

> In the past, we waged struggles in the rural areas, in factories, in the cultural field. . . . But all this failed to solve the problem because we did not find a form, a method, to arouse the broad masses to expose our dark aspect openly, in an all-round way and from below. The answer was the Great Proletarian Cultural Revolution.[3]

Yet even during the Cultural Revolution, Mao discovered that the two principal pillars of his program were themselves corroded by the self-seeking attitudes he was determined to eradicate. The Red Guards and other young radicals, urged by Mao to shatter the entrenched Party machine, quickly became as exclusive and autocratic as the *apparatchiks* they had ousted. The Army, instructed to direct the radicals in their mission, instead undertook to repress the youths in order to curb the tumult that threatened to weaken China—particularly at a time when the possibility of war with either the United States or the Soviet Union, or both, seemed to be growing.

A man of complex contradictions, Mao appeared to oscillate between doubt and confidence in his tactics during the Cultural Revolution. He was first encouraged by the dynamism of his acolytes as they assaulted the Party bureaucracy and smashed the symbols of past "feudalism." But when the turmoil reached gigantic proportions throughout China's cities, he sounded a note of regret at having uncorked forces that were spiraling beyond his control. Yet he never renounced his long-range aspiration. In one form or another, he forecast, the Cultural Revolution would continue for hundreds, perhaps thousands of years into the future. "The struggle in the ideological realm," he said, "will always exist." [4]

Pervading Mao's concepts and conduct, then, was his reluctance to concede to the reality that modern states, while ideally guided by lofty philosophies, actually operate on the basis of administrative routine and technical specialization rather than through exhortations, emulation movements, and mass enthusiasm. Though he did not wholly deny the value of scientific skills, his vision was essentially illuminated by the conviction that his brand of religious fervor constituted the prime ingredient in motivating man. In short, he held that "positive thinking" could be turned into material force. This belief found expression, for example, in his assertion that the "spiritual atom bomb" was more powerful than the real nuclear instrument, and in such parables as the tale of the Foolish Old Man whose sheer determination was sufficient to move mountains.[5]

Mao and his publicists proclaimed that this spiritual approach elevated Marxism-Leninism to a "higher and completely new stage." In many ways, however, Mao's thesis mirrored the extent to which the Marxist-Leninist dynamic had disintegrated. For his ideas were close to the romantic notions of Rousseau and the Jacobins that Marx had rejected in the mid-nineteenth century. As such, they represented the regression rather than the advancement of Marxist doctrine.

The genesis of utopian socialism in the nineteenth century had been part of the wider romantic revolt of the European intelligentsia against the beginnings of industrialization and its impact on human relations. Though he shared their hopes for an eventual utopia, Marx had rebuffed the romantics by affirming that salvation lay not in resisting modernization but in ruthlessly pushing through industrialization to the end and, at the same time, organizing the growing industrial proletariat. In other words, Marx contended, the climate for revolution would be ripe once a society had achieved abundance. And material progress could only be attained gradually through a historical process that evolved from well-defined economic and social conditions rather than from acts of will and displays of passion.[6] Accordingly, he predicted the triumph of communism in Germany, England, and France, the industrial nations of the time. In his view, the prospects for change in Russia were remote. He also minimized the importance of China and other undeveloped areas, arguing that disorders in those regions were significant only insofar as they deprived the imperialist powers of markets and resources, and thus would hasten the revolution in Western Europe.[7]

Lenin strayed from the Marxist orthodoxy. Seeing the opportunity to stage a *coup d'état* in Russia during World War I, he did not wait for the "objective" economic and social conditions in that backward country to mature. Yet he did retain certain Marxist precepts despite his violation of Marx's formula for revolution. His definition of communism as "Soviet power plus electrification" indicated, among other things, that he regarded industrialization and productivity as primordial. Moreover, he stressed the belief in a strong Communist Party organization that would serve as the vanguard of the industrial working class in its quest to establish the dictatorship of the proletariat.

While he inherited Marx's perception of class friction and Lenin's techniques for revolution, Mao effectively broke with both his precursors by tailoring their principles to fit what he called China's "concrete" situation. China lacked an industrial base from which Mao could hope to press toward the abundant society that Marx had envisaged as necessary for true communism. Therefore, just as Lenin seized power in 1917 before Russia's economic and social conditions for revolution were fulfilled, so Mao took advantage of the vacuum created by the prolonged Japanese invasion of China to topple Chiang Kai-shek's decrepit Nationalist regime. But in contrast to Lenin, who acknowledged the need for intensive industrialization, Mao focused on transforming the Chinese "soul" as a prerequisite to modernization. Hence he aligned himself less with Marx than with the romantic utopians who had interpreted history as a moral drama in which virtue rather than material progress was to be promoted.

One characteristic of the Maoist dynamic, especially in Mao's later years, was its shapelessness. Not once during the Cultural Revolution, for example, did Mao outline a clear-cut, practical program aimed at precise objectives. Instead, he exhorted his followers to destroy his opponents so that an undefined utopia might emerge at some unspecified point in the faraway future. In this respect, Mao held a good deal of appeal for New Left elements in the West and in Asia who were stimulated by the notion that disruptive action was an end in itself. Borrowing from Mao's *Quotations*, many American, European, and Japanese youths could declare that rebellion was justified even though they were unable to describe their ultimate aims. But if Mao's ambiguity seemed attractive outside China, it merely confused the Chinese themselves. Recalling the tumult of the Cultural Revolution, a Red Guard in Canton explained, "All of the factionalism, fighting, the shifting alliances, and the different positions arose because the instructions from Chairman Mao just didn't work. He might say that all members of the 'left' should unite, but we were never told how to determine who was 'left' or 'right.' His statements were so general that everybody, even those who opposed him, could find something to justify his own position."

Mao's ideas, however, at least evolved from a blend of Chinese traditions and his own observations of China's "concrete" situation. For all his preoccupation with revolution, Mao never entirely departed from the traditions of statecraft that reached back in Chinese history over two thousand years. Like every dynastic founder since the rise of the Ch'in empire in 221 B.C., he relied upon military strength to gain as well as protect his authority; hence his dictum that "political power grows out of the barrel of a gun." Like every Chinese emperor since the plebeian Liu Pang ascended to the throne and founded the Han dynasty, he consciously nurtured a personality cult designed to portray himself as a charismatic, infallible philosopher-king. And, like the "Sons of Heaven" who preceded him, he sought to govern without institutional checks and balances. Just as the emperors frequently circumvented their cabinets by appointing an Inner Court, so Mao bypassed the Communist Party structure during his most critical period by setting up a Cultural Revolution Directorate whose members included his wife, his secretary, his former bodyguard, and Lin Piao, then his trusted adjutant.[8]

Traditional Chinese attitudes and behavior also dictated Mao's external policies. Like their forebears, who viewed China as the "central kingdom" surrounded by predatory foreign "barbarians," Mao and his colleagues were always mindful of the danger of encirclement by the Soviet Union and the United States. Their alliance with Moscow, signed in 1950, was a temporary expedient that broke down within a decade, and not long afterward the two Communist giants were almost at the brink of war. At the same time, the Chinese felt themselves to be increasingly menaced by a growing American presence in Vietnam. Therefore, just as the early Ming rulers sought to assure China's security in the fifteenth century by dealing with rival Mongol princes, so Mao and his brilliant prime minister, Chou En-lai, maneuvered to play their principal enemies off against each other. They countered the Soviet threat by seeming to edge closer to the United States—and, with dramatic flexibility, even invited President Nixon to visit Peking. Meanwhile, they worked to "isolate" the United States diplomatically by reaching accommodations with America's allies in Western Europe and in the Western Hemisphere. Thus they demonstrated an extraordinary capacity for tractability, but without diluting their basic ideological belief in the inevitability of world revolution—a belief that corresponded to their conviction that they were the repository of absolute "virtue."

Despite his disavowal of Confucius, whose prescription for social harmony opposed his fixation on the need for protracted struggle, Mao nevertheless subscribed to the Confucian tenet of "virtue" as a key principle in public conduct. He owed to Confucius as well the notion that education was the only way to improve the human environment.[9] Mao's accent on education—broadened to embrace propaganda, indoctrination, and "thought reform"—was reflected in his portrayal of himself as the Great Teacher. For, as he saw it, one of his major roles was to remold the hearts and minds of China. This set him apart from his main communist contemporary, Joseph Stalin, who paranoiacally slaughtered suspected foes by the millions. Mao's method was to persuade his enemies to rectify their alleged errors. Cautioning his cadres to exercise leniency in dealing with their opponents, he said: "So long as a person who has made mistakes . . . honestly and sincerely wishes to be cured and to mend his ways, we should welcome him and cure his sickness so that he can become a good comrade. We can never succeed if we just let ourselves go and lash out at him." [10]

While Stalin was a Westerner whose despotism was basically Oriental, Mao was an Oriental whose authoritarianism was tempered by Western influences. He no doubt absorbed these influences from reading Rousseau, John Stuart Mill, Darwin, Friedrich Paulsen, and other Western thinkers, whose works were belatedly scratching the minds of Chinese youth around the turn of the twentieth century. In addition, as he would later admit, the example of Stalin's failure in the Soviet Union served to confirm his view that brutality would not suffice to implant communism in man's marrow.

In the Soviet Union, Mao observed, the Bolsheviks had taken power, eliminated their enemies, extended their hold over the country, and placed the means of production under state control. Yet Stalin had neglected to transform the Russian "soul." Nor had he properly prepared his heirs to carry on the real revolution. After his death, consequently, his successors proceeded to "revise" the true faith. Mao explained this to André Malraux:

> You remember Kosygin at the Twenty-third Congress: "Communism means the raising of living standards." And swimming is a way of putting on a pair of trunks! . . . It isn't simply a question of replacing the Tsar with Khrushchev, one bourgeoisie with another, even if it's called Communist. . . . If we decided to make of it what the Russians are now doing . . . everything will fall apart. Our revolution cannot be simply the stabilization of victory.[11]

But of all the influences that shaped Mao's thinking, the most important were those that stemmed from his personal experiences during the decades before the Communist movement conquered China. And perhaps the most profound of these experiences were the years he spent in Yenan, where he and the ragged remnant of his troops arrived in 1936 after retreating six thousand miles under harassment from Chiang Kai-shek's Nationalists. Here, sheltered in caves dug out of the yellowish loess cliffs, the Communists were not only forced to fight for survival, but compelled to manufacture arms and ammunition, grow food, and, among other activities, proselytize among the peasants of the region in order to collect intelligence, assure their defense perimeters, and recruit soldiers. Organized into compact guerrilla bands imbued with an all-for-one-and-one-for-all *élan*, they accomplished their tasks without complicated equipment, formal institutions, or a complex command hierarchy. They were much like the sympathetic rebels in *All Men Are Brothers*,* a Chinese equivalent of the Robin Hood story that Mao had read as a child.

This experience left Mao with the idea that many of the methods that had worked in the Yenan redoubt could be projected on a national scale. China, like Yenan, lacked capital, technology,

---

* Also known as *Water Margin*. The best-known English translation, entitled *All Men Are Brothers*, was done by Pearl Buck.

and adequate areas of arable land. Like Yenan, however, it had one resource—people. Accordingly, he calculated, the attributes of altruism and selflessness that had unified and actuated his heroic guerrillas in Yenan could be infused into China's huge population with similar results. Just as first he had regarded Yenan as a microcosm of China, so Mao later came to consider China as a macrocosm of Yenan.

CHAPTER 2

The Ailing Giant

*Direct your eyes downward, do not hold your
head high and gaze at the sky. Unless a person is interested in turning his eyes downward . . . he will never in his whole life
really understand things in China.*

—MAO TSE-TUNG, *March 1941*

MAO TSE-TUNG was confronted by a country whose problems
would have posed an enormous challenge to any leader.
For China since the late eighteenth century had been crumbling in
a variety of ways. Its population had grown dramatically, causing
severe economic and social strains that were partly responsible for
widespread peasant restiveness and rebellion. At the same time, the
imperial Chinese administrative system, which had shown remarkable stability for more than a century, began to deteriorate, undermined by its incapacity to respond to the burgeoning internal
pressures. Exacerbating this decay was the impact of the West,
which brought contemporary ideas to China yet humiliated many
Chinese by revealing the weaknesses of the Middle Kingdom that
they had so long revered as superior to all other nations on earth.
By the first decades of the twentieth century, China was disrupted,
fragmented, and confused—its decomposition serving to fertilize the
soil in which a diversity of new movements, among them Mao's
communism, could take root.

China's extraordinary population growth stemmed from a combination of factors that had been evolving for hundreds of years.
As far back as the eleventh century, the introduction of new varie-

ties of early-ripening and drought-resistant rice from Indochina had made double cropping feasible. The later introduction of such American crops as corn, sweet potatoes, and peanuts enabled the Chinese both to produce more crops in their valleys and plains and to improve cultivation of dry hills, mountains, and sandy loams. These innovations, which stimulated a substantial increase in food production, were paralleled after the Ch'ing dynasty finally established its authority in 1683 by a century of domestic peace and order that further contributed to a rise in living standards. So attractive did China seem by the eighteenth century that Voltaire hailed its morality and organization as "the best the world has ever seen." The cumulative result of this relative prosperity was, however, an unprecedented and disastrous demographic explosion. The Chinese population, estimated to have been 100 million in the middle of the seventeenth century, tripled by 1800 and soared to more than 400 million by 1850.[1]

The effects of the population boom proved, almost in exaggerated fashion, the validity of the theories then being propounded by Thomas Malthus, who was familiar with China. As the number of Chinese multiplied geometrically, the means to sustain them could scarcely keep pace, since the country's technological shortcomings limited its ability to attain required levels of efficiency.

Over the centuries, the Chinese had worked their soil so assiduously that there were very few areas that had not been touched by human hands. They had built canals and irrigation channels, some with elaborate systems of foot treadles, buckets, and wheels for lifting water up to terraced paddy fields spectacularly carved out of hillsides. They had opened virgin regions, planting them with cotton, tea bushes, and mulberry trees for silkworm cultivation. These and other developments were mostly accomplished by manpower alone, since equipment and draft animals were in short supply. But as the population increased and the amount of available labor expanded, the pressures on the land grew to intolerable proportions, for several reasons.

First, the Confucian ideal of large families in which there was no primogeniture meant that the patrimony was divided among the sons in the form of progressively smaller and less productive farming units. Second, the disdain of intellectuals for practical matters inhibited men of learning from contributing their intelligence and knowledge to technological inventions that would have helped to boost agricultural output. Third, in contrast to Europe and America during the early phases of the industrial revolution, there were virtually no urban factories in China to siphon off the surplus rural labor force. And finally, the imperial Chinese government was unprepared and unwilling to cope with the new economic situation and its social consequences.

Government inertia mirrored the obsolescence of China's ancient bureaucracy both in the provinces and at the center. Officials delegated to govern huge regions according to rigid codes of behavior discovered that it was safer for their careers to remain passive than to risk initiatives that might fail and thus blemish their records. They learned to accommodate to difficulties rather than to resolve them, and their potential creativity was dampened by rituals so formal that their calligraphic style was deemed more important than the contents of their reports. At the top of the pyramid, the emperor himself was less and less able to assert his rule as the volume of state business proliferated. Instead of serving as the infallible autocrat capable of dictating wise and just decisions on all matters, he became the chief bottleneck in the increasingly clogged bureaucracy.[2]

In all Oriental societies, even to this day, a plausible measure of corruption has been acceptable as the oil that lubricates the administrative gears. Throughout Chinese history, in fact, civil servants were expected to subsidize both their public and private establishments from funds obtained through their official positions. But the disintegration of the Ch'ing dynasty in the nineteenth century, like the decline of earlier and subsequent Chinese regimes, was characterized by excessive and oppressive graft and extortion.

Corruption was especially outrageous in the collection of the various levies exacted by the state. Government revenues, primarily derived from the land tax, grain tribute, salt tax, and customs duties, were collected through a system of "tax farming." Under this system, provincial officials were required to meet certain tax quotas, after which they could pocket further collections. This effectively mandated tax officials to bleed the people, which they generally did in collaboration with local landlords who acted as intermediaries in extracting payments from their tenant farmers.

Posts in the provincial bureaucracy were obviously lucrative, and they became increasingly in demand. According to government records, the proportion of appointments acquired by purchase climbed from 29 per cent in 1840 to 49 per cent in 1895. During the same period, the percentage of officials who qualified on the basis of merit dropped sharply.[3]

Another major source of corruption was the ancient salt monopoly, which was operated by private merchants under state license. Salt was an indispensable item to the Chinese masses living on a diet composed mainly of cereals. The original concept behind licensing private merchants was to save the government the large investment involved in transporting salt over vast distances. In practice, the merchants managed to cling to their permits by paying enormous bribes to the officials who supervised the trade. The merchants at Yangchow in northern Kiangsu province—where Marco Polo had served as a magistrate during his celebrated sojourn in China—are said to have paid the equivalent of $3 million a year to local functionaries in the late eighteenth century. These payments were often disguised as "donations" to public funds or "contributions" to military programs. The alliance between the merchants and officials was so mutually profitable that, on one occasion, an emissary detailed by the emperor to investigate the corruption was forced to abandon his effort because of obstructions thrown up by both the traders and the bureaucrats. Since the emperor himself received large gifts from the salt monopolists, it is unlikely that he was anxious to have their misconduct disclosed.

The tyranny of officials and landlords, combined with the privation caused by the growing population and diminishing opportunities, inevitably prompted banditry, riots, and other forms of dissidence. Revolt was nothing new in China. Striving to survive in a marginal economy, oppressed by feudal landowners and mandarins, plagued by floods, drought, and epidemic, disaffected peasants frequently turned into outlaws and, often joined by dissident officials, they sometimes mobilized sufficient strength to overthrow dynasties. The theme of insurrection was romanticized in classical Chinese poetry and in such novels as *All Men Are Brothers*.

Among the most persistent Chinese rebel institutions were secret societies that started as religious associations and gradually became subversive movements. Like groups of Freemasons, these societies had passwords, grand masters, and elaborate rituals that endowed them with a somewhat mystical flavor.

One of the oldest secret societies in China was the White Lotus Society, which was organized in the fourth century A.D. by eighteen acolytes of the Buddhist monk Hua Yin in the Lushan highlands, south of the Yangtze River. Their original purpose was to study the doctrines of Amitabha pietism, and they took the white lotus, a Buddhist symbol, as their emblem. In time, the cult lost its strictly religious cast. By the middle of the twelfth century, it had emerged as a powerful movement determined to oust the Sung emperors, and not long afterward it opposed the Mongol legions that had swept into China. One White Lotus leader at the head of the resistance against the Mongols was Chu Yüan-chang, a poor peasant from Anhwei province who had become a monk. By 1368, he had overthrown the Mongols and established himself as Emperor Hung Wu, the founder of the Ming dynasty. Knowing its capacities, he immediately banned the society.

The White Lotus Society played a less important role during the three hundred years of Ming rule. But it never disbanded and, as conditions in China deteriorated in the late eighteenth century, the movement rose again in opposition to the Ch'ing dynasty. It staged its first large-scale outbreak in northern Shantung province in 1774, and the insurrection, fueled by popular discontent, spread quickly in the years that followed.

Though it justified its rebellion as a reaction against official despotism—"the people are forced by the officials to revolt," ran its slogan—the White Lotus Society did not raise a rival dynastic standard, set up an administration in the areas it conquered, or offer a positive alternative to Ch'ing policies. Nor were its forces, roving bands rather than organized troops, able to stand up against the government army. Yet even after the movement's defeat, its adherents continued their activities against the dynasty. In 1812, for example, one of them who worked as a cook in the imperial household unsuccessfully attempted to assassinate the emperor. Two years later, posing as persimmon peddlers, a White Lotus group infiltrated into the palace but was fought off by the royal guards. In the years after that, the society went underground, splintering into factions with names like the White Clouds, the White Fans, and the White Eyebrows. Some elements surfaced again in 1900 as the Society of the Righteous and Harmonious Fists, better known in the West as the Boxers. The founder of the Chinese Republic in 1911, Dr. Sun Yat-sen, was said to have been associated with the White Lotus Society and other clandestine brotherhoods, as was his successor, Chiang Kai-shek.

The White Lotus Society was not the only movement to oppose the Ch'ing dynasty. Muslim minorities in northern Kansu had risen up in the late eighteenth century against Han Chinese domination, and their revolt mushroomed to other Islamic regions of China in subsequent decades. By 1856, a Muslim leader called Tu Weh-hsiu succeeded in setting up a separate state in southwestern Yunnan province, with himself as its sultan. Not until 1873, after fierce fighting and appalling losses of life among the civilian population, was he finally crushed by the government.

Simultaneously, the imperial regime was engaged in an effort to subdue another dissident movement, known as the Nien, which had gathered momentum in north and central China in the early decades of the nineteenth century as a coalition of five outlaw bands, each identified by the color of its banners. Comprised mainly of cavalry units, the Nien rebels struck out from fortified sanctuaries in which, in Maoist style, they had secured the allegiance of the peasants. They were eventually defeated in 1868 after the enlightened General Tsêng Kuo-fan won over the villagers by employing many of the counterinsurgency techniques that would become fashionable a hundred years later.

Still another rebellion was triggered by the Triad, or Heaven and Earth Society. Created in 1647 as a Buddhist blood brotherhood devoted to the overthrow of the Ch'ing dynasty, the Triad gradually became a loosely organized association of restive coolies, boatmen, petty officials, itinerant merchants, and others with grievances against the government, particularly in China's southern and coastal provinces. After sparking open revolts in the early nineteenth century, the Triad degenerated into a vehicle for racketeers, smugglers, and other assorted criminals, and it continued to operate a hundred years later among Chinese communities in Hong

Kong, Singapore, and Malaysia. Mao Tse-tung and several of his Communist associates indirectly sought Triad support during the days when they were seeking to recruit followers.[4] Chiang Kai-shek similarly relied on the secret societies in his attempts to eradicate the Communists in Chinese coastal cities.[5]

The biggest upheaval to devastate nineteenth-century China, however, was the Taiping Rebellion. Ignited by a mystic curiously exalted by Christianity, the insurrection rapidly inflamed vast numbers of Chinese desperate to free themselves from corruption, oppression, and poverty. By the time it was over, the episode had cost as many as 20 million lives.

The founder of the Taiping cult, Hung Hsiu-ch'üan, was born into a peasant family of the Hakka community, north Chinese who had migrated south centuries earlier but never fully assimilated into the local population. As a youth, Hung failed several times to pass the imperial examinations that would have given him an official position in the Ch'ing administration. His frustrations undoubtedly aggravated his psychological instability, and in 1837, prostrated by a high fever, he had a vision in which he claimed that God and Jesus Christ bade him to save mankind from the devil. His acquaintance with the Bible, Hung later recalled, came from religious pamphlets written by a Chinese Protestant missionary. These pamphlets inspired him with Old Testament zeal. For, as the story went, Hung awoke from his vision shouting: "Slay the demons! There is one and there is another. Many cannot withstand a single blow of my sword." [6]

The Orient has always been filled with mystics who wander from village to village, preaching their faith and hoping that propitious circumstances will win them followers. Hung fit this pattern. He drifted south into mountainous Kwangsi province, then beset by famine, urging peasants to destroy Buddhist and Taoist idols as well as Confucian ancestral tablets on the grounds that only his monotheism promised salvation. Soon his God Worshippers Society, as he called his sect, was attracting not only poor peasants but assorted bandits, dispirited scholars, and even landlords motivated to oppose the government. The movement also joined forces in some areas with members of the White Lotus Society and the Triad. Hung's cousin Feng Yun-shan, an unsuccessful scholar like himself, took over the military organization of the new cult. In one of his early public messages, Hung made it plain that his drive would be bloody. He wrote: "All who resist us are rebels and idolatrous demons, and we shall kill them without sparing. But whoever acknowledges the Heavenly King and exerts himself in our service shall have a full reward." [7]

Conferring upon himself the title of Heavenly King, Hung Hsiu-ch'üan named his chief lieutenants Northern, Southern, Eastern, Western, and Assistant Kings. And, after proclaiming his intention to establish a new dynasty, he called his movement the "Heavenly Kingdom of Great Peace." The term "Great Peace," used by other dynastic challengers throughout history, is *T'ai-p'ing* in Chinese.

At the outset of their ambitious campaign to conquer China, the Taiping forces probably comprised about three thousand men and women, most of them armed with spears and pitchforks and wearing red turbans. Like Muslim fanatics embarked on a holy war, they showed remarkable courage and discipline, and their puritanical aversion to looting and rape won them converts among villagers accustomed to plundering armies. Their ranks swelled, and by the spring of 1852 they had swept as far north as the Yangtze River and soon captured Nanking, the second city of the empire, bringing most of central China under their domination. Though they threatened Peking, their strength was inadequate to take the imperial capital.

In contrast to the other rebel movements of the period, the Taipings conceived a considerable array of programs based on a fascinating mixture of Christian and Chinese elements. Several of these programs, while never actually put into practice, were surprisingly similar to the reforms sponsored by later radicals, including Mao Tse-tung and his Communists.

Regulations in the Taiping army, like those promulgated by Mao for his soldiers, required that troops carry their own food and never enter private dwellings unless invited. Like the Communists, the Taipings also banned witchcraft, gambling, prostitution, and opium. In order to promote equality between the sexes, they abolished the old Chinese custom of foot-binding, mobilized women into military and labor units, and appointed them as officers and administrators. And borrowing from classical Chinese utopian thinkers, they worked out a system of primitive economic equality that included a blueprint to redistribute land among farming households, an agrarian scheme described in Christian rhetoric as a plan "to enable all under Heaven to enjoy the great blessings of the Lord God Almighty: land for all to till, food for all to eat, clothes for all to wear; money for all to spend. . . ." [8]

Despite its vigor and religious fervor, the Taiping movement began to weaken not long after reaching the peak of its power in the mid-1850s. Among other errors, its leaders failed to take advantage of the seizure of Amoy and Shanghai by their Triad allies and secure footholds in those important coastal cities. In addition, Hung Hsiu-ch'üan and his lesser kings fell to squabbling among themselves, fragmenting the Taiping hierarchy into rival factions. Finally, the imperial army was expanded and reorganized under Tsêng Kuo-fan, the great Hunanese scholar-soldier whose skilled tactics later crushed the Nien insurgents. In the summer of 1864, Tsêng's forces encircled the walls of Nanking. Anticipating defeat and a cruel death, Hung Hsiu-ch'üan committed suicide by poison. The city fell. All its defenders were slaughtered. The surviving Taiping leaders were executed, and the rebellion was effectively ended.

In the closing years of the Taiping insurrection, the imperial authorities adopted a policy unprecedented in Chinese history. They turned toward Western technology and, at the same time, sought the cooperation of the European powers in an effort to modernize and improve their defenses.

Dipping into tax and customs revenues, the Chinese Army purchased foreign weapons and built arsenals to manufacture Western-type guns and steamships. Early in 1862, when the Taiping rebels reached the outskirts of Shanghai, the British and French abandoned their neutral stance and began to help the Ch'ing regime to protect the area in which Europeans had substantial commercial interests. An American adventurer from Massachusetts, Frederick Townsend Ward, was commissioned to recruit, train, and command a unit of four thousand Chinese known as the "Ever Victorious Army." Ward was succeeded after his death by a British officer, Major Charles George "Chinese" Gordon, whose mixed battalion of foreign and native troops saw action in the battle for Soochow. A similar legion mustered by the French assisted the Chinese Army in the fight for Hangchow.

Commenting on the Taiping episode nearly a century later, Mao Tse-tung called it a "peasant revolutionary war against feudal rule and national oppression" that collapsed under the "combined onslaught of the Ch'ing government and the British, U. S., and French aggressors." [9] But the actual role of the foreign powers was less significant than the fact that the Ch'ing government accepted outside aid at a time of crisis. For this indicated the degree to which the emperor was compelled to concede that China, the theoretical center of the universe, was no longer superior to all other nations on earth. Only seventy years earlier, rejecting Lord Macartney's proposal to increase trade between England and China, the Ch'ien Lung emperor had declared that "our Celestial Empire possesses all things in abundance . . . and therefore needs not import the manufactures of outside barbarians in exchange for our own produce." [10] Now, reluctantly admitting to China's weakness, a successor to the haughty Emperor Ch'ien Lung decreed in 1862 that "for the time being, we have to make use of foreigners to train our soldiers, as a scheme for self-strengthening." [11]

China's temptation to borrow Western methods in order to strengthen itself was an idea that began to tantalize Chinese intellectuals as far back as the 1840s, following the Opium War. That war started in late 1839, when the British retaliated against attempts by a conscientious Chinese official, Lin Tse-hsü, to suppress Britain's efforts to bring Indian opium into Canton and other coastal cities. In reality, the war represented the first drive by a European power to open China to "free trade," and it dramatically revealed to perceptive Chinese both their own backwardness and the dynamism of the West. The Ch'ing government's so-called Army of the Green Standard, which supposedly numbered six hundred thousand men deployed throughout the provinces, was actually a rabble. The prime talent of its officers was to make money by doctoring their accounts. Like characters in a Chinese opera, its soldiers could only posture with swords and spears—except when given the chance to plunder hapless civilians. Thus it was no match for British warships and troops, which easily reduced the decrepit Chinese fortresses along the coast between Canton and Shanghai.

Their capitulation in the Opium War forced the Chinese to cede

Hong Kong to Britain as well as open the ports of Canton, Amoy, Foochow, Ningpo, and Shanghai to British residence and commerce. In the ensuing years, through pressures of one kind or another, Britain, the United States, and the other Western powers imposed a series of further "unequal treaties" on China that gave them considerable commercial and extraterritorial privileges. Under these inequitable treaty arrangements, Tsarist Russia also took over huge tracts of Chinese territory, thereby sowing the seeds of a bitter boundary dispute that would erupt a century later.

One of the consequences of the foreign encroachments on China was to incite strong xenophobic feelings among many Chinese. Despite Britain's victory in the Opium War, Canton officials refused to permit British merchants to trade freely until 1858. Elsewhere in the country, officials encouraged the population to attack foreign missionaries and their converts, and this anti-Christian sentiment was heightened during the Taiping troubles, which seemed to traditionalist Chinese to have been caused by Western influence.

But a small fraction of the Chinese intellectual community read the European incursions as a warning that China had to remodel itself by adopting at least some of the scientific knowledge and governmental institutions of the West. Among the early advocates of Westernization was Feng Kuei-fen, a prominent scholar. Confessing his shame that China could be defeated by small Western nations, he urged the Chinese to resist the blind impulse to expel foreigners, recommending instead that they "learn the superior technology of the barbarians in order to control them." He proposed that government schools teach mathematics and science, and that the ancient examination system for officials be revised to recruit more technicians into the administration. He also stressed the need for China to make better use of its people and economic resources within the framework of its own institutions. Borrowing a phrase from the *Classic of Changes*, he suggested that China strive to improve itself through "self-strengthening." [12] It was this phrase that the emperor employed in his edict calling for the training of Chinese soldiers by foreign advisers. In later years, a group of reformers formalized the phrase by creating the *Ch'iang-hsueh hui* —the Self-Strengthening Society.

Another important figure among the reformist thinkers of the period was Yen Fu, who translated Darwin's *Origin of Species* into Chinese while serving as a naval cadet in England. Returning to China, he went on to translate Adam Smith's *Wealth of Nations*, Huxley's *Evolution and Ethics*, Herbert Spencer's *Principles of Sociology*, and other books, annotating many of them with commentaries. Other works on Western science, technology, and current affairs were translated and published by European and American missionaries and scholars then in China. Among the more influential journals were those edited by an American Methodist, Young J. Allen. Published in the Chinese language, they stressed the progressive characteristics of Western culture and criticized the Confucian ethic for its obsolescence.

Hong Kong and Shanghai, port cities that looked out to the world beyond China, were especially lively centers of foreign ideas. One of the keenest advocates of Westernization in Shanghai was Cheng Kuan-ying, who divided his time between working for British commercial firms and writing essays on China's problems. Another was Wang T'ao, who served as an assistant to Christian missionaries and later became an editorialist for Chinese newspapers in Hong Kong and Shanghai. After a three-year sojourn in Britain under missionary auspices, Wang favored the creation of a bicameral Chinese parliament "elected equitably and universally." Both he and Cheng also emphasized the necessity for a free press that would expose official abuses. Similar views were expressed by Liang Ch'i-ch'ao, a scholar who became a Shanghai editor and gained a good deal of popularity among students in later years. These men were hardly radical by present-day standards. Loyal to the monarchy, they did not question the basic Confucian tenets. They believed, however, that Western techniques could profitably supplement traditional Chinese values. Or as one of their slogans held: "Chinese learning for the essential principles, Western learning for practical application." [13]

In about the middle of the nineteenth century, then, several Chinese officials began to attempt to put Western methods into practice. No less a personage than the emperor's brother, Prince Kung, outlined a program to establish a foreign affairs bureau, expand the use of Western advisers in new Maritime Customs Service at all ports, and, among other things, educate functionaries in foreign languages. Enlightened officials such as Li Hung-chang and Chang Chih-tung started the construction of modern shipyards, arsenals, telegraph lines, and railways. One of Li's major efforts was the creation after 1885 of China's principal fighting force, the Peiyang naval fleet based in the North, which included two German-built battleships among its twenty-five vessels.

This trend toward Westernization was limited, however. For one thing, it was mainly restricted to China's Westernized coastal areas. For another, the Chinese government lacked both the drive and the resources to push the modernization schemes through effectively. Such projects as a Shanghai textile mill and the railway linking Peking with the Manchurian border were completed only after long and costly delays. Li Hung-chang's northern fleet, though initially encouraged by the Ch'ing court, soon fell victim to official corruption as palace eunuchs and other courtiers siphoned off naval funds for themselves. Li's ships were disastrously defeated in 1894, when China and Japan went to war for control of the Korean peninsula. This war marked the failure of the Chinese hope for "self-strengthening." After that, had it not been for the rival ambitions of the imperialist powers, China might have become a European colony. Instead, it was opened to a scramble for concessions that put several of its regions and cities under the virtual control of various European nations.

Attempts at "self-strengthening" through the adoption of Western techniques were also inhibited by the deeply ingrained habits and customs of the Chinese bureaucracy. Officials might voice praise for modern scientific methods, yet they could not shake off the legacy of their Confucian education, with its emphasis on sterile ritual and detail. Cultural pride, combined with the struggles involved in seeking and holding office, militated as well against their receptivity to innovations. Toward the end of the nineteenth century, as the power of the narrow-minded, domineering dowager empress grew, conservatism and xenophobia became increasingly fashionable in court circles. Usually known as Tz'u-hsi, from the first two characters of her long title, the dowager empress had originally been a low-ranking concubine. She bore the emperor his only son, who died at the age of nineteen. After that, except during a brief challenge from her only nephew, whom she had placed on the throne after her son's death, her authority was absolute and reactionary—even though Western ladies who saw her, among them the wife of the American minister in Peking, were impressed by her "womanly tenderness."

The defeat inflicted by the Japanese followed by the seizure of various areas by Germany, France, Britain, and Russia, seemed to augur the dismemberment of China. The atmosphere of crisis that gripped the court in 1898 prompted the Emperor Kuang-hsü, by now an ardent young man of twenty-seven, to defy the dowager empress. He sought advice from K'ang Yu-wei, a classical scholar from Canton and one of the most daring iconoclasts of the time. To depend upon the conservatives to save China from catastrophe, K'ang replied, would be "like climbing a tree in search of fish." [14] The emperor, whose tastes included a fondness for Western gadgets, thereupon commissioned K'ang to submit a specific reform program. Thus, over a period of a hundred days from June through September of 1898, K'ang and his progressive friends drew up a list of more than forty proposals recommending changes in nearly every realm, from agriculture, commerce, and education to military affairs and the postal system.

K'ang's proposed reforms naturally threatened the entire Ch'ing establishment, including the dowager empress, who was still vigorous at sixty-three. Theoretically in retirement, she nevertheless controlled the army and the powerful palace eunuchs, and she reacted predictably. Without displaying a trace of "womanly tenderness," she deposed the emperor in a *coup d'état* and had six of K'ang's colleagues executed. K'ang himself escaped to Japan. The attempt to alter China from above by moderate, gradual means had failed and, as the twentieth century dawned, the prospects for violent revolution in the future seemed almost inevitable.

While far from revolutionary in the modern sense of the term, a serious outbreak of violence immediately followed the failure of the reformers. It was the uprising of the Boxers, the secret society whose activists were supposed to practice an ancient form of military calisthenics along with Taoist sorcery and other magic rites. Founded as an affiliate of the White Lotus Society, which opposed the Ch'ing dynasty, the Boxer movement was now encouraged by the dowager empress and the court reactionaries to exterminate the foreign influences spreading through China.

Like the rebellions that erupted earlier in the century, the Boxer rising gained its initial impetus from deteriorating economic and social conditions. The Yellow River—"China's sorrow"—had again flooded in 1898, causing extensive famine in Shantung province. Drought was also plaguing parts of north China. Aggravating these calamities were the dislocations created by the construction of new railways and the importation of foreign merchandise. The Boxers consequently attracted thousands of peasants, coolies, and other elements who could conveniently blame their poverty and frustrations on the "foreign devils."

The first alliance between the Ch'ing government and the Boxers took place in stricken Shantung, where the governor enlisted members of the movement into his militia and exhorted them to attack local Christians. By the spring of 1900, mobs of Boxers were roaming through north China, slaughtering Chinese Christians and missionaries. In June, they entered Peking and Tienstin, besieging the foreign legations and settlements in both cities. Inside the palace, meanwhile, the dowager empress was told by pro-Boxer courtiers that the foreign powers had demanded her abdication and were sending in troops to reinforce their demand. Her response was to declare war on the foreign powers.

Encircled by the Boxers, the eleven legations inside the Peking diplomatic ghetto mobilized nearly a thousand foreign civilians and guards as well as three thousand Chinese Christians into a defense force that was able to hold out for almost two months. It was one of those midsummer adventures that thrilled the world—especially since the press, lacking credible information from Peking, published fantastic tales of the event. After much bickering, an international contingent of some twenty thousand troops, about half of them Japanese, finally marched from Tientsin to the capital to rescue the beleaguered foreign community. Seventy-six foreigners had died during the siege of the legation quarter. Some two hundred fifty foreigners were killed in the surrounding provinces. The brutality was particularly severe in Shansi, where the governor personally presided over the execution of forty-six missionaries and other foreigners. The number of Chinese Christians slaughtered ran into the thousands.

As the Western invaders began to plunder Peking, the dowager empress and her closest courtiers fled the city in disguise. Li Hung-

chang, once the exponent of "self-strengthening" and now governor
of Canton, was left to retrieve the situation. Under the Boxer
Protocol, signed in September 1901, he acceded to the harsh demands imposed by the Western powers, including the payment of
a staggering indemnity to the eleven nations whose legations had
been assaulted. Despite her role in the episode, the dowager empress returned to Peking with her court soon afterward, supported
by foreign powers that considered her a symbol of "stability."
Unable to regain her former authority, she nevertheless continued
to act the monarch until her death in 1908.

Six decades later, at the height of his Cultural Revolution, Mao
Tse-tung took a curious retrospective approach to the Boxer uprising. He praised the Boxers while condemning the enlightened officials who had tried to change the Ch'ing government's reactionary
policies. As one of his publicists put it, the Boxers were a "great
anti-imperialist, anti-feudal revolutionary mass movement" that had
waged a "heroic patriotic struggle" against the foreign conspiracy
to partition China. The progressives of the period, in contrast, were
depicted as "bourgeois reformers" who had "cherished the illusion
that they could go completely to the side of imperialism and rely
on its strength to realize their aims of constitutional reform and
modernization." [15]

Mao's acclaim for the xenophobic Boxers was partly contrived
to arouse Chinese nationalistic emotions at a time when he was
attempting to isolate China from the outside world. Indeed, emulating the Boxers, his Red Guards stormed and burned a British legation building and harassed foreign diplomats in Peking during the
summer of 1967. But more significantly, Mao was using his own
version of history to vilify contemporary rivals who, he believed,
resembled the earlier reformers in advocating political gradualism
in opposition to his doctrine of "armed struggle." Yet Mao in his
formative years was swayed more by those early progressives than
by the Boxers he later claimed to admire.

CHAPTER 3

The Making of a Rebel

❦

*In a very short time, in China's central,
southern, and northern provinces, several
hundred million peasants will rise like a
mighty storm, like a hurricane, a force so
swift and violent that no power, however
great, will be able to hold it back.*

—MAO TSE-TUNG, March 1927

HUNAN PROVINCE, where Mao Tse-tung was born, is an area of
hills, lakes, and fertile farmland that had served for centuries
as a corridor linking north and south China. Insurgent and imperial
armies recurrently passed through this corridor in their drives to
conquer or defend dynasties, leaving a trail of destruction in their
wake. During peaceful interludes, the province was not only an
artery for commercial traffic but an avenue along which new ideas
flowed. Hence the Hunanese, insular yet exposed to outside influences, developed the skills of soldiering and scholarship as well as
a familiarity with civil strife. And perhaps, as Mao himself once
noted, the red peppers in their diet also contributed to their vigor.

In sharp contrast to other Chinese classicists whose approach
was largely academic, the scholars of Hunan tended to accentuate
the political, economic, and social aspects of Confucian texts. Wang
Fu-chih, the seventeenth-century Hunanese philosopher, laid the
foundations of this pragmatism by expounding the view that political systems, economic structures, social customs, and man himself
were all subject to change. Foreshadowing one of Mao's basic
dogmas, Wang argued that "there is not a single part of human
nature already shaped that cannot be modified." [1]

The pragmatic tradition initiated by Wang inspired much of the advanced Chinese thinking in the nineteenth century, and many of the most persuasive works of the period were produced by Hunanese scholars such as Ho Chang-ling, who compiled an anthology of political and economic essays, and Wei Yuan, who wrote a treatise on world history and geography. Local Hunanese officials, moreover, were among the most enlightened in the country. In addition to encouraging educational reform and modern industries, they invited both native and outside progressives to address students and other educated elements of the provincial population. The brilliant Hunanese radical T'an Ssu-t'ung, executed by the dowager empress in 1898 for his role in the reform movement, based his patriotic Southern Study Society in the province. The first girls' school in China was opened in 1903 in Changsha, the provincial capital. One of the earliest American educational programs in China, sponsored by Yale, was established as well in Changsha.

Hunan was also the source from which the Ch'ing government drew many of its ablest civilian functionaries and military officers for posts in other provinces throughout the empire. In 1865, for instance, five of China's eight regional governors were Hunanese. The most effective Chinese general of his time was Tsêng Kuo-fan, a Hunanese scholar who finally defeated the Taiping and Nien rebels. Another eminent officer of the period, Tso Tsung-t'an, who consolidated Peking's hold over Central Asia, was also from Hunan. This background may account at least in part for the Hunanese predominance in the twentieth-century Communist hierarchy. With its progressive intellectual ferment, the Hunan environment was certainly significant in shaping Mao.

Located almost exactly in the geographical center of the province, the village of Shaoshan is some thirty miles west of Hsiangtan, a busy market town on the Hsiang River. It is an area of isolated farms lying among hills and a few peaks, one of them the site of an ancient Taoist hermitage in which, according to legend, a monk composed the *shao* style of music that gave the village its name. Here Mao was born on December 26, 1893, in a hillside farmhouse overlooking a lotus pond. He was the eldest of three sons and a daughter. His brothers and sister would later die violent deaths as political activists.

Mao's father, Mao Jen-shêng, had been a dispossessed peasant who joined the army to escape heavy debts and returned to his native village to become relatively rich. As Mao afterward recalled, his father had gradually managed to acquire more than three acres of land, from whose yield the family succeeded in saving one hundred forty bushels of rice per year. Mao Jen-shêng converted this modest grain surplus into cash, which he lent out at usurious rates of interest. He also began to expand into cereal trading, until he was a full-fledged merchant with a substantial amount of monetary capital.

From all accounts, including those of Mao himself, Mao Jen-shêng was a badly educated, bigoted, solitary man who demanded total obedience from his sons in conformity with the Confucian notion of filial piety. He compelled his children to work hard, beat them frequently, gave them no money, and often deprived them of food. Mao's mother, in contrast, was a devout Buddhist who exuded love, generosity, and gentleness, and she usually sided with her children against her husband. Relating his life to Edgar Snow in 1936, Mao humorously described the household as having been split into two "parties"—the Ruling Power personified by his father, and the Opposition "United Front" comprised of his mother, his brothers, and himself. "My mother advocated a policy of indirect attack," he recalled. "She criticized any overt display of emotion and attempts at open rebellion against the Ruling Power. She said it was not the Chinese way." [2]

Several Western writers using psychoanalytical techniques have sought to attribute Mao's revolutionary vocation to his avowed hatred for paternal authority. Mao himself has lent substance to this thesis. He told Snow that he learned in his disputes with his father that he could defend his rights only by "open rebellion." [3] But, as Jerome Ch'en has pointed out, the relationships in the Mao family were normal in China of that era. The father expected to be strict master of the house, and the children resisted or eluded his control in coalition with their mother. [4] But hints in the autobiographical account he gave to Snow suggest that Mao was not entirely lacking in sympathy for his father. Therefore, while his tender years were impressionable, Mao's longer-range outlook was undoubtedly molded by an assortment of other experiences.

Mao was only five years old when he started working on his father's land. Three years later, though continuing to lend a hand in the fields, he began to attend the local primary school in order to learn enough reading, writing, and arithmetic to keep the family ledgers. The school curriculum, unchanged for centuries, consisted of reciting incomprehensible Confucian classics. Despite Mao's later claim to have disliked this arid fare, the frequent references to the Chinese classics in his writing indicate that he absorbed a good deal of it. Like all Chinese schoolboys of his generation, he also devoured such traditional novels as *Romance of the Three Kingdoms, The Dream of the Red Chamber,* and *All Men Are Brothers,* with their tales of historical heroes and villains and daring bandits. Mao was especially captivated by *All Men Are Brothers,* which glorifies revolt, even though its rebels seek to rectify the abuses of the imperial system rather than alter the system itself.

Compelled by his father to quit primary school at the age of thirteen, Mao labored long hours in the fields by day and on the family ledgers at night. He grew into manhood and, in customary manner, acquiesced to an arranged marriage with a girl four years his senior. The marriage, later repudiated by Mao, was never consummated. During these years, meanwhile, Mao found time to continue reading. One of his favorite books was *Words of Warning to an Affluent Age,* by Cheng Kuan-ying, a Shanghai merchant and scholar who pleaded for technical and economic modernization and a constitutional monarchy. According to Mao, the book inspired him to resume his education. He ran away from home, first to study with an unemployed law student in the village, and afterward to enroll against the wishes of his father at the Tungshan Primary School, a progressive establishment in nearby Hsianghsiang, his mother's native district.

An incident occurred in Hunan about this time that, in Mao's later words, "influenced my whole life." There had been a severe famine in the province as a result of floods. When hungry peasants protested to government officials in Changsha, many were arrested and decapitated, and their heads were displayed on poles to discourage others. Though Mao heard the story from merchants returning from Changsha, the event scarred his mind. "I never forgot it," he told Edgar Snow thirty years afterward. "I felt that there with the rebels were ordinary people like my own family, and I deeply resented the injustice of the treatment given to them." [5]

Mao and his schoolmates were also fascinated in those days

by an intermittent series of uprisings staged by a secret fraternity called the Society of Elder Brothers, which had many adherents among the peasants of Hunan. One of the leaders of the society, Huang Hsing, must have seemed to Mao to resemble a character out of *All Men Are Brothers*. After several thrilling exploits, Huang plotted to assassinate local dignitaries assembled to celebrate the birthday of the dowager empress in November 1904. The plan misfired. Helped by an Anglican missionary, he escaped to Japan, returning to China nine years later as a general in Dr. Sun Yat-sen's Kuomintang. Mao's imagination was also stirred by another attempted revolt by the Society of Elder Brothers against landlords in his own birthplace, Shaoshan. After defending a nearby mountain stronghold, the rebels were suppressed and their leader, known as P'ang the Millstone-Maker, was beheaded. Mao later recalled that he and his fellow students "all sympathized with the revolt" and regarded P'ang as a hero.[6]

At that stage, however, Mao understandably took a cautious attitude toward unrest that directly affected his family. During one period of serious food shortages in Hunan, his father ignored the pleas of starving peasants for aid until, in desperation, they seized a rice shipment he was transporting to the city. Mao recollected that he had been displeased by his father's selfishness. But, he added with unusual candor, "I thought the villagers' method was wrong also."[7]

Yet if Mao's social ideas at that time were ambiguous, his nationalistic sentiments were coming into sharper focus. He was aware of China's humiliating defeats by Japan and the European powers throughout the nineteenth century. Years later, he remembered that he first acquired "a certain amount of political consciousness" from reading a pamphlet deploring China's loss of suzerainty over Korea, Taiwan, Indochina, Burma, and other territories and tributary states. "After I read this," he recalled, "I felt depressed about the future of my country and began to realize that it was the duty of all the people to help save it."[8]

By his own admission, Mao was then not opposed to the monarchy or the imperial bureaucratic system. Like many young, literate Chinese of the period, however, he gradually adopted the view that Western technology, institutions, and thought had much to offer

China. The year he spent at the Tungshan Primary School, where he excelled as a student, was especially important in exposing him to contemporary Western trends. At the school he became acquainted with a teacher who had studied in Japan, deriving from that contact a vicarious pride in the Japanese defeat of Russia in 1905. There too he read about K'ang Yu-wei and Liang Ch'i-ch'ao, the Ch'ing government reformers he was later to repudiate— though he admitted to having "worshiped" them in his youth. His voracious reading during that year undoubtedly included as well some of Yen Fu's translations of Darwin, Spencer, and Mill. Another book, also translated by Yen Fu, was enormously popular among young Chinese at the time. Entitled *Principles of Western Civilization*, it was by an obscure English sociologist named Benjamin Kidd who argued that the individual must sacrifice himself for the sake of society in the struggle for progress. That belief would be echoed in Mao's credo more than a half-century afterward.

Another theme in Mao's thinking that had its origin in his schoolboy reading was his respect for martial strength and courage. He was impressed by George Washington and the American war for independence, about which he read in a now-forgotten volume called *Great Heroes of the World*. In 1964, he told a French delegation visiting China that he admired Napoleon the soldier more than Robespierre the revolutionary.[9] And his youthful imagination had been kindled by such ancient Chinese warriors as the legendary emperors Yao and Shun, and the king of Ch'in, who unified the empire in the third century B.C. In his first literary effort, published in 1917, Mao put forth a view that he continued to hold throughout his life: "The principal aim of physical education is military heroism."[10]

In the autumn of 1911, when he was nearly eighteen, Mao walked to Changsha in order to enroll in the secondary school there. He found the city bubbling with political excitement. Uprisings against the Ch'ing government had erupted at Canton to the south and in Wuhan to the north. The revolutionary effervescence spread to Changsha, where local radicals seized power. Mao was swept along in the ferment. Hardly had he arrived than he wrote a tract urging that Dr. Sun Yat-sen, the Kuomintang leader, return from Japan to head a new regime. Though he later described its thesis as having been "somewhat muddled," Mao remembered his tract as "my first expression of a political opinion." As a gesture of defiance against the Ch'ing dynasty, Mao also cut off his pigtail. And, about the same time, he quit school to enlist as a private in the new revolutionary army. His uneventful military career, which lasted only six months, gave him the leisure to read progressive newspapers and journals in which, he recalled later, he initially became acquainted with the notion of socialism.[11]

After leaving the army, Mao drifted until he entered the Hunan First Normal School in the spring of 1913, when he was almost twenty years old. His five years in this school, an institution for training teachers, constituted one of the most fruitful periods in his early life. For it was here that he laid the groundwork of his scholarship, began to shape his political ideas, and acquired his initial experiences in social action.

The curriculum and *ambiance* of the Normal School exposed Mao to a wide range of literature, both traditional and contemporary, Chinese and Western. One of his teachers, Yüan Liu-ch'i, persuaded him to discard his journalistic style in favor of the classical phraseology that would put sinews into his writing. Another professor, Yang Ch'ang-chi, was even more influential. Educated in Japan and England, he not only introduced his students to modern currents in European thought but inspired their devotion to China's national heritage. He also put them in touch with youth movements elsewhere in the country by encouraging them to read *New Youth*, the iconoclastic review then being published in Peking by Ch'en Tu-hsiu, later to become the first Secretary General of the Chinese Communist Party. Mao's first printed article, his appeal for physical fitness and military courage, appeared in *New Youth* in April 1917.

Faithful to his belief in a Spartan existence, Mao adhered to the rugged physical schedule he would observe for years to come. He took cold baths daily, swam as often as possible, walked tirelessly in all kinds of weather, climbed mountains, and even toyed with theories on nudism. During one summer vacation, he and a schoolmate hiked through the Hunan countryside with no money in their pockets, surviving on food given to them by peasants for whom, in exchange, Mao wrote scrolls in his bold calligraphy.

Meanwhile, plunging deeper into political activities, Mao became secretary of the Students' Society at the Normal School and initiated measures designed to break down its old-fashioned institutional regulations. Among other moves, he freed a student about to be forced into an arranged marriage, organized resistance to a levy on students to meet additional school expenditures, and created the Association for Student Self-Government, aimed at mobilizing opposition to unreasonable demands by the school authorities. In April 1918, a month before his graduation, he set up the New People's Study Society, a student discussion group, most of whose members were destined to join the Communist Party. By this time, Mao's opinions had grown increasingly radical. He decried religion, capitalism, autocracy, and Confucian morality as the "four evil demons of the empire." When his schoolmates discussed strategies to save China, he advised them to imitate the heroic rebels in his favorite novel, *All Men Are Brothers*, by taking to the hills to fight for equality and social justice.[12] Exactly a decade later, Mao himself would ascend the misty heights of Chingkangshan to pursue a similar path.

The years at the Hunan Normal School gave Mao the solid erudition that he displayed throughout the rest of his life. His essays were adorned with learned footnotes and his poetry rivaled that of T. S. Eliot for its classical references. During the Cultural Revolution, when students were being exhorted to smash traditional vestiges, he betrayed surprise that the campaign had gone so far as to proscribe the literature he had loved as a young man. When his niece, defending the ban, asserted that the students should have a "precautionary injection" before reading T'ang dynasty poems and novels like *The Dream of the Red Chamber* in order to protect them against contamination by the classics, Mao replied impatiently: "You are being purely metaphysical." [13]

Later, however, Mao developed a strong bias against the excesses of formal education. He repeatedly cited such figures as Benjamin Franklin and Maxim Gorki as men who had succeeded without schooling. "One who goes to school for several years becomes more stupid as he reads more books," he said at a Communist Party conference in 1965.[14] About the same time, he addressed cadets at a military academy: "A little reading of books is all right, but a lot of it harms people—it really harms them. It is revolutionary war that rears cadres; the battlefield is the school." [15] Even his own education, Mao pretended, had been a waste of time. "I only learned something at the school for brigands," he told two of his closest comrades. "What I learned in thirteen years of study was not usable for making revolution. . . ." [16]

For all their interest in Rousseau, Adam Smith, Darwin, Huxley, and other Western thinkers, Chinese intellectuals around the turn of the twentieth century paid virtually no attention to Karl Marx. The reason was simple: the Marxist concept of communism emerging in a highly developed industrial state bore no relevance to a society like China. Even so basic a document as the Communist Manifesto, issued by Marx and Engels in 1848, was not published in full translation in China until April 1920. By then, a cataclysmic event had occurred that gave communism a large measure of credibility. The event was the Russian Revolution. It struck many educated Chinese as a model to emulate in their own efforts to rise out of the dismal conditions that had overtaken China at the time.

The first Chinese Republic proclaimed by Dr. Sun Yat-sen in 1911 had disintegrated. The recognized Chinese ruler in Peking, Yüan Shih-k'ai, had died in 1916, leaving a vacuum that was quickly filled by warlords who fragmented the country as they built up their regional bases. Meanwhile, despite their rhetorical loyalty to President Wilson's principles of national self-determination enunciated at the close of World War I, the Western powers continued to carve up China. In particular, they secretly agreed to give Japan the special rights formerly held by Germany in the northern province of Shantung. This move ignited a student demonstration in Peking on May 4, 1919, that rapidly turned into a nationwide protest. Known as the May 4th Movement, it became the vehicle for a wide variety of political, economic, social, and nationalistic grievances that had been irritating Chinese intellectuals for years.

Within this context of discontent, ferment, and hope, then, the Russian Revolution had undeniable appeal. It was a welcome blow to the capitalist nations that were the cause of China's degradation. In addition, Lenin's seizure of power in Russia offered a lesson in the technique of staging a revolution that might serve progressive Chinese activists in their own attempts to bring about change in China. For those Chinese who still clung to the conviction that the methods of the West would save China, here was a Western "scientific" approach that could be imitated. Therefore, for many Chinese, the Bolshevik take-over in Russia was less the triumph of an alien and incomprehensible doctrine called Marxism than the victory of a system that could be employed to unify nationalism and eradicate imperialism in China. Indeed, the strategies that the Russians pursued in China were essentially aimed at eliminating the influence of their Western and Japanese rivals even more than establishing a Chinese brand of communism.

Significantly, the earliest enthusiasts for the Russian Revolution in China were two Peking University scholars who frankly admitted their ignorance of Marxism. One was Li Ta-chao, the university librarian and later history professor, who had evolved an abstract theory of man's relations with historic forces and the role of "the people" in society. The other was Ch'en Tu-hsiu, head of the University Literature Department and editor of *New Youth*, who had long believed that Western democracy and science could create a new order in China. In the spring of 1918, though not entirely convinced by communism despite their admiration for the Bolsheviks, they set up a Society for the Study of Marxism. It was the forerunner of the Chinese Communist Party, to be founded three years later. Among its members was Mao Tse-tung, who had just arrived in Peking and was employed as an assistant in Li's library.

Mao may have found the Marxist study sessions too tame. Perhaps he was troubled by his lowly status as a library assistant, which earned him rather humiliating treatment from the haughty university scholars. Sharing a bedroom with seven friends and trying to subsist on a monthly wage of eight dollars, he may have wanted to escape his miserable living conditions. Whatever the motive, he was restless. At one point, he considered going to France on a so-called "work and study" program—as did later Communist luminaries like Chou En-lai, Ch'en Yi, and Li Fu-ch'un—but evidently decided that he lacked the talent to learn foreign languages. Instead, he chose to return to Changsha as a primary-school teacher.

There he began to read the translations of Marxist texts, then being circulated in China for the first time. There, too, he formed youth groups and even mobilized a student strike against a brutal provincial warlord. Defying the warlord's ban on his writing, Mao also contributed articles to local publications, including a magazine sponsored by the Yale University educational mission to China. One of these articles, hailing the Russian Revolution, stressed that the organization of people according to their social class was the key to unity and ultimate success.[17] That thesis, clearly inspired by Marx, lent substance to Mao's later disclosure that he had come to consider himself a Marxist "in theory and to some extent in action" by the summer of 1920.[18] Soon afterward, he claimed to head a Communist faction in Hunan—even though a national Communist Party had not yet been founded.

In Changsha, having repudiated the marriage arranged by his parents when he was fourteen, Mao wed Yang K'ai-hui, the daughter of the Hunanese professor who had befriended him during his first year at the Normal School. A decade later, Yang K'ai-hui and Mao's sister, Tse-hung, were arrested by the pro-Nationalist governor of Hunan and executed. In 1957, sending condolences to the wife of a comrade who had also died, Mao recalled Yang K'ai-hui in a sentimental poem:

> My proud poplar is lost to me,
> and to you your willow;
> Poplar and willow
> soar to the highest heaven.[19]

If Chinese radicals and reformers were infected by the messianic message of the Russian Revolution, the Bolsheviks were beginning to be fascinated by the possibilities of political action in China and elsewhere in the Far East. In a heated strategy debate at the Second Comintern Congress in July 1920, it was determined largely on Lenin's insistence that the International and local Communist groups should collaborate with "national revolutionary" movements in colonial areas, regardless of their ideological coloration. This decision was to have far-reaching consequences in China, for it laid the basis from which the Kremlin could, in the name of a "united front," subordinate the Chinese Communists to Chiang Kai-shek's Kuomintang whenever Soviet interests so demanded. Even at the outset, Comintern agents sent to the Orient seemed to play a deceptive game with their potential protégés as they sought to muster a wide spectrum of "nationalist" sympathy for the Soviet Union.

The first of these Comintern operatives, Gregory Voitinsky, reached China in the summer of 1920. He went straight to Li Tachao and Ch'en Tu-hsiu, the founders of the Society for the Study of Marxism, and proceeded to guide them in the establishment of a Chinese Communist Party. It was by no means an easy task. Among other things, an organization was difficult to shape since so many candidates for Party membership were undisciplined radicals with only the vaguest notions of Marxist-Leninist doctrine. Finally, in July 1921, the first Chinese Communist Party Congress assembled at a girls' school inside Shanghai's French Concession. Among those present were two delegates from each of the six self-styled Communist factions in China, with Mao representing the Hunan contingent. Also attending were Voitinsky and a recently arrived Dutch agent, Henrik Sneevliet, alias Maring. The whole affair had a faintly comic character. Sniffed out by the police, the delegates fled the city and eventually, pretending to be taking a holiday excursion, completed their sessions on a boat in the middle of the famous lake near Hangchow, in nearby Chekiang province. The Congress announced the Party's intention to "overthrow the capitalist classes" while showing an "attitude of independence, aggression, and exclusion" that would "allow no relationship with other parties or groups." [20]

While the Comintern operatives had encouraged the Chinese Communist notion of exclusivity, they themselves had no such idea in mind for Soviet strategy. On the contrary, the Russian objective was to accept support wherever it could be found. Earlier, the Soviet Foreign Minister, G. V. Chicherin, had attempted a dual approach by simultaneously indicating a desire for normal diplomatic relations both with the recognized Chinese regime in Peking and with Sun Yat-sen's opposition Kuomintang based in Canton. Now, after the Congress of the new Chinese Communist Party had ended, Maring embarked upon a similar zigzag. Traveling south, he sounded out such figures as Wu P'ei-fu, the British-backed warlord of central China, and the governor of Hunan, Chao Heng-ti, later to become Mao's principal foe in the province. Eventually Maring met with Sun Yat-sen. The result of his mission, after lengthy negotiations, was an arrangement under which the Soviet Union would assist Sun's government with military aid and advisers, the most notable of whom would be Michael Borodin. In May 1924, the Kremlin broadened its options in China by establishing formal diplomatic ties with the very Peking regime that Sun was seeking to overthrow.

As for the Communists, they were directed by Moscow to cooperate by becoming a "bloc within" the Kuomintang—or, in effect, diluting their identity as a Party. When some Chinese Communists protested at a Comintern meeting held in Moscow in 1922, Karl Radek put them down with a blistering report: "Comrades, do not indulge in too rosy expectations, do not overestimate your strength. . . . You must understand, comrades, that neither the question of socialism nor of the Soviet Republic [in China] are the order of the day." [21] The Russians communicated virtually the same message in a different context to Sun Yat-sen when, seeking to allay his fears of Kremlin domination, they assured him that they did not regard China as suitable terrain for "the communistic order or even the soviet system." [22]

Several of the Chinese Communists who would prove to be most durable over the years were those who collaborated wholeheartedly with the Kuomintang during that period. The suave, skillful Chou En-lai, who had recently returned to China from four years in Paris, became chief of the Political Department of the Kuomintang's military academy at Whampoa, outside Canton, serving under Chiang Kai-shek. Mao also cooperated energetically with the Kuomintang, displaying such organizational talent that he was elevated to the movement's Executive Central Committee as an alternate member. This promotion brought him under attack from Communists who deplored the loss of their independence, and for a time, he was accused of having shifted to the right. Yet Mao evidently believed, as did the Kremlin, that the Chinese Communists would ultimately take over the Kuomintang from within through patient, prudent infiltration. The failure of that strategy later made him suspicious of "united front" arrangements he could not control. And, along with other experiences, it led him to doubt the wisdom of Soviet prescriptions for China.

It was in the mid-1920s that Mao, now operating as a professional political activist, began to perceive that tremendous revolutionary dynamism could be unleashed through the mobilization of China's vast, impoverished peasant population. The notion was neither so heretical as some students of communism have contended, nor so original as Mao's personal publicists have claimed. Both Lenin and Stalin had recognized that peasants could play a revolutionary role in underdeveloped areas. So had many early Chinese Communists, among them a landlord's son by the name of P'eng P'ai, who had created associations of discontented peasants in his native Kwangtung province in 1923. But in contrast and even in opposition to the Russians and many of his own comrades, who clung to the classical Marxist dogma that the urban proletariat must constitute the revolutionary vanguard, Mao introduced the proposition that the peasantry was potentially the backbone of the Chinese revolution. True to his dictum that theory is derived from direct observation, he first began to evolve this thesis from an examination of conditions in Hunan, his home province.

During the course of several visits to Hunan, Mao was impressed by the extent to which Hunanese peasants were rising in protest against local landlords and officials. This ferment accelerated in the autumn of 1926, when Chiang Kai-shek's Kuomintang legions, moving north from Canton in their expedition to eradicate warlords and unify China, inspired peasants in Hunan with the idea that a revolution had started that licensed them to overthrow their oppressive masters. Early in 1927, after a month spent investigating five counties in the province, Mao wrote a passionate report that laid the foundation for his lifelong conviction that rural rather than urban regions were the key centers of revolution not only in China but throughout the world. Predicting that the force of the peasants would "bury imperialism and militarism," he asserted that the value of any revolutionary party would be judged by its willingness to lead them. Further deviating from orthodox Marxism-Leninism, he neglected to affirm in his report that the peasants must be guided by the proletariat. Mao's report justified the "excesses" of peasant agitation in a celebrated passage expressing his doctrine that only "armed struggle" can bring about real change:

> A revolution is not a dinner party, or writing an essay, or painting a picture, or doing embroidery; it cannot be so refined, so

leisurely and gentle, so temperate, kind, courteous, restrained and magnanimous. A revolution is an insurrection, an act of violence by which one class overthrows another.[23]

Though the Kuomintang had initially encouraged peasant revolution in the southern province of Kwangtung, where destroying the propertied classes served its purposes, Chiang Kai-shek soon discovered as his armies moved northward that his officers were linked to local landlords. Thus he began to back away from the radical agrarian policies favored by the Communists. At the same time, he maneuvered adroitly through a period of confused political rivalries to unite both the right and left wings of his party against the Communists. He was helped in this by Stalin, who was persuaded that the Kuomintang had to be preserved for the sake of Soviet national interests as well as to reply to Trotsky's criticisms of his strategies. Increasingly isolated, the Chinese Communists were therefore easy prey for Chiang in April 1927, when he decided to suppress them completely. He delivered his most devastating blow in Shanghai. There, having secretly enlisted support beforehand from the foreign community and the city's underworld, he ruthlessly massacred the Communists, many of whom naïvely believed that he was still counting on their cooperation. Despite this debacle, Stalin continued to urge the remnant Communists to collaborate with the Kuomintang. Somewhat later, however, the Kremlin issued an ambiguous directive authorizing the remaining Communists to initiate military activities designed to set up "soviet" areas in the Chinese hinterlands.

In the summer of 1927, obedient to that directive, Mao mobilized four regiments of peasants, miners, and Kuomintang deserters, calling them the First Division of the First Peasants and Workers Army. Confident that the rural population would rally to his side at harvest time, he led these ragtag units into Hunan. Like the operation organized by Chou En-lai, Ho Lung, and Chu Teh a couple of months earlier against Nanchang, the capital of Kiangsi province, Mao's thrust ended in disaster. Expected assistance from workers in Changsha never materialized. Two of his regiments fell to fighting against each other, while two others were decimated by Kuomintang troops. Barely escaping capture himself, Mao managed to guide a thousand survivors up into Chingkangshan, a remote, precipitous mountain area that straddles the border between Hunan and Kiangsi provinces. There, in an impregnable fastness that recalled the rebel redoubt in *All Men Are Brothers,* Mao established a base. He was joined shortly afterward by other Communists seeking refuge. They included Chu Teh, the Szechwanese who had studied in Germany, as well as Ch'en Yi, who would become China's Foreign Minister in 1958, and Lin Piao, the brilliant soldier whom Mao in his closing years designated as his official successor.

The failure of the Autumn Harvest Uprising, as it became known, earned Mao a rebuke from the Communist Central Committee and dismissal from the Party's supreme Politburo. Undoubtedly reflecting Moscow's wishes, the Party also conferred the mantle of leadership on Li Li-san, one of Mao's former schoolmates from Hunan, who hewed to the Soviet line that the future of the revolution required the urban proletariat in the vanguard. For years after this, Mao's activities were so obscure that in March 1930, the Comintern published a long obituary reporting his death from consumption. During these years, however, Mao was using his enforced exile in the Chingkangshan wilderness to become familiar with the techniques of guerrilla warfare that would eventually give him the power to capture control of the Party. Lacking food and means of intelligence, he sought help from villagers in the mountain region. Accordingly, he devised his famous "three·rules and six injunctions," which warned his soldiers against such infractions as confiscating food and stealing "even a needle or a piece of thread from the people." Recognizing that he could not overcome the superiority of his adversaries by frontal assault, he devised the hit-and-run tactics summed up in his slogan: "The enemy advances, we retreat; the enemy halts, we harass; the enemy tires, we attack; the enemy retreats, we pursue."

Early in 1929, having decided that Chingkangshan was no longer suitable, Mao and Chu Teh led their force, now grown to about eleven thousand men, down to a new base area in southern Kiangsi province. There they proclaimed the formation of their "soviet." Meanwhile, other Communist groups were setting up bases elsewhere around the country. Ho Lung, who had been a bandit chieftain before becoming a Communist, organized his base along the border between Hupeh and Hunan provinces. A base under Fang Chih-min, another guerrilla leader, was created at the juncture of Chekiang and Anhwei provinces. By setting up these sanctuaries in provincial frontier regions, the Communists were able to slip into different jurisdictional areas in much the same way that American gangsters in the days before strong federal laws sought immunity by crossing state boundaries. The strategy of flexible, autonomous territorial bases proved to be effective. Between 1928 and 1933, Communist Party membership in China climbed from forty thousand to three hundred thousand. During the same period, the Communist Army's strength increased from roughly a thousand to about a hundred thousand rifles.

The growth of the Communist forces did not elude Chiang Kai-shek, who by then had jettisoned his Soviet advisers in favor of a German advisory mission headed by General Ludwig von Falkenhausen. Starting at the end of 1930, he launched a series of five so-called "bandit extermination campaigns" aimed at smashing Mao's Kiangsi sanctuary. The fifth and most intensive campaign was more than the Communists could endure. At least 2 million peasants in their region were killed or starved to death as the Kuomintang armies burned everything in sight. The Communists lacked a plausible strategy to counter this drive. Like Chiang Kai-shek, they were being counseled by a German—a Comintern agent named Otto Braun, who went under the Chinese *nom-de-guerre* of Li Teh. But unlike Chiang's adviser, Braun was a former schoolteacher with little military experience. He mistakenly convinced the Communists to defend every inch of their territory. As a result, Mao himself later conceded, they fought "stupidly" until they had no choice but to break through Kuomintang encirclement and embark without specific plans upon what would be hailed as their epic Long March.

The Long March has been compared to Hannibal's trek over the Alps and Napoleon's retreat from Moscow. It was probably more difficult than either. Lasting slightly more than a year, from October 1934 to October 1935, it propelled Mao and his followers six thousand miles from Kiangsi to northern Shensi province, where they established a temporary headquarters at Pao An before creating a permanent base at Yenan fourteen months later. During that year, the Communist force of ninety thousand men that had started out were reduced to about twenty thousand. For the journey was a series of running battles fought as the Communists crossed rivers, mountain ranges, and arid areas. "There were so very many battles," the veteran Communist General P'eng Teh-huai told Robert Payne. "Now, when I look back, it seems to be one enormous battle going on forever." [24]

Strenuous as it was, the Long March served Mao in several ways. It tested his senior officers, most of whom survived its ordeals to become the toughened elite of the Chinese Communist Party. It provided him with a truly heroic legend with which he could inspire later generations. It taught him valuable lessons in mobile warfare against a superior enemy. And it afforded him the opportunity to assert his unqualified leadership of the Chinese revolutionary movement. At Tsunyi, a captured town in the southern province of Kweichow, he convened a conference in January 1935 at which he finally subdued those who still favored urban revolution, and took over the Communist Party as Chairman of its Politburo.

In the closing years of his life, Mao would be depicted in millions of official posters, badges, and busts as an aging Adonis who combined the godlike attributes of infallible wisdom and unshakable strength. But at forty-three, when Edgar Snow encountered him at his northern Shensi base, Mao seemed "quite free from symptoms of megalomania." He was, as Snow described him, a "gaunt, rather Lincolnesque figure, above average height for a Chinese, somewhat stooping, with a head of thick black hair grown very long." He laughed easily at earthy jokes as he chain-smoked cigarettes, and he enjoyed nothing so much as Hunan's almost inedibly hot red peppers. Yet, in Snow's view, something about Mao suggested a "power of ruthless decision" when he deemed it necessary. Another American writer, Agnes Smedley, who saw Mao in Yenan, was similarly impressed. Initially repelled by Mao's inscrutable, faintly feminine characteristics, she found that "the sinister quality I had at first felt so strongly in him proved to be a spiritual isolation." Mao was respected rather than loved, Miss Smedley wrote, "as stubborn as a mule, and a steel rod of pride and determination ran through his nature. I had the impression he would wait and watch for years, but eventually have his way." [25]

Though he often gave an appearance of studied inactivity, Mao did more than wait and watch, especially after he shifted his base to Yenan in late 1936. Setting the example himself by tending a garden, he organized a system under which his soldiers farmed, raised livestock, sewed clothing, operated modest industrial workshops, and fulfilled other tasks. This drive for economic self-sufficiency was necessitated by the fact that the Yenan base was encircled and blockaded by Chiang Kai-shek's Nationalists. As they had in the Chingkangshan region, the Communists also expanded the area under their control by mobilizing peasant support. One of their methods for attracting peasants was an agrarian reform scheme designed to distribute land to tenants and to reduce rents. These and other such programs, carried out without the benefit of elaborate bureaucratic structures, confirmed in Mao the notion that spirit and will power could be more effective than institutions—and that notion remained with him through his later life.

Mao also read and wrote obsessively during the Yenan years. Edgar Snow reported that he would disappear for three or four nights of intensive reading whenever a visitor brought him new books. According to one of his aides, Mao worked almost steadily for nine days and nights in 1938 to complete his famous essay, *On Protracted War*. Virtually all his writing dealt with two broad subjects—military affairs and political questions. In the military realm, he emphasized many of his old principles of irregular warfare: that guerrillas must be fearless in their disdain for enemy weapons, yet cautious enough to avoid annihilation when confronted by a superior foe. In his political essays, Mao seemed to be groping to shape an ideological framework for the China he envisaged. Starting from Lenin's premise that revolution required a "bourgeois-democratic" stage before reaching socialism, he conceived of an initial phase called "new democracy." During this phase (which theoretically continued for at least two decades after Mao marched into Peking in 1949), the Kuomintang and other "bourgeois" movements were represented in the Chinese People's Political Consultative Conference even though that body was nothing more than an instrument of the Communists.

As the legend of Mao spread, more and more teachers, students, artists, and other educated Chinese streamed into Yenan. Their pilgrimage had one important effect on Mao's personal life—and, three decades later, on the life of all China. It brought into the region a minor movie actress from Shanghai by the name of Lan P'ing, who evidently believed that she could improve her career under Communist auspices. While not beautiful, she was tall, graceful, and infinitely more appealing than the unkempt female guerrillas in the area. Mao, then in his mid-forties, was roughly twice Lan P'ing's age. Their flirtation encountered complications, however. He was then married to Ho Tzu-cheng, his third wife, a former schoolteacher and Communist organizer who had borne him five children, one of them while making the Long March. Her rugged life had ruined her health. Whether Mao sent her to the Soviet Union for medical treatment before or after meeting Lan P'ing has never been clear. In any case, he eventually divorced Ho to wed Lan P'ing, to whom he gave the alias Chiang Ch'ing, or "green river," from a couplet in one of his favorite T'ang poems. It was under that name that she would become celebrated as the termagant of the Cultural Revolution.

The flow into Yenan of "intellectuals"—meaning, by Chinese measure, anyone with at least secondary schooling—also had important ideological consequences. These educated, urban Chinese contrasted sharply with the rugged, often illiterate peasants who had risen to posts of authority in the Communist ranks. Moreover, many of them were equipped with an academic knowledge of Marxism-Leninism that was largely alien to the "concrete" Chinese situation of the time.

Despite his revolt against Confucian tradition, Mao respected the role that intellectuals had played in reforming Chinese society over the centuries. But he recognized that one of China's ancient plagues was the wide gap that separated the educated classes of the cities from the majority of peasants. He therefore urged, as he would repeatedly in the years to come, that the intellectuals who had rallied to his side be indoctrinated so that "they gradually overcome their weaknesses, revolutionize their outlook, identify themselves with the masses, and merge with the older Party members and cadres, and the worker and peasant members of the Party." [26]

He also began to stress the need for the "Sinification of Marxism" in order to provide his Communist Party with an independent philosophy derived from the "concrete conditions and struggles of China" rather than Soviet doctrine. Criticizing comrades who "can only repeat quotes from Marx, Engels, Lenin, and Stalin from memory but . . . understand very little or nothing about their own history," he asserted that Marxism could only function in a "national form." He said: "We must discard our dogmatism and replace it by a new and vital Chinese style and manner, pleasing to the eye and to the ear of the Chinese common people." [27]

This effort to persuade his educated recruits to discard foreign models in favor of Chinese realities prompted Mao to launch a "rectification campaign" in February 1942, which, seen in retrospect, was an early forerunner of the Cultural Revolution. Its aim was "thought reform"—a therapeutic process through which, as Benjamin Schwartz has explained, the Chinese intelligentsia could undergo moral cultivation and thereby acquire what Mao considered to be proper "proletarian" attitudes.[28] For, unlike Marx and Lenin, whose ideas were basically materialistic, Mao came to regard "proletarian" as denoting a spiritual state of mind rather than an economic class. He had already begun to formulate his thesis that the mechanics of the Communist Party organization were far less vital than the quality of its members.

The attempt to give his concept of communism a distinctly national—and implicitly superior—flavor also induced Mao to promote himself as a new species of Chinese hero. He therefore initiated a cult of his own personality that was to build up to fantastic proportions in his final years. Though Edgar Snow had observed no hero-worship of Mao in 1936 in Yenan, Communist army publicists a few years later began to extol him as "our brilliant great leader, our teacher and our savior." This adoration was apparently not shared by the Communist Party apparatus, however. Central Committee resolutions omitted Mao's name, and the first edition of his *Selected Works* was issued in the period after 1944 by a regional branch rather than by the Party headquarters in Yenan.[29] Even in those days, there may have been incipient divisions between Mao and the Party stalwarts headed by Liu Shao-ch'i, as the Red Guards would allege during the Cultural Revolution.[30] Subtle differences also separated Liu from Mao at the Party's Seventh Congress in April 1945. The Party officially enshrined Mao's "theory of revolution" in its new Constitution, and Liu praised him as "not only the greatest revolutionary and statesman in Chinese history but also its greatest theoretician and scientist." [31] Yet Liu, the quintessential organization man, also affirmed in his report to the Congress that it was "impossible" that the Party could stray from the "correct political line"; the interests of the Party and the people were identical. In short, Liu adhered to Lenin's belief in the inviolable Party vanguard—and this would eventually bring him into collision with Mao's conviction that only the masses, with himself as their spokesman, were infallible.

On the battlefield, meanwhile, the Communists made phenomenal progress from the mid-1930s until 1945 as a result of three factors—their own strategies, Chiang Kai-shek's failures, and the devastation caused by the Japanese invasion of China. A combination of circumstances rather than Mao's purported infallibility propelled the Communists forward. Still, Mao was able to consolidate his gains by shrewdly taking advantage of those circumstances as they emerged.

A triangular conflict menaced China in late 1936, as Mao was moving his north Shensi base from Pao An to Yenan. The Japanese, having occupied the northeastern region of Manchuria five years earlier, were threatening to descend into China to challenge both Mao's Communists and Chiang's Nationalists, who were fighting each other. Mao, evidently expecting their initial attack to strike his territory, was anxious to respond to the Japanese in coalition with Chiang. The Comintern, then favoring "united-front" tactics throughout the world, also advocated this approach. But Chiang still gave priority to his "bandit-suppression campaign," as he labeled his effort to liquidate the Communists. Finally, a dramatic incident intervened to force Chiang's hand.

Marshal Chang Hsueh-liang, a Manchurian warlord saddened by the loss of his homeland and captivated by Mao's pleas for unity against the Japanese, kidnaped Chiang at Sian, the ancient capital not far from Yenan. Planning to prosecute Chiang, the Marshal invited the Communists to take part in the "people's trial." But Chou En-lai, then chief political commissar for the Communist

Army, took a different tack. Possibly acting on Kremlin orders,[32] he offered to spare Chiang on condition that the Nationalists halt the civil war and concentrate instead on a joint defense against the Japanese. In exchange, Chou pledged that the Communists would cease their attempts to overthrow the Nationalist regime and place their army, henceforth to be designated as the Eighth Route Army, under Chiang's command. Chiang accepted, and was freed. Later, though he remained loyal to the principle of an anti-Japanese alliance, Mao apparently recalled Chiang's betrayal of the Communists a decade earlier and refused to subordinate the leadership of his troops to the Nationalists. The wrangling over that point later blocked the formation of a coalition government and brought down the "united front."

If the deal between the Communists and the Nationalists seemed to favor Chiang in the short run, it proved to be a boon to Mao over the longer term. For, by operating in the countryside, he could use the patriotic and nationalistic appeal of the struggle against the alien Japanese to win the support of peasants who might otherwise have been unmoved by Communist ideology or its promises of social and economic justice. And the Japanese unwittingly assisted Mao by focusing on him as their primary enemy, as well as by pursuing a scorched-earth strategy that drove peasants into the Communist ranks. As a consequence, the strength of the regular Communist army grew tenfold in eight years—from some fifty thousand in 1937 to about a half-million by 1945.[33] During the same period, the Communists spread out from Yenan and a few other small base areas to extend their control over 100 million people, or more than one-fifth of the Chinese population. Years later, when a Japanese visitor to Peking expressed regrets to him for Japan's aggression, Mao replied that, on the contrary, the invasion had helped rather than hindered his cause. "So instead of your apologizing to me," he told the Japanese, "perhaps I should thank you." [34]

From its outbreak in July 1937 until the American atomic blow against Japan ended it eight years later, the Sino-Japanese war was largely a *drôle de guerre*. Both Chiang and Mao had envisaged a "protracted resistance" divided into three stages: first, the Chinese would inflict heavy casualties on the advancing enemy from defensive positions; second, after stabilizing the front lines, they would open flanking attacks against the Japanese; and third, having weakened the enemy, they would launch a general counteroffensive. But in reality, the war consisted of an initial push by the Japanese, in which they captured China's key coastal cities, followed by a long stalemate.

The Nationalists, though receiving the bulk of American and Soviet aid, failed to undertake a single major action against the Japanese during the entire conflict. Their officers and men became soft and corrupt. When the Japanese staged a final offensive in the summer of 1944, the Nationalists lost seven hundred thousand troops, one hundred forty-six towns, and about a hundred thousand square miles of territory containing 60 million people in a matter of seven months.[35] By the end of that year, Chiang's army was described by one observer as "a pulp, a tired, dispirited, unorganized mass, despised by the enemy, alien to its own people, neglected by its government, ridiculed by its allies." [36]

The Communists, meanwhile, not only expanded in numbers but improved their military capabilities and structure. In September 1937, at the outset of the war, they gained an enormous psychological boost and immense prestige by routing a long Japanese column at Pinghsinkuan, a mountain pass in northern Shansi province. Three years later, they made an equally dramatic impact with their famous Hundred Regiments Offensive, which foiled Japanese plans to seize the 1940 autumn harvest in north China. For the most part, however, the Communists fought behind the lines, harassing the Japanese from increasingly widespread guerrilla sanctuaries. In contrast to the demoralized Nationalist troops, Communist soldiers were disciplined, highly motivated, and extraordinarily rugged. While organized into regular divisions, their army had as its core small squads, headed by Communist Party members, which facilitated constant political indoctrination. This indoctrination was so intensive that Evans Carlson, a United States Marine colonel and the first foreign military observer to reach the Communist zones, noted that soldiers often wore tracts pinned to the back of their caps so that the man behind could study political lessons during marches.[37] Another American military expert has pointed out that from the early 1930s onward the Communist army gradually shifted from a collection of guerrilla bands to a centralized, specialized, conventional, professional army.[38] This trend, which accelerated during the civil war and especially during the Korean War, was to bring Mao into conflict with several senior Chinese officers who gradually adopted the view that guerrilla techniques had become obsolete.

Just before and immediately after the Japanese surrender in late 1945, the United States sought to prevent a Chinese civil war by encouraging the Communists and Nationalists to reconcile their differences. Stalin, apprehensive lest an internal conflagration in China provoke American intervention and thereby involve the Soviet Union, was reported to have gone even further by urging Mao to dissolve his army and join Chiang Kai-shek's government. It may be, as Mao's supporters charged during the Cultural Revolution, that Liu Shao-chi and other high-level Chinese Communist Party figures were also in favor of a settlement. But neither the American Ambassador, Patrick Hurley, who was miscast for the assignment, nor General George C. Marshall, whose talents were keener, nor Stalin, Liu, and others could persuade the two Chinese adversaries to agree. Playing for time in the hope that the corrupt Nationalist regime would collapse, Mao seemed moderate in contrast to Chiang, whose awareness that the Communists could only grow in strength prompted him to behave more aggressively. The Nationalists in fact sparked the formal outbreak of the inevitable civil war in July 1946 when, fearing that the Communists were seeking to reinforce their units in Manchuria, they blocked their attempt to withdraw from central China to north of the Yangtze River.

Like the conflict against the Japanese, the civil war demonstrated the Communists' military skill and Nationalist incompetence. It also showed the extraordinary ability of the Communists to expand from numerical inferiority to superiority over the Nationalists. With about a half-million regular troops under arms at the outset of the war, the Communist force was one-fourth the size of the Nationalist army. By the middle of 1947, the Communists had nearly half as many men as the Nationalists. A year later, the two sides were almost equal in numbers—though the Communists, with their higher morale and better generalship, were plainly stronger.[39] Only Chiang Kai-shek, with his blind faith in his own invincibility, was unable to see that the Communists had virtually won the war by the end of 1948.

The respective strategies adopted by Mao and Chiang in the civil war were dictated by essentially the same geographical considerations that had guided the military policies of ambitious Chinese factions from ancient times. Just as the kingdoms based in western China followed a "horizontal" design in their conquests by pushing across the Yellow River plain to the sea, so the Communists sought to drive to the coast from their sanctuaries in Shensi and other interior provinces. And just as the southern states traditionally pursued a "vertical" pattern aimed at stretching their command over the north, so the Nationalists tried to extend their control from Canton upward into Manchuria.

The Communists, in their retrospective analysis of what they called the "third revolutionary war," viewed the conflict as having passed through three successive stages. This analysis fit Mao's theory that an inferior force could only defeat a bigger enemy through a gradual process calculated to shift the balance of power in its favor. Largely because of Nationalist blunders, the process went faster in the civil war than Mao had anticipated. In November 1948, he noted that "the war will be much shorter than we originally estimated." [40]

The first stage, beginning with the eruption of hostilities in July 1946, was a "defensive" interlude for the Communists. Instead of striving to acquire territory, they worked to consolidate their own positions while reducing Chiang's numerical superiority by nibbling at his weakest points. Accordingly, they deliberately withdrew from several areas, including their celebrated Yenan headquarters—a tactic that the deluded Nationalists erroneously hailed as a sign of imminent victory. During this period, too, Chiang undertook a move that provided the Communists with a decisive advantage later. Defying American advice, he sent his best troops deep into Manchuria, thereby putting an enormous strain on his supply lines.

In the summer of 1947, the Communists entered their second stage by launching a limited counteroffensive against the provinces of central China and the principal railways used by Chiang to supply his forces in the north. This maneuver was prompted by the accurate assumption that Chiang had seriously overtaxed his communications capabilities by moving his troops into Manchuria, and consequently had increased the vulnerability of his rear areas. At the end of the year, though still engaged in mobile rather than positional warfare, the Communists captured the key railway juncture of Shihchiachung, in Hopei province south of Peking. Chiang could no longer move equipment or reinforcements northward except by air, an inadequate means of transportation in those days.

By mid-1948 the Nationalists were clearly on the defensive, their most effective units helplessly tied up in Manchuria and northern China, their troops weary and demoralized. While rampant infiltration and corruption ravaged his regime, Chiang committed such irreparable political mistakes as outlawing innocuous liberal movements and thereby driving their members into the Communist ranks. At this point, the Communists initiated their final strategic stage with a series of campaigns that carried them through central and eastern China. By this time, Chiang had fled to Taiwan, and Mao, disregarding the advice of Stalin as well as some of his own comrades, ordered the capture of Nanking, the Nationalist capital. A few months afterward, he would be in Peking, his own capital, as chief of state of the People's Republic of China.[41] Now, as he stood on the brink of triumph after nearly a whole life devoted to struggle, he paused to compose a poem in which a line would depict his future as it did his past:

> The true way that governs the world of men is that of
> radical change.[42]

CHAPTER 4

Cracks in the Monolith

There is no such thing as a perfect leader,
either in the past or present, in China or
elsewhere. If there is one, he is only pretending, like a pig inserting scallions into its nose
in an effort to look like an elephant.

—LIU SHAO-CH'I, July 13, 1947

ON A HOT EVENING in September 1964, a delegation of French
officials was ushered into the *salon* of an unpretentious bun-
galow near Hangchow, a scenic resort in central China. The room
was modestly furnished with overstuffed armchairs, small tea
tables, and a sprinkling of strategically located enamel cuspidors.
In contrast to nearly every dwelling in China, no portrait of Mao
Tse-tung gazed down from the wall. For this was Mao's summer
residence adjoining the same lake where, more than four decades
earlier, his embryonic Communist Party had held its first meeting
disguised as a holiday excursion. Soon Mao himself, the living legend, shuffled stiffly in to welcome his guests.

Mao was approaching the age of seventy-two at the time, and
one of the guests, observing him carefully, speculated that there
must have been a grain of truth in the rumors then circulating that
he had suffered a mild stroke or heart attack not long before. He
was much thinner than his photographs depicted him, his baggy
brown tunic and trousers reinforcing the impression that he had
lately lost a good deal of weight. Presumably defying doctor's orders,
he chain-smoked a Chinese brand of Virginia cigarette, his right
hand trembling as he lighted one after another. He walked with

difficulty, guided by a male nurse who tactfully held his elbow when he first entered the *salon* and again as the group later moved to an adjacent dining room.

If Mao looked unhealthy, the conversation that evening also suggested that he felt disappointed, perhaps even frustrated, as he sensed his life drawing to a close. For at dinner, slurping his soup, belching unabashedly, and picking his broken black teeth, he repeatedly focused on a subject that appeared to obsess him—the danger that China, growing soft and complacent in the absence of hardship, might betray his hopes following his death. He seemed to be worried that the Communist Party, after fourteen years in power, was degenerating into a bureaucracy as rigid and ritualistic as the ancient Chinese mandarinate. He seemed apprehensive as well that the People's Liberation Army, its very name now an anachronism, was becoming flabby for lack of combat experience. Above all, Mao made no secret of his fear that China's younger generation might fail to uphold his concept of perpetual revolution and turn instead to the Soviet type of revisionism that, he believed, would inevitably lead back to feudalism and capitalism.

When one of the Frenchmen described the "ardor and spirit" he had found among the Peking University professors and students with whom he had talked, Mao brushed aside the comment with unusual rudeness. "What they told you isn't necessarily the truth," he remarked. "It's not a good university." Another guest, who praised the students he had visited at the Sian Polytechnical Institute, provoked an equally skeptical reply. "Of course they sounded fine to you, but don't believe everything you hear," Mao grumbled. Then, his high-pitched nasal voice tinged with melancholy, he went on to catalogue the shortcomings of China's youth. "They know nothing of war and revolution, landlords and rich peasants," he said. "They must learn to struggle. Maybe they will learn. . . ." [1]

A similar note of uncertainty echoed through Mao's interviews with other foreign visitors to China during that period. Speaking with Edgar Snow in late 1964, for example, he deplored the fact that Chinese youth had never fought a war or been oppressed by imperialism and capitalism, and were only acquainted with the "old society" from history books. Thus it was possible, Mao said, that China's younger generation might negate the revolution after his disappearance.[2] He also complained to André Malraux that his adversaries inside China—"the bourgeois-nationalists, the intellectuals and so on"—were indoctrinating their children to oppose his policies. The "youth problem" had yet to be solved, he asserted, adding ominously, "Youth must be put to the test."[3] But perhaps Mao's feeling that he had to act quickly to reverse China's revisionist drift was reflected most clearly in a poem he wrote in early 1963:

> So many deeds cry out to be done,
> And always urgently;
> The world rolls on,
> Time presses.
> Ten thousand years are too long,
> Seize the day, seize the hour! . . .
> Away with all pests!
> Our force is irresistible.[4]

Though the pressures of advanced age and probable illness had undoubtedly exacerbated Mao's mood, his impatience was not merely a symptom of an old man's crankiness. For, it was later evident, he had ample reason to believe that his dreams for China were being subverted by many of his veteran comrades as well as by large segments of the Chinese people. In a sense, he had become a victim of his own success.

The Communist victory had given China in the years after 1949 greater domestic strength and international stature than that land had known since the zenith of the Ch'ing dynasty in the eighteenth century. In Mao's view, however, these accomplishments were insufficient. Hoping to shape a new human species cleansed of individualistic and materialistic tendencies, he sought to perpetuate his kind of spiritual revolution. But this aim soon met with passive and sometimes active resistance from numbers of Chinese peasants, workers, and particularly intellectuals who had supported the Communists less for Mao's ideological theories than for their ability to bring peace and order to China after decades of war and civil strife. More significantly, important factions in China's Communist Party, government, and Army also came to question and even reject Mao's principles, contending that the management of a country demanded organization, specialization, and bureaucratic routine rather than his mass-mobilization schemes, indoctrination campaigns, and moral exhortations. Still, Mao refused to alter his vision. The more he perceived real or imagined opposition to his ideas, the more he was confirmed in his conviction that the Chinese mentality needed a thorough transformation. Nothing less than a complete change in China's psyche—a "cultural revolution" that would "touch people to their very souls," as he put it—was imperative.

No ruling group, however monolithic it may seem, is without tensions capable of reaching the intolerable proportions that cause overt conflict. In the case of China, the Communist leaders succeeded in tolerating internal stresses and strains for years, even to the extent of appearing to the world to be an extraordinary model of unity. In fact, political, military, and economic strategy disputes had divided Mao and his associates more than once during the decades before they rose to power. And these disputes continued after the establishment of their regime in Peking.

In contrast to the Bolsheviks, who had no real political, economic, social, or administrative experience before seizing the Kremlin, the Chinese Communists had commanded territory and people ever since their retreat into their mountainous Chingkang-shan redoubt in 1927. After officially proclaiming the Chinese People's Republic on October 1, 1949, they were able to extend to a national scale many of the control methods they had employed for two decades.

With Mao as its Chairman, the Communist Party was the locus of power, exercising authority through its own apparatus as well as through the government and Army. Party representatives operated within state agencies, factories, and schools and, as commissars, inside every Chinese military unit. By liquidating a million or more landlords in the early 1950s, the Communists destroyed the rural gentry, thereby permitting the Party hierarchy to reach from the supreme Politburo in Peking down to the lowest village cadre. The Party also directed a formidable array of labor, youth, artistic, and other nationwide federations, each with millions of members, designed to manipulate public opinion every time a new policy was set in motion. The entire population was consequently exposed to continual study sessions, meetings, demonstrations, and rallies. Combined with "thought-reform" programs and vast mobilization movements, these exercises were essentially calculated to create a new environment in which, theoretically at least, the individual could not escape absorption into the "masses."

This complicated system initially appeared to be highly effective, for two main reasons. First, the new Chinese leaders had been forged in the same furnace. Almost all had served as soldiers, surviving the Long March and fighting the Japanese before finally conquering Chiang Kai-shek's Nationalists. As a result, they seemed to be an exceptionally solid group. Second, their functions overlapped and intertwined so intimately that it was difficult to discern possible splits among them. Most key Army officers and government figures were also Party dignitaries, while most Party members held Army or government positions. This was particularly true in the provinces, where Party, government, and Army organizations were closely related. Mao himself personified this multiplicity of roles, serving simultaneously until 1959 as chief of state and Party Chairman.

But this structure was less homogeneous than it seemed to be. A good deal of friction troubled the Communist movement prior to 1949 as the Party gradually acquired the bureaucratic trappings of a large, compartmentalized institution. As a consequence, it no longer fit Mao's Yenan ideal of a flexible guerrilla-style force adept at handling political, economic, and social as well as military tasks. In short, as he saw and deplored it, the romantic rebels of *All Men Are Brothers* had turned into prosaic functionaries.

The bureaucratic trend was especially pronounced in the Communists' Red Army, whose officers had grown inclined over the years to adopt what Mao persistently criticized as a "bourgeois military mentality." In the beginning, when they lacked manpower and matériel, Communist officers could make a virtue of necessity by accepting Mao's strategy of small-unit, hit-and-run warfare. But as their legions expanded in the early 1930s, they began to question Mao's emphasis on the importance of ideology and the primacy of men over weapons. Comintern advisers like Otto Braun, alias Li Teh, taught them conventional Soviet military tactics. They were also influenced by the idea prevalent among soldiers everywhere that rank, regulations, modern equipment, and professional status are desirable. Moreover, they learned from battlefield experience against both the Nationalists and the Japanese that large-scale deployments of trained, disciplined regulars were more effective than ragtag guerrilla actions. Even a general like Ho Lung, the prototype of the Maoist peasant soldier, had lost respect for guerrilla techniques by the time he was able to lead regular Eighth Route Army troops against the Japanese in Hopeh province in 1938.[5]

Disagreements over military strategy produced some of the earliest rifts between Mao and his comrades. In the late 1920s, for example, the prestigious Chu Teh disregarded his guerrillas, preferring instead to fight conventionally against the Nationalists, then attempting to dislodge the Communists from their Kiangsi base area. This "bourgeois" approach earned Chu a rebuke from Mao.[6] Questions of military policy were again involved in the early 1930s, when rival Party and Army figures, including Chou En-lai, temporarily stripped Mao of his authority.[7]

Professionalized officers also challenged Mao by rejecting or reducing whenever possible the power of political representatives attached to their units. The introduction of commissars into the Army, originally conceived in the mid-1920s by both the Communists and the Nationalists, reflected an ingrained Chinese suspicion that soldiers were men whose loyalties were only to themselves. Like the Catholic priests who accompanied the Spanish conquistadores in their conquest of America, the commissars were charged with guaranteeing fidelity to the cause—or, in Mao's imagery, with assuring that the Party "commands the gun." In practice, however, their presence in units frequently led to internal clashes of authority. During periods when Mao's line prevailed, commissars often nagged officers and even tried to direct their strictly military operations. At other times, when Army professionals had the upper hand, the commissars were relegated to minor assignments. Rarely did the two groups manage to work out a durable relationship, perhaps because their roles were basically incompatible.

Before 1949, meanwhile, there were other esoteric forewarnings of the cataclysmic dispute that would erupt later between Mao and the Communist Party *apparatchiks* headed by Liu Shao-ch'i.

Their rivalry was scarcely a simple contest for authority, though that was certainly part of the quarrel. It was largely rooted in divergent concepts of the function of the Party, and, consequently, the controversy had extremely broad implications. For the crucial question of which direction China would take fundamentally depended upon whether Mao or the Party predominated.

As Stuart Schram has written, Mao never really perceived the Party in the full Leninist sense to be a strong, self-sustaining central organization, a kind of Mother Church. Nor did he, like Lenin, view the Party's vocation to be the essentially political task of mobilizing and guiding the proletariat. Mao's belief, based on his experience, was that only "armed struggle" could achieve victory— or, as he put it, "political power grows out of the barrel of a gun." [8] Thus he attached enormous importance to the Army, without which, in his words, "the people have nothing." [9] If the Party "commands the gun," it was a Party that he considered to be his personal instrument. The Party line was his line. Allegiance to the Party signified obedience to him as the author of the correct ideology. [10]

In short, Mao was persuaded, pre-eminence belonged to the leader rather than to the Party machine. Just as in later years he obliquely attacked his Chinese adversaries for revisionism by criticizing Khrushchev, so Mao indirectly promoted the cult of his own personality by praising Stalin. He had no reason to revere Stalin, who had repeatedly tried to subvert his policies, yet, celebrating the Soviet dictator's sixtieth birthday in December 1939, Mao referred to him as the "commander of the revolutionary front," and "leader of the world revolution," adding, "Marx is dead, and Engels and Lenin too are dead. If we did not have a Stalin, who would give the orders?" [11]

Mao would demonstrate that concept of leadership most dramatically in 1959 when, facing censure by prominent Party and military comrades following the collapse of his ambitious "Great Leap Forward," he threatened to quit Peking, return to his Chingkangshan redoubt, raise a new peasant force, and fight his way back to power. [12] Though that tactic may have been a bluff, Mao still thought of himself as a unique figure towering above the Party apparatus. Perhaps it was no accident that, sounding like General de Gaulle, he said to André Malraux: "I am alone with the masses." [13]

Such a posture was plainly more than any bureaucracy could abide. Hence there was a certain plausibility to the documents issued during the Cultural Revolution indicating Liu Shao-ch'i and his Party colleagues for having persistently betrayed Mao. But these differences, to whatever degree they existed, were latent for years. Mao plainly would not have hailed Liu's contributions to the movement in his "revised" history of the Party had he suspected him of treason. Nor would he have left Liu in charge of the Yenan headquarters when he descended to Chungking in August 1945 to negotiate with Chiang Kai-shek. Moreover, Mao implicitly designated Liu as his successor in early 1950 by delegating him to serve as acting chief of state when he went to Moscow to sign a treaty with the Soviet Union. Yet there is no doubt that Liu did disagree with several of Mao's basic tenets at certain critical stages in their relationship. It seems clear that key figures within the Communist movement could develop sharply contrasting ideas despite similarities in background and experience.

Five years Mao's junior, Liu was also born of well-to-do peasant parents in Hunan province, just across a mountain range from the Mao family farm. Like Mao, he attended the Normal School at Changsha, the provincial capital, though there is no evidence that they knew each other there. In all probability, they did not become acquainted until 1922, when Liu was assigned to organize coal miners in the region of Hunan, where Mao was then secretary of the embryonic Party's district committee. Before that, Liu's activities in the Communist movement had been limited. He had helped to set up workers' schools in the suburbs of Peking, and, selected by the Kremlin agent in China, Gregory Voitinsky, he had spent less than a year in Moscow studying economics and labor questions at the so-called University of the Toilers of the East, a Soviet school for prospective Communist cadres from Asia. From all accounts, Liu was disappointed by his sojourn in Russia. He was there during a winter of severe famine, with little more than potatoes and black bread to eat. He could not speak the language, and found the Russians too preoccupied with their own dire problems to befriend a shy, awkward, lonely Chinese. In addition, the university courses created for Asians were mainly propaganda meetings in which nothing of real substance was taught. Nevertheless, Liu's visit to

Moscow was significant. For it introduced him to Leninist ideology, from which he derived a lifelong conviction in the primacy of the Party as the dominant force in the struggle to achieve revolution.

In contrast to Mao, who concentrated on mobilizing peasant support from the start of his revolutionary career, Liu devoted most of the fifteen years after returning to China from the Soviet Union in 1922 to organizing urban workers. He lived a furtive underground existence under an assortment of aliases, darting from one city to another to elude either Nationalist agents or European police, and occasionally going to jail. In 1928, he was elected to the Party's Central Committee and, four years later, to the Politburo. By the late 1930s, having repaired to Yenan, he appeared to be Mao's second-in-command.

Definite temperamental differences separated the two men. Mao's charismatic character exuded magnetism, but Liu was introverted, taciturn, and, as an old comrade recalled from their early days together, "a bit too glum and devoid of youthfulness." [14] Counterpointing Mao's dazzling creativity, Liu was a plodder who depended on sheer hard work rather than brilliance. For a long time, however, these differences complemented rather than contradicted each other. If Mao was the yogi, Liu was the commissar and, on the surface at least, they seemed to operate in harmony.

But this harmony, like the apparent cohesion of the Chinese Communist movement itself, was deceptive—or, at best, transient. According to Chang Kuo-t'ao, one of the founders of the Party and the only prominent Communist official to defect to the West, Liu was critical of Mao's strategies as far back as 1937, when he first reached Yenan. In a still unpublished report reviewing the Communist movement's conduct over the previous sixteen years, Liu indirectly blamed Mao for encouraging peasant uprisings and creating rural bases on the grounds that these moves represented "leftist adventurism." Chang also disclosed that Mao, unwilling to risk further trouble at a time when his own authority was shaky, sought to win Liu over to his side rather than dispute with him openly. He accepted Liu's criticism and guaranteed his Politburo position. In turn, Liu agreed to an accommodation.[15] However, in a series of lectures delivered in Yenan in July 1939, Liu made it plain that he still did not fully subscribe to Mao's notions of leadership or his populist principles.

Published as a book entitled *How to Be a Good Communist*, the lectures repeatedly referred to Marx, Engels, Lenin, and Stalin, and they even quoted lavishly from Confucius and Mencius. Yet mention of Mao's role in the Communist movement or his theories of "class struggle" was conspicuously absent. Instead, Liu stressed the Leninist orthodoxy that the Party must be upheld as a disciplined organization that demands obedience from all its members. "Every Party member must place himself within the Party in order to lead and urge forward the Party as a whole, and not outside the Party in order to lead it." In what would later be regarded as a shocking display of *lèse-majesté*, Liu did not hesitate to apply these rules to Mao himself:

> In our Party, there are no special privileges for individuals; any leadership which is not exercised in the name of the organization cannot be tolerated. Comrade Mao Tse-tung is the leader of the whole Party, but he too obeys the Party. . . .
>
> We obey the Party, we obey the Central Committee, we obey the truth; we do not obey individuals. No individual merits our obedience. Marx, Lenin, and Mao Tse-tung have done their work well; they represent the truth, and it is only for this reason that we obey them.[16]

In another passage, equally damaging to Mao's later claim to have inherited the mantle of Marx and Lenin and even to have surpassed them in creative originality, Liu singled out "some people" within the Communist movement who

> attempted to imitate in a superficial way certain styles of Marx and Lenin, picked up at random some Marxist-Leninist terminology, regarded themselves as the Marx and Lenin of China, posed as Marx and Lenin within the Party, and had the impudence to ask our Party members to respect them as we do Marx and Lenin, to support them as "leaders" and to offer them loyalty and devotion. They also made bold to appoint themselves as "leaders," climbed into responsible positions without waiting to be nominated by others, issued orders like patriarchs within the Party, attempted to teach our Party, abused everything within the Party and wilfully attacked, punished and rose roughshod over Party members. . . .

It is beyond doubt that this kind of people within the Party should be opposed, exposed and buried in oblivion by our Party members.[17]

Liu continued these veiled assaults against Mao in another series of lectures delivered in July 1941 and published later under the title *On Inner-Party Struggle*. Again, he made no mention of Mao's ideological contributions but inveighed against "some comrades" who regarded themselves as "revolutionary as revolutionary could be" and held that "the more bitter the inner-Party struggle, the better."

> To them, the more seriously the problem is brought up, the better; the more fault-finding, the better; the more high-sounding terms, the better; the more name-calling, the better; the more severe and the more rude the manner and the attitude, the better; the louder the voice, the better; the longer the fact, the better; the oftener the teeth are bared, the better.[18]

Within the next few years, however, Liu underwent a marked change. Evidently accommodating to new realities, he began to pay public tribute to Mao, who was then starting to glorify himself as he sought to endow his Communist movement with a distinctly national flavor. For the first time, in an essay written in 1943, Liu described Mao as a "resolute and great revolutionist" and urged Communists to "arm themselves" with his ideas in order to eradicate divisive "Menshevik" tendencies within the Party.[19] And at the Seventh Party Congress, held in April 1945, he extolled Mao in the loftiest language yet, calling him "not only the greatest revolutionary and statesman in Chinese history, but also its greatest theoretician and scientist." [20] His extravagant rhetoric notwithstanding, Liu subtly held back from total submission to Mao at the Congress by asserting the Party's infallibility as the vanguard of the masses and by scoffing at the Mao cult in colorfully pungent terms. On one occasion, he remarked, "There is no such thing as a perfect leader, either in the past or present, in China or elsewhere. If there is one, he is only pretending—like a pig inserting scallions in his nose in an effort to look like an elephant." [21]

When they proclaimed their People's Republic in 1949 in Peking, the traditional "northern capital," the Communists inherited a country in shambles. Since the turn of the century, China had been ravaged by revolution and internecine conflict, warlordism, foreign invasion, and chronic calamities like drought, flood, and famine. Unbridled inflation during the last days of Nationalist rule had paralyzed commerce and destroyed confidence in the money system. Such as it was, the Manchurian industrial base built up by the Japanese had been looted by the Soviet army of more than $2 billion worth of equipment. Dams, irrigation works, and canals had fallen into disrepair, and railroad lines had been cut and recut by contending armies. And the population, having suffered enormous casualties as a result of war and natural disasters, was dispirited, hungry, and exhausted. Still, the new Communist regime had important assets to bring to the immediate task of reconstruction.

First, large regions of rural China had escaped the turmoil, remaining relatively stable as they pursued their age-old patterns of agriculture, handicrafts, and internal trade. Second, because of its localized, cellular nature, Chinese society had a remarkably resilient capacity to rebuild itself after cyclical periods of turmoil. And finally, after years of governing the territories under their control, the Communists had experience as well as discipline, organization, and a sense of purpose. Thus they were able to meet the urgent challenge of rehabilitating China with extraordinary speed. It was during this phase of reconstruction, however, that Mao and his comrades began to revive many of the controversies that had troubled their earlier years and would later spiral into even more acerbic disputes.

The Communists scored impressive accomplishments soon after taking power. They stabilized the currency, repaired the railways, started an extensive public health and sanitation program, replaced corrupt local bureaucrats with relatively honest officials, and initiated a system for distributing available food and clothing equitably. Their hold on the nation consolidated, they embarked in 1952 upon a dynamic drive to develop heavy industry. Helped by the Soviet Union with loans, technical assistance, and blueprints, they went forth in dazzling style. Factory centers in Manchuria were restored and expanded, and new industrial areas were opened in Inner

Mongolia and the remote regions of the barren west. A town like Loyang, the ancient Han dynasty capital on the Yellow River, was transformed from a sleepy market place into a big city eight times its former size, its suburbs smoky with tractor, ball-bearing, and steel plants, its population a babel of Cantonese, Szechwanese, Mongolians, Hunanese—deliberately mixed up, as a European visitor observed, "like chemicals in a test tube." [22] So rapid was the industrial pace that coal could not be dug fast enough for the steel mills, and electric power was insufficient to satisfy the demands of textile plants and machine-tool factories. A British traveler to one booming town found workers at lathes while carpenters were still putting a roof over their heads.

This tremendous effort, announced in midstream to be China's First Five-Year Plan, yielded phenomenal industrial results. By 1957, when the Plan ended, iron and steel production had increased more than fourfold, while coal and cement output had doubled. According to the estimates of Western economists, the annual growth rate had averaged about 7 per cent—a performance so successful that India was inspired to shift the emphasis in its then forthcoming Five-Year Plan from agriculture to heavy industry. But despite the brilliance of their achievement, the Chinese leaders were locked at the time in serious policy disagreements that would ravage them in later years.

While not easily discernible as the Communists established their regime, one of the underlying problems in China from 1949 onward was the increasing authority of the People's Liberation Army in the provinces. The Army had fought the civil war against Chiang Kai-shek's Nationalists as a flexible conglomerate of disparate and autonomous "field" forces rather than as a monolith responsive to centralized orders. Each of these forces eventually conquered a particular area of the country, in which it created its own power base. Local officers developed vested interests in the regions under their command, and they were often able to exert decisive influence in the shifting disputes between Mao and the Party. In short, they became what Colonel William Whitson has called "Communist warlords"— even though, in contrast to China's earlier warlords, they were basically devoted to national unity.[23]

In some instances, the regional units of the People's Liberation Army were shaped by sophisticated figures like Ch'en Yi, the son of a wealthy Szechwanese landlord, who had studied in France before returning to China to join the Communist Party and acquire military experience. In other cases, disgruntled peasants, bandits, and others either anxious to right grievances or simply seeking adventure threw in their lot with leaders who in turn pledged allegiance to the Communist cause, frequently for expedient rather than ideological motives. Such a leader was Ho Lung, later to become a Politburo member and one of China's ten Marshals. The son of a poor Hunanese peasant, he was only sixteen when he killed a government official in a fight and fled into the mountains to begin years of wandering as a fugitive. By 1915, at the age of twenty-one, he had rallied a private army of twenty thousand men and was prominent in the Society of Elder Brothers, a secret fraternity active in Hunanese reformist movements. A decade later, with a short lifetime of rudderless rebellion behind him, Ho bequeathed himself and his troops to the Communists, assuming in the deal the title of commander of the Twentieth Corps of the Fourth Army Group. That this pretentious-sounding military unit was really Ho's private army under a formal designation was reflected in the fact that its officers included his older sister, the Annie Oakley of Hunan province.

After World War II, when the Communist struggle against the Nationalists intensified, the guerrilla bands of the type mobilized by Ho Lung had swelled into the five conventional Field Armies that comprised the Communist armed forces then demolishing Chiang Kai-shek's Nationalists. These Field Army formations were unique in two respects. First, virtually every senior Communist officer had spent his entire career in units that over a span of two decades had originated, expanded, and finally evolved into a single Field Army. A soldier like Wang Shang-jung, to cite an example, started out as one of Ho Lung's subordinates in 1927. More than twenty years later he was still associated with Ho as a Corps commander in the Third Field Army, a unit that traced its beginnings to Ho's private guerrilla band. Second, each Field Army remained attached to the regions in which it had first fought the Japanese and later the Nationalists. Having battled mostly in northwest and southwest China, members of the First Field Army were entrenched in those areas until the mid-1960s and even after. Similarly, Second Field Army officers were heavily represented in north-central China as well as in the border regions of Yunnan and Tibet, while Ch'en Yi's Third Field Army predominated in the coastal provinces it had conquered. The Fourth Field Army, headed by Lin Piao, had occupied Manchuria and the southern provinces. Nieh Jung-chen's Fifth Field Army, also known as the North China Field Army, was strong in the sector around Peking, where its precursor units had operated as far back as the 1930s.

One of the few veterans whose affiliations ranged well beyond a single Field Army formation was the tough, irascible P'eng Teh-huai. Like Ho Lung, with whom he was close, P'eng was a Hunanese peasant forced by poverty into banditry and later into soldiering. In 1928, with his own guerrilla band behind him, he joined Mao in the Chingkangshan redoubt, and though he quarreled with nearly everyone, his ability earned him promotion to deputy commander in chief of the Communist Army in the 1930s. As a result, P'eng was instrumental in organizing both the First and Second Field Armies, taking over as commander of the former. He later headed the Chinese "volunteers" sent into the Korean War, emerging in 1954 to become China's Defense Minister. But his devotion to the Army as a separate institution carried him into a fierce clash with Mao and, in 1959, P'eng was purged in the most critical shake-up to rock the regime until then. However, his relationships within the Army were so extensive that he remained a formidable adversary for Mao even after his dismissal.

Clearly, then, the Field Armies that constituted the main body of the Communist military force not only were composed of officers with tightly knit personal and professional ties built up over a generation, but were firmly implanted in the regions in which they had fought. The different regional commanders and their comrades represented potential "independent kingdoms," as Mao's propagandists later labeled those who opposed his authority. In most areas, moreover, local officers were intimately associated with the provincial Party apparatus, and their bonds were reinforced in the period after 1957 when, for a variety of reasons, political, economic, and military decentralization was accelerated. The intricate web that linked the Party the Army was not revealed until early

1967, however, when both resisted Mao and his Cultural Revolution from the regions in which their strength was so deeply rooted.

Some Western analysts have speculated that the Chinese decision to intervene in the Korean War in 1950 was partly prompted by Mao's determination to redeploy the Field Armies in order to dislodge them from their regional sources of power. If so, his elaborate effort was futile, since most of the Chinese officers and men who returned from Korea were reassigned to the areas they had left. In addition, all but one of the commanders appointed to head the thirteen Chinese military regions set up at the end of the Korean War in 1954 were still in office a decade later, and, in one way or another, most survived the turbulence of the Cultural Revolution.[24]

If the Korean War did little to uproot the army units from their provincial spheres of influence inside China, it did have a sharp impact on Chinese military thinking. After colliding with the dynamic American military colossus, professional Chinese soldiers emerged from Korea more doubtful than ever that the Maoist model of the invincible guerrilla armed primarily with proletarian *élan* could be effective. In the following years, senior Chinese officers treated Mao's precepts with increasingly open disdain as they turned to what he would later criticize as a "bourgeois military line."

Until October 1950, when their "volunteers" streamed across the Yalu River, the Communists had never engaged in contemporary warfare. Their conflict with the Japanese had been largely a stalemate interrupted by sporadic battles, while their war against the Nationalists was essentially against an enemy that was crumbling faster than it could be defeated. But in Korea, the Communists ran into American troops equipped with the latest weapons and backed up by an industrial machine able to give them enormous logistical support. Lacking tanks, artillery, and transport facilities, the Communists could only sacrifice huge numbers of men in "human-wave" tactics that, as one Chinese prisoner put it, were "indescribably miserable." [25] Even flying out of sanctuaries in Manchuria, which gave them the choice of both time and place of combat, the Chinese Air Force suffered losses at the rate of ten-to-one against American pilots. In short, the Communists were unable to match the superior firepower, technical skill, and supply system of the

United States, and the outcome was devastating. Though they held the United Nations coalition to a standstill, largely as a result of American restraint and eleventh-hour Soviet aid, the Chinese sustained more than a million casualties. Among the dead was one of Mao's sons, Mao An-ying, killed while piloting a fighter airplane. And in the end, what had been a relatively limited operation for the United States in twentieth-century terms was, as Frank Armbruster has observed, a "maximum, but obviously inadequate, effort" by the Peking regime.[26]

The Korean debacle prompted Chinese military leaders to reassess their strength and their strategies. No longer did they seriously credit Mao's thesis that American imperialism was a "paper tiger." Instead, urging "responsible officers" to give their men a "correct understanding of the American army," their directives began to stress more heavily the need for China to construct a "strong, modernized national defense." [27]

It would be a crude oversimplification to say that Mao totally disparaged the value of military expertise and that Chinese Army professionals rejected his focus on ideology. As early as 1949, Mao had underlined the necessity for China to develop a "completely modernized armed force," [28] approving programs to build nuclear bombs, missiles, and other sophisticated as well as conventional weapons. Meanwhile, even Chinese officers like P'eng Teh-huai accepted Mao's notion that political indoctrination was imperative for molding a soldier's spirit. Therefore, many of the differences between them were mainly a matter of emphasis. Yet these differences, exacerbated by related doctrinal, economic, and international problems, gradually polarized to the point at which Mao and a significant faction within the Chinese military establishment found themselves in bitter, irrevocable disagreement.[29]

One of Mao's fundamental ideas, based on his guerrilla-warfare concepts, was that the individual soldier could only understand "why he fights and why he must obey" if his discipline were self-imposed. Accordingly, the Communist Army throughout its insurgent days functioned without an official distinction between officers and men and, in principle at least, troops were encouraged to recommend tactics and even criticize their superiors. But if this symbolically egalitarian practice had actually died years before as the Army grew in size and specialization, it was formally buried in February 1955 when, following the Korean War, Communist military leaders set up a far more elaborate system of officers' ranks, pay-scales, and promotion schedules than they had ever had. They also expanded the number of China's military academies, lengthened training courses, and created a complex command structure—all of these innovations indicating that the Chinese Army bore only a scant resemblance to the rebel band of Mao's dreams. The Maoist ideal of the self-motivated soldier was further eroded that year when the Army ceased recruiting men by appealing for "volunteers" and began calling up conscripts under a new Military Service Law. Now, more than ever, the gap between amateur and career troops was sharply defined. As one of China's senior military specialists, Marshal Nieh Jung-chen, pointed out with approval, conscription "draws a distinction between privates . . . and professional officers."

Though Chinese officers themselves had long been moving toward military conventionality, Soviet influence during the first half of the 1950s propelled them faster in that direction. The Kremlin had rescued the Chinese from a disastrous defeat in Korea, mainly by providing them with MIG-15 jet fighter aircraft. After that, Chinese military leaders turned increasingly toward Moscow for the modern matériel that they could not manufacture at home or acquire elsewhere. The Russians were hardly generous. Their military aid, valued at some $2 billion until 1957, had to be reimbursed —and was, in fact, repaid by the Chinese by 1965. Moreover, they carefully avoided supplying Peking with any offensive equipment, such as medium- or long-range bomber aircraft, that might later threaten the Soviet Union. Nevertheless, Soviet assistance to China was extensive and decisive. It outfitted the Chinese infantry with its basic weapons, contributed to the development of a Chinese Navy and Air Force, and, in extremely cautious fashion, helped Peking to start its program to construct a nuclear arsenal. Several thousand Soviet military advisers were also assigned to China and their effect, while difficult to measure, undoubtedly was to reinforce the bureaucratic and professional tendencies of Chinese officers. It is likely, too, that these Russian advisers insisted on the primacy of weapons over ideology, thereby contravening one of Mao's basic theses. The degree to which this trend pleased Chinese career officers was reflected in a statement by General Su Yü, the Chief of General Staff, urging the Army to "strengthen our study in modern military science" by learning from the "advanced experience of the Soviet forces." But Mao was worried by this "blind faith in foreigners" that must have reminded him of the attitudes of Westernized Chinese earlier in the century. In his view, the Russians had little to teach China. "After defeating Chiang Kai-shek, Japanese imperialism and American imperialism," he said, "our experience is much richer than that of the Soviet Union, and it is wrong to regard it as worthless." He also complained that the Soviet military advisers in China were instructing the Chinese Army in offensive warfare, which violated his belief that a "defense-in-depth" was his country's best strategy. Soviet advice, he said, "does not conform to practical circumstances." [30]

Still, by the mid-1950s the Chinese military hierarchy showed signs of becoming a professional caste that emphasized technology, downgraded ideology, and paid only lip service to Mao's dictum that it must "cherish the people." Inevitably, Maoist spokesmen began to raise a cry of alarm that military modernization would be futile if not dangerous unless anchored in firm political foundations. This reaction mirrored Mao's fear, later justified by events, that the "gun" was slipping out of his grasp. A campaign of official newspaper articles, radio broadcasts, and oratory was unleashed against officers who "exaggerate the role of weapons . . . as the decisive factor in the outcome of war" while minimizing the importance of men properly motivated through political indoctrination. Underlining this thesis, a Chinese Army journal compared a modernized military organization to a "tiger growing wings," explaining that the wings of technology were merely an external appendage grafted onto a beast whose ferocity depended upon its revolutionary spirit. Professional officers failed to comprehend this, the journal complained: they rhetorically praised ideology but really believed that "modernization has no class character. . . . This is a fundamental point on which we differ from the bourgeoisie and the mono-military outlook." [31]

About the same time, political commissars responsible for maintaining ideological standards in the Army began to deplore the widening gulf between officers and men created by conscription and the new system of ranks. Marshal Lo Jung-huan, then the senior commissar as head of the General Political Department, criticized officers who exercised their powers "indiscriminately," thereby weakening the unity "between the upper and lower levels in our Army." Because they now wore braid and insignia, Lo went on, many officers "do not mix freely with the men, no longer show concern for their living conditions . . . and do not care for their ailments and individual difficulties." Longing for the all-for-one-and-one-for-all *élan* that inspired Communist guerrillas a generation earlier, Lo bemoaned the "bureaucratism and documentarianism, conceit and self-complacency" that infected Chinese officers as they sat in offices, neglecting their troops, and devoting "an excessive amount of their time to attending meetings, writing documents, directives, reports and plans. . . ." The remedy for this situation, Lo proposed, was increased "political consciousness." Otherwise, he affirmed, the "solidarity of our Army will be undermined, and its combat strength sapped." [32]

Similar commentaries published during that period aired additional shortcomings in the behavior of professional officers. One of these pointed out that officers declined to submit to criticism by their men, arguing that this would tarnish their prestige. Another asserted that Army specialists refused to educate troops, contending that modern science and technology were "very mysterious" and that "enlisted men must carry out orders much like a machine, since the era of military democracy is out of date." [33] Still another attack against the Army professionals accused them of one of the most heinous crimes that could be leveled against a Chinese soldier —"warlordism." [34]

If they were blamed for betraying the egalitarian principles of the Communist Army, career officers were also charged with adopting an aloof attitude toward the population, thus violating the Maoist catechism that revolutionary soldiers must immerse themselves among the people like "fish in water." In his indictment, Marshal Lo Jung-huan alleged that professional officers had misconstrued "modernization" of the Army to signify that their own living standards deserved to be elevated. He criticized them for turning their offices, barracks, and clubs into "places of splendor," and for displaying a taste for "extravagance . . . that divorces them from the masses." [35] Backing up this charge, Lo's General Political Department accused officers of such specific misdeeds as awarding themselves extra food rations, providing their families with luxuries, and seducing schoolgirls and married women.[36] This question of the Army's relations with the population was especially relevant to the tensions then developing between Mao and China's military leaders.

Mao's concept of the Army as a force available for economic, political, and social as well as purely military tasks meant that troops could be committed to everything from agricultural and industrial projects to educational assignments and police duties. In other words, recollecting his Yenan experience, Mao saw the modern Chinese soldier as a latter-day version of the all-purpose guerrilla. But his vision was not shared by China's professional officers, who maintained that the diversion of troops to nonmilitary activities would dissipate their energies and interfere with the full-time training schedules indispensable to the modernization of the Army. The debate between Mao and the Chinese military hierarchy over this issue escalated throughout 1958, when the Army was badly demoralized by the orders given out to pursue economic "human-wave" tactics in the ambitious Great Leap Forward. That dismal experience contributed to the clash between Mao and Defense Minister P'eng Teh-huai that led to P'eng's dismissal yet failed to erase fully the Army's suspicions of Maoist doctrine.[37]

Similarly, the Army was expected to commit itself to the population in order to fulfill Mao's notion that, under military tutelage, every Chinese could be made a soldier. Underlying this belief was Mao's conviction that China could best be defended by a "passive" strategy in which an aggressor invading the country would be drowned in an "ocean of people"—hence his repeated appeals for the formation of a vast citizen militia. But here again, professional officers balked for various reasons. First, persuaded that modern war had become a complex exercise to be waged by specialists, they no longer put much faith in the idea of the peasant fighter. Second, they were reluctant to enter into a program to organize a militia in which political commissars and other ideologues would play a key role. And finally, just as they felt that Army participation in economic construction detracted from their real vocation, so the mobilization of the militia struck them as a burden that would interfere with the training of regular soldiers. This dispute, which remained unresolved for years, gradually aggravated the discord within the Peking leadership. Indeed, one of the "crimes" attributed by Mao to General Lo Jui-ch'ing, the Chief of General Staff purged early in the Cultural Revolution, was his purported opposition to the militia.

Tensions between Mao and the upper echelons of the Army were also heightened in the late 1950s by the complicated issue of nuclear strategy. As far back as August 1945, after Hiroshima was obliterated by the American atomic bomb, Mao had reiterated his dictum that men rather than weapons counted in war. His statement, as he made clear at the time, was directed at Chinese Communist military men who "erroneously" held that atomic bombs could be decisive in a conflict.[38] A decade later, the subject of nuclear policy had expanded into a complex debate that touched on such larger questions as economic development priorities and Sino–Soviet relations.

At the core of the debate were divergent assessments of the significance of atomic weapons. Chinese career officers, like professional soldiers everywhere, were essentially concerned with tangible, practical, short-term tactics. Their opinion was expressed in 1957 by General Su Yü, when he worried aloud that the "tremendous destructive power" of nuclear arms, particularly in a first strike by the enemy, would cripple China.[39] While under no illusions about the devastation that atomic bombs could wreak, Mao contrastingly took the view that the longer-range effects of nuclear war might actually be beneficial. He explained this position to the Indian Prime Minister, Jawaharlal Nehru. According to one version, he said:

> If half of humanity is destroyed, the other half will still remain but imperialism will have been destroyed entirely and there will be only socialism in the world. Within a half-century, or a whole century, the population will again increase by more than half. . . .[40]

Mao's view of nuclear war coincided with a tough American posture that then alarmed Chinese officers. In March 1955, Secretary of State John Foster Dulles spelled out the Eisenhower Administration's "massive retaliation" doctrine as it applied to Asia by announcing that the United States would not hesitate to employ atomic weapons in the event of "open armed aggression" by the Chinese Communists in the region.[41] Interpreting this and similar warnings as evidence of an American nuclear threat, China's professional officers recommended a new defense posture. They proposed that China divert resources away from economic development in order to provide its armed forces with the most modern equipment. They also advocated closer ties with the Kremlin as a way of gaining the protection of the Soviet nuclear umbrella.

But neither of these suggestions appealed to Mao. Though he tried to convince Soviet Premier Nikita Khrushchev to harden the Communist bloc's line against the United States after the Russians launched their first earth satellite in 1957, Mao must have anticipated that China could not rely on the Kremlin. His forecast proved to be correct when Moscow reneged on an agreement to give Peking a "sample" atomic bomb and other assistance in building a nuclear arsenal. Second, both Mao and the Party bureaucracy were in accord in their opposition to attempts by career officers to have more of China's resources allocated to the modernization of the Army. By 1958, the Chinese Army brass had plainly lost the first round of its fight to place "expertise" over "Redness." Yet the clash between the proponents of professionalism and the advocates of ideological purity, by no means confined to military matters, would plague the Communist hierarchy for years to come.

During the mid-1950s, Mao and the Party leaders were rapidly moving apart over a wide variety of other questions that mirrored their essential disagreement on one central issue—the path that China should pursue in its economic development. If Mao believed that only the transformation of human consciousness could bring about material progress, the Party leaders believed that only material progress could transform human consciousness.

As they faced the challenge of elevating China from poverty and backwardness, the Party leaders contended that modernization could only be achieved through rational economic planning and practices based on organization, discipline, and technical proficiency. Above all, they argued, ruthless industrialization was the avenue to growth. Focusing their attention on the cities, they stressed the need to rely on urban workers as well as on the cooperation of scientists, engineers, managers, and other experts irrespective of their ideological credentials. Consistent with this "elitist" approach, they also insisted that the Party apparatus was best qualified to formulate and carry out economic policy. In other words, as Stuart Schram has suggested, the Chinese Party stalwarts were following in the footsteps of Lenin and Stalin in their affirmation that a "technocratic bias" was indispensable for the advance toward socialism.[42]

Mao favored a diametrically different strategy. Starting from the premise that change was impossible as long as "old ideas reflecting the old system remain in people's heads," [43] he maintained that priority be given to political and ideological programs calculated to purge men of their inherently conservative tendencies. "Revolutionaries are made, not born," he argued. Thus he asserted, in violation of the Party's principles, that the main emphasis be put on moral rather than material incentives, ideology rather than expertise, popular spontaneity rather than organizational discipline, will power rather than rules and regulations. He also held that industrialization would falter unless agricultural production were boosted but, in his view, the only way to increase farm output was by harnessing peasants in large collectives in order to guide and intensify their labor. And in promoting the "mass line," as he labeled his brand of populism, Mao sought to subordinate the Party bureaucracy to his own charismatic authority. In short, he regarded himself rather than the Communist Party as the source of wisdom capable of inspiring, motivating, and generating the energies of the masses.

Seen in perspective, there was remarkable continuity in the attitudes of Mao and his Party adversaries before and after the Communists took over China in 1949. Just as he had predicated his struggle to gain power on the mobilization of peasants, so Mao persisted in his conviction that the rural sector was the key to China's progress as a Communist state. Just as the Party, like the Army, had acquired respect for technical skills as it grew in size and complexity, so its leaders reinforced their belief that develop-been really settled yet. We still have to wage a protracted struggle against bourgeois and petty bourgeois ideology." [50]

The Party leaders flatly rejected this call for continued "struggle," however. "The question of who will win in the struggle between socialism and capitalism in our country has now been decided," proclaimed Liu Shao-ch'i in September 1956,[51] adding that bourgeois intellectuals and specialists who had helped the nation deserved to be praised rather than censured. And, without mentioning Mao by name, he attacked "some members of our Party who hold that everything should absolutely be of 'one color,'" describing their attitude as a "sectarian viewpoint." [52] This theme was echoed by Teng Hsiao-p'ing, the new Party Secretary General, in a statement criticizing the Maoist notion of "classifying . . . social strata into two different categories." [53] The official Party newspaper, the *People's Daily*, also berated "doctrinairism," while the chief of the Party's Propaganda Department, Lu Ting-yi, refuted one of Mao's basic tenets in a conciliatory appeal to intellectuals. "As everyone knows," Lu said, "the natural sciences, including medicine, have no class character." [54]

To a large extent, the simmering quarrel between Mao and the Party boiled up because of shortcomings in China's economic development drive. The First Five-Year Plan of 1953–57 was performing brilliantly in the field of heavy industry. But the records roken in iron, steel, coal, and other industrial production were ot being matched in the agricultural realm. Between 1953 and 55, the production of grains like rice and wheat repeatedly failed meet the targets set up by the government, while cotton output ually declined.[55]

This situation was critical, for the simple reason that Chinese strialization depended upon agriculture. Under a series of ements, the Soviet Union had contracted to provide China the blueprints, advisers, and low-interest loans to construct than two hundred major factories. However, the main bur f financing and meeting the other requirements of indus tion fell on the shoulders of the Chinese peasants. They wer ed to grow food for an expanding urban population; produc cent of the fibers, cotton, and other raw materials neede t industry and, at the same time, yield the additional su

ment could only be handled through specialization, industrialization, and modern management. This difference was expressed neatly in a pair of contrasting slogans. "Collectivization must precede mechanization," claimed Mao. On the contrary, replied Liu, "mechanization before collectivization."

One of the earliest controversies between Mao and the Party after the establishment of their regime focused on the role that scientists, engineers, and other intellectuals as well as "bourgeois" industrialists and managers should play in the Communist state. The industrial success of the First Five-Year Plan had been due in large measure to the ability of the Peking regime to enlist the collaboration of thousands of Chinese technical specialists, most of whom were uncommitted to communism. As a survey of the membership of the Chinese Academy of Sciences indicated, many of these experts had returned to China from the United States, Western Europe, and Japan.[44] In part, they were attracted by the integrity, patriotism, and efficiency of the Communists, especially after years of Nationalist corruption and ineptitude. In addition, they were reassured by the fact that the Communists, seeking a broad base of support, had initially set up a so-called "democratic coalition" government in which ideology was subdued. The new administration, with the durable Chou En-lai as its Premier, counted twenty-five representatives of minor non-Communist political groups among its fifty-six ministers and senior department heads. Serving under Mao in his capacity of chief of state were three non-Communist Vice-Chairmen of the Republic—among them Mme. Soong Ching-ling, the sophisticated, American-educated widow of Dr. Sun Yat-sen. Besides personifying the bridge between the two Republics, her prestigious participation was obviously contrived to present the Communists in a favorable light to the middle-class Chinese of the coastal cities.

This "united front" arrangement, officially entitled a "people's democratic dictatorship," seemed to be a liberal variation of Lenin's more exclusively proletarian "democratic dictatorship of workers and peasants." But soon disagreements arose over whether the relatively conservative experts and intellectuals posed a threat to the revolution.

Nearly two decades later, attempting to stress Mao's unswerving fidelity to the revolution, radical publicists in Peking asserted that he had terminated the "new democratic" phase and initiated the "transition to socialism" in 1949. This revision of events was designed to suggest, in simpler language, that Mao had opposed cooperation with bourgeois elements but had been betrayed by Liu Shao-ch'i and the Party bureaucrats, who had favored moderation toward "right-wing" intellectuals and capitalists. Documents dredged up from the early 1950s cited Liu as saying that "socialism is something for the future," and that "the bourgeoisie in China has a progressive part to play." [45] Liu was also alleged to have encouraged Chinese industrialists to build more private factories, advising them they would therefore help to stimulate the economy. Visiting the north China city of Tientsin, the home of his wife's wealthy family, he was reported to have told the owner of a local textile mill: "Your mill employs a thousand workers, so it would be much better if you had ten such mills employing ten thousand workers." [46] He was also quoted as having explained to a group of businessmen in the same city: "The government is calling for greater production efforts. To respond to the government's appeal, you must practice exploitation. This is not a question of who exploits whom. When you run factories, increase your production and pay taxes to the State, the State is thus exploiting you in turn." [47]

Though these and similar statements were unearthed in order to slander Liu as a long-standing "pro-capitalist," they were actually not so different from the theories voiced by Mao during that period. In his essay "On the People's Democratic Dictatorship," published in June 1949, Mao demonstrated far more flexibility than he would display in later years. He declared that the Communists merely intended to "regulate" rather than destroy capitalism, and he generously promised the "progressive" bourgeoisie the same rights that workers and peasants would enjoy under the "democratic dictatorship." Only when "the time comes to realize socialism," he went on, would the bourgeoisie be "educated and remolded." [48] But this matter of timing, never made clear, became a pivotal point in the quarrel between Mao and the Party. For Liu and his comrades, in their stress on industrialization, evidently felt that the "new democratic" phase should last a considerable length of time so that the technocrats could be encouraged to contribute to the economy.

Mao, on the other hand, began to have qualms about what he considered to be an unholy alliance between his unique style of communism and the ideologically dubious intellectuals.

These qualms stemmed in part from Mao's ingrained distr of the intelligentsia. Looking back across the centuries of Chir history, he was appalled by the gulf that divided the vast maj of the people from the educated minority. Even though their ary, artistic, and administrative accomplishments warmed h thetic feelings and national pride, he saw evil in the trad mandarins, whose long fingernails symbolized their disd manual labor. Scorning the value of formal education, he out that the two most successful Ming dynasty emperors illiterate while their incompetent successors had been me ing. [49] Perhaps Mao's hatred for scholars mirrored his experience serving them as a menial assistant in the Pel sity library. He had certainly observed in Yenan that th in common with his guerrilla ideal. He had also di they tended to be most resistant to his "spiritual" munism, with its accent on moral rearmament. school and university graduates even in China hav candidates for conversion to religious fundament held intellectuals in low esteem—unless, of cours to "thought reform," prostrated themselves be and acquired a genuine "proletarian" outlook. F their ability to undergo this process sincerely.

In 1955, Mao had personally conducted a Feng, an undistinguished Communist writer the political controls imposed by the regime Not long afterward, clearly concerned that from his revolutionary dream toward Sc Mao began to caution against "rightist fresh drives to intensify "class struggle." nese in one speech, he asserted that m support of Marxism since they came f Therefore, he said, they required "r future efforts to cleanse intellectuals he warned: "In the ideological field in the struggle between the proleta pluses for export to cover the cost of importing the capital equipment for heavy industry. By the spring of 1955, though, it was plain that the Chinese peasantry was not accomplishing this superhuman task. A Peking pronouncement issued in March warned that "if growth of agricultural production does not catch up, it is bound to affect . . . the speed of industrialization." [56]

Several factors conspired to hamper agriculture. Concentrating on heavy industry, the government had allocated only a tiny fraction of its development budget to the rural sector, leaving peasants without adequate draft animals, farm tools, chemical fertilizers, seed, and credit. These scarcities, coupled with the fact that the earlier agrarian reform had multiplied the number of privately owned farms, contributed to a rise in capitalistic tendencies in the countryside. Poor peasants, unable to settle their debts, were being compelled to sell their land and become laborers, with the result that distinct classes were re-emerging in the villages. Later, when the government moved to correct this trend by introducing measures to curb private activities, wealthier peasants reacted by cutting back production or even selling their property in order to elude controls. All this, exacerbated by the assorted pressures exerted on the rural population by zealous Party officials, combined to depress the Chinese agricultural scene.[57]

A possible solution to the problem might have been to scale down industrialization into line with agricultural production. But such a retreat was more than the Chinese leaders could have accepted. Mao therefore offered a remedy consistent with his theories—mobilize the people, China's primary resource. In July 1955, he proposed that the loose cooperatives then in operation be rapidly enlarged into big farm collectives in which peasants would be turned into an agricultural proletariat. That this recommendation met stiff resistance from the Party apparatus was evidenced in Mao's blast at the time against "some of our comrades who are tottering along like a woman with bound feet, always complaining that others are going too fast." [58]

These "women with bound feet," as later information would disclose, were Liu Shao-ch'i and other senior Party figures, and their resistance to Mao's idea was based on various apprehensions. Looking back at the dislocations caused by tamer collectivist efforts only a year or two before, they were concerned that peasant opposition to the new campaign would inhibit agricultural output even more. Recalling events in the Soviet Union in the early 1930s, they also feared a similar upheaval in China so soon after having established their regime. Moreover, faithful to orthodox Marxism, they contended that it was senseless to accelerate collectivization before China's industrial capacity had been raised, since large farms could only be operated efficiently with tractors and other machinery, chemical fertilizers, electrification, and such skilled personnel as engineers, agronomists, and economists. Liu had stressed this point as early as 1951 when, scorning "utopian" agricultural schemes, he had asserted that "the realization of socialism in the rural areas requires the development of industry." [59] Now, reiterating the same theme differently, he claimed that agriculture could only be collectivized "step by step . . . within a relatively long period." [60]

This debate intruded directly into the dispute between Mao and the Party over the role of intellectuals under communism. For Mao, with his view of collectivization as a fundamentally political and ideological process, was persuaded that the effort to socialize the countryside must be paralleled by a broader drive against "rightist conservatism . . . still causing trouble in many fields." [61] Hence he believed that his collectivization should not only convert the peasantry but simultaneously cleanse the bourgeois "technocrats" whose cooperation was needed by the Party bureaucracy in its thrust toward industrialization.

Despite the Party's resistance, Mao's collectivization policy prevailed and, by the end of 1956, roughly 100 million peasant families were incorporated into Agricultural Producers' Cooperatives, as the big collective farms were labeled. But the ambitious plan soon proved to be a failure. Facing the prospect of again becoming tenants, this time of the state, many peasants destroyed their farm implements, neglected their confiscated fields, and slaughtered their draft animals and livestock rather than surrender them to the collective. Food hoarding became widespread, and attempts by the government to attract produce to "controlled free markets" quickly led to unbridled speculation. Bad weather in many parts of the country aggravated these difficulties, and the upshot was an alarming decrease in the agricultural harvests, which in 1956–57 dropped far below the natural rate of population increase.[62] Famine, later reported in areas of Kwangsi province, probably occurred elsewhere as well. Many collectives were disbanded, and peasants in some regions fled to the cities, thereby imposing further strains on urban housing and food supply systems.[63]

Foreshadowing the dismal aftermath of the Great Leap Forward three years later, the failure of this major experiment in collectivization was conveniently blamed on local Communist cadres. They were accused of having committed such "errors" as beguiling peasants with false promises of improved income, inflating production targets in order to curry favor with their superiors and displaying "blind optimism" in claiming that those targets could be fulfilled.[64] But the real culprit in the eyes of the Party leadership was Mao.

Though they knew that Mao was no Stalin, the Party leaders were undoubtedly inspired by Khrushchev's denunciation of the late Soviet dictator's "crimes" in February 1956 to launch a similar assault against the personality who had encouraged a cult of himself in their own country. At their long overdue Eighth National Congress held in Peking in September 1956, Liu Shao-ch'i and his colleagues not only revamped the upper echelons of the Party hierarchy as a way of diluting Mao's authority, but subjected him to a thinly veiled and humiliating attack.

Under the Party Constitution promulgated in 1945, Mao had been given extraordinary power by being named to serve concurrently as Chairman of the Party Central Committee, Chairman of the Politburo, and Chairman of the Central Secretariat. At the 1956 Congress, however, he was deprived of the Central Secretariat, which controlled the Party's day-to-day operations. Henceforth, that vital Party organ would be under the supervision of a new Secretary General, Teng Hsiao-p'ing, a veteran *apparatchik* whose arrogance eventually earned him Mao's intense hatred. Formerly there had been no Vice-Chairman of the Central Committee. Now the Party created four Vice-Chairmanships for men who had never fully subscribed to Mao's theories—Chou En-lai, the suave, flexible Premier; Marshal Chu Teh, the old Army commander; Ch'en Yun, a pragmatic economic planner; and Liu Shao-ch'i. As First Vice-Chairman, Liu was delegated to share part of Mao's power to conduct "certain important conferences." The Party also established a Standing Committee of the Politburo, comprised of the Chairman, the four Vice-Chairmen, and the Secretary General. This meant, in effect, that China would be governed by a collegium in which Mao no longer ruled supreme.

Early in the Cultural Revolution, Mao sought to explain this reorganization of the Party hierarchy as having been undertaken at his own initiative. He had observed, he said, that the successors to Stalin were unprepared to rule following the Soviet dictator's death because they lacked experience. He therefore decided to divide the leadership into "first and second lines," placing Liu and Teng Hsiao-p'ing in the forefront while withdrawing himself to the background. "When I retreated into the second line by letting others handle the daily work," he said, "my purpose was to cultivate their prestige so that when I went to see God, the country would be spared great chaos. But I didn't expect that the situation would turn out differently." [65]

Mao's version of his downgrading seemed to have been an attempt on his part to "save face." For it was plain from Liu Shao-ch'i's Political Report at the 1956 Congress that the Party outvoted Mao on several key issues. Refuting Mao's notion of "protracted class struggle," Liu affirmed the Party's view that "the struggle between socialism and capitalism in our country has now been settled." Rejecting Mao's calls for campaigns to purify the conservative intelligentsia, he asserted that "we must enlist the services of bourgeois and petty bourgeois intellectuals in building socialism, and learn from them." Liu also criticized Mao's plan for rapid collectivization as typical of "leftists" who deviate from the Party Line "in demanding that socialism be achieved overnight." And, most significantly, he obliquely impugned Mao for having "tried to weaken the leading role of the Party" while authorizing himself to "go on taking arbitrary action." Conspicuously failing to extol Mao, as he had at the Seventh Congress in 1945, Liu insisted instead that the Party must respect the principle of "collective leadership." [66]

The Party Secretary General, Teng Hsiao-p'ing, echoed this theme even more strongly. Stressing that they stand "not above the Party but within it," he said that Party leaders should set an example "in obeying the Party organizations and observing Party discipline." Khrushchev's revelations of Stalin's misconduct, Teng pointed out, "showed us that serious consequences can follow from the deification of the individual." Obviously with Mao in mind, he went on to emphasize that the Chinese Party "abhors" the cult of the personality because "no individuals are free from flaws and mistakes in their activities." [67]

If this vigorous assault against Mao's belief in his own infallibility were not enough, the new version of the Party Constitution promulgated at the 1956 Congress deleted the reference to his "Thought" as the guide for all Communists, substituting in its place the assertion that the Party was "the vanguard of the Chinese working class, the highest form of its class organization." Years later, it was alleged by Mao's supporters that Marshal P'eng Teh-huai, then Defense Minister and a Politburo member, had plotted with Liu and Teng Hsiao-p'ing to make the blasphemous amendment to the Constitution.[68]

This was not the first or the last time that Mao suffered a setback. In the early 1930s he had been stripped of power by Chou En-lai and others, and, as the American Communist writer Anna Louise Strong put it, he would be placed "nicely on a shelf like a Buddha" by Liu and the Party leaders during the mid-1960s.[69] After the 1956 Party Congress, however, Mao's eclipse was brief. Within less than two years, he was well on his way toward launching the Great Leap Forward. What gave him the opportunity to revive his revolutionary momentum was a short but intensive interlude known as the "Hundred Flowers" campaign. This interlude, which turned the spotlight on the "bourgeois" intellectuals, owed its initial impulse to the reverberations reaching China from the Soviet Union and Eastern Europe following Khrushchev's posthumous denunciation of Stalin.

"Let a hundred flowers bloom" and "let a hundred schools of thought contend" had been slogans designed to inspire independent philosophical discussion in ancient China. Mao resurrected these slogans in the spring of 1957 as an invitation to China's academic, artistic, and managerial intelligentsia to criticize the Communist regime freely. Most Western analysts have suggested that Mao, sensitive to Khrushchev's de-Stalinization statement, felt the need to provide Chinese intellectuals with a safety valve through which to voice their complaints against Communist policies and practices. In a carefully documented study based on fresh information, however, Richard Solomon has concluded that Mao's real intention was to encourage the intellectuals to attack the Party. Mao's purpose in this tactic, according to Solomon, was to drive a wedge between the Party and the "technocrats" in order to rupture their alliance and undermine the economic development strategy they were pursuing in opposition to his own attempts to promote the "mass line." [70] Whatever his precise motives, the maneuver did in fact give Mao the chance to regain the revolutionary momentum he had temporarily lost.

In late 1956, ignited by Khrushchev's anti-Stalin speech at the Twentieth Congress of the Soviet Communist Party, the flames of dissent spread through Poland and erupted in a rebellion in Hungary. One of the first reactions in Peking was concern for the cohesion of the Communist bloc. Attempting to preserve bloc unity, Chou En-lai went to Warsaw in an effort to help the Poles gain a degree of autonomy from the Kremlin without impairing Moscow's hegemony in Eastern Europe. Essentially, however, the Chinese interpreted the cracks in the Communist monolith in terms of their own domestic tensions.

As they observed the post-mortem effects of Stalin's excesses, the Chinese Party leaders seemed to believe that China might be similarly nagged by internal ferment unless Mao's rigorous doctrines were checked and more temperate policies prevailed. So, through the medium of reproaching Stalin, they indirectly denounced Mao's attempts to perpetuate revolution.[71] Mao, in contrast, saw the Hungarian upheaval as proof of his view that tolerance of bourgeois intellectuals by the Party only fostered conservative trends that eventually eroded Communist ideology. His solution was increased tension rather than moderation.

Mao outlined this approach in a major address entitled "On the Correct Handling of Contradictions Among the People." It was, characteristically, a sweet-and-sour pronouncement. He hailed China's unity, minimized the danger that "counterrevolutionaries" menaced the regime, and even allowed that differences between the proletariat and the bourgeoisie could be resolved. At the same time, he repeated that "class struggle is not yet over," implying that "antagonistic" conflicts between the "people" and their enemies still existed within a socialist society.[72] His declaration, which would later provide him with the theoretical foundation to define his Party opponents as "enemies" during the Cultural Revolution, set the stage for the "Hundred Flowers" drama.

The appeal by Mao for free speech immediately uncorked a torrent of critical commentaries. The non-Communist Minister of Education, Chang Hsi-jo, accused the Party of "doctrinairism," charging that its members relied on rigid dogma as "their sole blueprint, their sole dictionary, all their capital, and their only support." Chu An-p'ing, the editor-in-chief of the non-Party newspaper *Kwangming Daily*, blamed Party officials for having "bungled their jobs to the detriment of the State," while other writers, artists, scholars, doctors, and even workers and peasants also expressed their dissatisfaction.[73] One of the angriest diatribes came from Ko Pei-chi, a young lecturer in economics at Peking University who indicted Party officials for granting themselves privileges while the people suffered from shortages of food and other commodities:

> China belong to 600 million people, including the counterrevolutionaries. It does not belong to the Communist Party alone. . . . If you carry on satisfactorily, well and good. If not, the masses may knock you down, kill the Communists, overthrow you. This cannot be described as unpatriotic, for the Communists no longer serve the people. The downfall of the Communist Party does not mean the downfall of China. . . .[74]

In the light of allegations he himself would direct against them years afterward, Mao was apparently delighted by this bitter assault on the Party *apparatchiks*. Indeed, some of the criticisms which iconoclasts leveled at the Party during the "Hundred Flowers" era were identical with those uttered by Mao a decade later. In June 1957, for example, a leader of the fellow-traveling Democratic League named Teng Chu-min indicted Communist functionaries for their self-righteousness, complacency and arrogance, hypocrisy, ostentation and extravagance, debauchery, vindictiveness and "subjective presumption," adding that their inability to appreciate the "sorrows of the masses" was incompatible with Marxism-Leninism.[75] In January 1967, in a speech entitled "Twenty Manifestations of Bureaucracy," Mao described the Party *apparatchiks* as truculent, arbitrary, brainless, corrupt, deceitful, egotistical, feudalistic, irresponsible, and "as slippery as eels," adding that "they are divorced from reality, from the masses. . . ."[76]

Another curious feature of the crescendo of criticism unleashed during the "Hundred Flowers" period was its focus against the Party rather than against Mao personally. Therefore, if Mao did not entirely orchestrate the attacks, he deliberately used them against the Party in a strategy that, in the jargon of the Cultural Revolution, was known as "right in form but left in essence."

Less than three weeks after announcing its start, Mao began to call a halt to the free-speech movement, asserting that "all words and actions that deviate from socialism are completely mistaken."[77] A month after, the Peking press officially signaled the end of liberalism and the beginning of an "anti-rightist" offensive. This "rectification" drive not only suppressed the unfortunate intellectuals who had been beguiled into venting their feelings publicly, but, more significantly, Mao channeled it into a campaign to purge the Party organization that, not long before, had humiliated him. In May 1957, in a statement that remained unpublished until the Cultural Revolution, Mao issued a broadside against "bourgeois" and "revisionist" elements within the Party who "echo the rightist intellectuals in society, and are united with them as closely as elder and younger brothers."[78] In addition to the arrest and imprisonment of dissident writers, artists, technicians, and other such types, a wholesale crackdown initiated inside the Communist apparatus also claimed as victims four alternate members of the Central Committee and some sixty other high officials, including the head of a Provincial Party Committee and four provincial governors.[79]

Thus, as Solomon has explained, Mao largely succeeded in breaking the relationship between the Communist bureaucrats and the "technocrats" by demonstrating that the Party could not rely on intellectuals. Implicit in this maneuver was the message that an economic-development strategy which depends upon experts rather than the "masses" presents great dangers for the Party. By extending his purge of the Party into rural regions of China, Mao's further purpose was to rid the countryside of officials who might interfere with his forthcoming program—the frenetic collectivization campaign called the Great Leap Forward.

CHAPTER 5

The Leap That Failed

*I have witnessed the tremendous energy of
the masses. On this foundation it is possible
to accomplish any task whatsoever.*
—MAO TSE-TUNG, *September 1958*

THE GREAT LEAP FORWARD was the biggest and most ambitious experiment in human mobilization in history. Though it lasted less than a year, it had deployed by its peak in the fall of 1958 more than a half-billion peasants into twenty-four thousand "people's communes" in which all private property was confiscated. Everything from food and clothing to child care and haircuts was guaranteed by the commune as peasants, formed into military brigades, were shifted from fields to dam sites and from makeshift factories to "backyard" steel furnaces amid a frenzy of slogans and exhortations urging them to work around the clock in order to perform economic miracles. "The achievements of a single night surpass those of several millennia," announced Chinese publicists, while the ideologues asserted that the Great Leap Forward had opened a "new historical era" signifying that China was outstripping the Soviet Union in the "transition to Communism." [1]

Peking propagandists, reflecting Maoist tenets, explained that the Great Leap had been "spontaneously started by the mass of the peasants on the basis of great socialist consciousness." [2] But the fantastic phenomenon flowed logically from Mao's implacable conviction that the only way to develop China was through the mobilization of its sole resource—people. As early as mid-1957, he had abruptly halted a birth-control campaign on the grounds that China's huge population "is an objective . . . asset." Soon afterward, he put forth the questionable thesis that the Chinese people, being "poor and blank," could therefore be easily guided into intensive revolutionary efforts.³ Undoubtedly impelling Mao, too, was a personal feeling of urgency. He was then nearly sixty-five, with not many years left to live, and he apparently felt that he had accomplished little to make China the powerful nation of his dreams. In short, he was impatient, and, speaking to a government conference in January 1958, Mao candidly expressed his restless mood.

"As much as we may brag about our large population and our thousands of years of history and culture, our country is no better than Belgium," Mao said, explaining that China's industry was embryonic, its agriculture primitive, and its people largely illiterate. His objective, then, was to raise China to the level of Great Britain within the next fifteen years. During that period, Mao forecast, Chinese steel production could be increased to 40 million from its present 5 million tons, and coal output to 500 from its present 100 million tons. Electric-power capacity could be boosted more than tenfold, he predicted, while the agricultural progress necessary to match these industrial advances could be attained in eight years. All this could be achieved, Mao asserted, through sheer determination and human energy. "Our nation is imbued with enthusiasm," he said. "It is like an atom, capable of releasing tremendous force." And, refuting critics who claimed that his ambitions were too lofty, he added:

> There is nothing wrong with the craving for greatness and success. There is also nothing wrong with yearning for quick success and instant benefits. . . . It is better to strike while the iron is hot. It is better to achieve something at one stroke than procrastinate. . . . One revolution must be followed by another, and the revolution must advance without interruption.⁴

Foremost among those who had criticized Mao's desire for "quick success and instant benefits" were the Party bureaucrats. To translate his beliefs into action, Mao had to override their objections, which were mirrored in a variety of cautious commentaries published in the Peking press in the latter part of 1957. "The power to change the objective world is limited," declared Feng Ting, a Party philosopher, in an obvious rebuttal to Mao. Vice-Premier Ch'en Yun, the most prominent of the moderate economic planners, warned that "one cannot reach heaven in a single step." Even Premier Chou En-lai favored temperance in opposition to Mao's "mass movements," voicing his views to an Indian agricultural mission then visiting Peking. As the Indians recorded the conversation, Chou was cited as saying that

> . . . from the organizational point of view, a big cooperative farm that tried to control a large number of workers perhaps could not really be so much more efficient than the small cooperative farm. . . . In fact, there was a possibility that this might lead to a lack of initiative on the part of individual workers and working teams, and hence be detrimental to efficiency. . . . There were some enthusiasts who wanted bigger and bigger cooperative farms but he had, indeed, serious doubts about large and complex farm cooperatives.[5]

The doubts voiced by Chou and others were officially reflected in a Party statement issued on September 14, 1957. Observing that the large collectives were "generally not adaptable to present production conditions," the Party leaders recommended reducing them in size to comprise about a hundred families—or about the dimensions of the "mutual-aid teams" organized five years before. They also proposed, in another step backward, that these smaller agricultural production units should "remain unchanged for the next ten years." [6] These suggestions, plainly designed to appease the weary peasants and give the regime a chance to consolidate its position in the rural areas, would have turned back the clock on collectivization had they been accepted. But within a month, two additional directives published in the name of the Party Central Committee took an entirely different tack.

Bearing Mao's imprimatur, these new directives referred to the impending Great Leap Forward for the first time in proclaiming a nationwide movement to channel the farming population into the construction and repair of irrigation systems, dams, dikes, and roads as well as the collection of organic fertilizers in various regions. Tens of millions of peasants were shunted around the countryside to the assorted projects from late 1957 through early 1958 and, as a European visitor to China then described one scene,

> Monumental ant heaps were busy on the sites of future reservoirs. Endless lines of blue-clad men and women were filing up moun-

tainsides like some unnatural stream changing its course. In the background, scattered all over the fields, multitudes of people were moving around with two buckets hanging from their shoulder poles. All together, they recalled the rhythmic breathing of some mythological colossus, suddenly awakened and flexing its milliard muscles in a supreme effort to change the face of the earth.[7]

In the midst of these convulsions, an unusual paradox for China suddenly occurred—a manpower shortage. The weather in early 1958 looked fine, promising good summer and fall harvests. But with multitudes of peasants engaged in construction tasks, labor was required to begin the spring planting. To meet this need, contingents of office employees, factory workers, students, and others were transferred from China's overcrowded cities to the villages. Peasant women had been recruited for farming tasks, and their enlistment necessitated the establishment of communal mess halls, nurseries, and other services formerly handled within the family household. At the same time, the deployment of tremendous labor brigades demanded the control and discipline that only a military-type system could assure.[8] Thus "a new social organization appeared fresh as the morning sun above the broad horizon of East Asia"—the "people's commune." In Mao's words, the commune would amalgamate "industry, agriculture, commerce, education, and the army," thereby becoming the "basic unit of society."

Though they had initially fought against the creation of big collectives, the Party leaders evidently went along with the new scheme. In part, they seemed to have no alternative solution to the baffling problem of maintaining agricultural production without curbing industrialization. As later documents indicated, the Party machine may have also come to believe that it could fortify itself through the Great Leap Forward by exercising control over the "people's communes." Whatever the reason, Liu Shao-ch'i publicly endorsed the campaign in the spring of 1958 in terms that differed totally from his statements of a year earlier. Repeating one of the slogans contrived to stimulate the peasants, he intoned: "Hard work for a few years, happiness for a thousand." [9]

Like most Communist innovations, the "people's communes" were first tested on a small scale before given ideological approval. The pilot area was a county of Honan province, the cradle of Chinese civilization, where experiments in rural cooperation had been carried on since the 1930s. Here, twenty-seven collective farms covering 53,500 acres and comprising 43,885 people were merged into a single unit in April 1958. By way of showing the Kremlin that China had a new weapon as powerful as the Soviet satellite, this pioneer commune was entitled the Sputnik Federated Cooperative. Other pilot communes were soon set up in the Liaoning, Szechwan, and Kwangtung provinces. In August, the decision was made to extend the communes to the entire nation and within forty-five days it was officially reported that virtually the whole peasant population—121,936,350 families—had been brought into the new collectives. Mao returned from an inspection tour of the countryside, convinced that his utopian vision was being realized. "I have witnessed the tremendous energy of the masses," he announced. "On this foundation it is possible to accomplish any task whatsoever." [10]

Coercion alone could not have conceivably marshaled a half-billion people. Large numbers of peasants were undoubtedly attracted to the collectives by the promise of equal food, clothing, and shelter or, as the Communist slogan put it, "to each according to his needs." Others were swept along by a fresh excitement that at least represented a change in their drab lives. For the most part, however, the enormous development was testimony to the ability of Party cadres at manipulating people. Local officials in many communes consciously created an intoxicating atmosphere by beating drums, clashing cymbals, and blowing horns as they called peasants out to work, and the movement in several places was organized along military lines. At the Chaoying commune in Honan province, as a correspondent for Peking's New China News Agency described it, the work day began at dawn with the ringing of bells and the shrill of whistles.

> In about a quarter of an hour, the peasants line up. At the command of company and squad leaders, the teams move to the fields, holding flags. Here one no longer sees peasants in groups of two or three, smoking or going leisurely to the fields. What one hears is the sound of measured steps and marching songs. The desultory living habits that have been with peasants for hundreds of years are gone forever. . . .[11]

But for all its dynamism, the Great Leap Forward seriously lacked management. Among other things, peasants were instructed to plow furrows as deep as six feet and to plant rice seedlings one or two inches apart as prescribed by Mao in his "eight principles" of agriculture. But these procedures were meaningless unless implemented under ideal conditions and so, in many instances, they led to crop failures. Misguided irrigation and dam projects also ruined the soil in several areas, while attempts to compel peasants to work day and night resulted in their exhaustion. Meanwhile, commune officials anxious to overwhelm their superiors and gain merit for themselves inflated production statistics, prompting the central government to raise output quotas which, in turn, actuated the further falsification of statistics. This focus on the overfulfillment of quotas was reduced to the absurd in June 1958 when, in a burst of zeal, the Association of Chinese Paleontologists pledged to cut thirteen years off its twenty-year program in order to overtake "capitalist" research in fossils.[12]

Though the Great Leap Forward was primarily concentrated in the countryside, it also reached into China's urban areas. How the episode affected the life of an individual in a city was recalled afterward by Albert Belhomme, who lived and worked in China during the Great Leap Forward and its aftermath.[13] Belhomme was one of twenty-one American soldiers who defected to the Chinese during the Korean War. Sent to the Shantung province capital of Tsinan, a city of more than a million people on the Yellow River, he was provided with a Chinese wife, whose peasant parents resided in the nearby countryside. After training, he was employed as an electrician in a local paper mill constructed by the Japanese during their occupation of the region in the 1930s. As a consequence, Belhomme had the extraordinary experience for a Westerner of sharing the existence of a Chinese worker.

Belhomme recounted that a mood of tension was deliberately created in Tsinan even before the Great Leap Forward officially began. Party cadres stepped up the frequency of meetings and rallies, festooning factories walls with posters and banners demanding accelerated production. At the same time, they inaugurated a campaign to "weed out doubtful elements" suspected of "bourgeois" or "capitalist" inclinations. This drive touched off a wave of suicides by people who presumably feared prosecution. In one week alone, Belhomme said, he saw three people throw themselves off a railway bridge in front of approaching trains. A schoolteacher of his acquaintance jumped from the upper story of a high building. A doctor, a Communist Party member, had been having a love affair with a nurse. Perhaps anticipating discovery, he killed himself by taking an overdose of sleeping pills.

As the campaign against "doubtful elements" became better organized, suspects were brought before "people's trials." Belhomme described the way these trials were conducted:

> We were all required to attend the proceedings, which were held in the factory auditorium. We sat on benches facing the stage. On the stage sat the judge, flanked by the prosecutor and the defense attorney. The defense attorney, appointed by the authorities, apparently considered the defendant guilty but would mention some of his good points in hopes of lightening the sentence. Every time I went to a trial I was certain the defendant would be found guilty, because there was always a large van with barred windows waiting outside to take the convicted person away.

As Belhomme recounted, the trials were invariably attuned to the current campaign. When "rightists" were under attack in early 1958, for example, those arraigned were accused of ambiguous political "crimes" like having belonged to pro-Nationalist or anti-Communist associations before 1949. One defendant at that time was formally indicted for theft but, Belhomme recalled, the principal charge raised against him was that he had served as an interpreter for the Japanese "Fascist aggressors" twenty years before. Later, as the emphasis changed to boosting production, the main "crimes" tended to be economic. Cheating on an output quota would be labeled "corruption," and "sabotaging production through deliberate neglect" might mean anything from mishandling a machine to indolence.

> As the defendant faced the judge, witnesses mounted the stage to speak out against him. The testimony against the defendant was generally vague. "He doesn't work well," or "he is lazy," or "he shows capitalistic tendencies," the witnesses would say. I never saw a witness speak in favor of a defendant.
>
> We in the audience were encouraged by the Party cadres among us to comment aloud during hearings. If a defendant tried to deny the charges against himself—which was rare—we would shout: "See how he lacks humility, refusing to acknowledge his mistakes."

Sometimes, if the judge allowed the defendant to sit down, which was also rare, the audience would protest: "Make him stand up." Of course, nobody in the audience really cared whether the defendant was guilty or innocent. We were shouting in order to show the Party officials that we were on the Party line. The people who shouted the loudest were probably those who were most afraid of being hauled up themselves on some phony charge or another.

A variation of the full-scale "people's trial," Belhomme related, were "criticism" sessions attended by roughly a hundred workers assembled by Party officials. These meetings were held to judge lesser offenses. A worker heard to complain that Communist Party members were "golden boys" who accorded themselves special treatment was brought before such a "criticism" session. He wisely confessed, and was sent out as a laborer on a road gang for three months. Another worker, a lathe operator in the mill's machine shop, was confronted at one of these sessions by a contradictory set of charges. After breaking a production record by turning out one hundred seventy-six bolts in a single day, he had been accused by Party officials of displaying "capitalistic" inclinations in striving to earn an increased wage under the piece-work system. He thereupon restrained his output but soon found himself under fire for failing to produce his capacity. Simultaneously damned for zeal and slackness, he sagely accepted blame on both counts and, amid much confusion, was let off with a reprimand.

As the Great Leap Forward gathered momentum, one of its most peculiar exercises was the revival of an earlier offensive against flies, sparrows, mosquitoes, and rats, the "four pests." Mao himself had blessed this offensive, viewing it as consistent with his concept that the masses could accomplish "anything whatsoever" under his guidance. "Not even Confucius called for wiping out the four pests," he said, "but now Hangchow is planning to eradicate them in four years, and other places plan to do so in two, three, or five years. Thus there is great hope for developing this nation of ours. It is groundless and wrong to be pessimistic, and we must criticize and repudiate the pessimists." [14]

In the drive against flies, Belhomme recounted, families were issued swatters and required to appear every Sunday morning to fill large collection sacks with the insects they had killed during the week. The amount of time consumed in this operation was considerable as Party cadres, mindful of targets, counted each dead fly as it was transferred with a pair of bamboo tweezers from the matchbox in which it had been saved to the large sack. But if the drive against flies was time-consuming, the anti-sparrow campaign proved to be an ecological boomerang. As Belhomme recalled:

> The strategy against the sparrows was to keep them flying until they dropped from exhaustion and could be killed. But then we began to notice something strange. The trees were covered with whitish webs made by some sort of worm or caterpillar. And soon there were millions of these goddam bugs about a half-inch long falling into your hair and down your neck. At the mill you had to carry your food across a courtyard from the kitchen to the mess hall. When you reached your table, you'd find these caterpillars floating around in your soup and mixed up with the mushrooms in your noodles. The Chinese aren't squeamish, but everyone was disgusted. It was a big loss of face for the Party.

A year later, a Ministry of Agriculture statement conceded that the war against sparrows had been a mistake. Henceforth, the Ministry statement said, the "four evils" marked for extermination would be flies, mosquitoes, rats, and—replacing sparrows—bedbugs.

The Great Leap Forward was rolling ahead at breakneck pace by the summer of 1958. Now, only production counted. Like Chinese "human-wave" tactics in warfare, machines and men were thrown into the battle to attain or surpass output quotas regardless of cost. As Belhomme related it,

> We worked day and night for a week in our shop to build seven 64-kilowatt generators. I must have slept standing up, because I never laid down once during that week. But our generators needed more power than the city could provide, so they got hold of a Polish-made 300-horsepower diesel engine to run the seven generators. A single 300-horsepower engine isn't powerful enough to run seven generators. The Party cadres refused to listen to reason. After all, didn't Mao say we could perform miracles? Well, the engine ate up too much oil under the strain, and finally its bearings wore out. They got another engine and wore that one out, and then found still another and ruined it too. In the end, we went back to using

municipal power, which meant that the whole mill would frequently stop because the city couldn't produce enough.

The paper-manufacturing machines were designed to turn out between seventy-five and ninety meters of paper per minute along a woolen conveyor belt. When the big production push started, the Party cadres said we could increase output by speeding up the belt. They cranked up the machine to one hundred-twenty per minute. No vibrations? One-fifty. No noise. Why not try two hundred? Up it went. Then the machine started rattling and shaking— even the building was rocking—and that was it. It wasn't built to take that kind of punishment. Its bearings were made of copper or babbitt metal instead of steel, and they couldn't stand the friction. Also, the conveyor belt wasn't designed to revolve at such high speeds. It slid off its track, getting tangled and torn. We had to stop the machine to order a new belt about every week. Not only were belts expensive, but deliveries were slow. The machine was idle while we waited and, of course, production dropped.

Toward the end of the autumn harvest in 1958, the Peking authorities sought to keep the labor force fully occupied without additional investments. Thus they launched the "backyard furnace" program, exhorting millions of peasants, workers, students, teachers, office employees, and others to produce pig iron and steel in makeshift ovens constructed in villages, factories, schoolyards, and other available sites throughout the nation. As Belhomme noted in Tsinan, its frenzy brought the Great Leap Forward to a climax.

We were told at a meeting in our factory in September 1958 that a country without steel was like a man without bones. So, to become strong, we must produce more steel. With that, we were ordered to build small ovens in which we would make iron that would be sent to bigger plants to be refined into steel.

This not only meant that we had to cut back on manufacturing paper at our mill, but as far as I could see, it put a terrible strain on the whole economy. Trains, trucks, and even hand-drawn carts were diverted to transporting bricks, coal, and iron ore for the campaign. People were taken off their jobs and put to work at the ovens. My wife and other women were given the task of cracking coal and ore with a cast-iron hammer, working twelve hours a day. About five hundred peasants were brought into our factory to help handle the furnaces. Many burned themselves badly. Besides, they should have been repairing dikes and irrigation ditches out in the country, as peasants do between harvests. I think that the floods that came later could have been avoided if the dikes hadn't been neglected.

Most Chinese found, moreover, that the metal produced by these primitive ovens was of such poor quality that it could not be used. Nevertheless, having decided to manufacture iron and steel in this fashion, the Communists refused to admit defeat. Rather than halt the campaign, they blindly urged people to intensify their efforts. In Tsinan, the sky glowed red in the night from the fires of the furnaces, and inevitably a shortage of iron ore developed. At this stage, futility was compounded by destructiveness.

Members of the Party street committees went from house to house confiscating pots and pans, ripping up iron fences, and even tearing locks off doors. When people complained, they were told that their utensils were unnecessary, since they would soon be eating in communal mess halls. After some people were caught trying to steal back their own utensils, Party cadres smashed up the pots and pans. They tore the radiators out of our shop at the paper mill and melted them down.

By now, Party officials could no longer deny that the "backyard furnace" drive was uneconomical. And though it was not formally ended before the spring of 1959, the campaign gradually faded away. Until then, Communist cadres would only concede privately that something had gone wrong. "You can expect a person who eats a lot to shit a lot," one of them observed to Belhomme, "but those ovens—we fed them and fed them, and nothing came out."

Years later, people had denuded the abandoned furnaces of their bricks and wooden scaffolds, leaving huge, cold, immovable chunks of iron incongruously adorning the landscape like grotesque pieces of sculpture. The Chinese wryly referred to these reminders of the Great Leap Forward as "monuments." They were, indeed, monuments to a demoniac dissipation of human energy.

If the Great Leap Forward had been reckless, its aftermath was costly, painful, and tragic. Not only had the episode arrested the formidable economic momentum generated by the Communists in their first eight years in power, but between 1959 and 1961 it plunged the Chinese people back into the kind of poverty they had begun to forget, making them increasingly cynical and apathetic. The abortive experiment also exacerbated conflicts within the Communist leadership that were to have severe political consequences.

The irrationality that had paralyzed Albert Belhomme's paper mill in Tsinan was only an example of the traumas that dislocated industry throughout China. Large quantities of coal and iron had been wasted in the "backyard furnaces." As a result, locomotive, machine-tool, and other plants were forced to burn wood scraps and sawdust for fuel, while campaigns were inaugurated to collect scrap metal for industrial purposes. In Liaoning province, the Machine Industry Bureau found in a survey of thirty-one key enterprises that forty thousand tons of equipment could not be finished for lack of parts. An electric generator plant in Shenyang, the Manchurian industrial city formerly called Mukden, was discovered to have some seven thousand motors unable to function because of sloppy workmanship. A Japanese engineer who had worked in a cement-manufacturing complex in north China revealed that the eight plants that comprised the complex completely ceased operations in March 1961, putting six thousand men out of work. A dearth of raw materials as well as widespread sickness among the workers due to food scarcities contributed to the stoppage. "The old spirit is gone," the engineer said at the time. "The Chinese are now engaged in a struggle for daily survival." [15]

Chinese industry suffered another crippling blow in the summer of 1960, when the Soviet Union abruptly terminated its aid and assistance programs to the Peking regime. Exasperated by its growing dispute with the Chinese, the Kremlin withdrew its entire contingent of 1390 Russian technicians from China, thereby suspending completion of about 200 modern industrial, scientific, and military projects scheduled to have been built with Soviet help. Though this action by Moscow eventually prompted the Chinese to become more self-reliant, Peking admitted that it "disrupted China's original national economic plan and inflicted enormous losses upon China's socialist construction." [16]

The industrial setback caused by the Great Leap Forward was reflected in a 25-per-cent drop in China's exports to Hong Kong from 1958 to 1959. More dramatically, the Communists were compelled to "revise" both their production claims and new output goals. In a report to a Party conference in August 1959, Premier Chou En-lai reduced the original steel production claim for the previous year from 11 to 8 million tons and scaled down the claim for iron output by 4 million tons. For the coming year, he said, "we are . . . adjusting economic targets in the light of realities." [17]

The havoc wrought in agriculture by the Great Leap Forward was even more critical. In many areas, spurious new farming techniques had ruined the soil. Dikes, irrigation systems, and other crucial water-control facilities were neglected. Mass mobilization campaigns upset traditional cultivation patterns and drove the peasants to exhaustion. These blunders, exacerbated by bad weather for three successive years, predictably led to a sharp drop in agricultural production. Lord Montgomery, visiting China during that period, learned from official sources that grain output in 1960 had been only 150 million tons—less than in 1952, when there had been 100 million fewer mouths to feed—and that the prospects for 1961 were not bright.[18] At the same time, Foreign Minister Ch'en Yi told another British visitor to Peking that living standards were "a little tight. We must," he added, "find substitutes for food grains." [19]

Through their strong, pervasive control network, however, the Communists were able to equalize the food shortages by maintaining a strict rationing system. Widespread famine, which had so often afflicted China in the past, when the death toll during lean years ran into the millions, did not occur. Still, in the wake of the Great Leap Forward, as many as seventy thousand people were reported to have died of starvation in areas of Kansu province, a marginal region even in the best of times. Belhomme also told of deaths among peasants in the villages across the Yellow River, north of Tsinan, where poverty was endemic. The casualties from food scarcities probably stemmed from the most part from diseases caused or aggravated by malnutrition. Refugees reaching Hong Kong from Kwangtung recounted that hospitals in Canton and other provincial cities were crowded with cases of tuberculosis, hepatitis, and edema.

In a country with the continental dimensions of China, conditions vary from region to region. Therefore, if the food crisis was severe in fertile areas, it was fair surmise that poorer parts of the country were worse hit. During the winter of 1960–1961, according to refugees arriving in Hong Kong, there was no meat, no fish, scarcely any vegetables, and only meager portions of rice in Kwangtung, one of China's richest provinces. Statistical evidence of the gravity of the crisis in Kwangtung was apparent in the number of food parcels sent by Hong Kong Chinese to their families in the province soared from fewer than 1 million in 1959 to nearly 12 million in 1961.[20] In the spring of 1962, when the Communist authorities temporarily relaxed controls on emigration, more than two hundred thousand people, almost exclusively motivated by hunger, fled from Kwangtung across the border into Hong Kong in the space of a few weeks. Reports from other parts of China told of similar food shortages. Even though the regime tried to put on a good face in Peking, the nation's capital, a French correspondent there at the time described the atmosphere as sadly reminiscent of "the darkest days of the German occupation in Paris," as people lined up for hours to receive only scanty rations.[21]

In their search for "substitutes for food grains," Chinese throughout the country attempted to nourish themselves on grass, corn stalks, and other flora. A girl from Hupeh province reported that peasants were eating cakes made from cotton seeds, a form of fodder normally reserved for pigs.[22] A common dish in north China in those days was a dumpling made from sorghum and sweet-potato flour and stuffed with a mixture of tree leaves and turnip tops.[23] In Tsinan, according to Belhomme, the police put on special patrols to prevent people from stripping leaves from the acacia and birch trees that lined the city streets. Meanwhile, the regime encouraged the population to experiment with strange edibles. The authoritative *People's Daily* featured an article on chlorella, a single-cell hydrophyte found in sewers, that was said to be rich in albumin. The Botanical Research Institute of the Chinese Academy of Sciences favored "a large variety of perennial wild plants," including the cinnamon rose and the monkey oleander, while other scientists advertised a "nonpoisonous, highly nutritious plankton" called "red worm" as a source of protein. And there were, of course, some gruesome food substitutes. During the worst period of scarcities, a nurse from Peking disclosed, her hospital canteen served placenta from the maternity ward disguised as beef.

Crime proliferated as the struggle for survival became acute. In several places, hungry peasants pilfered fields and even staged raids against state granaries. Many peasants fled from their communes, either wandering into the cities as beggars or roaming the country-side as outlaws, ambushing trucks and robbing travelers. For the first time since the Communists eliminated prostitution in the early 1950s, there were reports of girls selling themselves for food-ration coupons. In Tsinan, Belhomme related, the rate of petty theft and robbery rose as desperate townsfolk deliberately sought arrest in hopes of being fed in jail. But little evidence suggests any significant political opposition to the Communist regime. Instead, a mood of disillusionment set in, betrayed in some places by instances of sarcastic humor. In Kwangtung province, cynical peasants distorted slogans to describe diligent workers as those "who still expect a thousand years of happiness in the future," and the sneering response to a complaint was: "Keep quiet, you're in para dise." [24]

One serious kind of resistance to the regime took the form of "spontaneous capitalistic tendencies," as it was officially termed. Neglecting the "collective" crops cultivated for the state, such as rice, wheat, and other grains as well as cotton and fibers, peasants devoted themselves to raising and marketing vegetables and live-stock privately. The government later sanctioned limited private enterprise when it found that only material incentives could spur food production. But the lapse into profit-making activities was in fact a natural impulse that started as early as 1959, when the food shortages were initially felt. The way it evolved in most Chinese cities was probably similar to its emergence in Tsinan as described by Belhomme:

At first, peasants with grain, vegetables, or meat to sell were very timid. They came to the outskirts of the city at two or three o'clock in the morning, and transactions were carried on by the light of a match. People bought all kinds of things they didn't usually eat, like carrot and turnip tops, and the prices were high.

As conditions worsened, the peasants became bolder, coming right into the city in daylight. The police gave up trying to stop them, and soon parts of the city were so crowded with peddlers and customers that you couldn't ride a bicycle through certain streets.

Everyone who could raise some money patronized the black

market. Families sold heirlooms to buy food. I heard that very poor people even sold their children. My wife's parents dismantled part of their house to sell the beams as firewood so they could buy sweet potatoes.

The peasants who sold black-market food became rich. They bought bicycles and even radios in spite of the fact that their villages had no electricity. They also spent huge amounts eating in the "free" restaurants, where you could order good meals without ration coupons at high prices. Once, in one of these restaurants, I saw a peasant in patched, homespun clothes reach into his pocket and pull out a wad of cash that would have choked a horse.

Gradually, shrewd middlemen gravitated toward the thriving black market, improving and expanding its operations. Due to its proximity to Hong Kong, the Kwangtung province capital of Canton became a key black market center. Among other phenomena, a big business developed in cigarette-lighter flints, which became a parallel currency in much the same way that cigarettes had been a medium of exchange in Europe after World War II. Unrestricted in their travels, operators would buy flints in the south China city of Canton for about two cents apiece, returning to sell them in Tsinan for fifty cents each. Chinese who had resettled in China from abroad reaped profits by selling the food, clothing, and other merchandise sent to them by relatives in Hong Kong, Singapore, and other places. Inevitably, too, clerks at state stores passed on extra rations to their families and friends, prompting the regime to inaugurate a campaign to "close the back door" in the distribution system.

It is no surprise, then, that the disruptions caused by the Great Leap Forward led to demoralization, corruption, and an erosion of Communist principles and practices at the lowest village level. An insight into the extent of this erosion was provided in a collection of official Communist documents captured by Chinese Nationalist guerrillas in a raid on Lien Chiang, a county of some three hundred thousand people located on coastal Fukien province.[25] From February 1962 through April 1963, the documents disclosed, peasants reverted to capitalistic activities as well as to such old customs and superstitions as arranged marriages, fortune-telling, and idol worship. Warning that "exploitation of man by man has again appeared in the villages," one document revealed that peasants in some communes were cultivating as much as half of the collective land for private purposes. One peasant was reported to have acquired considerable wealth by speculation, profiteering, and contracting labor for construction projects. A certain Li Chao-fang, who had become affluent by lending money at usurious rates, was said to have built a new house and bought a wrist watch, silk, and gold bars. "Why should we go out to work when the weather is hot?" he was alleged to have asked his wife. "We wouldn't have to worry even if there should be three years of drought." [26]

Even more alarming, the documents said, Party officials in Lien Chiang county had slid into such "bad tendencies" as embezzlement, misappropriation of funds, and excessive consumption. Many had built new homes by stealing bricks, tiles, timber, and other building materials from state warehouses and commandeering peasants to perform the work. The documents also charged officials with staging elaborate parties at state expense to celebrate births, weddings, and other occasions. At one of these parties, a Party cadre made a profit by demanding "gifts" from the guests in time-honored Chinese fashion. The food for the party was taken from the commune. Commenting on this and other cases of extravagance, a Party investigator concluded that "a considerable number of persons do not have a clear understanding of the direction of socialism." [27]

The aftermath of the Great Leap Forward also touched off troubles within the People's Liberation Army. Appalled by reports of their peasant families suffering from famine, troops openly criticized the regime they were pledged to defend. Accounts of disaffection in the Army were disclosed in secret military documents distributed and published in the early 1960s. One of the documents revealed that four hundred eighty of the six hundred men in an engineering battalion, stationed in Wuhan, a city on the Yangtze River, had families in "disaster areas" of Honan, Shantung, and Kansu provinces.[28] According to another, sixteen relatives of sixty soldiers from Szechwan province, one of the wealthiest agricultural regions in China, had died between May and December 1960 as a result of food shortages. Recording the reactions of troops to the economic situation, the document said:

They expressed a great variety of opinions, made guesses, and showed suspicions. A few of them blamed their superiors and found fault with the local authorities. Last winter, the problem of food became the outstanding and most acute ideological issue of the company. Some soldiers, having read letters from home, complained bitterly, asking: "Where did the food go?" "Why did they not have enough to eat?" "Is it true that the State has held back food from the people? . . ."

Lei Tien-chung, deputy leader of the Fourth Squad, asked: "After the communes were established, why have the crops become worse than before? . . ." Other individuals expressed grave discontent. Some soldiers whose relatives died because of the disasters wept, became depressed, and refused to talk.[29]

At the same time, hunger among the troops themselves badly impaired the physical fitness, efficiency, and morale of the Army. Soldiers grumbled that they had only joined the Army to be better fed, but were now suffering along with the rest of the population. The number of instances of edema and hepatitis among troops rose alarmingly, and an entire unit was even afflicted with parasitic diseases of the blood. The lack of food in one armored unit was such that "when a man has driven a tank for more than an hour, he becomes dizzy and nauseated." In many companies, poor conditions drove men to suicide. One unit reported eleven suicides in 1960.[30]

The breakdown in discipline led to what one document called a "deterioration in the will to fight." [31] "The idea of revisionism" was spreading in the Army, some documents warned, suggesting that officers and men were losing respect for Maoist ideology. In several instances, soldiers hard hit by the food shortages spoke out acrimoniously against the regime. A deputy squad leader named Liu Sheng-hua, whose two sisters had died of edema, was one of those who could not restrain his bitterness. "During target practice last September, he said: 'At the time of my discharge, I shall not want anything but a rifle.' Someone asked him: 'Why a rifle?' He replied: 'To fight the Party!' " [32]

CHAPTER 6

The Marshal vs. Mao

*In the view of some comrades, putting poli-
tics in command was a substitute for everything. . . . But putting politics in command
is no substitute for economic principles,
much less for concrete economic measures.*
— P'ENG TEH-HUAI, *August 1959*

*If you don't follow me, I'll recruit a new Red
Army and begin over again. I think, how-
ever, that you will follow me.*
— MAO TSE-TUNG, *August 1959*

THE GREAT LEAP FORWARD left China with an economy in
shambles, a disaffected army, a famished population, and widespread apathy and cynicism. Yet Mao Tse-tung stubbornly refused
to concede that his concept had been at fault. Instead he claimed,
as he had on earlier occasions, that the bureaucracy had failed to
carry out his orders properly. In a memorandum issued in November 1959, for example, he criticized rural officials for having "misunderstood" his directives. Among other errors, Mao said, they had
bungled his instructions for planting crops, and he accused them
of "trumpet blowing" in having set unattainable output targets
and then falsifying production statistics.[1] The causes of the failure,
Mao explained later to Lord Montgomery, had been "inexperience,
waste, and bad organization at the lower echelons" of the Communist Party.[2]

These explanations lacked credibility. For the Great Leap Forward, as everyone in China was told from its inception, had burst forth from Mao's creative genius. His tours around the countryside to give the campaign its initial push had been punctuated by official press and radio announcements affirming that he was "like the sun giving light wherever it shines." His radiance, these pronouncements claimed, had generated the "great material force" that was propelling the program at its phenomenal pace.[3] "Heaven is here on earth" as a result of Mao's prophetic vision, said the *People's Daily*, and other newspaper articles extolled his bravery, selflessness, stamina, foresight, and love for the masses in their attempts to depict him as a godlike model for all Chinese to emulate. Indeed, as part of the effort to promote physical vigor, Mao's publicists reported that he swam the mighty Yangtze River on no fewer than seven separate occasions in September 1958—when he was approaching the age of sixty-five.[4] In the face of this extravagant propaganda, then, Mao's disavowal of responsibility for the devastation rang hollow.

At the end of 1958, therefore, the Party leaders who had curbed his authority in the past again moved to reduce his power. Meeting in December at Wuchang, part of the sprawling Wuhan industrial complex that spans the Yangtze River in Hupeh province, the Party leaders effectively halted the Great Leap Forward. Backtracking from the pledge to remove the "last vestiges of private ownership" in the communes, they permitted peasants to retain their houses, fruit trees, tools, livestock, and gardens. They also replaced the piecework system with regular wages supplemented by incentive pay. And, among other things, they dropped the ambitious ideological contention that China was hurtling into that nirvana known as communism.[5] At the same meeting, Mao handed in his resignation as Chairman of the Republic—though he would remain Chairman of the Party Central Committee. An official communiqué issued at the time declared that, having sought to resign on several previous occasions, he had retired voluntarily. Describing him in almost obituary language as the "sincerely beloved and long-tested leader of the people," the communiqué added that Mao would henceforth "concentrate his energies on dealing with questions of the direction, policy, and line of the Party and the state" as well as devote "more time to Marxist-Leninist theoretical work." [6]

The Party leaders had apparently persuaded—perhaps even compelled—Mao to relinquish his position as head of state. Years later, when the growing tensions between him and the Party had erupted into the open, Mao was quoted as recalling his dismissal bitterly: "I was most dissatisfied with the decision, but there was nothing I could do about it." Referring to the accolade that had accompanied his ouster, he was reported to have said wryly that his Party adversaries "treated me with the respect they would have shown their dead father at his own funeral." [7] But, then still concerned with protecting Mao's public image, the Party leaders directed rank-and-file officials to explain his demotion carefully to the people "so that the reasons for this may be understood by all, and that there may be no misunderstanding." [8]

A variety of considerations dictated this cautious approach. In contrast to the Russians, whose brutal methods reached insane proportions under Stalin, the Chinese Communists have been relatively humane in their internecine quarrels. Thus the Party leaders may have been genuinely deferential in their old chief. They were also, in the wake of the devastating Great Leap Forward, reluctant to trigger an internal squabble that would further weaken the country. In addition, they seemed to have believed that they could manipulate Mao's immense prestige in the pursuit of their own policies. This tactic, which they did in fact use for years afterward, was later described by Mao's publicists as "waving the Red Flag in order to oppose the Red Flag." At the same time, however, the Party leaders knew that Mao had substantial power to wield against them in a showdown. Indeed, Mao demonstrated this power in the summer of 1959 in a sharp and significant clash with a faction of opponents headed by Marshal P'eng Teh-huai, the Defense Minister.

A crusty old officer with the body of a bull and the face of a bulldog, P'eng was essentially a peasant. His ideological knowledge was limited—even though, as an old comrade recalled, his pockets were usually stuffed with political pamphlets that he read haltingly whenever he could spare the time. His military talent was also debatable. During the war against the Japanese and again in the Korean War, his impulsive, aggressive nature propelled him into several strategic errors. Moreover, he was a difficult, churlish individual who had squabbled with nearly every senior Communist, including Mao, at one time or another. One of his ambitions in the 1930s had been to replace Chu Teh as commander in chief of the Army, and, according to those who knew him, his disappointment at being passed over added to his surliness. Mixed with these shortcomings, however, was a quality that gave P'eng enormous influence in the Communist movement. He was, as one of his ex-comrades called him, a "soldier's soldier"—a stubborn, rugged fighter capable of enduring the worst kind of battlefield hardships along with his troops.[9] He was hugely popular with his men, and his cool courage even inspired Mao to compose a rather banal poem in his praise:

> Mountains are high, trails are long, valleys are deep;
> Large formations of troops rush in all directions.
> Who can calmly rein in his horse and sheathe his sword?
> Who else but our valiant great General P'eng! [10]

But P'eng's devotion to the Army, combined with his peasant instincts, were among the very traits that induced him to challenge Mao in the period following the Great Leap Forward. He had several grievances against Mao. As a professional soldier, he blamed the Great Leap Forward for setting back military modernization as well as aggravating Peking's dispute with the Soviet Union, the only source of China's sophisticated weapons. He was also troubled by the extent to which schemes to employ troops as farm laborers had hampered military training and eroded Army morale. And, remembering his peasant origins, he was shocked by the disruptions caused to the countryside by Mao's wild drive.

Personal vanity and ambition also aggravated the quarrels within the Chinese Communist leadership. Like many of his comrades, P'eng apparently resented the personality cult that Mao had built around himself and on one occasion, decrying the traditional slogan wishing Mao ten thousand years of life, was heard to grumble: "He won't even live a hundred years." [11] According to another report, P'eng vetoed the erection of busts of Mao in military installations on the grounds that "we will only have to remove them in the future." [12] P'eng was said to have complained as well that, as Defense Minister, he had to submit to the Military Affairs Commission of the Central Committee headed by Mao. "What kind of Defense Minister am I?" he was quoted as saying.

"I'm neither like the Soviet Defense Minister, who has the power to command, nor like the American Secretary of Defense, who controls the budget. I just welcome and bid farewell to people." [13]

In late 1958 or early 1959, therefore, P'eng put himself at the forefront of a group determined to defy if not overthrow Mao. Among his known allies were General Huang K'o-ch'eng, Chief of General Staff; Chou Hsiao-chou, the Party boss of Hunan province; and Lin Po-ch'ü, a seasoned and highly respected member of the Politburo. Like P'eng and Mao, these men were all Hunanese. Oddly enough for a barely literate soldier, P'eng counted among his other associates one of China's most cosmopolitan intellectuals, Deputy Foreign Minister Chang Wen-t'ien. A Politburo member and former ambassador to Moscow, Chang had worked in the United States and studied in the Soviet Union and had, among other sidelines, translated D'Annunzio, Oscar Wilde, Tolstoi, and Henri Bergson into Chinese. As later evidence made plain, the P'eng faction also had the sympathy if not the active support of the pivotal Peking Committee of the Communist Party headed by another Politburo member, P'eng Chen. If they were not actually part of the P'eng Teh-huai "clique," as subsequent allegations against them claimed, Liu Shao-ch'i, Teng Hsiao-p'ing, and other senior Party *apparatchiks* must have known of the plot against Mao and conceivably gave it their tacit blessing. Years afterward, assessing the assorted internal enemies he had faced, Mao described their different styles. Liu Shao-ch'i and Teng Hsiao-p'ing were "open and not secret," but P'eng Teh-huai, he said, had been a "double-dealer." [14] Given his chauvinism and profound ideological self-righteousness, Mao may have been offended less by P'eng's intrigue than by the old Marshal's connivance with the Soviet "revisionists."

Relations between Peking and Moscow were deteriorating rapidly at that stage, for a variety of reasons. Not the least among them was Soviet hostility to Mao's assertion, issued during the Great Leap Forward, that he was outstripping the Russians on the road to pure Communism. On a visit to the Chinese capital in the summer of 1958, Khrushchev bluntly told Mao that such "innovations" as the "people's communes" were nonsense.[15] Soon after that, the Kremlin leader abandoned all sense of fraternal propriety by telling an American politician, Senator Hubert Humphrey, that Mao's "communes" were an "old-fashioned and reactionary" experiment that had failed in the Soviet Union a generation before.[16] Increasingly worried by what they considered to be Peking's growing truculence in international affairs, the Soviet rulers also signaled their intention to abrogate an earlier promise to give the Chinese a "sample" atomic bomb and technical data for manufacturing nuclear weapons.[17] These moves apparently prompted P'eng Teh-huai to take the Russians into his confidence.

Both P'eng and Chang Wen-t'ien had been relatively close to the Soviet leaders for years. In addition to having studied and later served as ambassador in Moscow, Chang had been intimately linked to the Russians as Chinese representative to the Comintern. As late as November 1957, when Mao was urging the Communist bloc to stiffen its position against the "imperialists," Chang had contrastingly endorsed Moscow's plea for "peaceful coexistence." [18] P'eng, meanwhile, had been a frequent visitor to the Soviet Union to oversee the Kremlin's program of military assistance to the Chinese Army. In fact, it was P'eng who had negotiated the 1957 nuclear accord that now, less than two years later, the Russians were threatening to break.

In April 1959, P'eng embarked on a "military good-will" tour of Eastern Europe. While in Tirana, the capital of Albania, he met another traveler, Nikita Khrushchev. The encounter was deliberate. One of P'eng's objectives, if not his principal aim, was to dissuade Khrushchev from retracting his pledge to assist China in developing a nuclear arsenal. In the course of their conversation, much of which undoubtedly concerned conditions inside China at that time, P'eng showed Khrushchev the draft of a letter he planned to hand to Mao, criticizing the Great Leap Forward and its aftermath. Perhaps P'eng hoped to convince Khrushchev that the Chinese Army was opposed to Mao's adventurism and deserved to receive nuclear aid from Moscow. Though he had no intention of giving the Chinese an atomic bomb—and, indeed, broke the Sino-Soviet nuclear agreement a month later—Khrushchev presumably encouraged P'eng to proceed with his plan to challenge Mao.[19] When he heard of the talks between Khrushchev and P'eng not long afterward, Mao must have been reminded of the days, decades before, when Stalin had tried to replace him with Chinese rivals more receptive to Soviet dictates. Understandably furious, Mao later accused Khrushchev of having conducted "behind-the-scenes factional activity against a fraternal Party," [20] and charged the P'eng group with "betrayal of the fatherland" by having "sown discord at the bidding of a foreign country." [21]

Apparently anticipating P'eng's challenge on the eve of their clash, Mao was in an unyielding mood. A month earlier, he had returned to his birthplace of Shaoshan for the first time in thirty-two years, and there he composed a poem in which his remembrance of things past reinforced his present self-confidence:

> Red flags fly from the spears of the enslaved peasants,
> Black hands raise high the last of the tyrannical landowners.
> Only because so many sacrificed themselves did our wills
>   become strong,
> So that we dared command the sun and moon to bring a new day.

Soon after that, Mao wrote another, more esoteric verse in which he alluded to the celebrated fifth-century poet T'ao Yuanming, who had dreamed of a utopia that could not have matched the earthly paradise of the "people's communes" during the Great Leap Forward:

> Where has Magistrate T'ao gone now?
> Can one cultivate the land in the Peach-blossom Spring? [22]

The scene of the showdown between P'eng and Mao was, incongruously, the exquisite mountain resort of Kuling, in the Lushan highlands of central Kiangsi province. With its vista of gardens, lakes, and ancient temples perched atop craggy rocks, Kuling had long been an appealing spot for scholars and poets, who left inscriptions in steles that still dotted the landscape. The area was later a vacation retreat for Europeans from nearby Shanghai and there, too, Chiang Kai-shek had built a splendid summer residence. Now the Communist Party dignitaries were assembled at Kuling for meetings that would last through July and August of 1959. Among those present, along with the nearly two hundred full and alternate members of the Party's Central Committee, was a senior Soviet diplomat, F. N. Antonov. Officially billed as an "observer," Antonov was certainly aware of P'eng Teh-huai's intentions and, from his conveniently located pavilion, he may have even imparted advice to Mao's enemies.[23]

For six successive mornings in early July, probably before most of the delegates had arrived, P'eng put forth his views to a small conclave of comrades. Over the two previous years, he said, the Party had become so "highly elated" by its purported "victories" that it currently had "fever on the brain." During the Great Leap Forward, he had personally inspected the rural areas, among them Mao's native village in Hunan not far from his own birthplace, and found their production reports to be false. Each region should have told the truth without waiting for its lies to be exposed, P'eng emphasized. "You must take off your own pants, rather than let others pull them down." The heads of one province, Kiangsi, were still claiming to have boosted output by 67 per cent the previous year. "They should be stripped once and for all to save others the trouble," P'eng said. As for the failure of the Great Leap as a whole, he stressed, "everybody had a share of the responsibility, including Comrade Mao Tse-tung." [24]

Deploying themselves for a more formal assault against Mao, P'eng and his colleagues printed and distributed a polished version of the letter criticizing Mao that P'eng had shown to Khrushchev in Tirana nearly two months before. Written in the characteristically sweet-and-pungent style of a bold memorial to a bygone emperor, the memorandum was too clever for P'eng's primitive brush, and must have been the work of Chang Wen-t'ien and others in the conspiracy. But it was a salvo that would echo and re-echo for years to come.

In traditional fashion, the so-called "Letter of Opinion" opened on a note of fulsome praise for Mao's policies. Economic growth attained in China during the Great Leap Forward "has never been achieved in other parts of the world," it affirmed. Then, subtly criticizing Mao, the message went on to contrast the shortcomings of his experiment with its claims of success. Though capital construction projects "will gradually yield results," the memorandum said, they had been "too hasty and excessive" and had therefore created "imbalances and new temporary difficulties." Despite their "great significance," the "people's communes" had experienced "a period of confusion regarding the question of ownership." As for the "backyard-furnace" drive, it had served to "temper and improve" rural officials even though "material and financial resources were squandered" and the "tuition fee" of some 2 billion *yuan* for such an educational effort was rather exorbitant. Turning to the causes of these blunders, P'eng's letter directed its fire against Mao and his supporters.

They had encouraged the frenetic race to concoct phony statistics, the memorandum said, deluding everyone into believing that "the problem of food had been solved and that our hands would be freed to engage in industry." But even then, "there was serious superficiality in our understanding of the development of the iron and steel industry," with nobody properly able to cope with steel refining, transport, labor needs, and other such matters. Because no attempt was made to "seek truth from the facts," the letter asserted, "it seemed that communism was just around the corner, and more than a few comrades became dizzy." Extravagance, waste, and inefficiency proliferated because "we considered ourselves rich while actually we were still poor."

Accordingly, the P'eng faction complained, "it was not easy to get a true picture of conditions," and even as late as January 1959, Provincial and Municipal Party Committees were "still unable to find out the realities of the over-all situation." The trouble was that "there were only tasks and targets, but no concrete measures"—and this, as the memorandum put it in convoluted Communist jargon, prompted "petty-bourgeois fanaticism" that led to "leftist" mistakes. "Bewitched by the achievements of the Great Leap Forward and the passion of the mass movement," said the statement, "some leftist tendencies emerged, since we had always wanted to enter communism in a single step."

As a result of this "fanaticism," programs were not pursued on a "positive, steady, and reliable basis." Goals that required a decade to fulfill were supposed to be accomplished in a year "or even several months." In areas where bumper harvests were announced, quantities of food were wasted as "everyone was encouraged to eat as much as he could." New and untested techniques were adopted "without evaluation," and certain "economic and scientific laws were negated lightly." All these and other blunders, the P'eng letter made clear, stemmed from Mao's blithe assertion that his brand of ideology could perform miracles.

In the view of some comrades, putting politics in command could be a substitute for everything. . . . But putting politics in command is no substitute for economic principles, much less for concrete economic measures.[25]

Mao was overwhelmed by the ferocity of a bombardment that, as he later put it, "nearly leveled half of Lushan." He was also stunned by the attacks of other comrades, who accused him of being "despotic and dictatorial" and compared him to the paranoiac Stalin "in his declining years." [26] His initial instinct was to defend himself. At one meeting, therefore, he denied that there had been anything wrong with seeking "greater, faster, better, and more economical results," as one of the inspirational slogans of the Great Leap had proclaimed. The "shortcomings and mistakes" of the Great Leap had been minor, he contended, describing them in P'eng's phrase as the "tuition fee that must be paid to gain experience." Moreover, the setbacks had been transient, Mao said: "Come back in ten years to see whether we were correct." [27]

During the next week, Mao was apparently silent as he tried to measure the strength of his foes. As a youth, he later explained, he angered quickly at "bad remarks" against himself, but since then he had learned to listen before responding. Finally, on July 23, he counterattacked. At a plenary session of the Central Committee he delivered a long, rambling, disjointed reply to the P'eng group that was alternately humorous and solemn, apologetic and self-righteous, academic and earthy, sentimental and tough, persuasive and menacing. It was, with these contradictions, the real, elusive Mao, and it was climxed by the typical gesture of the charismatic leader—the threat to reject the bureaucrats and return to the masses in whose wisdom he would find support.

Opening on an ironic note, Mao reminded his audience that right-wring critics of his policies had likened him to the Ch'in emperor Shih Huang-ti, who fell because of his vast expenditures on the Great Wall of China. "Now we are about to collapse because of what we have done," Mao said. But such complaints were inconsequential, exaggerated.

China is not going to sink into the sea and the sky won't tumble down simply because there are shortages of vegetables and hairpins and soap. Imbalances and market problems have made everybody tense so that the people as a whole have become tense. But this tension is not justified, even though I'm tense myself. No, it wouldn't be honest to say I'm not tense. I'm tense before midnight, but I take some sleeping pills and then I feel better. You ought to try sleeping pills if you're tense.

He had urged speed during the Great Leap Forward, but now Mao admonished lower-ranking officials for having tried to set a rapid pace. "There can be no room for rashness," he said. "When you eat pork, you can only consume mouthful by mouthful, and you can't expect to get fat in a single day. Both the commander in chief [Chu Teh] and I are fat, but we didn't get that way overnight."

Mao then addressed himself to P'eng Teh-huai's charge that the Great Leap Forward had been a case of "petty-bourgeois fanaticism." Estimating the ideological coloration of the population, he calculated that 30 per cent of the people were revolutionary activists, 30 per cent opposed change, and 40 per cent "follow the tide." The one-third who actively favored the revolution, he said,

> . . . comprise 150 million people. They want to run communes and mess halls and undertake large-scale collectives. They are very enthusiastic. Can you call this "petty-bourgeois fanaticism"? They are not the petty bourgeoisie, but poor peasants, lower-middle peasants, proletariat, and semi-proletariat. . . . The "neutral" 40 per cent went along with them for a time and then 350 million people had the passion.

Mao urged that the communal mess halls be retained since, according to his estimate, 150 million "activists" wanted them. Indeed, he went on, communal eating arrangements should be extended rather than curbed, since they were "not invented by us, but by the masses." Those who criticized the mess halls and other innovations of the Great Leap Forward were only inflating its errors and neglecting its accomplishments. Errors were inevitable, Mao argued, pointing to the giants of history who, presumably like himself, had not been perfect.

> Everybody has shortcomings. Even Confucius made mistakes. So did Marx. He thought that the revolution would take place in Europe during his lifetime. I have seen Lenin's manuscripts, which are

filled with changes. He, too, made mistakes. . . . Have we failed? No, our failure has been only partial. We have paid too high a price, but a gust of Communist wind has been whipped up and the country has learned a lesson.

His own mistake, Mao explained, was his failure to perceive the errors being committed by the State Planning Commission and the government ministries, which abandoned attempts to manage the economy rationally during the Great Leap.

I am not trying to make excuses—even though this is still an excuse—but Premier Chou En-lai and I knew little about this business of planning. I am not Chairman of the State Planning Commission. Before August of last year, I devoted myself mainly to revolution. I am absolutely no good at construction, and I don't understand industrial planning. So don't write about my wise leadership, since I had not even taken charge of these matters. However, Comrades, I should take the primary responsibility for 1958 and 1959. It is I who am to blame.

Dramatizing his confession of guilt, Mao cited the ancient Confucian dictum that "he who first made clay idols to bury with the dead should have no posterity." This apothegm, originally intended to discourage a ritual associated with human sacrifice, had come to mean that evil deeds would be punished. Recalling that one of his sons had been killed in the Korean War and another was insane, Mao asked poignantly: "Am I, therefore, to have no posterity?"

Rank-and-file Communist officials were also guilty when they deprived peasants of their belongings at the height of the Great Leap Forward campaign to set up "people's communes," Mao emphasized. The "egalitarianism" of the communes had been wrong: "Nobody should say, what's yours is mine, take it and walk away. That is the law of underworld gangsters who steal and rob and exploit labor." Mao approved of the bandits in *All Men Are Brothers* who had "robbed the rich and helped the poor." But, he added, "what was taken from the peasants must be returned to them. We cannot confiscate the property of working people."

These failings proved once again, Mao continued, that insufficient attention had been paid to educating both local officials and peasants. "An illiterate person can be a Prime Minister, so why can't our commune cadres and peasants learn something about political economy?" he said. "Everybody can learn. Those who cannot read may also discuss economics and, through discussion, they will understand the subject more easily than the intellectual. I myself have never read textbooks!"

Thus, Mao conceded to P'eng, he shared the responsibility with the Party for the troubles caused by the Great Leap Forward. But if he admitted to his mistakes, so must the Party officials. "Comrades, you must also analyze your errors, and you will feel better after you have broken wind and emptied your bowels."

The real danger now, Mao stressed, was the rise of his enemies who, in their opposition to "adventurism," were becoming rightists under the influence of the imperialists and bourgeoisie. The "people's communes" and other features of the Great Leap Forward, "will never collapse" despite P'eng Teh-huai's desire to abolish them, he affirmed. Indicting P'eng as an "ambitionist" and a "hypocrite," he accused him of working to "sabotage the dictatorship of the proletariat, split the Communist Party, organize factions in the Party, spread their influence, demoralize the vanguards of the proletariat, and build another opportunist party of their own." Therefore, Mao asserted, their conflict at the Lushan meeting was a "class struggle"—a continuation of the "life-and-death struggle between the two antagonistic classes of the bourgeoisie and the proletariat in the revolution."

Apparently in response to warnings that the purge of P'eng would ignite a military revolt against him, Mao felt compelled to carry the quarrel to a showdown. He turned to the senior officers present. If outvoted, he said defiantly, he would go back to the countryside to recruit a new peasant army and return to overthrow the government. "If you don't follow me, I'll recruit a new Red Army and begin over again," he challenged them. "I think, however, that you will follow me." [28]

At that point the Chinese generals reportedly stood up in turn and pledged their allegiance to Mao.[29]

Still, P'eng stubbornly declined to yield. He warned that conditions in China were deteriorating so rapidly that a "Hungarian rebellion" was bound to erupt and that the Soviet Army would have to be summoned to restore order. As Mao sought to cut short the debate by adjourning the meeting, P'eng reminded him of a dispute between them in the wilderness two decades earlier. "In Yenan you fucked my mother for forty days," P'eng barked. "Now I've only fucked your mother for eighteen days and you're trying to stop me, but you won't." [30]

P'eng was correct—at least for the moment. Even though the generals lined up behind him, Mao seemed unable to rally the Central Committee to condemn P'eng and his group rapidly. He therefore turned to an assortment of persuasive tactics in an effort to dislodge his adversaries. Early in August, he addressed a firm yet conciliatory letter to Chang Wen-t'ien, P'eng's closest supporter, warning him of the implications of their conspiracy. Mao charitably attributed Chang's "error" to chronic malaria, but suggested that the illness might be beneficial if it sweated the wickedness out of him. Mao concluded: "Comrade, take my advice: rectify yourself thoroughly." [31]

Mao also wrote to another adversary, Li Chung-yun, a senior official in the State Planning Commission. Li was wrong to have underlined only the blunders of the Great Leap Forward, said Mao. But he commended Li for having "laid bare" his mind, saying: "Over the past ten years, we have not come across a comrade who dares to expose cogently, analytically, and systematically the shortcomings in our plans. . . . I have not come across such a person. I know that such persons exist, but they are afraid to go over the heads of their superiors." [32]

In short, Mao was striving to demonstrate, it was inaccurate to label him a despot who would not brook criticism. On the contrary, he welcomed criticism—provided, of course, that it did not represent an attack by the "rightists" and other bourgeois foes whose aim was to wreck the Communist movement. But the problem was how to distinguish between acceptable and hostile criticism. An equally difficult problem was how to recognize when prominent Party luminaries like P'eng Teh-huai and his associates had deviated from the official orthodoxy to become "enemies of the people." Mao assembled the conference delegates at a series of meetings in an attempt to give them the answers.

At one of these meetings, he reiterated his fundamental thesis that "class struggle" within the Party as well as in society would continue for a long time before pure communism was attained. Since this struggle was "full of twists and turns," Mao said, it was understandable for comrades to wonder why "the chief culprits of today were the meritorious statesmen of yesterday." The answer was that they had strayed from the "correct" line, refused to confess to their sins and mend their ways, and, as a result, became transformed from tolerable critics to adversaries beyond redemption.[33]

In the case of P'eng Teh-huai and his faction, Mao went on to elaborate, they had never been true Marxists but were "bourgeois and opportunist elements" who had managed to "sneak into our Party" disguised as "fellow travelers of Marxism." This was obvious from their behavior, Mao asserted. They had "employed conspiratorial means to split the Party," thereby violating discipline in their effort to destroy Communist unity. More important, they had consulted Khrushchev, which proved that they were "working hand-in-glove with a foreign country" in their plot to sow discord.[34]

Mao then carried his case back to the Central Committee with another speech. Unlike his discursive address of the previous month, this talk was short and sharp. A year before, he said, "there was no clear sign of a split" in the Communist Party, but now "such a sign" did exist. The task, then, was to separate the "mistaken" comrades whose errors could be corrected from those who adamantly refused to repent. The dizziness of the Great Leap Forward was over and there would be "no more pompous exaggeration," said Mao. The main thrust at the moment, he emphasized, was to "oppose the right"—as personified by P'eng Teh-huai and his cohorts.[35]

Just as his impetuosity had led him to commit battlefield blunders, so P'eng's impulsiveness compromised his challenge to Mao. He had struck too soon. Two years later, when the cumulative effect of the Great Leap Forward had plunged China into a deeper social and economic abyss, he might have succeeded. But in 1959, P'eng could not muster the support he needed to sustain his offensive against Mao. Compelled to retreat, he went through the ritual of confessing his alleged sins and appealing for absolution.

In his recantation, P'eng described his utterances as having been "a series of rightist absurdities" that had dealt a "blow to the activism of the broad masses and cadres, and damaged the prestige of the Party Central Committee and Comrade Mao Tse-tung." His "crime," he added, was all the more heinous for having been "prepared and organized" rather than "casual." [36]

On August 16, the Central Committee issued a verdict against P'eng and his associates in a lengthy document condemning them for their present deviation as well as for "divisive activities" purportedly committed more than two decades earlier. Their "mistakes," the verdict read, were not "isolated" or "accidental," but represented a "right opportunist line" they had pursued for years. They were officially dismissed from their respective government posts—but, pending admission of all their "errors," they could retain their places in the Party, and "we shall see how they behave in the future." [37]

P'eng's reaction to his ouster was a letter to Mao so passionately abject in style and substance that it constitutes almost a caricature of ceremonial self-abnegation. His dismissal was a "great victory" for the Party, he wrote, since it revealed "how horrible would be the danger if I were not exposed and criticized so thoroughly in time." "Bourgeois attitudes" had permeated him to such depths that for the past thirty years "I have been unworthy of your education and patience, so much so that I cannot express in words my regret and gratitude." Asserting that he had "failed the Party, failed the people, and also failed you," P'eng requested Mao's authorization to labor in the countryside in order to "steel myself and reform my ideology." [38] On September 17, he was officially replaced as Minister of Defense by Marshal Lin Piao, the brilliant Korean War commander. The Chief of General Staff, General Huang K'o-ch'eng, also dismissed, was replaced by General Lo Jui-ch'ing, who until then had been Minister of Public Security.[39] Chang Wen-t'ien was relegated to obscurity.

"Now that I'm out of office I feel free," P'eng was reported to have exclaimed, and, consistent with Mao's treatment of his foes, he was accorded an unusual degree of independence. Permitted to retain his nominal membership in the Politburo, P'eng was assigned first to serve as superintendent of a state farm in the northern province of Heilungkiang and later allowed to travel throughout China investigating agricultural conditions. These trips apparently confirmed his feeling that he had been justified in criticizing Mao's policies. In November 1961, P'eng prepared five separate studies on the situation in Hunan, all deploring the food shortages that persisted in that region. A year later, he produced an eighty-thousand-word-memorandum detailing the accuracy of his observations on the Great Leap Forward and demanding his "rehabilitation." Though never reinstated in the government, P'eng's Party position remained equivocal and even as late as December 1966, after a group of Red Guards arrested him in Chengtu, he defiantly defended himself. "I was no executioner of the masses," he said. "I was half right and half wrong. I made mistakes, but I rendered meritorious service as well." [40]

If Mao ostensibly emerged triumphant from his clash with P'eng, his victory was limited. First, P'eng had overtly voiced what most of the Party apparatus really thought of the Great Leap Forward and its blunders. Hence his disclosures marked a turning point that would be followed by a considerable Party effort to reverse Mao's past economic policies in favor of a more moderate approach to development. Second, as the official indictment against him had affirmed, P'eng's challenge did indeed damage Mao's prestige by shattering the Chairman's carefully cultivated mystique of omniscience, and this provided the Party leaders with a fresh opportunity to curb Mao's power. Finally, P'eng's daring assault against Mao had a striking impact on senior Chinese military officers, and it touched off a conflict between Mao and his adversaries for control of the Army that was never entirely resolved. Far from restoring Chinese Communist unity, the purge of P'eng and his "clique" was the beginning of a new phase in a struggle that would reach even more traumatic heights in the Cultural Revolution.

CHAPTER 7

The Party Takes Command

Liu Shao-ch'i and his confederates tried to put Mao nicely on a shelf like a Buddha so that people would blindly kow-tow to him while their clique managed the affairs of State in their own way.

— ANNA LOUISE STRONG, 1969

They treated me with the respect they would have shown their dead father at his own funeral.

— MAO TSE-TUNG, 1967

IN THE SPRING of 1961, accompanied by his wife, Liu Shao-ch'i traveled south from Peking into Hunan province. There he spend forty-four days investigating economic conditions in several areas, including the village of Huaminglou, his birthplace in Ning-hsiang county. A cold, aloof man hardened by years as a ruthless Communist organizer, Liu usually kept his emotions in check. But he was appalled by what he saw in Hunan. In one village, the population had decreased as a result of deaths from malnutrition, and food shortages still persisted. Irrigation systems, dikes, and water conservancy projects had fallen into disrepair, and peasants almost everywhere he visited were bitter, weary, and apathetic at having been compelled to labor like animals during the Great Leap Forward. Though government propaganda was officially attributing China's difficulties at that time to floods, droughts, and other natural calamities, Liu privately offered a different explanation. "The problems were not caused by natural calamities," he said. "They were man-made." [1]

The man was Mao and, in the early 1960s, the Party leaders headed by Liu moved quickly to reshape the strategies that had caused such damage to China. Henceforth, they announced, "all possible material, technical, and financial aid" would be funneled into agriculture in a crash program to boost farm production.[2] In contrast to the First Five-Year Plan, which bled the peasants to pay for heavy industry, factories would now serve the rural sector. Farm output would no longer be spurred through Maoist mobilization schemes but with technical investments. Urban capital construction was suspended, and factories were ordered to concentrate on turning out tractors, farm implements, insecticides, and irrigation equipment. Instructions went out to build small- and medium-sized chemical-fertilizer plants, and imports of chemical fertilizer from Japan and Belgium soared. Swallowing their Chinese pride and their belief in the superiority of communism, the Party leaders also took the unprecedented step of contracting to purchase 5 to 6 million tons of grain, principally wheat, from Australia, Canada, and other capitalist nations at an annual cost of $300 to $400 million. These grain purchases were partly intended to feed China's coastal cities and thereby to relieve the pressure on China's primitive railway system.

Fundamental in this new approach was an attempt to introduce rationality into Chinese economic operations. "We want to keep our two feet on the ground," advised the Peking directives stressing the need for pragmatism. For one thing, mechanization would no longer mean the serial production of heavy-duty tractors, but the manufacture of modest machinery suited to particular topographical conditions and job requirements. Efforts would be made to supplant human manpower with threshers, huskers, tillers, harrows, multi-share plows, and other simple tools that could be repaired on the spot. To help in this task, some twenty-five thousand small workshops were established under the auspices of the Second Ministry of Light Industry. Similarly, local Party cadres were told to stop setting ludicrous targets and to face realities. "We still cannot control nature completely," declared one Peking pronouncement. "Traditions that have come down to us from our ancestors all contain some truth. . . . What crops to plan, when to sow, how to cultivate, when to harvest—these cannot be changed by man's will." Another article, urging cadres to heed the wisdom of "sage old peasants," stated: "We must oppose that kind of leadership in production that does not start from real conditions, that claims to know and give orders without knowing. . . . If you do not know, do not pretend that you do."

An equally important shift in this new policy of "retrenchment," as it was euphemistically labeled, was a drastic alteration in the structures imposed on the countryside during the Great Leap Forward. Though the people's communes were theoretically left intact, they were radically modified to place power in the hands of "production teams," each comprising twenty to thirty families. These units, which resembled the "mutual-aid" groups set up six years before, were authorized to determine their own utilization of manpower, land, draft animals, and implements. Moreover, they were permitted to decide on expenditures and income distribution without interference from commune, provincial, and central government officials—provided, of course, that they produced negotiated quantities of grain, cotton, fibers, and other "cash" crops for the state.

Perhaps the most significant switch in agriculture, however, was to a liberal policy given the typical numerological slogan of "three privates and one guarantee." Now, peasants could legally cultivate limited private gardens, pursue their own handicrafts, and sell their produce at free markets so long as they fulfilled the grain and raw material output quotas recommended by the state. This was less an innovation than the legitimization of private farming and black-market activity that had sprung up spontaneously during the hungry days after the Great Leap Forward. To the Maoists it represented a great leap back to the capitalist laws of supply and demand, but the Party leaders, desperate to stimulate production, felt that any workable method was acceptable. "We must employ every possible means that contributes to the productive enthusiasm of the peasants," said Liu Shao-ch'i, adding that the prospect of capitalist tendencies appearing "is not so horrible." [3] Secretary General Teng Hsiao-p'ing expressed the pragmatic approach more colorfully: "Private farming is all right as long as it raises production, just as it doesn't matter whether a cat is black or white as long as it catches mice." [4]

These various calls for liberalism were echoed by economic specialists within the Party apparatus. Vice-Premier Ch'en Yun, a consistent advocate of moderation, asserted that only by "beating a retreat" to some sort of *laissez-faire* practice could the regime hope to improve peasant morale and thereby revive production." [5] And the Vice-Chairman of the State Planning Commission, Po I-po, reporting that "the situation in the countryside is worse than it was before the war," proposed that one way to raise their output was through "more income, more food, and more consumer goods for those who perform more work." [6] He said:

> It is wrong to think merely of production and not of the life of the people, to neglect harmony between work and rest, to disregard safety in production, to look simply at present-day production and ignore the next step, to eat up reserves in the warehouses, to use equipment and manpower to excess, and thus fail to maintain a steady productive rhythm. These things are bad for management. [7]

In parallel with this focus on temperance and practicality, the Party leaders emphasized the need for specialized skills, suggesting that bourgeois "technocrats" would be not only tolerated again but encouraged to join in the effort to pull the country out of its economic mess. "Questions of right and wrong in science are not decided by subjective 'convincing arguments,' but by their conformity . . . to reality," said a *Red Flag* article in January, 1961. [8] Speaking to graduates of Peking University a few months after that, Foreign Minister Ch'en Yi stressed the importance of professional knowledge to meet the challenge of "building up our country as a great socialist power with modern industry, modern agriculture, and modern science and culture." In a direct slap at one of Mao's tenets, Ch'en said that it was a "mistake" to judge people by their political leanings as long as "they are successful in their studies and contribute to socialist construction." [9] And, he added, "who wants to fly with a pilot who is ideologically pure but cannot manage the controls?"

Ch'en Yi's speech was welcomed by the Peking University students as a "liberation." Moreover, it was followed by real changes.

Professors who had been purged for political faults were "rehabilitated," and the educational curriculum was broadened. Closed fields of research, such as psychoanalysis, were reopened. Translations of Western authors began to reappear, and there was a marked relaxation in the control of Chinese poets, playwrights, and novelists.[10]

Apparently striving to consolidate their own position, the Party *apparatchiks* also began a thinly disguised literary onslaught against Mao and his policies. The authors and journalists employed in this effort were associated with either the Party's Propaganda Department or its Peking Committee—and were plainly, therefore, acting on behalf of Liu Shao-ch'i and his colleagues as well as for P'eng Chen, Party boss of the capital. Most of these literary broadsides aimed at three different targets. First, though accepting the idea of Mao as China's leader, they assailed the cult of his personality. Second, they underscored the devastation caused by the Great Leap Forward and demanded an end to such experiments. And finally, they contended that Marshal P'eng Teh-huai had been unjustly purged for having dared to say openly what numbers of Party officials personally believed. Liu Shao-ch'i probably favored a reversal of the verdict against the old Marshal, for he was quoted as having said that "some comrades also made speeches that more or less resembled those made by P'eng Teh-huai." [11]

Paradoxically, several of Mao's most vigorous literary opponents were the very men who had stifled intellectual freedom within the Chinese Communist movement since the early 1940s. Foremost among them was Chou Yang, a Hunanese whose experience as a left-wing writer and editor reached back thirty years. In August 1962, under the auspices of the Party's Propaganda Department, Chou organized a two-week conference of literary bureaucrats at Dairen, at which one speaker after another lashed out at Mao and the privations caused by the Great Leap Forward. The Vice-President of the Human branch of the Chinese Writers' Union, K'ang Cho, stressed the "contradiction between socialist ideological leadership and the actual needs of the peasants," urging authors to dramatize the pressures imposed by Mao on the rural population. In an assault against Mao's thesis that the proletariat be portrayed as flawless heroes, Shao Chuan-lin, Secretary of the Writers' Union, criticized "oversimplification, doctrinairism, and mechanical theories" in Chinese literature. Instead of depicting heroic and villainous extremes, Shao said, writers should describe the vast majority of the population as "people in the middle," as yet uncommitted to the revolution.[12]

At the same time, an even more withering if subtle fusillade against Mao came from the pen of the prominent historian and deputy mayor of Peking, Wu Han. In June 1959, obviously writing with the approval of his immediate superior, P'eng Chen, Wu had produced an essay on Hai Jui, a high official of the Ming dynasty who had served in the region of Soochow in the sixteenth century. Entitled "Hai Jui Scolds the Emperor," the analogy was transparently contrived to criticize Mao through the words of the ancient mandarin. In one passage, he quoted Hai Jui as bravely telling the emperor almost precisely what P'eng Teh-haui was preparing to say to Mao about the time the essay was published.

> In earlier times you did quite a few good things, but how about now? . . . Your mind is deluded, and you are too dogmatic and prejudiced. You think you are always right and refuse criticism. Your faults are too numerous. . . . The whole country has been dissatisfied with you for a long time, and the inner and outer ministers and officers all know it.[13]

After P'eng Teh-huai's purge, Wu Han went a step further. In February 1961, he staged a drama in the form of a Peking opera entitled *The Dismissal of Hai Jui*. In it, Hai Jui demanded that peasants be returned their illegally confiscated land, and was banished for his audacity. Though he certainly recognized the allegorical assault against him at the time, Mao did not respond until late 1965, when he mounted a campaign against Wu Han as his opening salvo in the Cultural Revolution. Only then did the *People's Daily*, under Mao's control for the first time in years, quote the Chairman's pronouncement: "Emperor Chia Ching dismissed Hai Jui. In 1959, we dismissed P'eng Teh-huai. P'eng Teh-huai *is* a Hai Jui." [14]

Mao's most acerbic literary critic, however, was the former editor of the *People's Daily*, Teng T'o, who in 1959 had been appointed chief of ideological and cultural activities in the Peking ment could only be handled through specialization, industrialization, and modern management. This difference was expressed neatly in a pair of contrasting slogans. "Collectivization must precede mechanization," claimed Mao. On the contrary, replied Liu, "mechanization before collectivization."

One of the earliest controversies between Mao and the Party after the establishment of their regime focused on the role that scientists, engineers, and other intellectuals as well as "bourgeois" industrialists and managers should play in the Communist state. The industrial success of the First Five-Year Plan had been due in large measure to the ability of the Peking regime to enlist the collaboration of thousands of Chinese technical specialists, most of whom were uncommitted to communism. As a survey of the membership of the Chinese Academy of Sciences indicated, many of these experts had returned to China from the United States, Western Europe, and Japan.[44] In part, they were attracted by the integrity, patriotism, and efficiency of the Communists, especially after years of Nationalist corruption and ineptitude. In addition, they were reassured by the fact that the Communists, seeking a broad base of support, had initially set up a so-called "democratic coalition" government in which ideology was subdued. The new administration, with the durable Chou En-lai as its Premier, counted twenty-five representatives of minor non-Communist political groups among its fifty-six ministers and senior department heads. Serving under Mao in his capacity of chief of state were three non-Communist Vice-Chairmen of the Republic—among them Mme. Soong Ching-ling, the sophisticated, American-educated widow of Dr. Sun Yat-sen. Besides personifying the bridge between the two Republics, her prestigious participation was obviously contrived to present the Communists in a favorable light to the middle-class Chinese of the coastal cities.

This "united front" arrangement, officially entitled a "people's democratic dictatorship," seemed to be a liberal variation of Lenin's more exclusively proletarian "democratic dictatorship of workers and peasants." But soon disagreements arose over whether the relatively conservative experts and intellectuals posed a threat to the revolution.

Nearly two decades later, attempting to stress Mao's unswerving fidelity to the revolution, radical publicists in Peking asserted that he had terminated the "new democratic" phase and initiated the "transition to socialism" in 1949. This revision of events was designed to suggest, in simpler language, that Mao had opposed cooperation with bourgeois elements but had been betrayed by Liu Shao-ch'i and the Party bureaucrats, who had favored moderation toward "right-wing" intellectuals and capitalists. Documents dredged up from the early 1950s cited Liu as saying that "socialism is something for the future," and that "the bourgeoisie in China has a progressive part to play." [45] Liu was also alleged to have encouraged Chinese industrialists to build more private factories, advising them they would therefore help to stimulate the economy. Visiting the north China city of Tientsin, the home of his wife's wealthy family, he was reported to have told the owner of a local textile mill: "Your mill employs a thousand workers, so it would be much better if you had ten such mills employing ten thousand workers." [46] He was also quoted as having explained to a group of businessmen in the same city: "The government is calling for greater production efforts. To respond to the government's appeal, you must practice exploitation. This is not a question of who exploits whom. When you run factories, increase your production and pay taxes to the State, the State is thus exploiting you in turn." [47]

Though these and similar statements were unearthed in order to slander Liu as a long-standing "pro-capitalist," they were actually not so different from the theories voiced by Mao during that period. In his essay "On the People's Democratic Dictatorship," published in June 1949, Mao demonstrated far more flexibility than he would display in later years. He declared that the Communists merely intended to "regulate" rather than destroy capitalism, and he generously promised the "progressive" bourgeoisie the same rights that workers and peasants would enjoy under the "democratic dictatorship." Only when "the time comes to realize socialism," he went on, would the bourgeoisie be "educated and remolded." [48] But this matter of timing, never made clear, became a pivotal point in the quarrel between Mao and the Party. For Liu and his comrades, in their stress on industrialization, evidently felt that the "new democratic" phase should last a considerable length of time so that the technocrats could be encouraged to contribute to the economy.

Mao, on the other hand, began to have qualms about what he considered to be an unholy alliance between his unique style of communism and the ideologically dubious intellectuals.

These qualms stemmed in part from Mao's ingrained distrust of the intelligentsia. Looking back across the centuries of Chinese history, he was appalled by the gulf that divided the vast majority of the people from the educated minority. Even though their literary, artistic, and administrative accomplishments warmed his aesthetic feelings and national pride, he saw evil in the traditional mandarins, whose long fingernails symbolized their disdain for manual labor. Scorning the value of formal education, he pointed out that the two most successful Ming dynasty emperors had been illiterate while their incompetent successors had been men of learning.[49] Perhaps Mao's hatred for scholars mirrored his humiliating experience serving them as a menial assistant in the Peking University library. He had certainly observed in Yenan that they had little in common with his guerrilla ideal. He had also discovered that they tended to be most resistant to his "spiritual" brand of communism, with its accent on moral rearmament. After all, high school and university graduates even in China have not been easy candidates for conversion to religious fundamentalism. Hence he held intellectuals in low esteem—unless, of course, they submitted to "thought reform," prostrated themselves before the "masses," and acquired a genuine "proletarian" outlook. Even so, he doubted their ability to undergo this process sincerely.

In 1955, Mao had personally conducted a campaign against Hu Feng, an undistinguished Communist writer who had objected to the political controls imposed by the regime on Chinese literature. Not long afterward, clearly concerned that China was drifting away from his revolutionary dream toward Soviet-style "revisionism," Mao began to caution against "rightist trends" while calling for fresh drives to intensify "class struggle." Singling out educated Chinese in one speech, he asserted that most were only tepid in their support of Marxism since they came from bourgeois backgrounds. Therefore, he said, they required "rectification" and, predicting future efforts to cleanse intellectuals and other dubious elements, he warned: "In the ideological field, the question of who will win in the struggle between the proletariat and the bourgeoisie has not been really settled yet. We still have to wage a protracted struggle against bourgeois and petty bourgeois ideology." [50]

The Party leaders flatly rejected this call for continued "struggle," however. "The question of who will win in the struggle between socialism and capitalism in our country has now been decided," proclaimed Liu Shao-ch'i in September 1956,[51] adding that bourgeois intellectuals and specialists who had helped the nation deserved to be praised rather than censured. And, without mentioning Mao by name, he attacked "some members of our Party who hold that everything should absolutely be of 'one color,'" describing their attitude as a "sectarian viewpoint." [52] This theme was echoed by Teng Hsiao-p'ing, the new Party Secretary General, in a statement criticizing the Maoist notion of "classifying . . . social strata into two different categories." [53] The official Party newspaper, the *People's Daily*, also berated "doctrinairism," while the chief of the Party's Propaganda Department, Lu Ting-yi, refuted one of Mao's basic tenets in a conciliatory appeal to intellectuals. "As everyone knows," Lu said, "the natural sciences, including medicine, have no class character." [54]

To a large extent, the simmering quarrel between Mao and the Party boiled up because of shortcomings in China's economic development drive. The First Five-Year Plan of 1953–57 was performing brilliantly in the field of heavy industry. But the records broken in iron, steel, coal, and other industrial production were not being matched in the agricultural realm. Between 1953 and 1955, the production of grains like rice and wheat repeatedly failed to meet the targets set up by the government, while cotton output actually declined.[55]

This situation was critical, for the simple reason that Chinese industrialization depended upon agriculture. Under a series of agreements, the Soviet Union had contracted to provide China with the blueprints, advisers, and low-interest loans to construct more than two hundred major factories. However, the main burden of financing and meeting the other requirements of industrialization fell on the shoulders of the Chinese peasants. They were expected to grow food for an expanding urban population; produce 90 per cent of the fibers, cotton, and other raw materials needed for light industry and, at the same time, yield the additional sur-

Party Committee. For almost a year and a half, Teng wrote a column called "Evening Talks at Yenshan," attacking Mao's policies in a language so Aesopian that only a restrained circle of Peking "insiders" could decipher his message. In one essay, Teng denounced the Great Leap Forward with the parable of a merchant who dreamed of amassing riches from a single egg and was therefore "just speculating" rather than pursuing the "proper and usual way of production in order to increase his wealth." Like Mao, Teng implied, the merchant "substituted illusion for reality." In collaboration with Wu Han and Liao Mo-sha, another Peking Party official, Teng went as far as to suggest that Mao was suffering from a psychosis that accounted for his irrational conduct. "A person afflicted with this disease must promptly take a complete rest," their article advised. "If he insists on talking or doing anything, he will make a lot of trouble." [15]

Teng T'o went beyond his other literary colleagues in assailing Mao's foreign policies. In an essay favoring a *rapprochement* with the United States, he put forth the dubious argument that the Chinese had actually discovered America and, consequently, the "long tradition of Sino-American friendship is an important historical fact." Teng also criticized Mao's alienation of the Soviet Union and the loss to China of Russian aid by warning that "if a man with a swelled head thinks he can learn a subject easily and then kicks out his teacher, he will never learn anything." In another essay, he ridiculed Mao's assertion that "the East Wind will prevail over the West Wind," an allusion to potential Communist superiority, calling the slogan "just hackneyed phrases without much meaning." His advice to Mao and other "friends who are fond of big talk," Teng wrote, was to "read more, think more, and talk less." [16] In September 1962, Mao moved to halt this criticism, and Teng terminated his series of articles with a final piece entitled "The Thirty-six Strategies." It recalled the old Chinese military saying that the best of the thirty-six strategies was retreat. Teng's retreat spared him for only four years, and he was bitterly denounced during the Cultural Revolution.

Meanwhile, Mao had plenty of other evidence to remind him that strenuous efforts were being made to weaken his authority. In 1960 the Party created six regional bureaus responsible directly to the Secretariat and clearly designed to reinforce the power of the Central Committee. Accompanying this structural change, numerous directives emphasized the virtues of order, routine, discipline, and other rules calculated to stiffen the Party bureaucracy and undermine Mao's concept of "mass" enthusiasm.[17] Not long afterward, the Central Committee convened a "work conference" at which Liu Shao-ch'i, Teng Hsiao-p'ing, P'eng Chen, and many others among the seven thousand delegates present spent nine days criticizing Mao's policies as having brought the Chinese economy "to the brink of collapse." [18] In August 1962, consistent with this trend, Liu Shao-ch'i published a new edition of his 1939 series of lectures, now entitled *On the Self-Cultivation of Communists*, which studiously omitted any reference to the "Thought" of Mao and even denounced him indirectly under the guise of criticizing "some comrades" who wanted "to have people sing their praises and flatter them . . . try to dress themselves up as 'great men' and 'heroes' in the Communist movement and . . . stop at nothing to gratify their desire." [19]

Mao must have been troubled as well about this time by various attempts to absolve P'eng Teh-huai of his "crimes." P'eng, then striving to vindicate himself, was apparently supported by several senior Party and Army figures, perhaps including Liu Shao-ch'i. These men had no particular affection for P'eng. But they may have felt that his "rehabilitation" would usefully serve to strengthen the Army during a period when China was approaching three simultaneous external security crises.

Information reaching Peking from Communist spies on Taiwan indicated that Chiang Kai-shek's Nationalists were planning to cross the hundred-mile strait in an invasion of the mainland. This intelligence was faulty. Still, sensitive to China's vulnerability, the Communist leaders deployed troops throughout the coastal provinces, and it was only after receiving assurances from American diplomats in Warsaw that the United States had no intention of backing Chiang that the Communists relaxed on the eastern front. But the illusion of a threat had been enough to unnerve them. Moreover, the crises in other areas in 1962 were quite real.

As the Sino-Soviet schism widened, Kremlin agents in Sinkiang, where the Russians had long been influential, began to stir up resistance to Chinese rule among Uighurs, Kazakhs, and other Muslim minorities resentful of Peking's political and cultural domination. In the spring of 1962, some sixty thousand of these Muslims, encouraged by Soviet propaganda, fled over the frontier into the Soviet Republic of Kazakhstan while others, unable to escape, staged abortive revolts in two or three Sinkiang cities.[20] This appeared to Peking, with much justification, to be a case of Soviet subversion, and it augured worse to come. Meanwhile, the Chinese were becoming embroiled in a border dispute with India, the international repercussions of which might be serious. Thus the Chinese leaders sought to assure the reliability of their Army.

None of these considerations swayed Mao into reversing his decision against P'eng Teh-huai. He could not take the risk of reinstating a known adversary in the Chinese military establishment. Faithful to his dictum that "political power grows out of the barrel of a gun," he had consistently concentrated through the years on winning military support. That had been his strategy in the 1930s and now, as he faced the challenge of regaining his authority, one of his principal objectives was to entrust the Army to officers of unequivocal loyalty to himself and to his concepts. But he was in no position to dictate terms. He was therefore compelled to compromise with his Party foes. After P'eng Teh-huai's dismissal, the Party leaders had accepted his choice for Defense Minister, Marshal Lin Piao. And Mao, in exchange, conceded to the Party's candidate for Chief of General Staff, General Lo Jui-ch'ing.

A tall, slightly stooped native of Szechwan province, then in his mid-fifties, General Lo was a secret police and espionage expert rather than a soldier. He had trained at a special Moscow academy run by the Cheka, the Soviet State security apparatus, and he later attended a similar Comintern school in France. On his return to China in the late 1920s, he was appointed an Army political commissar, and a severe wound he suffered in battle against Chiang Kai-shek's Nationalists left him with a face twitch befitting his sinister secret police role. As an undercover operative, Lo was careful in the course of his career to keep both his political and personal associations ambiguous. A former Chinese Communist official who knew Lo in the 1930s remembered him as a friendless, distrusted man, a "necessary evil" in the system.[21] Logically, Lo was appointed Minister of Public Security when the Communists established their regime. After 1959 his main function as Chief of General Staff was to protect the interests of the Party and its affiliated military professionals inside the Army—in short, to counterbalance Lin Piao.

In contrast, Lin Piao was a distinguished soldier whose military talents had repeatedly earned him praise from enemies and comrades alike. Born about 1908 as Lin Yu-jung—he later assumed the *nom de guerre* "Piao," meaning "tiger cat"—Lin was the son of a bankrupt textile manufacturer who had been forced to find employment as a purser on a Yangtze River steamer. Lin's birthplace, a village near the northern border of Hupeh province, was a center of peasant unrest in the early decades of the twentieth century. Inspired by the political ferment of the period, Lin went to Shanghai to join the Communist Youth League, and afterward moved to Canton to enroll at Whampoa, the military academy then operating under the Nationalists with Communist participation. Lin specialized in infantry training, received his commission in 1926, and promptly enlisted in the Communist Party as a full-fledged member.

During the following years, Lin was involved in nearly every major event in the evolution of the Communist movement. He participated in the abortive attempt in 1927 to seize Nanchang, the capital of Kiangsi province, and soon after that he accompanied Chu Teh's Army when it linked up with Mao Tse-tung in the misty heights of Chingkangshan. He later led the advance guard of the celebrated Long March and by 1936, at the age of twenty-eight, he was commander of the 115th Division of the Eighth Route Army.

Daring and courageous, Lin was seriously wounded while commanding his division against the Japanese in Shansi province in 1938. He was sent to Moscow for medical care and, according to some accounts, joined in the defense of Leningrad during its siege by the Germans in the winter of 1941–1942. In the civil war against the Nationalists, Lin suffered a series of setbacks until, devising a bold new strategy, his Fourth Field Army swept from Manchuria down to Hainan Island, China's southernmost territory. Not long after, he reportedly returned to the Soviet Union, either to recover from another wound or to be treated for tuberculosis. Long absences from view during subsequent years fueled speculation that his health was chronically poor. His occasional public appearances, in which he looked frail and spoke in a thin voice, further contributed to his image as a sick man.

Lin's political record over the years zigzagged within the labyrinth of Communist power rivalries, his chief opponent in bids for prominence apparently having been P'eng Teh-huai. Aware of their conflicting ambitions, Mao seemed to set Lin and P'eng against one another in order to secure his own authority. In 1937, for instance, Mao was reported to have deliberately slighted Lin by giving P'eng command of the First Front Army. In 1954, linking Lin to an alleged plot to carve out a semiautonomous Manchurian Communist state under Soviet tutelage, Mao again punished Lin by suspending him from the Politburo and naming P'eng to be Defense Minister. At the Lushan conference five years later, however, Mao cleverly turned the tables by using Lin as his spearhead against P'eng. Following that maneuver, Mao employed Lin to bring the Army under his control.

The political scene in China was in such disarray in the wake of the Great Leap Forward that Lin warned soon after taking over as Defense Minister, "We must ensure that the armed forces do not get out of hand," [22] and he quickly embarked on an intensive campaign to guarantee the Army's fidelity to Mao. He made an effort to appease officers and men by according them promotions and special food rations, and he laid particular stress on investigating the causes of their dissatisfaction. He also made some concessions to the military professionals by emphasizing his concern for modern weapons and techniques. But far more important was his drive to indoctrinate the Army along Mao's ideological lines.

On one hand, striving to deflect responsibility for the disasters of the Great Leap away from Mao, Army propagandists blamed the debacle on "confused" rural cadres. In addition, Lin Piao initiated a dynamic program to "rectify" the attitudes of officers and men. Introducing more than two hundred thousand new political commissars into Army units, he ordered that the ideological leanings and class backgrounds of troops be scrutinized and that their thinking be strictly supervised. Model heroes and units were either discovered or invented, and widely publicized as examples to be imitated not only by troops but by all Chinese. One of these ideal units was the "Good Eighth Company of Nanking Road," which had patrolled the main street of Shanghai without falling prey to prostitutes, black marketeers, and other bourgeois temptations that continued to flourish even after the Communists took the city. The most outstanding of the individuals offered for emulation was a soldier called Lei Feng, who had purportedly been a diligent student of Mao's works before being killed by, of all things, a falling telephone pole. The banality of Lei Feng's death was deliberately stressed. For, as the propaganda stated, heroes were expected to display their "revolutionary spirit" in "ordinary routine work" rather than in flamboyant exploits.[23]

In early 1964, Lin Piao escalated his campaign by launching a nationwide appeal to "learn from the People's Liberation Army." The purpose of this fresh effort was to portray the Army, in contrast to the Party apparatus, as the organization that truly fit Mao's ideals. Like the Army, Maoist spokesmen asserted, all Chinese must "resolutely oppose the bureaucratic working style that is divorced from reality and the masses," and rely on ideology rather than technocracy.[24] In February 1965, demonstrating the "extremely high proletarian character" of the Army even further, Lin erased the differences between officers and men by abolishing rank insignia and titles. This decision, with its stress on the egalitarian spirit that had inspired Mao's guerrillas in the Yenan days, was plainly calculated to undermine the Chinese career officers who had only a decade earlier transformed the Army into a formal, stratified structure.

Lin's campaign to shape the Army into a Maoist instrument marked the entry onto the public scene of a redoubtable personage —Mao's wife, Chiang Ch'ing, the former movie actress. She emerged from obscurity to make her political debut in the summer of 1961 with an article praising a "certain" Army company that years before had "shouldered the most honorable task of safeguarding our great leader, Chairman Mao." Though barely noticed outside China when it was published, the article was important both for its content and for its authorship. Using the technique of recalling the past to serve the present, the article implied that Mao again needed the Army to protect him against internal adversaries. And the fact that his wife was now playing a political role indicated that Mao distrusted the Party to such a degree that he felt compelled to turn to supporters whose loyalty was unquestioned. Indeed, Chiang Ch'ing later revealed, she had acted as a "roving sentinel" for Mao during this period, observing developments in culture, education, and even international affairs.

Chiang Ch'ing's appearance was paralleled by the emergence into Chinese political life of another woman—Wang Kuang-mei, the wife of Liu Shao-ch'i. Totally unlike Chiang Ch'ing, with her slightly disreputable background as a Shanghai movie actress, Wang Kuang-mei was a handsome, sophisticated lady whose father had been a Westernized industrialist in north China. Thus there was almost a "class struggle" between the two women, and their quarrel eventually degenerated into a bitterly feminine dispute.[25]

Lin Piao encountered substantial resistance from professional Chinese officers associated with the Party apparatus in his efforts to bring the Army into the Maoist orbit. Chief of General Staff Lo Jui-ch'ing often disregarded Mao's "Thought" in his statements, emphasizing instead the Army's purely military vocation. He organized weapons competitions in order to improve military skills while minimizing the importance of indoctrination sessions designed to raise the ideological "consciousness" of troops. And if Lin Piao's propagandists publicized models like Lei Feng as exemplary soldiers imbued with Maoist doctrine, Lo Jui-ch'ing and the Party glorified such "heroes" as An Yeh-min and Kuo Hsing-fu, who had excelled as fighters because of their technical talents.[26] Similarly, Mao and Lin ran into stiff opposition from the Party in early 1964, when they shifted former Army political commissars into trade, finance, and other government bureaus in Peking as well as in the provinces. Once again, the *apparatchiks* rejected Mao's attempt to put his ideology over expertise, and *Red Flag*, the Party's authoritative theoretical journal, explained: "Politics cannot take first place over economics, because the main task . . . is economic construction and, therefore, politics must serve the existing economic base." [27]

In the years that followed, as both men struggled to undermine the Party bureaucracy, Mao would promote Lin Piao to the prestigious position of his official successor. But in late 1971, Lin was purged in a mysterious episode that eliminated several key members of the Chinese high command.

By the early 1960s, Mao had perceived that he was making little headway in his revitalization of a revolutionary China. On the contrary, "spontaneous" capitalism was spreading throughout the country as a result of the liberal economic policies inaugurated by the Party. And, as economic conditions improved, peasants, workers, students, and other Chinese as well as Party officials were more reluctant than ever to subscribe to the principles that had led to the Great Leap Forward. Villagers and local cadres ignored central Party directives as they focused on earning money, eating better, building houses, and ameliorating their living standards. In Peking, writers like Wu Han and Teng T'o were airing their critical views with unusual freedom, and even senior Party and government leaders were lapsing into bourgeois if not corrupt practices. The Mayor of Canton, Tseng Sheng, was reliably reported to have imported everything from cameras and tape recorders to prostitutes and American films from nearby Hong Kong, and he regularly indulged himself in banquets that featured such Kwangtung province gastronomic delicacies as stewed seal, braised turtle, and chicken steamed in chrysanthemum petals.[28] According to charges later leveled against him, Party Secretary General Teng Hsiao-p'ing was so enamored of bridge that he commandeered private railway cars and special aircraft to transport his card-playing cronies to different parts of the country for foursomes.[29]

In September 1962, Mao made his first major move since the Great Leap Forward to arrest the erosion of his ideals. At a Party Plenum in Peking, he launched what he termed a Socialist Education Campaign with the ambitious objective of "educating man anew and reorganizing our revolutionary ranks." Plainly referring to the Peking literary set then sniping at him, Mao warned that a number of writers were "creating a climate of public opinion for the restoration of capitalism." He also focused on the problem of cultivating youths, asserting that their "class education . . . must be strengthened to ensure that our nation will remain revolutionary and incorruptible for generations and forever." Finally, he affirmed his intention to resurrect collectivist controls in order to repudiate the liberal economic trends that had been "incited by the bourgeoisie and its exponents within the Party." [30] In this program, then, Mao was already beginning to formulate the ideas that would later prompt him to unleash the more ambitious Cultural Revolution.

The first phase of Mao's counterattack against the liberals began with an effort to eliminate "harmful bourgeois influences" in fields of art and literature. He complained that "socialist transformation had by now achieved very little effect," calling it "absurd" that "many Communists are enthusiastic in promoting feudalist and capitalist art but are not enthusiastic in promoting socialist art." [31] Intellectuals were approaching the "brink of revisionism" and, unless halted, "would inevitably become like the Petofi Club of Hungary," the group of intelligentsia that had been instrumental in sparking the uprising against the Communist regime in Budapest in 1956.[32]

Mao's problem, however, was to find loyal activists to assist him in carrying out a purge of literary dissidents. He could count on his wife, Chiang Ch'ing, to serve as a cultural tsarina, but her authority was limited. When he looked to Liu Shao-ch'i and the *apparatchiks* for help, as he did in 1964, Mao must have known that it would be difficult to rely on them to strike down the writers and journalists who were actually operating on their behalf against him. The best he could do under the circumstances was to build up a case against the Party that he would unveil when he launched his Cultural Revolution a few years later.

Mao was confronted by a similar dilemma in the next phase of his projected counterattack, when he sought to reverse the "capitalistic" trends that were rapidly overtaking the countryside as the Party introduced liberal economic measures in order to repair the damage caused by the Great Leap Forward. To Mao, these trends were alarming. In some places, he noted in a document published in May 1963, "landlords and rich peasants" had regained power by manipulating local officials, and were putting out anti-Communist propaganda as well as "developing counterrevolutionary organizations." Elsewhere, the document said, "speculation and profiteering have reached serious proportions" as wealthier peasants "exploited" labor, engaged in moneylending, and made private land deals. Perhaps most distressing, lower-level Party committees in cooperation with village "capitalists" were subverting communism:

> In organizations and the collective economy, there have emerged a group of corrupt elements, thieves, speculators and degenerates who have ganged up with landlords and rich peasants to commit evil deeds. These elements are a part of the new bourgeoisie, or their ally.[33]

The Party leaders, considering themselves to be good Communists, were as determined as Mao to stop the slide toward capitalism and corruption in the countryside. But their methods for correcting the deteriorating rural situation opposed his approach in much the same way that their respective policy lines had diverged for years.

Consistent with his lifelong principles, Mao proposed that the "masses be set in motion" by permitting the poorer peasants to criticize local Party cadres and the re-emerging rural gentry. Wayward cadres would in turn be forced to confess their "errors" to peasant associations formed for that purpose. In short, just as he had provoked a conflict between intellectuals and the Party during the "Hundred Flowers" interlude nearly a decade before, so Mao was now trying to set dispossessed peasants against rural officials in order to weaken the Party *apparatchiks*.

But Liu Shao-ch'i and his comrades perceived that this strategy threatened the power of the rural Party organization. They also feared that fresh tensions in the countryside would undermine agricultural production, then beginning to recover after three lean years. Thus they countered Mao with a directive asserting that the effort to curb capitalism in the countryside be a slow, gradual process managed by Party investigation teams.[34] Liu also challenged Mao's tactic of using his wife for political activities by employing his own spouse, Wang Kuang-mei, to help draw up that directive. Disguised as a peasant woman, Wang Kuang-mei went to work with the Peach Garden Main Brigade at the Lu Wang Chuang Commune in Hopeh province, not far from Peking. Over a period of a year there, she gathered the experience to advise the Party on rural conditions.[35]

In early 1965, aware that his attempts to purify the rural Party structure were being blocked, Mao came back with a new edict.

Directing his fire against "those people in authority within the Party who take the capitalist road"—the formula he would later use over and over again to designate Liu Shao-ch'i and his colleagues—he reiterated his demand for a release of mass criticism "from below." Party officials must submit to supervision by the "masses," he insisted, evoking again the familiar image that "we must not be like women with bound feet" who prefer caution.[36] Here again, he was opposed by the Party bureaucrats even though they paid lip service to his appeals for mobilization of the masses. Compelled to confess his "crimes" during the Cultural Revolution two years afterward, Liu Shao-ch'i conceded that he had only played a charade in having appeared to support Mao, saying: "I committed the mistake of 'actually leaning to the right though seeming to lean to the left.' "[37] In Mao's view, even that confession was a charade.

If he was frustrated by his inability to impose his ideology on the countryside, Mao was equally disappointed by his failure to revamp the Chinese educational system, which in his opinion was increasingly losing touch with "proletarian" reality. The question of education obsessed him more than any other issue at that time. For Chinese youth represented the country's future leaders and, Mao feared, his brand of communism would be drastically altered if not entirely scrapped after his death unless he could mold a new generation of "revolutionary successors."

Mao's fears were largely justified. Many young Chinese were disillusioned in the wake of the Great Leap Forward, when educational and job opportunities were sharply curtailed. Unable to find employment after graduation, youths were becoming "delinquent," or so it seemed to Mao. The Army press, reflecting the Maoist view, repeatedly excoriated young "playboys and hooligans who do not want to hold decent jobs" and whose "extravagant clothing fits in nicely with their decadent and lustful style of living and their desire for sensual excitement."[38] As examples of "extravagant" dress, the radical journals singled out colorful, open-neck blouses worn by girls, and tight trousers and pointed-toe "rocket" or "peppercorn" shoes favored by young men.[39] Maoist publications criticized such "bourgeois" phenomena then in vogue as "beehive" coiffures for young ladies and "ducktail" haircuts for youths. One newspaper complained that the People's Park in Shanghai, which in pre-Communist days had been barred to Chinese and dogs, was now being "polluted" by "men wearing woollen jackets . . . and women with powdered faces and tinted lips" who discussed food, pleasure trips, and exchanged "reactionary stories." [40]

Mao's concern that young Chinese were becoming soft and complacent was also mirrored about this time in a series of scathing attacks in the Army press against Feng Ting, the prominent Party philosopher, who in lectures to youth groups had defined "happiness" as a "normal life in which there is peace without war . . . good food, good clothing, and spacious living quarters, and harmonious relations among members of the family." This definition of happiness "is almost identical with that of the Soviet modern revisionists," replied an Army journal, warning that "revolutionary youth should absolutely not be taken in by him" but must "severely condemn him and completely rid their minds of his erroneous influence." [41] Yet Feng Ting's materialistic view of happiness was undoubtedly shared by numbers of even the most radical Chinese youth. Interviewed in Hong Kong during this period, a former schoolteacher from Peking affirmed that all her students had been "revolutionary." But, she explained, they believed that the revolution would bring them higher incomes, better apartments, more food, a bicycle, and "maybe even an automobile some day." [42] In short, as Mao would put it, they were waving his Red Flag in order to oppose his Red Flag.

In universities and other institutions of higher learning, meanwhile, tensions were growing between the children of Party and government officials, who believed in "elitist" education, and students of worker and peasant origin, whose presence in classes lowered educational standards. Concerned with producing skilled technocrats, the Party favored a formal system of education. But this was anathema to Mao. In speech after speech, he inveighed against long schooling periods, heavy curricula, and examinations in which students were "ambushed by strange, remote questions" that resembled the "eight-legged essays" required of candidates for the mandarinate during the Ming dynasty. Such students, Mao said, were unable to distinguish between rice and wheat, or pigs and horses. In particular, he grumbled, it was criminal to force youths to sit through long, tedious lectures by boring professors. "Students should be permitted to doze off when a lecturer is teaching. Instead of listening to nonsense, they do much better taking a nap to freshen themselves up. Why listen to gibberish anyway?" [43]

Mao's obsession with the failure of Chinese youth to live up to his expectations was dramatically reflected in his talks with foreign visitors to China during that period. In an interview with Edgar Snow, he even went so far as to suggest that China's younger generation might "make peace with imperialism" after his death and conspire to "bring the remnants of the Chiang Kai-shek clique back to the mainland." [44] In July 1964, Mao boldly voiced his apprehensions in a significant essay entitled "On Khrushchev's Phoney Communism and Its Historical Lessons for the World." Written in his brilliant polemical style, the essay illustrated the degree to which Mao considered the dilution of "orthodox" communism in the Soviet Union since the demise of Stalin to portend the path China might take following his own death. His statement was a clear warning that the time was at hand for a major thrust to stop the slide toward "revisionism" in China.

In the Soviet Union, Mao wrote, Khrushchev had betrayed true Marxism-Leninism by promoting "material incentives," encouraging "free competition," "undermining the social collective economy," sponsoring "bourgeois liberty, equality, fraternity and humanity . . . and debasing socialist morality," and colluding with American "imperialism" in an attempt to place "the vested interests of a handful of people" above the interests of the Communist bloc. This had "opened the floodgates for the revisionist deluge" in the Soviet Union. The "historical lesson" for China was obvious.

> Let us look at the facts. Is our society today thoroughly clean? No, it is not. Classes and class struggle still remain, the activities of the overthrown reactionary classes plotting a comeback still continue, and we still have speculative activities by old and new bourgeois elements and desperate forays by embezzlers, grafters, and degenerates.[45]

Accordingly, Mao asserted, urgent efforts had to be initiated in China to defeat "spontaneous capitalist tendencies" and reinforce the collective economy, destroy the "bourgeois" attitudes of intellectuals, break down the power of the bureaucracy, and eliminate professionalism in the Army. Moreover, the Party apparatus required purification—or else "it would not take long, perhaps only several years or a decade, or several decades at most, before a counterrevolutionary restoration on a national scale inevitably occurred . . . and the whole of China would change its color." This was precisely what had happened in the Soviet Union, where Khrushchev's "goulash communism" had become "simply another name for capitalism." This was the dream of the "imperialist prophets" who, basing their predictions on the changes that had taken place in the Soviet Union, were hoping for a "peaceful evolution" in subsequent Chinese generations.[46]

To prevent this disaster in China, Mao affirmed, the Party must not only hew to his "correct line and correct policies," but it was imperative to "train and bring up millions of successors who will carry on the cause of proletarian revolution." Or, as he put it:

> In the final analysis, the question of training successors for the revolutionary cause of the proletariat is one of whether or not there will be people who can carry on the Marxist-Leninist revolutionary cause started by the older generation of proletarian revolutionaries, whether or not our descendants will continue to march along the correct road laid down by Marxism-Leninism or, in other words, whether or not we can successfully prevent the emergence of Khrushchevite revisionism in China.
>
> In short, it is an extremely important question, a matter of life and death for our Party and our country. It is a question of fundamental importance to the proletarian revolutionary cause for a hundred, a thousand, nay ten thousand years.[47]

Shortly afterward, when the Cultural Revolution erupted, Liu Shao-ch'i would be dubbed "China's Khrushchev" by the Maoists, and the millions of "revolutionary successors" would be known as Red Guards. So, as early as the middle of 1964, Mao had undoubtedly anticipated the storm that he himself would unleash. But the tempest was preceded by an intricate internal crisis which paralleled China's rapidly deteriorating relations with the Soviet Union and the rapidly growing potentiality of a threat from the United States.

Though the dispute between the Chinese and Russians until the mid-1960s was primarily over ideology, international strategy, and economic aid, other tensions were building up between the two Communist neighbors along a border region that stretched more than six thousand miles from the Pacific Ocean through Mongolia to the barren wastes of Central Asia. In the spring of 1962, the Russians were maneuvering to undermine Peking's influence in Sinkiang. In the years before and after that, other sectors of the frontier had been the scene of friction. According to Foreign Minister Ch'en Yi, the Soviet Union provoked more than five thousand incidents along the border between July 1960 and the end of 1965, and had deployed increasing numbers of troops in the frontier region in a manner that "presupposes China as the enemy." [48] At about the same time, attempts by China and the Soviet Union to settle their boundary differences through negotiations had collapsed. Clearly, the Chinese had reason to fear that their quarrel with Moscow could spiral into a shooting war. This fear was exacerbated, meanwhile, by events to their south.

In early 1965, Mao was rather sanguine about the situation in Vietnam. Speaking with Edgar Snow, he predicted with confidence that the United States would lose interest in the war there and withdraw its troops in a year or two.[40] But soon afterward, American bombardments of North Vietnam and the landing of combat troops in the South made it plain that the United States intended to escalate rather than reduce its commitment in Vietnam. Now, Mao realized, he was being flanked by the world's two most powerful nations—and the pressures they exerted on China were having a profound impact on his internal troubles.

As Mao perceived one part of this complicated dilemma, the expansion of the Vietnam war into a direct challenge to China's national security would require the use of Chinese troops for strictly military purposes. In that event, he could no longer count on the Army as an instrument in his political quarrel with the Party bureaucrats. In addition, a conflict with the United States would bring to the fore the Chinese Army professionals affiliated with the Party apparatus he was seeking to subdue. Confronted by the prospect of an enlarged Vietnam war, Mao's task was to avoid Chinese involvement at almost any cost.

A war with the Soviet Union, though it appeared to be less plausible at the time, would have also deprived Mao of the Army's services as a political weapon to wield against the Party. This too had to be averted. Yet Mao could not repair China's breach with the Kremlin without diluting his implacable hostility to the despicable "revisionists." Nor could he compromise with the Russians without courting the risk of having them again intrude into China's affairs in support of his rivals, as Khrushchev had done in the case of P'eng Teh-huai. While Mao eventually complied with a Russian request for transit facilities to ship Soviet supplies to Hanoi, he could not accept Moscow's repeated proposal for a Sino-Soviet agreement to act jointly against the United States in Vietnam. For he sensed that such an arrangement, which would have accorded airfield rights and other privileges inside China to the Russians, was also an invitation to the Soviet Union to exercise its influence among receptive Chinese Army officers.

Ideally, therefore, Mao had to maintain tensions with both the United States and the Soviet Union—but without allowing those tensions to carry China into full-scale conflict with either. This foreign policy was essential to his fundamental goal of eliminating his domestic foes and putting China on the track toward permanent revolution. To play his tricky and dangerous game successfully, however, Mao had to overcome the fierce resistance of his Party and Army adversaries.

The debate over strategy that raged in Peking through most of 1965 gradually polarized into two fairly clear-cut postures. On one side stood Mao and Marshal Lin Piao—"doves" in the sense that their aim was to side-step war in order to devote their energies to purging China of its alleged "revisionists." On the other side was General Lo Jui-ch'ing, representing Liu Shao-ch'i and the Party bureaucracy as well as the military professionals. Determined to wrest the Army from Mao's hands, they offered the "hawkish" proposal that China intervene in Vietnam—having first taken the precaution of resolving its dispute with the Kremlin in order to gain Soviet nuclear protection to deter an American atomic counterattack.

As early as February 1965, Lo Jui-ch'ing put forth the line that China must do its "utmost" to aid Hanoi, while a typical Party bureaucrat, the trade union boss Liu Ning-yi, went even further in asserting that Peking "will definitely not stand by idly without lending a help hand" if the Americans extended the war into North

Vietnam.[50] In contrast, the Maoists exuded extreme caution, saying that China would fight only if the United States "forces a war on us [and] we have no choice but to take it on to the end." [51] One of Mao's supporters prudently warned against "taking the enemy lightly and advancing in a reckless way," explaining that good soldiers "avoid battle" when they cannot be sure of victory.[52] That enunciation of Mao's guerrilla-warfare theories drew scorn from General Lo. Passive defense of the sort advocated by Mao was "a spurious kind of defense," he said, adding that "the only real defense is active defense." [53]

By the spring, as the American presence in Vietnam grew, the policy debate in Peking sharpened. In a speech commemorating the Soviet defeat of Nazi Germany in World War II, Lo Jui-ch'ing insisted that the United States was "playing a role more ferocious than that of Hitler" and suggested that the Americans could be beaten through concerted Sino-Soviet action. Pointing out that the American atomic monopoly had been "broken many years ago" by the Russians, Lo implied that the Soviet nuclear umbrella would serve to discourage the United States from counterattacking. His oration concluded on an emotional note that must have shocked Mao. Expressing his "full confidence in the great Soviet people and the great Soviet Army," Lo vowed that Peking and Moscow would be reunited to "fight shoulder to shoulder against our common enemy." [54] In reply, the Maoists made it clear that there could be no *rapprochement* with the Soviet Union, now headed by Leonid Brezhnev and Alexei Kosygin since the dismissal of Khrushchev in late 1964. According to the Maoist thesis, "revisionism" must be thoroughly eliminated "in order to promote the revolutionary struggles." [55]

An important feature in this debate were the arguments over the significance of nuclear warfare. Reflecting the professional military view, Lo Jui-ch'ing scoffed at Mao's old dictum that nuclear weapons were a "paper tiger" far less devastating than the "spiritual atom bomb" of the revolutionary masses. "We are materialists . . . who will continue to master the material atom bomb," said General Lo, implicitly rejecting Mao's guerrilla concepts as outmoded.[56] The Maoists responded that nuclear weapons had been rendered useless, since they could not be employed in revolutionary struggles in which targets were elusive. As evidence for this contention Mao disclosed to Edgar Snow that he had read General Maxwell Taylor's book, *The Uncertain Trumpet*, in which the prominent American opponent of "massive retaliation" had argued against the effectiveness of nuclear war.[57]

The strategy debate reached a climax in early September 1965, when the twentieth anniversary of Japan's surrender in World War II was celebrated in Peking. Addressing a rally in the presence of Liu Shao-ch'i and the other Party *apparatchiks*, Lo Jui-ch'ing reaffirmed his thesis that China could afford to take risks in Vietnam if the dispute with Russia were patched up because "the united front against United States imperialism today is much broader than the anti-fascist front in the past." He consequently urged immediate military preparations to "give more effective support" to the Vietnamese Communists, insisting that America's "much-vaunted 'air and naval superiority' is no longer of any avail." [58] At this stage, Mao unsheathed a monumental document. Appearing under the signature of Marshal Lin Piao, it was entitled "Long Live the Victory of People's War!" and it spelled out Mao's attitudes not only toward his domestic adversaries and his Soviet rivals, but toward the wider question of international strategy.

The Maoist essay flatly rejected General Lo's suggestion that any compromise could be reached with the Soviet Union. The Kremlin had "demoralized . . . revolutionary people everywhere" and had "greatly encouraged U.S. imperialism in its war adventures," the document declared. Therefore, it stated, Soviet "revisionism" must be opposed before the struggle against "imperialism" could be won. Expanding the attack against Russian "revisionism" to include Mao's internal foes, it emphasized that nothing could be done in the fight against bourgeois and capitalist trends at home and abroad until the Maoist ideology had emerged triumphant. Thus the top priority belonged to the domestic purges that Mao was about to inaugurate.

Lin Piao's essay also assailed the proposal by General Lo and the Chinese Army professionals that Peking turn to Moscow for nuclear protection. "Certain people," Lin Piao said, attributed the Communists' success against Japan and Chiang Kai-shek to "foreign assistance." But this assertion was "absurd," since the Communists had fought mainly with captured enemy weapons and foreign aid therefore could have played "only a supplementary role." In addition to rejecting the idea of a *rapprochement* with the Kremlin, this argument was contrived to refute Lo Jui-ch'ing's appeal for "more effective support" for Hanoi, as well as to advise the Vietnamese Communists and other guerrilla movements elsewhere not to expect much help from China. For Mao's whole theory of "people's war" was predicated on the notion, Lin affirmed, that such conflicts must be waged by peoples themselves, without external intervention.

> Revolution or people's war in any country is the business of the masses in that country and should be carried out primarily by their own efforts. . . . If one does not operate by one's own efforts . . . but leans wholly on foreign aid—even though this be aid from socialist countries which persist in revolution—no victory can be won, or consolidated even if it is won.

In response to Lo Jui-ch'ing's willingness to incur the risk of a clash with the United States, Lin Piao evoked Mao's principle that the wise guerrilla retreats in the face of overwhelming odds. Success was impossible, Lin explained, "without taking full account of the enemy tactically . . . and without being prudent." And, apparently addressing himself to the Chinese career officers who regarded Mao's concepts as obsolete, Lin said: "You rely on modern weapons and we rely on highly conscious revolutionary people. . . . It is adventurism if one insists on fighting when one cannot win." [59]

A hint that the debate was ending in favor of Mao was dropped in early September by that perennial weathervane, Foreign Minister Ch'en Yi, when he told a group of Japanese visiting Peking: "To tell the truth, America is afraid of China and China is somewhat afraid of America. I do not believe that the United States would invade present-day China." [60] Not long afterward, Lo Jui-ch'ing dropped out of sight, the first prominent victim of the Cultural Revolution. The charges issued against him later, even if partially accurate, made it clear that he had indeed sought to heighten the possibility of a collision with the United States. Between January and October 1964, according to these allegations, Lo had unilaterally ordered an increase in weapons production and traveled "at least thirteen times" to various regions "to supervise battle preparations." The indictment also disclosed that Lo provoked two clashes between Communist and Chinese Nationalist patrol craft in the Taiwan Strait in August and November 1965 in an attempt to escalate tensions. As the charge put it, Lo authorized the Foochow Military District headquarters commanding the central China coast to "attack the enemy on its own initiative" so that the Communists would "not lose the initiative in battle." [61]

Though they had backed up Lo Jui-ch'ing to varying degrees, the other Party leaders were apparently implicated in the Vietnam issue to a lesser extent. The mayor of Peking, P'eng Chen, had started out supporting Mao but, perhaps as his own position weakened afterward, he switched to the side of those who favored *rapprochement* with the Soviet Union. Liu Shao-ch'i displayed caution throughout the dispute. Yet his last public statement, a speech delivered in July 1966 advocating deeper Chinese involvement in Vietnam, revealed him to have been among the "hawks."

The entire episode was evidently a reflection more of China's domestic political troubles at the time than of its strategy toward Vietnam or even the Soviet Union. And the key issue at stake was the role that the Army would play. Party bureaucrats and professional officers were eager to spark a crisis in order to divert the Army toward purely military functions and thereby pull it out of Mao's grasp. Mao, on the other hand, needed peace in order to use the Army for his political purposes—and, most probably, would not have dared to launch the Cultural Revolution had he doubted the Army's loyalty.

But what guarantee did Mao have that the United States would not disrupt his plans by pushing the Vietnam war into China? It seems likely that, among other communications, the American ambassador advised Chinese representatives at the Sino-American talks in Warsaw in June 1965, that Washington had no intention of escalating the conflict beyond the borders of Vietnam. Mao apparently accepted that assurance—just as, in the spring of 1962, he believed President Kennedy's pledge, communicated through Warsaw, that the United States would not support a Nationalist invasion of mainland China.

One of the ironies in this tacit understanding between China and the United States was that by lowering the menace of Chinese intervention, Mao obliquely served as an American accomplice in the Vietnam war. At the same time, by minimizing the American threat to China, President Lyndon Johnson unwittingly provided Mao with the respite he required to trigger the Cultural Revolution. Even more ironically, propagandists in both Peking and Washington were striving during this period to portray the conflict in Vietnam as a struggle between Maoist revolution and American-style democracy.

By the fall of 1965, Mao was ready to launch a more ambitious campaign to impose his unique ideology on China than he had ever before attempted. The moment had arrived to translate into action the nervous lines of the poem he had written three years earlier:

> Seize the day, seize the hour! . . .
> Away with all pests!
> Our force is irresistible.

PART TWO

REVOLUTION
WITHIN
REVOLUTION

The Great Proletarian Cultural Revolution
now unfolding is a great revolution that
touches people to their very souls. . . .

Central Committee Decision,
August 8, 1966

CHAPTER 8

The Opening Salvos

❧

Who are our enemies? Who are our friends?
This is a question of the first importance for
the revolution.
— MAO TSE-TUNG, March 1926

M OMENTOUS HISTORICAL EVENTS do not begin according to
schedules. Mao Tse-tung's Great Proletarian Cultural Revolution was no exception. It took shape gradually—even though,
with their passion for precision, Chinese Communist publicists
would later date its origin at September 1965.

After spending the summer at his Hangchow retreat, Mao returned to Peking at that time to convene the Politburo Standing
Committee, technically the most powerful body in China. As he
surveyed the six other members of the Committee, Mao could dis-
tinguish his enemies from his friends. Liu Shao-ch'i and Teng
Hsiao-p'ing represented the entrenched Party apparatus that had
long opposed his personal rule, while Vice-Premier Ch'en Yun, the
liberal economist, had consistently resisted his collectivist schemes.
On the other hand, Mao could depend upon Defense Minister Lin
Piao, who had been working strenuously for six years to bring the
Army under his aegis. And he could probably trust Premier Chou
En-lai, though his past allegiance had been variable. The sixth
Committee member, Marshal Chu Teh, then nearly eighty, was an
honorific figure now nearly senile.

Mao's essential motive in convening the Standing Committee
was to reiterate his alarm at the "revisionist" trends that had been
growing since the aftermath of the Great Leap Forward. But he

realized that he could not launch a full-scale, frontal assault against the Party leaders whom he believed to be promoting these trends. For the Party stalwarts were strong enough to resist him—and might even, in a premature showdown, defeat him. Their authority was deeply rooted in their provincial and district committees and through P'eng Chen, the Party boss in Peking, they dominated the Chinese capital. They were intimately linked to senior officers in China's central military establishment, and were closely allied with Army commanders in various regions of the country. They also controlled a formidable and pervasive array of affiliated youth, labor, and other national federations as well as newspapers, radio stations, and other propaganda media. Indeed, as Mao himself later put it, "some departments and areas of our country were dominated to such an extent by revisionists that they . . . could not be penetrated even with a needle." [1] Thus Mao was isolated, despite his enormous prestige. And, consequently, he saw himself and his followers as "rebels" in a new revolution aimed at overthrowing the "power-holders" of the Party bureaucracy.

At the outset, the confrontation between Mao and his foes was not sharply defined. Respectful of his towering stature, Mao's rivals hesitated to challenge him directly but tried instead to subvert his plans. At the same time, aware of the heavy odds against him, Mao proceeded slowly and prudently, using deception rather than bluntness. The Cultural Revolution therefore opened with a series of elusive, cautious, and often confusing maneuvers.

Mao's first shot, fired at the Politburo Standing Committee meeting, was a surprisingly mild plea for renewed efforts to "criticize bourgeois reactionary thinking," particularly in art and literature. The target he offered for criticism was Wu Han, whose play, *The Dismissal of Hai Jui*, written four years before, had appeared to Mao to be an allegorical attack against his purge in 1959 of Marshal P'eng Teh-huai, then Defense Minister.

To Western observers of China, Mao's gesture seemed at the time to be merely another attempt to revive the faltering "socialist education" exercise he had inaugurated in 1962. In part, their inability to perceive the potential scope of Mao's objective stemmed from the failure of most foreign analysts—and probably most educated Chinese as well—to fathom the depths of the divisions within the ruling Communist hierarchy. Many outside specialists, with their tendency to interpret Chinese political dynamics in their own terms, were also unable to appreciate the extent to which Mao considered art and literature as crucial ideological instruments in his "spiritual" approach to revolution. Suggesting as it did that Mao was concerned only with artistic and literary dissent, the phrase "Great Proletarian Cultural Revolution" was a misleading English label for his movement, even though it was invented by official Chinese translators in Peking. For the literal meaning of the Chinese *Wu-ch'an Chieh-chi Wen-hua Ta Ko-ming* is "a full-scale revolution to establish a working-class culture." [2] Hence the word "culture" more closely approximated the German *"Kultur"* or the French *"civilisation"* in signifying that Mao's broader ambition was to alter China's whole way of life.

None of this was lost on the Chinese Communist Party "insiders." They quickly discerned that in singling out Wu Han, Mao was actually focusing his fire against P'eng Chen and the Peking Party apparatus. For Wu Han, a deputy mayor of the capital city as well as a historian, was one of P'eng's protégés. Hence it was plain to the Party bureaucrats, familiar as they were with the classical Chinese device of humiliating a subordinate in order to undermine his superior, that Mao's sights were leveled at a far more prominent foe. They sensed, too, that Mao's offensive would not stop with P'eng Chen.

The Party *apparatchiks* mobilized to voice their hostility to Mao at the strained meetings of the Politburo Standing Committee, which dragged on into October. Teng Hsiao-p'ing, the obstinate Party Secretary General, was reported to have expressed his opposition to Mao's call for changes in the Chinese educational system, and he was backed up by Liu Shao-ch'i. At another Party conference in Peking at the time, P'eng Chen also asserted that Mao had no right to claim infallibility. Lu Ting-yi, chief of the Party's Propaganda Department, obliquely added to the reaction against Mao with a diatribe against Stalin's "personality cult." [3] The Party press echoed this challenge to Mao by stressing the need for balance in the planned Cultural Revolution. In an obvious calculation to counter Mao's concepts of a protracted "life-and-death" conflict, in which his "proletarian" disciples would eventually eliminate the "revisionists" who had gained the upper hand in the Party, *Red Flag* urged that the campaign be carried out with "maximum reasoning," while the *People's Daily* warned against "exaggerating" the "class struggle." [4]

Time and again in the past, Mao had welcomed the emergence of an opposition as a "negative example" he could use to rally support for his cause. In late 1965 he may not have been entirely chagrined to see disaffection that would serve him as evidence that a thorough purge of the Party was imperative. But now, perhaps more than ever before in his career, his leverage was so limited that he could not even use the principal journals in Peking as a launching pad for his intended campaign. Indeed, there was scarcely anyone of stature he could trust. Thus he delegated his wife, Chiang Ch'ing, to go to Shanghai to enlist the help of sympathizers in that city. Later, explaining his motives for this extraordinary move, Mao candidly admitted that he had reason to doubt that P'eng Chen's Party organization in Peking would obey his instructions. As he put it, "My suggestions could not be implemented in Peking." [5]

Shanghai, China's largest metropolis, was a study in contradictions. As the former center of European imperialism in China and now the country's major port, it was rife with alien "capitalist" influences. Several Western banks and other firms continued to retain offices there, employing Chinese compradors who still functioned as they did in the days before the Communist take-over. As late as 1965, foreign visitors noted that many of the city's young people displayed "bourgeois" tastes in their dress and manners and were even acquainted with contemporary trends in Western music and movies. The Shanghai leadership also contained men like Ts'ao Ti-ch'iu, the mayor and the city's First Secretary, who sided with the Party bureaucrats in Peking and elsewhere in the resistance to Mao's policies. But there were also strong radical elements in Shanghai that fervently subscribed to the Maoist canon. One of these was Chang Ch'un-ch'iao, a veteran journalist who had risen to the post of Director of Propaganda in the local Party Committee. Defying his superiors in the municipal apparatus, Chang had been active within recent years in assisting Chiang Ch'ing to promote revolutionary operas, films, and other artistic endeavors in Shanghai. Quite naturally, she turned to him when she arrived.

Chiang Ch'ing's specific assignment in Shanghai was to find a writer capable of producing an article criticizing Wu Han in such a way that it would be understood by the Communist cognoscenti to be an attack against P'eng Chen. With the help of Chang Ch'un-ch'iao, she discovered Yao Wen-yuan, a young publicist who had earned himself a minor reputation as an ultraradical literary critic. If Maoist accounts of the episode are accurate, Chiang Ch'ing and her two cohorts went to work on the article in secrecy for fear that the Shanghai Party *apparatchiks* would obstruct them. There were even hints later that the trio had been in danger of assassination.[6] According to other accounts, the Party bureaucracy discovered the plot but could not decide how to handle it. In a document that appeared later, the Party First Secretary, Ts'ao Ti-ch'iu, was quoted as having explained his dilemma:

> What was mostly on our minds at the time was our relationship with Peking, with P'eng Chen in fact. Should we alert him? If we did not, he would be caught unawares. If we did, it would be against the wishes of Chairman Mao. What were we to do? Our Secretariat puzzled over the problem again and again.[7]

In the end, illustrating its real loyalties, the Shanghai Party signaled P'eng Chen that the disguised attack against him was imminent. And P'eng Chen, in turn, telephoned Chang Ch'un-ch'iao, complaining: "Why haven't you notified us? Where is your Party spirit?"

Whatever Chang Ch'un-ch'iao replied, the article denouncing Wu Han was published on November 10 under Yao Wen-yuan's signature in the Shanghai newspaper *Wen Hui Pao*. A long, tedious piece that went through at least six drafts before completion, the article argued that since Wu Han had glorified a Ming dynasty official for having distributed land to impoverished peasants, his drama deviously disseminated the view of those who sought to "demolish the people's communes and to restore the criminal rule of the landlords and the rich peasants" by favoring liberal economic programs in the wake of the Great Leap Forward. The play was therefore a "poisonous weed" that had been promoted by the "bourgeois opposition to the dictatorship of the proletariat and the socialist revolutionary struggle."[8] Implicit in this assertion was the charge that P'eng Chen, Wu Han's superior, was a leader of "bourgeois" opponents to the Maoist line.

Like the other senior figures in the Chinese Communist Party, P'eng Chen had undoubtedly been appalled by the damage caused by the Great Leap Forward. According to a later indictment against him, he was alleged to have described the hectic collectivization scheme as a "romantic" vision that violated the "objective laws" of economic development.[9] And he had been cool to efforts by Mao and Chiang Ch'ing to introduce "proletarian" themes into classical Chinese art and literature. In July 1964, for example, he had cautioned against attempts to purge the theater of its traditions quickly, saying that "reforming Peking opera is not like cooking chestnuts, which can be sold while they are still roasting." [10] He had also argued, in contrast to Mao's appeals for abrasive "class struggle," that China's political atmosphere should foster "discipline and freedom, unity of will and liveliness and ease of mind." [11] Now, however, P'eng Chen's primary concern was to protect his Peking apparatus against Mao's purges. For he recognized that the attacks being mounted against his underlings were really a threat to his own authority.

The conflict then developing in China was not a simple confrontation between Mao and his Party rivals. Factional disputes and personal feuds within the Communist movement made it difficult for individuals and groups to attack each other directly. P'eng Chen was therefore compelled to resort to a variety of dodges as he sought to cope with Mao's equally complicated assaults against him.

P'eng Chen's first move was to issue a directive to the editors of the *People's Daily* enjoining them from reprinting the article by Yao Wen-yuan. Soon afterward, however, P'eng was pressured by Premier Chou En-lai to reverse that directive. Realizing that Chou was speaking for Mao, whose desires could not easily be disregarded, P'eng switched to a different tactic. He instructed the *People's Daily* to print the Yao Wen-yuan article, but he personally wrote an "editor's note" depicting the polemic surrounding Wu Han's play as academic rather than political. Mao had always advocated free discussion as a "means of exposing and resolving contradictions," he emphasized, thereby implying that Yao Wen-yuan's assault against Wu Han would not be the final word on the subject.[12]

Following that gambit, P'eng Chen prompted the Party's stable of literary critics in Peking to defend Wu Han. He also encouraged the historian himself to explain his position in a ritualistic "self-criticism." Wu Han complied, conceding that his error had been his failure to understand that "proletarian literature and art must serve contemporary politics." In producing his drama, he said, he had "merely portrayed an ancient event for its own sake, and wrote a play only in order to write a play." [13]

By this time, evidently uncomfortable in the political climate of Peking, Mao had retreated from the capital. One of his last public acts before he left was to attend a banquet to celebrate the eightieth birthday of Anna Louise Strong, the American writer who served until her death in 1970 as a publicist for the Chinese Communists. Also present at the banquet were a number of other leftist Americans resident in Peking, among them Frank Coe, Sol Adler, and Sydney Rittenberg.

Mao's movements went unmentioned in the Chinese press for more than five months after his departure from Peking in late November. It was the longest period he had dropped out of public sight since 1949, and his absence naturally touched off speculation about the state of his health. A French visitor to China, who had observed Mao's trembling hands at a dinner a year earlier, unwittingly encouraged the notion that he was suffering from Parkinson's disease. Many Chinese were persuaded that he had died, and they continued to claim, even after his re-emergence, that he had been replaced by a "double." But Mao, very much alive, was strenuously maneuvering against his adversaries. In late December, assembling a group of disciples at a meeting in Shanghai, he rejected Wu Han's contention that the play about Hai Jui had been politically innocuous. Despite the historian's denial, Mao asserted, the drama had been a deliberate slander.

At the same time, turning to his faithful military supporters for assistance, Mao commanded Lin Piao to mobilize the Army for an intensive campaign designed to test the loyalty of cadres in low-level county committees as well as in the Party's powerful regional bureaus. Claiming that many Party functionaries were neglecting Mao's principles in favor of a more "professional" approach to their problems, a directive issued by Lin Piao prescribed that officials must henceforth take the Chairman as their sole guide—or else face "disqualification from leadership duties." [14] This message was reinforced by editorials in the *Liberation Army Daily*, the newspaper published in Shanghai under Lin Piao's aegis, extolling Mao's "Thought" as the "peak of contemporary Marxism-Leninism" and "our invincible banner." [15] In addition, acting under military auspices, Chiang Ch'ing stepped further into the limelight as head of a forum convened in Shanghai to publicize the Maoist dogma in art and literature. These moves were part of an escalating challenge to P'eng Chen and a warning to other Party figures that they still had time to swing over to Mao's camp. Now, more clearly than ever, the growing dispute between Mao and his enemies was being polarized.

Meanwhile, with Mao operating from Shanghai and his residence at nearby Hangchow, P'eng Chen began to reinforce his position in Peking. He reactivated a so-called Group of Five, comprised of himself and four other senior Communist officials, that had been organized in the fall of 1964 to supervise an earlier Party program to purify art and literature. His apparent aim in reviving this body, which had never actually functioned, was to create the impression that he was implementing the Cultural Revolution in accordance with Mao's instructions. This stratagem of "waving the Red Flag in order to oppose the Red Flag," as the Maoists later described it, would repeatedly be pursued by Mao's adversaries as a means of muddling the conflict.

A Maoist sympathizer inside P'eng Chen's Group of Five was K'ang Sheng, a Politburo member who specialized in security and intelligence affairs. A myopic man in his late sixties whose thick spectacles enhanced his sinister reputation, K'ang was a dogmatic and stubborn Communist veteran. At a meeting held in early February, he argued that the group should recruit known radicals to draw up an indictment of Wu Han for his veiled attack against Mao. But P'eng Chen rejected that proposal, reiterating that the historian's play should not be treated as "a political question." [16] Then, evidently without consulting K'ang Sheng, he directed his staff to prepare a lengthy study covering the events of the previous months and offering recommendations for the reform of art and literature. The announced purpose of the study, the "Outline Report on the Current Academic Discussion Made by the Group of

Five in Charge of the Cultural Revolution," was to guide Party Committees throughout the country in the reform effort.

The "February Outline Report," as it was abbreviated, was later vilified by Maoists as an attempt to exonerate Wu Han and other critics of Mao's policies, and this assessment was not incorrect. For the report suggested that Wu Han and others be given the same latitude to express their views as intellectuals had been accorded during the "Hundred Flowers" period. In an obvious swipe at Mao's cultural judges, it criticized "scholar-tyrants who are always acting arbitrarily and trying to overwhelm people with their power."

On the afternoon of February 5, P'eng Chen carried a draft of the "Outline Report" to Liu Shao-chi's home in the verdant Chungnanhai sector of Peking, where the Chinese leaders lived in surburban comfort. Liu advised P'eng Chen to clear the report with Mao personally. Two days later, P'eng Chen flew to Hangchow to see Mao, accompanied by three prominent Party propagandists, one of them being Wu Leng-hsi, who was then serving simultaneously as editor-in-chief of *People's Daily* and director of the New China News Agency. According to a Maoist version of the encounter, P'eng Chen sought to ingratiate himself with the Chairman by conceding that Wu Han was "not on the side of socialism." He also withheld the "Outline Report" from Mao but released it in Peking four days later, claiming that it bore the Chairman's seal of approval.[17]

Time and again throughout the history of the Chinese Communist movement, even the fiercest of Mao's foes refrained from attacking him openly, but instead attempted to appear loyal to the Chairman while shaping his writ to their own purposes. This was now P'eng Chen's ruse. His immediate aim was to demonstrate his fidelity to the Chairman while shielding his colleagues who had run afoul of Mao's line. In taking this approach, P'eng Chen may have estimated that he might eventually reach some kind of compromise with Mao. He may have also believed that the national Party apparatus would support his scheme to achieve such a compromise. If so, P'eng Chen erred in two respects. First, he failed to appreciate the extent to which Mao was determined to push through his campaign. And second, he failed to perceive that the other Party leaders were not above sacrificing him in order to consolidate their own positions as their confrontation with Mao grew in intensity. Indeed, one of the perplexing aspects of the Cultural Revolution in its later development was the way the powerful Party machine crumbled as the *apparatchiks* betrayed one another in apparent efforts to save themselves and their particular cliques. Whatever help he may have expected from the Party bureaucracy, P'eng Chen himself behaved no differently toward his own comrades in Peking as Mao's offensive against him escalated.

In late February, after P'eng Chen had released his "Outline Report" to the Party Committees, Mao countered with a withering riposte. The final communiqué of the forum on art and literature that had been held in Shanghai by his wife, Chiang Ch'ing, plainly announced that there would be no conciliation with his adversaries. Instead, the communiqué spelled out Mao's intention to launch the Great Proletarian Cultural Revolution as a dynamic campaign conducted under military auspices against the "revisionist" Party apparatus. The statement declared that China was headed toward an "arduous, complex, and long-term struggle" designed to eliminate the "dictatorship of the black line" that had "diametrically opposed" Mao since the establishment of the Chinese People's Republic nearly sixteen years before. This struggle "has a vital bearing on the future of the Chinese revolution and the future of the world revolution." It would "take decades, or even centuries" to achieve success. More ominously, the communiqué asserted that Mao's drive would be carried out by the Army—the "chief instrument of the dictatorship of the proletariat in China" and the "mainstay and hope of the Chinese people and the revolutionary people of the world." [18]

The Shanghai communiqué, then, was Mao's blueprint for action. Now on the defensive, P'eng Chen sent the controversial Wu Han out of Peking on a trip to inspect provincial agricultural projects, an assignment for which the historian was totally unqualified. Not long after, P'eng divested himself of another liability, Lu Ting-yi, the chief of the Party's Propaganda Department, by granting him a leave to "convalesce" in south China. A few weeks later, he also dropped Teng T'o, the Peking editor and writer who had cleverly assailed Mao in a series of articles in 1961. But if P'eng believed that he could escape repudiation by disassociating himself from these and other suspicious subordinates, he failed to realize that senior Party leaders were taking the same approach toward him. Late in March, for example, Liu Shao-ch'i, his wife, and Ch'en Yi left Peking without any official fanfare for a three-week state visit to Pakistan, Afghanistan, and Burma. Their only plausible motive for quitting China at that crucial juncture was to avoid involvement in the purge they surely anticipated.

Several other signs clearly indicated to Liu Shao-ch'i and other Party insiders that Mao was bracing for a major offensive. On March 11, Lin Piao had circulated a letter to China's industrial and communications departments stressing that the country could only "maintain vigorous revolutionary enthusiasm and a firm and correct political orientation" through "unified thinking, revolutionary thinking, correct thinking—that is, Mao Tse-tung's thinking." [19] The letter was significant. As the first message addressed by the Minister of Defense to a strictly civilian audience, it was consciously calculated to dramatize that Lin Piao was now playing a decisive political role. The letter was contrived to emphasize as well that Mao had the support of the Army in his campaign against his enemies. By identifying Mao's "thinking" as the only "unified, revolutionary, and correct" line, Lin Piao was also affirming that the Party no longer mattered. Almost pleased by the prospect of a bitter fight ahead, Mao said at the time: "The deeper the socialist revolution goes, the greater will be the resistance offered by the exponents of capitalism, and the better they will reveal their countenance." [20]

Taking advantage of Liu Shao-ch'i's absence from China, Mao triggered the attack against P'eng Chen. On March 28, two days after Liu's departure, Mao denounced the Peking Party machine and its boss by name for the first time. Characteristically adorning his statement with classical allusions, Mao told a group of his followers that the moment had arrived for Sun Wu-kung, the legendary "monkey king," to raise his "golden cudgel" against P'eng Chen's "imperial court." Then, speaking more bluntly, Mao called for P'eng Chen's dismissal, the dissolution of the Peking Committee, and the dismantling of the Party's entire Propaganda Department based in the capital.[21] Two days after that, abandoned by his senior comrades just as he had expended several of his own associates, P'eng Chen made his last public appearance in his capacity as Peking Party chief at an airport function. His downfall, though not officially announced for two months, marked the end of the first phase in Mao's preparations for the Cultural Revolution.

Nearly a year later, looking bloated and bedraggled after months of imprisonment and possibly torture, P'eng Chen and his wife, along with other key members of his apparatus, were dragged into a Peking stadium by soldiers and Red Guards and, their hands trussed behind their backs, forced to kneel in disgrace before the "masses." In accordance with Mao's techniques, however, their lives were spared. For they were more valuable as "negative examples" than as dead trophies.

By the early spring of 1966, the acute struggle between Mao and his rivals was intensifying in different ways. The various participants were publishing esoteric commentaries and making symbolic gestures or secretly maneuvering against one another. In the universities and secondary schools, students—guided by local leaders or acting spontaneously—were beginning to perceive the approaching disarray as an opportunity to make a broad range of demands. Not until later, when Red Guard journals, wall posters, and other documents poured forth in unprecedented profusion, was it possible to discern some pattern in the events of those hectic days.

Mao's strategy was, as it had been from the start, to create an atmosphere in which his enemies would become bold enough to reveal themselves. As his publicists put it, "a poisonous snake comes out of its hole under certain weather conditions." Thus Mao had waited for the propitious moment to "capture" the Peking boss and his cohorts.[22] Now he proclaimed P'eng Chen's deposition in an internal directive sent out in the middle of May to every echelon of the Party and government across China. This directive, the "May 16 Circular," formally revoked the "Outline Report" concocted by P'eng Chen in February. The circular also disbanded P'eng Chen's Group of Five, which had been trying to temporize the Cultural Revolution in order to defend the Party apparatus.

And it clearly indicated that Mao intended to initiate fresh purges. "People of the Khrushchev brand" were still "nestling in our midst" in the Party, government, and Army, and the circular urged that these "counterrevolutionary revisionists" be repudiated, dismissed, or transferred to less sensitive assignments.[23]

To carry out this ambitious program, Mao appointed a new Cultural Revolution Directorate, composed of disciples whose primary qualification was fidelity to his cause. The head of the new directorate, Ch'en Po-ta, typified these disciples. A native of Fukien province, then in his early sixties, Ch'en's only claim to importance stemmed from his many years' service as Mao's private secretary, speechwriter, and ideological adviser. In short, he was Mao's mouthpiece, without authority of his own. Similarly, his chief deputy was Mao's wife, Chiang Ch'ing. Along with several other radicals who had held only minor posts until then, the new group also included an obscure soldier by the name of Wang Tung-hsing, who had once been Mao's bodyguard. The new Cultural Revolution Directorate, then, was essentially a modern replica of the Inner Court relied upon by ancient Chinese emperors during troubled periods when they could no longer trust their official subordinates.

Mao mapped out an assortment of different tactics as he escalated his campaign. One of these, calculated to induce the Chinese intelligentsia to rally to his side, was particularly dramatic. He persuaded the aged *doyen* of China's writers, Kuo Mo-jo, to make a self-abasing "confession" that would provide intellectuals with a model they could emulate.

Kuo Mo-jo, who is only barely known in the West except to scholars, was as towering an eminence in twentieth-century revolutionary Chinese literature as Voltaire had been in the European Enlightenment. Trained as a medical doctor in Japan, where he later lived in exile for long periods, Kuo became a prolific poet, translator, novelist, playwright, essayist, and propagandist for the Communists. In the middle of April, he demonstrated his loyalty to Mao in spectacular fashion. Addressing a session of the National People's Congress, the rubber-stamp Chinese legislature, Kuo declared that all he had written in the past should be "burned to ashes, for it has not the slightest value." He had not studied Mao's works sufficiently, he explained, protesting that his ideological out-look was "muddled." The moment had therefore come to prostrate himself before the proletariat, Kuo said:

> Though I am over seventy, I still have a bit of ambition left. If I am asked to wallow in mud, I am willing to do so. If I am asked to cover myself with grease, I am willing. Even if I am asked to stain myself with blood and to throw hand grenades at the American im-perialists should they dare to attack us, I shall be willing to do so.
>
> I really mean what I have said. I should now properly learn from the workers, peasants and soldiers, and if possible I will do my best to serve them.[24]

This emotional apologia was matched by sharper assaults against cultural figures linked to the Party machine. Premier Chou En-lai called for a fierce onslaught against "bourgeois ideology in the academic, educational, and journalistic fields" as well as in art and literature. And Yao Wen-yuan, the rising young Maoist critic who had earlier attacked the historian Wu Han, now published a devas-tating diatribe against Teng T'o, who had mocked Mao a few years before. Alleging that Teng T'o was being protected by prominent Party figures, Yao appealed for broader and more daring revolu-tionary thrusts that would "show up all monsters and goblins in their true colors." [25]

Consistent with this line, Mao began in the late spring to focus his fire at Chinese educational institutions, which he considered to be centers of dissidence that required drastic change if they were to produce the "revolutionary successors" capable of shaping the future of China in accordance with his vision. Among other moves, he sent a directive to Lin Piao declaring that "the domination of our schools by bourgeois intellectuals should by no means be allowed to con-tinue." [26] This directive was an order to his military followers to start organizing the young activists who would afterward emerge as the Red Guards. Dissatisfied teachers and students were also encour-aged to agitate against the system, and their willingness to protest reflected both their own traditions and a variety of tensions then nagging them.

Students have always been a significant force in China. In an-cient times, they were the potential scholars whose mastery of the classics entitled them to the highest places in the imperial administration. By the turn of the century, the external pressures imposed by Western imperialism and the internal decay of the Chinese government combined to provoke youths into a search for new systems. They became an explosive element, spearheading the May 4th Movement, which erupted in 1919 as a patriotic demonstration and quickly expanded into a demand for wide reforms. But the students who agitated for China's modernization were betrayed by the leaders they helped to lift into power. Those who supported Chiang Kai-shek soon found his regime to be inept and corrupt. After Mao's victory, many also discovered that the Communists did not live up to their ideals.

One of the first outbursts of student unrest under the Communists appeared only eight years after the establishment of the Chinese People's Republic, when Mao inaugurated the "Hundred Flowers" experiment. Prompted not only by a desire to rectify abuses in education but to curb the injustices of the Party dictatorship as well, students took advantage of the temporary breath of freedom to manifest their feelings vociferously and often violently. As a later student generation would during the Cultural Revolution, they plastered the walls of universities and schools with crude, hand-painted posters demanding more liberalism in their curricula and denouncing such iniquities as favoritism for the children of Party members. Students in several cities staged strikes and fought with police. Three youths were publicly executed for engineering a riot in a suburb of Wuhan, the industrial city on the Yangtze River, and thousands of students were shipped off to labor in rural villages and remote border regions. The party further tightened its control by introducing dependable Communist officials into the educational system as university presidents and vice-presidents, school principals, and political instructors.[27]

Other problems continued to plague the students. The economic recession caused by the failure of the Great Leap Forward, for example, left large numbers of graduates without jobs to match their educational experience. Unemployed or underemployed young people crowded into China's cities, despite repeated campaigns by the authorities to transfer young people to the countryside to work with peasants. For those who found jobs, advancement was blocked as older employees clogged government, industrial, and academic positions. The Party apparatus was also top-heavy with aging Communist veterans unwilling to make room for the younger generation. At the same time, recurrent programs to infuse politically reliable "proletarian" youths into the educational system resembled the painful effort in the United States to open Ivy-League universities to black students. Like the blacks from America's urban ghettos and southern towns, the Chinese students of poor worker and peasant origin were unprepared to compete against the children of Party and Government officials, whose training had been superior. Attempts to lower the prevailing academic standards in order to accommodate the "proletarian" youths aroused the opposition of brighter students and their teachers. The poor youths, in turn, resented the privileges accorded "elite" students, many of whom attended special boarding schools, enjoyed preferential employment after graduation, and were even treated leniently when they misbehaved. By any measure, there were potentially explosive "class" tensions in China's educational institutions.

Thus Mao's Cultural Revolution seemed attractive to frustrated students regardless of their particular grievances. His call to oust the "bourgeois" administrations from the universities and schools could be interpreted by students of all political persuasions as a license to rebel. Therefore, though turbulence was deliberately encouraged, it spread rapidly because students were receptive to the need for change. Their conduct, however, was largely a confused reaction against authority that gathered momentum but lacked specific, clear-cut objectives.

The first clashes of the Cultural Revolution inside the academic community broke out at Peking University, familiarly known as Peita, the oldest and most prestigious institution of higher learning in China. Established in 1898 as Imperial University, Peita has been closely associated with China's political developments throughout the twentieth century. It was here that Mao had worked as a library assistant under Li Ta-chao, one of the founders of the Chinese Communist Party. The university had also been the scene of patriotic student demonstrations in the 1920s and 1930s. After the Communist victory in 1949, Peita remained relatively free from political pressures. Its president in the 1950s was Ma Yin-ch'u, an American-educated non-Communist and one of China's most famous economists. A stubborn advocate of such liberal notions as birth control, Ma was dismissed in 1960. His replacement was Lu P'ing, a robust and energetic man then about fifty, who had been a Communist youth leader for years. In addition to managing the university administration, he was also First Secretary of its Party Committee. If Lu was a dogmatist compared to Ma Yin-ch'u, he was still too pragmatic for Mao Tse-tung's radical disciples. For, like the Party *apparatchiks*, he believed in the primacy of technocracy over ideology. He emphasized the importance of academic excellence, selected his faculty on the basis of their professional ability, and even stressed that China had much to learn from Soviet, British, and American education.[28]

This line, with its accent on expertise rather than "Redness," ran into resistance from a faction of ultraleftists, among them a woman cadre in the philosophy department, Nieh Yuan-tzu, who had been admonished by Lu P'ing for her extremist views as early as 1961. How she survived in the years after that has never been made clear. By the spring of 1966, however, she and her comrades at Peita came into contact with Mao's wife, who was then recruiting radicals in the drive to intensify the Cultural Revolution on the campuses. Nieh, with her long record of opposition to the Party machine, was an obvious candidate to head the revolt at Peking University.

Mao's attack on P'eng Chen and the Peking Party Committee, going on at that time, had prompted a predictable response from other Communist officials in the capital and elsewhere across the country. Many went through the motions of assailing Mao's alleged foes while striving to maintain control over the campaign as a way of protecting themselves. Lu P'ing took essentially the same approach at Peking University. He voiced his support for the purge of Mao's adversaries but insisted that the "struggle must be conducted in a very careful manner," ruling out, for example, the use of wall posters and mass meetings. In the view of the radicals, this tactic was contrary to Mao's order to unleash the "masses." Early in the afternoon of May 25, Nieh Yuan-tzu and her comrades put up a poster on a wall outside the university dining hall addressed to Lu P'ing and his colleagues:

To hold meetings and to post big-character posters are mass militant methods of the best kind. But you "lead" the masses by preventing them from holding meetings and putting up posters. You have manufactured various taboos and regulations. By so doing, have you not suppressed, forbidden, and opposed the mass revolution? We absolutely will not allow you to do so!

You shout about "strengthening the leadership and standing fast at one's post. . . ." You still want to "stand fast" at your "posts" in order to sabotage the Cultural Revolution. We warn you that a mantis cannot stop the wheels of a cart and mayflies cannot topple a giant tree. You are day-dreaming!

Now is the time for all revolutionary intellectuals to go into battle! Let us unite and hold high the great red banner of Mao Tse-tung's thought . . . resolutely, thoroughly, totally and completely wipe out all monsters and demons and all counterrevolutionary revisionists of the Khrushchev type, and carry the socialist revolution through to the end.[29]

This passionate diatribe against Lu P'ing and his associates stupefied the Peking University students. Groups of them gathered around the poster, questioning its validity and wondering what would happen next. Their attitude for the most part was cautious. But a few hours later, when he learned of the attack against him, Lu P'ing mobilized members of the Communist Youth League to respond with posters excoriating Nieh Yuan-tzu and her faction as "renegades," asserting that their resistance to the Party in the university represented "opposition to the Central Committee of the Party." The same evening, Nieh was hauled before a meeting in the university dining hall. She was interrogated and accused of seeking to undermine the Party. When one of her comrades tried to come to her aid, according to his version of the incident, he was dragged out and manhandled.[30]

During the following week, fearing reprisals from the Party rather than acting out of real conviction, most of the students appeared to side with Lu P'ing and the university authorities. They besieged Nieh Yuan-tzu in her room, calling her a "rightist." At that stage, Mao brought his weight to bear with a gesture that was to give a fresh and decisive impetus to the Cultural Revolution.

Ensconced in his Hangchow retreat, Mao had kept abreast of

developments through his agents in the university. Indeed, his wife was in contact with Nieh Yuan-tzu while elements of the Army, obeying his instructions to Lin Piao, were helping to mobilize student activists. He therefore welcomed Nieh's poster, hailing it as "China's first Marxist-Leninist big-character poster," presumably because it represented a radical outburst rather than a recurrence of the liberal protests that had churned up the university during the "Hundred Flowers" episode.[31] A version of the "Paris Commune" could be created in China, he suggested, stressing that the significance of such an experiment would even "surpass" the brief and abortive power seizure by French workers in 1871.[32]

Mao's reference to the Paris Commune pointed in the direction he hoped to take. He believed that the Chinese "masses" could, through sheer energy, grasp the authority of the state and establish true "proletarian democracy," as the Communards had unsuccessfully tried to do. In this approach, however, Mao deviated from both Marx and Lenin. Though Marx supported their uprising after it started, he had warned the rebellious French workers beforehand that their planned insurrection was a "desperate act of folly," and Lenin, implicitly criticizing the "adventurism" of the Commune, condemned the notion of destroying all administration immediately as an "anarchist" dream.[33] Months later, after an attempt to emulate the Paris Commune in Shanghai had floundered, Mao would quietly abandon the idea as unworkable. But now the vision seemed captivating. He ordered that the text of the explosive poster written by Nieh Yuan-tzu and her comrades be broadcast to the nation and published in the press on June 1, 1966.[34]

Mao's endorsement of the poster electrified Peking University. Even though many students had read and discussed the text a week earlier, they crowded into the university dining hall on the evening of June 1 to hear it broadcast. One university official tried to prevent the assembly, advising the students against "listening blindly," while another threatened to have the Peking radio station "suppressed." But the students ignored them. According to a Reuters dispatch from Peking, the atmosphere at the university "seemed festive rather than tense."[35] The students sang revolutionary songs, chanted slogans, and, beating gongs, cymbals, and drums, paraded around a campus festooned with colored paper streamers.

Numbers of students from other universities and schools as well as mobs of inquisitive citizens joined the throng, and the excitement rose when an official from the revamped Peking Party Committee arrived to announce that P'eng Chen, the Communist boss of the capital, had been dismissed along with Lu P'ing and other members of the university directorate.[36]

The university campus soon began to resemble a fairground. Mounted on makeshift rostrums erected in Hyde Park fashion, student speakers poured out emotional tales of intimidation by the deposed Party apparatus. The oratory warmed to a feverish pitch when nearly six thousand students and teachers who had been sent to work in the countryside the previous autumn returned with accounts of the hardships they had suffered in the villages.[37] More than a hundred thousand posters went up on the university walls assailing not only Lu P'ing and other prominent figures but obscure professors and even fellow students. Inspired by personal feuds or sheer exuberance, many of the posters featured puerile attacks against officials and teachers for such alleged "counterrevolutionary" activities as "luxurious living" or displaying "lordly airs." As their appetite for denouncing the authorities sharpened, some students broke into the homes of professors, smashing their furniture and destroying their "bourgeois" books. Several faculty members were forced to march through the campus wearing dunce's caps and placards proclaiming their "crimes." A jocular note crept into the turbulence when a group of young people singled out an elderly American Communist sympathizer by the name of Robert Winter, who had taught English for years at the university and was then living in retirement on the campus. The youths pasted a poster on his door written in English: "Bob Winter stinks." [38] *

Many students, swept along in the general melee, must have simply seen the situation as an opportunity to raise hell. But many shared a genuine sense of elation at having been liberated from the oppressive controls of the Party machine, with its network of cadres and informers. Their surge of rebellion also reflected a release from assorted social tensions, not the least of which were the sexual prohibitions imposed by the puritanism of China's revolutionary

* Winter was afterward arrested and sent to a "labor reform" camp. He was released in 1970.

society. At the same time, the new freedom seemed to offer an escape from concerns about studies and jobs and the other frustrating uncertainties of an unpredictable system. Students appeared to be attracted less by the positive substance of Mao's dogma, if they understood it at all, than by his sanction of their right to kick over the traces. To a European journalist then visiting China, a Chinese girl explained the effervescence as a phenomenon that students anywhere in the world would have envied.

> We, the young, who will inherit this country, can go to our chief of government and tell him what bothers us and why. And in the wall posters we can now write about things that have been forbidden for twenty years. Do you really want to know what the Cultural Revolution is? It is *a feast of criticism*.[39]

The excitement at Peking University inspired students elsewhere in the capital and throughout the country to agitate for the removal of unpopular political and academic figures. Mao came forth with the new slogan, "Rebellion Is Justified," which encouraged them to assault officials and institutions indiscriminately. And the Peking press, now expressing the Maoist line, published daily exhortations to "sweep away all freaks and monsters," all "bourgeois 'specialists,' 'scholars,' 'authorities,' and 'venerable masters.' " As a *People's Daily* editorial put it:

> The fact that the Khrushchev revisionist clique has usurped the leadership of the Party, Army and state in the Soviet Union is an extremely serious lesson for the proletariat throughout the world. At present, the representatives of the bourgeoisie—the bourgeois scholars and authorities in China—are similarly dreaming of restoring capitalism.[40]

Despite these strident appeals to clean out adversaries of Mao's doctrines, very few important Party *apparatchiks* were actually dismissed from provincial posts that spring. Those who were purged included a handful of newspaper editors and a scattering of cultural figures, such as the composer Ho Lü-t'ing, whose anthem "The East Is Red" continued to be played long after his disappearance—and was even used as the signal emitted by the first Chinese earth satellite, launched three years later. Though the provincial university campuses appeared to be stormy, the peals of thunder far exceeded the strikes of lightning. Some prominent educational officials, like the president and upper echelon at Wuhan University, lost their posts. But the general ferment more typically resembled the commotion in the northern coastal city of Tientsin, where thousands of students from six universities and institutes staged a series of noisy demonstrations—only to dismiss one assistant professor of history.[41]

In short, much of the apparent animation at this point in the Cultural Revolution was a charade being enacted by the Party. Seeking to defend itself, the Party apparatus simulated agitation, even sacrificing some of its more expendable members in order to appease Mao. In the universities, the Party also revived so-called Work Teams in an ostensible effort to uproot "counterrevolutionary" professors and academic officials, but in reality to shield itself. At least as cunning as his adversaries, Mao was well aware of their duplicity—and probably encouraged them in order to trap the Party.

The Party Work Teams had been organized on a limited scale as far back as late 1962 as instruments to carry out the Socialist Education Campaign, a movement inaugurated by Mao to curb the trend toward liberalization then growing in the universities in reaction to the rigors of the Great Leap Forward.[42] Functioning as they did under Party auspices, however, the Teams carefully refrained from shaking the *apparatchiks* from their positions of control. Indeed, according to Maoist documents published later, the conflict at Peking University in the spring of 1966 had its origins two years earlier, when Nieh Yuan-tzu and her radical comrades sought to gain control of a Team investigating the alleged "revisionist" tendencies of Lu P'ing and his colleagues. At that time, the Maoists claimed afterward, the university leadership was protected by Secretary General Teng Hsiao-p'ing, who neutralized the leftists on the grounds that they were "carrying the struggle to excess." Though he then lacked the power to take action against them, Mao must have known that the Party was blocking his radical disciples. In a significant article written during that period, he underlined the importance of training China's youth to become "successors of the revolutionary cause" and cautioned against "conspirators and careerists like Khrushchev" who were trying to "usurp the leadership of the Party and the state." It was "essential to test and judge cadres . . . in the long course of mass struggle." [43]

In early 1966, Mao had "tested" his adversaries by delegating P'eng Chen and members of the Peking Party Committee to run the Cultural Revolution, and then purging them when they betrayed his aims. Now, in early June, Mao adopted the same strategy against Liu Shao-ch'i, Teng Hsiao-p'ing, and the other senior Party leaders by giving their Work Teams the responsibility for managing the Cultural Revolution in the universities. Mao was certain that he could discredit them, for he was confronting them with an impossible set of alternatives. If they permitted the radicals to speak out freely, they would face radical attacks for having opposed Mao in the past, and they would be compelled to recant ignominiously. If they attempted to prevent the radicals from criticizing them, they would be accused of repressing the "masses" and, like P'eng Chen, be subjected to further denunciations and possible dismissal as "revisionists." [44] Later, when he was sure that his strategy was succeeding, Mao would reveal that his maneuver had been deliberate. Speaking to Liu, Teng, and his other Party foes at a meeting in mid-July, Mao explained that the test of a true revolutionary leader was his willingness to "transform" himself under the tutelage of the "masses," the repository of ultimate wisdom. There was a tone of theological fundamentalism in his warning to his rivals that they had deviated from his truth:

> We should trust the masses and be their pupils before we can be their teachers. . . .
> Some comrades are very ferocious when they struggle against other people, but they are unable to wage the struggle against themselves. They will never be able to pass the test in this way.
> When you are told to kindle a fire to burn yourselves, will you do it—even in the knowledge that you will yourselves be consumed by the flames?
> Be prepared for the revolution to come down on your heads. Party and government leaders and responsible Party comrades must all be prepared. [45]

The Party leaders had courted this fate, as Mao calculated they would, by having used the Work Teams to stifle the radicals in the universities. They had therefore strayed from the "direction and line" of the Cultural Revolution. [46] But Liu Shao-ch'i and his Party colleagues originally believed that they could restrict the scope and focus of Mao's campaign, and shape it to their own advantage.

Months later, under pressure to make a ritual confession of his "crimes," Liu Shao-ch'i admitted that the Teams under his guidance had "adopted various methods to suppress the masses, such as prohibiting demonstrations and parades in the streets, and wall posters." [47] From the beginning of June into late July, Liu conceded, the Teams had operated to hinder rather than to stimulate the Cultural Revolution.

> The majority of the responsible members of the work teams neither understood the Great Proletarian Cultural Revolution nor properly learned from the masses. At the very outset, they asked the broad masses who had been aroused to act according to plans and steps which we and the work teams conceived on the basis of our subjective wishes.
>
> This ran counter to the law governing the development of the revolutionary mass movement, and many serious incidents occurred. In fact, we took a reactionary bourgeois stand, practiced bourgeois dictatorship, suppressed the great Cultural Revolution which was then vigorously developing, confused right and wrong, white and black, thereby inflating the arrogance of the bourgeoisie and demoralizing the proletariat.[48]

Stripped of its jargon—and allowing for the exaggerated contrition of an old Party veteran seeking to absolve himself of guilt—Liu Shao-ch'i's description of the role of the Work Teams was plausible. The Teams were fighting to preserve the Party's authority in that crucial period, and their rough tactics reflected the seriousness with which the Communist bureaucracy viewed the issues at stake.

Headed by Chang Ch'eng-hsien, an experienced Party official from Hopeh province, the Team that entered Peking University in early June was at first welcomed by the student radicals. Since the Team was functioning under the aegis of the new Peking Party Committee that had replaced P'eng Chen and dismissed Lu P'ing and the old university administration, the leftist teachers and students believed that their protests would be encouraged. Within a week, however, they perceived that the Team had different designs. Instead of promoting continued ferment, it halted demonstrations, banned student speeches, and assigned radical youths to such chores as scraping posters off the walls. The gates of the university were locked to anyone unable to show identification. About two weeks later, when the radicals tried to organize a meeting to denounce Lu P'ing and the other purged members of the university leadership, they were refused permission. When they defiantly held an unauthorized meeting, many were labeled "counterrevolutionary" by the Team and forced to confess to their "sins." [49]

At the same time, Team members tried to channel student energies by arbitrarily selecting victims whom the youths could attack. The Peking University Team singled out a woman professor in the Foreign Languages Department, and instructed one of her students, a young girl, to criticize her. When the young girl refused, she herself was brought before a board of political examiners and denounced as a "rightist." [50]

On July 12, five students in the university's Department of Geophysics, supported by Nieh Yuan-tzu, finally revolted by putting up a poster protesting against the Work Team.[51] The Team retaliated by assailing her and the other radicals. By now, in a chaos of rhetoric that would soon become even more confusing, the two camps were both pledging allegiance to Mao and indicting each other as "bourgeois," "reactionary," and "counterrevolutionary revisionist." Most of the students, baffled by this verbiage, were cautious. Recalling his inability to sort out the rival groups, one student later explained that his main concerns were his application for Party membership, his postgraduate job assignment, and his personal future. Consequently, he said, he was hesitant to take sides.[52] Many other students were equally prudent. Unable to remain neutral, the most dangerous position, they shouted slogans without conviction while watching carefully to judge which way the political winds were blowing. They were, in effect, the reluctantly vocal majority.

In another part of Peking, a similar tempest was brewing at Tsinghua University, China's foremost polytechnic institution. Founded in 1911 as a preparatory college for students planning to study in the United States, Tsinghua was raised to university status in 1925 as an important center of Sino-American educational cooperation. Under the Communists, it concentrated mainly on science and engineering and, by 1960, the university had some twelve thousand students and nearly two thousand faculty members.[53] The president, several department heads, and numbers of teachers and students at Tsinghua also served among the five hundred cadres on the university's panoply of Party committees.[54] In contrast to Peking University, however, Tsinghua had been relatively calm during the spring of 1966. For one thing, its scientific and technological focus made it a more conservative institution. And for another, the Tsinghua student body included many children of distinguished notables. When it erupted, therefore, the revolt at Tsinghua was apparently orchestrated by Mao's operatives for a specific purpose—to assail Liu Shao-ch'i's wife, Wang Kuang-mei, who had arrived at Tsinghua as a leader of the Work Team formed to bolster the Party machine there.

With Chiang Ch'ing a key figure in charge of the Cultural Revolution and Wang Kuang-mei a Party trouble-shooter, the two women were clearly engaged in a private vendetta. But in the ideological climate of the period, Wang Kuang-mei was at a disadvantage. Elegant, well-educated, and, above all, born into luxury, she could scarcely claim to stand for austere proletarian virtues in a system that measured the attitudes of people by the acreage of their grandfathers' farms. Even her name, Kuang-mei, was against her. Chosen by her father, who was traveling in the United States at the time of her birth in 1922, it signified "beautiful America." [55]

One of eleven children, Wang Kuang-mei was born and raised in Tientsin, the thriving cosmopolitan port city for Peking and northern China in those days. Her family—by Communist standards of the "bureaucratic capitalist" class—was wealthy, worldly, and powerful. Her father, after serving in lucrative official posts for the local warlord government in northern China of the early 1920s, parlayed his capital and contacts into a fortune by acquiring vast tracts of real estate, factories, and other holdings. One of her uncles managed the largest textile mill in the region. Another relative, Wang Shu-ming, became commander in chief of Chiang Kai-shek's air force and Chief of General Staff of the Nationalist armed forces. Her brother Kuang-ying—his name, reflecting her father's admiration for Great Britain, meant "beautiful England"—continued to run one of the family factories after the Communist victory and was hailed as a "Red capitalist" in those more tolerant days.

Wang Kuang-mei received an education befitting her family's

status and Western leanings and her own modern inclinations. She entered Fujen University, a Catholic-sponsored institution in Peking, and went on to Yenching, an American-subsidized university in the same city and the leading Christian college in China. Her English therefore was excellent and she had no trouble finding employment as an interpreter. Like many other idealistic young Chinese, she went to work for the Communists. Her first job was with their military procurement office in Peking. In 1946, she switched to the Communist mission then trying to negotiate a reconciliation with the Nationalists under the auspices of General George C. Marshall. Her cultivated style appealed to two senior members of the Communist group: Lo Jui-ch'ing, later Chief of General Staff and an early victim of the Cultural Revolution, and Yeh Chien-ying, the top figure in the group, who would survive the purges to become one of China's highest-ranking officers. When the negotiations collapsed, Wang Kuang-mei considered pursuing her studies in the United States, but Yeh Chien-ying persuaded her to go instead to Yenan. There, assigned to the Foreign Affairs Department of the Party Central Committee, she met Liu Shao-ch'i. At twenty-four, she was roughly half his age.

Having just discarded his fifth wife, Liu Shao-ch'i had an uneven marital record. One of his wives had been executed by the Nationalists in the early 1930s, and he had divorced four others. Now he fell in love with the "bourgeois" Wang Kuang-mei, and they married in 1948. She bore him two daughters in addition to serving as stepmother to several of his numerous children by previous marriages. With her grace and sophistication, she became a suitable "first lady" of China, a function she performed when Liu was elevated to chief of state in 1959. They traveled together to Pakistan, Afghanistan, and Burma, and she particularly impressed Indonesia's President Sukarno, a man easily charmed by pretty women. She was also effective as hostess to the many foreign delegations that streamed into Peking in the early 1960s. As a Party agent at Tsinghua University during the stormy summer of 1966, then, she was clearly miscast.

The Party Work Team, with Wang Kuang-mei prominent on its staff, arrived at Tsinghua on June 9 proclaiming in the rhetoric of the Cultural Revolution that the university administration required a complete overhaul. The Team thereupon dismissed the university's entire Party apparatus without examining the ideological credentials of individual cadres or giving those at fault the chance to "remold" themselves in accordance with Mao's teaching that all except "antagonistic" enemies can win redemption through self-criticism. One of the Team's motives for this maneuver, the Maoists alleged, was to promote its favorites into positions of authority. Thus Liu T'ao, Liu Shao-ch'i's daughter and a student of automation control, was made a deputy secretary of the Party branch in her department even though she was still only a candidate for Party membership. Similarly, Ho P'eng-fei, Marshal Ho Lung's son and a mechanical-engineering student, was appointed to the Party committee in his section. Other children of high officials were also given posts in the new Party bureaucracy.[56]

The chief radical to rise in opposition to this operation was an obscure young student of chemical engineering, K'uai Ta-fu. Probably encouraged by Mao's operatives, K'uai tried to mobilize a student group behind him. But the Tsinghua students were either too apathetic or prudent to support his cause. With extraordinary courage, K'uai acted virtually alone. He opened an offensive against the Party Team at the university by raising doubts about its claim to revolutionary competence. In a poster expressing these doubts, he said:

> Power is in the hands of the Work Team, and this must prompt every revolutionary leftist to ask: Does this power represent us? If it does, we must support the Team. If not, we must seize its power.[57]

Wang Kuang-mei apparently remained indifferent to this challenge, but the Party Team reacted immediately. At first its members tried to reason with K'uai. He could not decently accuse the majority of the Party of "revisionism," they said. But K'uai stubbornly refused to concede, sticking to his charge that the Party was a "gang of bourgeois royalists" resisting the Cultural Revolution.[58] At an ensuing series of meetings, he continued to hold his ground. Alleging that the Party bosses had fabricated evidence against him, he vowed, "I would still declare that I am a revolutionary even if I were dragged to the gallows." [59] Arrested in July, he staged a hunger strike punctuated by histrionic communiqués warning that his imminent death would be a curse forever on the Party "reactionaries." One of these communiqués, addressed to a senior member of the Party Team, reached melodramatic heights:

> I have fasted for more than fifty hours. I feel exhausted, disintegrated. I fear that I may not live through tomorrow. I therefore request that you talk with me while I can still speak. I have many things to say to the Party Central Committee, to Chairman Mao, to my parents, and to you people. If you are too busy, send a representative and a stenographer that I may dictate my last will and testament.[60]

K'uai Ta-fu did not die, of course. Released on condition that he admit his "errors," he confessed to having been "ultraleftist" in displaying "sectarian tendencies" and "revolutionary rashness" in his "political oscillations." His "petty-bourgeois world outlook" had led him to dramatize his "individual and personal heroism" in order to "put myself in the limelight." [61]

The confession was only a dodge, however. Not long afterward, when the Maoists had gained the ascendancy, K'uai resumed his radical stance and accused the Party Team of having "spread poison" among the Tsinghua students.[62] His charges were subsequently used as the basis for an indictment against Wang Kuangmei. And, in a ritual confession, she was compelled to concede that the Party team at Tsinghua had "suppressed democracy and differing opinions, creating a reign of white terror" in the university. By restricting the "enthusiasm, creativity, and initiative of the masses," she had been guilty of "right-wing opportunism." [63] Despite this *mea culpa*, which was apparently contrived to deflect a growing Maoist assault against her husband later in 1966, she was betrayed by her own children and subjected to a humiliating inquisition.

During the early weeks of the summer, events in the provincial cities echoed the pattern set in Peking as Party Work Teams penetrated regional universities in order to control the Cultural Revolution. This revealed, in part, that the Party was able to coordinate its defenses to a remarkable degree on a nationwide basis. But the extent of the activity also reflected the contagious ferment infecting young people in vastly different areas of the huge country.

In the ancient city of Sian, the capital of Shensi province, student restiveness became manifest as early as May in reaction to the campaign then developing against P'eng Chen and his allegedly "bourgeois" literary protégés. Students ceased attending afternoon classes, stopped doing homework, and dropped their extracurricular activities, devoting most of their time instead to political meetings. On June 1, when Mao ordered that the text of the radical poster put up by Nieh Yuan-tzu at Peking University be broadcast, the ferment intensified. Throughout the night, students in Sian painted wall posters and wrote statements in a disorganized "feast of criticism" against teachers, comrades, officials, and almost anyone else who came to mind.

The initial agitation in Sian lacked direction. But one group of young radicals at Chiao T'ung Ta Hsueh, the Transport and Communications University—known familiarly as Chiaota—was disciplined and purposeful. These students mounted a rhetorical assault against the university officials, charging them with promoting a "black line" against the Cultural Revolution. Their ambiguous accusations evoked an equally murky response from the university authorities, who quickly called a meeting to counterattack, branding the radicals "rightists" and denouncing their "wild actions." Within a few hours, fresh posters went up on the walls labeling the leftists "counterrevolutionaries." The next day, a Party Work Team arrived on the scene to take charge of the situation.

Headed by a senior member of the provincial Party apparatus, the Team moved rapidly to restore order. Students were prohibited from staging parades, putting up posters, and delivering speeches, and most of the youths, apparently respectful of the Party's power, observed the bans. The Team also sought to appease the radicals by mildly reproving one of the university officials and persuading him to confess to his "mistakes" at a public meeting. The episode might have ended there had not the radicals, either fired up by internal combustion or enflamed by outside fuel, escalated their protests against the Party Team. They telegraphed Mao, asking him to send a representative to Sian. They also defied the Party by plastering posters throughout the city complaining of "repression." In addition, they sent spokesmen to Peking to plead their case before the Central Committee and dispatched representatives to contact other student groups as far away as Szechwan.

Tensions in Sian were so acute by the first week of June that no less a personage than Huo Shih-lien, the First Secretary of the Shensi Party Committee and boss of the province, intervened. Calling on workers, peasants, and local officials as well as Party youth organizations to criticize the radical students, he even threatened to employ regional Army units, then passively standing on the sidelines, to maintain peace. Huo also mobilized a special squad to "investigate" the young radicals who were creating trouble.

The fate of one student activist singled out by the Party squad in the university has been described by an Englishman, Andrew Watson, who was teaching at the Foreign Languages Institute in Sian during the period.[64] A girl named Wang Yung-ting had imprudently signed twenty posters attacking the university's Party committee. Soon afterward, she was herself described in posters put up by Party members as a "witch" and a "drowning dog," while the university radio station labeled her "an enemy of the people." Arrested by the Party squad, she was interrogated for the names of her comrades and forced to write thirty-two separate statements acknowledging her "crimes." Despite her "confessions," the harassment continued. On June 8, she was put on public display in what was called an "animal exhibition." Her letters and private papers were confiscated, and seven students were assigned to guard her, presumably until she was brought to trial. But on July 9, she committed suicide by jumping from the window of the room where she was being held. According to Watson, hers was not the only suicide in those days.

In the southern city of Canton, meanwhile, local Party bureaucrats were similarly attempting to protect themselves by controlling the course of the Cultural Revolution. How their maneuvers appeared in microcosm was described by Dai Hsiao-ai, a student activist in a Canton secondary school prior to his defection to Hong Kong.[65]

As Dai recalled, the Cultural Revolution was first announced in his school by the principal, who also served as Party boss in the institution. At a meeting in late April, he instructed the students to paint posters, write articles, and mobilize discussions criticizing Wu Han, Teng T'o, and the other literary figures in Peking who were then being repudiated in the national press. The students knew nothing about these writers, but they followed orders. They copied phrases from the newspapers and invented trite slogans such as "Wu Han, you are a son of a bitch" and "Teng T'o, surrender or be destroyed." This activity was initially amusing as a change from school work, but after ten days, even the most active students in the school began to lose interest in the repetitious exercise.

But in the middle of May, when Mao moved openly against P'eng Chen and the Peking Party Committee, the principal in Dai's school felt constrained to revive the campaign. He selected two teachers to be criticized by the students. One had temporarily been in trouble during a drive against "rightists" in 1957, while another was reputed to have a "bad" family background. The students were now aroused, since the accused were real people rather than remote villains in Peking. Flimsy accusations against the two teachers were repeated for several days until the principal, anxious to keep the agitation going, urged the students to compel them to undergo a more cruel series of indignities.

> We forced the teachers to wear caps and collars which stated things like "I am a monster." Each class confronted and reviled them in turn with slogans, accusations, and injunctions to reform their ways. We made them clean out the toilets, smeared them with black paint, and organized "Control Monster Teams" to see that it was properly done. We would charge them with specific mistakes and not relent until they admitted that they were true. It took nearly a week of constant struggle to make the man admit he had said "Mao was wrong" in conversation with one of his fellow teachers. They had little rest and were forced to sleep apart from their fellow teachers. We would join into informal groups, raid their quarters, and begin to work on them again. They could not escape us.
>
> After about two weeks, we were afraid that the literature teacher would kill herself. We kept her under constant surveillance, and even wrote a poster and attached it to the mosquito net over her bed reminding her that she was being watched and could not succeed in committing suicide.

One of the peculiar features in this gratuitous terror was that Dai and the other students had actually respected the two teachers they were so brutally persecuting. However, as Dai recalled, their guilt was never doubted—the students could not possibly conceive that the sacrosanct Party might be wrong. As a consequence, even though he originally had compunctions about assailing the teachers, Dai quickly developed a genuine hatred for them. To attack them, he later said, "was our duty, and we showed no mercy."

In early June, as the rhetoric of the Cultural Revolution intensified with appeals to uproot "representatives of bourgeoisie" in the Party, government, and Army, Dai's school principal took a further step to insulate himself. He exhorted the students to repudiate seven more teachers, three as "rightists" and four as "bad elements" who had committed serious errors in the past. These teachers were all competent, popular, and dedicated, and Dai and his comrades were puzzled that they should have been chosen for criticism. They began to question the principal's motives, gradually perceiving that he and his associates were trying to defend themselves by victimizing subordinates. After discussing possible moves, the students sent delegates to the offices of the Provincial Party Committee to voice their suspicions. An official there politely listened to their story and promised to send a Work Team to investigate the school. In early July, therefore, a Team composed of sixteen cadres arrived to assume "all authority" over the school management. Within three days, the direction of the Cultural Revolution in the school was shifted.

Students were ordered to halt their attacks against teachers. Now their target was to be the school administration, including the principal, who was forced to wear a cardboard replica of a cow's head as he faced criticism. The fiercest assailants of the administration were naturally the teachers who had been persecuted earlier. They vilified the principal, who sought to ease the pressure by confessing lavishly to his mistakes. Amid this ferment, Dai noticed one phenomenon. Just as the principal had previously sacrificed his underlings in order to protect himself and his associates, so the members of the Work Team seemed to be denouncing the school administration in order to display the Party's zeal. The big fish, Dai observed, were merely eating the smaller fish. But in no way had the Team unleashed the "masses," in accordance with Mao's dictates. On the contrary, Dai concluded, the students' controlled activities bore little resemblance to Mao's vision of the Cultural

Revolution as a dynamic upheaval that would reach into the "souls" of the Chinese people.

Even though Mao's base of power in mid-1966 was Shanghai, the Cultural Revolution in that metropolis was also phony. For here, too, the local Party bureaucracy went through the motions of carrying on the campaign while actually working to keep it within bounds. According to Neale Hunter, a young Australian teacher who lived in Shanghai during that period, the most avid spokesman for the Cultural Revolution in the city seemed to be the mayor and First Secretary of the Party's Municipal Committee, a chubby little Szechwanese by the name of Ts'ao Ti-ch'iu. A quiet, unimaginative *apparatchik* concerned primarily with the management of a complex industrial center, Ts'ao had been the epitome of Party orthodoxy. Now, to shield himself against the radicals, he took the initiative in sponsoring Mao's drive. "The people who will be most criticized in this movement are those who hang up lamb but sell dog meat," he announced in a speech on June 4, warning that he would uproot Party members who "wave Red Flags as a cover for an attack on the Red Flag." But the student radicals believed that Ts'ao and his Party comrades were themselves waving the Red Flag to oppose it. They accused him of planning to "deceive the people" by attempting to "confuse the issue," and their charge was valid.[66]

Though Mao had decreed that students be given free rein, the Work Teams that went into Shanghai's universities under the auspices of Ts'ao Ti-ch'iu and the Party frequently behaved in dictatorial fashion. One of the most repressive of these Teams in Shanghai, according to Maoist accounts, was led by the Chief of the Security Police, Huang Ch'ih-po. An impatient, volatile man, Huang was reported to have lost his temper in several encounters with young leftists. Angered by one radical,

Huang, without letting him finish, sprang off the couch so fast that he left his shoes behind. Arrogantly placing his hands on his hips, he said: "Do you still want to argue the point, you stupid young punk? You've forgotten all about Party leadership! You don't give a damn about the Work Team! You say you want the Party to lead, but you really think we're not revolutionary enough. *You're* the only revolutionaries around here, I suppose. Do you think that just because you've fooled the workers you can pull the wool over *our* eyes too?

'You're not supporting Chairman Mao, you're supporting Chairman Chiang Kai-shek! . . . You haven't listened to advice from anyone—not even from your own wives! . . . You've tried to create chaos. You've made things so difficult for the Party cadres that their work has been paralyzed. What kind of people are you? If you thought about your position, you'd break out in a cold sweat!" [67]

On another occasion, sounding very much like the stereotype Party *apparatchik* in a bad movie, Huang was quoted as telling unruly students that "if you don't do as we say, then we have other methods, not such nice ones." In still another riposte to the radicals, he said:

You *still* insist on disobeying the Party! Chiang Kai-shek had eight million men, and he could not defeat us. . . . What chance have you got? . . . The Work Team *is* the Party. If you try to take power here, we will see that you lose power. . . . Has the Communist Party become an object of hatred in your eyes? If so, you are in grave danger.[68]

The Shanghai Foreign Languages Institute, where Neale Hunter taught, was considered too unimportant to warrant a Work Team, but it went through much the same experience as the city's larger colleges and universities. On June 3, just as the Cultural Revolution was beginning to escalate in Peking and elsewhere, a group of five young teachers at the Institute put up the first wall poster attacking its Party Committee for "lagging behind" in the movement. The Party Secretary responded quickly. Parrying the radical thrust, he called for a war against "bourgeois academics": "We must don the armor of Mao Tse-tung's ideas and root them out to the last man." Then, to appease the leftists, he quietly inspired the Institute's Communist Youth League to inaugurate a campaign against the Dean of English, a typical "bourgeois academic" who was said to have translated the complete works of Chaucer into Chinese. The choice of this obvious scapegoat seemed to satisfy most of the students, whose faith in the Party leadership was solid. But the radicals were unmoved. They raised the ante with an attack against the Vice-Secretary of the League, whom they accused of being the son of a landlord and a degenerate.[69]

Once again, instead of meeting the challenge head-on, the Party Secretary selected another "bourgeois academic," one of the Institute's vice-presidents, a jolly old Communist veteran with crew-cut gray hair and a passion for tennis and swimming. The indictment against him was a collection of ludicrous and petty complaints. But most of the students believed the charges, and their energies were for a time diverted. The leftists continued to press their offensive, however. They blamed the Institute for recruiting only a small percentage of students from "proletarian" backgrounds, and vilified the school officials themselves for having "landlord" and "capitalist" families. They even held the Institute's Party Committee responsible for the fact that one graduate, assigned to the Chinese diplomatic service, defected to the United States Embassy in Burundi in 1964.[70]

In Shanghai, as in other Chinese cities, though, the Party apparatus remained strongly entrenched despite the rising turbulence. As he observed this situation from his Hangchow retreat, Mao must have sensed that the real thrust of his Cultural Revolution was being blunted. After eight months of absence from the capital, he decided to return to Peking. And on the way, he staged a dramatic performance. On July 16, he dived into the Yangtze River near the city of Wuhan and broke all Olympic records by swimming nearly fifteen kilometers in sixty-five minutes.

This heroic exploit, if it actually took place as claimed, was no doubt contrived to quell speculation that Mao was ill and dying. Official press accounts insisted on his "wonderful health," reporting that "he was vigorous and showed no signs of fatigue" after his marathon swim.[71] His plunge also announced symbolically that he had emerged from the shadows to take personal charge of the Cultural Revolution. Press dispatches made this clear by quoting lines from a poem he had written on the occasion of an earlier swim: "I care not that the wind blows and the waves beat; it is better than idly strolling in a courtyard." [72] Moreover, the exercise was plainly designed to communicate to the "masses" that no obstacle, be it the tricky current of the Yangtze River or the powerful Chinese Communist Party bureaucracy, was too formidable to be overcome by those armed with Mao's doctrines. His defeat of the Yangtze, intoned an official Chinese commentator, proved "the splendor of Mao Tse-tung's thought." [73]

One of the many mysteries of that murky period was why Mao remained in Shanghai for so long when it was apparent that Liu Shao-ch'i and the Party machine were betraying his concept of the Cultural Revolution. Some analysts have contended that Mao lacked the strength to confront the Party *apparatchiks* before then, and chose to return to Peking in a desperate bid to retrieve his authority. Others have argued that he waited to return to Peking until the Party, having been delegated to manage the Cultural Revolution, could be criticized for the "errors" he was certain they would commit.

Mao reached Peking on July 18 to attend an improvised Party session. Judging from all the evidence, he dominated the meeting. He criticized the Party *apparatchiks* for their supposed supervision of the Cultural Revolution. They were "afraid of revolution," he said, and sat in their offices rather than going "to places where there are disturbances to take a look." Consistent with this theme, he decried the size of the Party bureaucracy, with its numerous clerks and secretaries, saying: "I am alone here and am doing quite well. . . . We did not have such mammoth offices in the past." Mao accused the Party Work Teams of obstructing the Cultural Revolution by restraining the free expression of students. Even the "rightists" should be allowed to speak out, he asserted. "Let them air their views! Why should we be afraid of a few big-character posters and reactionary slogans?" There was nothing wrong with conflict, he said, for "it tempers the leftists when they are beaten up." Above all, Mao told the Party bureaucrats, they must kindle the fires of revolution even though "you will yourselves be consumed by the flames." [74]

In the weeks following that session, Mao ordered the dissolution of the Work Teams in the universities, hoping to erode the Party's power. But the Party *apparatchiks* refused to surrender, and so, supported by Army elements, Mao mobilized a new weapon—the Red Guards.

CHAPTER 9

The Children's Revolt

> A revolution is not a dinner party, or writing
> an essay, or painting a picture, or doing em-
> broidery; it cannot be so refined, so leisurely
> and gentle, so temperate, kind, courteous,
> restrained, and magnanimous. A revolution
> is an insurrection, an act of violence by
> which one class overthrows another.
>
> —MAO TSE-TUNG, 1927

BY DAWN ON August 18, 1966, Peking's vast Tienanmen Square
—the Plaza of the Gate of Heavenly Peace—was packed with
more than a million young Chinese. Most were dressed in khaki,
their crimson arm bands bearing the inscription *Hung Wei Ping*—
"Red Guard." Shivering as they waited in the morning cold, they
sang songs and chanted catechisms from a small breviary bound in
bright red plastic entitled *Quotations from Chairman Mao*. Finally,
timing his appearance with theatrical precision to the rising sun
in the east, Mao Tse-tung emerged onto an upper gallery of the
Tienanmen Gate. He wore the olive-green uniform of a simple
soldier, a muffin-shaped military cap on his head. A thunderous roar
rolled through the hundred-acre square to welcome him—and a new
phase of the Cultural Revolution had begun.

Though he had not charted the course of his campaign precisely
from the outset, Mao's essential aim at this stage of the Cultural Revolution was to unleash the Red Guards against his rivals
in the Communist Party apparatus. Simply "dismissing people from
office" and other "pure organizational steps" would not suffice to

uproot "bourgeois" ideas, his spokesmen had asserted. Only by "boldly mobilizing the masses" could a real revolution be set in motion.[1] Thus, in his drive to overthrow the Party bureaucrats, Mao was also striving to inculcate his disciples with the proletarian *élan* that he feared the Chinese had lost. For that reason, he saw the Cultural Revolution as a crucial educational exercise as well as a decisive power struggle.

Since his return to Peking, Mao had been maneuvering to isolate and weaken the Party machine so that it might be swept away by the Red Guards, who supposedly represented the most activist elements among the "masses." Relying on loyal military units and Army political commissars under the command of Lin Piao to organize them, Mao encouraged young leftists to intensify their agitation. On August 1, he blessed two different Red Guard groups in Peking for their announced intention to "rebel against all reactionaries."[2] A few days later, further whipping up the spirit of revolt, Mao published his own "big-character poster"—the first and only time in the Cultural Revolution that he would issue so open a pronouncement. It was entitled "Bombard the Headquarters," and its contents left no doubt that his design was to smash the Party leadership. Praising the radicals who had initially shaken Peking University in the late spring, Mao's proclamation indicted "some comrades from the central down to the local levels" who had "diametrically" opposed his Cultural Revolution in the "last fifty days or so " These comrades were obviously Liu Shao-chi and his associates, and Mao's tirade against them was extraordinarily passionate.

> They have enforced a bourgeois dictatorship and struck down the surging movement of the great Cultural Revolution of the proletariat. They have stood facts on their head and juggled black and white, encircled and suppressed revolutionaries, stifled opinions different from their own, imposed a white terror, and felt very pleased with themselves. They have puffed up the arrogance of the bourgeoisie and deflated the morale of the proletariat. How vicious they are![3]

Once again, Mao's enormous prestige prevented his opponents from replying squarely to his attack. In a series of private talks delivered in early August, Liu Shao-ch'i resorted to other tactics. He echoed Mao's criticism of the Party Work Teams for their heavy-handed treatment of young radicals. But he emphasized that the Teams had been appointed with Central Committee approval, thus implying that Mao, as Chairman, shared responsibility for their "crimes." In addition, Liu blamed the Team members themselves for their excesses. He even conceded that the creation of the Teams had been a "mistake," and proposed that they be disbanded.[4] At the same time, however, Liu underlined the need for moderation. "Landlords, rich peasants, bad elements, counterrevolutionaries, and rightists" were "men and not animals," and to kill them was senseless, since their children and grandchildren would only "avenge their deaths" in the future.[5]

The whole thrust of Liu's strategy at this point, then, was to narrow the scope of the Cultural Revolution in the hope that, like so many past "rectification" drives, it would gradually lose momentum. And, contravening Mao's exhortations, he also stressed the sanctity of the Party. "At present we have a proletarian dictatorship," he said. "The Chinese Communist Party is Marxist. It is not justified to rebel against the Communist Party." [6]

Despite his disdain for formal measures, Mao evidently decided to lend a certain legitimacy to his assault against the Party bureaucracy. On August 1, he convened a Plenary Session of the Party's Eighth Central Committee in Peking. The Plenum was the first to be held since 1962, even though the Party Constitution required such meetings every two years.

It was the most momentous Party conclave since the founding of the Chinese People's Republic. Mao had undoubtedly hoped to swing most of the Central Committee behind him, thereby isolating Liu Shao-chi and the other senior Party figures. But, though he packed the hall with radical students and other sympathizers, he barely managed to rally a majority of those present to his colors. As he candidly admitted later, "Many people could not be converted to my view." Perceiving that his policies would have to be "tested in practice" rather than dictated officially, he therefore used the Plenum to lay down guidelines that his disciples could follow as they propelled the Cultural Revolution forward in the months ahead.[7] As usual, he welcomed resistance as further evidence that only the "masses" could purge the Party of its "revisionist" tendencies while simultaneously forging their own revolutionary character.

Lin Piao, soon to be revealed as Mao's heir apparent, delivered the keynote address at the Party conference, and his message was unequivocal.[8] Loyalty to Mao and his ideology was the only yardstick by which a true Communist could be measured, he asserted. Speaking in his thin, reedy voice, he combined protestations of humility with stern warnings:

> I am not equal to my task, and may fail in my duties. I may make mistakes. But to do the best I can to avoid mistakes, I shall rely on the Chairman. . . .
>
> With the Chairman as the axle, we are the milling stones and must do everything according to the thought of Mao Tse-tung. There is no other way. There cannot be two policies or two command headquarters. No wishful thinking should replace the thinking of the Chairman, and we cannot stage a rival drama in competition with that staged by the Chairman. We want monism, and closely follow the Chairman. . . .
>
> There are many ideas we do not understand. We must firmly execute the Chairman's directives. I have no special talent, but I rely on the wisdom of the masses, ask the Chairman for instruction when doing everything, and do everything according to his orders. I do not interfere with him on major matters, nor do I trouble him on minor matters. . . . The Chairman is the genius of the world revolution.

In the wake of the Cultural Revolution, five years later, as the decimated Communist Party machine was being rebuilt, Lin Piao would be excoriated for having thus portrayed Mao as a "genius." The argument used against Lin was that as Mao's heir he had attempted to promote his own personality cult at the expense of the Party. But now, as the Cultural Revolution accelerated, Lin sought to affirm Mao's infallibility—implying that only the Chairman and his close courtiers were in true communion with the "masses."

In explaining the necessity for the Cultural Revolution, Lin Piao did not deny the need for "developing production and raising the technological level" of China. But to "promote material incentives as the revisionist countries do," he claimed, would surely mean "retrogression and reversion to the old rule." Thus he reiterated the Maoist canon that "the important factor in productivity is man": "we must change ideas and concepts and heighten our sense of responsibility to society" in an effort to alter human nature. "When we win on the spiritual front, we shall also win on the material front." Hence the Cultural Revolution—the "large-scale struggle to transform men"—was imperative.

This ideological drive would not be easy, Lin Piao conceded, for "reversals, numerous struggles, and criticisms" lay ahead. Had Mao failed to intervene when he did, "the bourgeoisie would have gained the upper hand, and we would have lost the battle." Equally arduous would be the problem of educating the worker and peasant "masses" to understand the campaign, he said, since "they may have difficulty distinguishing fish eyes from pearls and must be taught that the thoughts of Mao Tse-tung are the pearls." Thus the urgent task at the moment was to launch a "general examination, a general alignment, and a general reorganization of the ranks of cadres" in order to overhaul the Party completely. Those who eagerly studied Mao, attached importance to ideology, and displayed revolutionary passion would be "promoted." Those who committed errors but "accept education and resolutely repent" might be "given a chance . . . to be tested in future work." As for the "incorrigibles"—those "who oppose the thought of Mao Tse-tung," those who "are impetuous by nature" and "upset" ideological policies, and those who lacked "revolutionary zeal"—they would be ousted. For unless they were purged, they would "carry out subversive activities once trouble flares up" and the Cultural Revolution would be threatened by a "stalemate" that would signify Mao's failure.

Ignoring the Party Constitution, which authorized structural changes only at Party Congresses, Mao used the August Plenum to revamp the Communist leadership. He demoted Liu Shao-ch'i, Chou En-lai, Chu Teh, and Ch'en Yun from their posts of Vice-Chairman and elevated Lin Piao to be his sole deputy. He also downgraded Liu to eighth place in the hierarchy while the relatively new face of T'ao Chu, who had risen meteorically from regional boss in south China to become chief of the Propaganda Department in Peking, now appeared in the Party's number four spot—where, however, it would remain only briefly. But these reshuffles were not really Mao's style, especially at this juncture in the Cultural Revolution. Rearrangements of the Party "from above" were only expedients, and Mao's aims went further. His mobilization of the

Red Guards, then, was aimed at launching a purge "from below."

Though Red Guard groups had formed in Peking and elsewhere as far back as May, the massive movement of youths that emerged in the capital in mid-August was plainly the result of precise and unusually efficient organization in which the Army played a major role—at least at the beginning. Only the Army had the means to transport thousands of young Chinese into the city as well as lodge, feed, and outfit them in khaki uniforms for their first demonstration. Only the Army could plan so monumental a demonstration and execute it down to such details as providing outdoor latrines to accommodate youths who would participate from dawn to midnight in the delirious pageant. Another clue to the Army's involvement was reflected in the fact that the "little red book" of Mao's *Quotations* distributed to the young radicals had been originally published in May 1964 under military auspices for the indoctrination of soldiers.[9]

Without specifically mentioning them by name, a Sixteen Point Decision issued by the Plenum on August 8 clearly indicated that the Red Guards would serve as Mao's principal weapon in the Cultural Revolution. The Decision, in which Mao outlined his hopes for the campaign, vowed to accomplish nothing less than a "great revolution that touches people to their very souls." This ambitious dream demanded the eradication of "old ideas, old culture, old customs, and old habits of the exploiting classes," and their replacement by "new ideas, new culture, new customs, and new habits to transform the spiritual aspect of the whole society." The "brave vanguards" in this offensive would be "large numbers of revolutionary youngsters" who had been "hitherto unknown," the Decision stated, adding:

> They have energy and wisdom. Using big-character posters and debates, they are airing their views and opinions in a big way, exposing and criticizing in a big way, firmly launching an attack against the open and covert representatives of the bourgeoisie.

But just as the delegates at the Party Plenum had been sharply divided, so the Sixteen Point Decision was scarcely a cohesive blueprint for the Cultural Revolution. For it contained such clouded and contradictory directives that it could only have been a compromise document patched together by an assortment of leaders with widely divergent views.

Premier Chou En-lai may have extracted concessions from the Maoists in exchange for swinging his invaluable support behind their cause,[10] since the Decision reflected his concern for insulating certain sectors of China from the rising storm. It stressed, for example, that the Cultural Revolution should not "impede" industrial and agricultural production. Similarly, with China's nuclear- and advanced-weapons' development in mind, it decreed that scientists and technicians be exempted from the struggles as long as they "love their country, work actively, are not against the Party and socialism, and do not secretly collaborate with any foreign power." Promising to protect the Chinese military establishment from disruption, the Decision also instructed the Army to conduct its own "socialist education movement" without external interference.

Mao must have pledged to certain senior Party figures that the Communist apparatus would not be totally disrupted. The Decision drew a distinction between "good" Party members who "encourage the masses" and those who "do their best to confuse the boundary line between revolution and counterrevolution" and therefore deserve dismissal. Moreover, it qualified the "majority" of Party cadres as "good and relatively good" while quantifying those who were beyond redemption as only a "small number:" In addition, the document asserted that no campaigns of criticism against alleged "reactionaries" could be undertaken without prior discussion and approval by Party committees "at the corresponding levels."

At the same time, however, the Decision was vague enough to permit the radicals to employ force. Though it urged the Red Guards to use persuasion rather than coercion, the document also asserted that "anti-socialist rightists must be fully exposed and knocked down" and "their influence must be eliminated." Warning that the Cultural Revolution would "unavoidably meet with resistance," it also affirmed that "if only the masses are fully aroused to action, such resistance will break down quickly." [11] This fiery rhetoric was paralleled by Maoist exhortations to the Red Guards to run rampant. Even in late July they had been told by Ch'en Po-ta to "be ready to fight," [12] and K'ang Sheng, another prominent Maoist, had advised: "Do not fear chaos." [13] And, of course, there was Mao's personal distum: "Destruction before construction."

Fogged by ambivalence from the start, then, the Cultural Revolution would seesaw between periods of turmoil when the radicals were in the ascendancy, and periods in which more conservative elements arose to impose law, order, and discipline. The weeks following the Party Plenum were a period of violence that had its beginning with Mao's huge reception for the Red Guards on August 18 in Peking. It was the first of eight such rallies in which, through November, a total of more than 11 million young people entered the capital.

Aware that a potentially volcanic force was bottled up in the frustrations of China's younger generation, Mao's aides consciously worked to build their emotions up to a fever pitch in the days before the rally. In a speech to Red Guards who had been brought to Peking for the demonstration from other regions of the country, Ch'en Po-ta spoke in the highly charged terms that were to become the common idiom of the Cultural Revolution for months to come. He reminded the provincial youths that they had been chosen as "successors to the cause of the proletarian revolution," urging them to "grow up braving storm and stress."

> Comrades, you must be absolutely fearless, you must steel and temper yourselves over and over again, and you must be able to withstand all trials and tribulations and all possible unforeseen setbacks. You must be able to bear all kinds of ordeals and the sharp conflicts between individualism and collectivism, between individualism and Communism.[14]

Exhortations of this kind were matched by less formal pep talks in which radical cadres, among them Army political commissars, cued Red Guards on how to behave during the scheduled rally. The youths were rehearsed in marching, advised which of Mao's aphorisms to read and what slogans to shout, and taught the lyrics of a stirring new song entitled "Sailing the Seas Depends on the Helmsman."

The décor for the mammoth rally resembled the settings for similar demonstrations staged in the Tienanmen Square in the sixteen years since the Communists took power. A huge image of Mao adorned the fifteenth-century Gate of the Heavenly Peace, while portraits of Marx, Engels, and Sun Yat-sen flanked the other sides of the immense enclosure. The Square was festooned with red flags and balloons and banners bearing such slogans as "Long Live the Chinese People's Republic" and "Hail to the Unity of the Workers of the World." And the multitude that filled the Square testified to the enormity of China's population.

Yet the August 18 rally differed significantly from the sort of demonstration choreographed in twentieth-century totalitarian states. It was not, in Nazi or Fascist style, an exercise in which the Führer or Duce harangued the mob, nor was it characterized by the cold solemnity of a May Day parade in Moscow. On the contrary, it seemed to be an almost religious ritual as Mao the god communed with the devotees of his cult.

From the moment he emerged onto the gallery of the Tienanmen Gate in the early morning sunlight until he retired after the evening's firework display, Mao played the part of a benign, paternal deity. He delivered no rousing address but left the oratory to his subordinates. Steered by a young nurse, he shuffled stiffly to and fro on the gallery, sometimes waving mechanically to the blur of faces below and, twice or three times during the day, descending into the "masses" to puff at his cigar and chat with selected Red Guards. Wearing a military uniform for the first time in public in order to symbolize his reliance on the Army, he designated Lin Piao to speak to the assemblage. As Mao peered over his shoulder like a faintly nervous parent watching his child perform, Lin stumbled through his speech in a manner scarcely calculated to inspire confidence in him as the Chairman's heir:

> Chairman Mao is the most outstanding leader of the proletariat in the present era and the greatest genius in the present era. . . . Mao Tse-tung's thought marks a completely new stage in the development of Marxism-Leninism. It is Marxism-Leninism at the highest level in the present era. It is Marxism-Leninism for remolding the souls of the people. It is the most powerful ideological weapon of the proletariat.[15]

Lin Piao's accent on "remolding souls" lent a theological tone to the Peking rally that must have mystified many of the young people present. But whatever they understood of the rhetoric, the Red Guards reacted as if intoxicated. They broke into rhythmic chanting of Mao's name, some weeping unabashedly as they waved their little red books like magic talismans at the object of their reverence. They screamed slogans, leaped into the air with excitement, and, when Mao descended into the Square like Zeus stepping down from Olympus, pressed forward against a cordon of soldiers for a glimpse of him. Much of this hysteria was genuine, but several scenes were carefully enacted for the benefit of official cameramen. In one episode, obviously contrived to portray his human qualities, Mao paused to sit among a group of Red Guards and discuss their problems. In another scene, recorded in a film of the rally shown throughout China and abroad, a pretty girl student from Tsinghua University came forth from the crowd to encircle his arm with a brassard reading "Red Guard." Then and there, a propaganda account of their dialogue related, Mao persuaded her to change her name from P'ing-p'ing, meaning "refined gentleness," to Yao-wu, signifying "will to do battle." [16]

Thus Mao identified himself with the Red Guards as his cry to them to "spread disorder" was given authoritative encouragement in *Red Flag*:

> The revolutionary youngsters are using Mao Tse-tung's thought to condemn and reform the old world, and to wipe out completely the old ideologies, culture, customs, and habits accumulated over thousands of years. They want to turn the old world upside down and to build a new world based on Mao-Tse-tung's thought. Is this fanaticism? No it is not. It is earth-shaking revolutionary ambition.[17]

Similar rallies resonated throughout China in the days that followed. Thousands of students braved a driving rainstorm to parade in Shanghai, and a half-million people were reported to have held outdoor meetings in Canton. Huge crowds streamed out in cities as diverse as Foochow on the coast, Harbin in the industrial north, and Lhasa, the capital of remote Tibet. Repeating the rhetoric broadcast from Peking, speakers at these demonstrations vowed to "answer the call of Chairman Mao" by promoting the Cultural Revolution. This nationwide convulsion, though it initially seemed simply to be orchestrated from Peking, was an extremely complex and often puzzling phenomenon.

Stimulated by appeals to rise up in revolt against Chinese traditions, Red Guard groups mushroomed around the country, and they assumed a baffling assortment of titles. Some, like the Ching-kangshan Red Guards, named their units for landmarks in Chinese Communist history. Others commemorated important dates in the Cultural Revolution, like the May 16th Detachment, so-called to honor the circular issued by Mao on that day, or the August 18th Red Guards, whose title celebrated the Peking rally. There were multitudes of Red Flag and Red Banner factions, and groups with militant slogans for names, like the Mao Tse-tung Thought August First Fighting Regiment, the Scarlet Guards for the Defense of Mao Tse-tung's Thought, and the Struggle-Until-Death to Defend Chairman Mao Combat Corps.

The titles of only a few of the Red Guard units that sprang up in Canton at the time illustrated the confusion that prevailed in that city. They included the Canton District General Headquarters of the Red Workers Militia Detachment, which had its offices at the Dawn Restaurant on Peking Road; the Students Joint Revolutionary Committee, with its headquarters at the First Workers' Cultural Palace, which included an assortment of primary- and secondary-school Red Guard factions; and the Card-Carrying Workers Revolutionary Rebels Headquarters, comprised mainly of young men who had drifted into the city from outlying villages. Later, when many of these factions became clustered in rival coalitions, the Canton scene grew even more complex. As part of the East Wind coalition, for example, the Canton Red Workers Revolutionary Rebels Headquarters opposed the Canton Red Workers Joint Revolutionary Committee, which belonged to the Red Flag coalition, while the Government Organs Great Alliance Revolutionary Committee clashed with the Government Organs Red Headquarters.[18] Understandably, one of the major difficulties encountered by the Peking leaders as they tried to conduct the Cultural Revolution was their inability to sort out the crazy quilt of Red Guard factions.

Some Red Guard groups contained thousands of adherents, while others had only ten or twelve members who had pledged allegiance to a single energetic chief. Many youths belonged to several units simultaneously or shifted from one faction to another, depending on circumstances. A young Cantonese worker, who estimated that there had been eighty-five separate Red Guard organizations in his factory, disclosed that he had switched affiliations in order to travel outside the city.[19] Operating through "liaison stations" in colleges and universities in different cities, a few Red Guard fraternities appeared to be national in scope. As the Cultural Revolution accelerated during the summer, thousands of radical activists left Peking to tour the country, dispensing advice to aspiring Red Guards in the provinces. At the same time, millions of youths were pouring into the capital.

Throughout August, most of the provincial Party leaders resorted to various devices to control the Red Guards. One was to suppress directives issued by Mao's subordinates in charge of the Cultural Revolution. The mayor of Shanghai, Ts'ao Ti-ch'iu, destroyed a document cataloguing the "crimes" of his Director of Education in order to prevent an upheaval in the city's schools and universities. The Red Guards later alleged that Mayor Ts'ao had acted on instructions from the Secretary General of the Party, Teng Hsiao-p'ing, who was then seeking to dampen the radical offensive.[20]

The *apparatchiks* also resisted the Cultural Revolution by placing self-protective interpretations on the Sixteen Point Decision issued by the Party Plenum in Peking on August 8. They emphasized its ban on violence and invoked passages describing the "majority" of Party cadres as "good" or "relatively good"—hence loyal to the Maoist line. The local Party leaders also tried to manage the Cultural Revolution by focusing the indignation of young leftists against helpless scapegoats.

At the Shanghai Foreign Languages Institute, for instance, eighty-one teachers and other officials were singled out by the Party for criticism in mid-August. Among them was an elderly woman who had been educated in the United States, an instructor whose father had been associated with Chiang Kai-shek, and a former Catholic nun who had quit the Church. As a teacher at the Institute recalled, these people made "perfect victims" because they were "no threat to anyone, and the Party authorities knew this very well." [21] At the same time, to create the impression that it was not above purging itself, the Party Committee at the Institute also chose to sacrifice ten from among its two hundred members. When a handful of radicals perceived this tactic for what it was, they tried to protest, but the Party machine succeeded in turning a majority of students against them.

As the Cultural Revolution intensified, youth groups splintered into smaller units that frequently fought each other less for ideological motives than simply to assert themselves. With rival factions all proclaiming their undying allegiance to Mao and his ideals, the situation appeared as confusing to Chinese as it did to the outside world.

Reminiscing on those days in August, a former Red Guard who had fled from Canton to Hong Kong said: "The whole business was too complicated for words. I didn't understand it then, and I don't understand it now." [22] He recalled that the students at his secondary school had been "excited beyond belief" by the news of the August 18 rally in Peking. Particularly inspiring to them was a photograph of Mao wearing a Red Guard arm band. The picture, far more effective than words, made it plain to the youths that they were authorized to create a Red Guard unit in their school. They immediately convoked a meeting, but discovered that they had no guidelines. They could not determine who would be eligible for membership, how to select leaders, or the nature of their relationship to the Party cadres in the school. Finally, after a night of discussion, they decided to form a group called the Mao Tse-tung Doctrine Red Guards, which would be open to all students whose political conduct had been "good" irrespective of their class background. This decision was reversed a day later, however, with the arrival of a student from Tsinghua University who had been sent south along with hundreds of other Peking youths to instruct provincial students in the organization of Red Guard units. Only truly "revolutionary" elements should be enrolled as Red Guards, he advised. He then defined these elements according to family lineage as the "Five Kinds of Red"— children of workers, poor peasants, revolutionary martyrs, revolutionary cadres, and revolutionary soldiers.

This formula, dictated as it was by a "veteran" Red Guard from Peking, was accepted by the Cantonese students. But it was to have a divisive effect on the Red Guard movement in the southern city. Not only did it alienate many students who could not qualify as authentic revolutionaries, prompt them to organize their own factions, and fragment the Red Guard movement further. It also disappointed many young radicals to observe that revolutionary Red Guards, by rejecting members of other classes, were becoming as "elitist" as the Party bureaucrats they were supposed to overthrow. For these among other reasons, the Red Guards never shaped a solid national or even regional organization, but continued to dispute among themselves.

Many of the early Red Guard groups in Peking, Shanghai, Canton, and other Chinese cities were being formed under the auspices of municipal Party committees intent on shielding themselves from attack. The *apparatchiks* worked to divert and dissipate the energies of youths by encouraging them to assault trivial symbols of the past. Issuing a "declaration of war on the old world," Red Guards in Peking poured forth to change the names of avenues, shops, restaurants, and other establishments. They urged that Legation Street, the thoroughfare that formerly housed foreign embassies, be called Anti-Imperialist Street, and they altered the name of the Eastern Peace Bazaar, a Peking department store, to East Wind Bazaar.[23] In Canton, youth groups compelled dress manufacturers to stop copying Western fashions, and they ordered barbers to cease cutting hair in what they referred to as "cowboy" and "airplane" styles. They broke into eating places, decorating one called the Peace Restaurant with posters denouncing it as a "nest of pleasure for depraved young men and ladies" and a "rendezvous for the drunken and daydreaming bourgeoisie." [24] One Red Guard faction in a Peking secondary school published a pamphlet entitled "A Hundred Rules for Destroying the Old and Establishing the New," proposing that regulations be promulgated to outlaw jewelry, prohibit folk songs, and authorize children to criticize their parents, a daring suggestion in a land where the Confucian concept of filial piety was still strong.[25] Amid this ferment, another group of young rebels demanded that traffic lights be "revolutionized" so that red would signal "go" and green "stop." [26]

One of the most vivid accounts of this destructive period has been provided by Dai Hsiao-ai, a Red Guard mentioned earlier who defected to Hong Kong from Canton.[27] He and his comrades sallied forth on August 23 to exterminate "old ideas, old culture, old customs, and old habits" by invading the homes of the "Seven Kinds of Black"—"landlords, rich peasants, counterrevolutionaries,

bad elements, rightists, monsters and freaks, and pro-capitalists."
Singing revolutionary hymns and shouting slogans, the students
went first to the nearest police station, where the residences of
their intended victims were indicated on a map of the precinct.
Using police records to guide them, the youths worked their way
up and down the streets of the neighborhood, hanging signs on
designated houses. Then they returned for their search-and-destroy
mission.

> In practice, we confiscated things like vases and furniture decorated
> in the traditional way. If there were revolutionary objects, like pic-
> tures of Mao Tse-tung, we left them alone. Usually we would
> smash something just for effect and confiscate everything else. . . .
> We took all foreign-made items, like blankets and quilts from Hong
> Kong as well as jewelry, scrolls, and even books that had been pub-
> lished before 1949.
> Because we were afraid that people would hide things, we
> searched their houses very thoroughly. Some of us would tear
> down the walls and look behind the plaster while others seized
> shovels and picks and tore up the cellars looking for hidden
> items. . . .
> While we searched each house, we made the occupants stand to
> one side while a few members of the group shouted that they must
> confess their counterrevolutionary crimes. If the women had long
> hair, we cut it. Sometimes we would shave half of the hair on a
> man's head and defy him to shave the rest. Our object was to hu-
> miliate these people as much as we could.

After two or three days, there was hardly an area of Canton
that had not been combed by Red Guards. Seeking to immunize
themselves, people covered their gates with Mao's quotations,
painted their furniture red, and themselves destroyed objects of
value. When private targets became difficult to find, however, the
students smashed other relics.

> Statues, paintings, and other such objects in public parks, temples,
> and cemeteries were quickly destroyed. We had no plan on these
> occasions, but simply roamed the streets looking for things. Some-
> one would shout, "Let's go to such-and-such temple," and we
> would all follow. Very often, some other group would have been
> there first and left nothing but a pile of ashes or a group of statues

smeared with paint. At least once a day, we would cart a statue to a large intersection and ceremoniously smash it to pieces. Passersby would stop and watch us. Some would congratulate us, but most lowered their heads and hurried by. . . .

In truth, this part of the movement was, in some ways, the most fun of all. We were free to do as we pleased, nobody checked on us, and we controlled ourselves. We felt like adults, really for the first time. I thought that what we were doing was important. Therefore, I enjoyed myself fully. It was a great deal of fun.

The Canton leaders were relieved to see the Red Guards direct their fury against innocent citizens rather than against the municipal authorities. No less a personage than Chao Tzu-yang, the First Secretary of the Kwangtung Province Party Committee, congratulated the youths for their vandalism. Less than four months later, Chao himself would face the wrath of the Red Guards, accused of having deceptively maneuvered to salvage his own power.

An authoritative clue to the number of persons rounded up by the Red Guards in the early stage of the Cultural Revolution was provided on October 2 by Hsieh Fu-chih, Minister of Public Security, when he disclosed that a total of 21,779 landowners, rich peasants, counterrevolutionaries, and other "evil" elements had been "arrested" by the radical youths. Hsieh claimed that the Red Guards had confiscated among other items more than 25,000 rifles, nearly 14,000 portraits of Chiang Kai-shek, close to 38 tons of gold, approximately 10 million silver coins, and a couple of million American dollars.[28] He also estimated that some 400,000 "reactionaries" had been subjected to some form of harassment by the Red Guards.[29] The validity of Hsieh's statistics has never been established, since neither Chinese nor Western sources inside China were able to observe more than individual instances of Red Guard brutality. Judging from the number of these instances reported during the later summer of 1966, however, the extent of violence must have been considerable. But it was probably far less than the turbulence that was to erupt in the summer of 1967 and again in the spring of 1968, when rival factions fought pitched battles in many parts of China.

Red Guards like Dai Hsiao-ai in Canton may have regarded their destructive activities as a "great deal of fun," but victims of the Cultural Revolution in its opening phase were humiliated, terrorized, and even killed or driven to suicide by the fanatical youths. In late August, diplomats in Peking witnessed Red Guards beat a man with ropes while a large crowd, many of them children, cheered and shouted approval.[30] Young activists broke into the Sacred Heart Convent, a Catholic school in Peking for foreign children, smashing its religious relics and forcing eight aged European nuns to run a gantlet of bamboo sticks. The nuns were subsequently deported to Hong Kong, where one of them, a woman in her seventies, died a day after their arrival.[31] Much later, when the tide had turned against the Red Guards, numbers of Chinese summoned up the courage to protest against the August holocaust. One man divulged in a wall poster pasted up in the capital that his wife, a woman of fifty, had been stabbed to death by Red Guards at a meeting in which she had presumably been accused of "capitalist" tendencies. Naming the Red Guard leader allegedly responsible for the killing, the man claimed that his appeals for justice had gone unheeded. In a similar poster, a youth charged that both his parents had been murdered by pupils of Peking's Kuang Street Primary School, where his mother had served as principal. A Chinese truck driver who worked in Peking that summer afterward reported that he had spent night after night carting away the corpses of citizens who had run afoul of Red Guard gangs.[32]

In several places Red Guard groups physically assaulted prestigious Chinese figures suspected of "bourgeois" or "revisionist" leanings. Early in November, for instance, radicals in Anhwei province arrested the region's Party boss, Li Pao-hua, whose father, Li Ta-chao, had been one of Mao's early patrons and an original organizer of the Chinese Communist movement in 1921. According to a report from the area, Li Pao-hua was flogged and tortured by the youths as they sought to force him to confess to his "sins." [33] Shanghai Red Guards even broke into the home of Madame Sun Yat-sen. Deploring this incident in a private speech somewhat later, Premier Chou En-lai admonished the radicals for attacking people solely on the basis of their "class" origin. "Some youngsters have acted like hooligans," he said.[34]

Among the many accounts related by Chinese refugees during those days were the personal experiences of two young people who escaped by swimming throughout the night across the bay that separates the coast of Kwangtung province from Macao, the quaint little Portuguese enclave on the edge of China. The woman, Li-han, had been a painter and stage designer in Canton. The man, Ling, was a cellist with a fondness for Western music.

A frail, shy man in his early thirties, Ling had two strikes against him. As the son of a French-educated economist, Ling had long been under suspicion because of his dubious "class background." And as a member of the Canton Symphony Orchestra, he was vulnerable to criticism for having performed the works of Western "bourgeois" composers like Mozart and Beethoven.

Until the early 1960s, Ling recalled, the Canton Symphony Orchestra had been relatively unmolested by politics. But after the inauguration of Mao's Socialist Education Campaign in 1962, ideological pressures gradually mounted. A Communist Party Committee was formed in the orchestra to pass judgment on the purity of its musicians. Several conductors and instrumentalists, dismissed for "bourgeois" proclivities, were sent out to the countryside to work as farm laborers. Nearly every night, after their performance, members of the orchestra were required to meet under the auspices of the Party Committee to criticize themselves and each other. The musicians were also called upon to debate the ideological significance of the orchestra's repertory, with Party cadres usually steering the discussion toward denunciations of Western composers. By the end of 1965, Western classics had been banned as "imperialist," Soviet compositions were prohibited as "revisionist," and even folk music was outlawed as "feudal." The last concert held under the aegis of the orchestra took place in April 1966. A visiting East German string quartet played Mozart, Dvořák, and Ravel. To prevent the public from being "contaminated," Ling related, attendance was by invitation only. Soon after that, the orchestra was disbanded.

Ling tried to earn a livelihood by giving violin and piano lessons. But as the Cultural Revolution intensified during the spring, Western musical instruments were declared to be "bourgeois," and his few pupils apprehensively peeled away. Frightened, he destroyed his violin, smashed his record collection, and burned his scores. His fears heightened as the ferment in Canton escalated sharply after Mao uncorked the Red Guards at the August 18 rally in Peking. On one occasion, Ling observed Red Guards taunting a schoolteacher whose face had been painted with chalk and ink to portray him as a "demon." The man stood silently, his head lowered and eyes closed, as the youths shouted and spat at him. On another day, Ling recounted, he watched a gang of adolescents terrorize the celebrated Cantonese opera star Hung Hsien-nu, who was charged with "opposing Mao" by having performed traditional dramas. It was rumored that her own daughter was among the youths tormenting her.

Unable to swallow the shame of denunciation, or perhaps anticipating worse, numbers of Chinese committed suicide. Ling testified to having witnessed four suicides during a two-week period. One afternoon he saw a middle-aged man dressed in the tunic of a Communist Party cadre fling himself from the fourth-floor window of a downtown building. Not long afterward, he saw another man leap from the roof above the Tai Tung Restaurant facing the Pearl River. And the same day, he watched as two bodies were dragged out of the river.

Strolling the streets one morning, Ling recalled, he was stopped by Red Guards. Finally, he thought, his moment had come. But the youths were mild, and they merely demanded that he get rid of his "peppercorns," as they called his "bourgeois" pointed shoes. Without hesitation, Ling walked into the nearest shoe store and bought a round-toed "proletarian" pair. But the incident served as a warning. His only salvation, he persuaded himself, lay in flight from China.

Canton, because of its proximity to capitalist Hong Kong, was filled with shady characters who managed to elude Communist controls. Through an acquaintance, Ling was introduced to a smuggler by the name of Tam who was willing for a fee to guide him to the coast opposite Macao. After arranging the escape plan, Ling contacted Li-han, the young woman painter and stage designer. He was certain, knowing her experience, that she would accompany him.

At twenty-nine, Li-han was an unusually beautiful young woman who had endured many tribulations in China. These tribulations, she frankly admitted, had been due to two errors in judgment. As a Catholic, she had made the mistake of believing the Communist claim that religious tolerance existed in China. And she had trusted friends without realizing that under duress they might have no choice but to betray her.

Born in Canton, the daughter of a merchant seaman, Li-han had been a child when her family emigrated to Hong Kong. Like thousands of Chinese residing in the British colony, she had frequently returned to Canton to visit relatives. But on one of these trips—it was during the hectic Great Leap Forward—she was suddenly arrested and charged with "espionage under the cloak of religion." Tried without benefit of counsel, she was sentenced to five years of "labor reform" to be served on a prison farm in the northern part of Kwangtung province. In retrospect, she attributed her arrest to a conversation with four Catholic friends in Canton to whom she had mentioned the names of priests she knew in Hong Kong. Their talk, however innocuous, had undoubtedly been reported to the authorities.

Presuming that "labor reform" had "remolded" her, the Religious Affairs Bureau in Canton asked Li-han to serve the Party by informing on her Catholic friends. In short, her assignment to "spy under the cloak of religion" exactly matched her own indictment five years earlier. Fearing a new imprisonment if she refused, Li-han agreed. But her reports lacked substance because, she claimed, her friends were too wary to speak candidly. In the view of the Party officials, however, she was being uncooperative, and they branded her a "bad element," imposing restrictions on her activities. She could not leave home for more than four hours without police authorization, her mail was censored, she was compelled to attend special political meetings, and she could be mobilized at any time for "voluntary" manual labor. She was therefore a natural target for the Red Guards as they swept through Canton in August 1966.

Unlike many of those classified as "Seven Kinds of Black," Li-han was somehow spared the indignity of being paraded through the streets wearing a dunce's cap. Instead, the Red Guards ordered her to print a sign with her name, address, and classification as a "counterrevolutionary," which she would have to hang from her neck if she left her house, and display on her door when she was at home. She was being watched, the youths told her, warning that she would be severely punished if she disobeyed them. "The first time I went out with that sign," Li-han recalled, "children surrounded me, spitting and jeering. I ran back home and stayed there. I refused to go out again, it was so terrifying."

Actually, it had been pointless for her to go into the city, since people designated as "Seven Kinds of Black" were banned from riding buses, entering restaurants, attending cinemas, and even strolling through parks. They were prohibited from making bank withdrawals—an academic rule, since their deposits had been confiscated—nor could they continue working. Li-han managed to earn some money, however, by designing toys at home. A few brave friends, Ling among them, took her designs to the toy factory and brought her food from time to time.

Day and night, Li-han recalled, her neighborhood resounded to the din of drums, gongs, and the shouts of Red Guards as they roamed the streets. She lay awake in the expectation that, any moment, the young vigilantes would break through her door. The nearest they came was an adjoining house, where they removed all the furniture except the bed, and burned every Chinese book published before 1949 as well as translations of "bourgeois" authors like Pushkin and Goethe. That close call coincided with Ling's proposal that they attempt to escape from China. Li-han accepted.

The smuggler, Tam, planned the escape carefully. He persuaded Ling and Li-han to join forces with two men, Chen and Liao, who were also seeking to flee the country. Itinerant patent-medicine peddlers who were being persecuted as "petty capitalists," Chen and Liao were familiar with the region between Canton and the coast. While Tam procured false documents to enable the party to travel beyond the Canton suburbs, he sent Liao ahead to wait with food, clothes, and plastic swimming tubes at a village on their way.

At five o'clock on the morning of September 9, Tam, Chen, Ling, and Li-han boarded a bus in Canton that took them to a village not far from the outskirts of the city. There they changed buses, rode to another village, again changed buses, descended at still another village—and continued in that zigzag fashion for four days, sleeping at country inns. Their object was to avoid main roads, where their papers might be examined by the authorities.

On the fifth day, they reached the rendezvous with Liao. From there they set off on foot across the terrain of barren hills toward the coast. After three days, their food ran out. Tam volunteered to find supplies in a nearby village. He never rejoined them. Whether he was captured by the police or soldiers or simply decided to abandon the group was never known. The others plodded on, surviving on sugar cane and sweet potatoes stolen at night from the fields of the few farms that dotted the desolate area. Finally, on the evening of September 19, they came within sight of the coast. It had taken them ten days to cover nearly a hundred miles. From the rocky shore they looked across to the lights of Macao, three thousand yards away. They could not risk waiting despite their fatigue. They slid into the water, clung to their plastic tubes, and paddled quietly, passing the shadows of sampans and junks riding at anchor in the bay. By morning, after eight or nine hours afloat, they had washed up onto a Macao beach. They were free. Yet their sense of accomplishment was mixed with faint abashment when they learned that more than two hundred Chinese had achieved the same feat in the preceding weeks.[35]

Not many Chinese were as fortunate as Ling, Li-han, and their companions. Particularly persecuted by the Red Guards during the first flourish of the Cultural Revolution were the older Chinese of the coastal cities who had been educated in the West. Many of these people were "technocrats" who, largely for patriotic motives, had chosen to cooperate with the Communists, and some had risen to important posts before the Cultural Revolution. In the eyes of the Maoists, however, they were "bourgeois" elements beyond redemption, and the suicide rate among them during the initial eruption of the Cultural Revolution was extremely high. The case of Madame Wong and her daughter Mei illustrated the fate that befell hundreds—perhaps thousands—of Chinese whose crime was to have been their association with a world Mao was seeking to destroy.

A Shanghai resident, Madame Wong was a sophisticated, brilliant, somewhat arrogant dowager who might, but for chance of birth, have presided over an English country house or an American women's club. Born into a northern family of great wealth, she had been educated at Oxford, where she met her future husband. An intelligent man dedicated to his country, he offered his services to the Chiang Kai-shek regime during China's war against Japan. He was assigned to diplomatic posts abroad and quickly rose to the rank of ambassador. Like many Westernized Chinese, he was soon appalled by the corruption and ineptitude of the Nationalists. In 1949, consequently, he opted for the Communists rather than join Chiang in exile on Taiwan.

The Communists at that time tolerated and even encouraged the presence in China of selected foreign firms whose operations were useful. Thus they registered no objection when former Ambassador Wong accepted the post of branch manager for a major British oil company in Shanghai. He was the first Chinese ever appointed to that position, and, in effect, his function was to serve as an intermediary between the Communists and the company's directors in London. The Wongs, classified as so-called "national capitalists," were permitted by the Communists to live in regal style. Their house in Shanghai, maintained by a legion of loyal servants, featured among its lavish furnishings a priceless collection of antique porcelains. They traveled abroad as they wished, relying for funds on bank deposits in Hong Kong, London, and Switzerland, and they were not alone in enjoying such privileges. Some ninety thousand "national capitalists" lived in Shanghai in comparatively luxurious fashion, drawing 5 per cent per year tax-free interest on bonds given them in compensation for their confiscated factories and other enterprises. Many held official jobs that employed their particular talents. One such gentleman, Yung Yi-jen, received an annual income of more than 2 million *yuan*, the rough equivalent of $1 million, as an indemnity for six textile mills nationalized by the Communists. Contributing his skills to the regime, he served as Vice-Minister of Textile Industry and a deputy mayor of Shanghai.[36] Like the Wongs, he lived in splendor. And, like the other "national capitalists," he could count on the protection of high Communist leaders—at least until the Cultural Revolution.

After former Ambassador Wong died of cancer in the mid-1950s, his wife effectively replaced him as manager of the British oil firm's Shanghai office. A shrewd and dynamic woman, she had the capacity for wise business decisions, and her contacts within the

Communist Party bureaucracy made her an invaluable "adviser" to the company. She occasionally expressed doubts about how long the regime would warrant her kind. But, though she could have probably emigrated from China, one predominant motive held her there. She was devoted to her only child, her daughter Mei. Training to be a dancer, Mei had left her mother's house to live in a student dormitory where, among her other duties, she attended political meetings at which she was compelled to denounce her mother in order to expiate her "class background." These denunciations did not trouble Madame Wong. She boldly called them a "charade" that did not represent Mei's real feelings.

Despite her sensitivity to political developments, Madame Wong believed, like many other Chinese, that the Cultural Revolution was merely another "rectification" drive that would eventually dissipate. By the summer of 1966, however, she realized her error. In a letter smuggled out to friends in Hong Kong, she conceded that she anticipated disaster—and that, for the first time in her life, events were beyond her control. There was nothing to do, she said, but to wait for the worst. In August, it came.

As friends who later fled Shanghai reconstructed the episode, Red Guards broke into Madame Wong's house. While some smashed her collection of antiques, others bound her hands behind her back, shaved her head, and, forcing her to kneel, ordered her to confess to her "sins." Declaring that she could redeem herself through menial labor, they assigned her to the task of charwoman in a government office.

What followed has been described in two different versions, both tragic. According to one account, Mei learned of her mother's ordeal and, despite her purported indoctrination, killed herself. On hearing of her daughter's death, Madame Wong committed suicide by taking an overdose of drugs. According to the other account, Madame Wong made an abortive suicide attempt and Mei, believing her mother dead, killed herself—whereupon Madame Wong succeeded, this time, in committing suicide.[37]

Squandering their passions in facile assaults against symbols of the past, the Red Guards were missing the primary objective of the Cultural Revolution—to topple Mao's adversaries in the entrenched

Communist Party bureaucracy. In a series of fresh exhortations at the end of August, therefore, Maoist spokesmen urged the youths to direct their attacks squarely against the Party *apparatchiks*. Speaking to a half-million young activists at Mao's second rally in Peking on August 31, Lin Piao congratulated them for "washing away all the sludge and filth left over from the old society." But, he reminded them, their principal target should be the "bourgeois" and "revisionist" leaders who "have wormed their way into the Party. . . . It is essential to hold fast to this main orientation." [38] In another Peking demonstration, two weeks later, Lin again stressed the need to strike at the Party. Mao's call issued in early August to "bombard the headquarters," Lin explained, meant: "Bombard the handful of persons in power who are taking the capitalist road." [39]

These appeals served to animate radicals in the provinces who were beginning to realize that their Party leaders had grabbed control of the Cultural Revolution in order to protect their own authority. Fire was now focused against regional Party machines that had hitherto managed to elude attack. In the meantime, the Maoist message to intensify the drive against the Party was being carried across the country by thousands of Red Guards from Peking, who streamed into China's cities with instructions to organize and direct local youth movements.

Party organs in different parts of China reacted in various ways to deflect the Maoist offensive. In several places they again resorted to their old tactic of sacrificing expendable officials. In the Manchurian industrial city of Changchun, for example, the Party Committee dismissed Sung Chen-t'ing, its Director of Propaganda, staging an elaborate meeting to vilify him as a "counterrevolutionary opportunist" who had "opposed the red flag while pretending to hold it aloft." [40] Another official thrown to the radicals by his Party comrades was P'eng Hsiao-ch'ien, vice-governor of Honan province, who was described as an "out-and-out reactionary land-lord-class element." [41] Party operatives engaged in similar maneuvers in other provinces, but in still other areas, Party bosses openly resisted the Maoists by forming rival Red Guard contingents and by mobilizing workers, peasants, and even soldiers to fight the radicals.

One of the most formidable foes of Mao's campaign at the time was the Party boss of southwestern Szechwan and its surrounding provinces, Li Ching-ch'üan, who derived his considerable political strength from connections in Peking as well as from the singularity of the area under his supervision. A bald, bespectacled man who looked as benign as a middle-class merchant, Li traced his revolutionary experience back to the 1920s, when he joined the Communist movement as a student at the Peasant Training Institute run by Mao in Canton. Years later, after surviving the celebrated Long March, he emerged as a political commissar in General Ho Lung's 120th Division of the Eighth Route Army. In addition to cementing a solid professional relationship, the two Communist veterans became brothers-in-law through marriage to sisters, and Ho Lung's rise as a dynamic military figure in Peking gave Li vital protection in the capital. Meanwhile, another of Li's important patrons was Teng Hsiao-p'ing, the Party Secretary General. Teng, who wielded enormous influence in his native Szechwan, had been instrumental in appointing Li to the post of the provincial Communist chief. By the early 1960s, then, Li was a powerful wheel in the Party machinery. As potentate of Szechwan, he ruled a province that was rich, populous, isolated, and particular enough to have existed as a separate nation. And he not only belonged to the Politburo in Peking, but directed the Party's Southwest Regional Bureau, which controlled Kweichow, Yunnan, and Tibet along with Szechwan.

With nearly 80 million people in the mid-1960s, Szechwan was exceeded in population by only seven nations in the world. It had long been China's leading grain producer, normally exporting some 2 million tons of rice to poorer provinces. Not only was Szechwan self-sufficient, but its defensive wall of mountains had traditionally made it an almost impregnable fortress. Rebels against imperial authority in ancient times frequently built their bases in Szechwan, and the province had been the site of Chiang Kai-shek's capital during World War II. Under Li Ching-ch'üan, the Maoists now claimed, Szechwan had become an "independent kingdom"—and that allegation was not wholly inaccurate.

But despite his power and autonomy, Li Ching-ch'üan was still an integral part of the national system. The days of the warlords were finished, and he could not secede from the People's Republic when he perceived the Cultural Revolution threatening his position. Like other Party *apparatchiks* elsewhere, moreover, he could not predict the scope and intensity of Mao's campaign. To defend himself and his comrades, Li resorted to the same subtle, complicated maneuvers being used by other regional Party figures at this juncture.

As early as the spring of 1966, when the Cultural Revolution was gathering steam, Li Ching-ch'üan had jettisoned a few subordinates in an effort to create the illusion that he dutifully subscribed to Mao's drive. Newspapers in Szechwan assailed obscure literary and propaganda functionaries in order to deflect radical attacks against more prominent Party officials. Li also sent some two thousand Party Work Team cadres into the universities, colleges, and high schools to keep students under control. In late July, when Mao decreed that the Teams be withdrawn from educational institutions, Li ignored his directive on the grounds that the situation in Szechwan was unique.[42]

Late in August, when Red Guards from Peking arrived in the cities of southwestern China to urge local youths to challenge the Party's authority, Li reportedly condemned their activities as "another Hungarian uprising." He instructed Party committees throughout the region to counter the Peking youths and their provincial allies by forming their own movements. One such movement, composed mainly of workers, was called the Industrial Workers Combat Corps. Another, made up of students at Chungking University, gave itself the romantic label of Spring Thunder.[43] Li allegedly financed these movements with Party funds, arguing that "it is impossible not to spend some money for such a great campaign."[44] He also infiltrated his own agents in the leftist Red Guard organizations. And, as the Army's senior political commissar in the region, he enlisted the aid of the area commander, General Huang Hsing-ting, to restrain the radicals. Huang and other military spokesmen addressed a meeting of more than three thousand Red Guards in the middle of September, exhorting them to "defend the interests of the Party and the state" by displaying a "high sense of discipline."[45] Meanwhile, sensitive to charges that he was suppressing the Maoist drive, Li ordered local officials to make ambiguous public confessions calculated to appease the radicals. He even appeared himself at a rally in the Szechwan capital of Chengtu, admitting to the crowd that he intended to repent his "errors."

Though Li had managed to navigate skillfully, the radical pressures gradually rose against him. While the Cultural Revolution was far from being a simple conflict among personalities, individuals often played important roles in the shaping of major events, and to a large extent this was true in Szechwan. The thrust against Li was propelled by a pair of relentless radicals called Liu Chieh-t'ing and his wife, Chang Hsi-t'ing. Former district Party officials in Ipin, a city in the southern part of the province, Liu and Chang claimed to have been suspended from their posts and later jailed for trying to criticize Li Ching-ch'üan's "revisionist" policies in the early 1960s. When they persisted, the couple alleged, Li had them expelled from the Party.

Like many minor officials with grievances against their superiors, Liu and his wife saw the Cultural Revolution as the chance to take revenge. Amassing a pile of documents indicting Li, they went to Peking to present their case to the Maoist leaders. After a month of fruitless lobbying, they finally gained access to Wang Li, a member of the Cultural Revolution Directorate. The material against Li Ching-ch'üan, he apparently perceived, could be used in the struggle against the Party bureaucracy.[46] But the effort to oust Li would not be easy.

The strife in Szechwan ultimately reached such proportions that, after much deliberation by the Maoist leadership, a military commander was assigned to the province to restore law and order. In the fall, however, Li Ching-ch'üan's tactic of turning the workers against intruding Red Guards was being used by Party *apparatchiks* all over China. This maneuver, known to Maoists as "hoodwinking the masses," led to widespread clashes that took a serious toll on China's economic production.

In the Shangtung province city of Tsingtao, for instance, at least two large skirmishes between Red Guards and Party-backed workers erupted within a week. The first occurred on August 16, when some four thousand workers battled students who had gathered to denounce a local Party cadre. Some days later, forty thousand workers and government employees were deployed in a demonstration in which more than a hundred Red Guards were reportedly injured. Another fight broke out in early September in the northern city of Shenyang, at the Anshan Iron and Steel Works, one of China's biggest industrial complexes, when Red Guards attempted to enter the plant to proselytize among workers. According to several accounts, troops were finally brought into the factory to quell the disturbance. About the same time, Red Guard and worker factions rioted in Canton when radical youths from Peking tried to pull down a bronze statue of Sun Yat-sen, celebrated in Canton not only as the founder of the First Chinese Republic but as a native of Kwangtung province.[47] Red Guards from Peking also met resistance in Sinkiang, where General Wang En-mao, who served as both Party boss and military commander, mobilized workers and troops to oppose them. One of General Wang's organizations, the August First Field Army Dedicated to Defend the Thought of Mao Tse-tung to the Death, was believed to harbor former Nationalist soldiers taken prisoner during the civil war and exiled as laborers to the remote frontier zone.[48]

In mid-September, recalling that the Sixteen-Point Decision issued on August 8 had proscribed attempts to "incite the masses to struggle against each other," the *People's Daily* pointed out that the directive was being "openly defied" by "responsible persons in some localities and units" who had "created various pretexts to suppress the mass movement . . . and even provoked a number of workers and peasants . . . to oppose and antagonize the revolutionary students" [49] But all these incidents, though unprecedented in China since the Communists had established their regime, were mild compared to what would grip the country in the months ahead.

Amid the ferment, however, there were signs that the Peking leaders then propelling the Cultural Revolution were at odds over how far and how fast to push the campaign. On one hand, Mao and his inner circle—including Lin Piao, Ch'en Po-ta, Chiang Ch'ing, and others—realized that the Cultural Revolution would lose momentum unless they persisted in stimulating the Red Guards. Thus they continued to bring young people to massive rallies in the capital. But Chou En-lai and his government associates as well as some military professionals seemed to fear that unrestrained turbulence would weaken China's economic and social stability and tried to keep the drive under control.

Heralded as the "great exchange of revolutionary experiences," Mao's reiterated call to Red Guards to visit Peking and other parts of China was eagerly greeted by young Chinese as a chance to travel beyond the narrow confines of their homes for the first time in their lives. Millions of young people therefore shunted around all over China from the middle of August through the end of November in one of the greatest human movements in history. The sheer weight of numbers placed an enormous burden on the fragile Chinese railway system, yet the regime's capacity to handle these multitudes was testimony to its organizational ability—at least within a short span of time.

The former Red Guard Dai Hsiao-ai later recalled that he and his comrades felt, as they embarked for Peking in late September, that they were escaping into an exhilarating "atmosphere of freedom." As they jammed into the train for the journey to Peking, none of the members of his Red Guard unit viewed the trip as a political exercise. One boy hoped that they might see snow in the north, another looked forward to eating Pekinese food, and a third remarked exultantly that he never imagined that he would travel across the country "without spending a cent." [50]

Arriving in the capital after forty-eight hours in a crowded train compartment, Dai and his comrades were taken by bus to a room in the First Ministry of Machine Building. There, they were shown their sleeping quarters—bamboo mats spread on a layer of straw. There, too, a Ministry employee was assigned to rehearse them for their performance in the parade to be staged on October 1, the anniversary of the founding of the Chinese People's Republic. The boys were instructed to march in columns of fifteen, some carrying Mao's *Quotations* and others displaying placards emblazoned with the Chairman's sayings. The rehearsals went on until the afternoon before the rally. The youths then slept for five or six hours, awakening at eleven o'clock that night. Each was given a small string bag with a couple of slices of steamed bread, a few pieces of fruit, and three hard-boiled eggs for the next day. Some boys ate the eggs immediately. At midnight, they started out to walk across the city to take their assigned places for the morrow's demonstration.

Soldiers were everywhere, directing Red Guards to their spots in the parade, which was scheduled to move from west to east through Tienanmen Square. As his unit marched to its position, Dai recalled, thousands of young people were in the streets, many of them running about and shouting hysterically. Some had accidentally strayed from their groups. Others, having slipped away in the darkness to relieve themselves at makeshift latrines, were desperately searching for their units. Those who had reached their places after hours of walking were so tired that they spread out newspapers and slept on the cold pavement, awakening to find their clothes damp with dew. As southern rice eaters, Dai and his comrades were unable to swallow their bread, which had hardened into inedible lumps. Hungry, thirsty, and exhausted, they waited, some singing songs to keep up their spirits. Finally, at ten o'clock, the revolutionary anthem "East Is Red" blared through the loudspeakers, followed by rhythmic chants of "Long Live Chairman Mao." The rally had begun.

For an hour before the procession got under way, the speeches of the Communist leaders boomed through loudspeakers located around the city. Dai observed that most of his comrades as well as other Red Guards were inattentive to the oratory. Some caught up on their sleep, others played games, and a few wandered around chatting with friends. Dai was impressed by Chou En-lai's eloquence, but neither he nor his comrades could understand Lin Piao. His voice was weak and hesitant, and his accent incomprehensible to them. "If his speech had not been published in the newspaper the next day, we never would have known what he said. We wondered why the Great Commander had chosen this kind of successor. Could Lin Piao really lead the Chinese revolution and the world revolution?"

Despite these misgivings, the Cantonese Red Guards were impassioned as they paraded quickly past the array of Chinese leaders reviewing them from the gallery of the Tienanmen Gate. Many of them wept at seeing Mao and, Dai recalled, they later recorded in their "little red books" the exact time that they had sighted him— 12:45 P.M.

Like millions of other Chinese youths, Dai and his comrades had been thrilled by the excitement of travel across China, and not long after returning to Canton, they embarked again on a trip to "exchange revolutionary experiences." By this time, however, hordes of Red Guards were wandering around the country. Railway stations were shaking with turbulence as different groups fought for trains, and departures were postponed for hours as the authorities tried to control the mobs. One night, a Japanese visitor boarded a northbound train at Canton's East Station, took a comfortable berth reserved for foreigners, and went to sleep. When he awoke next morning, the train was still in the station—delayed by the turmoil.[51]

The chaos on the railroads often left Red Guards stranded in faraway places that lacked the facilities to lodge and feed them. En route home after revisiting Peking in early November, for example, Dai and his comrades stopped for a few days at the northern port city of Tientsin. They and hundreds of other Red Guards there discovered as they decided to leave, however, that no passenger trains originated in Tientsin. They would have to find places on trains, already packed, passing through from Peking. Many of the people crowded into the Tientsin station had been waiting there for days—tired, hungry, dispirited. Dai and his friends eventually managed to board a train by smashing the glass of a coach door. Inside the coach, youths battled for space, cursing each other in a babel of dialects.

As they crisscrossed the country, the Red Guards rapidly learned how to survive without funds. They ate in restaurants, confessing to the manager afterward that they could not pay and offering to sign the bill. They applied to the authorities for "cost-of-living supplements," padding the rosters of their units with fictitious names in order to collect extra sums. In some cities, the Red Guards extorted money from officials by threatening to denounce them as "reactionaries" or "counterrevolutionaries," or even menacing them with physical violence.[52] Years later, when discipline had largely been restored to China, many Red Guards were held accountable for the debts they had incurred on these "exchanges of revolutionary experiences." Many were also tried and convicted for robbery, extortion, and other crimes committed at the time. The later crackdowns, mainly carried out by the Army, served to indicate that the Chinese bureaucracy must have continued to function at least partially despite the widespread confusion in the land during the autumn of 1966.[53]

It had already been evident, of course, that the Cultural Revolution threatened severe strains for the Chinese economy. In particular the movements of millions of Red Guards around the country was plainly bogging down China's feeble rail network. As early as mid-September, before the Red Guard tourists were out in full flourish, Chou En-lai disclosed that domestic transport of freight had declined by 10 per cent and that this was having a "tremendous impact" on China's foreign trade. Communications among various provinces had been impaired, and construction projects were being adversely affected, he also revealed.[54] The mobilization of state employees as guides for the Red Guards was also interfering with normal government functions. Industrial operations were being hampered by the skirmishes between radical youths and workers, and there was a danger that the Red Guards might carry the Cultural Revolution into the villages and disrupt agriculture as well.

No leader in Peking labored so strenuously during that period to keep the Cultural Revolution on an even keel as Chou En-lai. Despite his age—he was then approaching seventy—his energy was prodigious. In addition to formulating economic and foreign policy, directing the country's bureaucracy, and attending banquets and other ceremonies, he spent several nights a week with Red Guard groups, frequently staying up until dawn in efforts to convince them to restrain themselves.

Chou was not an opponent of the Cultural Revolution. On the contrary, he fully favored Mao's offensive. But believed that a victory for the Maoist cause would be hollow if China's basic stability were undermined in the process. Thus he endeavored to keep the drive sane and rational, and in his directives, speeches, and talks with Red Guards he repeatedly stressed the same themes. He advised the youths to organize their units along tighter lines, largely in order to make them easier to control. He urged them to rely on persuasion rather than force, pointing out that coercion would alienate segments of the population who could otherwise be won over. And he constantly emphasized the need to maintain industrial and agricultural production, without which China would face famine and a weakened defense establishment.[55]

On the subject of organization, for example, Chou admonished the Red Guards for having "sprung up like dandelions on a spring lawn." The units were not "compact" enough, he said, and required "strict" cohesion if they were to function as a "reserve" of the Army. It was essential that the wild assortment of Red Guard factions be shaped into an entity that could be managed. Accordingly, he called on the youths to "amalgamate" their different groups in order to achieve unity.[56] "We cannot suppress the student movement," he said, "but it must definitely be centralized." [57]

Chou also criticized the Red Guards for judging people according to "family lineage" and explained that "class analysis" was a complicated and difficult business. His own background was "feudal," and his father had been a minor magistrate who had certainly indulged in corruption. But redemption was possible, Chou asserted, if "one's objective acts are good and one has rebelled against his original class." [58] He also counseled the youths to exercise caution in their assaults against alleged "class enemies," pointing out that "bourgeois" revolutionaries like Madame Sun Yat-sen deserved "respect" for having collaborated with the Communists against Chiang Kai-shek, her brother-in-law. And it was important, Chou insisted, to distinguish between those "bourgeois elements" who were "making trouble" and those who were "law-abiding." Peaceable citizens should not be molested, irrespective of their political coloration. "Civilized" criticism in wall posters was acceptable, but "we need not pull [these people] down and confiscate their property." [59] Activities such as those of the Shanghai radicals who forced ten thousand "capitalists" to face their critics in a public demonstration were tarnishing China's image in the eyes of "world opinion," Chou argued, adding:

> Our country is strong enough to render such conduct unnecessary. Capitalists should not be dragged out to be paraded around. If we do that, the foreign news media will clamor that Chairman Mao has changed his policy, and that capitalists are to be liquidated physically. Classes are to be eliminated, but people are not to be killed.[60]

Upbraiding young "hooligans" among the Red Guards who were committing murder in the name of the revolution, Chou repeatedly emphasized that violence was not only illegal but ineffective as a weapon for transforming ideological attitudes.

> We all know that it is not difficult to kill a man with a gun—all that is necessary is to aim accurately. It is also not difficult to bruise a man with fists—all that is needed is brute strength. . . . But struggle by violent means merely touches people's flesh. Only struggle through reason can reach their souls.[61]

Above all, Chou tried to prevent the disruption of the economy. He instructed the Red Guards to refrain from attacking government ministries, for they had "work to do." [62] He also issued several directives ordering the young people to cease their nationwide train trips, exhorting them instead to emulate the Communists' celebrated Long March of the mid-1930s by traveling on foot.[63] And he repeatedly denounced the Red Guards for intruding into factories and farm villages. "The Cultural Revolution should be conducted only in middle-sized and large cities. . . . Industry and agriculture cannot take a vacation in order to stage revolution. . . . Production and the service trades cannot be suspended. Otherwise, what shall we eat?" [64]

These admonitions were echoed by Chou's government associates as well as in the official Chinese press and even in certain Red Guard newspapers. For example, Foreign Minister Ch'en Yi advised the Red Guards to behave "carefully" at the National Day celebrations on October 1, lest they trouble foreign guests and discredit China.[65] About the same time, a Peking directive disclosed that unruly youths were stealing "codes, files, and secret materials" from government and Party bureaus and warned that such felonies would be punished by law.[66] Newspapers were filled with appeals to the Red Guards to temper their excesses. *Red Flag* called on the "revolutionary young fighters" to restrain their "conceit and rashness" by adopting as their code the "three-eight" credo of the Chinese Army, conceived by Mao during the 1930s to discipline his peasant soldiers.[67] In a similar effort, a New China News Agency feature article described "model" youths who, like boy scouts, courteously helped old ladies to cross the street.[68] One Red Guard newspaper, possibly representing a conservative faction, published an unusual exclamation: "Insist on moderation." [69]

But for all his enormous energy and diplomatic skill, Chou En-lai was unable to hold back the storm. The Red Guards continued to invade government offices, break into factories, injure and sometimes kill their adversaries, and fight among themselves. They even launched verbal attacks against Chou himself, criticizing his "family lineage," assailing his speeches as "poisonous weeds," and forcing him on more than one occasion to deny charges that he was "counterrevolutionary." [70] In order to survive, Chou was compelled to shift to the left. By late November, he had surrendered to the radicals—at least for the moment. This was reflected in almost obsequious praise for Mao's wife, Chiang Ch'ing, whose power was then rising sharply, and in a remarkable admission he made to a group of Japanese visitors to Peking at the time. An individual's personal opinions should "advance or retreat" according to the will of the majority, Chou explained, making it plain that he had no choice but to accommodate to the Maoist view.[71] In addition, Chou like everyone else sought to protect himself and his more important colleagues by sacrificing lesser subordinates. Early in December, he authorized a rally to denounce Liao Ch'eng-chih, a key figure in Sino-Japanese relations, who had angered the Red Guards. Chou also allowed the Red Guards to stage a demonstration against Jung Kao-t'ang, a Vice-Chairman of the State Physical Culture Commission.[72] It became apparent afterward, however, that Chou's main motive in maneuvering as he did was to preserve his authority for a more propitious period. Faithful to Mao's guerrilla tactics, he was retreating in the hope of improving his position for a counteroffensive.

The decision to accelerate the Cultural Revolution during the autumn of 1966 was essentially inspired by Mao. He was not blind to the turmoil he had created. Yet he seemed to believe, even though he regretted the damage, that there was no turning back from the course he had charted. At a private meeting of the Party's Central Committee in Peking late in October, he reviewed the situation with extraordinary candor.[73]

"Something disastrously wrong was done by me," Mao confessed: he had blundered in the early stages of the Cultural Revolution by approving the radical attacks against the Peking University authorities in May and by publicizing his own exhortation to the Red Guards to "bombard" the Party apparatus two months later. After that, Mao said, the upheaval erupted so rapidly "as to surprise me." He had thus miscalculated in failing to anticipate that the "violent impact" of his gestures would "stir up the whole country" to such an extent. "I myself caused this trouble," he told the senior Communist officials at the meeting, "and I cannot blame you if you have complaints against me."

But errors were inevitable, Mao went on. "Many mistakes were made and many people died" during the twenty-eight years it took for the Communist Party to come to power. The Cultural Revolution was then only in its fifth month. "Experience can be gained only after at least five years," he explained.

In part, Mao said, the present difficulties were the result of his decision years earlier to relinquish authority to his comrades. His health had been poor, and he had learned a lesson from events in the Soviet Union, where Stalin had not properly prepared for his succession. So, Mao explained, he had retreated to the "second line" in order to permit his potential heirs to gain experience. "I wanted to have their prestige established before I died," he said. "But I didn't expect that things would turn out the other way."

What happened, Mao contended, was that his subordinates split into factions, setting up "independent kingdoms" and never discussing problems within the Central Committee. Even worse, they neglected him. The most independent of them all, Mao alleged, was Teng Hsiao-p'ing, the Party Secretary General. "He is deaf, but at meetings he would sit far away from me," Mao claimed. "He has not reported to me about his work since 1959."

Now the time had come to put the Cultural Revolution back on the track—meaning that the Party *apparatchiks* could save themselves by criticizing their errors, correcting their mistakes, and transforming their attitudes to conform to the Maoist canon. In short, Mao would give them the chance to capitulate peacefully. In that way, he promised, "all will go well again." But there was the hint of a threat. "Who wants to strike you down?" he said. "I, for one, do not want to strike you down, and I don't think the Red Guards want to strike you down either."

Liu Shao-ch'i appeared to accept Mao's offer by making a ritualistic confession of his mistakes.[74] He blamed other Party figures for having led him astray and tried to define his own blunders as faults that could be "rectified" rather than as hostile acts against Mao that would earn him condemnation as a heretic. It was an abject—and, as it turned out, futile—performance.

Reaching back to 1946, Liu allowed that he had believed in the "illusion of peace" between the Communists and Nationalists. He also conceded to charges that he had protected "bourgeois industries and commerce" as well as "urban feudal leaders" in the days after the Communist victory. In addition, Liu said, he had wrongly resisted Mao's agricultural collectivization programs in the mid-1950s. Following the collapse of the Great Leap Forward, he went on, he had erroneously favored moderate economic policies. In these and other deviations from the Maoist truth, he had made the mistake of having placed "too much confidence" in Ch'en Yun, the liberal economic planner, and had been misguided by Teng Hsiao-p'ing.

During the opening phases of the Cultural Revolution, Liu also confessed, he had "sanctioned the wrong decisions of others and made erroneous decisions myself" in having permitted the Party Work Teams in the universities to "suppress the masses." This mistake, he said, was shared by his wife, Wang Kuang-mei, who had belonged to the Team at Tsinghua University in Peking. He had failed to appreciate that the Cultural Revolution "marked a new stage of more intensive and extensive development in the socialist revolution" and, consequently, he had "distrusted the masses." He had erred because he had not learned to "grasp Chairman Mao's thought."

Liu therefore bowed to Mao's decision to downgrade him in favor of Lin Piao, whom he described as "better than I in every respect." Henceforth, he vowed, he would assiduously study Mao's "thought" and work "in the interest of the Party and the people."

If Liu had expected this self-abasing effort to gain him redemption, he miscalculated. For Mao's conciliatory invitation to his Party foes to air their errors had been a maneuver designed to achieve a triple purpose. First, it was aimed at isolating the "handful" of important Party leaders who had "put forward the wrong line," like Liu and Teng, from the larger number of cadres who could be "rehabilitated" if they corrected their mistakes. Second, it was contrived to stimulate internecine squabbling among the senior Party figures as they sought to salvage their positions. Finally, by inducing Liu and others to confess, Mao was able to expose them to further attack. Far from winning acquittal for his admissions, Liu soon found himself assailed more stridently than ever.

Lin Piao delivered the first major broadside against Liu. At the same Party meeting, Lin depicted the Cultural Revolution as a "fierce struggle between the proletariat and the bourgeoisie," in which Liu and Teng Hsiao-p'ing represented the "policy that suppresses the masses and opposes revolution." As far back as 1959, Lin alleged, Liu and Teng had plotted to "shelve" Mao and take control of the Party, and now they sought to "sabotage" the Cultural Revolution. The success of Mao's campaign, Lin indicated, depended upon their elimination.[75]

The indictment of the two senior Party leaders was endorsed by Ch'en Po-ta, Mao's ideological adviser and the head of the Cultural Revolution Directorate. He charged Liu and Teng with having attempted to "revise" the Maoist canon, asserting that they had "terrorized" Red Guards and other radical activists dedicated to the Chairman's cause. Ch'en reserved his angriest invective for Teng, denouncing him as an arrogant individual who "relied on his brilliance and considered himself a born encyclopedia." Discussing a question with Teng was "more difficult than climbing a mountain," Ch'en said. And, he declared, nothing less than the ouster of Liu and Teng would prevent China from sinking into "revisionism." "There will be a settling of accounts," he warned. "We are old, and it is important that we do this while we are still alive." [76]

These attacks against Liu Shao-ch'i and Teng Hsiao-p'ing were quickly publicized in Peking and elsewhere around China through the medium of the Red Guard press, and they served to signal to the radicals that Mao was as determined as ever to propel the Cultural Revolution forward. Maoist rhetoric took on a renewed tone of brutality. At a rally in Peking, for example, the radical Shanghai literary critic Yao Wen-yuan called for the ouster of all suspected adversaries of the Cultural Revolution. Borrowing a harsh image from Lu Hsun, a celebrated leftist Chinese writer of the 1930s, Yao urged Mao's followers to "beat the wild dog to death," for there could be no compromise in the drive to "overthrow the reactionary state power of the landlords and the bourgeoisie." [77] In a similar vein, a Red Guard faction in Peking vowed to "make the air thick with the pungent smell of gunpowder . . . turn the old world upside down, smash it to pieces, create chaos, and make a tremendous mess—and the bigger the better!" [78] Exhortations of this kind were matched by the increasing prominence of Mao's wife, Chiang Ch'ing. Besides appearing more frequently to whip up radical enthusiasm, she was promoted in late November to the post of "cultural adviser" to the Army, thus indicating that the Maoists were seeking to dominate the Chinese military establishment more fully.[79]

At the same time, in an address to Red Guards in the capital, Lin Piao put forth a new and explosive phrase that augured further tremors. Reviving the "principles" of the Paris Commune of 1871, which Mao had often cited as a model of proletarian egalitarianism, Lin announced the inauguration of "extensive democracy." From now on, the "broad masses" would be unleashed to "criticize and supervise the Party and government, leading institutions, and leaders at all levels." Nobody, with the presumed exception of Mao and his inner circle, would be immune to assault.[80] In effect, "extensive democracy" signified potential anarchy.

Throughout November and December, Red Guard and other activist groups ran rampant in their offensives against the authorities—and against each other. On November 10, more than two thousand Shanghai industrial workers, dissatisfied with the municipal administration, descended on the city's railway station, hijacked a train, and set off for Peking to present their case to Mao, thereby snarling up traffic along the China coast.[81] In Canton, resentful at having been deprived of opportunities to go around the country "exchanging revolutionary experiences," workers rioted against the factory management.[82] Paradoxically, the Maoist decision to encourage the "broad masses" to attack Party and government leaders had infuriated many radicals who had wanted the Red Guard movement restricted to youths whose origins were "truly" proletarian. In several places, the ultraleftists formed their own factions.

Some radical units in Canton felt so betrayed by what they considered to be a dilution of the ranks of the "revolutionary rebels" that, in one demonstration, they even threw stones at portraits of Ch'en Po-ta and Chiang Ch'ing.[83] At least one major Red Guard group later turned against Mao himself on the grounds that he "sold out" the revolution.

Meanwhile, the open season on criticism announced by Lin Piao produced unbridled denunciations of the highest central government officials. A partial list of Peking officials to incur the Red Guards' wrath, compiled by Western analysts in Hong Kong in late November, included five Vice-Premiers, seven Ministers, eleven Deputy Ministers, the Chief Justice of the Supreme Court, and four senior military members of the National Defense Council in addition to hundreds of lesser functionaries.[84] Not all those who drew fire were dismissed. Even though Chou En-lai was compelled to oust some of his associates, he managed to defend colleagues like Li Hsien-nien, Minister of Finance; Li Fu-ch'un, Chairman of the State Planning Commission; and Foreign Minister Ch'en Yi.

But one figure who did not survive was T'ao Chu. He had soared meteorically from Communist boss of south China to become the Party's propaganda chief—and then fell as rapidly.

Born in Hunan, like so many other Chinese leaders, T'ao Chu had served prior to 1949 as an Army political commissar in south China, gradually building up his authority and prestige in that area after the Communist victory. In 1961, when the Party reorganized its regional structure, he was appointed to head the Central-South Bureau, which controlled the vital corridor reaching from Honan province down through Hupeh and Hunan to Kwangtung and Kwangsi. This appointment made him, along with such figures as Li Ching-ch'üan of the Southwest Bureau, one of the most powerful Communists outside Peking. From all accounts, T'ao Chu was a vigorous, intelligent man, fundamentally faithful to the Party machine rather than to the cult of Mao's personality. He had undoubtedly shared the Party's disenchantment with the Chairman's economic policies following the Great Leap Forward, possibly feeling as well that the glorification of Mao had reached ridiculous proportions. He was later alleged to have slandered Mao by remarking that "the sun also has black spots." [85]

Therefore, though his phenomenal elevation in early 1966 seemed to observers at the time to mark him as one of Mao's loyal disciples, T'ao Chu probably owed his promotion more to his fidelity to the Party. For Liu Shao-ch'i and Teng Hsiao-p'ing were then very much in command of Party affairs. By the end of the year, however, T'ao Chu could no longer stand by Liu and Teng without drawing fire against himself. Thus he ostensibly sided with the Maoists, joined in the chorus denouncing the two Party leaders for having "distorted Chairman Mao's policies," and pursued a "bourgeois reactionary line." [86]

T'ao Chu's main aim was, it seemed, to defend his own Party subordinates in the south, upon whom he relied for his power. But that tactic proved to be his undoing. In late December, he was accused of having "stretched out his protective wings" to prevent the radicals from undermining his regional apparatus.[87] Soon afterward, according to reports from Peking, he was paraded through the streets of the capital by Red Guards cursing his name.[88]

The downfall of T'ao Chu and the regional leaders he had tried to defend meant that the Maoists, having been largely repulsed in their earlier attempts to topple the provincial Party bureaucracy, were trying another thrust into the Chinese cities and even into the countryside. On December 15, reversing the previous decision to prevent the Cultural Revolution from interfering with agriculture, the Maoist leadership issued a ten-point directive urging the Red Guards to invade villages in order to "revolutionize" peasants and "expedite" farm output. Henceforth, the directive stated, the "power structure" in the villages would be in the hands of local Cultural Revolution committees composed of poor peasants.[89]

Ten days later, similarly striving to destroy the Party leaders in charge of China's industries, the Maoists ordered the Cultural Revolution carried into mines and factories. Rejecting the argument that this would slow down industrial operations, radical publicists denounced Party officials who "seek to suppress the revolution under the pretext of taking a firm hold on production." [90] Matching these moves, Chiang Ch'ing and Ch'en Po-ta exhorted the Red Guards and other activists to seize control of the All-China Federation of Trade Unions, the Party's principal labor organization.[91]

These measures clearly augured an expansion of the Cultural Revolution. The *Red Flag* promised that the Maoist offensive would be pushed forward on a mammoth scale in 1967. "Hundreds of millions of people under the command of Mao Tse-tung's thought [must] launch a general attack on the enemies of socialism," the journal said, adding that "the leading organs and leading cadres at all levels" in the Party and government should expect to be targets of the "masses." [92] With that appeal, the stage was set for the "January Revolution"—and the months of widespread disorder and violence that followed would make the turbulence in China until then seem mild by comparison.

PART THREE

THE ERUPTION

We are paying a very high price in the great
Cultural Revolution.
— MAO TSE-TUNG, August 1967

CHAPTER 10

The January Tempest

There are casualties in all revolutions, so let us not exaggerate the seriousness of this situation. Many people have committed suicide or been killed. But these deaths are fewer than those incurred during the Japanese war and the Civil War, or in natural disasters. Thus our gains are greater than our losses.

—LIN PIAO, *March 1967*

ALTHOUGH HE HAD not initially plotted a precise timetable for his campaign, Mao Tse-tung instinctively conducted the Cultural Revolution like a guerrilla commander fighting a superior enemy. He was, after all, the "rebel" striving to overthrow the powerful Party leaders who had usurped his authority. Like a guerrilla, therefore, he attacked, retreated, retrenched, and attacked again as he sought to isolate his adversaries while building up his own strength. Describing his strategy to a group of foreign visitors to Peking, he later explained that the first phase of the Cultural Revolution had opened with assaults against literary dissenters in the fall of 1965 and lasted through the Eleventh Party Plenum in August 1966. This, Mao said, had been "primarily a mobilization stage" designed to rally support for his cause. From August until the end of the year, he went on, the second phase had singled out the targets of the Cultural Revolution and was, consequently, the "orientation" stage. Starting in January 1967 were the "crucial" stages in which his followers launched their offensive to topple the "bourgeois revisionist" Party bureaucrats.[1]

Throughout the first half of 1967, however, Mao would observe that his drive was running aground. On one occasion, he condemned Red Guard actions as "bordering on anarchy." [2] Later, deploring disunity of the radicals, he confessed that his hopes for their cohesion had been a "subjective wish that did not conform to the objective law of class struggle," since he had miscalculated the extent to which "different factions would still stubbornly seek self-expression." [3] The factional squabbling, Mao said, finally convinced him that his effort to shape the Red Guards and other student activists into "revolutionary successors" was a "fruitless task." Underlying this failure was the fact that China's educational system had been "dominated by revisionism" since the founding of the Communist regime. Hence students were infected with "bourgeois ideas" which were manifested in the "individualistic" tendencies that prompted radical organizations to divide into rival factions. In short, Mao asserted, his acolytes had demonstrated that they were "leftist in form but rightist in essence."

This did not mean, though, that the concept of the Cultural Revolution had been mistaken. On the contrary, Mao stressed, it merely confirmed his conviction that the route to real change lay in permanent revolution. Only a perpetual process of purification could cleanse human nature of egotism, the worst of the "bourgeois" tendencies, and make possible the emergence of a new species of "Communist man" dedicated to society. It was imperative, Mao said, that "two or three Cultural Revolutions be carried out every hundred years."

But if Mao regarded the Cultural Revolution as a recurrent necessity, many of his prominent comrades adopted a vastly divergent view as they witnessed the tumult that swept across China during 1967. During that year, the upheaval shattered civilian authority, paralyzed key sectors of the economy, provoked an Army mutiny, frayed the social texture of several regions, and nearly plunged some areas of China into civil war. Alarmed that China's very survival was in jeopardy, senior government and military leaders eventually insisted on measures to subdue the turmoil. After that, its forward momentum blunted, the Cultural Revolution gradually faded into a movement characterized more by rhetoric than reality. From January until early September of 1967, therefore, Mao's campaign went through its decisive stage.

FOUR VIEWS OF MAO TSE-TUNG

Mao when he was forty-two, in 1935, soon after his columns reached Yenan

Mao in Yenan, probably in the late 1930s, with the perennial cigarette

Mao in Peking shortly after the city fell to the Communists in early 1949

Mao during the Cultural Revolution in 1966

Mao and his wife, Chiang Ch'ing, in Yenan in 1945. She was then known by her real name, Lan P'ing

Lin Piao, in the uniform of a marshal in the People's Liberation Army in the period before adornments of rank were abolished. Lin was purged in 1971

Premier Chou En-lai

A rare photograph of Chinese Communist leaders in the summer of 1963. Front row (left to right): Huang Yen-pei, Vice-Chairman of the National People's Congress; Marshal Chu Teh, Vice-Chairman of the Communist Party Central Committee; Liu Shao-ch'i, Chairman of the People's Republic; Teng Hsiao-p'ing, Secretary General of the Communist Party; Mao; P'eng Chen, Politburo member and Mayor of Peking; Chen Shu-tung, Vice-Chairman of the National People's Congress; Premier Chou En-lai; K'ang Sheng, Politburo member and specialist in liaison with foreign Communist movements; and Teng Tzu-hui, Central Committee member and economic specialist. In second row, wearing white hat and dark glasses, is Foreign Minister Ch'en Yi. By 1971, only Mao and Chou En-lai were still active

Liu Shao-ch'i, former Chief of State

Marshal P'eng Teh-huai, Minister of Defense, who spoke out against Mao in 1959 and was purged

P'eng Chen, Politburo member and Mayor of Peking, one of the first major figures to be purged in the Cultural Revolution

General Lo Jui-ch'ing, the first prominent victim of the Cultural Revolution, who dropped out of sight in late 1965

Chiang Ch'ing, Mao's wife, the leading activist in the Cultural Revolution, addressing Red Guards

OTHER KEY ACTIVISTS IN THE CULTURAL REVOLUTION

Ch'en Po-ta, Mao's private secretary, head of the Cultural Revolution Directorate, purged in 1970

K'ang Sheng, member of the Cultural Revolution Directorate, purged in 1970

Yao Wen-yuan, reputed to be Mao's son-in-law, a young Shanghai official

Chang Ch'un-ch'iao, another Shanghai official

The Peking leadership welcomes Red Guards to the capital in the late summer of 1966; from left to right: K'ang Sheng, Chiang Ch'ing, Chou En-lai, Lin Piao, Mao Tse-tung

FOUR ARMY MARSHALS WHO SURVIVED RED GUARD ATTACKS

Chu Teh, venerated "Father of the Red Army"

The late Ch'en Yi, commander of the Third Field Army during the civil war and later Foreign Minister

Liu Po-ch'eng, the famous "one-eyed dragon"

Yeh Chien-ying, associated with Chou En-lai since the 1920s and believed to have replaced Lin Piao as Defense Minister

Teng Hsiao-p'ing, former Secretary General of the Chinese Communist Party

T'ao Chu, formerly the leading Communist in
south China, head of the party Propaganda Department during the Cultural Revolution, and in
disgrace by late 1966

Hsieh Fu-chih, Vice-Premier and Minister of Security, head of the Peking Revolutionary Committee during the Cultural Revolution and presumably purged in 1971

General Huang Yung-sheng, onetime Chief of General Staff, who disappeared in 1971 along with Lin Piao

General Wu Fa-hsien, commander of the Air Force, purged in 1971

General Li Tso-peng, chief political commissar of the Navy, another victim of the purge occurring in the wake of the Cultural Revolution

Marshal Yeh Chien-ying and Huang Hua (center), head of the Chinese delegation to the United Nations, welcome Henry Kissinger

Having set the direction of the Cultural Revolution in late 1966, Mao inaugurated 1967 with an impassioned call to the Chinese people to assault his foes across a wide front. His New Year's Day proclamation was military in both style and substance, and this feature revealed the extent to which he saw the drive against his adversaries as a form of revolutionary war.

The hour had come, Mao announced, for a "general attack" not only against the Party apparatus but against "monsters and demons anywhere in society." The Cultural Revolution, he said, should be pushed beyond "offices, schools, and cultural circles to the factories and mines and the rural areas" so that his followers could "capture all positions." Rejecting the warnings of Chou En-lai and others that Chinese industry and agriculture be protected against disruption, he denounced "some muddle-headed people" who feared that the Cultural Revolution would "impede production." These misguided "comrades," he explained, failed to appreciate a basic "truth" of the Maoist canon—that "revolution can only promote the development of the social productive forces." Those who argued for moderation sought "a pretext to repress the revolution" and they, along with other opponents of this "irresistible historical trend," would be dumped "onto the rubbish heap by the revolutionary masses."

Now, Mao also made plain, he expected workers and peasants to join with the Red Guards and other activists in a "mighty force" that would "storm the positions" held by the Party. "Extensive democracy," the phrase employed earlier by Lin Piao, was the new ideological slogan. It meant that there were no longer limits on either the participants or the targets in the Cultural Revolution. "Hundreds of millions of people" were authorized to assault the "enemies of socialism and, at the same time, criticize and supervise the leading organs and leading cadres at all levels." [4]

Mao's proclamation, like every Communist directive, was embroidered with caveats. It prohibited the radicals from resorting to "coercive measures," insisting instead that "different opinions among the masses should be debated" in a reasonable manner. It suggested, too, that the majority of Party cadres could be won over by carefully drawing a "strict distinction" between those who admitted their "errors" and the "few diehards who stick to the bourgeois reactionary line." But these nuances were lost as radical activists, interpreting Mao's call as a license to release their energies, rose up throughout the country with unprecedented dynamism.

In Peking, eager to demonstrate their zeal, radical youths immediately responded to Mao's exhortation by staging a public rally to disgrace the senior Communist Party officials already purged as "counterrevolutionaries." The most prominent figure hauled before the rally was P'eng Chen, formerly the city's Party boss. Also arraigned were Lu Ting-yi, who had headed the Party's Propaganda Department; Yang Shang-kun, a key member of the Central Committee Secretariat before his dismissal; and General Lo Jui-ch'ing, the ousted Chief of General Staff. Though he had lost his post in the spring, P'eng Chen had apparently been unmolested until the night of December 4, when eighty Red Guards broke into his Peking home, roused him out of bed, and drove him off in a truck. Perhaps underestimating their seriousness, P'eng Chen reportedly submitted to the youths as meekly as a "paper tiger." [5] Lo Jui-ch'ing, in contrast, had been under arrest for months. Evidently confined to a room in a Peking building, he had unsuccessfully attempted to commit suicide the previous spring by jumping from a window.[6] His leg broken, General Lo was dragged to the Red Guard rally in a cast.

The rally opened on the afternoon of January 4 at the Peking Workers Gymnasium, decorated for the occasion with a huge portrait of Mao and banners bearing his aphorisms. As they waited for the proceedings to start, the crowd chanted Mao's quotations and sang a stirring new song entitled: "We Crush Those Who Oppose Chairman Mao." The Red Guards led their victims onto a platform. The group of "reactionaries" included the wives of Lo Jui-ch'ing and Lu Ting-yi. All presumably had their hands bound behind them. According to a Maoist account,[7] the Red Guards forced the "sons of bitches" to turn their "canine heads" toward the "masses." And despite Mao's injunction against "coercive measures," the youths "knocked down" their victims and "put their feet on them" as the crowd applauded, cheered, and shouted slogans against the "despicable swine." The rally continued throughout the night into the next day as more than twenty orators read lengthy indictments against the former officials. Most of the speakers denounced P'eng Chen and the other victims as members of Liu Shao-ch'i's "clique," indicating that the Red Guards were priming themselves for an assault against the Chief of State himself.

At that stage, however, the group surrounding Mao seemed to be divided in its attitude toward Liu Shao-chi and Teng Hsiao-p'ing. Extremists like Mao's wife appeared to favor a direct personal attack against them, but Chou En-lai was anxious to avoid violence. The purpose of the Cultural Revolution, he argued, was to attack mistaken policies rather than individuals. "We should thoroughly criticize the bourgeois reactionary line represented by Liu and Teng, and we should smash it," he told a Red Guard audience, but "these two men still belong to the Standing Committee of the Party Central Committee" and deserved to be treated with the respect due their rank.[8]

While Chou En-lai tried to restrain the Red Guards, radicals in the Chiang Ch'ing camp were apparently stimulating the youths to harass Liu Shao-ch'i. Late in December, young activists at Tsinghua University had seized one of Liu's daughters, Liu T'ao, and compelled her to denounce her father. Herself a Tsinghua student, aged twenty-two, Liu T'ao had evidently had no choice but to comply with the Red Guard demand. She asserted that Liu Shao-ch'i had "opposed and resisted Chairman Mao for more than twenty years" and also called Liu's wife and her stepmother, Wang Kuang-mei, a "royalist."[9] Shortly thereafter, Red Guards captured Liu's second son, Liu Yun-jo, and put him through the same ordeal. A Soviet-educated aircraft technician in his mid-thirties, Liu Yun-jo was forced at a Peking rally to demand that his "dog's head" of a father "surrender unconditionally to Chairman Mao" and "bow to the people and admit his guilt"—or else face "extinction."[10]

About the same time, according to a Red Guard account, a group of forty Red Guards set a trap using another of Liu's daughters as bait to snare his wife, Wang Kuang-mei.[11] The Red Guards separated into two squads. One drove to the high school where Liu's teen-age daughter, P'ing-p'ing, was attending a political meeting. From there, they telephoned Wang Kuang-mei to inform her that P'ing-p'ing had been hit by an automobile and was in a

Peking hospital with "serious injuries." Meanwhile, the other Red Guard team drove to the hospital, took over its switchboard, and telephoned Wang Kuang-mei with the same story. Youths were posted at the hospital entrances to grab the woman who was, officially at least, still the First Lady of China.

To the Red Guards' dismay, however, the first of P'ing-p'ing's relatives to rush into the hospital was not her mother but her younger sister T'ing-t'ing, a girl of fourteen or fifteen, accompanied by one of her father's bodyguards. Quickly perceiving the trick, the bodyguard tried to telephone Wang Kuang-mei. But the Red Guards blocked him. They then "persuaded" T'ing-t'ing to call her mother to confirm that her sister's left leg had been injured and would require an operation. When Wang Kuang-mei asked to speak to a physician, a Red Guard took the telephone and, posing as the surgeon, described P'ing-p'ing's condition: "She is in bad shape. Her joint is broken. We are all set to take her to the operating room. Hospital regulations require the parent to sign approval. . . ."

Roughly an hour later, a small car pulled up at the hospital entrance. Out of it emerged not only Wang Kuang-mei, but Liu Shao-ch'i himself. Liu immediately realized that he and his wife had been deceived. The Red Guard version of what followed, though it is contrived to tarnish Wang Kuang-mei's image, unwittingly serves to bring her into focus as a lady of great pride, courage, and sensitivity. Assuring Liu Shao-chi that she could handle the youths herself, she sent him home and drove with Red Guards to Tsinghua University to confront a rally of radicals. On the way, she disclosed to one of them that she had suspected a trap from the beginning.

"Then why did you show up?" he asked.

"As soon as I got word that P'ing-p'ing had been injured," she replied, "I couldn't have cared less about this business."

Wang Kuang-mei stood before a kangaroo court of radicals at Tsinghua University from ten o'clock at night until five in the morning. In the end, she signed a statement praising the Red Guards for their "revolutionary action," vowing to submit herself to further "self-examination," and promising to send the students a regular report "exposing" Liu Shao-chi's "bourgeois reactionary line" as well as "things pertaining to his daily life and moral character." [12] There was no evidence, however, that Wang Kuang-mei ever fulfilled this pledge, and she would face a far more rigorous test at the hands of the Red Guards in April. Except for P'ing-p'ing, who was reportedly arrested in the spring of 1968, the fate of Liu's children has remained a mystery.[13]

Nowhere in China did Mao's call to the Red Guards to "storm the positions" of the Party apparatus "at all levels" have a more disorderly effect than in the sprawling metropolis of Shanghai.

In the fall of 1966, the city's mayor and Party boss, Ts'ao Ti-ch'iu, had shrewdly maneuvered to preserve his authority by sacrificing a few minor officials and thereby creating the impression that he was obeying Mao's exhortations. He had also mobilized his own Red Guard factions to defend himself and his colleagues against the radicals. By October, therefore, a fragile stalemate prevailed in Shanghai—and, for similar reasons, in most other parts of China.

But, inspired by the Maoist criticisms of Liu Shao-ch'i, the Shanghai radicals gradually intensified their pressure against the city's Party Committee. They were, in fact, directed by Maoist emissaries from Peking bearing specific instructions.

In mid-November, Chang Ch'un-ch'iao, one of the city's few Party officials to have initially sided with Mao, returned to Shanghai after more than four months in Peking. As a member of the Cultural Revolution Directorate, he was now a national figure. His mission was to organize the radical challenge to the Shanghai Party Committee. He gave his blessing to a coalition of radical students and workers, the Shanghai Workers Revolutionary Rebel Headquarters.[14] A week later, the Shanghai Maoists were further boosted by the arrival of Nieh Yuan-tzu, the woman who had sparked student protests at Peking University the previous May. Claiming to be Mao's personal representative—more probably she was operating on behalf of Chiang Ch'ing—Nieh Yuan-tzu denounced the Shanghai *apparatchiks* as supporters of Liu Shao-ch'i and Teng Hsiao-p'ing. On November 25, determined to escalate the offensive against the Shanghai mayor and his associates, she mobilized a demonstration whose militant tone was reflected in its main slogan: "We Swear to Rain Down Ten Thousand Bombs on the Bourgeois Reactionary Line of Ts'ao Ti-ch'iu and his Municipal Committee!" [15]

Such was the atmosphere in Shanghai—and elsewhere in China at the time—that the Party authorities could not overtly stifle the radicals without inviting the charge that they were "repressing the masses." Thus unfettered, the Shanghai radicals went into action. On December 2, strengthened by suburban students and workers, they occupied the offices of the *Liberation Daily*, the Shanghai Party's official newspaper. In reprisal, the Party formed a coalition of its own students and workers, the Scarlet Guards for the Defense of Mao Tse-tung's Thought. After two weeks of inconclusive skirmishing between the two groups, Mayor Ts'ao decided to appease the radicals, apparently in the belief that he would deflate their ardor. He publicly conceded that the *Liberation Daily* had indeed been guilty as charged of pursuing a "reactionary line." But the radicals, interpreting the Mayor's gesture as a sign of weakness, were emboldened rather than calmed. They intensified their verbal fusillades against him, finally compelling him to denounce the Scarlet Guards. Learning of Ts'ao's betrayal, the Scarlet Guards turned against him. Fighting broke out among rival factions in the city and suburbs and, amid the confusion, the Municipal Party Committee buckled. The Maoist troubleshooter Chang Ch'un-ch'iao, who had been shuttling back and forth from Peking, again returned to the city. Shanghai was now open to a take-over by the radicals under his command.

P'eng Chen's Peking apparatus had been removed in the spring of 1966 as a result of high-level machinations. In Shanghai, contrastingly, radicals appeared for the first time in the Cultural Revolution to have overthrown a local Party machine "from below." This achievement seemed to lend reality to Mao's vision of the "masses" rising to topple the "bourgeois revisionist" Party bureaucrats, and his publicists greeted the Shanghai episode with extravagant fanfare. Afterward, they would be compelled to recognize that their victory had been empty—but not before the Shanghai upheaval provoked a series of violent tremors throughout the Chinese provinces.

On January 4, acting with the approval of Mao's Cultural Revolution Directorate in Peking, eleven radical Shanghai groups coalesced under the leadership of the Workers Revolutionary Rebel Headquarters to assert control over the city. They seized the city's principal newspapers and its radio and television stations and, to publicize their supremacy, they arraigned Mayor Ts'ao and the defeated Shanghai Party bureaucrats at a public rally—held, appropriately, in a snowstorm. Also put on display was Ch'en Pei-hsien, the head of the Party's powerful East China Bureau, who until then had escaped direct criticism. Typically indiscriminate, the radicals vilified the Party officials for "crimes" ranging from "opposing the masses" to importing "pornographic films" from Hong Kong. Two deputy mayors, adorned with dunce's caps and placards identifying them as "reactionaries," were driven through the city streets in an open truck.[16] The senior Party *apparatchiks* were ordered to confess to their links with the "revisionist" conspiracy purportedly organized by Liu Shao-chi and Teng Hsiao-p'ing.[17]

The Maoist high command in Peking seemed delighted by this apparent triumph, for they hailed the Shanghai episode as a "brilliant example" for all of China to emulate.[18] "Internal rebellion is a good thing," Mao remarked. "The rise of the revolutionary forces in Shanghai . . . is bound to be felt throughout east China and in all the country's provinces and municipalities." [19] The *People's Daily* echoed this theme, calling on radicals to "seize power, seize power, seize power. . . . The mass of workers and peasants, revolutionary intellectuals and revolutionary cadres together should act as masters of their own affairs and establish a new proletarian order." [20]

But the Shanghai episode did not produce the effect that Mao wished. Though they successfully crippled Party organizations in a few places, the radicals were strongly rebuffed in most areas. The resulting eruption of complicated and confused clashes seemed to be propelling China toward an assortment of local civil wars.

In the southwest, the Party boss of Yunnan province, Yen Hung-yen, committed suicide by poison after coming under attack by Red Guards who had streamed into the region from Peking.[21] On January 25, the Great Alliance of Proletarian Revolutionaries claimed to have taken control of Kweichow, another province in southwestern China.[22] Radicals seized the Party newspapers and radio stations in Anhwei, Chekiang, Fukien, Hupeh, and Shantung provinces.[23]

The January upheaval also brought down Liu Lan-tao, the head of the Party's Northwest Bureau, whose headquarters were located in the Shensi province capital of Sian. According to Andrew Watson, a young English teacher who was resident there at the time, the downfall of Liu and his colleagues stemmed from an erosion of the Party bureaucracy in the area which had gone on steadily during the preceding months. In the fall, as Watson has described it,[24] the regional Party machine had managed to survive by relying on industrial workers to fight off rebellious youth contingents. Like "hard-hats" in the United States and Western Europe, the Chinese workers had no compunctions about beating up unruly students who threatened the Party apparatus to which labor owed its loyalty. But by mid-December, with increasingly shrill appeals for revolt emanating from Peking, many workers, government employees, and even policemen in Sian began to turn against the Party—even though they remained hostile to the student radicals. Thus the Party bureaucracy buckled for lack of support while students, workers, and others splintered into assorted factions that skirmished against each other. Amid this turmoil, the senior Party officials in Sian were detained in a special compound and forced to perform manual labor and write confessions of their "sins." The once prestigious Liu Lan-tao among them, they were also, in the usual fashion, paraded through the streets of the city wearing dunce's caps and compelled to face huge crowds at denunciation rallies. With the Party's controls broken, however, Sian slid toward anarchy. Not until the Army intervened later was a semblance of order restored. But the military move in Sian, as elsewhere in China, contributed to new problems that persisted throughout the spring.

In many other provinces, meanwhile, regional Party machines managed to mobilize continued support among workers, peasants, demobilized soldiers, and students to resist the onslaught of the radicals. The military authorities in several sensitive border areas, fearful that China's defense might be enfeebled by the turbulence, deployed troops to quell the disturbances. In some instances, this created tensions within the ranks of the Army.

Beginning in early January, fighting broke out between Party and Maoist factions in the Kiangsi province capital of Nanchang. This was the city where Communists headed by Chou En-lai and Chu Teh had staged an uprising against Chiang Kai-shek's Nationalists on August 1, 1927—a date since commemorated by the Communists as Army Day. Now, in Nanchang, the local Party bureaucracy organized six groups to oppose the radicals. The largest, known as the Workers Red Defense Corps, spearheaded an offensive against the radicals by storming their different headquarters throughout the city. Starting at three o'clock in the morning of January 9, the Workers Red Defense Corps raided colleges and high schools, confiscating loudspeakers, mimeograph machines, bicycles, and miscellaneous property belonging to radical students. During the raids, which continued for more than a week, some four hundred young people were reportedly hospitalized with serious injuries. Just as Red Guards of every coloration strove to portray themselves as Mao's true disciples, so now the Party *apparatchiks* in Nanchang did the same, and branded the radicals as "reactionaries." Army units afterward intervened, ousting the city's Party bosses—but without favoring the radicals.[25] Later the radicals would vent their wrath against the Army in a series of desperate assaults that reached a crescendo of violence in the summer.

In early January, factional clashes were even bloodier in Nanking, the former Nationalist capital lying on the south bank of the Yangtze River, in Kiangsu province. On January 3, the Party, evidently hoping to prevent Red Guards from coming into the city from Peking, ordered its supporters to block the railway at Chuhsien, a town north of Nanking. At the same time, the Nanking Party bureaucrats appealed to workers from nearby Shanghai and Wuhsi for assistance. An estimated hundred thousand workers took the offensive against the main radical group, the Red Rebel General Headquarters, primarily composed of students.

A leftist youth who escaped from the city during the turmoil reported that the workers started by attacking a radical stronghold at Chouyang, a suburb fifteen miles southeast of Nanking on the rail line to Shanghai. The workers captured twenty-three young radicals, he said, and confined them to the Kiangsu Hotel in Nanking. The battle was joined a day later, according to his account, when two thousand radicals streamed into the city to rescue their comrades. Both sides wielded bricks, clubs, and knives, and a Maoist version of the episode claimed that the workers met the counter-attack by flinging some of their hostages from the upper floors of the hotel. By the end of the first week of January, casualties in Nanking were said to be forty-three dead and more than five hundred seriously injured.[26] Subsequent evidence indicated that the Party sympathizers in Nanking were initially aided by the local Army garrison, under General Hsü Shih-yu, the commander of the region covering east China. Two years later, General Hsü was to emerge as a member of the new Politburo and one of China's most powerful military figures.

Violence also flared up in the remote region of Sinkiang. The turbulence there especially worried the Peking leaders, who had several reasons for considering the region to be extremely sensitive. First, China's nuclear and missile test sites were located in the vicinity of Lop Nor, a large lake in southeastern Sinkiang. Second, the majority of the population of 8 million consisted of Uighurs, Kazakhs, and other Muslims who had long resisted Han Chinese domination. Finally, bordering as it did on the Soviet Union, the area was regarded by the Peking leaders as the "front line in the struggle against revisionism."

As early as September 1966, four hundred Red Guards from Peking had arrived in the Sinkiang capital of Urumchi in order to "exchange revolutionary experiences" with local students. The Party *apparatchiks* in Urumchi went through the motions of welcoming the Peking youths, who proceeded to recruit university and high-school students into an organization entitled the Red Guard Revolutionary Rebel Headquarters.[27] But the Party bureaucrats were mistaken in believing that they could keep the students in line. The Red Guards soon began to criticize the "feudal" religious practices of the Sinkiang Muslims. They also denounced "those in power . . . who had sneaked into the Party and are taking the capitalist road." [28] That broadside was plainly aimed at General Wang En-mao, a veteran Army political commissar whose control over both the Party and military apparatus in Sinkiang since 1952 had made him virtual warlord of the area.

Originally a peasant from Kiangsi province, Wang had joined

the Communists in the mid-1920s as a guerrilla and later became attached to a unit in Ho Lung's 120th Division of the Eighth Route Army. He accompanied the Communist legions that pushed into Sinkiang in 1949, and he remained there to carve out his career like a powerful proconsul on the fringe of an empire. By his own admission, Wang governed the area with an iron fist, dealing "severe blows" to Party dissenters as well as against Muslims resisting integration into Chinese society.[29] In the spring of 1962, revolting against Wang's rule, some sixty thousand Uighurs and other Muslims had responded to Russian inducements to flee to Soviet Kazakhstan. That Wang escaped public censure for that episode may have been due to his connections with Ho Lung, who had risen to the rank of Marshal and membership in the Politburo. Ho Lung also had interests in Sinkiang as indirect boss of the Production and Construction Corps, a paramilitary force of nearly four hundred thousand men engaged in economic development in the territory. But now, as Ho Lung came under Maoist attack in January 1967, so did many of his old comrades, Wang En-mao among them.[30] Wang rushed to Peking to discuss the threat to his authority in Sinkiang. During his absence the region erupted.

The first large-scale clash in Sinkiang occurred on January 26 at Shih-ho-tzu, a military outpost of eighty thousand inhabitants lying in the shadow of the massive Tien Shan range that separates China from the Soviet Union. There, members of the Production and Construction Corps as well as active and demobilized soldiers had been incorporated into a region-wide organization elaborately called the August 1 Field Army Sworn to Defend the Thought of Mao Tse-tung to the Death. Wang En-mao had created this organization, known as the August 1 Field Army, in order to counter the Red Guards. Accordingly, when radical youths in Shih-ho-tzu made a foolhardy bid to seize power, the August 1 Field Army reacted brutally.

As a Red Guard account described it, the August 1 Field Army had earlier warned against creating disorder. But the youths persisted in calling for the overthrow of the Party "power-holders," and General Wang's supporters deployed ten truckloads of men armed with rifles and hand grenades. They encircled the Red Guards, who were staging a street rally, and opened fire. After that, the Red Guards claimed, members of the August 1 Field Army fanned out through the town in pursuit of suspected radicals. They stopped a bus, forced ten youths to descend, and shot them on the spot. Other youths were arrested and tortured. One Red Guard version of the event claimed that captured leaders had their eyes gouged out before being executed.[31] More than a hundred young activists were said to have been killed in the incident and hundreds more imprisoned in nearby labor camps.[32]

A Red Guard who escaped after seven months in detention later related that he and his comrades had been taken to a state farm run by the Production and Construction Corps. There, according to his account, several among them were tortured by Army officers trying to make them confess that their opposition to General Wang represented opposition to Mao. Students were flung from moving trucks with their hands tied behind their backs, as part of their punishment, he said, and officers stripped one girl and seared her breasts with a burning joss stick. The Red Guards were compelled to work sixteen hours a day and jammed into a vegetable bin at night. They were also subjected to "self-criticism" sessions at which, the youth said, they were told that they could only gain release by "transforming" their ideological attitudes.[33]

The Shih-ho-tzu incident reverberated in Urumchi and other parts of Sinkiang. In Peking, seeking to avenge their comrades in the border region, Red Guards raided the Ministry of State Farms and Land Reclamation, which was linked to the Sinkiang Party administration. They arrested Wang Chen, the Minister, an old associate of Wang En-mao.[34] Premier Chou En-lai ordered General Wang En-mao to return immediately to Sinkiang to impose a cease-fire in the region. Chou also advised General Wang that a special investigation team would be sent to the area.[35] Soon afterward, Peking issued a directive instructing the Red Guards to refrain from attacking either the political or the military apparatus in Sinkiang.[36] As elsewhere in China, however, the contending factions could not be pacified by mere decrees, and tensions continued to plague Sinkiang for months to come.

In the southern province of Kwangtung, meanwhile, radicals stimulated by Mao's call for rebellion succeeded in upsetting the local Party machine—but failed to gain power for themselves.

The Kwangtung apparatus, based in Canton, was seriously weakened in early January by the purge of T'ao Chu. Without his support, the Kwangtung Party bureaucrats maneuvered deviously to protect their authority. But they rapidly succumbed to the radicals. Yet the radical triumph in Kwangtung was only a brief prelude to a period of turmoil.

The Canton leftists were encouraged to escalate their activities in early January by both the Maoist exhortation to revolt and the apparent success of the radicals in Shanghai. Their cohesion was also cemented by the emergence of a dynamic young leader, Wu Ch'uan-p'in, a Hunanese student of physics at Canton's Sun Yat-sen University. A tall, articulate youth who always wore a neat khaki uniform, Wu had displayed unusual courage in the spring, when he openly attacked the Party chief at his university. In the fall, after returning from a pilgrimage to Peking, he formed two Red Guard units. One of them, the Sun Yat-sen University Red Flag Commune, was open to large numbers of students. The other, a tightly knit platoon called the August 31 Combat Detachment to commemorate the date Wu had passed in review before Mao, had only about two hundred members, most of them orphans—unconcerned that their unruly conduct might bring retribution against their families. These Red Guards were not only talented polemicists but skilled hand-to-hand fighters, and their elitist character contrasted ideologically with the Maoist concept of revolution by the masses. Nevertheless, Wu maintained close contacts with the Cultural Revolution Directorate through a liaison office he had established in the capital. On January 19, he received a long-distance telephone call from his Peking agent informing him that the Cultural Revolution Directorate now authorized the Kwangtung radicals to overthrow the Provincial Party Committee.[37]

Until then, Canton had been the scene of only sporadic, disorganized skirmishing. On January 11, for example, a radical group had taken control of the *Nan Fang Daily*, one of the city's Party journals.[38] In some neighborhoods, Red Guards had also clashed with workers defending their factories.[39] But when he received approval from Peking to assault the Kwangtung Party bureaucracy. Wu Ch'uan-p'in moved to meld the various cliques then active in Canton. With remarkable speed, he created a coalition of eight worker and student associations known as the Kwangtung Province Revolutionary Rebel Joint Committee—or, more simply, the Provincial Revolutionary Alliance. Included in the coalition were students and young workers from Peking, Harbin, and Wuhan who had come to Canton as delegates from their own Red Guard units.[40]

Soon, however, the Provincial Revolutionary Alliance was denounced by other Cantonese Red Guards who complained that the coalition was "monopolized" by northerners and therefore not truly representative of Canton. The Provincial Revolutionary Alliance, they alleged, had excluded many local organizations, thereby displaying "small-group" tendencies that violated Mao's appeal to "trust the masses." [41] This controversy, already acute in mid-January, foreshadowed the confused tensions that later gripped Canton as dozens of divergent factions asserted themselves. To a large extent, though, the dissension stemmed from the fact that the thrust by Wu's Red Guards to take power in Canton was outwitted by the local Party boss, Chao Tzu-yang.

The Canton radicals launched their *coup d'état* in classical style on January 22 by occupying the city's radio and television stations. They also took over the bureaus of both the municipal and provincial Public Security apparatus, which controlled the police, and they then proceeded to dismiss Chao Tzu-yang and his associates from office. But Chao, an experienced operative, maneuvered to deflate them. Instead of resisting their assault, he cheerfully capitulated by handing the Red Guards the symbolic seals of his authority.[42] He then issued a statement conceding that his Party machine had committed a "grave error of orientation and line" by following the orders of Liu Shao-ch'i and Teng Hsiao-p'ing. Henceforth, he vowed, he and his colleagues would strive for redemption by acceding to the "supervision of the . . . broad revolutionary masses." [43] Chao even offered to face criticism at a public rally.

Wu Ch'uan-p'in's Provincial Revolutionary Alliance was prepared to accept this surrender, but rival radicals considered it to be a charade, a "sham seizure of power" staged by "out-and-out royalists" and "servile tools" of Chao Tzu-yang.[44] Within a matter of weeks, the rhetorical quarrels among competitive Canton factions had escalated into serious physical conflicts, and the Army stepped in to restore order. The violence intensified into a long period of civil strife.

Nor was Peking spared the rebellious ferment. Hardly a day passed during January without its Red Guards assailing Party, government, and Army figures, clashing among themselves or splitting into rival factions. For nearly a week, Red Guards demonstrated against the Soviet Embassy compound, hanging effigies of Leonid Brezhnev and Aleksei Kosygin from trees in front of its gates and denouncing the "revisionist renegades of the international Communist movement." [45] A Red Guard unit affiliated with the College of Geology closed the Peking zoo as well as the celebrated Summer Palace, northwest of the city, while youths from Shanghai desecrated the famous tombs of the Ming dynasty emperors, causing "incalculable losses." [46] One of the most extraordinary incidents to occur during this stormy period was an uprising staged by a Muslim group resident in Peking. Though claiming fidelity to Mao, these Muslims protested against national and religious persecution by the Han Chinese, and their agitation was symptomatic of the extent to which the Cultural Revolution provided a pretext for different segments of China's population to express their grievances.

Indigenous to Sinkiang and Kansu, where they numbered about 5 million in the mid-1960s, the Muslim Huis are a Turkic people ethnically akin to the Uighurs and Kazakhs. Many had emigrated over the years to Peking, clustering in the Hsuanwu district, where they lived amid their own small shops, their restaurants and coffee houses, and their mosques. But in the fall of 1966, infected by the dissident mood of the Cultural Revolution, some of them formed an organization called the General Headquarters of the Peking Hui Nationality Rebel Regiment for the Thought of Mao Tse-tung. Despite this revolutionary title, the real purpose of the movement was to agitate for the religious and cultural rights of Muslims. Hui activists plastered up wall posters in their neighborhood irreverently proclaiming their faith in Allah along with their devotion to Mao. They also skirmished frequently with Red Guards who intruded into their ghetto in forays aimed at eradicating Islamic "feudalism."

On January 18, some four hundred Huis stormed a police station in the Hsuanwu district, injuring several policemen in the scuffle. The police arrested three of their leaders, and a large Muslim crowd returned to attack the police station again. "Crush the dogs' heads of the police," they shouted as they broke windows and smashed furniture. The police repulsed them, and the Muslims retreated to one of their mosques. Besieged there by the police for nearly two weeks, they were finally subdued. But, minor as it was, the Muslim resistance served to confirm radical allegations that anti-Maoist "dark forces" were "still powerful." [47]

The general turbulence in Peking by this time had spiraled to such proportions that, with the exception of Mao and Lin Piao, no Chinese leader was immune to Red Guard attack. Radicals forced the closure of several offices of the Public Security Bureau, the repository of police authority, and denounced Hsieh Fu-chih, the Minister of Public Security.[48] Chiang Ch'ing had earlier inspired this assault by asserting that the Public Security Bureau was "riddled with bad characters." Now, in late January she came to Hsieh's defense, calling him a "good comrade" who had earned his revolutionary chevrons in the initial offensive against Liu Shao-ch'i, Teng Hsiao-p'ing, and the other senior Party bureaucrats.[49] She also admonished the radicals for assailing such figures as Hsiao Hua, chief of the Army's political department, and Foreign Minister Ch'en Yi, who was then in the process of confessing his "mistakes."

Yet even as she sought to protect these leaders, Chiang Ch'ing and her colleagues on the Cultural Revolution Directorate were themselves being decried by certain Red Guard factions. She and her associates had been "slandered," she said, in wall posters throughout Peking. While conceding that she might have "shortcomings," she lashed out at her critics, claiming that they were trying to "isolate" Mao by attacking his disciples.

Much of the criticism against Chiang Ch'ing and her comrades came from Maoist radicals who, given license to revolt, apparently felt that nobody except Mao was sacred. Attempting to describe their ideological error, Chiang Ch'ing tortuously argued that these factions had swung so far to the left that they had become "reactionary." In other words, as she put it, they were showing "manifestations of extreme democracy and liberalism" that reflected an alarming trend toward anarchy.[50]

The turbulence shaking China was now aggravated by the emergence of a nationwide coalition of student groups dedicated to defending the Party against the Red Guards and Maoists. Known as the *Lien Tung*, or United Action Committee, this coalition differed from the many youth and worker factions set up by local Party machines in that it was mainly composed of the children of officials. As such, it heightened the element of authentic "class struggle" in the conflicts between the upper and lower echelons of Chinese society.

First mobilized under the auspices of the Party Work Team that entered Peking's Tsinghua University in the spring of 1966, the United Action Committee had initially included such members as Liu T'ao, the daughter of Liu Shao-chi, and Ho P'eng-fei, the son of Marshal Ho Lung.[51] As the Cultural Revolution gained momentum, the organization attracted other groups and individuals with similar aims. In Peking, for example, it became associated with a faction of high-school students called the Hsicheng Picket Team, whose leaders included Ch'en Hsiao-wu, the son of the Foreign Minister, and Tung Liang-ko, the son of Tung Pi-wu, one of China's two deputy chiefs of state.[52] An affiliated group in Canton, the Doctrine Red Guards, counted among its leaders Huang Chun-ming, the son of General Huang Yung-sheng, the regional Army commander.[53] Other factions in the United Action Committee came from a number of secondary schools especially created for the children of high-ranking Party, government and military figures. One such institution, the October 1 School in Peking, catered to fifteen hundred privileged youths in a gardenlike atmosphere. Unlike ordinary Chinese schools, where one teacher handled thirty-five or forty pupils, the ratio of students to faculty at the October 1 School was seven to one. Its staff included gardeners, drivers, and other servants, and its state subsidy was reportedly ten times larger than the allocation provided to regular schools.[54] At a similar Peking institution called the August 1 School, students were told: "You will be generals, ministers or premiers in the future. . . . You are not meant to peddle bean sauce or vinegar in the streets." [55]

The fight between the United Action Committee and the radicals, as it began to take shape in late 1966, was symptomatic of the struggle that had pitted the Party elite and Mao against each other for decades. Maoist strategy was designed, of course, to topple the Party apparatus. The Party, on the other hand, intended to prevent an upheaval that might shatter its organization throughout the country, and the United Action Committee was conceived as an instrument to defend that cause. Its fundamental conservatism, however, was clouded by the leftist rhetoric of its spokesmen as they "waved the Red Flag in order to oppose the Red Flag."

The policy of the United Action Committee was publicized in the fall of 1966 by T'an Li-fu, the head of a Red Guard faction at Peking Technical University. The son of a senior official in the Chinese judicial establishment, T'an had been associated since the summer with the children of Liu Shao-ch'i and Ho Lung in founding the organization. Speaking in Peking in October, he put forth the proposal that Red Guard membership be limited to "Five Kinds of Red"—the children of workers, peasants, revolutionary martyrs, revolutionary cadres, and revolutionary soldiers. Youths with other family backgrounds were to form separate units to be led and trained by the Red Guards. This proposal, though seemingly radical, was denounced by the Maoists. They saw it as a violation of Mao's design to uncork the "broad masses." In their view, T'an would have turned the Red Guards into an exclusive organization kept under close Party supervision. Although T'an disappeared not long afterward, and Red Guard units were opened to youths of all persuasions, the United Action Committee maintained its cohesion as a movement composed of "elitist" students.[56]

After a period of quiescence, the Peking branch of the United Action Committee surfaced again in early December. In all likelihood, the Party machine had revived the Committee for defensive purposes as the Maoist attacks against Liu Shao-ch'i and Teng Hsiao p'ing grew in intensity. Employing wall posters, tracts, and flimsy newspapers, the Committee protested against the persecution of the Party leaders, contending that it was criminal to derogate prestigious Communist veterans.[57]

On the evening of January 6, several hundred of the Committee's members marched into the headquarters of the Peking Municipal Party Committee, then under Maoist control. They boldly denounced the Cultural Revolution Directorate and shouted

"Long Live Liu Shao-ch'i." [58] United Action Committee posters went up around the city accusing the Directorate of pursuing a "left opportunist" line and claiming that Chiang Ch'ing, the most illustrious of the Maoists, was "going crazy." [59] This rhetoric was matched by increasing violence as United Action Committee squads clashed with Red Guard units.

An indication of the brutality shown by conflicting factions to each other was described in one document that charged the Hsicheng Picket Team with having "inhumanly" maltreated its rivals. [60] A nineteen-year-old student, Wang Kuang-hua, the document said, had been kidnaped by the Hsicheng Team. Taken to the Team's headquarters at the No. 6 Middle School in Peking, Wang was tortured by his captors as they tried to make him sign a statement denouncing his Red Guard unit. They clubbed him with rifle butts until his face was a pulp, his ribs were broken, and he was urinating blood. According to the document, Wang finally died, and his corpse was secretly cremated. Another victim of the Hsicheng Picket Team, the same document disclosed, was a retired worker by the name of Hsu Pei-lin who had been tortured and then hanged, the team claiming that he had committed suicide. Other documents revealed similar instances of savagery, and the violence spiraled in the months ahead.

Speaking to Edgar Snow in late 1970, Mao himself confirmed that these factional battles had been fierce. Conveniently forgetting that he had originally encouraged the ferment, Mao deplored the Red Guards' lack of discipline. [61] It was implicit in his disclosure, however, that he had simply lost control of the Cultural Revolution by early 1967. Certainly the Maoist leaders recognized that the situation had become desperate. In several talks with Red Guards during January, Premier Chou En-lai criticized their "seizure and control of everything," and warned that their continued unruliness would "wreck the social order and production, and thereby make us a laughing stock." He recommended what he called a "much better and more practical" policy—the "supervision formula," under which Party and government cadres would not be ousted by radicals but, rather, would perform their functions under the Red Guards' nominal aegis. [62] Even Chiang Ch'ing now also tried to halt the turmoil, telling the Red Guards that "blowing the wind and sparking the fire . . . is no longer effective." [63] In contrast to Chou, however, she did not caution the Red Guards against purging the administration, but merely urged them to pursue the campaign in a more orderly fashion.

By this time, though, the Red Guards had acquired a momentum of their own that could not be stopped or slowed down by oratory. They had gone to extremes—and only extreme measures would halt them.

CHAPTER 11

The Revolt of the Proletariat

To sabotage the Great Proletarian Cultural
Revolution and shift the target of the struggle, a small handful of power-holders in the
Party . . . try to lead some of the masses
onto the evil road of economism, where they
would pursue exclusively personal and temporary interests in disregard of the interests
of the State and the collective.

—Central Committee Circular,
January 1967

IN EARLY 1967, the Maoist leaders were deeply troubled by a new
phenomenon potentially more critical than clashes among rival
Red Guard factions. Workers in nearly every major city and
province of China had begun to express their dissatisfaction with
economic and social conditions. In many areas, they were being
joined by discontented peasants and a wide assortment of other
elements in China's labor force. Maoist propaganda condemned
these revolts as an ideological deviation labeled "economism,"
asserting that the rebellious workers, peasants, and others had been
"hoodwinked" by "reactionary" Party officials into agitating to satisfy their "personal and short-term interests." [1] There was a measure of truth to this allegation, for Party cadres in several places
did in fact attempt to win the support of workers by giving them
bonuses. But many workers and peasants were prompted to agitate
for reforms by genuine grievances that stemmed from serious labor
problems.

One of these problems was unemployment. Though precise statistics were never made available, hundreds of thousands of urban workers probably lost their jobs in the early 1960s, when the failure of the Great Leap Forward had forced the government to cut back on industrial production and capital construction. The slowdown in industry and construction also contributed to unemployment among school graduates trying to enter the labor force. In Canton, for example, it was estimated in the mid-1960s that the majority of secondary-school students remained idle from three to five years after graduation—unless they were sent to do manual labor in provincial villages or in Sinkiang and Inner Mongolia.[2]

The practice of sending superfluous graduates to rural regions —a movement known as *Hsia-fang*, or "down to the countryside"— was supposed to fulfill Mao's dream of closing the traditional Chinese gap between intellectuals and peasants. But the movement created other kinds of labor problems. Accustomed to urban comforts, the city youths adapted badly to the rigors of primitive village life.

Several of these rusticated students, who later fled home to Canton, recorded their experiences in a report descriptively entitled "Three Years of Blood and Tears."[3] They related that many of their comrades, too weak to put in long hours of heavy manual labor, had collapsed from exhaustion, fallen sick, and even died. Their inability to work hard, they recounted, inevitably provoked the resentment of the peasants, who had little use for "city slickers" under any circumstances. The peasants deprived them of food rations and, in some instances, beat them. An account of conditions in another village said that educated youths assigned to a labor brigade were deliberately accorded low wages under a complicated "work point" system, with the consequence that they ended each month in debt. When they complained, according to the report, the students were told to ask their families for money. Eight of these students ended by committing suicide. Others clashed constantly with peasants and rural cadres. Most, however, were appalled by the sheer tedium of rural existence. As the account commented: "Could life be duller, more monotonous, more uninteresting?"[4]

With the breakdown of controls during the Cultural Revolution, thousands of young people who had been sent to the countryside grasped the opportunity to escape, and they poured back into the cities on the pretext of participating in Mao's revolutionary drive. If they had been troublesome in the villages, they now became even more disorderly as they swelled the ranks of protesting workers in the cities.

Industrial apprentices were another source of labor discontent. These youths, usually adolescents with only primary-school educations, were recruited to serve three-year terms on half wages, at the end of which they were theoretically scheduled to be elevated to full worker status, with commensurate salary increases. But in the mid-1960s, they began to show signs of disappointment. They were generally able to master their simple jobs within five or six months, yet they could not expect promotion before the completion of their training. This meant that they were committed to thirty months of regular labor at half pay until they reached the lowest rung of the wage scale. One of their demands, therefore, was a reduction in the apprenticeship period.

The industrial apprentices who finished their terms in late 1966 were irritated by what they considered to be an even bigger injustice. At that time the authorities, apparently for budgetary reasons, decided to postpone promotions. Instead, apprentices faced two alternative prospects. They could be ordered to continue working at half pay. Or, under an industrial decentralization scheme then taking shape, they could be transferred to the countryside as employees in rural factories. These equally unattractive choices understandably put the apprentices in a rebellious mood, and their dissidence contributed significantly to the outbreaks in China's cities in the new year.[5]

Still another—and more volatile—source of labor unrest lay in the legions of underprivileged, insecure contract workers who had been shunted into Chinese cities throughout the previous decade. In an effort to recover from the disastrous Great Leap Forward, the Peking regime had cut wage and welfare expenditures by contriving a so-called "worker-peasant" system under which unskilled urban jobs could be filled by labor imported from rural regions on a seasonal or rotational basis. This system, the reverse of the *Hsia-fang* movement, was also purported to conform to Mao's doctrine of erasing differences between the cities and the countryside. In fact, it was largely designed to exploit cheap manpower as well as to save state funds in a variety of other ways.

For one thing, peasants could be substituted in urban industries for higher-paid workers, who were then sent to rural areas at lower salaries. During the 1965–1966 winter season, for example, nearly eight thousand permanent workers were dismissed from the country's sugar refineries and replaced by peasant laborers, thus reducing wage costs by 2.5 million *yuan*. Peasants accustomed to hard physical labor could also be employed as railway and dock coolies—jobs shunned by more sophisticated urban workers. Moreover, peasants assigned to temporary work were usually required to provide their own food and lodgings. They received neither medical benefits nor family allowances, and they could be returned to their villages before they became eligible for retirement pensions.[6] In short, then, the temporary contract workers were the "niggers" of China. And their rebellion, when it first erupted in late 1966, came as a revelation that the Chinese Communist regime had clung to a system that would have shocked the most egregious capitalist.

Even though they would later berate them for having chosen the "evil road of economism," the Maoists gave the workers the initial impetus to revolt. On December 26, Chiang Ch'ing and her comrades hailed the formation of a new revolutionary labor organization called the All-China Red Workers General Rebellion Corps, which had taken over the Ministry of Labor and planned to dissolve the National Federation of Trade Unions, an instrument of the Party bureaucracy. At the same time, asserting that they had "suffered the most" and therefore had the "greatest spirit of revolt," she exhorted the contract workers to rebel against the "political oppression and economic exploitation" to which they had been subjected under the system allegedly created by Liu Shao-chi, Teng Hsiao-p'ing, and the Party machine.[7]

This appeal to the most alienated elements of the Chinese labor force to participate in the Cultural Revolution was purposely timed to coincide with Mao's decision to push his campaign into the farms and factories. But it was a decision that backfired badly.

The rebellious workers at first seemed to be joining the Red Guards in the drive to topple the Party apparatus. Appropriating the language of the Cultural Revolution, they extolled Mao while denouncing his "counterrevolutionary" adversaries. But soon it became apparent that these militant phrases were only rhetorical cosmetics to camouflage a basically economic labor revolt. Most of the workers wanted higher wages, lower working hours, better housing, improved medical care, and other benefits. The contract workers in particular sought the abolition of the onerous system under which their status was, at best, second-class.

By no accident did one of the earliest outbursts of labor unrest occur in the Shanghai port, where many stevedores were peasants brought from the countryside. The labor force in the harbor also included many apprenticed youths, salaried at eighteen *yuan* per month, half the pay of a permanent worker.

At the end of December, these dock workers began to mobilize. In one area of wharfs and warehouses, where the labor force numbered fewer than three thousand, workers formed fifty-seven separate groups to agitate for improved wages and working conditions. The harbor officials, fearful of being branded as "revisionist counterrevolutionaries," promised to satisfy every demand. But the more the authorities sought to placate them, the higher the workers escalated their claims. At one point, according to an eyewitness description of the scene, harbor officials appeared to be playing hide-and-seek as irate workers pursued them around the docks.[8] Amid this upheaval, operations in the port of Shanghai slowed down and eventually ceased.

The Shanghai dock strike, the first overt labor protest to occur in China since the Communists took power, had a contagious effect. Similar disturbances spread to the northern Chinese ports of Tsingtao, Tientsin, and Dairen. Foreign ships scheduled to unload chemical fertilizers, machinery, and other merchandise and pick up such Chinese export commodities as rice, coal, and soybeans were condemned to long and costly delays. The captain of a Japanese vessel stranded in Shanghai telegraphed an angry complaint to Peking, while a European ship held up in that port signaled its impatience by flying the Chinese flag upside down.[9] Local Chinese, interpreting these gestures as insults, squabbled with foreign seamen on several occasions. Foreign firms, worried by the ferment, instructed their ships to divert course, and China's external commerce began to slide. Tokyo businessmen, especially alarmed by the tumult, decided to send a delegation to Peking to discuss the problem with Nan Han-chen, head of the Committee for the Promotion of International Trade. A distinguished banker and commercial specialist, Nan had long enjoyed the confidence of Japan's financial community. But before the Japanese delegation could embark on its mission to consult him, it received startling news. Indicted by Red Guards as a "bourgeois revisionist," Nan had committed suicide. He was seventy-five years old at the time.[10]

The storms whipping through China's ports also dealt a blow to the *amour-propre* of the Peking regime. Until this point, the Chinese Communist regime had been proud of the correctness of its commercial relations with the outside world. Underlying the Communists' sense of propriety was an intensely nationalistic impulse to live up to China's claim to be equal to other nations. Though they bargained hard, they had consistently endeavored to honor their commitments. But now, with their ports in disarray, they could not meet their obligations. Once again, it seemed to them, China presented a spectacle of disorder and unreliability, as it had in the past. Sensitive to this image, the Chinese leaders strenuously attempted to revive normal port activity, and dispatched truckloads of sailors and soldiers to break the harbor strikes in Shanghai and elsewhere. Unfamiliar with the ports, however, the troops were ineffective, and the restoration of order was difficult. The strike in Tsingtao, for example, dragged on for six weeks.[11] Afterward, when the tumult had begun to subside, harbor officials were singled out as having been responsible for the episode. Significantly, they were charged with "damaging the international prestige of China." [12]

Apparently inspired by the port upheavals, railway workers throughout east China also struck for better working conditions. China's railway network was vital for the transport of people, food, and raw materials as well as for troops and military supplies. Thus the railway disturbances, when they broke out, crippled the country far more severely than the port upheavals.

The first of the railway strikes, evidently timed to follow the harbor disorders, was planned for the final days of December by the Scarlet Guards for the Defense of Mao Tse-tung's Thought, the workers' faction that had been organized in Shanghai by the Municipal Party Committee. On the morning of December 30, employees in the Shanghai Railway Control Office pulled the switches that halted all rail traffic in the vicinity of the city. Service abruptly stopped on the main rail lines running northwest to Nanking and southwest to Hangchow, leaving more than fifty passenger and freight trains stranded along the route.[13] An official account, published to celebrate the heroism of two engineers who managed to steer the No. 14 Express from Shanghai to Peking, inadvertently provided a glimpse of the turmoil on the tracks. Strikers had blocked the tracks and smashed signals along the line in an effort to stop the train, according to the account. At one stage, the two thousand passengers packed in the train were near panic when the lights went out—sabotaged, presumably, by strikers who had somehow climbed aboard. Farther along the way, passengers fainted as the crowded train encountered fresh difficulties. But despite adversity, the No. 14 Express chugged forward until it finally reached the capital several days after leaving Shanghai. Normally, the trip should have taken twenty-three hours.[14]

The railway strikes did more than inconvenience passengers. Coal shipments were delayed throughout China, for example, and at one period the Yangshupu thermal power plant in Shanghai was down to a two-day supply.[15] Coming as it did in the middle of winter, the coal shortage imposed serious hardships. Steel, textile, and other industries were affected as well when rail deliveries of raw materials failed to reach factories. Food supplies carried by train from Kwangtung province to Hong Kong—China's principal source of foreign exchange earnings—dropped sharply. Other commodities, due to be transported from the interior to ports for export abroad, were also held up. In early January, for example, Japanese freighters arriving in the northern port of Chinhuangtao were advised that scheduled shipments of soybeans had been diverted to Dairen. The ships steamed back across the Gulf of Liaotung to Dairen—only to discover that the soybean cargoes had been delayed somewhere along the railway down from Manchuria and might not reach the port before February.[16]

The trains that were functioning, in the meantime, were strained to the limit as hundreds of thousands of workers poured into Peking from provincial cities. Their ostensible objective was to present their grievances to the central government. In reality, most were simply taking advantage of the confusion to enjoy more trips to the capital—just as Red Guards had freely roamed the country months earlier under the guise of "exchanging revolutionary experiences." Factories, mines, and other enterprises were badly disrupted as workers quit their jobs. At the Pingtingshan colliery in Honan province, for example, when more than seven thousand miners left for Peking, the output of coal declined.[17] Production stopped from late December through mid-January at the Tsingtao Szu Fang Locomotive Works in Shantung for the same reason.[18] Even the Taching Oil Field in northern China, long celebrated as a model Maoist enterprise, was hit as its managers sent some ten thousand young workers to Peking on the pretext that they deserved to participate in the Cultural Revolution. Chou En-lai called this gesture, which he said had partially paralyzed oil-drilling operations, "counterfeit revolution." The vast migration of workers to Peking, he further charged, was a form of sabotage by "bourgeois reactionary" elements striving to subvert the Maoist leadership.[19]

Chou En-lai's allegation was not entirely unfounded. Local officials in several areas had indeed advanced considerable sums of money to protesting workers in hopes of appeasing them, and the workers promptly left their jobs for tours of the country. In Shanghai, the Municipal Party Committee instructed the city's banks to disburse millions of *yuan* in state funds to agitating labor groups in an attempt to satisfy their demands.[20] Party bureaucrats and factory managers also raised salaries, dispensed bonuses, and even handed out free merchandise. One Shanghai workshop distributed bicycles to its thirty employees, while another small plant gave each of its workers three dozen bath towels. Other enterprises in Shanghai sought to placate workers with such items as leather shoes and winter overcoats, and one factory allocated four million *yuan* in "premiums" to its staff.[21] In Harbin, the authorities paid every employee in the transport department "back wages" of a thousand *yuan*—the equivalent of two years' salary.[22] Using the excuse that they had not been paid for supplementary labor performed in 1958,

] 268 [

the directors of a Peking marketing agency accorded themselves and their staff some forty thousand *yuan* in "retroactive" overtime pay.[23]

Mao's publicists referred to these material inducements as "sugar-coated bullets" that threatened to kill the true proletarian spirit of austerity. Their attacks against Communist officials alleged to have fostered "economism" not only provided an insight into the extent to which government money was squandered, but offered a glimpse of the way pilgrims to Peking passed their sojourns in the capital.

Among those accused of wasting state funds was Hsiao Wang-tung, Vice-Minister of Culture. According to an indictment against him, he spent nearly 4 million *yuan* to subsidize visits to Peking by assorted art, literary, film, and other groups that did little to promote the Cultural Revolution once they reached the capital. The indictment charged, for instance, that he footed the bill for a troupe of actors that whiled away its time in Peking in typical Thespian style by eating, drinking, and playing poker. On one occasion, Hsiao mobilized the actors to stage a phony demonstration against him so that he could go through the motions of "self-criticism" and thereby display his revolutionary ardor. After the demonstration, the indictment claimed, he served tea and cakes to his "critics." [24]

Another Peking dignitary accused of riddling workers with "sugar-coated bullets" was Lü Cheng-ts'ao, the quiet, respected Minister of Railways and one of China's foremost communications specialists. A lengthy diatribe issued by one Maoist faction charged him with having "incited a great multitude of workers to leave their production posts" by offering them free train trips to Peking. Railway traffic had been hampered by delays, accidents, and other "tremendous difficulties" as a result. The attack against Lü also alleged that he had provided cheap food and lodgings for workers coming into the capital, encouraging their disruptive movement.[25]

Assaults of this kind against Lü Cheng-ts'ao and other Chinese administrators placed Chou En-lai in an awkward position. The Premier was loath to lose these skilled technicians, without whom the nation's essential services might well be endangered. Yet he could not risk his credibility with the radicals. Thus he sought to

appease the Maoists while simultaneously protecting his subordinates by urging men like Lü Cheng-ts'ao to confess their shortcomings. The Railway Minister accordingly admitted his "mistakes,"
pledging that he would henceforth carry out his functions in a
"responsible manner." [26] But the Red Guards were not satisfied.
Late in January, forcing him to wear a white dunce's cap as a sign
of his humiliation, they paraded Lü through the streets of Peking.[27]
After that, he disappeared from public view, presumably to do
penance in a labor camp.

Though the Maoist allegations accusing Party officials of bribing
labor were frequently exaggerated, workers did in fact explode in
a frantic spending spree with huge sums acquired from the government treasury. Until they were closed by Red Guards in mid-
January, department stores in Peking were jammed with workers
purchasing almost everything in sight. According to a Japanese dispatch, daily sales of wrist watches tripled and sales of woolen
yarn soared twentyfold above the previous month. A worker who
had come into the city from north China was observed buying a
dozen shirts for the equivalent of his annual wage. Other workers
were seen carrying away bicycles, sewing machines, and radios.[28]
And the drive for commodities was not confined to Peking. A report
from the Yunnan provincial capital of Kunming described the
hectic scenes there as workers, their pockets bulging with cash,
indulged in shopping orgies.[29] This rush for consumer goods was
short-lived—primarily because the supply of merchandise was soon
exhausted. But, if he was aware of it, the episode may well have
confirmed Mao in his conviction that China would require several
Cultural Revolutions before "spontaneous tendencies toward capitalism" could be eliminated from its people.

Nor were workers the only Chinese to show "capitalistic tendencies." Peasants in several regions plundered government grain
stocks, pilfered commune funds, refused to deliver cereals to state
purchasing agents, slaughtered livestock, and, among other things,
abandoned collective rice and wheat fields in order to cultivate private crops.[30] Those living in suburban areas streamed into the cities
to sell their produce illicitly at high prices and to join in the revolutionary ferment. Though the Maoists predictably accused the
"bourgeois revisionist" Party bureaucrats of encouraging them to

agitate, the peasants themselves had sufficient cause to revolt. The kind of dissatisfaction troubling them was mirrored in a list of grievances set down in mid-January by villagers from Nanhui, a county south of Shanghai. To some degree, their complaints were probably shared by peasants throughout China.

"We are second-class citizens," the Nanhui peasants complained. They grumbled that the countryside was considered a "general rubbish heap" to which reactionaries, criminals, and "anyone else in need of reform is sent." Rural areas lacked schools, cultural facilities, newspapers, medical services, and competent officials, they protested. It was difficult for young men to find wives, as country girls preferred urban workers—and with good reason, since city workers lived in apartments and earned high salaries while badly paid peasants lived in thatch-roofed huts "exposed to wind and rain, and often about to collapse." Factory workers received meat, bean curd, and other special rations, but peasants were not even allowed to retain the very food they had cultivated. Above all, the protesters argued, the rural population was unable to express itself. "Workers, soldiers, and Party members have associations to represent their interests," they pleaded, "but the peasants have no voice." [31]

Meanwhile, the workers, students, office employees, and others whom the regime had transferred to rural areas took advantage of the turmoil and confusion to drift back to the cities. Several factories that had been shifted to the interior of the country for defense purposes were abandoned as workers returned to their homes.[32] By far the biggest movement to the cities, however, was undertaken by young people who had been sent to the far off reaches of Kansu, Inner Mongolia, and Sinkiang to work on state farms or construction sites.

During the mid-1960s, more than a hundred thousand youths had gone from Shanghai to Sinkiang, either as volunteers or as forced exiles. Many had been appalled by their experiences in that vast, arid border region, where, instead of being assigned to modern agricultural projects equipped with tractors and other machinery, as advertised, they were herded into barbed-wire compounds and compelled to work like coolies under military supervision.[33] Now, seizing the chance to escape, they streamed back to Shanghai.

Some claimed that they had been unjustly banished by Liu Shao-ch'i's Party "revisionists," while others asserted that they had come back to participate in the Cultural Revolution. But whatever their justification, they created a new problem in Shanghai. Not only were they swelling the city's population, already bursting with hundreds of thousands of displaced Red Guards, peasants, and other outsiders. As volatile rebels, they also contributed to its instability. Moreover, having returned illegally, they lacked residence permits, ration coupons, and all the other documents required as Chinese citizens. They could only survive by stealing, black marketeering, and engaging in other shady activities. In the Shanghai tradition, they gradually banded together into outlaw gangs and, for many years afterward, one of the main tasks of the city authorities was their arrest and deportation.

Throughout January, the Maoist leaders in Peking and the provinces made repeated attempts to restore order to the Cultural Revolution. On January 5, the eleven radical organizations in Shanghai that had attempted to seize control of the city from the Municipal Party Committee published a declaration calling for discipline. It charged "reactionaries" in the Municipal Party Committee with having provoked the labor revolt, conspired to paralyze Shanghai's water and electricity supply, and plotted to bring public transport to a standstill. Faithful disciplines of Mao, the declaration said, should "serve as the vanguard and backbone not only in grasping revolution, but also in stimulating production." Workers should therefore "make a clear distinction between right and wrong, avoid delusion, quickly wake up, return to your production posts, and rejoin the proletarian revolutionary line." [34] Four days later, thirty-two Shanghai organizations issued a ten-point "Urgent Notice" that was even stronger in tone. The notice warned workers that they could be prosecuted for "sabotaging production" if they stayed out on strike. It also warned all agitators, whatever their political coloration, that they could face punishment for seizing public buildings, committing acts of violence, or "undermining social order." [35] At the same time, in an effort to put teeth into these directives, the Shanghai radicals announced that the metropolitan police would henceforth suppress unruly elements, even to the extent of inflicting the death penalty for certain crimes.[36] In an effort to reactivate the city's municipal services, some youth groups occupied the Railway Control Office and other Shanghai administrative bureaus.

But the Maoist strategy in Shanghai rapidly proved to be ineffective—if not actually disruptive. In the first place, the threat to unleash the police was largely bluff. For the city's Public Security Bureau was just as divided as every other municipal department and could not be considered reliable.[37] There were also growing indications that the Shanghai radical movement itself was fragmenting into a multiplicity of factions despite the propaganda proclaiming its unity. Several of the thirty-two groups that signed the "Urgent Notice" on January 9, for example, were offshoots of the eleven organizations that had published the similar message only four days earlier.[38] In addition, even though the radicals blamed the local Party apparatus for "economism," it was plain that the real targets of their attack were the workers, peasants, and others who had gone out on strike in December to seek redress for genuine economic and social grievances. This approach, ironically, served to alienate the Maoists from a significant segment of the proletariat.

The potential dangers in the Shanghai situation were not immediately visible to the Maoist leaders in Peking. On the contrary, as earlier described, they initially praised the city's radicals for their "forceful counteroffensive" against the "bourgeois reactionaries." Underlying this unusually rapid endorsement was Mao's apparent conviction that, as his vision held, the "masses" were really capable of assuming and exercising power in a responsible manner. He saw the radical take-over of Shanghai as a resurrection, Chinese-style, of the Paris Commune of 1871. But it soon became clear that the notion of a Shanghai Commune was chimeric. As disorders persisted in the city throughout January, it also became obvious that Shanghai could not be held up as a model of revolutionary stability. The leaders in Peking now turned to less imaginative measures to curb the turmoil that was now overrunning nearly every city as well as many rural areas of China.

Judging by the series of almost daily decrees they issued in January, the Maoist leaders were desperate. They directed that stores be closed in an effort to halt the sale of consumer goods, and they instructed the Army and police to prevent the public from withdrawing money from banks.[39] They declared a moratorium on the payment of back wages, bonuses, welfare benefits, and other special allowances, promising workers that their complaints would be reviewed.[40] They ordered a stop to the movement of rusticated students and laborers from the countryside to the cities, urged peasants to cease their protests, and put out numerous pleas to youths to return to Sinkiang and other border regions.[41] They commanded radicals to withdraw from the radio stations they had seized, ordaining that stations would henceforth only broadcast programs initiated in Peking.[42] And, among other edicts, they canceled the traditional Lunar New Year holiday in order to reduce the strain on the country's disrupted financial and transport systems.[43]

Premier Chou En-lai was characteristically in the forefront of this strenuous effort to stabilize the nation. No subject was too trivial to command his attention and, despite the enormous pressure on him, he apparently handled himself with almost superhuman equanimity. He listened to complaints from parents whose children had been banished to Sinkiang, promising to investigate their grievances.[44] He frequently stayed awake until dawn as he talked night after night with students, workers, provincial representatives, government officials, and Army officers. He passed judgment on the ideological purity of Red Guard units and their leaders.[45] At five o'clock on the morning of January 10, he addressed an assembly of transport workers, informing them that free train travel was being suspended and appealing for their cooperation in restoring normal railway traffic.[46] At another meeting, he asked radical youths to stop squabbling, explaining that the Cultural Revolution was "not an individualistic power struggle nor the power struggle of small cliques." [47] Chou repeatedly stressed in his speeches that there was no need to overthrow China's entire political and economic structure. Instead, he emphasized the importance of carrying out a selective, surgical purge by eliminating a few "reactionaries" while encouraging others to reform. Consonant with that approach, he protected his close subordinates against Red Guard harassment— even though, in the process, he exposed himself to criticism.

From time to time, Chou's admonitions were echoed by the

senior radicals, among them Ch'en Po-ta and Chiang Ch'ing, even though their motives differed from his. They were aware of the dangers of prolonged turmoil to the Chinese economy and, too, they knew that the fragmentation of the Red Guard organizations would subvert the Cultural Revolution. But they realized that moderation would blunt the forward thrust of Mao's drive. They therefore adopted an ambivalent position. They appealed for radical unity, but pressed the Red Guards to take stronger action against suspected Party "revisionists." They urged their followers to "struggle through reason," but also authorized them to defend themselves "with force." Reiterating the Maoist slogans publicized at the outset of the Cultural Revolution, they continued to assert that "rebellion is justified" and that "destruction must precede construction." The ambiguity of these directives effectively gave local radicals the freedom to pursue their own campaigns.

By the end of January, then, China resembled a spastic whose limbs were unresponsive to its brain. Central authority in Peking was largely intact. But the provinces writhed in chaos as Red Guards, having shattered the regional Party structures, were unable to erect new political mechanisms. Only one institution had the capacity to fill the power vacuum—the Army. Thus the next attempt to impose order began under military auspices. Yet it brought on a period of further conflicts.

CHAPTER 12

Out of the Barrel of a Gun

❧

The Chinese Red Army is an armed body
for carrying out the political tasks of the
revolution.

—MAO TSE-TUNG, December 1929

The attitude toward the People's Liberation
Army is in fact the attitude toward the dictatorship of the proletariat, and an important criterion for determining whether or not
a person is a genuine revolutionary.

—Red Flag, May 1967

MAO TSE-TUNG had unleashed the Red Guards at the start of
1967 with instructions to "storm the positions" held by the
Communist Party in China's political, economic, and social institutions. But now, only a few weeks later, the "irresistible historical
trend" destined to defeat the "enemies of socialism" was faltering.
The Maoist radicals were meeting stiff resistance in many areas as
local officials counterattacked with their own legions of students,
workers, and peasants, or staged confusingly deceptive demonstrations of fidelity to the Maoist cause. Even in the places where they
had managed to topple the Party bureaucracy, like Shanghai, the
Red Guard groups were fragmenting into rival factions. Despite
Mao's inspirational appeals, the radicals could neither seize power
nor wield it effectively. Instead of forging a new revolutionary order,
they were creating chaos.

At this critical juncture, Mao might conceivably have conceded that his campaign had miscarried and abandoned its more ambitious objectives, as he did when the Great Leap Forward stumbled. But such a policy would have been extremely hazardous. For if his adversaries had cut down his authority after the collapse of the Great Leap, they would now retaliate even more fiercely against him. Retreat meant not only the defeat of his dream but, quite possibly, his very downfall. His only plausible alternative, then, was to turn to the sole force that had the sinew, the prestige, the discipline, and the organization to swing the balance in his favor—the People's Liberation Army. On January 23, he publicly instructed China's military commanders to go to the aid of his radical followers.

Until then, though instrumental in mobilizing the Red Guards, China's troops had been under orders to remain neutral in the drive against the Party machine. Those orders were now rescinded. Mao directed the Army to give "active support" to "genuine" radicals in need of assistance. "Counterrevolutionaries" must be "resolutely suppressed," and he authorized the Army to "strike back with force" against them should they resort to violence. In addition, he warned that the Army itself might be subjected to a purge if it shielded "diehards who persist in the bourgeois reactionary line." [1]

Much later, in justifying his call for Army support, Mao explained that the radical students had proved themselves unreliable. They were "intellectuals"—a species he had long disdained—who suffered from "wavering character" and the lack of will to pursue "thorough revolution." For that reason, Mao claimed, he had entrusted the most crucial stage of the Cultural Revolution to soldiers who were "merely workers and peasants in military uniforms" and therefore constituted the true proletariat.[2]

Whatever the validity of this rationale, Mao's decision to rely on the Army scarcely brought the results he had anticipated. Chinese soldiers, like soldiers everywhere in the world, were essentially dedicated to the preservation of stability. Their basic impulse was to impose law and order, the very antithesis of revolution, and hence their intervention served mainly to frustrate the Maoist radical movement. The upheavals that ensued, moreover, further prompted the Army to strengthen its political authority, notably in the composition of the so-called Revolutionary Committees that were gradually created to govern the Chinese provinces. After April 1969, when a new national Communist Party structure was established, the Army plainly emerged in a predominant position—at least for a time.

For all his purported omniscience, Mao could not have predicted these consequences. Yet his move to enlist the Army in the Cultural Revolution was made with apparent reluctance. Signaling his plan to a group of senior Chinese officers beforehand, he seemed to communicate a feeling of desperation. He had opted to commit troops to the side of the floundering radicals, he explained, because he saw "no other recourse." The struggle against his Party enemies had grown so "extraordinarily acute," that it was too late for "compromise." It was also too late to discuss the pros and cons and whys and wherefores of military intervention. The situation demanded drastic measures, he asserted, suggesting in effect that troops should act first and ask questions later. "Power must be seized before anything else is done. We can no longer continue to deal in abstractions. Otherwise, our hands will be tied." [3]

Mao had undoubtedly been contemplating the notion of positive military involvement in the Cultural Revolution for some time. During the previous months, he appeared to be developing increased concern for the ideological purity of the Army. In early October, his Defense Minister and heir-apparent, Lin Piao, had emphasized at a rally of soldiers the necessity for the Army to reinforce itself with Mao's "Thought." [4] At Lin Piao's orders, teams of Army political activists were sent to Peking for special training. Mao soon afterward hinted symbolically that troops needed stronger ideological guidance by appointing Chiang Ch'ing to be the Army's "adviser" on artistic and literary matters. The possibility of military intervention was also mirrored in the fact that both Party and Army elements began to betray their hostility to the idea.

The Party feared military participation in the Maoist campaign for the obvious reason that its apparatus was no match for the Army if regional commanders undertook to dismantle it. A prominent official who probably voiced opposition to the scheme was T'ao Chu, who had become the Party's propaganda chief in 1966. The exact nature of his resistance to the new Maoist line has never been clear. But one esoteric sign that his prestige was waning in late 1966 was perceptible when in November a Peking opera company and three other artistic troupes that had functioned under his supervision were shifted to the control of Chiang Ch'ing in her new capacity as cultural "adviser" to the Army.[5] A few weeks later, T'ao Chu was purged amid Red Guard denunciations accusing him of almost every imaginable crime.

Several senior Chinese military figures were equally reluctant to sanction the Army's involvement in the Cultural Revolution. These veteran Communist officers were closely linked to central and provincial Party *apparatchiks* who were being singled out for attack by the radicals, and they were naturally inclined to stand by their old comrades. The professional soldiers, among them were also worried that a deeper Army commitment to the Maoist campaign would weaken China's national security, particularly as Soviet and American pressures seemed to be mounting.

Resistance to involving the Army in the Cultural Revolution —or thrusting the Cultural Revolution into the Army—was apparently led by officers like Marshal Ho Lung. Ho was intimately connected with many key Party officials, especially in southwest China, where his First Field Army had operated for years. As a professional soldier, he was also sensitive to China's defense priorities, and he was wary of engaging the Army in an ideological drive that might divide its leadership and reduce its effectiveness in the event of war. Ho Lung's views seemed to have been shared in varying degrees by other members of the Peking military hierarchy, including Marshal Chu Teh, the aged and illustrious "father" of the Chinese Communist Army.

But the Army chiefs, like the Party bureaucrats, could not openly oppose Mao without seeming to be guilty of heresy. Their strategy was thus to contrive an impression of enthusiasm for the Cultural Revolution while taking steps to restrict the Army's real role in the drive. Typical of these steps was an "urgent directive" issued on October 5 by the Military Affairs Commission and the Army's General Political Department and couched in the fashionably fierce rhetoric of the period. The directive urged cadets and young officers to join in the Maoist offensive to uncover "counterrevolutionaries." More significantly, however, it specified that this agitation should be strictly limited to military schools and academics —in which, quite clearly, it could be controlled.[6] To prevent the turmoil from disrupting its ranks, moreover, the Army set up its own

Cultural Revolution Directorate, separate from the civilian group headed by Ch'en Po-ta and Chiang Ch'ing. Predictably, the officer appointed to manage this Army directorate was General Liu Chih-chien, a senior military commissar who had long been associated with Marshal Ho Lung.[7]

Throughout the autumn of 1966, top Chinese military men went through the motions of genuflecting to Mao while cautioning troops against involvement in his campaign. Ho Lung himself exemplified this dual approach in a speech he delivered in mid-November to Army instructors and cadets then visiting Peking. He lavishly praised Mao as the Army's "greatest inspiration" and the "reddest sun in the heart of each and every revolutionary fighter," recommending that all soldiers arm themselves with the Chairman's portrait as a symbol of their "infinite love and adoration" for him. Switching from hyperbole to reality, however, Ho then told the troops that they should "neither take part in nor interfere with local Cultural Revolution activities, and shall not participate in such pursuits as bombarding [Party] headquarters, making rebellion, confiscating private property, and holding parades." [8]

Early in October, to take another instance, Marshal Yeh Chien-ying, a Vice-Chairman of the Military Affairs Commission, had warned troops against "interfering" in the Cultural Revolution. "We must confine ourselves to our own campaign," he said, adding that soldiers should "not carry out Red Guard activities." Minimizing the need for a purge within the Army, Yeh estimated that only 3 per cent of military cadres could be classified as "bad elements." [9] This plea for moderation was echoed by Marshal Hsu Hsiang-ch'ien, another Vice-Chairman of the Military Affairs Commission. Chinese defenses might be damaged if the Army was shaken by internal discord, he observed in November. American escalation in Vietnam and the Soviet build-up in Siberia were combining "to menace the security of China." So the Army "must be certain that there is no threat to its command structure," since "we would be in a plight if the enemies took us by surprise." Thus Hsu urged young soldiers to refrain from harassing their superiors:

> Give consideration to the very arduous administrative tasks shouldered by the leading cadres. You must give them time to direct their troops and to handle routine work. . . . Many are old men be-

tween the ages of fifty and sixty. Many are sick, yet they must make preparations for war at any time. You must have regard for their work and their health. This is not meant to impede your revolutionary action, but you should show concern for them whenever you can.[10]

But by the turn of the year, Mao was maneuvering to overcome the Army's recalcitrance by dividing its senior officers. On one hand, he encouraged the radicals to assail Ho Lung and the generals whom he considered to be his most implacable adversaries, while at the same time he undertook to reassure Yeh Chien-ying, Hsu Hsiang-ch'ien, and the professional soldiers that an Army commitment to the Cultural Revolution would not impair China's defense capabilities. In short, his design was to isolate a minority of his military opponents while appeasing a majority of the Army's leadership. This design was disclosed early in January in an editorial in the *Liberation Army Daily,* the military journal published under Lin Piao's guidance. The editorial announced that a "handful" of purported "reactionaries" who had "wormed their way into the Army" would be ousted. But because the Army "has the important responsibility of defending the motherland," the editorial cautioned, its "arrangements" for conducting the Cultural Revolution "should be different from those of other units." [11]

A Red Guard offensive against Ho Lung initiated in late December quickly attained large and somewhat ludicrous proportions. In Peking, wall posters, pamphlets, and other literature denounced Ho for everything from slandering Mao to indulging in sexual perversions. One brochure claimed that he had described Mao's doctrines as "no better than dogshit" and had forbidden his subordinates to study them. Another recalled that his older sister had been an opium-smoking bandit and, consequently, an "exponent of pure fuedalism." He was also accused of such "bourgeois" tastes as keeping pet monkeys and feasting on fat puppies. One Red Guard attack even asserted that Ho frequently slept with several prostitutes simultaneously.[12]

Though most of this vilification was distorted, there was probably some truth to the charge that Ho protected numerous relatives whom he had placed in influential positions. One of his sons had been instrumental in organizing the United Action Committee at

Tsinghua University early in the Cultural Revolution. Two of his nephews were high-ranking Army political commissars in Peking, and his brother-in-law, Li Ching-ch'üan, controlled the Communist Party apparatus in southwest China.[13] Trying to blacken Ho's image even further, Red Guards alleged that he had plotted a *coup d'état* against Mao in February 1966. The Maoist leaders knew this accusation to be false, yet it served their purpose to let it spread for several months before issuing a denial.[14]

Ho Lung was finished by the middle of January. Whether he was actually arrested has never been made clear. In early May, however, Red Guards arraigned him before a kangaroo court and, after briefly admitting his "errors" in customary style, he disappeared from public view.[15]

A similar assault was staged against Marshal Chu Teh, then eighty years old and the most venerated officer in the Communist movement. Chu Teh had been exalted in the past almost as highly as Mao—and even by Mao himself. But now he had apparently voiced misgivings about committing the Army to the Cultural Revolution, and this resistance exposed him to a spate of denunciations. The Red Guards labeled him a "swine" and a "big warlord," addicted to such "feudalistic hobbies" as raising orchids.[16] These Red Guard attacks also revealed, undoubtedly with some measure of accuracy, that Chu Teh had criticized the excesses of the Great Leap Forward in 1958. It was also likely, as the radicals claimed, that he had advocated increased reliance on military specialization in opposition to Mao's theories of guerrilla warfare.[17] The extent to which this assault could go was limited, however, since Chu Teh's prestige in the Army was enormous. Hence the campaign against him gradually faded, and he continued to appear at ceremonial occasions, mainly as a symbol of unity. In April 1969, when the Communist Party structure was revamped, he remained in the Politburo—though no longer on that body's powerful Standing Committee.

The campaigns against Ho Lung and Chu Teh were matched, meanwhile, by a sweeping purge of senior officers presumed to have opposed Army intervention in the Cultural Revolution. Among those dismissed were Hsu Kuang-ta, commander of the Armored Forces; Li Shou-hsuan, head of the Army's Railway Corps, and Wang Shang-jung, Director of Operations on the General Staff. These along with an impressive array of other officers had been associated with Ho Lung. One of them, Liao Han-sheng, a Vice-Minister of National Defense and First Commissar of the Peking Military Region, was Ho's nephew.[18] Paralleling this move, Mao fired the entire membership of the Army's own Cultural Revolution Directorate, including its head, Liu Chih-chien, who was specifically accused of having resisted the Chairman's plan for military intervention in his campaign.[19] In its place, Mao named a new group with Marshal Hsu Hsiang-ch'ien as its boss. The appointment of Marshal Hsu, who had been cool to the idea of Army involvement in the Cultural Revolution, was plainly aimed at placating the military professionals. Beyond that, Mao packed the group with his loyal disciples, among them Hsiao Hua, chief of the Army's General Political Department and a protégé of Lin Piao; Kuan Feng, a radical theoretician; and Yu Li-chin, political commissar of the Air Force. Another member of the group was Lin Piao's wife, Yeh Chun, who was then emerging as a dynamic leftist. And of course, there was Mao's wife, Chiang Ch'ing, an "adviser" to the new body.[20]

Mao was able to eliminate such a panoply of powerful foes because he had carefully taken measures beforehand to win the acquiescence of officers who were uneasy about the effects of the Cultural Revolution on China's defenses. He assured them that the Army's political role would not extend to sensitive frontier regions, and, to allay their fears of prolonged disruptions elsewhere in the nation, he apparently promised to put the Cultural Revolution on a more orderly course. Moreover, he issued written guarantees to back up these promises.

On January 28, five days after directing the Army to intervene in his drive, Mao decreed that the Cultural Revolution "should be postponed for the time being" in the coastal provinces facing Taiwan, in the southern areas adjacent to Vietnam, and along the northern border sector contiguous to the Soviet Union.[21] Though public Chinese propaganda was then still focused primarily against American "imperialism," Mao divulged in a private message to the Army leaders that he believed Soviet pressures on China were growing. Soviet air as well as ground operations in the vicinity of Sinkiang were increasing, he pointed out, and Chinese troops in that neighborhood "must be on guard and in a state of preparedness."[22]

Also in late January, Mao approved an eight-point directive

prohibiting the Red Guards from ransacking homes, compelling people to wear dunce's caps and placards, parading them through the streets, forcing them to kneel, and submitting them to other indignities.[23] The Red Guards were once again told to stop traveling around China, and were given deadlines to return to their native towns.[24] These orders had been issued before, but now the Army was authorized to enforce them. In addition, it was authorized to take control of provincial radio stations and the nation's civil airlines.[25]

While Mao saw military intervention in the Cultural Revolution as a positive boost to his radical followers, Chou En-lai apparently viewed the Army's involvement as a chance to restore order. But Chou had to exercise the same kind of delicate tact and diplomacy during this period that he had frequently displayed in earlier crises. He could not openly advocate military repression of the Red Guards without exposing himself to radical attacks, yet he could not encourage the radicals without intensifying the tumult he sought to avoid. His task, then, was to appear to stand on every side on all questions. He met this challenge with consummate skill, by making himself indispensable to Mao's inner circle as well as to the senior Army officers who were eager to keep the Cultural Revolution in check.

Judging from available evidence, both Mao and Lin Piao repeatedly relied on Chou to negotiate complicated problems with local military commanders. It was Chou, for example, who worked out a temporary settlement in late January among rival Army elements in Sinkiang.[26] He also played an important role in resolving similar disputes in Honan, Szechwan, and Kwangtung, and he was to serve as the key intermediary in the dramatic Army mutiny that erupted in July in the Yangtze River industrial complex of Wuhan. Mao may partly have depended upon Chou to deal with the Army because Lin Piao, who should have been supervising his military subordinates, lacked the Premier's diplomatic talents. Lin Piao was also a chronically sick man, often absent, and scarcely able even when available to devote long hours to tortuous talks with diverse factions. Lin's disappearance from public sight during the crucial months between November 1966 and April 1967 was apparently due to an illness that, according to his own disclosure, left his nerves badly frazzled.[27]

Mao could also count on Chou as a go-between with the Army because the Premier had many long-standing associations with the upper echelons of the Chinese military establishment. He had been head of the Political Department at Chiang Kai-shek's Whampoa Military Academy in the mid-1920s, at a time when the school's staff and student body included such future Communist military leaders as Marshals Yeh Chien-ying, Nieh Jung-chen, Hsu Hsiang-ch'ien, and Lin Piao. Chou had also been a major figure in the famous Nanchang Uprising on August 1, 1927, the first Communist attempt to seize and hold a Chinese city. His ties with China's senior officers were further cemented during the 1930s, when he served as the Red Army's chief political commissar. And, probably more important than these common experiences, Chou and the military high command tended to share a concern for maintaining China's stability in the face of recurrent Maoist adventures.

Although Mao issued his call to the Army to help the radicals on January 23, troops had actually begun to go into action weeks earlier—and, contrary to the Chairman's hopes, they did little to advance his cause. In fact, they either suppressed unruly Red Guards or tried to arrange compromises between rival factions. So, well before Mao's order was proclaimed, the Army had already started to contravene his wishes by restoring discipline to troubled areas. From the beginning, therefore, the Army's intervention significantly altered the direction of the Maoist campaign.

In early January, as clashes between radicals and Party *apparatchiks* spread, the Army had mobilized to protect various government installations and enterprises against the growing violence. On January 11, for instance, troops took over the banks in order to prevent workers, office employees, and others from withdrawing their deposits.[28] They also moved to guard local roads, bridges, factory warehouses, and, particularly, rural granaries, which were then being stormed by peasants in quest of rice, wheat, and other cereal stocks.[29] Soldiers assigned to these missions were assaulted by disorderly factions despite directives from Peking insisting that "no person or organization may attack" the Army.[30] Their patience worn thin, military units in several places reacted by cracking down on their assailants without regard for ideological nuances.

One of the first military thrusts aimed at disciplining unruly youths occurred in mid-January in the Hunan province capital of

Changsha, where Mao himself had been a radical student more than a half-century earlier. Soldiers there arrested Red Guards who had broken into the city's Party headquarters and were trying to besiege the local Army garrison.[31] A similar episode took place in the town of Fangshan, thirty miles southwest of Peking, where leftist youths were confronting the local Party machine. On instructions from Hsieh Fu-chih, the Minister of Public Security, truckloads of troops based in the capital drove into the town, halted the skirmish, and assumed police duties.[32] In both instances, Maoist spokesmen announced that the Army had intervened to suppress "counterrevolutionaries." In reality, the troops had moved mainly to stop the turmoil.

Far more crucial at the time, meanwhile, was the Army's involvement in two other regions—Heilungkiang province, in the heart of industrial Manchuria, and the northern province of Shansi. Military intervention in these areas had a drastic impact on the future shape of the Cultural Revolution.

Mao saw the Army's commitment to his radical disciples as a means rather than an end. His ultimate hope was that the radicals would overthrow the Party apparatus with Army support, and would then proceed to establish a Chinese equivalent of the Paris Commune—a system which in his view would make the state bureaucracy constantly responsive to the "masses," enfranchised as they were to revoke the mandates of their elected delegates at any moment. In short, he saw it as the perfect vehicle for perpetual revolution. Mao had welcomed the uprising at Peking University in the spring of 1966 as a portent that a new Commune was in the making. He had referred to the Commune again when he outlined the objectives of the Cultural Revolution. Now he observed developments in Shanghai, where the radicals were currently preparing to inaugurate their version of the Paris Commune.

But the Shanghai People's Commune, as its name would be, was having serious birth pains that would eventually make it stillborn. The vast number of radical factions were unable to unite as each group demanded representation in the Commune's potential ruling committee. Clamoring for power, each faction fought against the others and also against Chang Ch'un-ch'iao, the local Maoist leader, who was saddled with the unenviable task of putting the Commune together.[33] In the midst of this confusion, the creation of the new body was postponed day after day until February 5, when its formation was finally announced at a noisy rally.[34] By this time, though, the Commune concept was dead. For it was clear to everyone, including Mao, that the radicals were hopelessly inept unless firmly guided. Soon afterward Mao described the Shanghai situation as "bordering on anarchy," explaining that "we cannot manage without cadres and specialists." The Paris Commune was no longer his ideal—except, perhaps, for the remote future. Instead, he now advocated the establishment of so-called "triple alliances," formations that had initially been imposed by the Army in Shansi and Heilungkiang provinces to supplant the collapsing Party apparatuses.[35]

These coalitions were intended to comprise veteran officials, young radicals, and Army officers. The officials would provide indispensable administrative experience. The radicals would add revolutionary coloration. And, since power grows out of the muzzle of a gun, the officers would be responsible for setting up the new coalitions and preventing them from falling apart.

Formalized as Revolutionary Committees, the "triple alliances" were quickly endorsed in Peking as the model to be emulated everywhere, and, with great difficulty, they were gradually erected across China in the years that followed.

If the impulse for establishing the "triple alliances" plainly came from the Army, precisely how the formula was contrived has never been clear. The effort to create the new bodies was too swift, too uniform, and too coordinated to support the notion, widely publicized in the Maoist press, that local military units acted spontaneously. More likely, the regional commanders who set up the "triple alliances" in January were responding to directives from the highest echelons of the Chinese military establishment in Peking. According to one thesis, senior officers in the capital as well as moderate leaders like Chou En-lai conceded to Mao's call for Army intervention on condition that troops be used primarily to enforce discipline. If so, then Mao must have agreed to allow the Army to curb the radicals—even though his appeal for military involvement exhorted soldiers to support them.[36] And his agreement could have been contingent upon the Army's conduct in handling the situation in Shansi province.

Lying on a mountainous plateau more than four thousand feet above sea level, the Shansi provincial capital of Taiyuan had been the scene of intermittent clashes between Red Guard and Party groups for months. As elsewhere in China, the conflict there began to polarize more sharply in early January. The Party mobilized workers, students, peasants, and others against the Red Guards, reportedly strengthening them with money and, in some cases, weapons. The radicals, in turn, welded together twenty-five different factions. Fighting between the two sides escalated. The Party organizations encircled radical strongholds, routing out and beating their foes. In reaction, the Red Guards streamed through the city streets, breaking into the homes of suspected enemies and, according to their version of events, confiscating arms and ammunition.[37]

Local Army units had remained neutral throughout this turbulence. Finally, on January 12, some two thousand troops wheeled into action across the city. As a team of German engineers working in Taiyuan at the time later recalled, these troops bore automatic weapons and others carried rifles with fixed bayonets as they rode on trucks mounted with machine guns. Artillery and antiaircraft pieces were set up at strategic street corners. But not a shot was fired.[38] The provincial Party bureaucracy crumbled. And the radicals proclaimed that they had seized power.[39]

Oddly enough, this instance of military intervention went unpublicized until January 25, when Peking hailed it as an example of the Army's response to Mao's call. The delay suggests that the Shansi operation had been a test case, initiated to measure the Army's effectiveness in helping to topple a Party apparatus.

But despite claims by the radicals that they now wielded authority, it soon became apparent that real power in Shansi was invested in its military force. When the region's Revolutionary Committee was officially inaugurated in the middle of March, its chairman was not a newly emergent radical imbued with Maoist fervor but a veteran Party figure, Liu Ko-p'ing, a Muslim who had been the province vice-governor and chief political commissar of its military garrison. His deputies on the Committee included other Army commissars and local Party officials.[40] In short, though it purged certain Party *apparatchiks*, the Cultural Revolution in Shansi was less an overthrow of the old bureaucracy than a reshuffle of its members. And, while they would squabble among themselves for months to come, these leaders made it plain from the beginning that they had no intention of tolerating radical effervescence. Or, as a military spokesman described the Army's role in the province, troops had "strengthened the proletarian dictatorship and insured the establishment of revolutionary order." [41]

Even more decisive than Shansi was the birth of the Revolutionary Committee in Harbin, a key industrial and communications center in Manchuria. Developments there were important in two respects. The provincial Revolutionary Committee, set up on February 1, was the first "triple alliance" publicly endorsed by Peking, and it consequently superseded the abortive Shanghai Commune as the model formula for the nation. Moreover, its composition was unusual. The Committee's chairman, P'an Fu-sheng, not only was the former Party boss of the area, but years before had been purged as a "right-wing opportunist." Thus he hardly personified the Marxist orthodoxy. Yet his appointment to head the new Committee was deliberate—and it reflected an attempt to resolve a serious problem troubling the more moderate military and civilian leaders then coming to the fore in Peking in the wake of the destructive January upheaval.

Though the Army was moving to restore order in different regions, there was a pressing need for experienced officials to help to revive China's paralyzed administration. But officials who had faced Red Guard attacks were understandably afraid to expose themselves again to humiliating assaults. Like turtles sensing danger, they hesitated to stick their necks out. In addition, the young Maoist radicals were reluctant to relinquish their newly acquired authority to bureaucrats they had overthrown. And they, too, were in no mood to see the old officials stage a comeback. On one hand, therefore, the choice of a man like P'an Fu-sheng was calculated to demonstrate to wary officials that they were welcome to return to their posts. At the same time, his elevation served to remind the Red Guards that nobody was beyond redemption. This fresh policy of leniency for officials was spelled out in an authoritative *Red*

Flag editorial. "It must be soberly recognized that most cadres are good," the editorial declared, explaining that even those who had committed "serious mistakes" could "make amends" through education by the "masses." Moreover, the editorial went on, experienced officials were "more mature politically," had "greater organizational skill," and displayed "the ability to exercise power and administer work for the State." Without their guidance, the radicals resembled a leaderless "herd of dragons, each going his own way." Hence the moment had come for the Red Guards and other activities to cooperate with former officials.[42]

P'an Fu-sheng, then in his early sixties, did indeed exemplify the "renovated" Party *apparatchik*. As a senior official in Honan province, where Mao initially tested the Great Leap Forward in 1958, P'an had run into difficulties for resisting the Chairman's intensive collectivization program. According to an indictment published at the time, he had argued that the province was too poor and its population too apathetic to support accelerated collectivization. He reportedly complained that peasants were being turned into "beasts of burden," that "oxen are tied up while human beings are harnessed in the fields." As a result, P'an disappeared from sight until late 1962, when he emerged as head of the nation's Federation of Supply and Marketing Cooperatives.[43] By May 1966, he had regained stature as First Secretary of the Heilungkiang Communist Party Committee.

As elsewhere in China during the late summer and fall of 1966, Red Guards in Heilungkiang held mammoth rallies to denounce the local Party machine. And, as in other Chinese cities, the Party leaders in Harbin went through the motions of demonstrating their zeal for the Cultural Revolution. According to his own account, P'an Fu-sheng allowed himself to be criticized by the Red Guards and even went without food or sleep for four days as he submitted to the "remolding" of his ideological attitudes.[44]

By the turn of the year, the situation in the province had gotten out of hand. Student groups had been agitating for months. Demobilized soldiers, unreconciled to the rigors of farming and land reclamation in the northern parts of the region, now mobilized a so-called Glorious Veterans Army to demand improved conditions. Similarly, rusticated youths returned to Harbin to form a War

Preparedness Army. Industrial and transport workers created other movements, and soon Harbin was plunged into chaos.

Inevitably, the Army stepped in to halt the strife. As an official report made clear, it was the Army that put up P'an Fu-sheng as the head of the new Revolutionary Committee.[45] The Army's presence was also apparent not only in the person of the Vice-Chairman of the Committee, General Wang Chia-tao, military commander of the province, but in the keynote speaker at the ceremony inaugurating the Committee, Sung Jen-ch'iung, the Army's chief political commissar in the sector.[46]

Hailing the creation of the Heilungkiang triple alliance, Peking publicists emphasized that law, order, and discipline had triumphed. The *People's Daily* explained that it represented the "consolidation of the proletarian dictatorship" and, in a distinct switch from the days when Red Guards were being told that "rebellion is justified," the newspaper warned radicals to behave themselves. "It is entirely wrong," said the *People's Daily*, "to oppose everything, cast out everything, and strike down everything." [47]

Illustrating the advantages of stability, a document issued in Peking described the improvement that took place in the Harbin railway system after order was restored. Inadvertently, the document also disclosed the extent of the damage that had been inflicted on that same rail system by the riots that had roiled the city before the Army take-over. Prior to January 25, the document revealed, passenger train service between Harbin and the Shantung province city of Tsinan had been suspended for two months. Strikes by engineers and other workers put fifteen locomotives out of action for periods up to eighteen days, with the result that eight hundred freight cars were inoperative. More than six thousand tons of merchandise had piled up in one of Harbin's stations during the month of January. The disturbances also caused more than half of the freight and passenger traffic to run late, sometimes by a whole day. The Army presumably exerted considerable pressure on the Harbin transport workers to return to work and make up for the losses. For after the founding of the Heilungkiang Revolutionary Committee, the document claimed, railway operations in Harbin broke "the highest level in history." [48]

Matching its intervention in Shansi and Heilungkiang, the Army moved swiftly to impose order in Peking and elsewhere in China. On the night of February 12, for example, troops in the capital marched in formation to the headquarters of the Municipal Public Security Bureau, the city's central police authority, and occupied it amid the beating of drums and clashing of cymbals. The Peking military garrison then issued a communiqué announcing that police and public security personnel would henceforth function under Army auspices.[49] On the same day, the Army set up its first Military Control Commission in Peking, and similar bodies were quickly established in Shanghai, Canton, and other cities, where they effectively authorized local commanders to exercise police powers.[50] About the same time, the Army initiated military and ideological training programs in universities and schools.[51] Army control stretched out into the countryside as well, as soldiers obeyed instructions to supervise peasants and rural cadres in the spring plantings.[52] Not long afterward, troops moved into factories, mines, and other enterprises in order to enforce "labor discipline" and assure the rhythm of production.[53]

As a former employee of a paper mill in Canton has described the Army's involvement, soldiers succeeded in halting the turbulence that had inhibited industrial activity. But they also troubled the workers and interfered with management.[54] The East River Paper Mill, with nearly two thousand workers, was one of the largest and most modern in Canton, and its operations had been frequently interrupted in December and January for many reasons. Once, the mill stopped for three days for lack of electricity when a local power complex was reportedly sabotaged. It also slowed down from time to time as young workers, who had organized several Red Guard factions inside the factory, left to "exchange revolutionary experiences around the country." Production often ceased as workers staged demonstrations, attended rallies, or squabbled among themselves. Finally, in late February, a so-called Military Work Team arrived, comprised of two hundred unarmed soldiers. Their chief was an Army political commissar, and he rapidly asserted his command over the plant. One of his initial acts was to demote both the factory's Party boss and its personnel director to common workers on the vague grounds that they had "abused their authority." He then established a plant committee along the lines of a "triple alliance," with twelve soldiers among its thirty members. He also dispersed troops throughout the mill, assigning two or three men to every dormitory and putting two noncommissioned officers in each of the plant's five workshops as monitors.

But if this military presence in the East River Paper Mill served to maintain order, it failed to inspire the workers. Most of the soldiers were from Hunan and other provinces north of Canton and, speaking an alien dialect, could not communicate with the plant employees. In addition, though they were not harsh, the troops behaved like overseers. The commander of the Military Work Team also interfered with the management of the mill. Eager to increase the plant's production in order to dramatize the virtues of Army control, he instructed the mill superintendent at one point to turn out an inferior grade of paper more quickly. The superintendent initially refused but under pressure finally complied. Still, there had seemed to be no plausible alternative to Army supervision of the mill. "Conditions were so confused," the former employee said, "that the place would have fallen apart if the soldiers had not come in."

The Army's intervention elsewhere was bolstered by a series of admonitions from Peking telling the radicals to restrain themselves. In early February, Chou En-lai openly castigated an assembly of Red Guards for their chaotic and "arrogant" conduct. He said that their violence had alienated a "great many people" who might have otherwise been won over to the Maoist cause. It was better to "conquer the hearts" of adversaries than to "scratch their skins," Chou explained, and warned against tormenting officials whose "errors" could be "reformed." [55] Somewhat later, Chou criticized a group of young radicals even more forcefully when he disclosed that Red Guards had killed Chan Lin-chih, Minister of Coal Industry, after submitting him to forty days of public criticism and torture.[56]

Similar expressions of concern were echoed by Maoist zealots in Peking. Even the most dogmatic members of the Cultural Revolution Directorate, like Wang Li, cautioned that "anarchy is the biggest danger at the moment." [57] Mao himself voiced disappointment in the "little red generals," as he had originally called the Red Guards. Among other things, he remarked in one talk, they were being corrupted by "money" and "cars," wasting their time at "too many rallies," and displaying "sectarian" tendencies as they squabbled among themselves for power.[58] On another occasion, urging the radicals to show "more dignity and justice" toward their foes, Mao said:

> Slogans put up in Peking are of low quality. They refer repeatedly to "smashing the heads of dogs." There surely cannot be so many dogs' heads. They are all human heads. Posters of this sort are difficult for the masses to understand. Pictures of people being pilloried, with their arms twisted behind their backs like jet airplanes, have been published and transmitted abroad by foreign correspondents.
>
> The level of the struggle is too low. We must educate the next generation. If not, it will resort to the same low tactics. What is important is to fight on the political level.[59]

Expressing the Peking hierarchy's disenchantment with the Red Guards, an article published jointly in the *People's Daily* and the *Liberation Army Daily* diagnosed the radicals' principal shortcomings. They suffered from "ultra-democracy and liberalism," which were "corrosives" that "eat away unity, subvert organization, cause apathy, and create dissension," as well as damage "strict discipline and alienate the leadership from the masses." Another affliction of the Red Guards was their "pursuit of the limelight," which drove factions and individuals to assert themselves rather than work "anonymously." The Red Guards also displayed symptoms of a "mountain-stronghold mentality," defined as the obsession of certain radicals to "control a small unit and proclaim themselves the rulers" as they strove for "hegemony and power." In addition, the article said, there was the "sectarianism" of radicals who "tend only to see the things under their noses and concern themselves only with their own small groups" while disregarding the interests of the entire nation. These propensities could be summed up in a single word—"ego." And, the article warned, "they cause the revolutionary ranks to disintegrate, to waver, to lose their fighting power, and to fail to unite, and they may eventually lead the revolution to doom." [60]

The authorities in Peking did more than merely speak out

against the more virulent young activists. They also decreed the dissolution of several Red Guard organizations, and their switch to moderation was punctuated by a baffling change in ideological labels. Groups like the Red Worker Rebels and the National Construction Army Rebels were now disbanded for such allegedly "reactionary" activities as intruding into government offices, plundering state property, and raiding private homes.[61] Directives also commanded the radical young people not only to return to their universities and schools but, once there, to undergo a "painful process of protracted ideological struggle" in order to overcome their "egotistical inclinations.[62] In late February, moreover, Peking instructed the panoply of diverse factions in the capital to merge in a single Red Guard Congress.[63] Publicized as a move to cement and strengthen the radicals, the formation of the Congress was obviously contrived to facilitate control over the disparate Red Guard splinter groups then resisting efforts to restrict their freedom. In short, having uncorked the Red Guards, the Chinese leaders were now trying to force them back into the bottle.

A stream of fresh decrees also poured forth from Peking urging forgiveness for most Party officials, whose services were desperately needed to stabilize the country. Effectively reversing the earlier exhortations to youths to "bombard" the Party bureaucracy, Mao and his associates now stressed that seasoned officials must be respected and even obeyed. In a major policy declaration published in late February, for example, *Red Flag* unequivocally laid down this line. Extremists were laboring under the "misconception" that "all those in authority are not good . . . and should therefore be overthrown," the journal said. The tendency was to assault an official for a "single fault" without considering his merits, "to seize only his mistakes, willfully exaggerate them, and carelessly brand him with unwarranted labels." But this approach was "completely wrong. . . . It would be very dangerous if the scope of attack were erroneously expanded and the spearhead of the struggle were directed against the broad sections of cadres." *Red Flag* demanded, consequently, that the Red Guards accept the guidance of the Party *apparatchiks* they had formerly been cited to denounce. "If the masses alone are active without a strong leading group to organize their activity properly, such activity cannot be sustained

] 295 [

for long, or carried forward in the right direction, or raised to a high level." [64]

Variations on this theme were repeated throughout China's provinces. In the city of Tsingtao, for instance, radicals were derided for spreading the "fallacious view" that all officials were opposed to Mao.[65] A directive issued in the southern province of Kweichow condemned the Red Guards for indiscriminately assailing local functionaries, claiming that most officials had "good backgrounds" even though they may have "made some mistakes" early in the Cultural Revolution.[66] The new line was also publicized in Shanghai, where the radicals now conceded that they had aborted their attempt in January to create a Commune. The purpose of the Cultural Revolution, they now said, was "not merely to dismiss people from office." [67] Somewhat reluctantly, they echoed the exhortation to welcome selected officials into a "triple alliance" to govern the city.[68]

Though they had recognized the necessity for disciplining unruly Red Guards, the Maoist leaders in Peking were certainly not in favor of eliminating the radicals from positions of power. Yet, by early March, it was becoming apparent that military commanders in many areas were taking advantage of their new authority to ostracize and even suppress the Red Guards and other radical activists. Noting this trend, the Maoists warned that even though some radicals displayed "shortcomings or errors," it was "imperative" to give them "full weight," heed their "opinions," and "never regard them as simply the supporting cast" in the drama of the Cultural Revolution.[69] But the Army had extended its domination across the country and showed no signs of placating the radicals.

CHAPTER 13

The Army Attempts to Rule

The situation in China today resembles the situation in 1949, when the country was under military control.

—CHOU EN-LAI, *February 1967*

"THE PROLETARIAN POLITICAL POWER was seized by us with rifles, and it will be defended by us with rifles," a military unit in Shantung province had announced on January 28, and that proud proclamation summed up the Army's attitude throughout China.[1]

Troops had moved into factories and rural communes to supervise industrial and agricultural production. Since February 11, when they took over the Public Security Bureau in Peking, soldiers had assumed police duties in several cities. Military Control Commissions, designed to formalize the Army's influence, were also being set up in almost every provincial capital. Troops were running radio stations in Peking and other places and, in late February, they were reported to be in control of four provincial newspapers as well as the *Peking Daily*, the organ of the Party's municipal apparatus in the national capital. They were managing airports and railway stations, guarding warehouses, and even handling freight in the port of Shanghai.[2] On March 30, Lin Piao estimated in a private speech that more than thirty Army divisions—nearly four hundred thousand men—were being deployed to run China's essential services. "Nothing like this has happened in the past seventeen years," he remarked.[3]

In addition, the five tripartite Revolutionary Committees which had been established by early spring were basically dominated by Army officers with veteran Party officials as their main subordinates. The Shantung Committee, founded on February 3, was headed by Wang Hsiao-yu, the local Army political commissar, with the regional military commander as his deputy. The chairman of the Kweichow Committee established ten days later, Li Tsai-han, was also the Army political commissar in his area—as was Liu Ko-p'ing, the boss of the Shansi province "triple alliance" set up on March 18. Created on February 24, the Shanghai Revolutionary Committee was led by a prominent Maoist civilian, Chang Ch'un-ch'iao, who had been instrumental in ousting the city's old Party apparatus. But seven of the Shanghai Committee's thirteen "leading members," as they were called, were infantry, Air Force, and Navy officers.[4] There was nothing illusory in the Army's contention that it constituted "the pillar of the proletarian dictatorship." [5]

Plainly an illusion, however, was the propaganda that sought to disseminate the myth that the Army was boosting the Red Guards into positions of authority, as Mao had hoped. For in fact, local commanders in several regions were cracking down on disorderly youths in most vigorous fashion. In many provinces, the casualties inflicted by the Army on Red Guards and other radicals ran into the thousands. This brutality created the impression, particularly among observers in the West, that Chinese Army troops were no different from, say, the Indonesian soldiers who had slaughtered an estimated half-million suspected Communists in Java and Bali in 1965 and 1966. But the Chinese military establishment was different, and its participation in the Cultural Revolution was complicated.

The Chinese Army was far from a police force. Decades of indoctrination, combined with their unique experience, had endowed its officers with a sense of dedication to revolution. At the same time, however, Army commanders believed in the necessity of a strong China. Only to a certain degree would they tolerate disruption. As they strove to organize the tripartite Revolutionary Committees, therefore, Army officers found themselves caught in a dilemma. By and large they welcomed the compromise arrangements, yet they could not overcome a whole array of problems that made truly authentic "triple alliances" almost impossible to achieve.

Innumerable radical factions were still as undisciplined as a "herd of dragons." Despite the many efforts to unite them, they could not agree on acceptable representatives to sit on the Revolutionary Committees. Meanwhile, Peking's appeals to the Red Guards and to Party officials to cooperate on the Committees were predictably falling flat. Confronted by this fragmentation of Red Guard and Party factions, the Army was unable to form more than six Revolutionary Committees in China's twenty-nine provinces and municipalities from the formation of the Heilungkiang Committee on January 31 to the birth of a triple tripartite body in Peking on April 20, and these were essentially façades concocted to camouflage military control. Regional Army commanders in most other parts of the country could not even erect such façades. For their efforts to appear devoted to the revolution were basically incompatible with their determination to impose order. Hence they aggravated the chaos they were seeking to curb.

In several areas, the Army backed relatively conservative factions, often offshoots of groups that local Party machines had mobilized months earlier, when they were going through the motions of subscribing to the Cultural Revolution. Sometimes, Army commanders deliberately chose to support these factions because of their own close ties with the Party apparatus. But this tactic inevitably intensified friction at the provincial levels. For one thing, rival factions assailed the military-supported groups and even attacked the Army itself. On occasions, too, the Army was itself divided about which faction to back, and clashes would erupt among military units loyal to competing groups. Elsewhere, the turbulence was exacerbated by the Army's sincere inability to distinguish between "true" and "false" radicals, since everyone spouted the Maoist litany with equal fervor. Commanders who favored one faction courted the risk of drawing fire from other groups, while officers who tried to remain neutral were accused of opposing the Cultural Revolution.[6] In Canton, the military garrison conceived a simple solution to this problem. It set itself up as the sole arbiter of ideological purity, declaring that "the difference between a genuine and a fake revolutionary lies in his attitude toward the Army."[7] And, on the basis of that tenet, the Canton commander proceeded to suppress any element that seemed to resist his dictates.

Years later, Mao would concede that it was difficult even for him to "sort out" his foes from his followers during the zigzags of the Cultural Revolution.[8] In the spring of 1967, however, he must have perceived that his dream of spawning a new species of "Communist man" was as far from attainment as it had ever been. Many Party officials remained unresponsive to his efforts to win their allegiance out of fear that they might be subjected to renewed denunciation. The Red Guards were no longer model "revolutionary successors" but a collection of mobs struggling to fulfill individual ambitions. The Army, against its own principles, had been largely reduced to a constabulary. In a talk to a Red Guard assembly in late March, Lin Piao said:

> There are casualties in all revolutions, so let us not exaggerate the seriousness of this situation. Many people have committed suicide or been killed. But these deaths are fewer than those incurred during the Japanese war and the Civil War, or in natural disasters. Thus our gains are greater than our losses.[9]

Much of the initial fighting between radicals and military units during the late winter and early spring of 1967 had been concentrated in China's coastal and border provinces. In deference to the Army's professional officers, who were concerned by the threat of external attack, Mao had decreed that the Cultural Revolution "should be postponed for the time being" in these vulnerable areas. But just as Mao's word was insufficient to deter extremist Red Guards aflame with the fires of rebellion, so it offered a convenient pretext to the Army to repulse the radicals ruthlessly.

One of the most prolonged of the provincial civil wars to rage during the Cultural Revolution started about this time in the Kwangsi-Chuang Autonomous Region, an area of southern China adjacent to Vietnam. The Kwangsi region is a poor, mountainous subtropical province partly populated by the Chuangs, a people ethnically akin to the Thais, and it had long been noted for its instability, its dissident secret societies, and its bandit sects. It was from Kwangsi, for example, that the Taiping rebels launched their devastating insurgency in the middle of the nineteenth century. Later in the nineteenth century, the province was a cockpit for European imperialist competition as the British moved down from Hong Kong to set up river trading stations at Wuchow and

Nanning while the French, their missionaries in the vanguard, pushed up from Indochina. The rebellious Chuang spirit surfaced again in January 1967, when local Red Guards attempted to wrest power from the region's Party apparatus. But they met a formidable adversary in Wei Kuo-ching, an ethnic Chuang who, as both Party boss and the Army's political commissar there, had ruled the region virtually single-handedly. Apparently anxious to avoid trouble in a province adjoining Vietnam, the Maoist leaders in Peking endorsed Wei Kuo-ching's decision to suppress the radicals. But in his crackdown on the Red Guards, Wei Kuo-ching unwittingly solidified widespread radical opposition to his military establishment. A conflict thus began in Kwangsi between the Red Guards and the Army that, among its other effects, disrupted the flow of Chinese Communist supplies to North Vietnam. A year later, the conflict would reach a dramatic climax in a battle which destroyed half of the city of Wuchow and took thousands of lives.[10]

A similar sequence of events took place during the same period in Yunnan, another province bordering on Vietnam. Here the Party boss, Yen Hung-yen, had committed suicide in January 1967 after unsuccessfully trying to resist Red Guard harassment. His death spelled the collapse of the provincial Party apparatus, and local radical factions coalesced quickly to fill the power vacuum. But like the Army in Kwangsi, the Yunnan military garrison moved swiftly to curb the radicals while claiming that it was "supporting the left" in conformity with Mao's instructions. Under the command of General Chin Chi-wei, Army officers dissolved or reorganized local Red Guard factions, and dispatched the most incorrigible radicals to remote rural villages to work as laborers.[11] But the Red Guard groups were strong enough to respond, and, according to some evidence, they were supported by troops that had broken away from the garrison. Armed clashes involving youths, workers, peasants, and soldiers gradually grew in intensity through the spring until, in late May, a major battle erupted in the province capital of Kunming. By early 1968 as many as eighty thousand lives were said to have been lost throughout the province.[12]

In Fukien province, long considered by the Communists to be the logical beachhead for an invasion by Chiang Kai-shek's Nationalists, local Army units were evidently sanctioned by Peking to repel the Red Guards with comparable ferocity. As elsewhere in China, the Fukien radicals had gone into action around the turn of the year, seizing the Party newspaper and the main radio station as well as government offices, factories, and other enterprises. Emboldened by their success, they had gone on to assault the region's Army installations. On two occasions in late January, radical youths stormed the military headquarters in Fuchow, the province capital, kidnaping and beating up soldiers. The Army counterattacked in early February, compelling various Red Guard factions to lay down their weapons and unite under military control. This brief restoration of order was initially welcomed by the Maoist leaders in Peking, in the mistaken belief that the diverse Fukien groups had formed a "triple alliance." But the temporary truce between the Army and the radicals in the area soon crumbled, and chronic strife continued to nag the region.[13]

Meanwhile, three especially worrisome frontier areas were Sinkiang, Inner Mongolia, and Tibet. These areas were not only vulnerable to foreign threats, but each had a background of internal instability stemming from the resistance of its ethnic minorities to Han Chinese rule. To a degree that seriously troubled the Peking leaders, moreover, this ethnic resistance was related to the external threats. In northwestern Sinkiang, the Uighurs, Kazakhs, and other Muslim minorities had long been encouraged by the Soviet Union to oppose Chinese cultural assimilation and political domination. Similarly, the inhabitants of Inner Mongolia were constantly exposed to propaganda from the People's Republic of Mongolia, a Soviet satellite, evoking the glories of Genghis Khan and the heritage of Mongol nationalism. Recurrent insurgencies had plagued Tibet ever since the Communist conquest in 1951, and in more recent years, the Peking government had reason to suspect, Tibetan rebels were being inspired by India and perhaps armed and financed by the United States Central Intelligence Agency. As they saw it, in short, national interest took precedence over ideology where China's security was concerned. Thus they tolerated the Army's repression of Red Guards and other young extremists.

In an effort to stop the violence that had erupted in Sinkiang in January, the Peking leaders had issued a directive on February 11 calling a halt to the Cultural Revolution there. Red Guards and other student radicals were told to return to school and prohibited from political proselytizing outside their own institutions of learning. They were also forbidden from attacking Army units, such as the Production and Construction Corps. The directive flatly declared that "elements that have seized power and stolen weapons and ammunition shall be treated as counterrevolutionaries and arrested." [14] The ordinance prescribed as well that military units cease their political activity, contending that this would interfere with "war preparations," presumably to defend China against the Soviet Union.

This edict effectively lent support to General Wang En-mao, the Sinkiang Party boss and Army commander. With Peking's obvious approval, Wang proceeded to crack down on the radicals. Troops took over the region's newspapers, radio stations, and railways and the Army staged a rally in Urumchi, the Sinkiang capital, at which seven alleged "counterrevolutionaries" were paraded before a crowd of forty thousand. [15]

But the Sinkiang situation did not remain stable for long. Frustrated by the curbs imposed upon them, the radical Red Guards continued to assail Wang En-mao and his supporters. Clashes between rival factions broke out, and, aggravating the tension, the regional military establishment split as General Tso Chi, the Army's First Deputy Political Commissar, sided with the radicals against Wang. Thousands of young people who had been exiled to Sinkiang fled back to their native cities. In the meantime, as it had in the spring of 1962, the Soviet Union accelerated its attempts to incite the Muslim minorities to rise up against their Chinese rulers. Beamed across the border from Tashkent and Alma Ata, where there were large Muslim communities, Uighur-language radio broadcasts denounced Mao's "Han chauvinism" and urged the Sinkiang minorities to escape to the "happy life" in the Soviet Union. [16] According to some evidence, the Soviet authorities secretly began to infiltrate weapons, portable radios, and other equipment to Muslim guerrilla bands operating in the Tien Shan range of Sinkiang. [17]

Inner Mongolia, like Sinkiang, had long been beset by problems arising from the fears of its indigenous Mongols that they would lose their ethnic identity. These fears had a basis in reality. Since 1958, Peking had been carrying on a program of assimilation aimed at eradicating what was called the "local nationalism" of the Mongols. Instruction in the Chinese language was made mandatory in the area's primary schools. Mongol officials were replaced by Chinese functionaries. And, through an intensive immigration policy, Chinese were moved into the province until, by the late 1960s, they outnumbered the Mongols by an estimated ratio of twelve to one. As an incentive to emigrate into the region, Chinese farmers were given land confiscated from Mongol shepherds. This added to Mongol resentment and contributed to the potential volatility of the province.[18]

One local leader who sensed these dangers was Inner Mongolia's Party boss, Ulanfu, a veteran Mongol Communist who had been educated in Moscow and Peking. As early as 1951, he had urged the Han Chinese to "respect the equal rights and opinions of national minorities," and he worked strenuously throughout the mid-1960s to protect the rights of Mongols.[19] His nationalistic attitudes inevitably made him the target of Maoist attacks when the Cultural Revolution gathered momentum in the fall of 1966. But supported by the Army in Huhehot, the regional capital, Ulanfu fought back.

In the middle of January, inspired by Red Guard actions in other parts of China, Maoist radicals in Huhehot occupied the telegraph office, the railway station, the principal newspaper office, and several government buildings, proclaiming that they had "seized power." Faced with this threat to his authority, Ulanfu instructed the Army to react. Bristling with machine guns and artillery, troops from the city garrison surrounded the local Red Guard headquarters and forced the youths to surrender.[20] In the days after that, soldiers and radicals clashed frequently. On February 5, when the Red Guards staged a rally to protest against Army repression, soldiers fired into their ranks, killing several students. This ignited new Red Guard riots, and again the Army responded with force. Fresh military units wheeled into Huhehot, arresting both local leaders and agitators who had come into the city from Peking. The troops also smashed the Red Guards' propaganda equipment and decreed a ban on their activities.

Alarmed by this situation, Chou En-lai instructed representatives of the different Inner Mongolian factions to meet with him in Peking. In contrast to General Wang En-mao, the Sinkiang commander who had confidently gone to the capital, Ulanfu suspected a trap. He refused to attend Chou's meeting, but instead sent a delegate. The result of the parley, held on February 16, was a truce that lasted only two weeks. Calculating that Chou's intervention had merely been a ruse designed to gain time, Ulanfu again ordered his troops to arrest the radicals who had been released following the truce. His next step was to establish an Inner Mongolia Revolutionary Committee under his own leadership—and without Peking's approval.

In the view of the Peking Maoists, there was only one answer to this challenge—military force. General T'eng Hai-ch'ing, Deputy Commander of the Peking Garrison, was directed to lead the Twenty-first Army from neighboring Shensi province into Inner Mongolia. Other Army units were deployed in the area. The operation now had all the aspects of a civil war. By April 7, apparently having encountered little resistance, T'eng Hai-ch'ing had taken control of Huhehot. Martial law was declared and a curfew imposed. A week later, the government in Peking removed Ulanfu from office and placed General T'eng in command of the province. Thus Inner Mongolia came under the supervision of military men apparently loyal to the Maoist leadership.[21] For months, these officers coped with the dual problem of repressing radicals who refused to submit to discipline and of fighting off supporters of Ulanfu, many of whom were stimulated by a spirit of Mongol nationalism to continue the struggle against Han Chinese domination. This spirit was well expressed in the name that Ulanfu's sympathizers gave to their resistance organization. They called it the Genghis Khan Combat Corps.[22]

In Tibet, meanwhile, the Army headed by General Chang Kuo-hua worked consistently to restrain both local radicals and Red Guards who had come there from Peking. Having commanded the first Chinese Communist troops to conquer Tibet in 1951, General Chang had been there ever since—and he may well have regarded the area as his personal domain. During the summer of 1966, he had permitted Red Guards to release their revolutionary energies by invading ancient Tibetan temples and monasteries, destroying religious paintings, books, printing blocks, statues, and treasures that the Communists considered to be "feudal relics." But drawing the line at any challenge to his own authority, he kept the radicals on a tight political leash, warning them against "making trouble" and, rephrasing Mao's earlier slogan, told them that "it is forbidden to bombard our proletarian revolutionary headquarters." [23] Like entrenched Party officials and Army officers elsewhere in China, he also mobilized his own student organizations to counter his radical adversaries.

Despite the distance between Lhasa and Peking, there were leaders in the capital who appreciated Chang Kuo-hua's attempts to keep peace in Tibet. One was Premier Chou En-lai. In October 1966, Chou had decreed that young radicals from Peking and other parts of the country were not to enter Tibet to "exchange revolutionary experiences." But Mao's wife, Chiang Ch'ing, quietly countermanded Chou's decree by authorizing five Peking youth groups to go to Tibet, where they formed a coalition called the Metropolitan Revolutionary Rebels. Apparently at Chang Kuo-hua's behest, Chou issued another directive ordering the Peking radicals to return home. The young people appealed to Chiang Ch'ing for permission to stay, and once again undermining Chou, she granted their request.[24] By early 1967, claiming that he was trying to turn Tibet into a "watertight independent kingdom," the radicals were clamoring for Chang Kuo-hua's dismissal.[25] With the same idea in mind, Chiang Ch'ing and her comrades on the Cultural Revolution Directorate summoned Chang to Peking for "consultations." No doubt because he sensed a maneuver to purge him, he refused.[26]

Throughout the fall of 1966, the war between Chang Kuo-hua and the Red Guards in Tibet had been primarily verbal. In late January 1967, however, Mao's edict to the Army to intervene in the Cultural Revolution provided Chang with the pretext to direct his troops against the obstreperous Red Guards. On February 7, he brought the Army's 155th Division into Lhasa and proceeded to arrest four hundred youths, killing one and wounding a number of others in the roundup. He also imposed martial law, set up military checkpoints at the city gates, and closed traffic on the roads leading east to Szechwan and north to Tsinghai.[27] When the Red Guards attempted to counterattack, Chang deployed Chinese and Tibetan troops against them, killing scores of youths in several days of street fighting.[28] One witness to the repression, though biased in favor of the radicals, described the treatment meted out by soldiers to a captive Red Guard. His hands pinioned behind his back, the youth was brought into the Lhasa military headquarters and then, according to the witness,

> Ten men surrounded him, and began to beat him savagely. Some pulled his hair, others grabbed him by the neck and still others struck his head with their pistols. They punched his face, his chest, and his back. Soon his face was a mass of blood and flesh swollen out of shape. They tore his clothes and kicked him in the groin until he fell to the floor, and then they trampled on his stomach and chest. After that, they carried him away to a cell.[29]

During the ensuing month, according to reports from Lhasa, Chang Kuo-hua's troops systematically cracked down on the Red Guards, seizing their documents, cameras, and printing presses, and arresting their leaders.[30] On February 26, the Peking leadership confirmed that Chang was really a faithful Maoist, and instructed all Red Guards in the region to give him their cooperation.[31] A week later, the Army command in Lhasa staged a victory celebration at which one speaker, in a skillful demonstration of Communist mirror-language, denounced the radicals for having "colluded with landlords, rich peasants, bad elements, counterrevolutionaries, rightists, and American and Chiang Kai-shek agents . . . in their vain attempt to rebel against the proletariat." [32] On March 8, complying with a Peking order, the Metropolitan Revolutionary Rebels who had invaded the area finally embarked for home as Army-supported factions shouted at their send-off: "Farewell to the god of plague." [33] Two months later, General Chang Kuo-hua was transferred to a more important and far tougher assignment—as political and military boss of turbulent Szechwan.

Szechwan was also experiencing an extraordinary upheaval during the early months of 1967, and the self-sufficient nature of the province made its disorder crucial. For Szechwan had all the attributes of a separate state. To the Maoist leaders in Peking, the specter of an autonomous Szechwan serving as an enemy base of operations was real and frightening. Moreover, the power of the Szechwan Party machine seemed to lend plausibility to this prospect. The Szechwan Party chief, Li Ching-ch'üan, was Marshal Ho Lung's brother-in-law, and he was also close to Teng Hsiao-p'ing, the Party Secretary General, who had formerly served in Szechwan. The Maoists therefore made a special effort to topple Li's apparatus.

But Li was a formidable foe. In November, he had gone to Peking to pledge his loyalty to Mao, obtaining the Chairman's blessing in exchange for the vow that he would "obey the masses." [34] With that endorsement, Li had mobilized his own worker and student factions as a defensive force, claiming that they were the real Maoists. He also went through the motions of submitting to the rituals of the Cultural Revolution, explaining to his associates that the key to survival was "unlimited patience and sham confessions." [35] Demonstrating this stratagem on one occasion, he played out a scene that might have come from a Chinese opera. He allowed himself to be marched through the streets of the province capital to a meeting at which he abjectly admitted his "sins." That the performance was a subterfuge was clear from the fact that it was held under the auspices of one of Li's own organizations.[36]

By late January, however, Li Ching-ch'üan no longer felt it necessary to rely on such subtle maneuvers. Mao's edict to the Army gave him the authorization he needed to direct troops against his opponents. Beginning in early February, the Army in Szechwan inaugurated a series of forays against the Red Guards that gradually escalated into a crescendo of violence by the middle of spring. Most of the initial action occurred in Chengtu and Chungking, the former Nationalist headquarters on the Yangtze River. Troops set up checkpoints at the gates of both cities, arresting Red Guards as they tried to leave or enter. In some instances, they strafed vehicles filled with youths attempting to break the cordon, and they reacted strongly against counterattacks on police and military installations. When a contingent of Red Guards stormed the Public Security Bureau office in Chengtu, soldiers quickly quelled the assault and went on to punish a number of youths publicly in order to discourage others. They stripped them naked, bound their hands behind their backs, paraded them through the city, and, as an added touch, compelled the captive youths to wear their Red Guard arm bands.[37]

On February 8, Li Ching-ch'üan staged another charade by prompting his faithful factions to proclaim that they had "seized power" in the province in accordance with Mao's dictates.[38] A week later, skillfully employing Maoist phrases to justify its repressive measures, the Szechwan military command declared that anyone attempting to "turn the spearhead of the struggle against the Army" would be subjected to "all the serious consequences arising therefrom." [39] Though the Peking leaders later denounced the declaration as a forgery—Chiang Ch'ing burned it publicly— they probably approved it at the time. For, in all likelihood, they believed that Li Ching-ch'üan and the Army were carrying out their instructions. The rare references to Szechwan in the official Peking press during February noted with satisfaction that provincial troops had organized so-called Mao Tse-tung Thought Propaganda Teams to help the "masses" understand the need for discipline.[40] Peking also appeared to be pleased with an Army program to assist peasants in the spring planting. Early in March, indeed, one of the members of the Cultural Revolution Directorate was even reported to have praised Li Ching-ch'üan and his comrades as "comparatively good people and able men." [41]

During this period, however, Li Ching-ch'üan and his Army colleagues in Szechwan were strenuously consolidating their position. They rounded up thousands of Red Guards, compiled dossiers on them, and staged rallies against their leaders. Provincial soldiers made a special effort to arrest Liu Chieh-t'ing and his wife, Chang Hsi-t'ing, who had been squabbling with the local Party apparatus for years. Troops ransacked their home and lavishly labeled Liu "the greatest counterrevolutionary in the southwest." But, as he had before, Liu managed to elude capture by fleeing to Peking, where he later succeeded in persuading the Maoist leaders to alter their benign attitude toward the Szechwan situation.[42] By the end of March, though, more than twenty thousand Red Guards had been jailed in Chengtu, and an estimated hundred thousand were imprisoned throughout the province. According to radical accounts, so many young people were under arrest that the Army kept them confined in old temples or corralled in city parks.[43]

An extremely complex tangle developed at about the same time in Honan province, the rich wheat-growing province straddling the

Yellow River in central China. Here, as elsewhere in the country, Red Guards and other young radicals had harassed the local Party bureaucracy throughout the fall of 1966, but with little success. The Honan Party had been largely able to withstand the assaults because its former boss, Liu Chien-hsun, had been appointed Secretary of the Peking Municipal Party Committee in September and he presumably used his influence in the capital to protect his provincial comrades.[44] But in early 1967, the political situation in Honan became almost indescribably complicated. A wide array of youth factions formed two rival alliances. One of them, the Honan Provincial Revolutionary Rebels Command, was evidently backed by the local Army garrison. The other was apparently created by the provincial Party.

On February 7, the Party-supported coalition grabbed control of the newspaper as well as government bureaus in Chengchow, the province capital, claiming to be the new authority in the province. To commemorate its purported *coup d'état*, the coalition baptized itself the February 7 Commune. The leaders of the Cultural Revolution in Peking, possibly recalling the miscarriage of the highly publicized Shanghai Commune, greeted the event with silence. But in Honan, the Revolutionary Rebels Command charged immediately that this was a hoax staged by entrenched Party *apparatchiks* anxious to preserve their positions. They also alleged that Liu Chien-hsun had deviously manipulated the coup in an effort to defend his own predominance.[45] At that, the rival groups began skirmishing. In the first fight, which broke out at the office of the *Honan Daily* as members of the February 7 Commune seized the newspaper, more than three hundred people were injured.[46] During the following weeks, the February 7 Commune went on to assail the region's senior Army officers, calling them a "handful of swine" for suppressing students. Even more daringly, its activists attacked military installations at an air force base outside Chengchow and attempted to infiltrate an artillery school located in the city.[47] The violence continued to escalate.

As viewed by Mao's inner circle in Peking, the Honan predicament was difficult to resolve. On one hand, the provincial military commanders could not be censured, since they had carried out the current Maoist line of imposing law and order. Some of the Peking leaders may have also believed that condemning the Army might provoke a military mutiny—as would indeed occur in the city of Wuhan only a few months later. But at the same time, they could not indict the February 7 Commune, since it was closely linked to Liu Chien-hsun, who stood in favor in Peking. Finally, Chou En-lai undertook to mediate the dispute—and his effort was a dismal failure.

On February 17, Chou telegraphed an order to Chengchow instructing the Army to separate the rival factions in the city, take over the *Honan Daily* and suspend publication, and select delegates from the competing groups to be sent to Peking to meet with him.[48] When they assembled in the capital ten days later, however, spokesmen for the squabbling Honan organization could not reconcile their differences even under Chou En-lai's diplomatic auspices. Instead, they accused each other of "bourgeois" and "counterrevolutionary" heresies, and they all chanted Maoist catechisms to prove their ideological purity.[49] Despite its failure, though, the meeting in Peking worked in favor of the Army in two respects. First, it punctured the February 7 Commune's claim to have secured authority in Honan. And second, it gave the Army commanders the time to reinforce their hold over the region. By mid-April, therefore, the Army had effectively assumed the responsibilities of the Honan Party Committee, and it proceeded to arrest thousands of youths on such ambiguous charges as "attempting to subvert the Cultural Revolution."

If the Honan military commanders had been actively involved in their region's dispute from the start, the Army in the southern province of Kwangtung did not apparently intervene in the local situation until early February. In the weeks before their move, senior officers in Canton had watched provincial authority dissolve as rival Red Guard factions fought against local Party bureaucrats and among themselves. At first the confusion had baffled and paralyzed them. They could not follow Mao's directive to assist the radicals, for the simple reason that they were unable to discern which among the vast variety of groups then swirling around Canton deserved their support. Their safest course was to remain neutral—unless, of course, young agitators attacked military installations. Mao's edict had clearly forbidden assaults against the

Army, and this meant that troops could retaliate against assailants regardless of their ideological complexion. But activists in the Provincial Revolutionary Alliance, headed by the student leader Wu Chuan-pin, made the mistake of violating the injunction, and their blunder ultimately weakened the whole radical cause in Canton.

The Alliance contended that it represented the true Maoist gospel and, in accordance with the Chairman's decree, deserved Army support. On February 8, seeking to accentuate their contention, a number of Alliance activists therefore invaded the Army headquarters in Canton, cut its telegraph lines, and occupied the premises until ordered out by the Military Commission in Peking.[50] The Red Guards also criticized General Huang Yung-sheng, the military chief of south China, and accused him of neglecting them.[51]

This diatribe against General Huang was imprudent, for he was not only the most powerful individual in Kwangtung at the time but, with his later appointment as Chief of the General Staff, he would become one of the most influential figures in the country—until, along with Lin Piao, he fell in disgrace in mid-1971.

Then in his early sixties, Huang Yung-sheng was a career officer with nearly forty years' experience as a soldier. As a young peasant in Kiangsi province, he had enlisted in a Nationalist unit that defected to the Communists, and he eventually joined Mao at his Chingkangshan redoubt. Huang made the celebrated Long March—which act established him as a member of the Communist elite—and he later saw action against the Japanese in north China. Afterward, as a corps commander in Lin Piao's Fourth Field Army, he fought against the Nationalists from Manchuria down to Kwangsi. He remained in south China following the victory in 1949, becoming boss of the Canton Military Region, which controlled more than two hundred thousand troops stationed in Kwangsi, Kwangtung, and Hunan. Huang was elected to the Communist Party's Central Committee as an alternate member in 1956.[52] As a soldier, however, his major preoccupation was the maintenance of law and order, especially in a city like Canton, whose proximity to Hong Kong made it easily corruptible.

High Party officials in Canton, as elsewhere, defended themselves by encouraging their own children to form loyal Red Guard groups. One such group—possibly affiliated with the United Action

Committee in Peking—was the Doctrine Guards. Among its members was Huang Yung-sheng's son, Huang Chun-ming, a secondary-school student. According to Maoist accounts, the Doctrine Guards served to protect local functionaries by breaking up radical demonstrations, and these plainly "counterrevolutionary" activities were undoubtedly sanctioned by General Huang.[53] In February, after the Provincial Revolutionary Alliance raided the Canton military headquarters, Huang extended the Army's support to a wider array of relatively conservative factions which came to be known as the East Wind coalition. Meanwhile, the Provincial Revolutionary Alliance expanded into a broader movement under the name of the Red Flag.[54] Huang's task, as he saw it, was to tame the Alliance—but in such a way that he would not be vulnerable to charges of suppressing the "masses."

On March 15, in conformity with a nationwide trend, Huang Yung-sheng set up a Military Control Committee as the instrument of Army authority in Kwangtung province. But that gesture was merely the official expression of an accomplished fact. For Army units labeled Military Training Platoons had been rapidly moving into factories, offices, schools, and other enterprises throughout the latter half of February.[55]

One student from Canton has described the platoon assigned to his secondary school. It comprised twenty soldiers headed by an officer and a political commissar, and their main duties were to hold meetings and write wall posters. The troops were clearly briefed to denigrate the Red Guards, for they selected passages for study from Mao's writings that implied criticism of the Provincial Revolutionary Alliance and they often convened sessions to denounce radical teachers. The radicals felt crushed. The student, himself a radical sympathizer, put it this way: "After nearly a year of making revolution, we were to receive no reward at all, only 're-education.'" Protest was futile, since it was "counterrevolutionary" to assail the Army.[56]

Huang Yung-sheng further sought to emasculate the Provincial Revolutionary Alliance by keeping its leader, Wu Ch'uan-p'in, under surveillance by the Military Training Platoon assigned to Sun Yat-sen University. Even so, Wu was free to receive his disciples and, according to one visitor, he vowed that he would continue fighting against the Army at the risk of imprisonment.[57] The young radical agitator kept his word—and met the fate he predicted. Backed by extremist members of the Cultural Revolution Directorate in Peking, he mobilized several assaults against the Army throughout 1967 and into the spring of 1968.[58] After that, Wu disappeared from public view, perhaps to undergo "labor reform" in some remote camp.

In February, as he accelerated his campaign to restore order in Kwangtung, Huang Yung-sheng took the daring step of flatly outlawing the more turbulent Red Guard movements. One of these was the August 1st Combat Corps, an affiliate of the Provincial Revolutionary Alliance. But Huang's decision to ban the August 1st Combat Corps backfired, for the group was shortly to be vindicated by Chou En-lai. The perplexing problems that faced the Maoist leaders in Peking as they tried to judge the ideological leanings of various factions were reflected in two documents concerning the controversial organization. One, the Army's opinion of the movement, was published by the Canton military garrison on March 1, the day the August 1st Combat Corps was proscribed. The other, the Corps' view of itself, was issued later, following its vindication.

To the Army, the August 1st Combat Corps was a "counterrevolutionary" organization whose members included former labor camp inmates, escaped convicts, speculators and market manipulators, landlords, rich peasants and their children, all of them having "committed towering crimes against the people" under the "cloak" of revolution. Among their alleged crimes, members of the faction kidnaped officials in the Haichu and Liwan districts of Canton, and stole their seals of office. In one neighborhood, the document went on, they smashed open the safe belonging to a Party street council and robbed eighty thousand *yuan* as well as the official records. On more than one occasion, members of the August 1st Combat Corps were supposed to have stormed police stations and attempted to release prisoners, whom they described as "victims" of the police. The Army also charged that they wantonly arrested people and ransacked their homes, set up kangaroo courts, conducted illegal trials, and incarcerated their enemies in underground cells. These "reactionaries" also disguised themselves as soldiers in order to provoke hostility against the Canton military garrison. And in addition to furnishing "intelligence information" to espionage agents in Hong Kong, members of the August 1st Combat Corps "insulted females and even raped young girls." In short, said the Army denunciation, "they were born rascals." [59]

The Corps' self-portrayal was predictably different. Its hundred thousand members were factory workers whose "revolutionary character was relatively firm." The "democratically elected" leaders of the Corps were demobilized soldiers employed in industry and government departments. Far from sowing discord as the Army alleged, the Corps pointed out that its members had intervened on three occasions to halt labor unrest and, on February 24, had joined in putting out a fire at a Canton oil depot. On the day the Corps was banned, the document went on, troops arrested thousands of its adherents, jailing many of them for months without trial. Those imprisoned were beaten and compelled to confess to "crimes" and their families were deprived of welfare benefits, the document asserted. The document also claimed that several members of the August 1st Combat Corps, crippled Army veterans among them, were forced to face denunciation rallies wearing placards identifying them as "counterrevolutionaries." The Canton military garrison's refusal to rehabilitate the Corps proved that the local Army commander "stubbornly clung to the bourgeois reactionary line." [60]

General Huang Yung-sheng eventually changed his attitude toward the August 1st Combat Corps, conceding that his garrison's understanding of the Cultural Revolution had been "inadequate." [61] But that switch did not come until the following October, when the Kwangtung radicals no longer seemed to represent a threat.

During the spring, however, the confusion in Kwangtung province became so great that China's semi-annual International Trade Fair, scheduled to open in Canton to thousands of foreign businessmen on April 15, appeared to be in jeopardy. To adjourn the Fair—as Peking was forced to do under extreme pressure a year later—would have constituted an acute "loss of face." But ugly Red Guard incidents in Canton once the Fair opened would be equally humiliating. Thus urgent action was necessary to calm the city, and inevitably, Chou En-lai stepped onto the scene.

Whether Chou was acting on his own initiative or in response to a request from General Huang Yung-sheng has never been clear. In either case, he flew to Canton on April 14, accompanied by ten aides who promptly investigated the situation throughout the city. Chou convened representatives of the diverse Canton factions to a meeting at the Sun Yat-sen Memorial Hall. Though his objective was mediation, his talk tended to favor the radicals. He had a few kind words for the Army, but he bluntly criticized the military garrison for having committed "errors" in manhandling student activists. He also exonerated several radical organizations, the August 1st Combat Corps among them, that had been outlawed by General Huang. And he went out of his way to praise Wu Chuanpin, then under military surveillance, lauding his "political prescience" and devotion to "revolutionary truth." [62] The net effect of Chou's speech was to arouse the radicals, and they erupted soon afterward in a fresh burst of violence that would again plunge Canton into chaos. He may have also alienated Huang, and their conflict might well have contributed to a later dispute that ended with the general's dismissal in 1971.

For Chou En-lai to have deliberately stimulated the radicals was uncharacteristic, since he had consistently labored to prevent the Cultural Revolution from destroying all vestiges of China's social and economic stability. During February, he had maneuvered assiduously to protect his own cabinet of ministers, upon which the management of the country depended. And he had persuaded key technicians to stay at their jobs and restored those who had been ousted, arguing tirelessly that the nation could not afford to lose its skilled officials. He had even gone so far as to revive the old Party structures that had existed within such vital government agencies as the National Commodity Price Commission, the Central Administrative Industry and Commerce Bureau, and the Ministry of Finance. But toward the end of March, there were signs that Chou was under pressure to shift to a more radical posture.

This shift was hardly capricious. It must surely have reflected Mao's view that the Army had swung the pendulum too far and, as a result, the dynamism of the Cultural Revolution was flickering and might even fade out completely. Voicing just such an apprehension, *Red Flag* asked rhetorically whether Mao's campaign would be "carried through to the end or abandoned halfway." For Mao, the answer to that question was predictable. Like a guerrilla fighter, he had retreated temporarily. Now the time had arrived to counterattack.

PART FOUR

FROM REVOLUTION
TO REACTION

*Fight, fail, fight again, fail again . . . till
their victory; that is the logic of the people.*
—MAO TSE-TUNG, *August 1949*

CHAPTER 14

The Radical Resurgence

✿

*The enemy still has strength and will not
concede defeat. Whether we can mobilize
the force to defend Chairman Mao to the
death is the challenge that we revolutionary
rebels now face. Thus we must cast away
illusions and prepare for battle.*

—K'UAI TA-FU, March 1967

ON MARCH 16, 1967, a perceptive Japanese correspondent in
Peking filed a long dispatch to his newspaper that differed
sharply from his reports of only a few weeks earlier. Though political posters still adorned walls everywhere and theaters remained
closed, he observed, calm had largely returned to the capital. Days
passed without noisy demonstrations, and mobs of youths no longer
blocked traffic and harangued pedestrians. Buses once crammed
with Red Guards now had space for ordinary citizens and were
running on schedule. Tiantan Park, where hordes of provincial Red
Guards had camped during their pilgrimages to glimpse Mao Tse-
tung, was again open to the public, and the Temple of Heaven
was intact—except that a sign that formerly identified it as a "house
of worship" had been removed. Shops and markets, plundered by
briefly affluent workers in January and then shut, were doing business as usual. Restaurants functioned as they had before. In one of
Peking's narrow lanes, the journalist paused at an old gray house,
the sun gilding its tiled roof. An ancient woman with bound feet
stood in the doorway, chatting with her grandchild. Drying laundry
draped the cobblestone courtyard, where another woman sat on a

stool mending the sole of a cloth shoe. Down the lane came a peddler, his cart laden with cabbages and radishes and potatoes, singing a song of vegetables. Quite suddenly, the Japanese correspondent felt himself back in a city he once knew. Peking, he speculated, would soon regain its past tranquillity.[1]

Though the journalist's description was vivid, the prediction could not have been more inaccurate. For a revival of normality was precisely what troubled Mao and his comrades—and that possibility prompted them to rekindle a fresh conflagration.

The Maoists had staked all on a cataclysmic upheaval that would shake every Chinese "soul." Yet now not only had Mao's dream of inspiring a Chinese version of the Commune evaporated in Shanghai but, by the beginning of April, Revolutionary Committees had been established in only four provinces and one city. Even in these places, power was primarily in the hands of the Army and veteran Party cadres, with tamed radicals serving mainly as revolutionary window dressing. Army officers and their Party associates also dominated most other regions of China. Central governmental authority had declined to such an extent that spokesmen in Peking referred to several dissident areas as "independent kingdoms" ruled by local "emperors" and "warlords." In a private meeting in late April, Chou En-lai revealed that the Peking hierarchy was striving to "negotiate" settlements with military and civilian officials in twelve provinces and was totally out of contact with seven other regions.[2] In Maoist rhetoric, this trend represented an "adverse current of counterrevolutionary restoration" that had to be halted lest the Cultural Revolution collapse.

Probably still at his Hangchow retreat, where he annually spent the winter, Mao appeared to have little to say during this period. Actually, there was little he could say. After all, it was he who had ordered the Army into action and had called for leniency toward Party officials, and he could not openly concede that these policies had backfired. Thus he turned to one of his time-honored tactics. Operating through intimate aides like Ch'en Po-ta and Chiang Ch'ing, he authorized his more radical disciples to express alarm at the conservative drift that seemed to be overtaking the country. In that way, the impression could be created that the "masses" were clamoring to regenerate the Cultural Revolution.

One of the earliest cries of alarm came in mid-March from Nieh Yuan-tzu, the radical woman cadre who had initially triggered the revolt at Peking University a year before. At a conference at the university, she claimed that Party "reactionaries" were creeping back into their old positions. This augured a "capitalist" resurgence that could only be stopped by a radical counteroffensive.[3] Ch'i Pen-yu, a left-wing extremist in the Cutural Revolution Directorate, sounded a similar theme two days later in a speech warning that efforts to subvert Mao's campaign were being encouraged at the very highest levels in Peking.[4] The same line resonated even more strongly in a gloomy article by K'uai Ta-fu, the first Red Guard leader at Peking's Tsinghua University. Liu Shao-ch'i "refuses to accept defeat," and his wife, Wang Kuang-mei, "is active everywhere," K'uai wrote, adding that "reactionary slogans" were again proliferating, and "the political wave against Chairman Mao is running high." Unless this tide was stemmed, he forecast apocalyptically, "the enemy will launch political, economic, and military attacks, and imperialism, revisionism, Chiang Kai-shek, natural calamities, and human disasters will befall us simultaneously." Therefore, radicals "must cast away illusions and prepare for battle." And, K'uai made plain, the battle should be fought with guns.[5]

This interpretation of events was echoed in the official Chinese press. In early March, *Red Flag* declared that "a big question now confronting the people of the whole country" was whether the Cultural Revolution would be "carried through to the end, or abandoned halfway." Shortly afterward, it contended that Mao's drive should be propelled forward regardless of its cost to industry, agriculture, and other sectors of the economy, "revolution must be put in command of production." [6] While admonishing the Red Guards to cease their internecine squabbling, other editorials also warned against the Army's attempts to quell the young radicals. "We will absolutely not tolerate slinging mud at the Red Guards, and must resolutely hit back," announced the Shanghai newspaper *Wen Hui Pao*. One radical publicist exhorted young activists to prime themselves for renewed turbulence. "The enemies will never lay down their butcher knives and become Buddhas," he asserted, and called on the Red Guards to "launch resolute attacks against the open and hidden representatives of the bourgeoisie." [7]

A revolutionary upsurge began to take shape at the end of March as the Maoists opened a three-pronged offensive destined to unfold with extraordinary speed and fervor. On one flank, they would escalate their assault against Liu Shao-ch'i, his wife, and his colleagues. On another, they planned to denounce Party and government officials who had clung to their old positions or had returned to them. And most significantly, they intended to push through measures to curb the authority of the Army, then the biggest single obstacle to radical ambitions.

In verbal intensity, Mao's onslaught against Liu Shao-ch'i makes Stalin's campaign against Trotsky seem mild. Yet nowhere is the difference between Mao and Stalin illustrated so dramatically as in their drives against their respective rivals. Stalin simply marked Trotsky for liquidation and, in 1940, finally had him assassinated. To Mao, in contrast, it was imperative that Liu Shao-ch'i be kept alive. For Mao's far-reaching objective was not merely to eliminate his adversaries but to convert the Chinese people to his brand of spiritual Communism. Mao needed Liu as the "negative example" that personified "bourgeois revisionist counterrevolutionary" evil. Had Liu not existed, Mao would have been compelled to invent him. As a tactical maneuver, moreover, Mao hoped that his focus on Liu would encourage the majority of Party cadres whom he considered to be "good or comparatively good" to join with the radicals in supporting his cause. As he saw it, most Party officials would abandon Liu rather than face dismissal for his sake, and could therefore be won over. As he issued orders for the fresh assault against Liu in the spring of 1967, Mao said: "Isolate and attack the smallest minority." [8]

Mao's earlier efforts against Liu and his closest colleagues had run aground after January. In the first place, the attempt to portray Liu as a villain for having advocated private gardens, free markets, and other material incentives had not only failed to tarnish his image but, on the contrary, suddenly made him popular. For the first time, peasants could identify the gray, faceless figure they had hardly known as the man who had eased their suffering after the Great Leap Forward.[9] In addition, though he had made a ritual confession, Liu stubbornly refused to capitulate to the Maoists and demanded his right to arraignment before the Party Central Committee.[10] This shrewd argument won him a respite, for it reminded the other Peking leaders, some of Mao's stanchest acolytes among them, that they too might be vulnerable to summary dismissal unless legal formalities were observed. Chou En-lai underscored this point in a heated dispute with a group of Red Guards in early January, when he told them that it was permissible to criticize the "bourgeois reactionary line" symbolized by Liu and Teng Hsiao-p'ing, but that they could not personally indict the two men since "they are still members of the Politburo Standing Committee." [11]

Mao, in further contrast to Stalin, was also concerned with legitimacy. But to convene the nearly two hundred members of the Party Central Committee to impeach Liu Shao-ch'i was too risky a venture. Mao had barely scraped through the Eleventh Central Committee Plenum held in August 1966, and resistance to the Cultural Revolution within the Party since then had clearly increased. Toward the end of March, he contrived another device. Returning to Peking from Hangchow, he convoked a meeting of the Politburo Standing Committee to censure Liu and Teng Hsiao-p'ing informally. He had enlarged the Committee from its original complement of seven to eleven members, three of the four additional faces being his supporters. As the Committee assembled, crowds of Red Guards somehow appeared in the streets outside, denouncing Liu and Teng as "counterrevolutionary revisionists."

Even so, Mao managed after much persuasion to mobilize a majority of only one vote in favor of his motion against Liu and Teng. Those who voted with him, besides Lin Piao and Chou En-lai, were Ch'en Po-ta and K'ang Sheng, both in the Cultural Revolution Directorate, and Li Fu-ch'un, a Vice-Premier and one of Chou's protégés. Backing Liu and Teng were the old Marshal Chu Teh, the liberal economist Ch'en Yun, and T'ao Chu, who was still functioning despite the fierce attacks against him two months earlier.[12] Only a plenary session of the Central Committee could legally remove Liu and Teng from their Party positions, and such a meeting would not be held until two years later. But the narrow vote gave Mao the support he needed for a public campaign against them.

] 323 [

As early as March 26, twenty Red Guard factions in Peking formed a "preparatory committee" to organize the offensive against Liu Shao-ch'i.[13] Within a week, the committee had mobilized a massive demonstration in the capital. At dawn on April 2, hundreds of thousands of Red Guards, schoolchildren, soldiers, and others converged on Tienanmen Square carrying huge portraits of Mao and chanting his slogans. Beating drums and clashing cymbals, they marched toward the ornate red and gold gate to the Chun'gnanhai compound inside the ancient imperial city, where the official residences of Liu and the other Chinese leaders stood behind high gray walls. With loudspeaker trucks guiding their movements and cueing their slogans, the marchers passed in procession for six hours—and they repeated the demonstration day after day for nearly a week while similar parades were staged in Shanghai, Harbin, and other provincial cities.

Peking's walls were plastered with hostile posters assailing Liu and his wife, Wang Kuang-mei. Some demanded that Liu be executed for alleged "collusion" with the Soviet "revisionists," while others caricatured him as a monstrous oppressor of the "masses." One caricature depicted him as a cannibal devouring virtuous workers and peasants, and cartoons invariably portrayed his wife wearing Western clothes and high-heeled shoes to denote her "bourgeois" tastes.[14] At the same time, the official Peking press began to publish a series of critical commentaries on "the top Party person in authority taking the capitalist road," or "China's Khrushchev."

The opening shot in this barrage was a lengthy *Red Flag* article published on April 1 which, though signed by Ch'i Pen-yu, the radical historian and publicist, bore the imprint of Mao's brilliant polemical brush. It offered a revealing analogy between the present time and the closing years of the Ch'ing dynasty, when the abortive attempt by Westernized Chinese reformers to modernize China's crumbling imperial institutions had given way to the xenophobic Boxer uprising against the foreign community in Peking. Mao's aim in reaching back to that historical episode was plainly to draw a parallel between his Red Guards and the Boxers, both of whom the article glorified as "heroic revolutionaries." Just as the Boxers had been correct in having attacked "bourgeois reformers," Mao argued, so the Red Guards were justified in denouncing Liu Shao-ch'i and his "revisionist" comrades. And just as the "bourgeois reformers" had believed in constitutional change and "modernization from above," so Liu had tried to subvert the Maoist revolution by introducing liberal economic measures following the Great Leap Forward. Therefore, the article declared, Liu had exposed his "ugly bourgeois soul" by having advocated "the development of capitalism and the safeguarding of the bloody system of exploitation of man by man." Challenging Liu's claim to being a "veteran revolutionary," the article indicted him with eight charges, ranging from the allegation that he had favored a compromise with Chiang Kai-shek's Nationalists after World War II to the assertion that he had resisted the Cultural Revolution two decades later.[15]

Liu refuted these charges not long afterward. The entire Chinese Communist Party, including Mao himself, he pointed out, had decided to sign a "cease-fire agreement" with Chiang's Nationalists in January 1946. He also denied the charge that he had attempted to cripple the Cultural Revolution. But he would study Mao's works, Liu promised, since "only then shall I be able to reply as to why I committed errors." [16] This "confession" amounted to a rejection of the Maoist indictment, and as a consequence, the drive to defame Liu escalated to extravagant proportions. Beginning in April, a proliferation of newspaper articles and radio discussions focused on *How to Be a Good Communist*, the lectures that Liu had originally delivered to Communist cadres in Yenan in July 1939 and had reprinted in revised book form in mid-1962. Typical of the diatribe against the book was a *People's Daily* editorial that condemned it as a "pernicious influence" not only in China but "also throughout the world." [17] The criticism was valid from a Maoist angle. Liu's basic approach, consistent with Leninist orthodoxy, held that every Communist subordinate himself to the Party organization, which was by definition infallible. This thesis not only undermined Mao's dogma that each individual could perfect himself, but defied the Chairman's claim to be the sole spokesman for the "masses." Moreover, republished at a time when Mao's authority was waning, the revised edition of Liu's book had seemed to be an attempt to demean Mao. One passage, for instance, spoke of "some comrades" who "regarded themselves as the Marx and Lenin of China . . . and had the impudence to ask our Party members to respect them as we do Marx and Lenin. [They sought] to appoint themselves as 'leaders' . . . abused everything within the Party and wilfully attacked, punished, and rode roughshod over Party members." Such comrades, Liu urged, must "be opposed, exposed and buried in oblivion"—which was precisely what Mao, now seeking revenge, was trying to do to him.[18]

The Red Guards now resorted to every imaginable device to blacken Liu's reputation. A radical Peking faction called the Chingkangshan Fighting Corps alleged that Liu's grandfather had been a landlord, his father a "rich peasant," and his eldest brother in the employ of a warlord. Liu, they said, had "sneaked into the Party" in 1921. The document then went on with a list of Liu's purported crimes so devastating that it unwittingly reflected on Mao's blindness to the culprit at his side. When the Party underwent a reshuffle in 1935, it asserted, Liu managed to hang on to his position in the Central Committee by "opportunistic means." During a famine in the early 1940s, he had feasted daily on chicken and even demanded oranges while his hungry comrades survived on corn pudding. The Red Guards also charged Liu with having brutally mistreated his numerous wives. And they heaped scorn on his present wife, Wang Kuang-mei.[19] She had been subjected to humiliating Red Guard interrogation in January. Now, she was forced to submit to even worse abuse.

On April 10, Red Guards affiliated with Tsinghua University set up a kangaroo court to judge Wang Kuang-mei. With two brief interruptions, the proceedings rambled on from six-thirty in the morning until ten o'clock at night. Apparently expecting to be jailed immediately, Wang Kuang-mei had brought a towel, a toothbrush, and other toilet articles to the "courtroom," a hall on the seventh floor of one of the university buildings. From time to time during the interrogation, she was given tranquilizers by a soldier, presumably one of Liu Sho-chi's military aides. Despite her admitted nervousness, however, she tenaciously fought back against her young inquisitors.

The weather was still cool in Peking in early April, and Wang Kuang-mei arrived at the trial in a fur coat, a gift she had been given when she went on a state visit to Afghanistan with Liu Shao-ch'i in the spring of 1966. The Red Guards, anxious to dramatize her "bourgeois" tastes, had brought as evidence a thin silk dress and the high-heeled shoes she had worn while on official trips to Indonesia and Pakistan. They demanded that she change her clothes. She refused, and the dialogue between the Red Guard prosecutor and herself reflected the absurdity of the entire episode:

PROSECUTOR: You must put on that dress!

WANG KUANG-MEI: I will not!

PROSECUTOR: You have no choice in this matter!

WANG KUANG-MEI (of the dress she is wearing): This is good enough for receiving guests.

PROSECUTOR: Receiving guests? You are under attack here today!

WANG KUANG-MEI: I am not going to put on that dress. It is not presentable.

PROSECUTOR: Then why did you wear it in Indonesia?

WANG KUANG-MEI: It was summer at that time, and I wore it in Djakarta.

PROSECUTOR: Why did you wear it in Lahore?

WANG KUANG-MEI: I am not going to put it on, whatever you may say.

PROSECUTOR: Let me repeat. You are under attack here today. If you are not honest with us, take care!

WANG KUANG-MEI: Even if I must die, it does not matter.

PROSECUTOR: Death? We want to keep you alive. Put on the dress!

WANG KUANG-MEI: Shouldn't we be discussing serious subjects?

PROSECUTOR: Who wants to discuss things with you? Let me tell you again that you are under attack!

WANG KUANG-MEI (angrily): On no account can you encroach upon my personal freedom.

PROSECUTOR (amid the sound of laughter): You are a member of the reactionary bourgeoisie and a class dissident. You will not be given an iota of minimum democracy, let alone extensive democracy! Dictatorship is being exercised over you today, and you are not free.

WANG KUANG-MEI: I will not put on that dress, come what may. If I have committed mistakes, I am open to criticism.

PROSECUTOR: You are guilty! You are under attack today, and you will face further attacks in the future. Put on the dress!

WANG KUANG-MEI (evasively, pointing to the fur coat she was wearing): This was a gift from Afghanistan. They said I was fashion-minded.

PROSECUTOR: We want you to put on that dress you wore in Indonesia.

WANG KUANG-MEI: That was summer. There is winter clothing for winter, summer clothing for summer, and spring clothing for spring. I cannot put on a summer dress now.

PROSECUTOR: Skip that nonsense. We know nothing about such bourgeois stuff as what is good for summer, winter, or spring or for receiving guests or for travel.

WANG KUANG-MEI: Chairman Mao has said that we must pay attention to climate, and change our clothing accordingly.

PROSECUTOR (amid laughter): What Chairman Mao said refers to the political climate. And the way you stand in that respect, you will freeze to death even though you're wearing a fur coat. Now, are you going to put on that dress?

WANG KUANG-MEI: No.

PROSECUTOR: All right! We'll give you ten minutes. See what will happen at a quarter to seven. Try to defy us by not wearing that dress. We mean what we say. (Changing subject.) What do you think of the unhorsing of Liu Shao-ch'i?

WANG KUANG-MEI: That is fine. Then there will be no revisionism in China.

PROSECUTOR: We still want to drag him out for attack. That will take place some day, don't you think?

WANG KUANG-MEI: You are at liberty to attack him if you wish. (After a pause.) Your methods of attack are not really very good. You ought to do better at criticism and repudiation.

PROSECUTOR: Ignore her! In ten minutes you will see.

WANG KUANG-MEI: You . . . I can ring someone up and ask for a spring dress.

PROSECUTOR: That won't do!

WANG KUANG-MEI: This dress is made of silk. It's too cold.

PROSECUTOR: Put it on and wear your fur coat over it.

WANG KUANG-MEI: If I were really opposed to Chairman Mao, I would deserve to freeze to death.

PROSECUTOR: You are opposed to Chairman Mao.

WANG KUANG-MEI: I am not against him now, and I will not oppose him in the future.

PROSECUTOR: No more nonsense with her. Well, there are seven minutes left.

WANG KUANG-MEI (after a pause, pointing to the pair of high-heeled shoes they had brought): How about my just putting on the shoes?

PROSECUTOR: That isn't enough. You must wear everything.

WANG KUANG-MEI: You have no right.

PROSECUTOR: We do have the right! You are under attack today. We are at liberty to attack you however we wish, and you have no freedom. We are of the revolutionary masses, while you are a notorious and counterrevolutionary woman. You cannot confuse the class line! [20]

When the ten minutes ended, according to a Red Guard account, a group of students pushed Wang Kuang-mei to the floor and tried to change her clothes. She struggled against them, alternately evoking Mao's injunction against force and complaining that the silk dress was too small. But the youths continued awkwardly to disrobe her as the audience chanted such slogans as "a revolution is an act of violence," and "die-hards will eventually turn into dogshit spurned by mankind." Exhausted, Wang Kuang-mei finally surrendered. She donned the silk dress and the high-heeled shoes and the Red Guards mockingly added a necklace of ping-pong balls around her throat. As they photographed her humiliation, she repeated her warning that they had violated Mao's rule against coercion. "Nonsense!" replied the Red Guard prosecutor. "Coercion is justified when dealing with such a reactionary bourgeois element as you." The audience supported his remark by chanting another of Mao's aphorisms: "Everything reactionary is the same. If you do not hit it, it will not fall."

During the marathon inquisition that followed, the Red Guards faced a tough and resilient adversary. When they accused Wang Kuang-mei of having "disgraced" the Chinese people by lighting President Sukarno's cigarette during her visit to Djakarta, for instance, she was quick to remind them that the Indonesian leader had been one of Peking's close allies at the time. When they charged her with "sneaking" into the Communist movement, she recalled that one of her first jobs for the Party had been as a translator for Premier Chou En-lai. She also denied that she had persecuted Red Guards at Tsinghua University during the early days of the Cultural Revolution. And when her Red Guard interrogators called her work as a rural investigator in 1964 "scandalous," Wang Kuang-mei snapped back at them: "Where do you get your information? You've spent no more than five days at the grass-roots level, while I stayed there for almost a year. I understand things better than you do."

Knowing that her interrogation was calculated to discredit her husband, Wang Kuang-mei defended Liu Shao-ch'i with rare valor and unusual skill. She allowed that he had committed errors, quoting Lenin to the effect that "it is impossible to work without making mistakes." But she rebuffed charges that Liu's career had been a series of "crimes." When he had proposed marriage to her in 1947, she reminisced somewhat sentimentally, he "honestly" told her about his former wives and several children. She denied that Liu had favored capitalism, asserting that his primary concern during the initial phase of the Communist regime had been to boost the "prosperity of the country" through the development of private industry. She brushed aside the tale that Liu alone had urged a compromise with Chiang Kai-shek following World War II, pointing out that Mao and others had also advocated a truce with the Nationalists. Similarly, she recalled, though Liu was blamed for sending Work Teams into the universities to control the Cultural Revolution during its opening phase, the entire Politburo Standing Committee had approved that decision. "Liu Shao-ch'i is not Chiang Kai-shek," she insisted. "He is not in any way a counterrevolutionary."

As her trial droned on into the evening, Wang Kuang-mei's endurance and polemical talent plainly frustrated her young assailants. They repeatedly lost their tempers as she evaded their questions or threw back quotations from Mao to prove her case. During one hot exchange, she silenced her interrogators by referring to Mao's dictum that good revolutionaries "must listen to the views of others whether or not they are favorable." When the Red Guard prosecutor impatiently demanded that she "hurry up and make a clean breast of Liu Shao-ch'i's misdeeds," she replied cooly: "How can I tell you his misdeeds if he has none?" But when the youth claimed that she was unworthy of membership in the Communist Party, she flew into a rage, barking at him: "Don't you bully me!" Still, at the end, Wang Kuang-mei conceded that the attacks against Liu and herself had driven her to tears. Their fall from grace meant, she suggested, that they would be disowned by their children. Thus her extraordinary sixteen-hour ordeal curiously ended on a Confucian note of concern for filial relations.

The Red Guards directed Wang Kuang-mei to submit a written

"self-examination" within ten days after her trial. But she side-stepped this order by requesting a verbatim transcript of the testimony so that, she claimed, she could study the record and gain "a deeper understanding of the seriousness and wickedness" of her alleged mistakes. She continued to circumvent Red Guard pressures until late June, when she finally produced a "confession." Once again, however, it was an evasive document. She admitted to personal "errors" but declined to provide the radicals with what they really wanted—evidence against Liu Shao-ch'i.[21]

In early April, paralleling their revived campaign against Liu Shao-ch'i, the Maoists renewed their drive to denounce senior Party and government officials. The most prominent of those to come under fire were Foreign Minister Ch'en Yi, Finance Minister Li Hsien-nien, and Li Fu-ch'un, Chairman of the State Planning Commission. They also directed an especially virulent attack against T'an Chen-lin, the country's foremost agriculture specialist.[22] These men were all Politburo members as well as Vice-Premiers under Chou En-lai, and the assault against them had one essential purpose—to oust officials who had taken advantage of Mao's earlier appeal for leniency toward veteran cadres to suppress radical elements in their departments. The real target of the offensive, however, was Chou En-lai.

Confronted by the new challenge to his authority, Chou En-lai resorted to three tactics. He tried to protect deputies like Li Fu-ch'un, an old comrade from his Paris days, whose technical skill as an economic planner was indispensable and whose ideological credentials were beyond reproach. He permitted limited though sometimes severe criticism of other associates, notably Ch'en Yi, whose cooperation he appreciated but whose outspoken scorn for the Red Guards made him difficult to defend. And he agreed to sacrifice T'an Chen-lin, whose utility he apparently considered marginal.

In short, by providing the Maoists with victims, Chou hoped that he could salvage enough power to keep China's administration operating with a measure of efficiency. But this approach worked unevenly. For the radicals voraciously chewed up officials, and the more they were fed the hungrier they became. Within half a year, Chou would lose eight of his fifteen Vice-Premiers, three out of six chairmen of the vital Staff Offices, seventeen of the government's thirty-two ministers, and other important functionaries.[23] Many of these figures returned three or four years later, however, when the Cultural Revolution had become a memory.

The most surprising feature of the campaign against Ch'en Yi was that he succeeded in surviving it—just as he had weathered a series of previous assaults and would endure future attacks. For Ch'en, despite his hedonistic propensities, was a rugged Communist veteran quite capable of handling his adversaries. The son of a well-to-do magistrate, Ch'en had acquired—both in China and abroad—tastes that scarcely fit the Maoist ideal of proletarian austerity. As a Szechwanese accustomed to one of the finest provincial cuisines in China, he indulged in exquisite Chinese banquets and, on one occasion, agreed to dine at a foreign embassy in Peking only on condition that he be served French pastry and Napoleon brandy.[24] He delighted in traditional opera and dancing, played excellent chess, and composed poems in praise of flowers.[25]

Beneath this elegant and refined manner, however, Ch'en Yi was an experienced and able soldier. In the spring of 1949, as commander of the Third Field Army, he was responsible for the capture of Shanghai, and he later forged a powerful political base in east China. Afterward, as Foreign Minister, Politburo member, and one of China's nine living Marshals, he raised his voice for rationality in the midst of some of Mao's more visionary episodes. In one of his most celebrated pronouncements, later to be used against him, Ch'en had cautioned Peking University students in 1961 that it was a "mistake" to judge people solely on the basis of their political orientation.

In the spring of 1966, Ch'en Yi had sought to restrain the ferment in the Foreign Ministry by organizing fifteen Work Teams similar to those sent by Liu Shao-ch'i into the universities.[26] Not long afterward, when the Red Guards denounced him for preventing them from purging "bourgeois reactionaries" under him, Ch'en slapped back. "I'll give you some cold towels to cool your hot heads," he told one radical faction and, resisting another Red Guard group, he said: "If you attack me for forty-eight days, I'll attack you for forty-nine, and if you use ten abusive words, I'll use eleven." [27]

Later, however, Ch'en Yi was compelled to retreat—at least temporarily. On January 24, 1967, addressing a large Peking audience in the presence of Chou En-lai, Ch'en Po-ta, Chiang Ch'ing, and other leaders, he confessed that he had misunderstood the Cultural Revolution because he "seldom went deep among the masses to learn humbly from them" and had consequently "lost sight of their revolutionary enthusiasm." Henceforth, Ch'en Yi vowed, he would throw himself "into the furnace of this great mass movement and burn away my mistakes." [28] The confession won him redemption. Ch'en Po-ta declared him "vindicated," and Chou En-lai praised him for the "painful recognition" of his errors.[29] But in the weeks that followed, as the Red Guards persisted in their efforts to oust Foreign Ministry officials, Ch'en Yi again exploded. He retracted his confession and now claimed that it had been "forced" on him, asserting that he was innocent of any misconduct.[30] And he resumed his counterattacks against unruly radicals. On February 12, he scolded Red Guards who had intimidated a returning Chinese ambassador: "If you want to fight so badly, why don't you go to Vietnam and fight the Americans?" [31]

Early in April, Ch'en Yi joked about the Red Guard campaign against him. He cheerfully told an Australian delegation that if he weren't so busy he would publicly respond to his critics. "I can put up posters, too," he said. In a similarly jocular vein, he told a group of Japanese, "If the foreign ministers of other countries were criticized like me, the world would be a more peaceful place." [32]

But the war between Ch'en Yi and the Red Guards was no laughing matter. The radicals repeatedly staged demonstrations against him until, in the middle of April, the Maoist leaders felt compelled to support them at least partially. Ch'en Po-ta now approved the denunciations of Ch'en Yi but argued against his dismissal, while Chou En-lai announced that he would personally assume the supervision of the Foreign Ministry. The radicals interpreted these concessions as signs of weakness, however. They continued their offensive against Ch'en Yi until, on May 13, mobs of rampaging youths armed with knives and crowbars broke into a Foreign Ministry building. The mob, led by a student faction from the Foreign Languages Institute, the training school for Chinese diplomats and interpreters, occupied the building for six hours, beating up officials and soldiers who stood in their way and stealing classified documents. One youth was reported to have shouted: "What's so terrific about secrets? To hell with them." [33]

This unprecedented outburst of violence against the Foreign Ministry partly reflected the Red Guards' impatience with the restraints imposed on them by Chou En-lai. Indeed, at a meeting following the assault against the Ministry, they handed Chou an ultimatum bluntly demanding that Ch'en Yi and two Vice-Ministers of Foreign Affairs, Chi Peng-fei and Ch'iao Kuan-hua, be dismissed and arraigned before a Red Guard tribunal.* When Chou rejected this ultimatum, posters went up around Peking criticizing him. And a Red Guard contingent staged a return raid against the Foreign Ministry on May 29, again removing confidential documents.[34]

The Foreign Ministry radicals were inspired as well by a dynamic and ambitious new chief, Yao Teng-shan. A middle-ranking diplomat who had served in Finland and Ceylon, Yao was stationed in Djakarta during the abortive attempt by Indonesian Communists to take power in the fall of 1965. Peking's alleged involvement in this attempted coup—combined with the Indonesian Army's slaughter of thousands of Chinese resident in the archipelago—led to a deterioration in relations between Indonesia and China, and the Chinese diplomatic mission was eventually expelled from Djakarta. Yao, by then its *chargé d'affaires,* was given a hero's welcome on his return home on April 30. He was greeted at the airport by the entire Peking hierarchy except for Mao and Lin Piao, and they accorded him an audience the next day.[35]

Perhaps as a result of these experiences Yao had delusions of grandeur. He spearheaded the Red Guard raids against the Foreign Ministry, and in the summer he tried to elevate himself to the position of Foreign Minister. He failed and, by September, would be denounced as a "thug" and a "political gambler." [36] But before his downfall, Yao and his comrades almost totally disrupted the Chi-

---

* Chi was appointed Foreign Minister after Ch'en Yi's death in January 1972. Ch'iao led the Chinese delegation to the United Nations in the autumn of 1971.

nese Foreign Ministry and certainly aggravated the heart condition that later brought Ch'en Yi's career to an end. Ch'en died of cancer in January 1972. The publicity accorded his furneral obliquely symbolized his complete "rehabilitation" and also served as an indirect criticism of the radical.

If Chou En-lai had tried to protect Ch'en Yi, he found it expedient to make T'an Chen-lin a sacrificial offering to the Red Guards. Indeed, T'an's symbolic value as a scapegoat for the Red Guards lifted him into a position of importance that far exceeded any authority he had actually exercised. In early spring, therefore, he was publicized as the ringleader of the "counterrevolutionary current" that had undermined the Maoist cause during the two previous months.

One of the few authentic "proletarians" in the upper echelons of the Communist movement, T'an Chen-lin was born around the turn of the century into an extremely poor peasant family in Hunan, Mao's native province. Having learned to read while working as a printer's apprentice, he enrolled in the young Communist Party in the mid-1920s. T'an participated in peasant uprisings in Hunan and then retreated to Mao's Chingkangshan redoubt, where he rose rapidly as a political commissar in the Communist armed forces. He fought almost everywhere in the country during the wars against the Japanese and the Nationalists, serving at the time of the Communist victory as deputy political commissar in Ch'en Yi's Third Field Army, which conquered east China. Ironically, in light of his subsequent fate, T'an had been a foremost advocate of the Great Leap Forward. His support for Mao's intensive collectivization program in 1958 in fact earned him membership in the Politburo and a Vice-Premiership. He later became Director of the Agriculture and Forestry Office, and it was in that job that he ran afoul of the Red Guards. For T'an apparently resisted attempts by the young radicals to take over his organizations. In short, despite his past fidelity to the Maoist line, T'an evidently felt compelled to defend himself against Red Guard interference. In the early summer of 1966, for example, he had created Work Teams to supervise the Red Guard units then mushrooming in the Agriculture and Forestry Office and its ancillary agencies. He also persisted in voicing his allegiance to Liu Shao-ch'i and the Party machine, declaring on more than one occasion that it was wrong to "dispense with Party leadership and rely on the masses for everything." [37] Later, he mobilized his own Red Guard factions, reinforcing them with Mao Tse-tung Thought Propaganda Teams. But the radicals were undeceived by these maneuvers. And they were encouraged by Mao's wife, Chiang Ch'ing, who had bluntly accused T'an of plotting to "erase the achievements" of the Cultural Revolution.[38]

In January, 1967, T'an Chen-lin resorted to the same tactic being used by other Chinese officials. He directed his own Red Guard groups to "seize power" in his agencies.[39] This tactic bought him time. For soon afterward, when Mao called for a "lenient" policy toward government officials, T'an not only was able to claim that his efforts to shield his subordinates had been justified, but proceeded to suppress his leftist enemies. From early February until late in March, his supporters arrested, beat up, and arraigned radicals in the Ministry of Agriculture, the Central Meteorological Bureau, and other departments under his control. At mass rallies the young radicals, bound and trussed, were forced to bow their heads and confess to being "counterrevolutionaries." [40] T'an also dissolved leftist movements within his apparatus, exiling their members to "labor reform" camps or construction gangs in remote rural areas.

The facility with which T'an carried out these crackdowns indicated that he must have enjoyed the tacit support or at least tolerance of the Army, then engaged in imposing law and order in Peking and the provinces. And, judging from his silence at the time, Mao himself probably approved of his drive. In any case it did not contradict his disapproval of unruly extremists.

But when Mao's tactic on the Cultural Revolution shifted, T'an Chen-lin's position changed quickly. On March 14, acting on instructions from the Cultural Revolution Directorate, thousands of university and secondary-school students flooded the streets of Peking, denouncing T'an and demanding that the Maoist cause be rescued from "reactionaries." Mao's personal imprimatur on these demonstrations was assured by Ch'i Pen-yu, then emerging as the leading spokesman for the Maoist hierarchy. Ch'i described T'an as a "representative figure" in the "anti-revolutionary" wave that had taken hold in February, and that "all statements made in his defense must be retracted." [41] In other words, Ch'i plainly suggested, T'an Chen-lin had been singled out as the symbol of a trend that was subverting the Cultural Revolution. The new indictment of T'an was also a veiled warning to Chou En-lai, who had pleaded that his senior associates be spared.

Chou now switched his stand. He labeled T'an a "traitor" and endorsed the campaign to dismiss him. From then on, the vilification of T'an Chen-lin surged ahead in its monotonously typical manner. Red Guards dredged up "evidence" disclosing that T'an's father-in-law had been an "industrial-commercial capitalist," that his brother-in-law had served Chiang Kai-shek and that, among his other sins, he had sheltered landlords, rich peasants, and other "bourgeois parasites." [42] But along with these familiar bromides, the radicals presented a valid case against T'an in their contention that he had maneuvered to immunize his government bureaus against the Maoist purge.

T'an managed to survive through the month of April, and even appeared atop the Tienanmen Gate with Mao and the other Chinese leaders at the annual May Day celebration. Then he faded from public view, undoubtedly to one of the "labor reform" camps to which he had exiled his Red Guard foes. Yet his name became synonymous for the duration of the Cultural Revolution with any adversary of the radicals. Red Guards throughout China referred to their Party, government, and Army enemies as "local T'an Chen-lins."

CHAPTER 15

The Troubled Spring

❧

*There cannot be peaceful coexistence in the
ideological realm. Peaceful coexistence cor-
rupts.*

—CHIANG CH'ING, *April 1967*

IN THEIR THREE-PRONGED EFFORT to regenerate the Cultural Revolution early in the spring, the Maoists had been relatively successful in their offensive against Liu Shao-ch'i and their stepped-up
assaults against Party and government officials. Now they were confronted by the far more complicated and sensitive problem of the
Army.

Late in January, after committing the Army to the Cultural
Revolution, Mao had quickly observed that local commanders were
concentrating on maintaining stability rather than helping the radicals to overthrow local Party machines. Military crackdowns
against Maoist agitators were reported to be so severe that the
Chairman dispatched investigative missions to several areas to find
out what precisely the situation was.

In Anhwei province, which straddles the Yangtze River in central China, one such mission concluded that the region's Military
Control Committee had banned Maoist factions, "indiscriminately"
arrested radicals, and was "monopolizing" authority to the exclusion
of the "masses." Representatives of Anhwei's Army command
were summoned to Peking and ordered to release "without exception" all radicals who had been jailed and to exonerate those
who had been labeled "counterrevolutionaries." A mission sent to
Inner Mongolia revealed a similar case of Army repression after

General T'eng Hai-ch'ing, Deputy Commander of the Peking Garrison, had led the Twenty-first Army's three divisions into Inner Mongolia in February and taken control of Huhehot, its capital. Since then, the mission found, troops had eradicated "large numbers of revolutionary masses" while backing "conservative" groups linked to the "revisionist" provincial Party organization. Still another mission returned with an even more damaging account of the Army's activities in Tsinghai, the large, mountainous, sparsely populated province lying between Tibet and Sinkiang in western China. On February 23, the mission reported, the deputy Army commander in Sining had "usurped military power" in a "counterrevolutionary coup" and then, claiming that Red Guards had opened fire on his men, killed and wounded numbers of them, including many teen-age girls. The Peking authorities ordered the Tsinghai officer and two of his subordinates placed in solitary confinement pending trial, and absolved the Red Guards from any guilt for the incident.[1]

Mao knew that to permit the Army to continue quelling his young Red Guard supporters meant the end of the Cultural Revolution, a prospect he abhorred. Yet it was also clear that, with virtually all of China's government and political system in shambles, any move to restrain the Army would license fresh outbursts of violence, an alternative that was equally undesirable. Mao contemplated this dilemma throughout the month of March—and then came up with a solution that was almost fanciful. On April 1, he renewed his instructions to the Army to assume responsibility for controlling the country and assisting in the establishment of tripartite provincial Revolutionary Committees. But, in order to prevent military commanders from quashing the radicals, he curtailed their real authority. As a consequence, presuming that they now had Mao's sanction to behave as they pleased, the radicals went on rampages, while the Army, confused by contradictory directives, acted according to its own dictates. The result was unparalleled chaos.

The first of these directives admonished the Army for having judged the ideological complexion of diverse Red Guard movements. Henceforth, no faction could be branded "counterrevolutionary" without Peking's prior assent. The directive also instructed local officers to liberate "without exception" not only youths arrested for criticizing the Army, but even those activists who had been jailed for raiding military installations. Many officers had overreacted to Red Guard attacks against the Army, the directive said, and had taken these assaults "too seriously." Finally, the Army was prohibited from further crackdowns and commanders were urged to give the Red Guards free rein in the future. Plainly reflecting Mao's deeply rooted belief that the "masses" by their very nature cannot err, the directive declared:

> Chairman Mao has more than once taught us that "it is not a crime to make revolution," "it is not a crime to speak out," and "it is not a crime to practice extensive democracy." To force the masses to admit guilt is extremely wrong. Suppression of the revolutionary masses under the pretext of "suppressing counterrevolution" is strictly forbidden.[2]

Less than a week later, the leaders circulated an even more stringent directive that circumscribed the Army's power in two more ways. First, it forbade the Army from shooting at unruly elements—even in instances in which troops themselves were under fire. Second, asserting that a "small handful" of officers were pursuing the "bourgeois reactionary line," it warned that a purge might be carried out within the ranks of the Army. In order to emphasize its importance—and perhaps to dispel doubts as to its authoritativeness—the directive bore this rare annotation: "Comrade Lin Piao. This document is very good. Mao Tse-tung. April 6." [3]

These decrees temporarily emasculated the Army. By depriving commanders of the right to judge the ideological leanings of Red Guard factions, for example, Mao withdrew his confidence in the Army's ability to serve as a political arbiter. By compelling officers to release Red Guards imprisoned for acts of violence, he undermined the Army's prerogative to enforce law and order. And by preventing soldiers from using their weapons even in self-defense, he was indirectly encouraging armed mobs to run riot. Lastly, by hinting that the Army was tainted with "bourgeois reactionary" tendencies, he was implicitly encouraging his followers to assail China's military establishment with the same zeal that they had assaulted the Party bureaucracy.

If these directives were not sufficient, Mao took additional steps to weaken the Army's position. In early April, he removed Marshal Yeh Chien-ying as Vice-Chairman of the powerful Military Affairs Commission, replacing him with General Hsieh Fu-chih, Minister of Security and apparently more sympathetic to the radical line.[4] He also dismissed Marshal Hsu Hsiang-ch'ien, who had been appointed in January to manage a modified version of the Cultural Revolution inside the Army. An old professional soldier primarily concerned with national security, Marshal Hsu had evidently maneuvered to keep Mao's campaign from disrupting the armed forces at a time when the danger of war with the United States or the Soviet Union, or both, was believed to be growing. That effort now cost him his position—at least for the present. He was supplanted by General Hsiao Hua, one of Lin Piao's closest subordinates and head of the Army's General Political Department, who quickly brought intensive ideological pressures to bear on military commanders and their troops.[5]

These pressures took ·the shape of a political indoctrination program endorsed by Mao and personally inaugurated by Lin Piao, designed to rid the Army of its "malignant elements" and "correct mistakes" made by officers who had cracked down on radical extremists.[6] Starting in April and continuing through May, a series of newspaper articles and radio broadcasts exhorted the Army to support the Red Guards even though, as one journal put it, "they have some shortcomings."[7] The Army should not "exaggerate" offenses by the Red Guards, another journal said, explaining that the "errors" of the young radicals "must be condoned" and the youths themselves be "trusted to rectify" their own faults.[8] The indoctrination program also required that military commanders atone for their alleged misconduct by openly admitting their failings and asking the radicals whom they had wronged for forgiveness.[9]

This procedure, again predicated on Mao's tenet that the "masses" were the fountain of virtue, caused serious dissension within the Army. In Shantung province, according to one official document, several officers hotly argued against conducting public self-criticism sessions on the grounds that such demonstrations would "dampen" military morale, "upset" troops, provoke "splits" within the regional command, and make the Army vulnerable to attack.[10]

Meanwhile, a spate of Maoist pronouncements reproved the Army for its failure to advance the radical cause. Predictably, the most prolific of the Army's critics was Chiang Ch'ing, whose prominence if not survival depended upon a continuation of revolutionary ferment. Like any politician, Chiang Ch'ing tailored her style to fit her audience. Speaking to student activists in Peking on April 4, she whipped up their enthusiasm by reproaching the Army for suppressing Red Guards and other young militants, stressing that it was the "duty" of military commanders to back radical factions.[11] Ten days later, she delivered essentially the same message to the Military Affairs Commission, the nation's highest Army council —but in a long, rambling discourse that, with its digressions and historical analogies and protestations of humility, seemed to typify classical Chinese persuasive oratory.

She opened her speech to the Military Commission by commenting that she and Mao "live together" and therefore, "though there are many things I do not know," her credentials as his most intimate associate lent weight to her remarks. Lest the senior officers misconstrue her address, however, she emphasized her devotion to the Army. She had always loved the Army, she insisted—even if the Army had not always loved her. She recalled the commanders in Yenan who had refused to permit her to wear the Army's red star insignia on her cap. Nevertheless, she went on, she had persisted in trying to gain acceptance by China's officers, and even now, whatever they thought of her, "my heart still belongs to the Army." Chiang Ch'ing then meandered through an ancient parable and emerged with the real point of her speech—it was not enough for the Army to have fought the Japanese, defeated the Nationalists, and resisted the United States in Korea. Commanders could not rest on their laurels. "They must come out of their barracks and their offices, and return to our old tradition of mingling with the masses," she said. They must respect the Red Guards and other representatives of the "masses," and join with them in the construction of new revolutionary power structures to replace the shattered Party administration.[12]

The new restraints on the Army, combined with exhortations to the radicals to resume their momentum, had immediate, widespread, and devastating repercussions throughout China. Multitudes of rival Red Guard groups again fell to squabbling, either in renewed drives to seize local power or in attempts to settle old scores. At the same time, regional Army commanders were exposed to fresh attacks from factions they had suppressed earlier. Military garrisons in many areas fought back in self-defense, disregarding Mao's directive. In several places, Army units swept up in the ferment squared off against each other. As a consequence, the country was quickly in what the Maoist press later labeled "unprincipled civil wars"—meaning, according to the official definition, sheer anarchy.[13] In an alarmed editorial, the authoritative *People's Daily* warned that the nation was being devoured by flames fanned by "a sinister gust of wind." The conflagration was "wrecking production, destroying State property, and threatening the lives of people," the paper cautioned, and unless the violence was checked it would "upset the orderly process of revolution"—a curious phrase in light of Mao's original concept of the Cultural Revolution as a cataclysmic episode that would reach into the "very souls" of the Chinese population.[14]

Mao and his associates had hoped that, beginning in February, this "orderly process of revolution" would rapidly spawn tripartite Revolutionary Committees in all of China's provinces and special municipalities. General Hsieh Fu-chih, Minister of Security, disclosed that the Maoists had expected the "triple alliances" to have been established everywhere in the nation before the end of May. But, Hsieh remarked gloomily in early May, "the deadline may need to be extended." [15] In Peking alone during the first ten days of the month, he revealed, there had been one hundred thirty-three bloody incidents involving sixty-three thousand people, a "two-figure" number of whom were killed. He also divulged that industrial output in the capital had fallen 7 per cent in April as a result of labor protests and "armed struggles" among rival worker and student factions.[16] At a private conference in the capital on May 7, Hsieh said candidly: "The situation here at the moment is not good. There are fights and splits . . . and the tendency is toward anarchy." [17]

Reports of turbulence emanated from Peking almost daily through the spring. On May 3, for example, three workers were killed and sixty seriously hurt in scuffles between labor groups at the Peking Watch Factory, located in a northern suburb. The factory was forced to suspend operations for two days until troops could restore order.[18] Soon afterward, more than two hundred Red Guards stormed Peking's main government building in an attempt to kidnap high officials, injuring seven soldiers who tried to block their way.[19] Meanwhile, at Peking University students broke into two hostile coalitions. An organization led by Nieh Yuan-tzu, the University's veteran radical activist, mobilized some seven thousand students to combat a rival movement of five thousand students and teachers directed by Chou P'ei-yüan, a vice-president of the institution, who had received his Ph.D. at the California Institute of Technology. In one skirmish, following a memorial service for a young girl who had been driven to suicide by repeated denunciations, four young people were reported killed and three hundred wounded as partisans on both sides wielded clubs, knives, and meat cleavers, a popular amateur weapon among Chinese. The fighting escalated to such proportions that Ch'en Po-ta had to be rescued by police when he ventured into the university in an attempt to reconcile the competing factions.[20]

Similar clashes among student organizations also broke out in Tientsin. There, on April 27, thousands of Red Guards ended a demonstration protesting against the mistreatment of Chinese in Indonesia by fighting for three hours among themselves. Troops and workers finally quelled the riot—but not before more than two hundred young people had been injured. When the Red Guards in Tientsin again started skirmishing almost immediately afterward, Chou En-lai rejected requests from the city's authorities for help, saying in effect that he was too busy coping with far more tumultuous situations elsewhere.[21]

Much more serious than intramural Red Guard disputes were the increasingly frequent and fierce collisions between youth factions and military units. In the Kansu province capital of Lanchow, the site of China's main nuclear research laboratories, the Army garrison went into action against radical groups attempting to grab control of the regional Party apparatus. On April 18, eight truckloads of soldiers encircled the offices of the *Kansu Daily* and proceeded to shoot at young activists occupying the newspaper building, reportedly killing and wounding "several hundred" of them.[22] Troops also struck at Red Guards in Chihsi, a city in the Manchurian province of Heilungkiang. As related in Peking wall posters, soldiers armed with grenades, rifles, and machine guns surrounded a rally being held there by sixty thousand Red Guards on the morning of May 14. Presumably determined to punish the youths for having raided factories, coal mines, and other enterprises in the heavily industrialized area, the soldiers fired into the crowd, continuing their repression in the days that followed by rounding up more than a thousand young agitators. The Army's intervention against the radicals had plainly been authorized by the Heilungkiang Revolutionary Committee—a significant indication that the first provincial "triple alliance" formed in China scarcely qualified any longer as a model of fidelity to the Maoist cause.[23]

In a number of places Red Guard factions appeared to be taking the initiative in attacking military units and installations. In some instances, radical youth groups represented Army political commissars whose Maoist leanings pitted them against regional commanders striving to maintain law and order. Such was the case at Shihchiachung, a pivotal railway junction in Hupeh province, south of Peking. Evidently mobilized by Army political commissars in the district, a Red Guard movement known as the May 1st Rebel Corps assailed the local garrison on eight separate occasions in May, climaxing its offensive with a raid on June 3 against a military hospital situated in the city. Some three hundred young activists flung bricks, tiles, and medicine bottles at the patients, sprayed them with high-velocity water hoses, and smashed the laboratory. More than two hundred patients and participants were said to have been injured.[24] A similar skirmish between Red Guards acting on behalf of contending Army factions also occurred in late May in Chinhua, another important railway center in Chekiang.[25]

Battles between rival military groups and their satellite Red Guards flared up with growing intensity as summer approached. A particularly savage episode occurred in early June in the Hunan province capital of Changsha, where Mao had been a student. There, incensed that old Party and government officials were still exercising authority with military protection, radical factions had staged a series of protest demonstrations beginning in late April.

Operating under Army auspices, labor groups had moved against the young radicals. Skirmishing between the two sides gradually intensified. On June 6, when a coalition of radical students planned to hold a rally at the Sino-Albanian Friendship Hall, workers ambushed them as they arrived for the meeting. What followed makes the student–hard-hat conflict in America seem pale by comparison. Armed with clubs, knives, bayonets, crowbars, and chains, the workers first destroyed three loud-speaker trucks belonging to the students and, in their initial assault, killed five youths. When the students retreated into the hall, the workers besieged the building, then set it afire and slaughtered the young people who fled the flames. According to one account, they killed fourteen or fifteen students trying to escape through the west wing of the hall. The same account claimed that they grabbed one girl, stripped her clothes, gouged out her eyes, and clubbed her to death. Other students died as they leaped from the burning building. Employing a ruse used in confrontations elsewhere, workers posed as doctors and nurses and helped the injured students into ambulances, drove them outside the city, and murdered them in cold blood.[26] Altogether, sixty students were slain during that day in Changsha, and many more were listed as missing.[27] One student described the corpse of a comrade of twenty-two whose "face had been beaten to such a pulp that he could not be recognized." In his pocket, along with his identity card, was half a cucumber that the boy had carried to quench his thirst during the conflict.[28]

Shortly afterward, the Hunan Red Guards published a long indictment of the Army for having violated Mao's instructions by suppressing "true revolutionaries." [29] But despite this complaint, the man who emerged as boss of the area was General Li Yuan, commander of the Forty-seventh Army.

Frustrated by what they considered a betrayal of their cause, the Hunan radicals subsequently formed a coalition called the Provincial Proletarian Revolutionary Great Alliance Committee—abbreviated in Chinese as Sheng-wu-lien—and published one of the most remarkable documents of the Cultural Revolution. Entitled "Whither China?" the document audaciously excoriated Mao on the grounds that his failure to fulfill his promise to support the seizure of power by the "masses" permitted old Party officials and Army officers to retain their authority—and therefore encouraged the rise of a "red capitalist class" of whom Chou En-lai was "the chief representative." [30] A year later, desperate efforts by these and similarly disappointed Red Guards elsewhere in China to assert themselves were to lead to the last major gasp of the Cultural Revolution.

Another area where the chaotic conditions of the spring were particularly marked was Honan, in central China. There, earlier in the year, despite attempts by Chou En-lai to reconcile the Army and its Red Guard adversaries, the provincial military garrison had suppressed the largest local radical movement, the February 7 Commune. Though dismayed by this blow to their disciples, the Maoist leaders in Peking feared antagonizing the region's commanders—or as Hsieh Fu-chih, the Minister of Public Security put it: "The Honan problem involves the Army, and it cannot be solved quickly." [31] Indeed, faced with a *fait accompli*, the Peking authorities issued an edict on April 12 giving full authority to the military command to rule Honan and to arrest Red Guards regardless of idcological persuasion who violated "public security rules and regulations." The edict also endorsed the past conduct of Honan's scnior officers who, it said, had "consistently backed true revolutionaries" and were "correct in the general orientation of the struggle." The Peking leaders pledged not to interfere in the Army's decisions concerning the February 7 Commune, declaring euphemistically that the "broad masses" of Honan would determine its fate.[32]

Early in May, however, Mao reversed that edict. He had reportedly examined the Honan question personally and concluded that the February 7 Commune represented his line and deserved total support.[33] Accordingly, he dispatched a squad of agents to the Honan capital of Chengchow with instructions to direct the Red Guards to wrest authority from the provincial military command. Mao apparently did not expect trouble. He probably estimated that the sheer weight of his supreme judgment would suffice to prompt the Honan Army officers to surrender or, at least, to concede to some kind of face-saving compromise. But he miscalculated. Bluntly disobeying his order, the provincial military establishment inflicted a severe setback to the radicals in one of the bloodier clashes of a bloody period.

This challenge to Mao in Honan was unprecedented—and far-reaching in its consequences. Until now, regional commanders had rarely defied the Chairman directly but would, in the traditional style of Chinese officials responding to the emperor, genuflect to his decrees while maneuvering to evade them. But the Honan garrison had established a new pattern for insubordination, and it would be imitated during the weeks ahead elsewhere in China—and most dramatically, in late July, in Wuhan. The Army's virtual act of sedition in Honan was both a cause and an effect. It inspired other military units throughout China to rebel openly against Mao, and it reflected the degree to which the turmoil of the Cultural Revolution had already eroded his prestige and power.

Given a new lease on life by Mao, the Honan radicals sought to personalize their opposition to the provincial garrison by focusing their fire against General Ho Yun-hung, the deputy political commissar of the regional command. They claimed with considerable justification that "the hangman of Honan's Cultural Revolution" had imprisoned, tortured, and killed numerous members of the February 7 Commune.[34] In response to these charges, the Honan garrison blamed the Red Guards for "sowing social chaos" by having "pointed the spearhead of the struggle" against the Army, thereby undermining its endeavors to impose the "dictatorship of the proletariat." As tensions grew, General Ho himself convened a "political work conference" in Chengchow at which he accused the radical activists of trying to "hoodwink the masses" by staging "bogus shows of power" designed to display their strength.[35] These exchanges of rhetoric ultimately led to a showdown on May 26, when the February 7 Commune and its affiliated factions assembled twenty thousand followers at a rally in the Chengchow stadium to denounce General Ho for his "crimes."

The Army could have plausibly banned the demonstration. But the local commanders devised other plans. They alerted their own "mass" organization, the Provincial Revolutionary Rebels, whose ranks included an estimated ten thousand tough industrial workers only too eager to vent their wrath on students. In preparation for close combat in city streets, the workers pasted identifying strips of white adhesive tape on their wrists, and divided themselves into flexible six-man teams outfitted with clubs, crowbars, chains, belts, and other improvised weapons as well as rattan helmets. Uniformed soldiers, presumably acting as "advisers," were dispersed among them. Apprised in advance that the radicals intended to parade through the factory district of Chengchow following their rally, the workers waited.[36]

Night had fallen as the thousands of February 7 Commune members and sympathizers spilled out of the stadium. With Mao's special envoys at their head, they marched across the bridge spanning the Chinshui River, past the remains of earth ramparts that once enclosed the ancient city, over railway tracks, and into Chengchow's industrial suburbs. Chanting Maoist slogans, singing revolutionary hymns, and shouting epithets against General Ho Yun-hung, they turned into Mienfang Lu—Cotton-Spinning Road—the site of the city's numerous textile plants. Suddenly the whistle of the Chengchow Cotton Textile Mill No. 6 screamed "like the wail of a ghost" in the eerie darkness, as a Red Guard later recalled. It was the signal for the Army-supported workers to spring their ambush.

Strategically poised on the upper floors of factories overlooking the road, the workers bombarded the paraders with bricks, tiles, stones, and other missiles, then poured out onto the street swinging their weapons. The youths, caught by surprise in the narrow street, panicked. Many pleaded for mercy. Others, unable to distinguish friend from foe in the darkness, hit back at their own comrades. Still others tried to resist. Some four hundred young people took refuge in a nearby mill, but workers laid siege to the building and finally forced them out by launching tear-gas bombs and grenades provided, presumably, by the Army. At one point, a survivor related afterward, a six-wheeled truck roared at full speed into the fray, mowing down people in its path. No match for the well-organized labor platoons, the young radicals were decimated. By dawn, according to their own rough count, "scores" had been killed, more than a thousand were wounded or missing, and the macadam surface of Mienfang Lu was "smeared with blood." [37]

The turmoil in Chengchow was far from finished. During the following days, riots continued to lash the city. Students, workers and soldiers as well as peasants from rural suburbs ran amuck—looting shops, invading factories, smashing schools, and fighting among themselves in skirmishes undoubtedly motivated more by personal than political quarrels.[38] Breaking discipline, a few military units fragmented into rival factions, and clashed.[39] Hospitals issued desperate appeals for medicine and plasma.[40] Corpses piled up at the local crematorium.[41] On May 27, the outbreaks disrupted China's two main railway lines traversing Chengchow, halting vital east-west traffic between the coast and the interior, and north-south traffic between Peking and Canton.[42] Amid this turbulence, the city garrison made plain its intention to tame leftist elements by force. Military spokesmen proclaimed that the "counterrevolutionaries" would be shown "no kindness," warning: "It is necessary to depend upon guns . . . to maintain and consolidate political power."[43]

Meanwhile, fighting erupted in other parts of Honan province. In the town of Loyang, the military garrison mobilized local industrial workers and suburban peasants in an offensive similar to the thrust against radical students in Chengchow. One of the strongest labor contingents formed under Army auspices was recruited from among the twenty thousand employees of the Loyang Tractor Plant, one of China's showcase factories.

On June 5, for example, some four thousand Loyang workers assaulted students at a vocational-training institute attached to the Loyang Glass Factory, setting fire to the building and rounding up the youths as they emerged. Next day, with the late spring temperature in the inland city registering nearly a hundred degrees, the students counterattacked at the Loyang Ball-Bearing Plant, another one of China's industrial showpieces.[44] The almost daily fighting apparently reached a high point of violence on the afternoon of June 19, when a battle broke out between Tractor Factory workers and students enrolled in a technical school run by the plant. Unable to dislodge the students who were holed up inside the school, the workers brought in local construction experts armed with a five-ton demolition ball, and simply proceeded to wreck the building, leaving dozens of youths buried in the debris.[45] About that time, macabre testimony to the carnage in Honan appeared in Peking, where Red Guards who had escaped to the capital displayed the blood-stained shirts of comrades killed in the provincial strife on a truck parked outside the city's main department store.[46]

More than six months later, after further outbreaks of violence, the tensions in Honan would be eased by a tenuous compromise between the region's old Party officials and the Army. But like other such accommodations elsewhere in China at that stage, the Honan arrangement frustrated the radicals, and they continued to clamor for the power that they claimed to be their due. As late as spring of 1968, the Honan military garrison was still suppressing Red Guards under the guise of eradicating "wicked elements" and "counterrevolutionaries." [47]

Probably no region troubled the Peking leaders more acutely during the first half of 1967 than did Szechwan, the immense granary lying in remote splendor beyond the gorges of the Yangtze. In February and March, the Maoist leaders had apparently approved the crackdown on unruly radicals conducted by Li Ching-ch'üan, the provincial Party boss, and his local military associates. Though Li and his colleagues had imprisoned an estimated hundred thousand Red Guards and other leftist militants, they were hailed as "comparatively good people and able men," and that endorsement encouraged them to continue their repression.[48] But in April, as Mao and his subordinates moved to reverse the trend toward stability, they took special steps to promote a radical resurgence in Szechwan.

The zigzagging fortunes of the Szechwan radicals could be traced in the adventures of Liu Chieh-t'ing, a Party official from Ipin. Liu Chieh-t'ing and his wife, Chang Hsi-t'ing, had been purged by Li Ching-ch'üan for having opposed his liberal economic policies after the Great Leap Forward. Viewing the Cultural Revolution as an opportunity to avenge themselves, Liu and his wife went to Peking to present their grievances to Mao's inner circle. From then on, their ups and downs and ins and outs were like a veritable barometer of the changing political climate in Szechwan. The Maoists would neglect Liu during the calmer interludes of the Cultural Revolution, even to the extent of raising no objections to his imprisonments by the Szechwan Party apparatus. When they needed a symbol of radical dynamism, however, they would restore him to favor. In early April, therefore, they turned to him as a convenient lever to revive the Szechwan radical movement.

Having again escaped from Li Ching-ch'üan's clutches, a feat he seemed to perform with almost magical dexterity, Liu Chieh-t'ing had reached Peking in late March and presented the Maoist leaders with a catalogue of "crimes" committed by the Szechwan Party machine and its military cohorts against the region's "true revolutionaries." [49] Had they not been planning to regenerate the radical drive in Szechwan, the Maoists would have probably ignored him. But Liu's appearance was now expedient—if not contrived.

On April 1, Chou En-lai, Chiang Ch'ing, Ch'en Po-ta, and other members of the Peking hierarchy convened a meeting to assess the Szechwan issue. Present, besides Liu Chieh-t'ing and his wife, were two senior officers representing the Szechwan Army command. After a good deal of heated discussion the Peking leaders criticized the two officers for having oppressed the radicals and instructed them to confess their faults. [50] The conference then exonerated Liu Chieh-t'ing, his wife, and a number of other Szechwan radicals, and directed that the Red Guards who had been jailed by the provincial Party apparatus be released. The decree also retracted the earlier Maoist commendation for Li Ching-ch'üan and, branding him a "pro-capitalist," called for his dismissal. [51]

These widely publicized decisions had an electrifying impact in Szechwan. Interpreting the exoneration of Liu Chieh-t'ing to signify their own vindication, Red Guards throughout the province rose up with renewed vigor. Moreover, the judgments rendered against Li Ching-ch'üan and the Szechwan Army command had licensed them to focus their fire on the region's political and military establishment.

Starting in early April, leftist factions unleashed a series of forays against Party-backed organizations in Chengtu, Szechwan's capital and one of China's loveliest cities. In the first of these attacks, on April 5, four radical groups disrupted an outdoor rally being held by the Industrial Workers Combat Corps, the labor movement that had been mobilized under Li Ching-ch'üan's auspices. During the following week, the rival sides fought five more skirmishes, leaving some four hundred participants injured. [52] After that, the violence rapidly spread to other parts of the province. On May 1, in one of the rare naval encounters of the Cultural Revolution, two hundred youths were drowned in the Yangtze near Chungking when their boat was rammed and sunk by a vessel steered by their foes.[53] Fighting also erupted in Ipin, a town up-river from Chungking that is the uppermost point accessible to Yangtze steamers. There, more than a hundred people were reported to have been killed during the first four days of May.[54] But the biggest battles in Szechwan during that period were centered in Chengtu, and they spiraled to a scale that was virtual civil war.

In the heart of the fertile Szechwan basin, Chengtu had been transformed by the Communists from a charming provincial city into a thriving industrial complex of more than a million inhabitants, its suburbs humming with textile mills, iron and steel works, and several sensitive armaments plants, among them factories producing tanks and frames for jet fighter aircraft. In early May, the fiercest conflicts to roil Chengtu occurred in the city's industrial district. The Szechwan Cotton Mill served as the stronghold of the main radical faction, the Red Flag Combat Division, while the Industrial Workers Combat Corps had its bastion in a weapons plant cryptically designated for security purposes as Factory No. 132.

Starting on the afternoon of May 1, the Industrial Workers staged probing attacks against the radical groups in the Szechwan Cotton Mill, abducting a number of youths and putting them through the ritual of torture and confession. The radicals mobilized squads to rescue their comrades, and soon thousands of Chengtu workers, students, and masses of suburban peasants had joined in the melee. On May 5, contingents of the Industrial Workers stormed the radical positions in the textile factory. The fighting dragged on through the day, abating inconclusively at dark with some two hundred participants seriously injured.[55] Mobs continued to roam around the city throughout the night, clashing sporadically.

The Industrial Workers Combat Corps had held several wounded Red Flag youths as hostages in their headquarters at Factory No. 132. The next morning, eight nurses drove to the plant in an ambulance to retrieve the injured. Though seven of the nurses were women clad in white uniforms, the Industrial Workers regarded them as the enemy. According to one account, they pulled them into the factory and, stripping off their clothes, beat them. News of this brutality spread quickly, bringing Red Guards to the plant from all corners of Chengtu. They encircled the buildings and, wheeling loudspeaker trucks into place, appealed to the Industrial Workers to capitulate. By noon, Factory No. 132 was under siege. But the plant was a weapons factory—and that made the difference. At 2:45 P.M., workers in a factory workshop squeezed off two bursts of gunfire, probably from AK-47 automatic rifles being manufactured for delivery to Vietnam. A few minutes later, two more bursts echoed from another part of the plant. Nobody was hit. Yet the shots gave the skirmish a new and fatal dimension.

The weapons in their hands seemed to endow the workers with a fresh sense of power. When a Red Flag loudspeaker truck called on them to lay down their arms, the workers responded by firing at the vehicle. Two young people in the truck, one of them a schoolgirl, were killed instantly. All restraints gone, armed workers in other sections of the factory opened fire against the mobs outside. Most of the crowd scattered, but a few youths managed to break into the plant. They stormed up stairways and fought amid upturned desks and filing cabinets in the factory's offices. A clash inside the building destroyed the plant laboratory, and, at one point the fighters nearly touched off an explosion as they smashed the plant's fuel tanks.

The Chengtu military garrison, fearful of exposing itself to charges of supporting the wrong side, had avoided open involvement in the battle. Later documents would allege that its commanders secretly aided the Industrial Workers Combat Corps. But finally, acting on instructions from Peking, troops intervened to restore order on the evening of May 6. By that time the recorded casualties totaled forty-five dead and nearly three thousand hospitalized with serious injuries. Countless others had been slightly hurt, and numbers were missing.[56] But the casualties were overshadowed by the fact that guns had been used heavily by civilian activists for the first time in the Cultural Revolution.

This phenomenon alarmed everyone but the most intransigent of the Maoists in Peking. For despite their commitment to revolution, the Chinese Communist leaders could recall that civil strife had torn China apart for a century before the Communist rise to power. And they must have felt that, perhaps in different form, history might repeat itself. Moreover, the prospect of dissidence in

Szechwan was an especially sensitive one, since the province's separatist tendencies had traditionally concerned China's rulers for centuries.

In late April, even before the Chengtu battle, the Peking leaders had been trying to alter Szechwan's administrative structure. They perceived that they could no longer tolerate Li Ching-ch'üan and his Party apparatus without risking protracted turmoil. But they could not hand control over to the radicals, who lacked the experience and discipline to manage such a vital area. Hence they sought to work out a compromise arrangement and, on May 7, they announced it in a ten-point directive.

Entitled "Red Ten Articles," the directive dismissed Li Ching-ch'üan and two of his principal Army associates, and it placed Szechwan under the command of two seasoned officers—General Chang Kuo-hua, the boss of Tibet, and General Liang Hsing-chu, deputy political commissar in south China. This reshuffle seemed peculiar, since both men had been strongly opposed by Red Guards in their former areas. But the appointments had a three-fold purpose. First, as veterans of the First and Second Field Armies that had conquered Szechwan for the Communists, the two generals had old ties with officers still serving in the region and could therefore be expected to maintain a hold over the garrison. Second, they presumably carried weight with the Szechwan conservatives, whom Peking regarded as the main source of the trouble. And finally, they could always be relieved, in the event of failure, much more easily than figures closer to Mao. Meanwhile, to placate the Szechwan leftists, the directive promoted Liu Chieh-t'ing and his wife to a four-member "preparatory group," headed by General Chang, commissioned to establish a tripartite Revolutionary Committee to govern Szechwan.[57]

When General Chang Kuo-hua was summoned from Tibet to receive his new appointment, the Maoist hierarchy convened a conference. Present were Chou En-lai, Chiang Ch'ing, and Hsiao Hua, chief of the Army's General Political Department. They made it plain to Chang that they considered the Szechwan military command to have been grievously at fault in its handling of the earlier situation. Chang would have to perform better.

Almost patronizingly, Chiang Ch'ing told General Chang that

the Army could redeem itself in Szechwan. "We have such a fine Army, and must not jump to the conclusion that it is always wrong just because it makes mistakes in one area or over a particular question," she said, explaining sweetly that troops "are boys of the people" who must be treated "leniently" when they commit errors. The correct role for the Army in Szechwan, she prescribed, was to "minimize internal strife" and to isolate Mao's enemies by unifying the radicals and winning over the "masses" allied to "conservative" factions whose "force . . . is not negligible." [58]

Hsiao Hua, in contrast, bluntly denounced the Szechwan garrison. The Army's duty was to "safeguard the gains of the Cultural Revolution and defend the people," but the Szechwan commanders had deployed troops "to suppress the revolutionary masses" and, as a consequence, "the Cultural Revolution has suffered a setback. How grave this mistake is!" The Army's consistent failure to support the Szechwan leftists had served to strengthen the "reactionaries," he said, with the result that the "sharp and complicated class struggle" in the region could not easily be resolved. Referring to the Chengtu armaments factories damaged the day before, he warned that the violence was especially serious since the province "is an important base of national defense construction." Unlike Chiang Ch'ing, he had few kind words for Szechwan's senior officers. They must "criticize themselves, examine their errors, mend their ways, really join Chairman Mao's revolutionary line," and, above all, Hsiao Hua insisted, they must "resolutely back the true proletarian revolutionaries." [59]

Chou En-lai spoke calmly. "Some comrades" considered conditions in the province to be "chaotic," he said. But viewed "dispassionately," the Szechwan situation "is excellent and is taking a turn for the better." Li Ching-ch'üan had been "unhorsed" and "the liberation of the southwest has begun." In his practical fashion, Chou urged General Chang to be prudent when he reached Szechwan. "Don't expect to change everything at one stroke," he advised, pointing out that Szechwan was so huge and diverse that all its problems together added up to an unduly "dark picture " A solution to the region's complex questions would "take time " With an extraordinary eye for minutiae, Chou concluded his talk by settling a few details. There was the case, for example, of two Peking Red Guards who had been killed in Chengtu. "Why ship their bodies when they can be cremated in Szechwan and their ashes sent home?" Chou asked. Someone present replied that the Chengtu crematorium was being held by the "reactionary" Industrial Workers Combat Corps. "Then telephone orders to the Army to capture it," said Chou.[60]

General Chang Kuo-hua had little to say when his turn to speak came. In good soldierly style, he vowed to fulfill his assignment "one hundred per cent" even though he was "not acquainted" with the Szechwan issue.[61] But in reality his mission would be almost impossible to carry out, and he barely managed to survive it.

Several fundamental flaws marred the Szechwan compromise. In the first place, General Chang Kuo-hua instinctively sympathized with the provincial military commanders and shared their impatience with the students. Second, faced with the task of restoring law and order, Chang would be compelled to seek help from Szechwan's *apparatchiks*, whom the young militants were striving to overthrow. And finally, because of his basically conservative inclinations, he would inevitably clash with Liu Chieh-t'ing and Chang Hsi-t'ing, now the area's foremost radicals. In other words, jointly assigning General Chang and Comrade Liu to the job of managing Szechwan was as unrealistic as expecting that George Wallace and Huey Newton would cooperate in governing Alabama. Their interests and aims were wholly incompatible and the arrangement was bound to founder—unless one or the other prevailed. Not until ten months later, in one of its periodic conferences on Szechwan, did the Peking hierarchy reveal the extent to which the attempt to reconcile the divergent regional factions had failed.

At that conference, held in Peking on March 15, 1968, Chiang Ch'ing accused General Chang Kuo-hua mercilessly of having encouraged "reactionary" groups while suppressing "true revolutionaries" in Szechwan. She charged that he had failed to promote the campaign to defame Li Ching-ch'üan and the region's Party bureaucrats, and really favored Mao's enemies, had ignored directives from Peking, and had worked with his associates to create their own "independent kingdom." In the cruelest cut of all, she denounced him for "bourgeois objectivity." Referring to one of his speeches, Chiang Ch'ing said scornfully: "You talked like a newspaper reporter. We don't know where your sympathies lie."

Premier Chou En-lai was reluctant to lose Chang Kuo-hua,

however, and he came to the general's rescue. "He is familiar with the Szechwan situation, but he has a habit of muttering and mumbling," Chou explained to the others. Turning to Chang, he advised, "You should speak up boldly." He reminded the general that he had formerly been regarded as one of Mao's most resolute disciples, "Why is it that you no longer have the same determination?" [62]

Underlying General Chang's ambiguity, in part at least, was sheer bewilderment. An honest soldier with no great diplomatic skill, he had been caught in an incomprehensible political tangle. Indeed, Chang confessed, he and his staff had been confused from the moment they assumed their posts in May. "Hardly had we arrived in Szechwan than we were attacked from all sides." [63]

The ferment that had greeted Chang on his arrival in Szechwan dramatized the unresponsiveness of China's provinces to Peking's decrees at the time. The so-called "Red Ten Articles," designed to revamp the provincial administrative structure, was having virtually no effect. Chengtu continued to be the scene of bloody skirmishes. On May 8, the Industrial Workers Combat Corps counterattacked radical strongholds in two factories, leaving seventy dead in an encounter that lasted three days.[64] Over the following week, violence enveloped the city's outlying farm districts as the rural population joined in the fighting. In the suburb of Loshan, nearly a hundred people were killed in one incident.[65] In Chungho, a village six miles outside Chengtu, workers and peasants captured some two thousand students who had evidently gone into the countryside in quest of support. Afterward, it was reported, the headless bodies of thirty-four youths were found in a stream near the village.[66]

According to many documents, large numbers of activists on both sides were armed—and determined to remain so. Rejecting demands by the local military garrison that it hand over its weapons, one group of Chengtu radicals declared: "We must use our guns to defend the Cultural Revolution and the proletarian dictatorship. We will not surrender them lightly." [67]

Meanwhile, the violence spread like an epidemic to other parts of Szechwan. It particularly shook Chungking, the largest city in the province. It had not been easy for the Peking leaders to appraise the political map of Chungking. After several futile meetings devoted to deciphering the Chungking puzzle, they resorted to a facile expedient. They reshuffled the city's Army commanders, creating a temporary committee empowered to work out a compromise.

This approach infuriated the Chungking University August 15th Combat Regiment, an important student group supported by the local military garrison. It resented the idea of sharing the spotlight with other factions, and its activists inaugurated a resistance campaign.[68] They plastered up posters openly denouncing Peking and, in a refreshing change from the solemnity of most Red Guards, resorted to satirical criticism of the Maoist leadership. Recalling a statement by Lin Piao that Mao's edicts must be obeyed even if not understood, the youths formed a faction labeled the Fail-to-Understand Combat Group and staged a burlesque rally at which speakers read Peking directives as the audience shouted in reply: "We fail to understand." [69]

The resistance in Chungking was more than satirical, however. On May 19, more than two thousand students invaded the railway station and blocked train traffic for two days.[70] Tensions grew during the ensuing weeks, and in early June youths were armed with rifles and bayonets besides such improvised weapons as clubs, crowbars, and vials of sulphuric acid. A few Army units split into competing cliques, while peasants and apprentice workers as well as rusticated students streamed into Chungking to vent their grievances.

There were hints amid this ferment that Li Ching-ch'üan, Szechwan's former Party boss, was still wielding a measure of power. Local security agents loyal to him were said to be operating in several areas. Significantly, too, radio broadcasts attacking him originated in neighboring Kweichow, where the Maoists were strong, rather than in Szechwan.[71] By August, the province was in the throes of almost complete civil war. The following year, Chou En-lai would be prompted to quote an old Chinese adage:

> Long before the world fell into chaos,
>   Szechwan was chaotic.
> Long after the world became calm,
>   Szechwan was still chaotic.

Nearly every other region of China was experiencing something close to civil war during the late spring of 1967. Radio broadcasts from Anhwei disclosed that different factions there were fighting among themselves as well as indulging in theft, murder, and other forms of lawlessness.[72] In the Kiangsi province capital of Nanchang, production in thirty-three factories had stopped or slowed down as a result of clashes among workers, while rail service to nearby Fuchow halted for ten days in early June following a skirmish in which twenty-nine youths were killed.[73] At the end of May, a battle in the Yunnan province capital of Kunming left close to three hundred dead and more than a thousand wounded.[74]

Exalted by this frenzied atmosphere, reckless Red Guards in a paroxysm of xenophobia even attacked foreign diplomats stationed in China. On May 24, truckloads of Red Guards broke into the British Consulate compound in Shanghai and harassed the British Consul, Peter Hewitt, his wife, and two children, who were under orders to leave China within forty-eight hours. Chinese youths tore Hewitt's clothes, spat in his face, and smeared him with glue as he ran the gantlet to his aircraft.[75] In Peking not long afterward, two Indian diplomats were kicked, punched, and forced to their knees as they also departed the country on an expulsion order.[76] Soviet, French, Yugoslav, Indonesian, and Mongolian diplomats were also assaulted by unruly radicals. Even envoys representing China's sole ally, Albania, were mistakenly mistreated. At the same time, Chinese diplomats abroad went on rampages inside their missions to display their revolutionary zeal.

Despite efforts by moderate leaders in Peking to keep the Cultural Revolution confined to China, the Maoist drive spilled over the borders of Kwangtung province into the tiny Portuguese enclave of Macao and, somewhat later, into the British Colony of Hong Kong. While relatively restrained, the Hong Kong episode resembled the real Cultural Revolution in at least two important respects.

Though a British possession, Hong Kong was pervaded by a Communist bureaucracy of banking, commercial, and propaganda agents serving as China's representatives to the outside world. These operatives, many of whom live in "bourgeois" style in the Colony, now came under pressure from younger militants in much the same way that Party officials in China had been subjected to Red Guard assaults. As in China, moreover, the Cultural Revolution in Hong Kong gave many local Chinese workers, students, and others a chance to express valid as well as imaginary grievances. But three factors saved Hong Kong from the turmoil that convulsed China. First, British-led police and troops maintained firm control over the situation. Second, the radical activists failed to gain support from Hong Kong's population of 4 million, a large percentage of them Chinese refugees anxious to avoid political involvements. And finally, Peking never gave the agitators more than rhetorical encouragement—for the simple reason that China relied on Hong Kong for nearly half its foreign-exchange earnings and its leaders were reluctant to slaughter the goose that laid its golden eggs.

In November 1966, Premier Chou En-lai had issued instructions to a group of Hong Kong Communist *apparatchiks* invited to Peking. Chou told them that he contemplated no change in the Colony's status—unless it were turned into an "active" base for American naval vessels engaged in the Vietnam war. More significantly, he advised them that Peking expected the Colony's Chinese population to be "patriotic" and "productive"—in other words, to pledge their allegiance to the homeland while earning hard currency for China.[77] But just as Chou was unable to curb the excesses of the Cultural Revolution inside China, he could not prevent its disruption of Hong Kong.

Several events combined to stimulate the Hong Kong radicals in the spring of 1967. The purge of T'ao Chu, the Communist boss of adjacent Kwangtung province, weakened the Colony's Party machine and correspondingly reinforced its radical fringe. The capitulation of the Portuguese authorities to leftist agitators in Macao also fired the Hong Kong radicals with ambitions to inflict the same humiliation on the Colony's British administration. In addition, a variety of legitimate labor protests persuaded the Hong Kong leftists that the Colony's "proletariat" was ripe for revolution.[78]

Under radical guidance, some workers added an ideological touch to their protests. In late April, for example, employees at a Hong Kong cement plant waved Mao's "little red book" and chanted his catechisms as they complained about labor conditions, and they were imitated by striking workers at an artificial flower factory. These incidents led to limited clashes between strikers and police.[79] Soon afterward, the radicals organized demonstrations—in which several respectable Communist figures, compelled to keep pace with the "masses," uncomfortably participated. The Hong Kong colonial establishment handled them with characteristic British aplomb—and a dash of condescension. A typical confrontation occurred on May 18, when some five hundred Communist militants assembled at the handsome mansion of Sir David Trench, K.C.M.G., C.M.G., M.C., the Governor.

The solemn young activists all wore badges bearing Mao's profile, and they clutched the red-covered *Quotations.* Braving the intense heat of the day, the hardier among them had trudged up Garden Road, past the Hilton Hotel and the United States Consulate. Others arrived in automobiles and chartered sight-seeing buses that traffic officers politely directed to a lot marked "Petitioners' Special Car Park." Finally, lined up under the Queen's emblem E2R emblazoned on the mansion gate, the youths began waving their red books and chanting such Mao aphorisms as "Unity is Strength" and "Patriotism is Guiltless and Violence is Justified."

Behaving as coolly as they looked in their crisp khaki shorts, a scattering of colonial Chinese policemen and British constables watched quietly. They were under orders not to react—or, as one of their superiors had put it, "Jolly useful to let the Communist 'glee clubs' sing off a bit of steam." And passive they remained while agile youths plastered the Governor's sentry boxes with Peking-style wall posters denouncing "British brutality" and "Trench's atrocities."

Inside his mansion, Sir David was conferring with the Colony's military garrison commander and other advisers. He decided against receiving any Communist delegations, since "reasonable dialogue" with them was impossible. "Even when we've tried to ring up a Communist headquarters," a colonial civil servant said, "the girl at the other end simply sings Mao Tse-tung over the telephone."

But despite his exterior composure, Sir David was perturbed by the impact of the demonstration on his poodle, who was upset by the noise and had been taken to a kennel after staging a tantrum. A British official later explained that "the animal was frantic with indignation."

At the gates outside, meanwhile, the crowd was warming up as a four-car motorcade appeared, led by a sleek black Mercedes-Benz. At first it seemed like a Chinese wedding party had somehow gone astray. But when the occupants emerged, the crowd cheered. For these were Hong Kong's Communist leaders, the most distinguished among them Fei Yi-min, the urbane editor of the newspaper *Ta Kung Pao*. A slight, bespectacled gentleman in his fifties, Fei Yi-min had been Shanghai correspondent for Agence France-Presse in his youth, before he rallied to the Communists, and he sent his children to school in Paris. He had acquired a good deal of real estate during his years in Hong Kong, and though he was not as wealthy as some other Chinese Communist sympathizers in the Colony, his fortune was considerable. Perhaps for these reasons, Fei demonstrated louder and lustier than anyone else. He demanded to see the Governor and, brandishing his volume of Mao's *Quotations*, he cried: "We want Trench."

The Governor's aide-de-camp, a slim British Army major, descended the steps of the mansion, strode across the courtyard and stopped inside the iron gate. He detailed a Chinese policeman to approach Fei Yi-min with the message that Sir David was "too busy" to see him. Recovering quickly from this rebuff, Fei called to the major to step outside to receive a petition. The major agreed on condition that Fei bring it to the gate. There was a pause as the two men, twenty yards apart, stared at each other. Face was at stake. Neither budged.

Suddenly the silence was shattered as Fei Yi-min held up two fingers, a signal to the Communists to open Mao's missal. With the crowd chanting slogans on cue, he read aloud a lengthy statement assailing the Governor for his "fascist attitude." It was nearing one o'clock when he finished and climbed back into his Mercedes, which needed a push to start. The other demonstrators marched back to their vehicles in the "Petitioners' Special Car Park." A British constable glanced at his watch. "They keep union hours," he observed, "it's time for tiffin." [80]

As the weeks wore on, the confrontation between the Communist militants and the British authorities in Hong Kong slid down toward violence. In early July, more than a thousand Chinese stormed a British frontier post, killing five colonial policemen and injuring twelve others.[81] The next day, a crowd attacked a police patrol, killing one officer with a cargo hook as the others, opening fire, fatally wounded two youths.[82] For weeks after, gangs roamed the Colony's downtown sections, raiding police stations with acid-filled bottles, bricks, and other objects as the police retaliated by ransacking Communist offices throughout the city.

As long as the Communists fought the police, the apolitical Hong Kong population remained largely neutral. But in mid-August, two incidents lost the Communists whatever tolerance they may have enjoyed. In the first incident, two small children were blown to pieces by a terrorist bomb.[83] A couple of days later, radical youths attacked a popular local Chinese radio performer, burning him alive.[84] Not long afterward, in a face-saving statement calculated to curb his followers, a Communist spokesman urged activists to switch to a "practical" approach by concentrating on the "political struggle." [85] In short, his statement implied, armed violence had failed.

Throughout the Hong Kong episode, Peking's conduct was ambivalent. Mao's publicists had constantly exhorted the Colony's Chinese to overthrow the British administration and recover territory "occupied by the imperialists." Yet Chinese military units stationed along the border strenuously prevented mobs from crossing the frontier, and Peking's repeated diplomatic protests to London were as toothless as they were vociferous. Though it had been feared that they would try to dehydrate the Colony into submission, the Chinese scrupulously resumed the water supply to Hong Kong on October 1, in accordance with their contract.

But this ambivalence on the part of Peking's leaders was not limited to their Hong Kong policy. In many ways, it reflected their confusion as they sought to cope with the immense national problems created by the Cultural Revolution. As summer approached, the leaders in Peking saw a country whose social and administrative fabric was being frayed by the traumatic impact of Mao's campaign. One sign of the deterioration was apparent in the rise of common crime. For the first time in years, foreign visitors were advised to lock their hotel doors and carry their valuables with them. In many cities, young people were taking advantage of the political disorder to rob, steal, and even murder. Reports from Shanghai disclosed that discharged soldiers, vagrant students, escaped prisoners, and other alienated elements were operating as outlaw gangs.[86] On June 9, the Shanghai authorities held a rally calling for "tighter public security" at which speakers warned against the recrudescence of "hoodlums and juvenile delinquents" of the kind common to that coastal metropolis prior to the establishment of the Communist regime.[87]

Equally critical was the breakdown of law and order in the countryside, as rival groups organized armed peasants to set up roadblocks, sabotage rail lines, and destroy other transport facilities. In several provinces, peasants were induced to invade urban areas to fight in factional disputes, with the result that agricultural production was suffering.[88] The strategy of mobilizing peasants had been Mao's great innovation in his struggle to attain power in China. But now, the Chairman personally decreed, that strategy was "reactionary." "Surrounding the cities" had been a "correct" doctrine in the past, but, he insisted, "circumstances have changed." Now, Mao said, "to encircle cities is to encircle the proletarian class." [89] In plainer language, this meant that peasants should be excluded from the Cultural Revolution.

On June 6, the Peking leaders issued yet another impressive and somewhat contradictory edict. Henceforth, it declared, Red Guard organizations must not make arrests or conduct "private" trials. The directive forbade youths from stealing official files and documents, wrecking State installations, and raiding the strongholds of rival factions. In addition, "it is strictly prohibited to carry on armed struggle, to beat up people, to fight in groups . . . or to rob properties belonging to individuals." And the directive empowered military garrisons throughout the country to impose law and order.

On its face, the June 6 edict looked like the beginning of a return to normalcy—except for one crucial detail. Nothing in it suggested that the Army could employ force against unruly factions or individuals.[90] Thus commanders remained powerless to stop trouble unless they acted on their own initiative—which many were hesitant to do for fear of exposing themselves to Peking's censure.

The dilemma confronting the Peking leaders at that time, then, essentially resembled the problem they had faced throughout the Cultural Revolution: how to push Mao's drive forward without destroying the country. But now, the pervasive violence made the problem more acute than ever before. "Anarchy," the Maoists warned, "must be overcome without fail." Yet they refused to direct the Army to use its muscle, recommending instead that soldiers "patiently" strive to preach good conduct to the "masses." [91]

Early in the summer, the Peking hierarchy met yet again to discuss ways to meet the challenge of continued tumult. Chou En-lai and the senior military commanders spoke in favor of permitting the Army to suppress disorderly factions, while Chiang Ch'ing, Ch'en Po-ta, and the other prominent radicals predictably advocated more militancy. After "heated discussions," the debate ended with a compromise decision to try a new approach. High-ranking government and Army delegations would be dispatched to investigate specific provinces in an effort to determine which local factions were "legitimate" and therefore deserved support. The touring teams were also commissioned to enjoin radical groups to stop their internecine fighting and unite in "revolutionary alliances." [92] At the head of the most prestigious of these delegations were Hsieh Fu-chih, Minister of Security, and Wang Li, the radical publicist. In July, they embarked on a trip that would trigger the most dramatic chapter of the Cultural Revolution.

CHAPTER 16

Explosion on the Yangtze

❧

*Some people say there is no civil war in
China. But I think this is a civil war. It is
not a foreign war. It is a violent struggle.*
— MAO TSE-TUNG, *September 1967*

ON JULY 14, 1967, Hsieh Fu-chih and Wang Li flew into the
Hupeh province capital of Wuhan to negotiate an end to the
turbulence that had troubled that city for months. They had every
expectation that their mission would succeed. They were personal envoys of Mao Tse-tung. In addition, Premier Chou En-
lai had preceded them to Wuhan and had persuaded the various
factions there to cease their internecine fighting—or so he believed.
Moreover, Hsieh and Wang had just spent eleven days in Kunming,
capital of Yunnan province, contriving a formula to paste over the
differences between Red Guards and the Army garrison there.[1]

But their arrival in Wuhan, far from restoring peace, provoked
an unprecedented mutiny on the part of workers and soldiers
headed by General Ch'en Tsai-tao, the regional military commander
—and the revolt would have decisive consequences for the Cultural
Revolution and for the ultimate political shape of China. Indeed,
among the many upheavals that disrupted communities all over
China during the Cultural Revolution, none occurred in more surprising and spectacular fashion than this event. Nor did any other
have so significant an impact on the eventual outcome of Mao's ambitious campaign. Until then, the Cultural Revolution had largely
featured clashes between various local factions, each claiming to be
faithful to Mao and his doctrines. At Wuhan, in contrast, a military commander and his supporters overtly defied Mao—challenging

not only the Chairman's sanctity but the concept of central authority that the Communists had strenuously tried to secure since 1949, when they extended their control over a land that had been fragmented by internal strife and foreign invasion for more than a century.

That gesture of defiance, reminiscent as it was of the "warlordism" of a generation before, had immediate repercussions throughout China. Red Guard groups and military legions fought against each other and among themselves with unbridled ferocity. The month of anarchy that followed was so devastating that, by early September, the Peking leaders were compelled once again to direct troops to take drastic measures to save China. This brought the Army to the fore and spelled the beginning of the end of the Cultural Revolution. Thus, while it represented the height of turmoil, the Wuhan uprising also marked a turning point, after which Mao's drive never fully recovered its momentum. In a matter of weeks, the Cultural Revolution went from a Reign of Terror to the equivalent of Brumaire.

Wuhan was a plausible scene for such high drama. Composed of Wuchang, Hankow, and Hanyang, three cities facing each other at the confluence of the Yangtze and Han rivers, the Hupeh capital had long been one of China's most sensitive urban areas. During the late nineteenth century, its location on the Yangtze halfway between Shanghai and Chungking made it a natural trading post for British, French, Russian, Japanese, and other foreign commercial firms seeking to penetrate the interior of China. Local Chinese reformers also endowed Wuhan with factories and arsenals, and its economy further burgeoned in the early twentieth century when it became a key junction on the newly constructed Peking-Canton railway. After 1949, the Communists transformed Wuhan into a major industrial complex featuring a huge iron and steel mill, heavy machine-tool plants, and metallurgical installations. One of their most impressive achievements, completed with Soviet aid in 1958, was a mile-long bridge spanning the Yangtze between Hanyang and Wuchang that turned Wuhan into a strategic communications center—as Mao phrased it in a poem celebrating the structure, "a chasm becomes a thoroughfare."

Over the years, Wuhan's increasing economic importance was

matched by its growing vitality as a political crucible. The foreign companies that opened offices in Hankow in the nineteenth century inadvertently imported Western ideas along with Western merchandise. And the railway had encouraged the growth of a proletariat receptive to the radical nationalism spreading through China during the early years of this century. In 1911, the revolution that resulted in the creation of the first Chinese Republic began in Wuchang when elements in its garrison revolted against the Manchu authorities. The city's students and workers were frequently active in the next decade, and in the mid-1920s Wuhan was the seat of a short-lived national government that included Communists. In 1927, Chiang Kai-shek abandoned it to set up his own Nanking regime. During that period, too, Mao based his Institute of the Peasant Movement in Wuhan. Hence the city had a tradition of dissidence that persisted even after China came under Communist rule. In 1957, three Wuhan youths were publicly executed for having staged a riot in protest against rigid university controls.[2]

Against that background, there were several new social and political stresses and strains that were crucial in Wuhan during the Cultural Revolution. For one thing, the city's early industrialization had spawned an elite labor force that was closely linked to the provincial Party apparatus. These workers, like veteran trade unionists in the United States and Western Europe, perceived that they had much to lose from the destruction of the local political bureaucracy. They therefore became stanch defenders of the *status quo* in opposition to the Red Guards and other militants striving to overthrow the Party machine.[3] Similarly, the Army garrison had become firmly implanted in Wuhan since 1949, when it had occupied the area during the Communist take-over of China. Its senior officers, intimately affiliated with the regional Party Committee, were committed to protecting the bureaucracy against Maoist assaults. Moreover, as some Western analysts have suggested, the Wuhan commanders were associated with certain figures in Peking who had consistently resisted Mao's purge.[4] Thus, among its many causes, the Wuhan uprising in 1967 reflected a desire on the part of the provincial Party and Army hierarchy to preserve its autonomy, and so it was a rebellion for the sake of conservatism.

In that respect, the Maoists accurately portrayed the Wuhan episode as "counterrevolutionary."

The Wuhan events also dramatized the importance of the human quotient in the Cultural Revolution. The Peking leaders, scarred by the memory of "warlordism," may have overreacted to signs of regional resistance in the belief that the fragmentation of China they had worked so hard to avoid was returning to threaten national unity. Judging from their public and private statements, too, Mao and his comrades seemed to have been persuaded that their enemies had mounted an extensive and intricate conspiracy against them, and this may have prompted them to respond to the Wuhan dissidents more forcefully than was necessary. And, finally, the age-old Chinese preoccupation with "face" undoubtedly played a key role in the episode. For the Peking leaders apparently abandoned diplomacy and confronted the Wuhan commander with an ultimatum that made graceful retreat impossible. Thus cornered, he rebelled.

To label Ch'en Tsai-tao a "warlord," as the Maoists did, was gross exaggeration. But he typified the entrenched provincial commander. Born in Hupeh in 1908, he was a peasant of nineteen when he joined a Communist guerrilla band operating near his village, and he served throughout the rest of his career in central China. In 1954, he was put in charge of the Wuhan Military Region, with responsibility for Hupeh and Honan provinces, and he was still in that post thirteen years later. As part of a Communist system in which political and military affairs overlapped and intertwined, Ch'en developed a complex web of Party and Army relationships. Starting in the mid-1930s, for example, he formed close links with Liu Po-ch'eng, the celebrated "one-eyed dragon" later to become one of China's ten Marshals, who was an early critic of Mao's guerrilla doctrines and a foremost advocate of military professionalism.[5] Afterward, as the senior soldier in the Wuhan region, Ch'en also forged ties with the area's Party *apparatchiks*. These included T'ao Chu, and Wang Jen-chung, the Communist boss of Hupeh.

During the summer of 1966, as the Cultural Revolution was getting under way, Ch'en Tsai-tao and the other Wuhan leaders had reason to be optimistic for their future. T'ao Chu was then achieving prominence in Peking as national propaganda chief, and he was using his influence to promote his old comrades. Wang Jen-chung not only had taken over the Party's Central-South Bureau but was given a place in the Cultural Revolution Directorate. Wang's elevation, in turn, assured the authority of Chen and other key figures in Wuhan.

Like Party officials and Army officers elsewhere in China during that period, Wang and Chen went through the motions of sub-scribing to the Cultural Revolution in order to control the Maoist campaign and shield themselves in the process. They sent Work Teams into Wuhan's universities as a way of checking student agi-tation and, along with other maneuvers, directed local Red Guard attacks against convenient scapegoats. Among their targets was Li Ta, one of the founders of the Chinese Communist Party, then president of Wuhan University.

Seventy-six years old and suffering from a bleeding ulcer, Li Ta addressed a personal message to Mao, pleading: "Please save me." Mao eventually received the message and issued orders to the Wuhan Red Guards not to "kill Li Ta by persecution." But that order allegedly was intercepted and withheld by Wang Jen-chung, and Li Ta was forced to face a kangaroo court that branded him a "black gangster" and recommended his expulsion from the Party. Other Red Guard assaults against the old man continued until, on the morning of August 13, he suddenly collapsed. For nine days after that, Red Guards refused to permit his hospitalization, even though he was spitting blood and running a high fever. On August 22, now realizing that Li was nearing death, the youths rushed him to a clinic, registering him under a pseudonym. Li died two days later.[8]

The disappearance of Li Ta compelled the Wuhan leaders to find other victims for the Red Guards, and they arraigned several minor functionaries in the following months. They also strove to keep pace with the rhetoric of the Cultural Revolution. On one occasion, Hupeh Governor Chang T'i-hsueh told a youth rally: "The more chaos the better. Only through chaos can we cultivate and stiffen our ability." [7]

But during the fall of 1966, as they sought to curb Red Guard excesses, the Wuhan Party leaders turned more and more to the Army for help. General Ch'en Tsai-tao, who until then had remained behind the scenes, appeared repeatedly at rallies. He exhorted Red Guards and other militants to carry on the Cultural Revolution, promising them that the Army would serve as a "defender of the people's interests." [8]

Whatever his long-range design, Ch'en's growing prominence put him into a pivotal position. For T'ao Chu's collapse in December brought with it the downfall of Wang Jen-chung and his associates in the Party's Central-South Bureau, and Ch'en filled the vacuum created by their purge. In January 1967, when Mao issued the call to his followers to "seize the bourgeois strongholds," Ch'en simulated obedience by organizing Red Guard groups to storm Wuhan's factories, banks, radio stations, newspapers, and other enterprises. As became clear later, his action was calculated to convince Peking that he was responding to Mao's decree directing the Army to support the radicals. In reality, like other regional commanders. Ch'en appeared to believe that he could prevent the Red Guards from causing irreparable damage by controlling their destructive appetites.

At that stage, however, controlling the Red Guards was almost impossible as the youths, once unleashed, refused to submit to discipline. On January 9, for example, a report from Wuhan disclosed that thousands of young men and women had blockaded the Yangtze River bridge and occupied the airport, disrupting traffic of all kinds into and out of the city. Referring for the first time to a problem that was to become increasingly serious—and would later have critical international implications—the same report revealed that the turmoil in Wuhan was interrupting railway shipments of Soviet and Chinese military supplies to North Vietnam.[9]

Other indications of growing turbulence were to be contained in the Wuhan garrison's attempts to impose law and order. On February 3, the Army published a thirteen-point edict criticizing the city's radical factions for "sabotaging" industrial production, cutting communications, and, among other things, inciting peasants to leave the surrounding countryside to participate in the urban ferment. While paying lip service to the Cultural Revolution, the edict plainly tried to limit the campaign. Red Guards and other activists, it asserted, should pursue the Maoist drive only "in their spare time," adding that meetings and rallies must be conducted in a "rational manner" that would not impede the economy.[10] These and other admonitions were futile, however. The situation in the city gradually polarized as two rival coalitions mobilized their forces.

One of these coalitions, put together by Ch'en Tsai-tao as his instrument for preserving order, was called the Wuhan Area Proletarian Revolutionary Liaison Center of Mao Tse-tung Thought Million Heroic Troops—or, in familiar abbreviated form, the Million Heroes. Included in this "conservative" movement were groups of skilled workers, office employees, minor officials, militiamen, older students, and others who had most to lose from a revolutionary purge. They were backed up by the 9th Independent Division, an Army unit used for internal security purposes.[11]

The Million Heroes, which comprised about a half-million activists, outnumbered its rival coalition, the Mao Tse-tung Thought Fighting Team's Wuhan Workers General Headquarters—or, in shorthand, the Workers Headquarters. This movement, considered to be radical, was mainly composed of workers from the Wuhan Iron and Steel Company as well as university and school students. In its ranks, too, were Red Guards sent to Wuhan from Peking.[12] The Workers Headquarters was also supported by certain military units loyal to Li Ying-hsi, a local Army political commander determined to challenge Ch'en Tsai-tao's authority.[13] The split within the Wuhan garrison had been widening since February and, like the polarization of the city's political factions, became increasingly acute as summer approached.[14]

Throughout the late spring the rival coalitions escalated their attacks against each other from verbal exchanges to physical clashes. On May 17, for instance, some two thousand members of the Workers Headquarters assaulted the Army garrison, seriously injuring ten soldiers.[15] Sporadic fighting continued after that until June 14, when skirmishes again led to the closing of the Yangtze River bridge.[16] After this, in an attempt to restore order, Ch'en Tsai-tao drastically cracked down on the city's radical youth groups. The radicals fought to defend themselves, and by the latter half of June, Wuhan had degenerated into anarchy.

Ch'en Tsai-tao began his operation against the radicals on June

17. At one o'clock in the afternoon, according to several versions of the event, the Wuhan garrison deployed a number of trucks filled with members of the Million Heroes armed with spears, axes, and pitchforks against a student hostel in Hankow. The battle raged all night and by the next morning more than a hundred were dead and some three hundred injured. On the same day, the Army sent thousands of peasants against youths gathered at the site of a suburban water-reservoir project, and the toll in that battle was nearly two hundred killed and more than a thousand injured.[17] The next morning, when a group of young people tried to visit their hospitalized comrades, they were kidnaped and beaten, and their Polish-made automobile was confiscated. In another part of the city, seven students were clubbed to death by a Million Heroes group when they tried to negotiate a truce to end the fighting at a railway office.

Wuhan's hospitals were crowded with wounded, and the water and electricity supply in several districts had broken down.[18] Yet the rioting continued. Night after night, opposing gangs fought at different places in the sprawling metropolis. On the afternoon of June 23, at the Hanyang Steel Rolling Mill, rival factions used improvised weapons, homemade incendiary bombs, and vials of acid in a clash that claimed eight dead and more than a hundred injured. About the same time, buildings of the Water Transport Engineering College were gutted by fire as opposing student groups battled for control.[19] Other skirmishes erupted daily, and reports in Peking estimated that some two thousand factories, mines, and other enterprises in the Wuhan area either had suspended their activities entirely or were operating only part-time.[20]

Alarmed by the havoc wrought on one of China's key industrial sectors, the Peking leaders telephoned Ch'en Tsai-tao on June 26, commanding him to halt the fighting. But Ch'en, apparently convinced that he had to suppress the radicals in order to protect his own authority, refused to comply. Finally, Chou En-lai himself reportedly flew to Wuhan to examine the situation.

Precisely when Chou went to Wuhan, how he conducted his investigation, or how he reached his conclusion has never been made clear. But on July 14, he convened a meeting at the local Army headquarters at which he decreed that Ch'en Tsai-tao had erred in backing the "conservative" Million Heroes and should shift his support to the truly revolutionary Workers Headquarters. At noon of the same day, Hsieh Fu-chih and Wang Li arrived in Wuhan, together with several Red Guards from Peking and General Yü Li-chin, chief political commissar of the Air Force. Chou returned to Peking, leaving Hsieh and Wang to persuade the city's assorted factions to accept his verdict.[21] *

During their first few days in Wuhan, Hsieh and Wang met with delegates of the various Red Guard movements. On the evening of July 15 they accepted arm bands and badges from Red Guards of the Central China Technical College, an affiliate of the Workers Headquarters, thus endorsing their organization. When they convened representatives of the Million Heroes two days later, in contrast, Hsieh and Wang blamed them for making trouble. This tactless approach divided the rival groups even further, and recurrent skirmishes occurred around the city despite the presence of Mao's two emissaries. One afternoon, for example, during demonstrations staged to hail the envoys, eight people were killed when a fight broke out between members of the Million Heroes and the Workers Headquarters.[23]

On the evening of July 19, the explosion came. Hsieh and Wang, having compiled sufficient documentation to substantiate their case, summoned Ch'en Tsai-tao and other senior military officers to a conference at Wuhan Army headquarters. Their message essentially repeated Chou En-lai's earlier verdict. They urged Ch'en and his associates to support the Workers Headquarters and disband the Million Heroes, telling them, "You must only correct your mistakes and all will be well." According to Hsieh's own account, that decision particularly infuriated one officer, Niu Hai-lung, commander of the 9th Independent Division. Niu refused to believe that Chou En-lai had issued the instructions and claimed that Wang Li had invented them.[24] After much argument, he jumped up and walked out of the conference, shouting: "I am prepared to risk my life." [25]

It was nearly midnight when Hsieh and Wang returned to

* According to one account, Mao also went to Wuhan, and remained there after Chou's departure. This account claimed that the Chairman anticipated an attempted *coup d'état* and spoke with Ch'en Tsai-tao on July 18 in an attempt to "give him a chance to rein in on the brink of the precipice." But Ch'en "did not listen, being a reactionary." The account claimed that Mao stayed in Wuhan until the night of July 21, narrowly escaping capture by the mutineers.[22] The authenticity of this sole version has been questioned. It may simply have been contrived to dramatize Mao's prescience.

their suite at Tung Hu Hotel. As they were preparing for bed, trucks, fire engines, and loudspeaker vans suddenly swept into the hotel compound. According to several versions, including Hsieh's own, two hundred men descended from the vehicles and encircled the building while others sealed off nearby streets. Armed with rifles, spears, and knives, many were troops of Niu Hai-lung's 9th Division even though they wore arm bands identifying themselves as members of the Million Heroes. As they milled around in the compound, the loudspeakers broadcast slogans denouncing Hsieh and Wang and proclaiming loyalty to Mao.

Ch'en Tsai-tao, summoned by telephone, arrived to explain that the situation was beyond his control. His explanation was probably sincere, for a dozen agitators shortly burst into the hotel room, threw him to the floor, and began to kick him—until one of them discovered they were attacking the wrong man,[26] whereupon they turned on Hsieh Fu-chih and Wang Li. Leaving Hsieh in the room, they took Wang to the Wuhan garrison headquarters, where they tore off his clothes and beat him. At about two o'clock in the morning, meanwhile, Hsieh Fu-chih managed with the help of sympathetic Red Guards to escape from the hotel. He made his way to the Hydroelectric Institute, a radical stronghold. There, he learned of Wang's whereabouts and went to the garrison headquarters to rescue him—only to be placed under guard himself. By now, the episode was changing from a confused political dispute into a direct military confrontation between the Wuhan command and the Peking authorities.[27]

Anticipating a reaction from Peking, Ch'en Tsai-tao's military and civilian followers reinforced their defenses. They replaced the regular guards at the garrison headquarters, seized the radio station, took over vital positions along the railway, occupied the airport, and blocked the approaches to the bridges across the Yangtze and Han rivers, thus isolating their adversaries in each of Wuhan's three cities. They also staged forays against the main radical strongholds, killing and injuring those who resisted them. And, to justify their actions, they broadcast declarations asserting that their goal was to eradicate Mao's "counterrevolutionary" foes.[28]

The Peking leaders received news of the abduction of Hsieh and Wang at dawn on July 20, and they responded swiftly and forcefully. An airborne division and three infantry divisions were ordered to move toward the city from posts in the province, and five gunboats of the East Sea Fleet were sent from their Shanghai naval base up the Yangtze to Wuhan.[29] At the same time, Chou En-lai left Peking by airplane—convinced, apparently, that he could persuade Ch'en Tsai-tao to free Hsieh and Wang.

By now, however, Ch'en could not retreat. Apprised of Chou's imminent arrival, he sent twenty-five truckloads of troops and civilian vigilantes to take the Premier into custody as his airplane landed. But loyal Air Force elements radioed Chou's plane of this maneuver, and the pilot set down at an alternate field south of Wuhan.

In the meantime, Hsieh Fu-chih and Wang Li, incarcerated in separate rooms at the garrison headquarters, were in danger of being transferred by the mutineers to a more secure place outside Wuhan. According to some reports, Ch'en Tsai-tao planned to transport them by boat up the Yangtze to Chungking, then also in chaos, to hold them there as hostages.[30] He could then use the two captives as bargaining counters to negotiate a compromise with Peking—in much the same way that the Communists had imposed a settlement on Chiang Kai-shek after kidnaping him in Sian in 1936.

At this critical juncture, a daring officer known only as Chang made his appearance. The chief political commissar of a regular Army division stationed near Wuhan, Chang had been aligned against Ch'en Tsai-tao for months. On the evening of July 20, according to his own story, he led three men into the garrison headquarters, overcame the sentries, and discovered the room in which Wang Li was being held. Taking Wang with them, they fled into the Hungshan highlands outside Wuhan, eluding capture by Ch'en Tsai-tao's men. In the morning, they were able to contact other loyal troops, and finally escorted Wang to the airfield at which Chou En-lai had landed.[31] There they found Hsieh Fu-chih, who had been rescued by an airborne contingent. Leaving the two men at the airfield, now under regular Army control, Chou returned to Peking to arrange for their reception. At two o'clock in the morning of July 22, Hsieh and Wang departed Wuhan, reaching the national capital at dawn.[32]

The rescue of Mao's emissaries did not bring the Wuhan mutiny immediately to an end. On July 21, as Chou En-lai was returning to Peking, no less a figure than Lin Piao visited Wuhan to organize the offensive against the dissidents. He appointed General Yü Li-chin, the Air Force political commissar who had originally accompanied Hsieh and Wang, to command the operation. By July 23, the loyalist forces had gone into action. Gunboats of the East Sea Fleet, joined by additional vessels, cruised into position and trained their cannon on targets in the three Wuhan cities while airborne troops, some of them reportedly parachuted into the fray, seized the bridges, the radio station, the main telegraph office, and other strategic points. Units of the Fifteenth Army moved into the city from their base near Hsiaokan.[33]

Confronted by this awesome display of military muscle, many of the dissidents capitulated without a fight and, according to one report, the weapons they surrendered filled thirty trucks.[34] Ch'en Tsai-tao and his staff were arrested and sent to Peking, and the Wuhan Military Region was placed under the command of General Tseng Ssu-yü, former deputy Army chief of Manchuria. Under his aegis, local officers promptly issued a series of statements admitting their errors and pledging to pursue the "correct" line in the future.[35]

But the rebellion persisted in one form or another into early August. On July 27, the Maoist leaders were still calling on the Wuhan garrison to overthrow the insurgents,[36] and the Peking press two days later said that the struggle for the city had moved "into a new stage" as opposing factions were deployed on "battlefields along both banks of the Yangtze."[37] On July 31, the Peking radio disclosed that aircraft had showered Wuhan with leaflets urging radicals in the city to intensify their attacks against remnant dissidents.[38] Wuhan's hospitals were crowded with wounded soldiers and civilians, and thousands of refugees were disrupting railway service as they tried to flee south to Canton.[39] Another sign that Wuhan remained unstable for weeks was that the gunboats of the East Sea Fleet did not finally return to their Shanghai base until October.[40]

On July 26, meanwhile, China's principal civilian and military leaders met in Peking for nine hours to question Ch'en Tsai-tao and his comrades. The next morning, Red Guards invaded the hotel where Ch'en was being held and dragged him out for the first of a series of unofficial interrogations.[41] At one of these sessions, convened on August 4, Army representatives grilled Ch'en for ten hours. The disgraced general was compelled to bow to his inquisitors as the hearing began. But he stubbornly denied having engineered the mutiny—until, in the end, his exasperated interrogators forced him to repeat that he had been "the manipulator and ringleader of the incident." Thus they were able to announce that Ch'en had confessed.[42] Apparently anxious to avoid aggravating the dissension in the Army, however, the Chinese leaders treated Ch'en with surprising lenience. Some months later, Chou En-lai quoted Mao as having said that Ch'en "may come forward again"—but only after he had "mended his ways in all seriousness," presumably through "labor reform." [43]

Ironically, when the Army was suppressing radicals throughout China a year later, Ch'en Tsai-tao's Wuhan rival, Li Ying-hsi, would be among those brought to trial. He was accused of having attempted an unauthorized seizure of power in February 1967, labeled a "typical soldier ruffian," and, like Ch'en, condemned to redeem himself at hard labor—once again demonstrating the tendency of the revolution to devour its most devoted activists.[44]

Inglorious though it was, the Wuhan uprising heartened the most militant advocates of the Cultural Revolution. For by dramatizing that Mao's doctrines still faced widespread opposition, they were able to clamor for intensified purges not only in the Party but in the Army as well. The extremists also urged that Red Guards and other radical activists across China be armed. But this prospect of increased violence inevitably prompted the regional Army commanders and their supporters to respond with force. From late July through early September, China seemed dangerously close to civil war.

Nobody encouraged the revival of violence more openly than did Mao's wife, Chiang Ch'ing. She cautioned the Red Guards against disarming, and her exhortations were echoed by Ch'en Po-ta. "Prepare for protracted war," he said, insisting that the struggle will not be resolved merely by the exchange "of a few words." [45] Most important, Mao himself circulated various decrees authorizing the distribution of arms. "Issue weapons to the leftist masses," one read, and another declared: "Everyone should be prepared to take up bayonets." He was also quoted as saying: "We are now carrying pens, but we should be ready to carry rifles." [46]

Maoist leaders also utilized the Wuhan rebellion to initiate a series of demonstrations and rallies calculated to whip up fervor among the Red Guards, many of whom had been earlier showing signs of weariness with the Cultural Revolution. Starting on July 22 with the airport reception for Hsieh Fu-chih and Wang Li on their return from Wuhan, the organized excitement reached a high point three days later, when a million people were mobilized to fill Tienanmen Square. Mao was absent, but Lin Piao and nearly every other Chinese leader appeared on the balcony of the Tienanmen Gate, and the rhetoric that pervaded the rally was belligerent. Speakers called for fresh efforts to "strike down" Mao's adversaries and warned that the Cultural Revolution would be subverted unless it was defended "with blood and life." [47] The same emotional tone vibrated in the press. One *People's Daily* editorial, portraying Mao's enemies as "rats running across the street," cried out: "Kill them! Kill them!" [48]

Amid these passionate pleas for a radical resurgence emerged a new and significant theme—the demand for a thorough purge of the Chinese armed forces. Demands for the elimination of individual officers had been put forth before. But now, for the first time, the entire Peking press and radio resonated with strident allegations that the Army was riddled with Mao's foes. Recalling the "betrayals" of P'eng Teh-huai and Lo Jui-ch'ing, the commentaries contended that their sympathizers in the Army were engaged in a wider conspiracy inspired by Liu Shao-ch'i and the "revisionist" Party machine. It was imperative "for the proletariat to keep a firm hold over the Army" in order to "destroy the bourgeois reactionary line." [49] Some radicals even favored the cancellation of Army Day, since Mao had not participated in the historic episode which it commemorated.[50]

Though the attempt to purge the Army was at the outset plainly endorsed by Mao's closest subordinates, its most dynamic advocate in Peking was a group of ultraleftists known as the May 16th Detachment, named after the date of the important circular issued by the Chairman early in the Cultural Revolution. One of the leaders of this movement was Wang Li, who had apparently become embittered against the Army as a result of his experience in Wuhan. The May 16th Detachment also included Ch'i Pen-yu, the radical journalist who had triggered the offensive against Liu Shao-ch'i in April, and Yao Teng-shan, the Chinese diplomat who had been expelled from Indonesia. Several of these extremists belonged to the Cultural Revolution Directorate and, in that capacity, were intimately affiliated with Chiang Ch'ing, Ch'en Po-ta, and other figures in charge of Mao's campaign.[51] They were probably associated as well with General Hsiao Hua, the Army's chief political commissar, whose main function was to eradicate military professionalism. Thus their attacks against the Army—along with the other disruptive activities they promoted during the turbulent month of August—may have initially been tolerated if not actually approved by Mao.

Ultimately, however, the May 16th Detachment would be branded "counterrevolutionary" by the professional military commanders, who realized that the country could not withstand endless turmoil. Worried by both the growing Soviet threat on China's northern borders and the escalating American presence in Vietnam, the commanders apparently warned Mao and the other Peking leaders that they had reached the limit of their endurance. The commanders may have also resented Lin Piao's association with the radicals who, in the wake of the Wuhan mutiny, called for a purge of the Army. And their resentment may have been at the origin of Lin's downfall four years later.

The Wuhan revolt and its aftermath, like the Cultural Revolution itself, served to bring to the surface tensions which had plagued China even before the establishment of the Communist regime. These tensions illustrated the degree to which the "souls" of the Chinese people, which Mao had sought to transform, remained unchanged.

CHAPTER 17

The Guns of August

As revolutionary masses, you should take up
arms to defend yourselves. . . . Don't be
naïve. Don't lay down your weapons when
your enemies use pistols, rifles, spears, and
big swords against you.
                    —CHIANG CH'ING, July 22, 1967

Under the dictatorship of the proletariat,
there is no reason whatsoever for the working class to split into two big irreconcilable
organizations.
                    —MAO TSE-TUNG, September 1967

T HE MONTH OF AUGUST 1967 was the most dangerous period of
the Cultural Revolution—indeed, perhaps of the entire Communist regime. Inspired by the Wuhan mutiny, factions throughout
the country rose to the attack—their agitation further encouraged
by official criticisms of the Army. And Mao's directive to "arm the
leftists," published in late July, significantly contributed to the
turmoil. Every faction regarded itself as truly revolutionary, and
many now felt licensed to acquire weapons. In some areas, the Army
mobilized armed groups to suppress them. Elsewhere, extremist
organizations were given guns by military units trying to perpetuate
the ferment for their own purposes. In several places where militant
youths were denied arms, they broke into arsenals to steal rifles and
heavier equipment, and many even ambushed soldiers in order to

seize their weapons. In south China, trains transporting Soviet and Chinese military supplies to North Vietnam were looted more and more frequently, thus aggravating the already strained relations between Peking and Hanoi and deflating China's claim to being a "reliable rear area" in the struggle against the United States.

On August 10, the Army command in Kiangsi province issued weapons to special vigilante groups directed to "protect State property and maintain revolutionary order." [1] For similar motives, the Hunan military commander armed some three thousand members of two civilian organizations formed under Army auspices.[2] In Peking, in contrast, more than two thousand youths affiliated with the Aviation Institute's Red Flag faction, one of the most radical movements in the city, were furnished with rifles and mobilized into a paramilitary regiment that would "strengthen the morale of revolutionary groups . . . and guarantee the smooth development of the Cultural Revolution." The Chingkangshan Red Guards at the Peking Normal College, another extremist faction, were also armed.[3] Hence the potential for violence was enlarged to a degree that Mao had never envisaged. And that potential rapidly became reality.

Shantung was one of the first regions to react directly to the events in Wuhan. There, local dissidents abducted a team of Mao's emissaries investigating the political situation in the city of Linyi. Radio broadcasts from Shantung disclosed that the dissidents had brought "large numbers of ignorant peasants" into the city, inciting them to "encircle, attack, and beat up" the visiting investigation team. Similar outbreaks also erupted at Tsaochuang, another Shantung city on the main rail line to Peking, where rebels unsuccessfully attempted to overthrow the Municipal Revolutionary Committee loyal to Mao. In both places, the radio broadcasts claimed, the revolts were "coordinated with the recent Wuhan incident." [4]

By the middle of the month, the ferment had spread to other parts of Shantung. Rival labor factions in the port city of Tsingtao were reported to be battling each other with the usual assortment of crowbars, knives, and axes. Here, the radicals' apparent objective was to topple the local Revolutionary Committee, which had evidently excluded the more militant Maoist groups when it was founded earlier in the year. In short, the Revolutionary Committee had become as entrenched and conservative in office as the former Party apparatus it had displaced. As its spokesmen declared: "Our stand is clear-cut. No matter whether it is rightist subversion or leftist attack, we must resolutely counter them." [5]

Insurgent elements also rose up in Honan province, an area under the jurisdiction of the Wuhan Military Region. Led by General Ho Yun-hung, the Army's deputy political commissar there, the Honan activists were reportedly joined by allies sent into the region from Szechwan. This suggested a measure of collusion among military commanders throughout the Yangtze River valley from Wuhan to Chungking, and the nationwide implications of this frightened the Peking leaders. A committee of Honan representatives was convened in Peking in late July, where one of Mao's aides advised them that the "devious, complicated, and arduous" fight for control of the province had reached a critical level. He warned them against emulating the Wuhan dissidents: "The schemes and tricks of those who cooperate with the mutineers will sooner or later be brought to light." [6]

The uprising in Wuhan also ignited a fresh explosion of violence in Szechwan, where, according to several reports, weapons were being shipped down the Yangtze from Hupeh province.[7] By early August, Szechwan Army units, Red Guard factions, and other groups were armed with everything from rifles to tanks and artillery. During one period of fighting in Chengtu, hundreds of buildings were leveled by artillery fire, and communications in and out of the city were cut off completely. Similar battles destroyed sections of Chungking, Nanchung, and other cities, and the provincial Army commander, General Chang Kuo-hua, narrowly escaped death when snipers fired at him in Chengtu.[8] Though casualty figures were never published, the toll in Szechwan was illustrated in Peking on August 20 when hundreds of Red Guards, each carrying a chrysanthemum, marched silently through the city in mourning for their comrades killed in the province. "Szechwan is Swimming in Blood," their banners pleaded, "the Central Committee Must Act." [9]

As in other provinces, the rival groups in Szechwan had inflated their ranks with peasants from nearby villages. According to one report, a half-million peasants poured into Chengtu alone during August.[10] The peasants apparently welcomed this opportunity to break out of the rigors of their "people's communes" and, in the general confusion, to loot urban shops and warehouses for merchandise that was unavailable in the rural regions.

Mao had conceived of this strategy of "surrounding the cities by the countryside" decades before during his wars against both the Japanese and the Nationalists. He had later broadened the concept to form the basis of his strategy for world revolution, arguing that the underdeveloped areas of the globe would eventually defeat the industrial nations. Now he perceived that his strategy was being used by his opponents against him, and he tried to stop it. His private secretary, Ch'en Po-ta, undertook to explain the doctrinal shift in almost scholastic style. The mobilization of peasants had been "correct" during the struggles to take over China, he said. But since the establishment of the "dictatorship of the proletariat, conditions have changed." Therefore, Mao had decreed that peasant deployments should be judged "reactionary." Speaking in Peking on July 21, Mao said: "To mobilize peasants to flock to the cities is a crime—a crime—a crime against the proletariat, against the people, and, from the viewpoint of the peasants, against themselves." [11]

Aggravating the ferment in Szechwan were serious schisms in the military establishment. The most distinguished unit in the province was the Fifty-fourth Army, which had served in both the Korean War and the Indian border conflict. Afterward assigned to Szechwan, the Fifty-fourth Army was divided into forty smaller units by Li Ching-Ch'üan, the regional Party boss who doubled as the Army's political commissar in the province. Li dispersed these units to different districts in order to integrate officers with local Party officials. In theory, this policy conformed to the Maoist dogma which favored civic action by the Army among the "masses." But in practice, close affiliations between Army officers and Party apparatchiks worked against Mao's goals. For the officers not only acquired a vested interest in defending the Party machine, but soon developed a concern for their own authority. In many instances, their wives were employed in local government or Party agencies and their children attended local schools. Thus, as a study of the Army's behavior in the Szechwan city of Tzukung concluded, officers stationed there instinctively tended to side with the entrenched "power-holders" against the Red Guards and other radicals.[12]

Another Szechwan force, the Fiftieth Army, adopted a somewhat different posture. Based almost entirely in the region around Chengtu, the province capital, it was more responsive to General Chang Kuo-hua, the regional commander. Though nominally faithful to the Maoist line, Chang regarded the imposition of law and order as his primary function. His detachments were therefore detailed to suppress various factions irrespective of their ideological leanings and, as a result, they frequently clashed with military units backing troublesome groups. As a Peking analysis of the situation pointed out, many rival movements in Szechwan distorted Mao's old slogan "Support the Army" to suit their own purposes. "Certain people," the analysis said, "support only the military units that back up their faction. . . . This practice of bourgeois and petty bourgeois factionalism . . . has served to split the Army." [13]

By late August, a crazy quilt of Army and Red Guard factions were engaged in battles throughout Szechwan. Some had formed into guerrilla bands fighting in the hills and mountains. To the delight of the Chiang Kai-shek regime, which consistently claimed to have sympathizers within the People's Liberation Army, some of the irregulars were described by Peking propagandists as remnant Nationalist troops.[14] General Chang Kuo-hua, unable to cope with the disorder, was finally compelled to ask Peking for reinforcements in the hope that soldiers from outside the province, unfettered by links with local factions, could restore peace.[15] The device of deploying outside troops was used elsewhere, too—notably in Kwangtung, where the turbulence during the summer became too difficult for the local Army garrison to handle.

In mid-April, during his quick visit to the Kwangtung province capital of Canton, Chou En-lai had criticized the military command there for having manhandled student activists. He had also exonerated the main radical organization, which the Army garrison sought to suppress. These moves seemed to restore calm to the city, but the differences dividing the factions were too acute to permit more than a temporary peace. Hardly had Chou departed than they began to prepare for another round. By then, two large coalitions were forming, distinguished from each other primarily by their past relationship with the Army. Those that had been suppressed by the Army formed a loosely knit movement known as the Red Flag. Those favored by the Army designated themselves the East Wind, the name borrowed from a couplet that had celebrated the period of military control in early spring as the "March east wind." [16] The leaders of the East Wind were said to include the son of General Huang Yung-sheng, commander of the Canton Military Region, as well as the sons of a half-dozen other senior officers stationed in the Kwangtung. [17] The rival movements mobilized forces in anticipation of a pretext to resume fighting. That pretext was provided by the mutiny in Wuhan.

On July 21, the Canton Army garrison and its civilian supporters struck first at their radical adversaries, imitating the military dissidents in Wuhan. East Wing vigilantes, aided by troops, besieged a hundred Red Flag activists in a Canton sugar refinery. Armed with improvised weapons, they killed four young radicals during the skirmish. Two days later, the Red Flag organized a service to mourn its fallen comrades, and this ignited a bigger battle. As Red Flag members marched from a local stadium to the Sun Yat-sen Memorial Hall to hold the service, East Wind activists attacked them. The two sides fought all day to gain control of the hall. By evening, thirty-three Red Flag and an undetermined number of East Wind supporters were dead. After the battle, according to one participant, the East Wind contingent retreated to safety under Army protection. [18]

If the radicals harbored grievances against the Canton military authorities for that incident, they were quickly given doctrinal justification to assault the Army openly. On July 22, Chiang Ch'ing warned Red Guards and other militants against surrendering their weapons, and the official Peking press was calling for a purge of the Army. The Canton radicals began to refer to General Huang Yung-sheng, the local military chief, as "Canton's Ch'en Tsai-tao." Both they and their rivals also started to raid arsenals for weapons, and the violence rapidly escalated. [19]

A new series of clashes broke out on August 13, when the Army killed eighteen young people aboard a boat transporting guns to a Red Flag stronghold on the Pearl River. The Red Flag faction retaliated two days later by assaulting the headquarters of the Kwangtung Province General Trade Union, which was occupied by East Wind members. As a participant in that skirmish later related, the defenders of the building fought from the roof, bombarding their foes with bottles and spraying them with pistol, rifle, and machine-gun fire. Using mortars to open the way, Red Flag activists stormed into the building and up the stairs as East Wind fighters shot down at them from above. In Peking, Chou En-lai received reports of the fracas. He immediately directed the rivals to compose their differences. But soon afterward the Red Flag took over the contested building and the fighting resumed.[20]

The brief rise of the Red Flag faction in the center of Canton prompted East Wind activists to retreat to the suburbs, where they sought support from workers in the industrial sectors outside Canton. Many of them also fled to nearby villages to mobilize the assistance of peasants. Pursuing their enemies, Red Flag groups attacked and occupied suburban schools, using them as strongholds. At the suburb of Kaochung, for example, one Red Flag band took over a school, cemented up its entrance, encircled it with an electrified fence, and put up a sign reading: "If anyone dares to encroach upon our school property, his wife will be called a widow and his filial son will pay homage to a dead father." [21]

By this time, Canton was in total chaos. Thousands of its residents were fleeing to the countryside, disrupting suburban bus traffic. Skirmishes near the municipal airport delayed scheduled flights, and with the main railway station in the midst of the combat zone, travelers had to drive or walk to the outskirts of the city to board trains. A Hong Kong Chinese, returning from a family visit in a town north of Canton, reported that he had had to make his way south by walking, hitching rides in trucks, or hiring pedicabs. Crime in Canton spiraled as the police left their posts and criminals took advantage of the situation to rob and even murder. One Canton resident recounted that groups of outlaws were descending from nearby hills to attack warehouses and homes for food. Such accounts, exacerbated by rumors of similar lawlessness, plunged Canton deeper into apprehension and insecurity.[22]

The turmoil in Canton was even visible to foreign visitors, whom the Chinese usually shield from sights that reflect unfavorably on China. In mid-August, after a two-week tour of China, Japanese Communist students were confined to their hotel for safety's sake and later reported that they had heard shooting in the streets during the night. They were prevented by the fighting from boarding the train for Hong Kong and were taken to the border by bus under Army escort. Even so, they recalled, they were stopped en route by armed Red Guards, interrogated and permitted to proceed only after their escorts explained that they were "honored guests" of the People's Republic.[23] Also in Canton at that time, a group of German tourists accidentally came upon a body hanging from a lamp post. Their embarrassed guide told them, "It is a bandit who has been executed by the people." [24]

Nothing so weakened the Army's prestige and thus intensified the violence in Canton than Peking's demand that General Huang Yung-sheng submit to a "self-examination" of his "mistakes." The purpose of this demand was not clear. Perhaps the Peking leaders believed that, by holding Huang responsible for the unrest, they might appease the Red Guards and thereby calm them. Or they may have been convinced that having failed to curb the disorder, he genuinely deserved censure. In any case, Huang and his staff made ritual confessions. They admitted that their "dictatorial measures" had placed them "in a position antagonistic to the masses," and they not only pledged to vindicate the factions they had banned but promised to release numbers of young people who had been arrested for disruptive activities.[25] But far from placating the radicals, this show of weakness on the part of the Army only encouraged them, and the ferment in Canton grew. Finally, in mid-August, troops from other provinces began to move into Canton to restore order. They included elements of the Forty-seventh Army stationed in Hunan. By September, eleven divisions were reported to be in the Canton region.[26]

In Peking, meanwhile, the Maoist leaders again turned to Liu Shao-ch'i and his wife, Wang Kuang-mei. Though nominally still China's chief of state, Liu no longer exercised authority either in that capacity or within the national Party apparatus. Yet he remained the symbol of opposition to Mao—the personification of all evils of bureaucratic "revisionism." Moreover, Liu was conveniently located to serve as the prime target of Maoist invective, for he had been permitted to continue living in Chungnanhai, the closely guarded residential park reserved for dignitaries of the Chinese government.

Liu had written three "confessions" since the previous October, when he produced his first formal "self-criticism" at a Central Committee meeting in Peking. In the last of these, completed on July 9, he had reiterated his "mistakes" in having tried to dominate the Cultural Revolution in the universities a year before, apologizing to the radicals "who have been suppressed and harmed by the erroneous line which I represent." He invited his comrades to "expose and criticize freely" the "evil influence" he was accused of exerting at the outset of the Cultural Revolution.[27]

But the Maoist faction in the government could not accept Liu's *mea culpa* without conceding that his "crimes" had been less horrible than their frenetic propaganda had been claiming for months. Nor could they liquidate him without losing a valuable target for their campaign against "bourgeois revisionism." Thus their strategy was to keep up the rhetorical drive against him while protecting him against physical assault. In late July, however, with the radicals' emotions stirred by the Wuhan mutiny and their tempers shortened by the midsummer heat of Peking, this tricky approach was not easy to manage.

Hundreds of Red Guards began to demand that Liu and his wife face a public denunciation rally on August 5, the first anniversary of Mao's initial appeal to his disciples to "bombard" the Communist Party bureaucracy. Youths streamed by the thousands to the area outside the walls of the Chungnanhai compound. They put up tents and makeshift huts, and they constructed an ingenious plaster effigy of Liu, its cheeks pierced by a pen and its eyes consisting of blinking blue and yellow electric lights. They also draped their sprawling encampment with banners and posters asserting their determination to place Liu on public display by their August 5 deadline. One placard proclaimed: "We Will Never Retreat Until We Drag Out Liu the Bandit." [28]

Anxious to avert a direct confrontation with Liu, the Maoist leaders delegated Ch'i Pen-yu to dissuade the Red Guards from carrying out their threat. One of the most radical members of the Cultural Revolution Directorate, Ch'i had published a virulent diatribe against Liu in April and was presumed to enjoy the respect of the young militants. Visiting their encampment on the night of August 2, he warned them against invading the forbidden Chungnanhai area. He also urged them to remove their huts and tents, pointing out that they could continue to denounce Liu from the headquarters of their various organizations.[29] Disappointed by this lack of support, the Red Guards countered with an alternate proposal. They would hold a huge rally without Liu's presence—on condition that their representatives be allowed to interrogate him whilst the demonstration went on. The Maoist leaders agreed.

On the afternoon of August 5, this singular episode began with a million people in formation in Tienanmen Square listening to orators haranguing them with speeches hostile to Liu Shao-ch'i and his wife. At the same time, in the garden of their Chungnanhai residence not far away, Liu and Wang Kuang-mei were forced to listen to a broadcast of the rally as a group of Red Guard inquisitors grilled them with familiar accusations. Liu had praised Chiang Kai-shek, conspired to overthrow Mao, and plotted to subvert the Cultural Revolution, the young prosecutors charged. They also blamed him for favoring capitalism, betraying the proletariat, and seeking to promote himself.[30]

Though nearly seventy and undoubtedly numbed by the campaigns against him, Liu nevertheless held his ground. He had indeed praised Chiang Kai-shek, he conceded, but as a "tactic" at a time when the Communists and Nationalists were allied against the Japanese. The charge that he had planned a *coup d'état* against Mao was false. He had certainly made mistakes, Liu went on, yet his errors could not be construed to signify opposition to either Mao or the Communist Party. Finally, exasperated by the old man's intransigence, the youths turned to Wang Kwang-mei and insisted that she expose her husband's lies. "He and I have lived together for more than twenty years," she responded calmly. "I have never heard him tell a lie." [31]

Elsewhere in the Chungnanhai enclosure, other Red Guard teams were questioning Teng Hsiao-p'ing, the Party Secretary General, and T'ao Chu. Here the youths fared better. With almost no prodding, Teng Hsiao-p'ing bleated that he was a "counterrevolutionary" who had eluded Mao's control for years. T'ao Chu was equally unheroic. He admitted to having pursued a "reactionary" line, but pleaded that he had been forced to obey Liu Shao-ch'i. "And what kind of person is Liu Shao-ch'i?" the Red Guards asked. To which T'ao Chu predictably replied: "He is the biggest capitalist in the Party." [32]

Somewhat appeased by the opportunity to harass Liu Shao-ch'i face-to-face, the Red Guards grudgingly folded their tents and slowly went away. But hardly had this interlude faded when even more dynamic radicals inaugurated a fresh thrust. Their main objective seemed to be to gain control over China's foreign relations. This paroxysm nearly ruptured China's diplomatic ties with several nations, among them Burma and Cambodia, and it served to damage what little was left of Peking's international reputation at the time.

Official Peking sources later attributed the nihilistic outburst to the May 16th Detachment, headed by Wang Li and a group of ultraleftists that included Ch'i Pen-yu and Yao Teng-shan, the former Chinese *chargé d'affaires* in Indonesia who had been active in the demonstrations against the Foreign ministry in May. Also associated with them was an improbable figure, Sydney Rittenberg, an American in his late forties who had resided in China since the end of World War II and, under the Communists, become an "adviser" to the central radio station in Peking.

A rebel since his youth, Rittenberg was born into a distinguished Jewish family that had emigrated from central Europe to South Carolina in the seventeenth century. His grandfather had been Speaker of the state legislature, and his father mayor of Charleston. Rittenberg left home while still young to organize cotton-mill, public-utility, and tobacco-plantation workers. A remarkable linguist, he learned Chinese in an Army training program and later made his way to Peking as an employee of the United Nations Relief and Rehabilitation Agency. When he disappeared from sight in 1949, his name was inscribed among the war dead in Charleston's historic Synagogue. [33]

But Rittenberg was very much alive. His homespun American

voice soon became a feature on Peking's English-language propaganda broadcasts, and he enjoyed prominence in that community of "foreign friends" in China known as the "Three-Hundred Percenters" because of their excessively zealous devotion to the Communist cause. Rittenberg displayed even greater zeal during the Cultural Revolution. He delivered speeches denouncing Liu Shao-ch'i and, according to some accounts, went as far as to mobilize a faction of Red Guards under his own leadership.[34] Along with Wang Li and other radical activists, Rittenberg was later branded a "reactionary" and "counterrevolutionary" and indicted for plotting to overthrow both Lin Piao and Chou En-lai.[35] But in early August, he and his comrades were still riding high.

Though China's diplomacy had been gradually paralyzed by the Cultural Revolution during the preceding months, a bigger fight for command of the Foreign Ministry began on August 7. That evening, Wang Li convened Ministry employees to a meeting at which he announced that the time was ripe for authentic revoluaries to direct China's foreign affairs.[36] Mao had personally instructed him, he subsequently intimated, to play a key role in that realm.[37] Wang's principal aim was to challenge the authority of Chou En-lai, who had taken responsibility for the management of the Foreign Ministry in April, when Foreign Minister Ch'en Yi was being subjected to increasingly severe Red Guard attacks. Now, as he had before, Chou reacted with characteristic caution. He encouraged Red Guards to renew their assaults against Ch'en Yi in the hope that they would cease to trouble him. But the militants only intensified their offensive.

In mid-August, Wang Li and his comrades stormed and occupied the Foreign Ministry—this time for about two weeks, installing Yao Teng-shan as Foreign Minister. China's diplomatic behavior during this period became ludicrously paranoiac. On one occasion, the new Foreign Ministry formally protested to the Danish Government against a Copenhagen newspaper cartoon of Mao. A similar complaint was sent to the Swiss Government protesting against the presence of Tibetan refugees in the Alps. After a Burmese crowd jeered Chinese diplomats in Rangoon, an official Peking statement described the incident as an "outrage unparalleled in the annals of international relations." [38] The Foreign Ministry also incited overseas Chinese residents in Cambodia to stage Maoist demonstrations. Infuriated, Prince Norodom Sihanouk threatened to break off relations with Peking, thus depriving the Chinese of a pivotal post in Southeast Asia. At the last minute, however, Chou En-lai retrieved the situation with a virtual apology.[39]

In Peking, Red Guards victimized diplomats of almost every foreign mission. They compelled a Russian to face a kangaroo court for having accidentally broken a glass in a restaurant, and they put the Italian commercial attaché through a similar ordeal in retaliation for Italy's ban on Chinese propaganda activities in Venice. The French Ambassador, Lucien Pye, was trapped and abused, and even a North Vietnamese diplomat found himself being insulted by fanatical youths.[40] This xenophobic frenzy reached a climax on August 22, when mobs of Red Guards raided the compound of the British mission in Peking.[41] Stimulated by the suppression of their compatriots in Hong Kong, they bombarded the British Chancery with bottles of gasoline, setting it aflame. They then pounced on the British fleeing the burning building, beating and kicking both men and women. Grabbing Donald Hopson, the *chargé d'affaires*, by the hair, they forced him to bow his head and confess his "sins." Chinese troops eventually arrived to rescue the diplomats. Though reportedly appalled by the savagery, Chou En-lai remained silent at the time. More than a year later, however, he quietly expressed his regrets for the incident to a British envoy.[42]

Even more crucial to China's political future was the outcome of the struggle between the radicals and the Army. In late July, Mao had called for a purge of the Army. But the regional commanders, assembled in Peking for the Army Day celebrations to be held on August 1, were cool to the idea of an ideological drive that might disrupt their units. In a series of private sessions with Lin Piao, they undoubtedly argued that any move which undermined the Army's prestige or power could only incite the Red Guards to further violence.

Indeed, these senior officers could point to the turbulence already threatening provinces across the entire nation. Virtual civil war was cutting transportation and communications networks as well as obstructing the flow of military supplies to Hanoi. The interruptions in rail traffic were also slowing down China's nuclear and missile development program, and disorder menaced the border defenses against the Soviet Union. Equally worrisome was the damage being inflicted on industry in general and on military industries in particular. In Szechwan, for example, an aircraft factory had reportedly been gutted, and production at defense plants elsewhere throughout the provinces was slipping.[43]

On the afternoon of August 9, Lin Piao called a conference in Peking that would prove to be one of the watersheds of the Cultural Revolution. Among those present, in addition to Chou En-lai, were prominent Maoists like Chiang Ch'ing and Ch'en Po-ta as well as such ultraleftists as Wang Li and Ch'i Pen-yu. The key regional commanders there included Huang Yung-sheng, military chief of south China, and Ch'en Hsi-lien, Army boss of Manchuria. Also present was Tseng Ssu-yü, who had taken over Wuhan after the dismissal of General Ch'en Tsai-tao and his dissident comrades. The divergent attitudes of these figures underlined the dilemma that Lin Piao faced. He was sensitive to Mao's determination to purge the Army. But he also appreciated the apprehensions of the commanders. He therefore sought to appease both the radicals and the military professionals—and satisfied neither.

In typical Maoist fashion, Lin Piao stressed that the "educational significance" of the Wuhan mutiny had been "tremendous," since the incident had revealed "the acuteness and complexity of the class struggle." Such episodes were really welcome, he went on, for they made it possible to expose "bad people and bad things."

> The victory of the present great Cultural Revolution is very great. The price we paid is the smallest, smallest, and smallest, but the victory we gained is the greatest, greatest and greatest. On the surface, everything seems so chaotic, but the chaos is the result of having upset the reactionary line. . . . This upheaval is necessary and normal. Had there been no upheaval, reactionary elements would not have been exposed.[44]

Having thus spouted Mao's doctrine, Lin turned to the soldiers. Beseeching the commanders to avoid another Wuhan revolt, he advised them against taking sudden initiatives that cause trouble. "Let us not have another Ch'en Tsai-tao," he pleaded, adding in peculiarly persuasive language:

We must not have the idea that we needn't report to the Central Committee because we ourselves understand the situation. Nor should we think it unnecessary to seek instructions because the matter is small and we are intelligent enough to handle it. We must not hesitate to disturb the Central Committee. . . .

Send a telegram or make a telephone call, or take an airplane and you'll be here in an hour or two. Don't act on your own because you think your ideas are right or you are clever.[45]

In contrast to the radical statements of only a week earlier demanding that the Army be cleansed of "counterrevolutionaries," this was unusually mild. Officers had inevitably made "mistakes," he said, because their intervention in the Cultural Revolution had been "rather hasty," and he recommended instead that "we should solve problems slowly and step-by-step."

Evidently hoping to win the favor of the professional officers, Lin Piao castigated the Army political commissars whose position he himself had strengthened. The commissars had been initially successful, he explained, but had "performed badly and failed to keep abreast of the situation" during the Cultural Revolution. In particular, he blamed Hsiao Hua, the head of the Army's General Political Department, who had "made one mistake after another." Now, Lin asserted, the country could only rely on "the various military districts, armies, divisions, regiments, battalions, and companies." In short, the commanders would become the principal repository of power. "The old leadership group fell, and it has been supplanted by the military," he proclaimed.[46] But despite his recognition of their authority, the regional commanders never forgave Lin for having encouraged the radicals against the Army. Four years later, in tandem with Chou En-lai, they would move to eliminate him.

Lin Piao's statement heralded the rise of military influence in China. In the following weeks, a series of measures was initiated to reassure the regional Army commanders. The Peking authorities publicly condemned more than fifty Army political commissars who had actively promoted the Cultural Revolution to the detriment of the military professionals.[47] At the same time they refrained from punishing Ch'en Tsai-tao publicly, and Mao was even quoted as saying that the rebel officer might win redemption if he "mended his ways." [48] Simultaneously, a nationwide campaign was launched to "support the Army and cherish the people," with rallies throughout the country thumping the theme of solidarity and mutual trust between soldiers and civilians. [49]

This major reversal of policy must have irritated the left-wing members of the Cultural Revolution Directorate like Chiang Ch'ing and Ch'en Po-ta, who were insisting only a few weeks earlier that the Army be purified. But they prudently remained silent and delegated radical subordinates like Wang Li to voice protests. Whether or not they realized they were being used as lightning rods, Wang and his comrades of the May 16 Detachment spoke out boldly for a purge in the Army. One of them, a radical writer named Kuan Feng, reportedly sent a student group from Peking to Canton with instructions to abduct Huang Yung-sheng. [50] Wang Li himself assailed Hsü Shih-yu, commander of the Nanking Military Region, for "opposing Mao's leadership." [51] The futility of radical efforts to topple these and other officers was later reflected in the fact that Huang Yung-sheng was elevated to the post of Chief of General Staff, and both he and Hsü Shih-yu were promoted to the Communist Party's revamped Politburo.

During August, then, China was buffeted by two conflicting winds. On one hand, the regional commanders were determined to resist radical onslaughts. At the same time, persistent criticism of the Army on the part of Wang Li and other members of the Cultural Revolution Directorate stimulated the Red Guards and other activists to new heights of violence. By late August, armed factions were raiding arsenals for weapons and fighting pitched battles in nearly every province.

Finally acknowledging the gravity of the situation, Mao and his colleagues were compelled to concede that the restoration of order was imperative. This prompted them to initiate two related measures. The first was to disassociate Mao himself from blame by finding scapegoats on whom to pin responsibility. Thus the Peking leaders singled out Wang Li and the May 16th Detachment. These radicals had only advocated policies that Mao himself originally favored. But since Mao's policies could not be criticized, it was necessary to sacrifice his more expendable subordinates. In late August, therefore, the May 16th Detachment came under fire, and some of the accusations directed against members of the movement were characteristically exaggerated. Simultaneously describing them as "ultraleftists" and "reactionaries," Peking publicists not only linked Wang Li and his comrades to Liu Shao-Ch'i and the Party bureaucracy but charged them with "working closely with United States and Chiang Kai-shek secret agents and Soviet revisionists." [52] The fate of Yao Teng-shan was typical. He had been given a warm airport welcome after his expulsion from Indonesia, and even accorded an audience with Mao. Now he was branded as a "schemer of the Khrushchev type" who was "mad with ambition and blinded by the lust for gain." [53] Yao faded from public sight until June 11, 1971, when he was brought to trial before a crowd of four thousand at a Peking stadium [54] and sentenced to a jail term.

In addition to jettisoning these radicals, Mao made a far more significant move. On September 5, for the first time in the Cultural Revolution, he agreed to authorize the Army to shoot at unruly "mass organizations or individuals." Though this directive was specifically designed to discourage the seizure of weapons, ammunition, vehicles, and other military supplies, it gave troops the latitude to open fire on any elements they deemed beyond their control. The test of the directive, however, seemed to betray Mao's extreme reluctance to take this step. As the operative passage read:

> Local garrison forces must first patiently carry out political and ideological work, carefully reason with offenders in order to dissuade or stop them from committing offenses. When such dissuasion or prevention proves ineffective, shots should be fired in the air as a warning, and they should be ordered to withdraw. When such warnings prove ineffective, their behavior may be declared counter-revolutionary, and action should be taken to arrest the few bad ringleaders and trouble-making murderers so that they may be dealt with according to law.
>
> When such persons resist arrest or fight back, the Army may act and retaliate in self-defense.[55]

Chiang Ch'ing began to publicize the new line to Red Guard groups, and it was no accident that she had been selected for this task. As Mao's wife and a confirmed extremist since the start of the Cultural Revolution, she carried enormous weight with the radicals. Her credibility was bound to be enhanced by the fact that she had formerly been a most outspoken opponent of moderation.

Chou En-lai may well have prodded Chiang Ch'ing into undertaking this assignment. For she indicated in one of her speeches that the role she was performing had not been her idea. She had been "unexpectedly" summoned to utter "a few words," she explained, apologizing that she had "not prepared herself for this" and inviting criticism "if what I say is wrong." But, old actress that she was, Chiang Ch'ing played her part—with feeling.[56]

Emphasizing the new plea for temperance, she blithely contradicted the very slogans she had earlier promoted. On July 22, she had urged the Red Guards to "take up arms" to defend the Maoist cause "by force," but now she denounced "armed struggle" that would "ruin the nation." Six weeks before, in the wake of the Wuhan mutiny, she had clamored for a purge of the Army. Now, she declared, the Army was the inviolable "cornerstone of proletarian dictatorship," and chaos would follow were it "thrown into disorder." Moreover, she pointed out to the young radicals, the Army's "deadly" directive meant business. Troops would indeed shoot at Red Guards and other youths who abashed them. "The penalty for stealing weapons is death," she said, adding: "If I were a soldier and someone tried to grab my rifle, I would certainly retaliate."

Chiang Ch'ing further backtracked by repudiating radical attempts to topple all authority as a dangerous "left wind." Absent from her speeches, too, were emotional exhortations to the Red Guards to defeat Mao's adversaries. "It is mistaken to run through the streets," she said. "This is the time to sit down, mobilize your brains, and study documents, however difficult and painful that may be." She told the radicals to "criticize and reform themselves," and she advised rival Red Guard organizations to hold "dispassionate" discussions in order to "seek agreement on major issues while tolerating differences over minor issues." In contrast to her previous declarations, which consistently boasted of triumphant progress, Chiang Ch'ing now conceded that the Cultural Revolution was losing momentum. The Peking leaders were now striving to solve the problems of "one province at a time and one city at a time."

In that way, she concluded, regional Revolutionary Committees that had failed to develop in the spring could be "set up gradually" in an atmosphere of peace and unity.

Chiang Ch'ing was not alone in her appeal for temperance. Ch'en Po-ta, another fierce Maoist, now assailed "extreme leftists" who were spreading anarchy. "We must not allow factionalism to dominate everything. . . . Ransacking does not constitute a revolutionary act." And Hsieh Fu-chih, the Minister of Security who had been abducted at Wuhan, echoed the same theme. Calling for an end to "civil war" and "violent struggle," he cautioned the Red Guards, "Do not let your minds become overheated." [57]

In early 1966, Mao had advanced the argument that "destruction must precede construction." By the fall of 1967, the Communist Party bureaucracy that once ruled China had been shattered from top to bottom. The Politburo was decimated. Of the ninety-three full members of the Central Committee, only thirty-six were still active. The Party's six Regional Bureaus had virtually ceased to exist. Among the twenty-eight provincial Party bosses functioning at the start of Mao's campaign, only five were still in office.[58] Equally devastated were the trade unions, youth associations, women's movements, and other organizations that had underpinned the Party apparatus. Many officials who disappeared later surfaced, either at their old jobs or in different positions. For the Cultural Revolution, with all its tumult, was not a Stalinist terror. But in late 1967, it remained for the Army to pick up the pieces of a country in disarray. Thus from early September onward, military commanders sought to fill the vast power vacuum throughout China.

Conspicuously eclipsed in the new power structures that painfully evolved during the next two years were the Red Guards. Mao had conceived of his cataclysmic drive largely as a training exercise for "revolutionary successors." The more he observed the Red Guards, however, the more he was convinced that they had failed to pass the test. In the summer of 1968, after a brief period of renewed violence, he would disavow them in a poignant scene. But even now, he could not conceal his disappointment with them—and perhaps, too, with the course taken by the Cultural Revolution.

In mid-August, just one year after the great Peking rallies had introduced the Red Guards to China and the world, Mao was asked by an aide if the militant youths might some day be able to take over the provincial Party committees. "In my opinion," Mao replied sourly, "they won't even be fit to take over county committees." [59]

PART FIVE

THE PENDULUM SWINGS

Some comrades have come to regard themselves as "most revolutionary and most advanced" because they had made some contributions during the Great Proletarian Cultural Revolution. This shows that they fail to view themselves correctly, and lack the spirit to remold themselves. Others have desperately exaggerated the role of the former mass organizations, incorrectly handled relations between mass organizations and the Party, and tried to put themselves above the Party in an attempt to challenge its leadership. This is an expression of reactionary anarchism.

—Red Flag, January 5, 1970

CHAPTER 18

Dialectics in Action

Under the dictatorship of the proletariat,
there is no reason whatsoever for the working class to split into two big irreconcilable
organizations.
— MAO TSE-TUNG, September 1967

Chaos is another expression of the eruption
of class contradiction, and the culmination
of the struggle between the two lines in violence. There is nothing wrong with sowing
chaos in the enemy ranks.
—Shanghai Radio, June 11, 1968

ON APRIL 14, 1969, addressing the Chinese Communist Party's
Ninth Congress midway through its deliberations, Lin Piao
announced that the Cultural Revolution had achieved a "great victory" despite its chaotic "twists and reversals." [1] That claim,
though debatable, was significant, for it signaled that Mao Tse-
tung's tumultuous campaign was officially finished. But in reality
the Cultural Revolution had begun to die in the fall of 1967, when
the Army embarked upon its vigorous drive to stamp its rule on
China. And years later, the repercussions of the period would still
be felt.

China's high military officers, as their behavior demonstrated,
had never fully subscribed to the Cultural Revolution. As soldiers,
they were instinctively conservative men suspicious of grandiose
schemes. As veterans who had fought for decades to unify their

country, they were dedicated to national cohesion, and their sense of nationalism also dictated a desire for political stability, social equilibrium, and vital economic development. In short, they favored the construction of a strong China whose domestic solidity would serve as a defense against external enemies.

Mao shared this objective. Yet he and his commanders differed in one important respect. They advocated pragmatic policies while he, in contrast, was convinced that China's avenue to greatness lay in permanent revolution that would release the energies of the "masses."

Though Mao's propensity for episodic upheavals may have dismayed them, most senior Chinese commanders at least acknowledged his leadership. They were mesmerized by his charisma and captivated by his immense prestige. They undoubtedly felt as well that he personified the national cohesion they cherished, and they seemed to believe that any overt action against him might jeopardize China's unity.

By August 1967, however, the Army's tolerance was exhausted. In their view, the foreign threat was present again. The United States was within striking distance of their southern borders. Russian's military build-up along the northern and western frontiers was reaching alarming proportions. And Japan, the old enemy, had become the most powerful nation in Asia. On September 1, at a meeting of the Peking Revolutionary Committee, one Chinese leader reflected the apprehensions of his comrades at what he described as the growing "encirclement" of China by its foes. The Soviet "revisionists" and their Mongolian satellite, he said, were now colluding openly with American "imperialism" and the Japanese "militarists." To assure China's security, the imposition of internal order under Army auspices was imperative.[2]

This concern on the part of China's military officers was fully appreciated by Chou En-lai and, to a certain extent, by Lin Piao. But the job of imposing order on China would not be easy. To tame the millions of Red Guards and other militants was a gigantic challenge. Equally difficult was the task of disciplining workers and peasants who in the past years had tasted real freedom for the first time since the Communists established their regime. Also, in a society where conciliation is an alien concept, months of bloody clashes between rival clans and factions had left a residue of feuds and vendettas that promised to persist, making a return to social peace extremely difficult.

Moreover, there was no guarantee that Mao would continue to cooperate. He had oscillated throughout the past year between encouraging ferment and calling for order. Now, he had acquiesced in the Army's assertion of power, but he was capable of reviving the "masses" at any moment.

Despite these obstacles, Chou En-lai and the Army commanders managed in the next few years to put China back on the road to recovery. Their success was partly due to their ability to exercise authority. They were also helped by the extraordinary resilience of the Chinese people, whose capacity to survive cataclysms had shown itself throughout history.

Late in 1958, when the Great Leap Forward was devastating the Chinese economy, Mao had gone on one of his rare inspection tours of the provinces, and he concluded from his observations that the program required "tidying up." In September 1967, under somewhat comparable circumstances, he took a similar trip. He traveled to Shanghai and around to Honan, Hupeh, Hunan, Kiangsi, and Chekiang, the particularly troubled areas along the Yangtze River, talking with local officials and regional commanders. His conclusion, he candidly admitted, was that the turmoil plaguing the country was serious. Summing up the situation in Kiangsi, for instance, he said: "Some people say there is no civil war in China. But I think this is a civil war. It is not a foreign war. It is a violent struggle." [3]

His first-hand impressions evidently persuaded Mao of the urgent need for moderation, at least for the present. His alarm was reflected in a new set of "supreme instructions" handed down after his return to Peking.

One of these was essentially a repetition of the edict, issued in the spring, which had urged the Red Guards and other activists to stop their wanton attacks against Party and government officials and collaborate in creating unity. The "ferocious" and "inexperienced" Red Guards would have to stop their practice of "beating up cadres, making them kneel, hanging signboards from their necks, and forcing them to wear dunce's caps." Officials "as a rule" should not be condemned, Mao said, and even the "most stubborn" among them "must be given a bowl of rice." Loyal to his concept of "thought reform," he emphasized that careful indoctrination rather than brutality was the only technique for transforming attitudes. "Cadres should not be punished without being educated, nor should they be punished by way of education." [4]

This call for leniency toward officials reflected the Army's need for experienced cadres to help manage the country, and it touched off an extensive campaign publicizing the cases of veteran Party workers who were "rehabilitated" after recognizing their "errors." Some of these accounts, however, inadvertently explained why many officials whom the Red Guards had denounced and mistreated were reluctant to undertake their duties again. One Shanghai Party cadre was said to have been handled "a bit excessively" by the Red Guards, who had refused to exonerate him even after he had admitted his mistakes.[5] The report had a happy ending, but it suggested that many officials must have declined to resume their former jobs for fear that they might again become targets for the radicals.

Mao also urged rival groups to compose their differences amicably. "Really promising men are those who think, not those who show off," he said, explaining that "people who are now making trouble and noises are merely flashing across the stage of history." With that, he uttered a quotation that would become the slogan of the movement:

> There is no fundamental clash of interests within the working class. Under the dictatorship of the proletariat, there is no reason whatsoever for the working class to split into two big irreconcilable organizations.[6]

Along with this plea for unity, Mao underlined the pre-eminence of the Army, a key instrument for the restoration of order. "The chief danger at the moment is that some people want to crush the Army," he warned, asserting that "the Army's prestige must be resolutely safeguarded." Problems nagging military units should be negotiated "within the scope of each individual province," he said—in effect conceding to the regional commanders' demand for autonomy by telling them to resolve their own difficulties rather than responding automatically to Peking's directives.[7] On September 26, back in Peking, Mao expressed his renewed faith in the Army by holding a reception for a number of provincial officers.[8] About the same time, the press initiated a supportive campaign. "Without a people's Army, the people have nothing," proclaimed the *People's Daily*. "The Army is the chief component of State power. Whoever wants to seize and retain State power must have a strong Army." [9]

Chou En-lai echoed the same theme in a series of talks with different youth groups. On September 17, he scolded Red Guards for having continued to attack military units even after the "erroneous" call to purge the Army had been retracted. "You did not listen," he told them, "but instead went on attacking the Army until, by the end of August, the situation had become impossible." Describing the present time as a "transitional period," he said that "we need the Army" to serve as "the Great Wall that protects our frontiers." In a further effort to discipline the young radicals, he ordered them to return to school within a month. Those who disobeyed, he warned, would be expelled and refused jobs by the State, the country's sole employer.[10] That order, like others before and after it, went largely unheeded—since most of China's schools, closed in the spring of 1966, had not reopened.

Chou delivered a similar speech at an all-night meeting of Red Guard representatives from Canton. "There is no need to divide people into the Red Flag faction and the East Wind faction," he said. Such factions were "man-made" and could be dissolved. Their rivalry mainly represented "petty bourgeois" egotistical ambitions, he said, urging the youths to forge an alliance with their adversaries. Chou also told the Red Guards to refrain from interfering with workers, while he stressed that workers must remain in their factories and stop political agitation. Finally, on the question of relations between the Army and the radicals, Chou underlined the new policy he had undoubtedly helped to shape.

During his visit to Canton in April, Chou had sided with the radicals. But now, attuning himself to the new trend, he reproved them for having followed the line he had then favored. He denounced their assaults against Huang Yung-sheng, the Canton commander, and ordered them instead to acknowledge the General's leadership. Conditions in Canton and elsewhere had so deteriorated that military rule had become imperative, he disclosed. Police authority had collapsed, ports were paralyzed, and lawlessness was rampant. The Army was therefore taking control of internal security agencies, airports, railways, warehouses, and wharves. "Revolutionary order should be improved," he went on. Communications and transportation must be guaranteed so that "coal is delivered and electricity generated." To maintain order in the cities, squads of soldiers would take on police duties and patrol the streets. He called on the Red Guards to cooperate with the local commanders and reiterated that the appeal to purge the Army, issued after the Wuhan mutiny, had been "a wrong slogan." To emphasize this point, Chou resorted to a familiar device. Knowing that the young radicals admired Chiang Ch'ing, he claimed that she had been the first person to oppose the "ultraleftist" plot against the Army.[11]

Nothing dramatized the new influence of the People's Liberation Army more vividly than the positions occupied by senior Chinese officers during National Day celebrations on October 1. Though they had been bitterly denounced by Red Guards, the old Marshals like Chu Teh, Ch'en Yi, Hsu Hsiang-ch'ien, Nieh Jung-chen, and Yeh Chien-ying were to be seen in prominent places along with such military professionals as General Su Yü. Six regional commanders were also placed favorably, among them Huang Yung-sheng of Canton; Hsü Shih-yu, the top officer in central China; Ch'en Hsi-lien, military chief of Manchuria; and Han Hsien-ch'u, Army boss in Fukien. All of these Army men had been targets of the Red Guards in the preceding year, as were a number of other figures on the Tienanmen Gate. The appearance of Yu Ch'iu-li, Minister of Petroleum Industry, along with that of other protégés who had been defended by Chou En-lai against severe Red Guard attacks, testified to the Premier's success in protecting his subordinates.[12] Their re-emergence also mirrored the attempt to return to stability.

Most of the rhetoric that now resonated in official press and radio statements bluntly contradicted the earlier slogans of the Cultural Revolution. In July, Chiang Ch'ing had been urging the Red Guards to "take up arms" to defend Mao's cause "by force." Now, as a provincial radio commentary put it, "to stress 'defending by force' deviates from the general orientation of the struggle and this is extremely wrong." [13] Earlier declarations had affirmed that those who emphasized economic output were traitors to the Cultural Revolution. Now *Red Flag* intoned that to ignore production was to "undermine the mass revolutionary alliance and . . . cause unnecessary damage" to the economy." [14] With the same passion once directed against "reactionaries," demonstrations and rallies now denounced "ultraleftists." At one rally held in Changsha in mid-October, the Hunan Army commander, General Li Yuan, used language that would have been heretical eight months before. He criticized the radicals for their attacks on "middle-of-the-roaders" and their resistance to the Army and, rephrasing one of Mao's celebrated exhortations, he reproached them for "bombarding the proletarian headquarters." Soon afterward, the Hunan military authorities singled out a typical "ultraleftist" in much the same way that the Red Guards had once humiliated alleged "bourgeois revisionists." Put on display before a crowd of sixty thousand, an obscure figure by the name of Tsai was charged with crimes ranging from "making rebellion" and "striking down everyone" to seizing weapons and promoting violence.[15] His mistake, of course, had been his overzealous allegiance to the Maoist cause.

In several places, the suppression of radicals took a harsher form. On September 12, for instance, a crowd of ten thousand assembled under Army auspices at a Peking stadium as speakers pronounced the death sentence on four "counterrevolutionary murderers" who had been convicted by the Peking Municipal People's Court of having "hoodwinked the masses, incited struggle by force, sabotaged production, and even committed murder." They were summarily executed at the end of the rally.[16] Other trials and executions took place during September in Shanghai, Tsingtao, Hangchow, and Harbin. Variously described as "enemy agents," "looters," "thieves and hooligans," and "counterrevolutionaries," many were presumably Red Guards or other militants whose criminal activities had once been an accepted part of the turmoil of the Cultural Revolution.[17] Years later, large numbers of former Red Guards were still being punished. Ironically, many of these young radicals in South China fled for safety in Hong Kong.

As part of the drive to impose law and order, meanwhile, the Peking leaders inaugurated a major offensive against the May 16th Detachment. The case of the May 16th Detachment was a significant example of the process by which the Peking leaders sought to absolve Mao and themselves of responsibility for the excesses of the Cultural Revolution by pinning the blame on convenient scapegoats.

That the May 16th Detachment had existed was undeniable. But in September 1967, Chou En-lai advised against "exaggerating its importance," since the movement consisted of "only a few hotheads who cannot do much harm." [18] A lesser Chinese official later described it as a radical "state of mind" rather than a real movement. By the end of 1970, however, Peking publicists were portraying the May 16th Detachment as a vast network of military and civilian conspirators whose objective had been to overthrow Lin Piao and Chou En-lai and govern China with Mao as their figurehead.[19] The basic pattern underlying this change was simple. The campaign had apparently been mounted to shield Mao from criticism for the radical strategies he had initiated. In later years, as Peking's policies became more moderate, the need to explain the wild turbulence of the Cultural Revolution became greater and the importance of the May 16th Detachment was proportionately inflated. By mid-1971, in still another reverse, Lin Piao himself would be assailed as the "black hand" behind the "ultraleftist" conspiracy.

In September 1967, however, it was Chiang Ch'ing who fired the opening salvo against the May 16th Detachment. In a rather unconvincing polemical display, she accused the movement of having attempted to topple Chou En-lai and described it as an "ultraleftist" faction that was serving American "imperialism" and Soviet "revisionism." [20] Her charges were amplified by Yao Wen-yuan, the radical Shanghai writer who had been Mao's charter publicist in the Cultural Revolution. He accused the May 16th Detachment of "creating dissension and exploiting confusion," alleging that it was linked to T'ao Chu.[21] By December, the movement's most prominent members had disappeared: Wang Li, the Maoist troubleshooter who had been abducted in Wuhan; Ch'i Pen-yu and Kuan Feng, *Red Flag* editors and deputies to Ch'en Po-ta; and Mu Hsin, a radical Peking propagandist. All had belonged to the Cultural Revolution Directorate which, by the end of 1967, was down as a result of purges to six of its original thirteen members.[22]

The purge of the radicals in late 1967 also took a devastating toll on Mao's seven-man "brain trust" of theoreticians in the Department of Philosophy and Social Sciences at the Chinese Academy of Sciences. The entire group—including its head, Chang Chi-ch'un—was dismissed and, presumably, sent to "labor reform" camps. Purged as well were Chiang Ch'ing's literary and artistic advisers on the staff of the Cultural Revolution Directorate. The most influential among them was Cheng Kung-tun, head of the literary and art department of *Red Flag,* who was arrested in November and charged with a familiar assortment of crimes, ranging from "ultra-leftism" to operating as a "secret agent" for Chiang Kai-shek. With him fell a number of his comrades who had been associated with Chiang Ch'ing's programs to "purify" Chinese literature and art.[23] Chiang Ch'ing herself dropped from public view for nearly two months, inspiring speculation that her star had waned. Chou En-lai fueled this speculation. "Arduous struggle" had impaired her health, he explained, adding ominously that "spiritual consolation and inspiration will certainly make up for the loss." [24] Whether real or diplomatic, her illness was brief, and she was to resurface with a vengeance in the spring.

Throughout the Cultural Revolution, Mao periodically revived the idea of a Chinese version of the Paris Commune. This notion, which had been frequently suggested by Ch'en Po-ta in his ideological essays over the years, had commended itself to the more visionary Maoists as a free-flow political system "spontaneously" responsive to the "masses." In mid-January 1967, Ch'en Po-ta and Chiang Ch'ing had actually proposed that Peking be governed by a People's Commune composed of a constituent assembly whose leaders could be elected or recalled at any time by the "masses." Soon after, radicals in the Shansi province capital of Taiyuan had announced that they had formed a Commune to replace the Party Committee they had overthrown, and the Shanghai radicals did the same. But the Commune concept, so attractive in theory, was subverted in practice by the very principles it sought to promote. Licensed to reject their leaders or assail their rivals as they chose, innumerable worker, student, and other factions tore apart the Commune even before it could be built. For that reason, the new prototype structure was declared to be the tripartite Revolutionary Committee. And the

Commune concept was quietly buried, perhaps to be resurrected at some future date, when Mao's doctrines had "purified" the people.

Coinciding as it did with Mao's directive to the Army to intervene in the Cultural Revolution, endorsement of the Revolutionary Committees rather than the Commune may have been the price exacted by China's military commanders for their assumption of a political role that threatened to be both difficult and risky. In any case, the Revolutionary Committees were patently a device to permit soldiers and veteran cadres to discipline the fractious radicals. Thus the formation of Revolutionary Committees proceeded mainly during periods in which the Army had the upper hand and when, as the topical slogan held, the "consolidation of revolutionary order" was imperative. Revolutionary Committees were created in Heilungkiang, Shantung, Kweichow, Shanghai, Shansi, and Peking in early 1967, when the Army was pre-eminent. To the radicals, however, those months represented a "counterrevolutionary adverse current," and when they returned to the fore in late spring and summer, the program to set up Revolutionary Committees foundered as the Army's authority foundered. The only Committee formed during the summer was in Tsinghai, a huge, arid, sparsely populated province in western China that was virtually a military domain.

In the fall, as the Army regained power, one of its priorities was to regenerate the drive to implant the Revolutionary Committees in the provinces. This priority fit into a longer-range plan. Charting the future, the leaders in Peking hoped to convene a Party Congress, out of which would emerge a new Politburo and Central Committee that would, in turn, appoint new provincial Party Committees. In this way, the national Party structure shattered during the Cultural Revolution could be rebuilt.

Mao himself was undoubtedly suspicious that the Army might become a substitute for the Party—and might even, indeed, try to subvert his own authority. During the first half of 1967, when he had purged and reorganized nearly half the regional and district commands in the country, he was constantly grumbling that officers lacked "education" and "experience" and needed "training classes" to correct their deficiencies.[25] Even so, as Chou En-lai observed, Chinese military commanders had effectively assumed the "monistic leadership" of China.[26] Thus Mao saw the Revolutionary Committees as instruments by which he would shape a new Party apparatus more submissive to him than the old bureaucracy headed by Liu Shao-ch'i and Teng Hsiao-p'ing. He therefore insisted that Revolutionary Committees be set up throughout the provinces before the end of January 1968 so that he could proceed to convene the Party Congress. By that deadline, as he put it, the "whole situation" should be "put onto the normal track." [27]

Hsieh Fu-chih, the Minister of Public Security, reflected Mao's sense of urgency. In a speech delivered in late October, he anticipated that the Ninth Party Congress might be held by the spring of 1968, or at the latest before October 1, China's National Day. The prerequisite to assembling the Congress was the formation of provincial Revolutionary Committees throughout the country, he stressed. For one thing, as the basic organs of power, the Committees would select the delegates to attend the Party Congress. For another, they were the only bodies capable of governing China until a renovated Party machine could be installed.[28]

The Chinese Communists normally had the capacity to make remarkably rapid institutional changes. During the Great Leap Forward, they had organized twenty-four thousand People's Communes within months. But forging the Revolutionary Committees for China's twenty-nine provinces and special municipalities was a slow process, and Mao's timetable would be stretched by eight months.

Only two Revolutionary Committees were created from August until the end of 1967. One of these, set up on November 1 to rule Inner Mongolia, was headed by General T'eng Hai-Ch'ing, who had been sent to pacify the region in the spring and only succeeded by bringing several fresh Army divisions into the province. The other Committee, formed in Tientsin on December 6, came under the chairmanship of Hsieh Hsueh-kung, a former member of the Party's North China Bureau. He, too, required at least two additional Army divisions to restore order.[29]

After the turn of the year, Revolutionary Committees were organized at a faster pace, with nine new committees created by the end of March. Most of them shared the predictable characteristic that they were headed by generals, some of whom had only recently arrived into the provinces to quell disturbances. The Kiangsi Committee, for instance, was inaugurated on January 5 under the chairmanship of General Ch'eng Shih-ch'ing, a tank commander and political commissar who had brought two Army units into the province in mid-August. The Hupeh Revolutionary Committee, established on February 5, was headed by General Tseng Ssu-yü, who had been transferred from Manchuria to replace General Ch'en Tsai-tao, the instigator of the Wuhan mutiny. In other areas, the new Revolutionary Committees were simply taken over by entrenched local commanders. General Huang Yung-sheng took charge of the Kwangtung Committee, General Hsü Shih-yu became Chairman in Kiangsu, and General Nan P'ing, the Army commander in Fukien, broadened his powers there. One of the few civilians designated to direct a Revolutionary Committee during this period was Li Hsueh-feng, the former First Secretary of the Party's North China Bureau, who became Chairman in Hopeh, the province surrounding Peking. However, four of his seven senior deputies were officers.[30] Not long before the Hopeh Committee was inaugurated on February 3, the Thirty-eighth Army was moved into the province to put down an attempt by local radicals to challenge military rule.[31]

Part of the delay in forming the Revolutionary Committees stemmed from the reluctance of veteran Party officials to cooperate. China's official press and radio urged cadres to contribute their services, saying that their "richer experience, better organizing and working ability, and higher understanding of policy" would make them the "backbone of the revolutionary provisional organs of power." [32] These exhortations were matched in Peking propaganda by moralistic tales of old functionaries who mended their "errors" and were once again playing important roles. But the frequency of these pleas suggested that many local officials who had survived the worst excesses of the Cultural Revolution were still in no mood to expose themselves again.

The reluctance of experienced officials to become involved also contributed to the breakdown of administrative controls, thereby eroding the entire national economy. Humiliated by repeated criticism, many cadres simply refused to perform their duties on the grounds that they could no longer command the respect of workers and peasants. In the farming areas around Shanghai, regional radio broadcasts disclosed, rural production was "abandoned" and "the collective economy disrupted" as agriculture officials shunned the countryside, contending that they "cannot firmly wield power." [33] Similarly, an account from Honan province revealed, spring planting was "going very slowly" because rural cadres formerly victimized by Red Guards were "afraid to make mistakes and thus do not dare to lead boldly." Many of these cadres, the Honan report added, "even lie down and do nothing. None of them cares about collective production." [34]

Meanwhile, as they had the year before, urban workers were taking advantage of the unrest and confusion to reassert demands for higher salaries, improved welfare benefits, and better labor conditions. In the Anhwei province capital of Hofei, according to an official report, a special congress was convened in January to demand that workers return "extra wages, incentive money, subsidies, overtime pay, public funds, and welfare benefits that they were accorded or acquired illegally." [35] An account from Inner Mongolia warned that "economism is again rearing its head" and that the "demons and monsters" were reaping financial gains.

> Some of them have scooped up fat profits through speculative business ventures. Some created rumors to create a rush on the market for daily commodities. Some have set up factories and stores without permission, upsetting the system. Some have acted as contractors and middlemen. Some have even opened gambling houses in broad daylight. . . .[36]

Work stoppages, transport difficulties, and other problems combined to cause shortages of food, fuel, and other necessities. Reports from Peking and Shanghai disclosed that private homes in both cities were suffering from a lack of coal. The dearth of coal was also impairing the electricity supply, compelling factories to slow down. According to one account, peasants in Kwangtung province intercepted a freight train and looted large quantities of grain. In December, another account revealed, peasants near Canton staged a demonstration to protest against a decision to ship five thousand tons of rice to Chinese radicals then still struggling against the British authorities in Hong Kong.[37]

Predictably, no Peking leader was more outraged by the damage being inflicted on the economy than Chou En-lai. At a gathering of Red Guards in Peking on January 17, he flayed the youths mercilessly for having obstructed production in various sectors and blamed them outright for industry's failure to meet the quotas for 1967. He deplored the conflicts then disrupting the Seventh Ministry of Machine Building, a defense agency, where the employees "often turn to fighting among themselves" because "they have nothing else to do after meals." He also demanded a halt in the disputes nagging the Scientific and Technological Commission, the department responsible for China's nuclear and advanced military development. He angrily divulged that Red Guards had seized rifles, cannons, ammunition, and other equipment destined for Hanoi and, in a factional clash, "fired into the air thousands of shells that should have been sent to Vietnam." Uncharacteristically, he concluded his remarks in a burst of temper, exploding: "I am indeed very much upset, very very upset." [38]

In addition to impeding production, the discord among rival Red Guard and other groups was subverting the Army's efforts to recruit representatives of the "masses" to serve as window dressing on the Revolutionary Committees. One aspect of the factionalism fragmenting the multitude of Red Guard movements was described in a Shanghai newspaper article written to urge militant youths to cease their squabbling and merge into alliances.

> Some say, "Since our organization was the earliest to rise up, we should be the nucleus." Others say, "But we made the greatest contribution, so we should be the nucleus." Still others say, "We should be the nucleus since our group is the largest." And so on and so forth. . . .
> Thus nobody serves as the nucleus, and each unit occupies a mountain peak, claiming to be heroic master of its own territory. The result of this is disintegration.[39]

As the drive to restore order accelerated throughout the fall and into early 1968, the strident campaign to curb factionalism grew in intensity. An Anhwei province account depicted factionalism as "a malignant political epidemic" whose most visible symptom was the determination of rival groups to defend only their own interests.[40] Employing a different image, a Shanghai journal called factionalism "a huge poisonous snake . . . that has already encoiled some comrades and is drawing tighter and tighter around them." [41]

In another denunciation of unruly Red Guards, a Honan radio broadcast described them as "imperial inspectors" who "give directives on this and that and monopolize everything, assuming that they alone are revolutionaries." Underlining the change that had occurred since the start of the Cultural Revolution, the Honan broadcast conceded that the Red Guards had once been justified in "whipping up the wind and kindling fires," but now their agitation was "splitting our ranks and causing great disturbances." [42]

Far more dramatic—and, in some ways, rather poignant—was the disillusionment of many Red Guards with what they considered to be a betrayal of the Maoist revolution. Only a year before they had been extolled as "little red generals" and encouraged by Mao himself to believe that they represented the most dynamic force in China. But now, they perceived, the revolution that was supposed to have transformed the "very souls" of the people had altered the appearance rather than the reality of China's political structure. They had only to examine the composition of the Revolutionary Committees to appreciate this bitter truth. Among the eighty-nine Vice-Chairmen of the Committees, only twenty-nine could be classified as "revolutionary rebels," Mao's label for his young acolytes.[43] The rest were either officers or old *apparatchiks*, and these bureaucrats were to become even stronger in the years ahead.

No document to emerge from the Cultural Revolution more vividly illustrated the frustrations of the disappointed radicals than a rambling essay published on January 6, 1968, by the *Sheng-wu-lien*, the Proletarian Revolutionaries Great Alliance, an admittedly "ultraleftist" movement in Hunan. Composed in October 1967 of about twenty factions, most of them secondary-school student groups, the Alliance also included at least one civil-service organization and counted two former Army officers among its leaders.[44] The essay, "Whither China?," sounded an anguished cry of protest against the conservative trend then gathering momentum. Essentially, the Alliance concluded to its dismay that *le plus ça change, le plus c'est la même chose.*

> The form of political power has only superficially changed. The old Party Committee and the old Military District have become the Revolutionary Committee [and] old bureaucrats continue to play

the leading role. Thus, as the masses say, everything remains the same after so much ado.

When the radicals were riding high at the beginning of 1967 and again during the summer, the Alliance asserted, "the whole country had a sense of vigorous growth," and it was believed that the Cultural Revolution would be "carried through to the end," smashing "all traditional ideas that had fettered the minds of people." But in the autumn, with the rise of Army officers and veteran Party cadres to positions of authority, an "adverse current of counterrevolutionary reformism" appeared to create "an atmosphere of class compromise." This was first felt by "extrasensitive" young intellectuals and students, the Alliance said, and its members drafted their essay in an attempt to explain the development.

In a rare swipe at Mao, the Alliance argued that his guidelines for the Cultural Revolution had merely been an "abstract prediction." He had initially recommended the establishment of a Commune, for instance, inspiring the hope that China was headed toward "utopia." But in fact China had drifted away from the Commune concept and was edging closer to the "revisionist" Soviet model. To "expose" this "deception of the masses," the essay reached back to analyze events in 1967.

During the stormy month of January, the Alliance's analysis pointed out, almost the entire Party and government apparatus was overthrown, leaving the management of the country in the hands of the "masses." Despite warnings by the bureaucrats that "production would collapse and the society would fall into chaos," the essay claimed, "productivity was greatly liberated. . . . Workers for the first time felt that it was not the State that directed them, but they who directed the State." But then Mao "suddenly" reversed his line. He abandoned his plan to set up a Commune, and he called for Army intervention, which inevitably brought back the Party *apparatchiks*.

In February and March, the bureaucrats returned to power, suppressing the "masses" by the "most urgent and savage means." The chief engineer of this "counterrevolutionary" thrust was Premier Chou En-lai, excoriated by the Alliance as the "general representative of China's red capitalist class." His ally in this drive was the Army.

The Alliance analysis argued that the radicals had originally harbored "very childish ideas" about the Army, believing as they did that military commanders would join with them to crush the Party machine. But in reality, Army bureaucrats would always side with Party bureaucrats, for one clearcut reason: the Army had undergone a process of *embourgeoisement* since the days when it was a guerrilla force. Living in barracks and enjoying special privileges, soldiers "have not only changed their blood-and-flesh relations with the people . . . but they have become tools for suppressing revolution." This was evident, the Alliance contended, in the turmoil that ravaged China in August. By attacking troops and seizing their weapons, the essay continued, the "masses" were displaying their hostility toward an Army that had lost its revolutionary fervor. The Alliance therefore suggested that only a purge "from the lower level upward" could free the Army of its domination by the bureaucrats and restore its good relations with the population.

But since September, the Party bureaucrats and their military cohorts had come back stronger than ever. They had authorized the Army to shoot at radicals. They had revived the program to establish Revolutionary Committees—a device for imposing a "new bourgeois dictatorship" on China. And they were planning a national Party Congress in order to legitimize their "bourgeois reformism." Consequently, the Alliance charged, the "contradictions" in the society "remain fundamentally unresolved."

> The overthrow of the new bureaucratic bourgeoisie, changes in the armed forces, the establishment of communes and other basic social changes that were supposed to be fulfilled by the Cultural Revolution have not been fulfilled. . . . The fruit of victory has been usurped by the bourgeoisie.[45]

With all their frustrated indignation, however, the Hunanese extremists offered little in the way of a positive strategy beyond advocating that the dynamism originally released in the Cultural Revolution be prolonged. In that sense, they seemed more akin to student activists in the United States, Western Europe, and Japan than to the orthodox Red Guards first mobilized by Mao. Moreover, their "ultraleftism" contravened Maoist doctrine. For Mao, despite his exhortations to youths to rebel against authority, had never favored anarchy. The Hunan Alliance was therefore too revolutionary even for the Peking radicals, and it was denounced by Chiang Ch'ing as a "hodgepodge of rubbish" operating on behalf of the American "imperialists" and the Soviet "revisionists." [46] Curiously, though, the movement was not disbanded. By early 1968, the disenchantment with the course taken by the Cultural Revolution was shared by more distinguished radicals, including Chiang Ch'ing herself. To have banned the Alliance, they apparently believed, would have been to play into the hands of their adversaries.

Though they had criticized the Hunan students for their "ultraleftism," the Maoist leaders themselves began to show concern at some aspects of the conservative trend developing in early 1968. Like the young Hunanese, they were troubled by the predominance of military commanders and old *apparatchiks* in the Revolutionary Committees, and they were alarmed by the Army's efforts to exclude Red Guards from positions of responsibility. Equally worrisome was the Army's frequent mobilization of labor vigilante groups, militia units, and special security teams charged with suppressing Red Guards and other agitators in the name of enforcing law and order. In another device calculated to discipline Red Guards while strengthening the country's defenses, regional commanders had been stepping up a program to conscript youths into the Army. Starting in February, registrations and examinations of draftees met with little overt opposition, and this testified to the progress made by the Army since September in imposing routine administrative procedures. [47]

Hints of dissatisfaction with these developments first emerged from Shanghai, where the Cultural Revolution had received its initial impulse in the fall of 1965. In late December, a newspaper there published a plea for workers, peasants, students, and "advanced elements" who had "distinguished themselves during the revolutionary struggle" to be given places in the future Party apparatus and that officials "devoid of revolutionary zeal" be expelled. [48] By March, this relatively mild request had escalated into a major counteroffensive aimed at regaining prominence for the radicals.

As the radicals perceived it, the country was then going through a repetition of the so-called "adverse current" that had subverted their revolutionary push in early 1967, and they were determined to block it. Only a few months earlier, one of the main themes in Peking's propaganda had been leniency for reformed Party officials. Now, in contrast, the radicals inveighed against the exoneration of "black cadres" who had been ousted during the Cultural Revolution. Not long before, there had been proposals that Red Guard groups had fulfilled their "historic task" and should be dissolved as the new Revolutionary Committees assumed power. "This view is completely wrong," the radicals now asserted, demanding instead that their organizations "be further strengthened" and given "effective roles in the class and production struggle." [49] And in response to the Peking publicists' strenuous campaign discouraging factional disputes and urging rival movements to resolve their differences, the radicals contended that "the factionalism of the proletarian revolutionaries is very good, very good indeed. There is no room whatsoever for reconciliation" with the "bourgeoisie." [50]

Challenging the entire effort by the Army and its allies to pacify China during the previous months, the radicals also revived their appeals for a recrudescence of violent conflict. As one of their spokesmen put it:

> Chaos is another expression of the eruption of class contradiction, and the culmination of the struggle between the two lines in violence. There is nothing wrong with sowing chaos in the enemy ranks by attacking and purging the handful who have burrowed deep among them. These hidden enemies cannot be uprooted without creating chaos.[51]

This crescendo of appeals for radical resurgence could not possibly have occurred without the approval of Mao and Lin Piao. By early spring, apparently persuaded that the pendulum had swung too far in the direction of stability, they were convinced that a radical push was necessary—even if its costs might be high. Loyal to the Maoist dialectic, Lin cautioned against fearing disruption: "the situation will improve when disorder has reached its extreme." "Even if heaven collapses," he went on, Mao and his "invincible thought" could "prop it up and mend the cracks." [52] Mao himself, meanwhile, gave his blessing to the radicals in one of those ambiguous yet pregnant pronouncements favored by charismatic leaders:

"To protect or oppress the masses—that is the fundamental difference between the Chinese Communist Party and the Kuomintang, between the proletariat and the bourgeoisie, and between the dictatorship of the proletariat and the dictatorship of the bourgeoisie." [53]

Now back in the limelight after a winter's absence, Chiang Ch'ing also stepped forth with a series of speeches in mid-March, warning that the "main danger all over the country" was coming from the conservatives. This tendency "has not just sprouted" but had been emerging for "several months," she said. And in a tortuous attempt to justify her diatribes against the "ultraleftists" only a few months earlier, she argued that they had really been "rightist in essence" and appealed for a fresh attack against the "class enemy." [54]

That summons to action was echoed by the entire Peking leadership, including Chou En-lai. Ch'en Po-ta, head of the Cultural Revolution Directorate, especially welcomed the new line with the announcement that the Maoist campaign was now entering its fifth "major round." The first round, he said, had been the dismissal in early 1966 of P'eng Chen and the Peking Party machine. The second had been the denunciation of Liu Shao-ch'i, Teng Hsiao-p'ing, and their "revisionist" colleagues. The third was the defeat of the "counterrevolutionary adverse current" in the spring of 1967, and the fourth round had been the ouster of Wang Li and the "ultraleftists" who were really "rightists." [55]

On March 22, the fifth round officially opened with the purge of three senior Army officers—General Yang Ch'eng-wu, Acting Chief of General Staff; General Yü Li-chin, political commissar of the Air Force; and General Fu Ch'ung-pi, commander of the Peking garrison. All were formally indicted for having committed "extremely serious mistakes." General Huang Yung-Sheng, controversial military boss of south China, was appointed to succeed Yang as Chief of Staff. [56]

A native of Fukien province, then in his mid-fifties, Yang Ch'eng-wu was one of the most experienced field commanders in the Chinese Army. After fighting in several critical battles during the Long March, he had played a prominent role in both the Sino-Japanese war and the conflict against the Nationalists, and was probably engaged as well in the Korean War. By 1959, he was Deputy Chief of General Staff and, six years later, he filled the post vacated by the dismissal of Lo Jui-ch'ing.

Running true to form, Red Guard publicists now charged Yang, once his indictment was announced, with every imaginable crime. They linked him with elements as diverse as the "ultraleftist" May 16th Detachment, the Soviet "revisionists," and the American "imperialists," claiming that he had even gone so far as to install bugging devices in Mao's residence and office in his plot to overthrow the Chairman.[57] Lin Piao, however, offered a more authoritative if not necessarily accurate account of the circumstances surrounding Yang's ouster in a talk with Army officers in Peking on March 25.[58]

Among other maneuvers, Lin said, Yang and his comrades had conspired against both Chou En-lai and Chiang Ch'ing, employing "secret police methods" to compile a dossier of "black materials" with which to incriminate them. In addition, Yang had jockeyed to eliminate a number of key field commanders as well as the chief of the Air Force so as to put his own protégés into their positions. Lin portrayed Yang as an overweeningly ambitious man who "believed only in himself and his tiny group of men" and therefore violated the basic premise of communism—"devotion to public interest." And in the same moralistic vein, Lin added a piquant anecdote. As part of his plot to gain control of the Air Force, Lin related, Yang had delegated his own daughter to have "illicit sexual relations" with a high-ranking officer in that service whose marriage was then in trouble. This only became known, Lin divulged, when the jealous wife reported the love affair to her husband's superiors—who promptly transferred him to another post "to protect his honor."

Judging from Lin's speech and other documents, the purge of Yang Ch'eng-wu and his two colleagues was prompted by an assortment of factors—some related to events of the moment and other reflecting deeper stresses and strains within the Chinese leadership.

Contrary to allegations linking them to the "ultraleftists," Yang and his comrades had clearly been in the forefront of the Army's efforts to subdue the Red Guards. For one thing, Yang had been closely associated throughout his career with Marshal Nieh Jung-chen, the director of China's nuclear development program and one of the most conservative officers in the Chinese Army.[59] Months later, in fact, the Red Guards denounced Nieh for having tried to protect Yang.[60] Yang Ch'eng-wu's concern for law and order was also mirrored in his behavior immediately after the Wuhan mutiny. While Peking's entire propaganda machine was appealing for a purge of the Army, Yang pursued a significantly different line, declaring that the purported "counterrevolutionary" plot to "usurp control of the Army" had been "discerned in good time and smashed," and that "all the commanders and fighters . . . are boundlessly loyal" to Mao. And, at a moment when events within China were of the utmost importance, Yang deliberately diverted to foreign affairs, even disgressing so far afield as to discuss the "Afro-American struggle in Detroit." [61]

Yang's concern for internal "peace" inevitably inspired his hostility toward Chiang Ch'ing and the radicals, and there was undoubtedly a large measure of truth in Lin Piao's charge that he strove to neutralize them. On one occasion, Yang reportedly sent two truckloads of armed troops to the headquarters of the Cultural Revolution Directorate in Peking in an attempt to arrest some of its minor functionaries. He evidently tried as well to curb the Red Guards at Peking University, who in the late winter of 1968 were seeking Chiang Ch'ing's support for a resurgence.

Like establishments everywhere in the world, the Chinese military hierarchy was riddled with personal, professional, and regional rivalries. Hence Yang Ch'eng-wu may well have maneuvered to displace several senior officers in favor of his own protégés, as Lin Piao charged. Or he could have fallen victim to the ambitions of his opponents within the Army. In any case, two of the men Yang had allegedly tried to eradicate went on to become members of the Politburo. One was General Hsü Shih-yu, commander of central China. The other, Yang's replacement as Chief of Staff, was Huang Yung-sheng. Their later promotions contained important clues to the motives underlying the dismissal of Yang and his colleagues.[62]

Men like Huang Yung-sheng and Hsü Shih-yu were no more sympathetic to the radicals than Yang. Indeed, Huang had persistently suppressed Red Guards in Canton, and Hsü had repeatedly come under fire from extremists in his area. Thus Yang's purge, whatever its later effect would be, was not intended to encourage the radicals to initiate fresh rampages. Instead, it seemed to represent a compromise worked out by Lin Piao to placate both the Maoists and the commanders. While they accepted the compromise at the time, the commanders may have later held the purge of Yang, one of their kind, to Lin.

Lin made it clear that the decision to oust Yang had involved a good deal of intricate negotiating. The subject had been discussed at four separate meetings held at Mao's private residence before those present—presumably selected Maoist leaders and Army officers—finally agreed to dump Yang. Philosophizing somewhat sadly on the move, Lin later explained that "the objective situation changes independently of man's will" and so, faced by the necessity for perpetual "struggle," they had "no choice but to expose and resolve the conflict. . . . The abcess must be punctured, and fire cannot be wrapped up in a piece of paper." [63]

At the same time, Lin took pains to stress that Yang's dismissal by no means signified a wholesale purge of the Army. Just because Yang had been wrong was no reason to eliminate his past supporters, subordinates, and acquaintances. Lin generously allowed that these relationships may have been dictated by "historical conditions," or that Yang had perhaps "deceived people." At any rate, "we must continue to trust those comrades," and Lin assured them that "they shall have our full confidence" as long as they repudiate Yang and "stand under Chairman Mao's banner." [64]

One effect of this compromise was to give the radicals larger representation in the Revolutionary Committees formed thereafter. Radicals had accounted for about 20 per cent of the leading members of the Revolutionary Committees created from August 1967 through March 1968. In contrast, the proportion of Red Guards and other activists jumped to more than 30 per cent between April and September 1968. Still, the Committees essentially remained under Army control. And the roles played by the field commanders showed the reinforcement of the power of the regional military authorities. This was to become even more dramatically apparent with the emergence of the new Party Politburo a year later.[65]

The other consequence of Yang's ouster was a fresh explosion of violence throughout the provinces. In part at least, simmering factional tensions had never eased. But there was no doubt that

Chiang Ch'ing and her radical comrades in Peking and Shanghai helped to ignite the new outburst. As usual, they interpreted the willingness of regional commanders to strike a compromise as weakness, and this prompted them to push ahead. As faithful Maoists, they believed as well in the Chairman's dialectical thesis that "the situation will improve when disorder has reached its extreme."

CHAPTER 19

The Storm Before the Calm

*You have let me down and, moreover, you
have disappointed the workers, peasants, and
soldiers of China.*

—MAO TSE-TUNG
to Red Guard leaders, July 27, 1968

EMPOWERED SINCE SEPTEMBER to shoot at fanatical agitators, the Army had managed to make some progress toward the restoration of order during the fall and winter of 1967–1968. Many local commanders formed special vigilante groups to help troops maintain peace. One such group in Shanghai—called the Attack By Reason Defend By Force Great Column, its name ironically borrowed from one of Chiang Ch'ing's bellicose slogans—was composed of thousands of armed workers, and it claimed to have staged seven major actions against "renegades, secret enemy agents, counterrevolutionaries, and incorrigible hooligans" during the month of December.[1] Similar teams were mobilized under military auspices in Canton, Nanking, and other cities.

Nevertheless, the Army encountered enormous difficulties in its efforts to impose discipline and even Peking, patrolled by soldiers day and night, was not immune to violence. In mid-January, four people were killed and eighteen injured in a village near Peking when Red Guards wielding knives and clubs attacked peasants in an attempt to steal food.[2] A clash broke out in the heart of the city itself between textile workers and laborers engaged in constructing the capital's new subway.[3] By late March, factions of every stripe were again skirmishing openly.

One major scene of conflict in the national capital was Peking University, which had been recurrently torn by discord ever since the Cultural Revolution erupted there two years before. Underlying the new outburst was a disagreement between the institution's two main student movements, both of which had originally been regarded as radical. One, the Chingkangshan, had taken its title from Mao's celebrated mountain stronghold of the late 1920s. The other was called New Peita—"Peita" being the familiar name for Peking University. Their dispute had arisen out of the Chingkangshan's opposition to Nieh Yuan-tzu, the radical woman activist who had risen during the Cultural Revolution to become a Deputy Chairman of the Peking Revolutionary Committee. During the last week of March, Chingkangshan activists raided their rivals' offices, wrecked a radio station, abducted several New Peita leaders, and invited students from other Peking schools and colleges to participate in demonstrations denouncing Nieh Yuan-tzu and demanding her resignation.

On March 25, the Minister of Public Security, Hsieh Fu-chih, visited the university in his capacity as Chairman of the Peking Revolutionary Committee in an effort to halt the tumult. He ordered the students to stop fighting and unite behind Nieh Yuan-tzu. But the students ignored him. Finally, on the morning of March 29, a senior Army officer arrived at the campus, flanked by soldiers and accompanied by Nieh Yuan-tzu. As they entered one of the buildings, students armed with daggers ambushed them. They stabbed Nieh Yuan-tzu in the back of the head, and escaped in the ensuing melee.[4] Nieh Yuan-tzu survived. The daring students, however, were apparently never found, despite pleas by the authorities that they surrender or be handed over by their comrades.

Troops deployed to control Peking University were unable to prevent continued skirmishing there throughout April. One of the few foreigners to observe the actual fighting, Jean Vincent, Peking correspondent for Agence France-Presse, witnessed on the afternoon of April 28 a battle in which competing students fought each other from fortified buildings on the university campus. Barricading smashed windows with mattresses, radiators, and furniture, the rival factions conducted an "artillery" duel from the rooftops—the artillery consisting of improvised catapults with which they hurled bricks, tiles, and other projectiles at their foes as loudspeakers on both sides kept up a fusillade of propaganda.[5]

Radical zealots were also reported to be killing suspected "bourgeois" and "revisionist" elements or driving them to suicide in a new wave of terror. At a session of the Peking Revolutionary Committee on May 15, Hsieh Fu-chih revealed that activists in one suburb had rounded up and slaughtered a number of alleged "counter-revolutionaries" and their families, children included. He disclosed as well that suicides were proliferating as a result of Red Guard harassment of Mao's purported adversaries. Acknowledging that many people had committed suicide "out of fear of punishment for their crimes," Hsieh nevertheless urged the Red Guards to restrain themselves, explaining that "even counterrevolutionaries must be given a chance" to redeem their sins. Touching on a point that would increasingly preoccupy the Peking leaders, Hsieh warned that continued violence would complicate the country's future social and political problems. "Feudal" family and clan relations in China were still strong, and bloodshed now would create vendettas for years to come. Or as he put it: "When the father is killed, it is difficult to remold his children. This is a serious question." [6]

If Peking was in ferment, turbulence in the provinces was even more acute. In several areas, the establishment of Revolutionary Committees had merely exacerbated the frustrations of the radicals. Two other factors combined to heighten the level of violence: Thousands of young militants were now armed with weapons they had stolen or been issued the previous summer. And troops were still authorized to shoot at agitators. Thus the provincial clashes that broke out in the middle of 1968 were especially bloody, particularly in south China.

Reports during the spring indicated that frontier regions like Sinkiang, Tibet, and Inner Mongolia were being plagued by persistent turmoil. In Szechwan, despite the introduction of outside troops, local conflicts reached critical proportions as rival Red Guard and Army factions fought each other with modern antiaircraft guns and artillery pieces presumably manufactured for shipment to Vietnam.[7] But the worst violence of that period gripped the volatile provinces of Kwangtung and Kwangsi.

On September 27 of the previous year, Chou En-lai had convened a meeting in Peking at which he exhorted delegates of competing Kwangtung factions to resolve their differences and rally behind General Huang Yung-sheng, the regional military commander.[8] A few weeks later, the delegates returned to Canton with a set of agreements to merge their organizations and respect the authority of the local Army garrison.[9] But the settlement quickly collapsed as rival groups asserted themselves anew. In mid-December, student gangs fought to occupy a school in the town of Chiangmen, about fifty miles south of Canton.[10] Soon after, Red Guards in a Canton suburb abducted a student in a rival gang and, according to one grisly account, smashed his knee-caps and finally murdered him by driving nails into his forehead.[11]

The conflicts in Kwangtung inevitably intensified. On February 18, after one youth movement tried to prevent another from pasting up wall posters, a battle erupted that spread through Canton.[12] Three days later, the provincial Revolutionary Committee was established under General Huang Yung-sheng, who bluntly emphasized in his inaugural address that he would "resolutely punish all class enemies" in a determined drive to restore order in the province.[13] Even as he spoke, rival Red Guards attending the inauguration ceremony at a Canton stadium began fighting among themselves, and hundreds were reportedly injured.[14]

In the spring, the increasing number of Red Guard clashes in Canton seemed to be simply a confused assortment of local struggles for power. A typical explosion of passions flared up on May 25 in the five-story office building of the state-owned Canton Electric Company, located in Sea Pearl Square, not far from the exhibition hall where China's biennial international trade fair is held. Like workers, students, officials, and nearly everyone else in Canton, the employees of the company belonged to factions affiliated with either the East Wind or the Red Flag. Complying with the numerous directives to resolve their differences, their delegates were meeting that day to choose representatives to a joint committee to be set up in the Electric Company. By noon, the debate had degenerated into emotional name-calling and table-thumping, and the delegates agreed to adjourn for lunch.

The East Wind group was conferring in its second-floor office when a band of thirty Red Flag activists swept down the stairs in an attack. Flinging rice bowls, flasks, and light bulbs, the East Wind drove them back. Then both factions barricaded their offices and sent out for reinforcements.

At about four o'clock in the afternoon, some three hundred Red Flag fighters arrived on the scene, armed with improvised weapons. They cordoned off the streets around the building and occupied its ground floor. Soon afterward, three truckloads of East Wind youths appeared, many of them wearing steel helmets. Greeted by a hail of stones, the East Wind responded by throwing vials of sulphuric acid and homemade incendiary bombs at their opponents, forcing them to retreat into the building. From the third floor, meanwhile, members of the Red Flag bombarded their foes with bricks, tiles, and even a few grenades.

An hour later, a battalion of troops encircled the area in an attempt to prevent more youths from pouring in. The soldiers, restrained by their officers from shooting, instead attempted to cool the mob by chanting Mao's dictum to "struggle with reason, not with force." But they were ignored. At one point, a group of East Wind youths broke through the Army line in a stolen bus containing ten barrels of gasoline and set the Electric Company building aflame. Eventually, their patience exhausted, the troops opened fire, killing three young activists and wounding several others.[15]

But the fighting continued all night, spreading in the weeks that followed into other parts of the city and suburbs. On June 3, armed Red Flag students stormed the Physics Building on the Sun Yat-sen University, then serving as an East Wind stronghold. After nearly three days of battle, the Red Flag had killed ten students and abducted sixty others. One captive was said to have been drenched with gasoline and burned alive.[16] Students and workers were reported to be fighting in shipyards, steel mills, and other industrial enterprises.[17] By the middle of June, the Army had imposed a dusk-to-dawn curfew on the city, and troops were patrolling its streets in armored cars.[18]

The situation was aggravated, meanwhile, by severe monsoon floods which not only threatened to inundate Canton, but were forcing thousands of peasants to seek asylum in the city. These peasants, suffering from food shortages, reportedly took advantage of the disorder to loot and pillage. In addition, rural youths joined disparate Red Guard factions in Canton, further contributing to the ferment.

At the same time, the floods brought grim evidence to view of the troubles in south China. Swept down to the sea by swollen rivers, more than a hundred corpses washed onto the shores of Hong Kong and Macao. The bodies, despite their various degrees of decomposition, all appeared to have been murdered. A few were headless, some showed traces of gunshot wounds, many were mutilated, and most had their hands trussed behind them, suggesting that they might have been executed in Oriental style by decapitation or by a bullet in the back of the neck as they knelt. One, believed to be a girl of thirteen or fourteen, bore strands of a rope around her throat.[19] They had evidently come from the Kwangsi-Chuang Autonomous Region, bordering on Vietnam, a region that was perhaps most devastated by the upheavals of the Cultural Revolution.[20]

Over the centuries, the Han Chinese had emigrated into the Kwangsi region until, by the time of Communist victory in 1949, the native Chuangs comprised only about a third of Kwangsi's population of 20 million. The Han Chinese became urban merchants, workers, and officials, leaving the Chuangs to cultivate their hillsides as they had for millennia by their slash-and-burn farming methods. But the Communists initiated a special program to bring Kwangsi deeper into the national fold by Sinicizing the Chuangs. This led to ethnic frictions that undoubtedly were exacerbated during the Cultural Revolution.

Kwangsi had been ruled almost single-handedly since 1954 by Wei Kuo-ch'ing, veteran Army officer and Party *apparatchik* who served simultaneously as the region's military commissar, political boss, and administrative governor. A Chuang by birth, he was one of the few members of an ethnic minority to have risen to the Central Committee. Wei had joined the Communist movement as an adolescent and became a general by the time he was in his early thirties. As a senior officer in Ch'en Yi's Third Field Army during the war against the Nationalists, he participated in the capture of Fuchow and remained in that sensitive coastal sector opposite Tiawan until his assignment to Kwangsi five years later.

Despite his stature and skill, Wei Kuo-ch'ing had apparently lagged behind in carrying out Peking's *mission civilisatrice* among the Chuang aborigines of Kwangsi. For in 1957, an outside official by the name of Wu Chin-nan had been sent into the region to speed up the assimilation process. A veteran of the Long March with impressive credentials as a Party cadre, Wu had served most of his career in his native Kwangtung province. Wei Kuo-ch'ing may have resented Wu's intrusion, and there could have been some tension between the two men even before the Cultural Revolution. In any case, a sharp dispute divided them in January 1967.[21]

That month, Wu Chin-nan had mobilized some forty thousand Red Guards in Nanning, the Kwangsi capital, in an attempt to oust Wei Kuo-ching and his associates. Like many other provincial Party leaders at the time, Wei defended his apparatus while seeming to obey Mao's directive. He dissolved his old Party machine and proclaimed himself the head of a new Maoist-style committee to govern the province.

But Wu Chin-nan and his Red Guards, perceiving the maneuver, accelerated their offensive, and the various Kwangsi organizations soon polarized into two broad coalitions. Wu's group of five large youth factions was formally mobilized on April 22, 1967, and hence called itself the April 22 Revolutionary Rebel Grand Army. Its supporters included a few senior officers, among them General Sun Feng-chang, commander of the Fifty-fifth Army, and its main strength lay in the city of Kweilin, the United States military headquarters in China during World War II. Wei Kuo-ch'ing's movement, comprised largely of workers and backed by most of the Army in the region, was the Kwangsi Proletarian Revolutionaries Alliance Command. Its sympathizers included General Ou Chih-fu, the Kwangsi Military District chief and, like Wei, a Chuang, and the local Air Force and public security commanders.[22]

The rival Kwangsi factions attacked and counterattacked each other during most of 1967, their battles ending inconclusively and blending into fresh turmoil. At one point, possibly seeking to win over some of his adversaries with a ritualistic display of contrition, Wei Kuo-ch'ing appeared at a public rally in Nanning to confess his "sins." But this did nothing to halt the fighting and finally, in late 1967, Peking intervened.

Kwangsi's location adjacent to Vietnam gave them special cause for concern. Several new airfields had been constructed in the province, both for China's defense and also to service North Vietnamese fighter aircraft engaged in the Vietnam war. Equally important, the railway that transported Soviet and Chinese military supplies to Hanoi ran through Kwangsi, and China's leaders could not afford disruptions that would impair their relations with North Vietnam and make them vulnerable to Russian criticism. With these considerations in mind, they summoned Wei Kuo-ch'ing and Wu Chin-nan to Peking to negotiate a settlement.

On November 8, the Kwangsi rivals signed an accord pledging to cease their conflict "immediately" and to disarm their respective factions.[23] Ten days later, the Peking leadership issued a document approving the accord and expressing the "hope" that the opposing movements would honor the agreement "in earnest." The document bore Mao's personal endorsement as an indication that he was troubled by the unrest in Kwangsi.[24]

But hardly had the truce been signed than fighting again began to convulse the province. On November 26, members of Wu Chin-nan's Grand Army attacked a cotton mill and a bus depot in Kwei-lin, killing three of their foes in the melee.[25] At the same time, Grand Army partisans were reported to be bracing for a major battle in Wuchow, a sprawling city on the West River. They had moved large quantities of guns, ammunition, grenades, bombs, and land mines into the People's Hospital, their stronghold, and they were constructing trenches and pillboxes in the vicinity of the Municipal Council Building, the headquarters of the Alliance Command.[26] On December 6, the first of several Wuchow skirmishes began as a gang of youths assaulted troops patrolling the city and seized their weapons. By evening, nine soldiers had been wounded, and sporadic fighting continued for weeks, gradually intensifying into what would be, in the spring, a full-scale battle.[27]

During the following month, the rival factions signed new cease-fire agreements and promptly violated them. Meanwhile, anticipating an eventual showdown, Wei Kuo-ch'ing rapidly deployed his forces throughout Kwangsi. In February, for instance, he reportedly dispatched five thousand troops and irregulars to take over positions held by the Grand Army in Jungan county.[28] He also placed members of his Alliance Command in charge of all the new county committees then being set up around the region. To establish the committee in Kuei county, for example, he sent more than three thousand militia into the area, imposed martial law, and proceeded to round up Grand Army activists who showed signs of resistance. By late April, he controlled seventy-three of the region's eighty-six county committees, and one of his spokesmen proclaimed that "the situation is excellent." [29] On April 26, apparently ready for the showdown, Wei Kuo-ch'ing virtually declared war against the Grand Army. He said: "We must not be soft or hesitant in dealing with the enemy. We must mount a fierce attack against the class enemy, and not give him breathing space. We shall not rest until complete victory is won." [30]

With that, a round of battles erupted in Kwangsi's principal cities. The first—in Liuchow, in the center of the region—lasted a month. Starting on April 28, Wei Kuo-ch'ing's troops assaulted the city with rockets and incendiary bombs that demolished more than a thousand buildings, among them a steam turbine plant, a hospital, and two schools. Led by his Alliance Command, thousands of peasants poured into the city, and the fighting was savage. More than a hundred participants and countless innocent civilians were killed, and finally, outnumbered and outgunned, the decimated Grand Army forces retreated to the outskirts of the city.[31]

The Liuchow battle was overshadowed by a simultaneous and even bigger clash in Wuchow. As they had in Liuchow, Wei Kuo-ch'ing's forces in Wuchow strengthened their ranks with armed peasants and some seven hundred recently demobilized soldiers, and they could count for further support from the local Army garrison. They installed loudspeakers in different districts of Wuchow and, on April 13, they proclaimed their adversaries to be "counterrevolutionaries," and that the struggle between themselves and the Grand Army was "between Communists and the Kuomintang." Four days later, Alliance Command activists opened their offensive. Using high explosives, they blew up the offices of the State Sugar, Tobacco, and Alcohol Corporation, a Grand Army stronghold, and seized the city's Central Post and Telegraph Bureau. They then encircled the Tsaofan Building, the headquarters of the Grand Army, ordering residents of the neighborhood to leave the area within twenty-one hours or "face the consequences." That night, evidently equipped by the Army, the Alliance Command wheeled light howitzers, antiaircraft guns, mortars, and machine guns into range of the Tsaofan Building. On April 18, the attack began.

The Tsaofan Building collapsed under the first artillery barrage, and the Grand Army forces streamed into the streets, seeking protection elsewhere. But Alliance Command vigilantes pursued them. The two factions skirmished in alleys and lanes, public buildings and private homes. On the night of April 19, when a band of Grand Army youths took refuge inside a compound, the Alliance Command hurled napalm bombs over the walls to flush them out. The next day, surrounding some fifty Grand Army activists inside the offices of a government trading company, Alliance Command cadres appealed to them to surrender, explaining that they had been "hoodwinked" and would be shown leniency. But when they emerged, the Grand Army youths were bound and taken to the local Culture Hall, now a temporary Alliance Command prison.[32]

By May 3, according to one version of the episode, more than two thousand Wuchow buildings were in ruins and some forty thousand inhabitants of the city had been rendered homeless. With the Grand Army routed, Alliance Command vigilantes began mopping up. Assisted by local troops and police, they conducted a house-to-house manhunt, arresting hundreds of their rivals. Finally, with more than three thousand captives crowded into the Culture Hall and other makeshift jails, the Alliance Command leaders proceeded systematically to interrogate, torture, and execute their prisoners. They staged at least three mass executions, evidently by firing squad, and three hundred seventeen bodies were reported to have been dumped into shallow graves at the Palungli cemetery. Other bodies were thrown into the West River and some of these corpses later washed ashore in Hong Kong and Macao.[33]

In a post-mortem report, the defeated Grand Army described the "fascist atrocities" committed in Wuchow as "even worse than those of the Kuomintang and the Japanese devils." The report estimated that fifty thousand Grand Army members had been massacred throughout the region, and that twenty thousand others fled to the neighboring provinces of Yunnan, Kweichow, and Kwangtung.[34] Whatever the reliability of those statistics, the devastation in Kwangsi was dramatic—and the fighting did not cease with the victory of Wei Kuo-ch'ing's Alliance Command.

Members of Grand Army remnants, seeking asylum in Kwangtung, were arrested by troops there and shipped by river boat back to the Wuchow military authorities.[35] Calling themselves an "accusation mission," several members of the Grand Army even made their way to Peking in hopes of expressing their grievances to China's top leaders. Neglected, they wandered aimlessly around the capital for weeks, searching for an audience to hear their protests. Their money soon ran out and some, caught stealing, were branded "bandits and hooligans" and imprisoned.[36] In contrast, Wei Kuoch'ing and his comrades were summoned to Peking in grand style and, on July 3, they were photographed with Mao to illustrate that they enjoyed the Chairman's "greatest support." Wei's visit to Peking was marred, however, when frustrated activists in the Grand Army "accusation mission" broke into his hotel, denounced him as a "capitalist" and, according to one account, "made a great hullabaloo." Soldiers intervened to restore order and the rioters were "arrested on the spot." [37]

Mao's accolade for Wei Kuo-ch'ing came as a hint that, perceiving anew that China could not sustain continued turmoil, he was once again swinging to the side of moderation. His shift may well have been a measure of the growing influence of Chou En-lai and the regional commanders, who were alarmed by the chaos sweeping through South China.

Though their comrades in Peking had been subdued, frustrated Grand Army agitators in Kwangsi could not be easily checked. Following their defeat in Wuchow, they again struck out in passionate and often indiscriminate attempts to retrieve their momentum. Other local factions emulated them, and Kwangsi was soon slipping toward fresh turbulence. With no apparent motive, for example, Red Guards stormed Hanoi's consulate in Nanning on June 2, forcing the puzzled North Vietnamese diplomats out of the building and assailing them as they emerged.[38] Desperate for weapons, youths also ambushed, derailed, and raided trains carrying military supplies to Vietnam.

The extraordinary amplitude of these raids was first revealed on June 13 by the Peking leaders in a stern directive calling for a halt to the tumult obstructing the Kwangsi railway system. The directive said that rival factions had "looted our country's aid-Vietnam supplies . . . carried out armed attacks against trains and damaged railways, completely disrupting traffic" in the vicinity of Liuchow. The document insisted that "no time be lost in restoring communications and transport," and it decreed that all stolen weapons and equipment be surrendered to the Kwangsi military authorities.[39] Some idea of the magnitude of the pillage was contained in other disclosures by the Peking leaders that one Kwangsi faction had seized more than eleven thousand cases of ammunition while another had stolen six thousand rifles.[40]

The June 13 directive was ignored. A week later, Chou En-lai telephoned the Kwangsi military headquarters to demand that law and order be imposed in Kweilin and Nanning, and he issued an ultimatum insisting that rail traffic in the Liuchow area be returned to normal within three days.[41] But the Kwangsi factions went on running rampant. Peking issued another directive along the same lines on July 3, and this edict was stronger in two respects. It bore Mao's personal imprimatur and it warned that prolonged resistance would be "severely punished." [42] Again, there was no sign of compliance from Kwangsi. Indeed, three weeks after the directive was issued, rail service near Liuchow remained paralyzed as youths continued to attack and pillage trains.[43]

On July 24, the Peking leaders put out yet another appeal for order to the entire nation. Their edict disclosed the extent to which China's social fabric was torn. For it revealed that "counterrevolutionaries" in several regions were robbing banks and warehouses, burning or blowing up public buildings and private homes, stealing automobiles and trucks, disrupting rail traffic, killing soldiers and seizing their weapons—and refusing to obey Peking directives. While again threatening the guilty with "severe punishment," it added a sweetening promise that those who had been "coerced" or "hoodwinked" into committing crimes would be pardoned.[44]

The lengths to which the Peking leaders were compelled to go in their efforts to restore order illustrated not only the extent of anarchy within China but the degree to which central authority had collapsed. This critical state of affairs resonated as well in the exasperation of the Chinese leaders with the Red Guards and other young militants. Gone were lavish phrases extolling the "little red generals" and hailing them as "revolutionary heirs." Now they upbraided the youths like old-fashioned cops scolding juvenile delinquents.

K'ang Sheng, China's security chief, was the most archetypical exemplar of the new line. In a talk with a group of Kwangsi militants in Peking on July 25, K'ang bluntly warned that they had not been convened to "submit a lawsuit" and were in no position to "discuss terms." They were there to listen and obey. "Do you know who you're making happy?" K'ang asked them. "The American imperialists, the Soviet revisionists, the traitors, and special agents— that's who you're making happy. You shout about wanting revolution, but you oppose revolution. I want no more double-dealing. Some of you have reached the edge of the cliff. One more step and you'll go over." And though himself a university graduate, K'ang infused the meeting with an air of Maoist anti-intellectualism: "You students never fought the Kuomintang or the Americans in Korea. Yet you think you're superior just because you've been educated." [45]

Two days later, in an attempt to destroy the monster he had invented, Mao himself repudiated the Red Guards. Speaking to five radical leaders, among them Peking University's Nieh Yuan-tzu and K'uai Ta-fu of Tsinghua, he catalogued their blunders. They had failed to unite, and their persistent fighting was ruining the country. Besides, they had not even begun to transform their inner selves in the process that was supposed to shape them into truly "Communist men." Then, reportedly with tears in his eyes, Mao disavowed them: "You have let me down and, moreover, you have disappointed the workers, peasants, and soldiers of China." [46]

Even before that scene was played, regional commanders had been taking steps to suppress the Red Guards. In Canton, Army officers staged a rally on July 11 to endorse the authority of the Workers Provost Corps, a labor vigilante force. The next day, the local Revolutionary Committee published a ten-point decree on "stopping armed struggle," enfranchising the Army and the Workers Provost Corps to "take compulsory action against those who refuse to comply" with the directive. A week later, the Committee announced a new program to transfer thousands of students to rural areas, and soon after that the first batch was reported to have "joyfully" entrained for Army-run farms, repudiating the bourgeois notion that "it is better to go to college first." [47] At the end of the month, the Revolutionary Committee indicted Wu Ch'uan-p'in, the dynamic Red Guard who had done most to promote the Cultural Revolution in Canton during the spring of 1966.

A year before, when Wu had come under fire from the military authorities in Canton, Chou En-lai had personally exonerated him, praising his "political prescience" and devotion to "revolutionary truth," and that plaudit won the student activist a prominent place in the Kwangtung Revolutionary Committee.[48] Now Chou stigmatized him as a "black character." [49] At a meeting held in Canton on July 31, Wu was further denounced as an "overbearing and arrogant scoundrel" whose crimes included espionage and violence. He was blamed as well for sexual promiscuity with young girl Red Guards and this, speakers at the meeting said, had "left a big stain on his moral reputation." [50] The Revolutionary Committee also arrested a number of radical professors who had been active during the early stages of the Cultural Revolution in Canton, predictably charging them with being American or Kuomintang agents, or both.[51]

Army-dominated Revolutionary Committees in several provinces now began to dissolve the large Red Guard coalitions that had held sway at the peak of the Cultural Revolution. In Changchun, a major Manchurian industrial city, a Red Guard movement known as the August 10 Commune proclaimed on July 23 that it had "voluntarily" disbanded, quoting Mao to the effect that "an organizational form that no longer conforms to the needs of the struggle must be abolished." [52] Other Red Guard factions that ceased functioning included Honan's troublesome February 7 Commune. The public rationale for this move held that the revolutionary cause would be "strengthened and consolidated" by replacing the big Red Guard movements with smaller occupational and school groups. In reality, smaller groups were easier to control. County and other local administrative bodies were also directed to "streamline" by reducing staff—advice that authorized them to oust their disruptive elements.[53]

By the middle of summer, the trend toward moderation was firmly established, and it was publicized by a lexicon of mirror-language phrases. What had formerly been justifiable "rebellion" now became "counterrevolution." Red Guards were now "anarchists" poisoned by "bourgeois factionalism" and "leftist opportunism." The restoration of law and order by the Army and its auxiliaries was no longer a "reactionary adverse current," but the imposition of "revolutionary discipline" designed to defend the "dictatorship of the proletariat" against its "class enemies." And the rationale for the new line, like the rationale for the exhortations that had launched the Cultural Revolution, would be found in Mao's immense body of doctrine.

CHAPTER 20

The Road to Recovery

❧

The People's Liberation Army is the mighty
pillar of the dictatorship of the proletariat
. . . the main component of the State.

— LIN PIAO, *April 14, 1969*

IN LATE JULY, immediately after Mao Tse-tung's tearful disavowal
of the Red Guards, troops surrounded Peking's Tsinghua University, and a veil of silence fell over the campus. It was broken ten
days afterward by a bizarre announcement.

On August 6, the *People's Daily* covered its entire front page
with the news that, the day before, Mao had sent a basket of mangoes to workers and peasants engaged in promoting his doctrine
among Tsinghua University students. The mangoes had been a
gift to Mao from Pakistan's Foreign Minister Arshad Husain,
who had just ended a visit to China and, the *People's Daily* related,
their delivery to the Tsinghua campus was greeted with "seething
jubilation." The recipients of the fruit were reported to have
cheered, wept, and chanted Mao's slogans, describing his generous
gesture as the "greatest inspiration" to proletarian militants. The
mangoes then sat on a red table in the middle of the Tsinghua
campus for several days, until they began to rot. Thereupon, according to one official account, experts placed them in a glass jar of
formalin, to be preserved for posterity like a hair from the beard of
the Prophet.[1]

This extravagant fuss over a basket of fruit was enormously
significant. For Mao's presentation of the mangoes to workers and
peasants—rather than to students—symbolized in exquisitely
esoteric style a totally new tactic: the introduction of so-called

Mao Tse-tung Thought Propaganda Teams into universities and schools throughout the nation. While nominally composed of workers and peasants, the real backbone of these teams were soldiers. Their essential purpose was to impose military control over the Red Guards and other young activists—though the sinister connotation of Army rule was camouflaged by rhetoric claiming that the "working class" would henceforth play the "leading role" in the Cultural Revolution.[2]

The Army's real power was visible, however, in the final Revolutionary Committees created during August and September in Yunnan, Fukien, Kwangsi, Sinkiang, and Tibet. All were headed by generals, and each featured a high percentage of officers among its leading members.[3] The renewed importance of the Chinese military establishment was also apparent in the Army Day celebrations held on August 1 in Peking, heralded by the issuance of a special set of postage stamps which celebrated the Army as an "invincible force." [4] The keynote speaker, General Huang Yung-sheng, emphasized that the Army's "glorious" function was, among other things, to exercise "military control" of the country.[5]

Though it comprised some five thousand workers and peasants, the Mao Tse-tung Thought Propaganda Team that entered Tsinghua University in mid-July was under the direction of an Army unit. The Team's first task, according to an order issued by Hsieh Fu-chih, Chairman of the Peking Revolutionary Committee, was to separate the rival university factions "until their hostility has disappeared" and then, through persuasion rather than force, disarm the students and urge them to resume their studies.[6] But in several areas, aware that their heyday was over, the youths put up resistance.

In Shanghai, where some ten thousand soldiers and workers moved into universities, colleges, and other educational institutions in August, resentment among student activists ran high. They complained that China's younger generation had been "discredited" and had "fallen out of favor" and, in some parts of the city, the youths physically fought against the intruders.[7] On August 6, students beat up six members of a Mao Thought Team who had entered the Shanghai Foreign Language Vocational School to conduct an investigation.[8] Students in Szechwan reportedly opposed similar teams on the grounds that soldiers and workers "do not understand education" and would create "an awful mess if they try to lead the schools." [9] In the Shensi province capital of Sian, tensions between youths and workers were reflected in the remark of a speaker at a meeting held to endorse a newly formed disciplinary Mao Thought Team. "We will never," he said, "allow young students and intellectuals to wave their hands and feet and interfere with the workers' movement." [10]

Clashes between Red Guards and the Army-run Mao Thought Teams were especially severe in the southern parts of Chekiang province. In mid-September, a serious skirmish broke out in Wenchow when workers and soldiers intervened to stop a fight between rival youth factions. But instead of quelling the disturbance, the workers and soldiers reportedly sided with one faction while the police came to the aid of the other, and the fight spread through the city. A Wenchow resident wrote to his sister in Hong Kong that "several hundred" people had been killed and "the sound of gun shots can be heard every night." [11] A clue to the degree of turbulence was contained in news of a series of mass trials held in Chekiang's cities from early August through late September. The defendants were variously portrayed as murderers, hooligans, corrupt officials, thieves, and speculators, and one group was accused of "attempting to wreck our steel wall—the People's Liberation Army." [12] Two of the trials ended in executions.[13]

Mao's most massive effort to restore order, meanwhile, was conducted through a revival of the *Hsia-fang*, or "Down to the Countryside," program. Variations of this program had been initiated and abandoned on several occasions. But now, undertaken with almost desperate urgency, it became the biggest and most intensive migration scheme in human history, as an estimated 20 million people were moved from China's cities to rural and remote border regions during the winter of 1968–1969.

One reason for the effectiveness of the movement was its acceptance, for different motives, by assorted groups within the ruling Chinese hierarchy. Moderate leaders in Peking viewed the scheme as a tactic for ridding urban areas of disruptive Red Guards and other youths. They also saw the program as an opportunity to alleviate the congestion of China's crowded cities, solve the problem of unemployment caused by sluggish economic development, and streamline and rationalize factories, commercial firms, offices, and other enterprises that had become clogged with superfluous employees. At the same time, the Army welcomed the population shift as a chance to decentralize China and strengthen the self-sufficiency of its provinces, thereby reinforcing their capacity to resist an enemy invasion. Concerned mainly with the growing Soviet threat, senior Chinese military strategists particularly emphasized the importance of populating the frontier areas of Sinkiang, Inner Mongolia, and Manchuria.[14] Later, when much of the country's defense system had been restructured around the network of "people's communes" created earlier during the Great Leap Forward, the Chinese boasted that an invader would be confronted "not by one China but by twenty-four thousand Chinas."[15]

Significantly, the *Hsia-fang* program had Mao's overwhelming support. For it promised to fulfill his lifelong vision of eradicating what his publicists termed the "three disparities" that had traditionally separated workers from peasants, intellectuals from manual laborers, and the urban from rural sectors. Until these barriers were obliterated, Mao believed, China could not advance. And, consistent with his faith in peasant revolution, he further held that it was the duty of teachers, students, doctors, engineers, scientists, office employees, officials, and similar "mandarins" to acquire a "proletarian" outlook by soiling their hands in the good earth of China. On December 22, therefore, Mao gave fresh impetus to the *Hsia Fang* movement by proclaiming that city youths should be "re-educated" by the peasantry. Uurging urban residents to send their children to the countryside—and appealing to peasants to accept them—Mao intoned: "Let us mobilize."[16]

Hardly a day passed without the Peking and provincial press and radio reporting migrations. By February 1969, official Chinese sources claimed, more than two hundred thousand youths had been transferred out of Peking and, by the end of the year, nearly a half-million "young intellectuals" had migrated from Shanghai to Kiangsi villages, Yunnan labor camps, and Manchurian forestry projects.[17]

The Chinese authorities resorted to all kinds of publicity devices to whip up enthusiasm for the program. An Academy of Sciences employee told an interviewer that she had persuaded her daughter to "live in the countryside until the last day of your life" by describing the sufferings of peasants before the Communists took power.[18] A female engineer from Shenyang was quoted as saying that the rigors of farm life had taught her the futility of her "bourgeois" education.[19] Inevitably, publicists glorified model heroes like Chin Hsun-hua, a Shanghai student who drowned in an attempt to save "state property" while working on a project in Heilungkiang.[20] Official press agents even resurrected Mao's son An-ying, who had died in the Korean War. Returning from school in the Soviet Union in 1946, he volunteered to work as a peasant and, as the story went, proudly announced afterward that he had graduated from a genuine "agricultural college." [21]

In many cities the need to send young people "down to the countryside" was largely dictated by the disruption of the educational system during the Cultural Revolution. The suspension of classes for three and even four years in some places had created a backlog of thousands of students who could no longer make up for lost time since the schools had to make way for new candidates, and for whom there were no jobs. Except for certain specialized defense research-and-development institutes, almost all of China's universities, colleges, primary and secondary schools had ceased to function in the spring of 1966. The lower-level schools began to resume classes in late 1967, but higher institutions only started to operate again in mid-1970—and even then, many still remained paralyzed.[22] The repeated delays in reactivating the universities and colleges were in part due to recurrent ferment in the cities. In part, too, the Chinese leaders encountered difficulties as they sought to implement Mao's reform program, which called for shortened schooling periods, formal studies integrated with physical labor, the elimination of examinations, and other changes designed to destroy the remnants of the rigid, narrow, elitist educational system that had produced the mandarins of ancient China.

In any case, during the Cultural Revolution, China's educational institutions had served primarily as headquarters, dormitories, and fortresses for Red Guard factions. Classes, such as they were, featured little more than genuflection to Maoist doctrine and adoration of the Mao cult. At Tungshi Engineering University in Shanghai, for example, the day began at six in the morning with loudspeakers broadcasting revolutionary songs, after which students devoted most of their classroom hours to chanting Mao's slogans and confessing their "failure" to apply the Chairman's wisdom to their daily life. A visitor to Tungshi in early 1968 was told by students that scholarship was "bourgeois" and "revisionist," since high achievement in examinations represented surrender to "vulgar self-interest." [23] A second-grade Shanghai pupil later recalled that her school day included reciting Mao's proverbs, singing his aphorisms, and dancing to music composed as settings for Mao's quotations. Younger children in her school were assigned to such tasks as counting pills manufactured at a nearby pharmaceutical plant while the older boys and girls were given the privilege of working on farms in the Shanghai suburbs.[24]

For all their excited rhetorical allegiance to the Cultural Revolution, students were not generally enthused by the prospect of rural labor. In Canton, for instance, the local authorities had to take measures to induce—or coerce—young people to leave the city. School committees set up daily indoctrination sessions at which cadres outlined numerous reasons for students to volunteer for farm work. Among their other arguments, the cadres appealed to patriotism, explaining that the resettlement scheme was of "vital strategic significance" in stiffening China's defenses. In November, Mao Tse-tung Thought Propaganda Teams conducted a house-to-house campaign, striving to persuade students and their parents that voluntary enlistment was advantageous. Volunteers could select rural areas near Canton, and thus visit their families on holidays. Those who lagged behind or refused soon felt pressure from Army representatives and, virtually forced to comply, they were usually sent to difficult spots like Hainan Island or to distant regions such as Sinkiang or Inner Mongolia. Students reputed to be troublemakers could also expect faraway assignments—and these youths, ironically, included many Red Guards who had been most active during the early stages of the Cultural Revolution in Canton.

Two devices were employed by the municipal authorities to discourage students from attempting to flee back to Canton. Their identity cards, revised to show their new rural address, now prevented them from claiming the city to be their legal residence.

And their urban ration cards were canceled, thus precluding them from rice and other food staples if they returned home.[25] Strong resistance to the resettlement program nevertheless came from students and their families as well as from peasants in the regions to which the youths were assigned. In a Kansu province commune, according to an official account, peasants rejected a contingent of city youths on the grounds that they were difficult to manage, lacked farming experience, demanded more food than they deserved and, in sum, represented a "burden." [26] When a trainload of students arrived in one Kwangtung commune, peasants simply sent them home. Elsewhere in Kwangtung, peasants arrested four students who had accidentally broken farm equipment while working, and charged them with "counterrevolutionary" sabotage.[27] To many youths, the program represented a form of punishment that fit no discernible crime. Reporting on the resettlement of thirty-four thousand city teachers and students in an area of Kiangsi province, a Peking commentator denounced them for floundering in lethargy, squabbling with peasants, and criticizing rural life as "monotonous and distasteful." [28]

Faced with the prospect of rural exile, several doctors, professors, and professional men in Canton reportedly committed suicide. In a few places, rusticated students were said to have escaped from their assigned communes into mountainous areas to form guerrilla bands, raiding Army posts for weapons and villages for food. More of a problem, however, were youths who made their way back to the cities, where they had no choice but to go underground as virtual outlaws. It was to these youths that newspaper articles and radio broadcasts often referred in their periodic attacks against "juvenile delinquents and hooligans." In the spring of 1970, the Canton authorities would initiate a severe crackdown against them, publicly judging and executing more than a hundred within a one-month period.[29]

Despite its shortcomings and difficulties, the *Hsia-fang* movement nevertheless scored notable achievements. Among these was the extension of public health services to the countryside by the transfer of thousands of so-called "barefoot doctors" to rural areas. Given a few months of rudimentary medical training, these "doctors" were commissioned to treat common ailments and practice preventive medicine—and one of their key functions was to promote birth-control information and techniques in an effort to curb the growth of China's huge population.[30] The *Hsia-fang* movement also contributed to the decentralization of China's resources —and this would be especially crucial as the threat of a war with the Soviet Union loomed.

The massive migration was matched during the winter of 1968–1969 by a number of economic experiments somewhat reminiscent of the years during and after Great Leap Forward. Peasants in a few provinces were deprived of the private gardens they had been granted as a means of stimulating food production after the Great Leap. Several areas also introduced a radical "free supply" system, under which peasant families would receive a large portion of income in the form of food, medical care, education, and essential services.[31] On one hand, these experiments may have reflected an effort on the Army's part to restore the rural controls that had broken down in the course of the Cultural Revolution. At the same time, the ideologues appeared to believe that the moment was ripe for a fresh campaign along the lines of the Great Leap Forward. But the caution with which these innovations were introduced —and the fact that they were limited to only a few regions of the country—indicated that the Peking leaders were trying to test new policies rather than initiate sweeping changes. Their prudence, then, suggested that they were locked in a debate over economic strategy.

Expressions of an eagerness for grandiose Maoist schemes could be seen in statements by Yao Wen-yuan, the radical Shanghai publicist, calling for the unleashing of "social productive forces" in a "vigorous technical revolution." [32] And signs of a revived Great Leap Forward mentality were also contained in a rash of patently fraudulent production statistics and output targets.[33] In contrast, the moderates publicized their views by reprinting an old essay by Mao, originally published in March 1949, that stressed the virtues of temperance, warned against "blind and haphazard" programs, and insisted that economic growth should proceed "step-by-step." And in strange contrast to the rhetoric of the Cultural Revolution, it urged that the "positive qualities of urban and rural capitalism" be mobilized "as far as possible in the interests of developing the national economy." [34] Mao's essay was significant for another reason. It had been written at the end of the civil war against the Nationalists —and it was now being reprinted at the end of another civil war.

The economic debate was paralleled by a similar political debate. Mao and his associates held a full-scale Central Committee Plenum during late October—their first such session since the hectic days of August 1966—at which they summarily expelled Liu Shao-ch'i from both his Party and government posts, declaring that he had been thrown "onto the garbage heap of history." They also stated that the Ninth Party Congress, which Mao had hoped to convene much earlier, would be assembled "at an appropriate time" in the near future.[35] Both the dismissal of Liu and the persistent ambiguity shrouding the date of the forthcoming Congress were indicative of differences within the Peking leadership.

Though they usually adhered strictly to legal form, Mao and his comrades had acted unconstitutionally in their expulsion of Liu from his positions. For under the Party Constitution, he should have been arraigned before a Congress of the Party. Nor could he be officially removed as Chief of State except by the National People's Congress, the rubber-stamp Chinese legislature. Thus it appeared that Mao had moved hastily against Liu out of fear that a trial of his adversary would turn into a protracted, messy spectacle that might exacerbate divisions within the hierarchy.[36]

A year earlier, discussing plans for the Ninth Congress, Hsieh Fu-chih had candidly stated that delegates would be appointed by the central authorities in Peking in order to "guarantee" that the radicals would "be in the majority" and hence assure a Maoist success.[37] Now, however, the Army-dominated provincial Revolutionary Committees were determined to designate the delgates, making it almost certain that representatives dedicated to moderation would be pre-eminent. That the provincial Committees intended to control the radicals was apparent in various statements demanding that "intellectuals"—a term synonymous with Red Guards and other student activists—must accept the leadership of workers, peasants, and, of course, soldiers. Replying to Red Guards in Honan province who were seeking representation, for example, the local Revolutionary Committee asserted:

> Can you represent the working class? No! Absolutely not! You vainly attempt to vie for leadership power with the working class.

This shows that you do not resemble the working class in the slightest. On the contrary, by resisting the leadership of the working class, you are representing the interests of the bourgeoisie, the extremely reactionary bourgeois authorities and the landlords, rich peasants, bad elements, counterrevolutionaries and rightists. . . . Improperly reformed intellectuals and scholars belong to the petty bourgeoisie. They can by no means become the leading force of the proletarian revolution.[38]

The dispossessed radicals, in the meantime, were protesting with increasing vehemence against their exclusion. In many places, they inveighed against what they called "the restoration of the old" —implying that veteran Army commanders and Party bureaucrats supposed to have been purged in the Cultural Revolution had instead regained power or never lost it.[39] As usual, the loudest complaints came from Shanghai. In one editorial, the city's foremost newspaper pointed out that many Revolutionary Committees were "composed entirely of former personnel," while the Red Guards and other "new proletarians" had been "squeezed out like toothpaste from a tube." [40] Another article criticized officials who were concerned only with "production" and "labor discipline," warning that such attitudes threatened to sabotage the drive to convert the Party into "a militant, vigorous and vital organization of vanguards." [41] Therefore, the Shanghai radicals insisted, the new Party should be built on a "crash priority basis," with its ranks open to "outstanding revolutionary rebel fighters who have been tested in the fires of the Cultural Revolution." [42]

Much of the debate over representation in the future Party revolved around a declaration that Mao had issued not long before. Comparing the Party to a human being, he had warned that it would lack vigor unless "it eliminated waste and absorbed fresh blood." [43] To the radicals, "fresh blood" signified the Red Guards.[44] To the military commanders and old *apparatchiks*, the Party's "fresh blood" would be "primarily the advanced elements among industrial workers." [45]

By the spring of 1969, the debate had been more or less resolved in favor of cohesion and stability. Peking directives urged that "class struggle" be dampened, emphasizing that "the target of attack must be narrowed and more people must be helped through education." [46] Key editorials stressed the importance of pragmatic economic and social policies, quoting Mao's latest instruction that planning and production be pursued with "enough leeway" to permit flexibility.[47] And still another epitaph was written for the Red Guards. They had made "tremendous contributions" but, as "intellectuals," they "often vacillate and lack a thoroughgoing revolutionary spirit." Therefore, said the *People's Daily*, they must "overcome their weaknesses" by "integrating themselves with the masses of workers and peasants." [48]

The Ninth National Congress of the Chinese Communist Party, which finally did open on April 1, 1969, eight months later than Mao had anticipated, was unique in many ways. In violation of the Party Constitution, which called for a new Congress every five years, it was the first such conference to be held in more than a decade. In contrast to past Party conclaves, it was closed to foreign Communist observers. And unlike previous Party Congresses, which merely ratified decisions reached beforehand, the April meeting seemed to have been organized without careful preparation—as if the Peking leaders, impatient after repeated delays, felt that they could wait no longer.

Various indications testified to hasty preparation. The unusually large size of the Congress—more than fifteen hundred delegates were present—suggested that the selection process had not been easy. The fact that the Congress dragged on for twenty-four days reflected the difficulties encountered by delegates as they worked to choose the new Central Committee. In addition, the Central Committee was greatly expanded, perhaps as a result of compromises.

The principal speeches at the Congress and at the Central Committee Plenum that followed were less than inspiring. Mao's address to the Central Committee seemed defensive, and Lin Piao's Political Report failed to have an immediate impact. Delivered on April 1, it underwent two weeks of discussion before its adoption and was not finally published until April 27.

As one perceptive observer has noted, Lin Piao's performance was essentially an attempt to reconcile what happened in the Cultural Revolution with what should have happened.[49] In short, it sought to provide a rationale for Mao's campaign, whose origin Lin traced back to the mid-1950s. At that time, he said, Mao had observed two disturbing trends: one was the growth of a Chinese Party bureaucracy that was increasingly "divorced from the masses," and threatening to stifle their "revolutionary initiative." The other was Khrushchev's abrupt doctrinal switch at the Soviet Union's Twentieth Party Congress, which revealed the "rampancy of revisionism in the international Communist movement," convincing Mao that the struggle between capitalism and socialism was "still not really solved."

The relationship between these two trends, in Mao's view, was that China would degenerate into Soviet-style "revisionism" unless he intervened. Thus, Lin Piao recalled, Mao delivered his celebrated speech in 1956 on "contradictions among the people," in which he tried to define the nature of the real enemy. Implicit in this thesis was the assumption that the people would rally to his cause if liberated from bureaucratic restraint. That assumption prompted him to initiate a series of nationwide campaigns designed to revitalize the different sectors of Chinese society. But each effort ended in disappointment.

Lin Piao described how Mao had pitted the intellectuals against the Party in the Hundred Flowers episode, only to find that the intellectuals themselves were tainted with "bourgeois rightism." He launched the Great Leap Forward in an attempt to release peasant energies, only to discover that peasants responded more enthusiastically to free enterprise than to his appeals for self-sacrifice. He initiated the Socialist Education campaign in 1962 in an effort to purify low-level Party officials, only to be confronted by their determination to preserve their ossified, corrupt bureaucracy.

Still clinging to his faith in the "masses," Mao concluded that the real culprits were entrenched in the upper echelons of the Party apparatus. His final strategy, then, was to mobilize the "masses" against Liu Shao-ch'i and the *apparatchiks*—which he did by unleashing the Red Guards. In a hitherto unknown speech delivered in February 1967, Lin Piao disclosed, Mao had outlined the process that led him to launch the Cultural Revolution:

> In the past, we waged struggles in the rural areas, in factories, in the cultural field, and we carried out the Socialist Education movement. But all this failed to solve the problem because we did not find a form, a method, to arouse the broad masses to expose our

dark aspect openly, in an all-round way and from below. The answer was the Great Proletarian Cultural Revolution.

When Lin Piao turned to the events of the Cultural Revolution itself, however, he was less precise. Mao had been almost as confused as everyone else by the turmoil, he concluded, explaining that intractable heretics became "mixed up" with misguided sinners, and it was "hard to sort them out." Amid the chaotic "twists and reversals" of the Cultural Revolution, Lin implied, the opposition to Mao had changed. The Red Guards who had represented Mao's "revolutionary successors" in the summer of 1966 became a "reactionary evil wind" a year later, when they went on uncontrollable rampages. As a consequence, Lin said, Mao switched his trust to the "working class," saying it with mangoes.

That switch had taken place eight months earlier, yet Lin closed his account without suggesting whether the "working class" had yet fulfilled Mao's trust. His assertion that the Cultural Revolution had resulted in a "great victory" indicated that the upheavals of the past four years were formally finished. Yet, Lin hinted, Mao's optimism in the power of the "masses" remained unquenched. When he had asked Mao what to do "if bad people go wild again," the Chairman had replied that he would "just arouse the masses and strike them down."

Though his Report had been advertised in advance as a "great program" to guide China's "production," Lin devoted only two paragraphs to the economy, and these offered little more than vague generalities. He appealed for "new leaps forward" in economic output. But stressing that "production would not be replaced by revolution," he made it clear that there would not be another Great Leap Forward of the kind that had disrupted China in 1958. He emphasized the importance of economic moderation, reiterating that agriculture would take precedence over industrial development. The guarantor of temperance was, of course, the Army, which Lin again described as "the mighty pillar of the dictatorship of the proletariat." As for the Communist Party, it still required major reform —and that task would be a key challenge in the years ahead.[50]

The deliberately muted tone of Lin Piao's Report was matched by Mao's equally sober statement. Speaking to the new Central Committee at its first plenum on April 28, he focused on the need for unity and, though justifying the Cultural Revolution, he almost apologized for its excesses. "You must operate with discretion," he told the new Party leaders, pointing out that brutality and indiscriminate arrests compounded rather than rectified "mistakes." There were conflicts between and within groups, between the Army and civilian organization, and inside military units. But most of these were "internal contradictions among the people" rather than "antagonistic" differences between the people and their implacable enemies, Mao said, therefore they could be resolved. The Party was large and flexible enough to tolerate divergent opinions as long as "people of all circles unite," Mao concluded, again underlining that "our goal is solidarity that will strengthen the dictatorship of the proletariat." [51]

One of the principal documents to emerge from the Ninth Congress was a new Party Constitution. The document had been drafted either in late 1967 or early 1968 by a ten-man commission headed by Chang Ch'un-ch'iao and Yao Wen-yuan, the radical Shanghai leaders, and it was afterward circulated in Peking and throughout the provinces for comments before its adoption by the Congress. Predictably, it contrasted drastically with the 1956 Constitution, which had been the product of a highly structured Party apparatus. Influenced by de-Stalinization in the Soviet Union, the 1956 document had been careful to avoid any hint of devotion to the "cult of personality," emphasizing instead the Party's collective leadership. The new Constitution changed all that. It equated Mao's doctrine with Marxism-Leninism as the "theoretical basis" of China's political, social, economic, and military policies.* Moreover, it confirmed Lin Piao's status as Mao's "close comrade-in-arms and successor." Conforming to Mao's preoccupation with "spiritual" renovation, the new Constitution also dropped the passage in the 1956 document that had called for the "gradual and continuous improvement of the living conditions of the people," stressing instead the necessity for protracted "class struggle." Absent from the new Constitution as well was the Party's table of organization, such as had been detailed at length in the 1956 charter. And

* Mao's elevation to the Communist pantheon was marked by the omission of the hyphen in the English transliteration of his name, which now became Mao Tsetung in official documents. This permitted the slogan Marxism–Leninism–Mao Tsetung Thought. In Chinese, however, the characters *Tse* and *tung* remained distinct.

among its other contents, the new Constitution denounced Russian "revisionism"—a notable switch from the 1956 referrence to the Soviet Union as the leader of international communism.[52]

In essence, then, the new Constitution was more an impressionistic political platform than a durable code of laws, and its amorphousness seemed to have been intended to negate the existence of a Party bureaucracy. But its very fuzziness appeared to suit the Army commanders controlling most of China. For they would not be restricted by sharp definitions of their authority and could, consequently, exercise their power with considerable flexibility. Thus the Politburo and Central Committee elected by the Ninth Party Congress simply ratified the Army's predominance, while it elevated several regional commanders who had been the targets of Red Guard attacks during the Cultural Revolution.

Mao, of course, remained Chairman of the Central Committee, with Lin Piao as his deputy. And they, along with Chou En-lai, Ch'en Po-ta and K'ang Sheng, comprised the Politburo Standing Committee. The new Politburo also featured prominent Maoists like Chiang Ch'ing and the two Shanghai radicals Chang Ch'un-ch'iao and Yao Wen-yuan, as well as Lin Piao's wife, Yeh Ch'ün, and Mao's former bodyguard, Wang Tung-hsing. Most significant, however, was the rise of Army representation in the ruling body. Three old Marshals—Chu Teh, Liu Po-ch'eng, and Yeh Chien-ying —regained their former places on the Politburo, but among the new military faces were such men as Huang Yung-sheng, Chief of General Staff; Ch'en Hsi-lien, commander of Manchuria; Hsü Shih-yu, senior officer in central China; Li Tso-p'eng, Navy political commissar; Wu Fa-hsien, the Air Force commander; Li Teh-sheng, Army chief of Anhwei province; and Ch'iu Hui-tso, head of the Army's Logistics Department. The Politburo also included one old Party official, Li Hsueh-feng, now Chairman of the Hopeh Revolutionary Committee.[53]

Almost twice the size of its predecessor, the new Central Committee contained two hundred seventy-nine full and alternate members, and, like the provincial Revolutionary Committees, it was overwhelmingly weighted in favor of Army officers and Party cadres who had survived the Cultural Revolution. Indeed, the Red Guards ended up with derisory treatment. Two of Chiang Ch'ing's female firebrands, the Peking University activist Nieh Yuan-tzu and Chang Hsi-t'ing of Szechwan, were elected only as alternates. In contrast, figures like Yu Ch'iu-li, the Minister of Petroleum Industry who had been desperately defended against radical assaults by Chou En-lai, rose to full membership. Another sign that very few drops of "fresh blood" had been infused was that the average age of its full members was fifty-nine, and most had been affiliated with the Party before the Communists attained power in 1949.[54]

But the new central hierarchy would not endure for long. In the summer of 1970, apparently seeking to eliminate the radicals who had become prominent during the Cultural Revolution, the Peking leaders were to purge Ch'en Po-ta, who had guided the Maoist campaign. A year after that, no less a figure than Lin Piao was dismissed. With him fell Huang Yung-sheng, Wu Fa-hsien, Li Tso-p'eng, and Ch'iu Hui-tso, all generals and members of the Politburo. Unlike Liu Shao-ch'i and the Party *apparatchiks*, whose lives were spared during the Cultural Revolution, these men were reportedly liquidated in a short but bitter power struggle that reached its climax in the autumn of 1971.

Nor did the establishment of a new leadership structure at the top automatically bring stability to the Chinese provinces. Though nothing in the period following the Ninth Party Congress resembled the turmoil of the two preceding years, a number of incidents nevertheless erupted in various parts of the country, most of them the result of resistance by Red Guards and other youths to military efforts to impose law and order. In Fukien province, for example, students clashed with soldiers striving to deport them to the countryside and, on one occasion in August, several participants were killed in a skirmish.[55] The biggest outbreak during the summer occurred in the Shansi province capital of Taiyuan, where Liu Ko-p'ing, Chairman of the Revolutionary Committee, was challenged by General Chang Jih-ch'ing, a local Army political commissar. Their rivalry ignited factional fighting of the kind that had nagged the province before and, on July 20, troops surrounded the city, issuing an ultimatum to its opposing groups to cease their conflict. Liu and General Chang were then invited to Peking to resolve their differences, but their compromise settlement remained tenuous.[56]

Apparently convinced that the Ninth Party Congress had

spelled the end of the Cultural Revolution, the Revolutionary Committees showed confidence as they initiated measures to restore or maintain discipline around the country. In Shensi province, they mobilized "command groups" to scour factories, schools, and rural communes for cases of disobedience and, in the Hunan capital of Changsha, they organized mass meetings to denounce "class enemies" suspected of fomenting trouble. The civilian vigilante movement in Canton known as the Workers' Provost Corps was reinforced by other amateur police outfits, among them the Little Red Sentinels, schoolchildren assigned to spy on citizens and perform other minor security jobs.[57] A new wave of public trials and executions also began, with most of those singled out for punishment accused of "ultraleftism." More than forty persons were sentenced to death in Canton on March 10, and similar trials were held about the same time in Peking and other cities.[58] In a few instances, those convicted seemed to be the victims of old clan feuds, family vendettas, and personal grudges. In Fukien province, for example, an aged dentist and his son were executed for having raped a local woman twenty years before.[59] That incident, underlining as it did the length of the Chinese memory, suggested that the social tensions generated by the Cultural Revolution might remain fresh long after a surface appearance of calm had returned to China.

The authorities in many areas also now began to compel Red Guards and other agitators to compensate for the damage they caused at the outset of the Cultural Revolution, when they had responded to Mao's exhortations to smash "feudal" and "bourgeois" vestiges throughout China. A Canton schoolteacher whose five sons and daughters had been Red Guards was required to pay the equivalent of a year's salary to cover the cost of "feudal" antiques and "reactionary" books destroyed by his children. A former Red Guard from Kwangtung recounted that he had been billed by the provincial apparatus for 600 *yuan* in expenses he had incurred in Peking, Shanghai, and Chungking while "exchanging revolutionary experiences" during the fall of 1966. The itemized bill included the precise costs of food, lodging, and travel and the youth, who fled to Hong Kong to escape his creditors, expressed amazement that the Chinese accounting system had functioned so efficiently during that chaotic period.[60]

Further evidence of moderation was seen on October 1, 1969, in the Peking celebrations marking the twentieth anniversary of the Chinese People's Republic. Striving to publicize their preoccupation with unity, the Peking leaders displayed several figures who had been denounced during the Cultural Revolution, among them the liberal economist Ch'en Yun, Marshals Hsu Hsiang-ch'ien and Nieh Jung-chen, Foreign Minister Ch'en Yi and Madame Sun Yat-sen.[61] Conspicuously absent from the list of twenty-nine official slogans was the familiar exhortation to "carry the Cultural Revolution to the end." The accent instead was on "socialist revolution" and, in his keynote speech, Chou En-lai modestly praised China's "rudimentary prosperity" and called for a "new high tide in industrial and agricultural production, culture, and art." [62]

The new sobriety was especially pronounced in efforts to recuperate the lost economic momentum of the mid-1960s. An important *People's Daily* editorial published in November, for example, offered an assortment of pragmatic recommendations for improving working methods. Among other proposals, it urged economic officials to plan carefully, reminding them that "experience gained in selected units cannot be spread to the whole area at once." The editorial also insisted that labor be given time to relax, and it advised cadres to cease wasting days in marathon political rallies and preparing long reports, saying that "meetings, documents, and forms should be drastically cut down and simplified." [63] Matching this revival of pragmatism, *Red Flag* even went so far as to suggest that China might accept foreign aid and learn from "good foreign experience," provided it could "keep the initiative in its own hands." [64] Later directives would also stress the importance of technical skills and even material incentives, once considered to be "revisionist."

This changed attitude was illustrated as well at Canton's international trade fair held in the fall of 1969. Before, foreign trade representatives visiting the biennial fair had been nagged constantly by songs, speeches, and meetings extolling Mao and the Cultural Revolution, and several had even joined in the ferment in hopes of pleasing the Chinese. But now, when a Swedish importer tried to engage a Chinese commercial specialist in an ideological discussion, the official cut him short, saying: "We're here to talk business, not politics." [65]

Amid all these shifts, however, China's leaders still faced the gigantic task of rebuilding the decimated Chinese Communist Party. One problem complicating this effort was the reluctance of former officials to participate in the renovated Party apparatus. In many areas, officials continued to be harassed by remnant radicals who claimed prominent places in the new Party machine. At the same time, persistent struggles for power by rival factions impeded the establishment of Party Committees, even at the lowest echelons. This struggle for power was paralleled at the highest level by a growing dispute between groups headed by Chou En-lai on the one hand, and Lin Piao on the other. Not until September 19, 1969—nearly five months after the end of the Ninth Congress—did the first regional Party Committee materialize, and it was merely at the level of a commune in Hunan province, Mao's birthplace.[66] More than a year would pass before the first provincial Committee emerged, again in Hunan. Even by then, fewer than a hundred of China's two thousand counties had succeeded in forming Committees.[67]

In December 1969, endeavoring to speed up the process of Party reconstruction, Peking publicized the ideal procedure recommended for emulation throughout China, selecting as its model the Committee set up in the printing plant of the New China News Agency in the national capital. At the start, former cadres, "outstanding" workers, and soldiers at the plant created a Revolutionary Committee whose function was to unify the employees, then divided by "bourgeois factionalism, sectarianism, mountain-stronghold mentality, and anarchism." Unity was largely achieved, the report claimed, by an intensive campaign to persuade the plant officials and staff to confess their "errors" and pledge to mend their ways. But the key role in this operation was played by an Army unit that had apparently assumed the direction of the plant in the summer of 1968. Moreover, the report divulged, Army officers would continue to exercise authority in the plant as members of both the Revolutionary Committee and the new Party Committee.[68]

This pattern of military predominance was dutifully applied to the Party Committees germinating in the provinces. A Party-building conference held in the Honan province capital of Chengchow proclaimed: "The Army is the chief component of the State, and its strength determines the degree of consolidation of political power." [69] Fresh directives made it clear that the Red Guards and other radical activists would be given minimal functions, if any, in the new Party Committees. An official announcement from Kwangtung province stated that "revolutionary mass representatives" were being barred from working sessions of an embryonic county Committee in order to curb their "unnecessary upper-level activities." [70] In early January, the Peking leadership dealt a severe blow to the radicals with a decision denying them any real position in the new Party apparatus. The decision, contained in a *Red Flag* editorial, was couched as a reply to elements claiming to be "most revolutionary and most advanced" and demanding pre-eminence in the reformed Party:

> This idea is extremely wrong. . . . Some comrades have come to regard themselves as "most revolutionary and most advanced" because they had made some contributions during the Great Proletarian Cultural Revolution. This shows that they fail to view themselves correctly, and lack the spirit to remold themselves. Others have desperately exaggerated the role of the former organizations, incorrectly handled relations between the mass organizations and the Party, and tried to put themselves above the Party in an attempt to challenge its leadership. This is an expression of reactionary anarchism.[71]

Most significantly, the *Red Flag* editorial went on to negate a fundamental tenet of Mao's doctrine. To rely on the Red Guards and other radicals as the "foundation" of the new Party, it said, would be to "reduce" the Communist apparatus from a "vanguard" movement to simply "the level of a mass organization." This portrayal of the Party as the "vanguard" effectively sounded the death knell of Mao's ideological aspirations. For, by returning to the Leninist concept of the Party as an "elitist" hierarchy, it subverted his dream of perpetual revolution in a society free of bureaucratic routine. In short, if Mao's misty vision of a Chinese equivalent of the Paris Commune had died during the Cultural Revolution, it was now being unceremoniously buried.

The last of the new Party Committees were finally established in late August 1971, twenty-one months after the first new provincial apparatus had been set up in Hunan, and the Army's predominance throughout the country was dramatic. Twenty of the twenty-nine First Secretaries were military officers, and all but one of the nine civilian Committee heads concurrently assumed positions as political commissars of provincial military commands. Of the one hundred fifty-eight Committee leaders down to the rank of Deputy Secretary, nearly 60 per cent were soldiers, 25 per cent civilian *apparatchiks*, and only about 5 per cent radicals who had emerged during the Cultural Revolution. The exception to this pattern was Shanghai, where the new Party Committee was headed by Chang Ch'un-ch'iao and his deputy, Yao Wen-yuan. But as Politburo members, these men spent most of their time in Peking, leaving the administration of Shanghai to two subordinates—an Army officer and a veteran Party cadre.[72]

Another indication of the Army's pre-eminence was to be found in the slowness of Party reconstruction, which was largely due to the refusal of radicals to submit to military domination. In Tibet, one of the last areas to form a Committee, a serious dispute had developed between General Jen Jung, the Army commissar, and General Tseng Yung-ya, the military commander and Chairman of Tibet's Revolutionary Committee. Tseng had apparently shifted to the left, and he was ousted three months before the Party Committee emerged under General Jen's leadership. Another late-forming Committee, in Heilungkiang, was delayed by a fight in which General Wang-Chai-tao, the local Army commander, ousted P'an Fu-sheng, the former province boss. In contrast the areas that established Committees most rapidly were those where military authority had been preponderant from the start—such as Kiangsu, Anhwei, and Chekiang, all of them under the jurisdiction of the Nanking Military Region commanded by General Hsü Shih-yu, a Politburo member and one of China's senior officers. Similarly, the early formation of Party Committees in Hunan and Kwangtung testified to the power of the Canton Military Region and its former boss, General Huang Yung-sheng.

Along with being a vehicle for the Army's authority, the new Committees also featured veteran Party figures who had dropped from public view during the Cultural Revolution and no doubt underwent "thought reform" before staging a comeback. One such figure was Cho Tzu-yang, former First Secretary of the old Kwangtung province Party Committee. Initially denounced by Red Guards in Canton in January 1967, he was purged the next month and disappeared not long afterward. By mid-1971, however, he had been resurrected in a senior capacity on the Inner Mongolia Party Committee. Similarly, the former First Secretary in Hunan, Cheng Ping-hua, reappeared on the Shansi Party Committee, and T'an Ch'i-lung, who had been dismissed as Communist boss of Shantung, surfaced four years later in a key post in Fukien province.[73]

Nothing vindicated these "bourgeois revisionists" more vividly, however, than the eventual humiliation of one of the Cultural Revolution's foremost activists, Ch'en Po-ta. Mao's private secretary and chief ideological counselor since Yenan days, Ch'en had managed the Cultural Revolution Directorate from its inception, capping his rise in influence with membership in the Politburo's supreme Standing Committee. But if his record was pure by Maoist standards, it evidently appeared spotty to the Army commanders and Party officials who now had assumed control over China. Like so many of those he had helped to eliminate, Ch'en fell from public sight in the summer of 1970 and, ten months later, hints emerged to indicate that he was in serious trouble. On May 25, 1971, for example, a Peking journal reached back into history to assail the author of an essay written nearly forty years before as a "sham Marxist." The journal did not identify the author by name, but it was Ch'en Po-ta.[74] Not long afterward, in an editorial marking the fiftieth anniversary of the Chinese Communist Party, *Red Flag* denounced "the type of person who claims to be a 'humble little commoner' but is actually a big careerist." [75] The reference, though esoteric, was plain to Peking insiders. In a speech delivered on April 13, 1967, Chiang Ch'ing had described Ch'en as a "humble little commoner"—and she depicted herself as an "even smaller one." [76]

A more dramatic—and still largely mysterious—episode unfolded late in the summer of 1971. On the night of September 12, a British-built Trident jet airliner belonging to the Chinese Air Force crashed about a hundred miles inside the People's Republic of Mongolia, a satellite of the Soviet Union. The seven men and two women aboard were killed, their bodies charred beyond recognition. At the same time, a helicopter that had taken off from Peking's Tsinghua University campus in an apparently desperate attempt to reach the Mongolian border, was forced down. All but one of its occupants committed suicide.

The Peking authorities immediately grounded all air traffic

throughout China. They also let it be known that the National Day celebrations marking the twenty-second anniversary of the Communist rise to power, scheduled to be held on October 1, would be canceled. Soon afterward, almost unbelievable tales of intrigue and conspiracy began to be heard inside China.

Confidential documents circulated among Party officials related that Lin Piao, his wife, Yeh Chun, and their son Lin Li-kuo, an Air Force officer, had been killed in the crash of the Trident along with General Huang Yung-sheng, Chief of General Staff; General Wu Fa-hsien, the Air Force Commander; and General Li Tso-p'eng, chief Commissar of the Navy. The documents alleged that Lin Piao had attempted unsuccessfully on three occasions to assassinate Mao—the last time in early September by ordering a senior officer in central China to bomb a train carrying the Chairman from Nanking to Peking. The officer refused and, according to the account, informed the Peking leadership of Lin's plot. As the story went, Lin was also betrayed by his daughter, whose nickname "Tou-tou," meaning "beans," stood for her father's favorite dish. Fearing arrest, the documents continued, Lin and his fellow conspirators commandeered the Trident in an effort to escape to the Soviet Union. But the aircraft crashed, either for lack of fuel or because of bad weather.

Though fascinating, those details of Lin's attempted escape and death were probably fabricated. Both Soviet and Mongolian investigation teams examined the remains of the crashed Trident, reporting that its occupants all seemed to have been below the age of fifty. The teams further reported that some of the bodies contained bullet holes, and speculated that a fight could have taken place aboard the aircraft. This suggested that the Trident, one of four such airplanes purchased by China from Pakistan and used exclusively by high-ranking Chinese officers, may have been the scene of a clash between rivals—some trying to flee the country and others striving to prevent their flight. The helicopter that attempted to take off from Tsinghua University no doubt carried other potential defectors.

But whether or not Lin Piao and his comrades were victims of the crash, the fact that the Peking authorities asserted that they were killed was significant. For it indicated that they were dead—

perhaps from other causes. They may have been shot in an abortive bid for power.[77]

One of the earliest hints that Lin Piao was slipping into disfavor with Mao was communicated in a strangely esoteric form. During the summer, Chiang Ch'ing distributed a collection of photographs that she had purportedly taken. A portrait of Lin showed him hatless and almost completely bald—a condition about which he was known to be extremely sensitive.[78] By autumn, it was clear that Lin and his associates had been defeated in some kind of power play. Lin dropped out of sight after having last been seen publicly at a Peking reception for Rumanian President Nicolae Ceaucescu on June 3, and foreign embassies in the capital were later instructed by Chinese protocol officials to cease mentioning his name in toasts and congratulatory messages.[79] Veiled attacks against him also became apparent in official Chinese newspaper articles and radio broadcasts.

On October 20, for instance, Peking Radio quoted a passage by the writer Lu Hsun, who died in the 1930s, that seemed to mirror Mao's chagrin toward the man he had designated as his "close comrade-in-arms" and heir. "The enemy is nothing to fear," it said. "What hurt and disappointed me most was the sinister arrow fired by my ally, and his smiling face after I was wounded." [80] An analogous theme was featured in another broadcast that appeared to equate Lin's alleged opposition to Mao with Khrushchev's betrayal of Stalin. Khrushchev had "pretentiously praised" Stalin while the Soviet dictator was alive but "viciously denounced" him after his death, the broadcast said. It warned against those who "pretend to be good people but actually commit evil deeds," and, describing them as "sham Marxists," it called them the "most dangerous, ferocious, and wicked enemies of the dictatorship of the proletariat." [81] A spate of other articles and broadcasts also assailed Lin obliquely by harking back to his portrayal of Mao as the "genius of the world revolution." The implication here was that Lin, as Mao's successor, was claiming to have inherited the right to be considered as infallible as the Chairman. Or as a *People's Daily* editorial put it: "By pretending to acclaim someone else as a genius, renegades from the Communist movement present themselves as 'geniuses.' " [82]

If one pieces together the available evidence, the dispute between Lin Piao's group and the faction headed by Mao and Chou En-lai was apparently confined to Peking, and did not, therefore, augur another nationwide upheaval of the kind that erupted during the Cultural Revolution. It was, in short, essentially a limited power struggle at the leadership level—even though its outcome would determine the future course of China as a whole.

Some analysts have contended that the quarrel represented a continuation of the conflict between professional soldiers and political commissars that had long plagued the Chinese Communist Army. This conflict reached a peak during the Cultural Revolution, when the commissars tended to side with the radicals against the professionals, who sought to maintain law and order. According to this thesis, Lin Piao tried to perpetuate the authority of the commissars in the provincial Party committees being reconstructed after the Cultural Revolution. His objective was to reinforce his own power, which he had built up since his emergence as Defense Minister in 1959. But he was opposed by Chou En-lai and the regional commanders, who worked to put the new Party machine under the control of an alliance of civilians and professional soldiers. Their aim was to prevent another Cultural Revolution, which they believed would cause irreparable damage to China.

Lin Piao apparently reached the height of his power in April 1969, when he managed to have himself appointed Mao's official successor in the new Party Constitution. After that, however, his position was slowly undermined by Chou and his supporters among the professional officers. In late 1969, for example, the Army's General Political Department, which had traditionally been headed by a commissar, came under the tutelage of General Li Teh-sheng, a veteran commander. During the following year, almost all the commissars in charge of provincial Revolutionary Committees were removed.[83] And in August 1970, the radicals were further weakened with the purge of Ch'en Po-ta.

By the middle of 1971, the renovated Party was strenuously working to impose its authority over the Army elements inspired by Lin Piao that still sought to exercise power. Time and again, reflecting this effort, the official Peking media asserted that placing the Army "under the absolute leadership of the Party" was imperative. Propaganda also publicized a song entitled "Three Main Rules of

Discipline and Eight Points for Attention," which stressed the need for soldiers to obey the Party. Lin Piao and his comrades presumably tried to resist, and the showdown between them and Chou En-lai's faction apparently arose as the Chinese leaders approached the convocation of a National People's Congress to select a new Chief of State to replace the dismissed Liu Shao-ch'i. Fearing that Lin would attempt to grab that post, Chou evidently moved to block him.

The quarrel was probably complicated by a dispute over the allocation of China's meager resources. Judging from the evidence, Chou and the regional commanders favored investment in industry and agriculture. They also sought to concentrate on support for the Chinese Army's ground forces. Lin Piao and his comrades, among them the heads of the Air Force and Navy, apparently advocated a larger focus on the development of sophisticated weapons.

Underlying this debate over budgetary questions was the issue of China's foreign policy at the outset of the 1970s. Chou and his group were plainly partial to a *rapprochement* with the United States as a way of countering the growing Soviet threat to China. Lin and his colleagues were not entirely opposed to that strategy. But they must have argued that a reconciliation with the United States might provoke the Russians, and thus they contended that the Chinese armed forces be fortified for the possibility of a pre-emptive Soviet attack. When their views were rejected, they may well have attempted to balance Chou's move toward the United States by seeking a *détente* with the Kremlin. After their purge, official propaganda excoriated them as "bourgeois careerists and conspirators having illicit relations with foreign countries." [84] The phrase had been used in 1959 to describe P'eng Teh-huai. Now, ironically, it was being used against Lin Piao, who had succeeded P'eng as Defense Minister.

How this conflict reached its climax may one day be elucidated. By early 1972, it was only clear that Chou and his group had won.

Mao undoubtedly watched the squabble from the sidelines, finally swinging over to the victor. But his own prestige could not have gone unscathed. Just as he had earlier extolled Liu Shao-ch'i and afterward found him to be a traitor, now he had been betrayed by Lin Piao, the man he had hand-picked as his heir. The omniscient deity had proved to be fallible.

By 1971, then, Mao's second revolution had devoured its most prestigious offspring, and China was moving in a direction that would have been considered unthinkable only a few years before. The direction was toward *rapprochement* with the United States, and Peking was steering a triangulated course.

CHAPTER 21

Rejoining the World

How to give "tit for tat" depends on the situation. Sometimes, not going to negotiations is tit for tat; and sometimes, going to negotiations is tit for tat.
—MAO TSE-TUNG, *October 17, 1945*

ON THE NIGHT OF July 15, 1971, in a brief television address, President Richard Nixon revealed that he had accepted an invitation from Premier Chou En-lai to visit Peking at an "appropriate date" within the next ten months. The purpose of his "journey for peace," as the President termed it, was not only "to seek the normalization of relations" between the United States and China, but "also to exchange views on questions of concern" to both countries. He expressed his "profound conviction" that "all nations will gain from a reduction of tensions and a better relationship between the United States and the People's Republic of China." [1] Less than seven months later, Nixon arrived in Peking, and his week of discussions there put Sino-American relations on a totally new course.

That sensational sequence of events would have been impossible four years earlier, when Mao Tse-tung and his comrades were encouraging Red Guards to storm foreign embassies and assault foreign diplomats in Peking, and China appeared to be receding into the xenophobic isolation that had characterized its attitudes toward the world in centuries past. The willingness of China's rulers to negotiate with the "ugly imperialist chieftain," as their publicists had portrayed Nixon, illustrated the degree to which the fanaticism of the Cultural Revolution had evaporated. It also dramatized the rise of Chou En-lai and the Army commanders, who had long advocated sobriety in the interests of China's foreign relations.

Yet this stunning switch did not signify any fundamental reversal of the Chinese leaders' long-range aspirations and ambitions. As dynamic Communists, they still clung to their faith in the inevitability of world revolution. As Chinese, they were still determined to defend their nation's security, retrieve its lost territories and win it international recognition as a major power. What had essentially changed was their tactics. Diplomatic tractability now promised to be more effective than intransigence. As usual, they found the ideological rationale for the new approach in one of Mao's apothegms: "Our principles must be firm. We must also employ all permissible and necessary flexibility to serve our principles." [2]

The Chinese leaders saw this tactical flexibility working to their advantage on a number of foreign-policy issues. For one, a thaw in their frozen relations with the United States would dilute American support for Chiang Kai-shek's regime on Taiwan, thereby inducing elements among the Nationalists to concede to an accommodation with Peking. They estimated as well that a Sino-American *détente* might prevent the rearmament of Japan and, in particular, forestall the development of a Japanese nuclear arsenal. Motivating their effort to achieve a modus vivendi with the United States, too, was their hope of playing a role in Southeast Asia following the withdrawal of American forces from Indochina. And finally, they viewed a *rapprochement* with Washington as a unique opportunity to counter the Kremlin. They had come close to war with the Russians in 1969, and even though a full-scale conflict was averted, the Chinese were by no means certain that the Soviet threat had abated.

All these foreign-policy issues were crucial to the Chinese, but the most urgent concerned their dispute with the Soviet Union—a quarrel that had its origins in a wide range of ideological, national, economic, and even racial differences. An important ingredient in Peking's fear of the Soviet Union was the primacy of Inner Asia in traditional Chinese strategic thinking. Rebels and pirates had chronically marauded China's maritime provinces, but no major enemy had ever penetrated the country from the sea. In contrast,

China had been invaded time and again over the centuries by the "barbarians" of the interior, many of whom were absorbed into Chinese civilization. Indeed, half the emperors who reigned during the last thousand years of imperial China were not Chinese.[3] Starting with the Khitan Mongols, who established the Liao dynasty in the tenth century, the "barbarian" cavalry thrusts grew more powerful until, in the seventeenth century, the Manchus swept into Peking to found the Ch'ing dynasty.

As they built an empire that stretched from Tibet and Sinkiang through Mongolia and Manchuria down into Southeast Asia, the Manchus themselves became obsessed by the strategic significance of Inner Asia. Even after the British demonstrated China's coastal vulnerability in the Opium War, the Manchu rulers still continued to be preoccupied with the menace of continental aggression. In 1875, faced by the choice of constructing a navy to resist Japan's rising influence in Korea or sending an expedition three thousand miles to block Russian advances into Sinkiang, the Manchus opted in favor of protecting their western frontier.

The Chinese Communists inherited this inward focus. Just as the Manchus had banished dissidents and criminals to remote border areas, the Communists shipped contingents of demobilized troops, students, and refractory intellectuals out to populate and cultivate Sinkiang, Tibet, and Inner Mongolia, and to convert their indigenous peoples to Han Chinese culture. One of the Communists' top military priorities after coming to power, for example, was to restore Chinese hegemony over Tibet—an objective that met with Chiang Kai-shek's envious approval. And in their earliest negotiations in Moscow, the Peking leaders sought to curb Soviet influence in Sinkiang by setting up "joint-stock companies" with the Russians to develop the region's resources. These companies were transferred to Peking's exclusive ownership in 1952. But the Chinese continued to be worried by the Soviet shadow hovering over them from the north and west. In 1954 and again in 1957, both Mao and Chou En-lai raised the question of borders with Khrushchev. On each occasion, the Chinese disclosed, the Soviet Premier had either declined to discuss the subject or refused to give them a "satisfactory answer."[4]

From the seventeenth century onward, Peking claimed, Tsarist

Russia had annexed a half-billion square kilometers of Chinese territory reaching from the vicinity of the Amur River adjoining Manchuria to the Pamir mountains adjacent to the southern corner of Sinkiang. Much of this territory was acquired by the Soviet Union under what Peking termed "unequal treaties" forced by Tsarist Russia on the decaying Ch'ing dynasty in the mid-nineteenth century, when China had fallen prey to foreign imperialists. The Chinese insisted that Moscow acknowledge these treaties to have been "unequal" even though, they said, they were prepared to "respect them . . . as the basis for a reasonable settlement." [5] To bolster their case, Peking recalled Lenin's pledge in 1920 to return "gratis and forever everything the Tsarist regime and the Russian bourgeoisie rapaciously stole" from China.

Against these arguments, the Russians contended that Lenin's statement had been a "declaration of principles" rather than a promise.[6] They flatly rejected Peking's demands that the old treaties be qualified as "unequal," asserting instead that the boundaries had been "fixed by life itself, and treaties concerning the border cannot be disregarded." [7] Kremlin spokesmen pointed out that the Chinese emperors had taken over Sinkiang and other parts of Central Asia by "aggression" and, in one area, had slaughtered more than 2 million local inhabitants in an unparalleled instance of "mass brutality." [8]

By 1964, the Sino-Soviet boundary problem had begun to escalate, and Russian statements charged for the first time that the Chinese had been "systematically violating the Soviet frontier" since 1960.[9] In reply, Peking alleged that the Kremlin had carried out "large-scale subversive activities" in Sinkiang in the spring of 1962 by "enticing and coercing" tens of thousands of Uighurs, Kazakhs, and other indigenous Muslims to go over the border into the Soviet Union.[10] As other accusations and counteraccusations flew back and forth between Peking and Moscow, Mao himself weighed into the dispute with a blunt complaint against the Russians. To a group of Japanese visitors to Peking in mid-1964, he declared that "there are too many places occupied by the Soviet Union." And, he added ominously: "We have not yet presented our account for this list." [11]

Aggravating the border issue were ideological and political differences between the Russian and Chinese Communists that dated back decades. Either through errors of judgment or efforts to promote Soviet interests, Stalin had repeatedly sought to subordinate Mao and Ch'ü Ch'iu-pai, Li Li-san, Wang Ming, and other Chinese Communist rivals who were more responsive to Moscow's dictates. In the late 1920s, Stalin had tried to compel them to preserve a "united front" with the Nationalists even after they had been decimated by Chiang Kai-shek. Twenty years later, apprehensive lest the United States intervene in the Chinese civil war and thus involve the Soviet Union, he attempted to restrain the Communists from pushing on to victory and, according to one source, proposed that China be partitioned along the line of the Yangtze River. Years afterward, disclosing Stalin's pressures on him, Mao said: "But we did not obey, and the revolution succeeded." [12] The trouble with Stalin persisted after the Chinese Communist triumph. Increasingly paranoiac, Stalin stalled signing an alliance with them for two months in 1950 because, as Mao himself recollected, he "feared that China might degenerate into another Yugoslavia, and that I might become a second Tito." [13] About the same time, Stalin was said to have conspired to extend his control over Manchuria through its Chinese leader, Kao Kang, whom Mao purged soon after the Soviet dictator's death in 1953.[14]

But in the minds of the Chinese, the memory of Stalin's maneuvers was pale in contrast to their experience with Khrushchev. The three years from Stalin's death until the Soviet Communist Party's Twentieth Congress in February 1956 was the only real period of friendship between the Russians and Chinese. The new Soviet leaders, less secure than Stalin had been, were eager to have Peking's support, and therefore endowed China with economic and military aid and assistance. Now committed to industrialization and military modernization along Russian lines, the Chinese were reliant on Moscow and willing to pay tribute to Soviet leadership of the Communist bloc. But the seeds of discord were germinating beneath this apparently harmonious relationship. Among other things, Chinese pretensions to big-power status rankled the Russians. Chinese self-confidence had also been boosted by economic and social progress at home and successes abroad. They had fought the United Nations to a stalemate in Korea, and they had played a key role at the Geneva Conference of 1954 and at Bandung the following year. Now, they felt, they were surpassing the Soviet Union in prestige and influence, particularly in Asia and Africa. "When we speak," asserted Madame Sun Yat-sen, "we speak not only for ourselves, but for all of Asia." [15]

According to an official Chinese recapitulation, the Sino-Soviet honeymoon ended with Khrushchev's revelations of Stalin's "crimes" at the Russian Party's Twentieth Congress. The Chinese were not surprised by the catalogue of Stalin's excesses, but in their view, Khrushchev's denunciation signified that he aspired to replace his former boss as the uncontested ruler of world communism. This represented a challenge to their own ambitions. In addition, Mao perceived that Khrushchev's policies, especially his efforts to ease tensions with the United States, threatened to weaken international Communist unity. As Mao analyzed the world situation at that point, Soviet technological advances had swung the balance of power in favor of the Communist camp—in his celebrated phrase, "the East wind is prevailing over the West wind." Thus he argued for a rougher rather than moderate stance toward the United States, even if such a strategy provoked nuclear war. "If worse came to worse and half of mankind died," he said, "the other half would remain while imperialism would be razed to the ground, and the whole world would become socialist." [16]

This logic sounded to Khrushchev like the rantings of a madman, and he behaved accordingly. During the Middle East crisis of 1958, in which American and British troops landed in Lebanon and Jordan, he proposed a summit meeting of the major world powers, including India but pointedly excluding China. Soon afterward, when the Chinese Communist leaders began preparations for a military offensive to "liberate" Taiwan from Chiang Kai-shek's control, Khrushchev rushed to Peking in an attempt to dissuade them from an adventure that he feared might ignite a wider war. In the course of that visit, he reportedly rejected a Chinese request for Soviet nuclear warheads to deploy in the offensive. Less than a year later, the Kremlin retracted its 1957 agreement to provide China with a "sample" atomic bomb and "technical data concerning its manufacture." That decision, the Russians explained, stemmed from their "serious doubts regarding the aims" of Chinese foreign policy.[17]

At the end of September 1959, Khrushchev infuriated the Chinese even more. After completing a visit to the United States, he flew directly to Peking for the tenth anniversary of the Chinese Communist regime, and there, in a banquet speech, he publicly extolled President Eisenhower as a sincere advocate of peace.[18] The Chinese replied by describing Eisenhower's conduct as a "smoke screen" designed to camouflage his intensification of the cold war.[19]

Now the dispute between Russia and China was plainly visible, and it was escalating at a rapid pace. Khrushchev and the other Soviet leaders openly denounced the Great Leap Forward and backed Marshal P'eng Teh-huai, the Defense Minister, in his assault against Mao. And in the summer of 1960, in his most dramatic gesture of hostility, Khrushchev abruptly withdrew more than a thousand Russian technicians then in China under Soviet assistance agreements, and canceled the Soviet aid program. This move hit the Chinese during the dismal aftermath of the Great Leap Forward and, they conceded, "caused our construction to suffer heavy losses, thereby upsetting our original plan for the development of our national economy and greatly aggravating our difficulties." [20]

By 1962, the rupture between the two countries seemed beyond repair. Late in that year, when Chinese and Indian forces clashed in the Himalayas, the Russians effectively sided with India. While adopting a posture of neutrality, they continued to deliver military aircraft to the Indians to be used against the Chinese and in addition supplied India with twelve MIG-21 fighter airplanes—an advanced model they had refused to give the Chinese.[21] Not long afterward, in the summer of 1963, Peking stressed a theme that was to dominate its propaganda against Moscow in the coming years. Excoriating the Russians for signing the Nuclear Test-Ban Treaty, the Chinese accused them of "colluding" with the United States against China and other Communist countries. "The real aim of the Soviet leaders is to compromise with the United States in order to . . . maintain a monopoly of nuclear weapons and lord it over the socialist camp." [22]

Peking's charges of Soviet-American collaboration became more vociferous after the United States dispatched combat troops to South Vietnam and began bombing North Vietnam in early 1965.

For the Vietnam war was intensifying a complex triangular relationship involving China, the Soviet Union, and the United States. This relationship was further tangled by stresses and strains within China as Mao launched his Cultural Revolution. And it was significantly influenced by changing policies in Hanoi.

During the first years following the 1954 Geneva Conference, which concluded their war against the French, the North Vietnamese tended to emulate the Chinese. Among other things, they slavishly imitated Peking's land-reform program—and with disastrous consequences. But in 1957, beset by severe economic problems largely caused by their inability to rely on traditional rice supplies from South Vietnam, the Hanoi leaders turned to the Soviet Union for assistance. Within a year, Moscow had replaced Peking as Hanoi's principal source of aid, and the North Vietnamese, now subscribing to Khrushchev's pleas for "peaceful coexistence," toned down their talk of "liberating" South Vietnam by force and urged instead that priority be given to economic development in their zone. The neutralization of Laos in 1962 strengthened the partisans of restraint in Hanoi. They argued that the Laotian settlement could serve as a model for South Vietnam, and thus eventual unification could be achieved through diplomatic rather than military means, an approach favored by the Russians. But when it became clear that the United States had no intention of accepting a neutral South Vietnam, the Hanoi hierarchy veered away from the Soviet Union and began heeding Chinese advice to pursue a tough line.[23]

By 1964, the North Vietnamese were firmly lodged in the Chinese camp—even to the extent of denouncing Soviet "modern revisionism." [24] Khrushchev's impetuous reaction to this switch was to disengage completely from Indochina. But after his ouster in October 1964, the new Kremlin leaders tried to rebuild Soviet influence in Hanoi. First, with the United States plainly escalating the war, they could not abandon North Vietnam without courting the risk of losing prestige in the eyes of Communist countries and movements for whom Hanoi's struggle symbolized the fight against "imperialism." Second, worried by the danger of a wider war, the Russian leaders were anxious to persuade the North Vietnamese to come to terms with the United States. Early in February 1965, Premier Alexei Kosygin went to Hanoi with a dual proposal. He would increase Russian military and economic aid to North Vietnam, but he counseled the Hanoi leadership to help the United States to "find a way out" of the conflict through negotiations.[25] In the middle of Kosygin's visit, however, the United States raided targets north of the seventeenth parallel in retaliation for Vietcong assaults against American installations in the South. Kosygin had no choice but to accelerate Russian aid to Hanoi, perhaps hoping that he might temper the North Vietnamese in the future.

The Chinese view of the Vietnam situation at that stage was complicated by the rivalries then dividing Mao and his adversaries in the Communist Party and Army. Mao's primary concern was the forthcoming Cultural Revolution, in which he would require the services of the Army. He was therefore determined to avoid Chinese involvement in Vietnam. His opponents, in contrast, favored a direct military commitment to Vietnam as a way of depriving Mao of the Army for domestic political purposes. Thus the debate that arose in Peking over the question of Chinese help for Vietnam was intimately tied to the growing tensions then building up between Mao and his foes. In this debate, Liu Shao-ch'i and the Chief of General Staff, Lo Jui-ch'ing, favored intervention, while Mao stood for caution. In short, they were "hawks" and he was a "dove."

The Vietnam issue was in turn intricately linked to China's dispute with Moscow. Consistent with their willingness to risk intervention, Mao's opponents called for a *rapprochement* with the Soviet Union that would discourage the United States from counterattacking China. But Mao rejected any arrangements that might restore Soviet influence in China. He rebuffed several Soviet proposals for "united action" on Vietnam, contending that they were "designed to meet the needs of American imperialism." [26] He also denied the Russians the use of Chinese airfields and the right to fly supplies over China to North Vietnam. His motives were simple, he told them:

Frankly speaking, we do not trust you. We and other fraternal countries have learned bitter lessons in the past from Khrushchev's evil practice of control under the cover of aid. . . . China is not one of your provinces. We cannot accept your control. Nor will we help you to control others.[27]

For all his criticism of the Kremlin for colluding with American "imperialism," however, Mao made it clear that he would do nothing to deter United States escalation in Vietnam so long as China was not directly threatened. To be sure, he briefly deployed a squadron of Chinese aircraft in Hanoi in August 1964 to help defend North Vietnam against the possibility of American raids, and he constructed airfields in south China as alternate bases for North Vietnamese fighter aircraft. Beginning in the fall of 1965, he also sent some fifty thousand labor troops into North Vietnam primarily to maintain railway communications between Hanoi and China.[28] But he indicated plainly on several occasions and through different channels that he was as anxious to avert a clash with the United States as President Lyndon Johnson was to avert a clash with China.

Throughout late 1964 and early 1965, for example, there were no Chinese troop movements toward the Vietnam border of the kind that preceded the entry of China's "volunteers" into the Korean War. And Chinese representatives at the Sino-American ambassadorial talks in Warsaw signaled to United States diplomats that Peking was striving to avoid involvement in Vietnam. Mao's prudence was also reflected in the fact that he barred North Vietnamese aircraft from using Chinese bases for operational purposes lest the United States invoke the right of "hot pursuit." [29] And he further transmitted his desire to keep out of Vietnam through the medium of Lin Piao's famous essay, "Long Live the Victory of People's War!" Though labeled Mao's *Mein Kampf* by facile analysts in Washington and elsewhere, Lin Piao's essay was really an announcement that China had no plans to intercede militarily in Vietnam. "Revolution or people's war in any country is the business of the masses in that country," it said, "and should be carried out primarily by their own efforts." [30]

Even American bombing flights near or over their borders evoked essentially cautious reactions from the Chinese. When American aircraft attacked a North Vietnamese target ten miles from their frontier on August 13, 1967, for example, Peking's spokesmen waited nine days before warning, rather lamely, that "if you impose war on the Chinese people, we will accommodate you to the end." [31]

Hence there was little evidence to substantiate such alarmist statements as the observation of Secretary of State Dean Rusk that China was poised to "overrun" Southeast Asia.[32] On the contrary, Mao's Vietnam strategy was founded on the principle of nonintervention, for several reasons. Not only did he believe that "people's war in any country is the business of the masses in that country," but he viewed the Vietnam conflict as his "war by proxy" against "imperialism," in which the United States would be drained and ultimately defeated at virtually no cost to China. And finally, as his exhortations to the Vietnamese Communists to continue fighting revealed, he favored a protracted struggle that would eventually leave Vietnam exhausted, weak, and in no position to resist Chinese influence.

The North Vietnamese were fully aware that the Chinese, despite their protestations of friendship, were mainly concerned with advancing their own interests. As a consequence, relations between Hanoi and Peking were often tense, particularly in 1967 and 1968. Appalled by the excesses of the Cultural Revolution, the North Vietnamese criticized Mao for shattering the Chinese Communist Party, calling him a "Don Quixote tilting against windmills." [33] And they were outraged by Red Guard attacks against trains transporting Soviet and Chinese military supplies to Hanoi, even though Chou En-lai repeatedly tried to reassure them of China's devotion to their cause. They were also irritated in early 1968 by Peking's awkward attempts to dissuade them from entering into talks with the United States in Paris. With these and other differences, relations between Hanoi and Peking reached a low point in the fall of 1968, and the two Vietnamese Communist officials chosen to attend the Chinese National Day celebration on October 1 were so obscure that they were ranked behind a Maoist from Auckland, New Zealand.[34]

Chou En-lai did much to improve China's relations with North Vietnam when he rushed to Hanoi to pay his condolences on the death of Ho Chi Minh in September 1969. He also went to considerable lengths to cultivate the Vietnamese Communists following the allied invasion of Cambodia in the spring of 1970. But by the summer of 1971, the Chinese appeared to have downgraded the importance of Vietnam. For the chances of a *rapprochement* with the United States now seemed to offer a broader spectrum of gains more tempting than their narrow commitment to Hanoi.

In contrast to the dispute between Peking and Moscow, which was rooted in deep historical, national, and ideological animosities, the tensions that separated China and the United States for two decades after 1950 were largely the result of mutual distrust and misunderstanding that might have been overcome. And indeed, the Chinese were able to alter their attitude toward the United States in 1971 with remarkable rapidity and ease. Official reassessments in Washington at that time, similarly, were quick to argue that, after all, the Chinese menace had perhaps been exaggerated.

During World War II, the leaders of the Chinese Communist Party had been fairly cordial toward the United States as they sought American support for their resistance against Japan. In 1944, for instance, Mao praised the United States and expressed the hope that Americans might play a more active role in China. His senior military leader, Chu Teh, even proposed that an American officer be appointed to command the Communist and Nationalist forces.[35] But this cordiality soured after General Marshall's failure to arrange a political compromise between the rival Chinese movements. With the revival of the civil war against the Nationalists, the Communists publicly aligned themselves behind the Soviet Union in the "international struggle against imperialism" and proclaimed their mission to foment revolution throughout the world. Coinciding as it did with the emerging Cold War in Europe and elsewhere, this stance prompted the United States to view the Chinese Communists as an instrument of aggressive and expansionist Soviet policy. When they took power in 1949, Washington refused to recognize them immediately and unsuccessfully attempted to dissuade allies such as Great Britain from establishing diplomatic relations with the new Peking leadership. The United States also opposed the Communist claim to represent China at the United Nations.

At the same time, however, the United States was cautiously

receptive to the idea of an eventual accommodation with Mao. When the Communists were capturing China's major urban areas in the last days of the civil war, for example, American diplomats stationed in those cities were instructed to stay at their posts and make contact with new local regimes. Significantly, the American Ambassador, John Leighton Stuart, remained in Nanking when the Communists seized Chiang Kai-shek's capital—while the Soviet envoy accompanied the Nationalists as they fled south. But the Communists, flushed by victory, showed few signs of conciliation toward the United States, mistreated several American diplomatic representatives, and arbitrarily grabbed U.S. consular property in a move that finally prompted Washington to withdraw all its officials from China.[36]

Despite these indications of Communist hostility, the United States disengaged from the Chinese civil war. In January 1950, the Truman Administration declared that it would cease to aid the Nationalists on the grounds that the civil war was, as Secretary of State Dean Acheson put it, "the product of internal Chinese forces" that were "beyond the control" of the United States.[37] Though the rapid establishment of formal relations between the United States and the Communists seemed to be precluded, the logic of the situation suggested that Washington's recognition of the Peking regime was probably only a matter of time. In June 1950, however, the North Korean Communists invaded South Korea, and the consequences of that event were to set back any *rapprochement* between the United States and Communist China for years to come.

The North Korean invasion was primarily instigated by the Soviet Union, perhaps in the expectation of a quick victory. For in the spring of 1949 and again in early 1950, both General Douglas MacArthur and Secretary Acheson had publicly excluded Korea from the American defense perimeter in the Pacific, and their statements constituted a virtual invitation to Communist aggression.[38] But in June 1950, when the North Koreans initiated their thrust, President Truman reversed American policy. Along with sending American forces to Korea under the banner of the United Nations, he ordered the Seventh Fleet to "neutralize" the Taiwan Strait and subsequently revived military aid to the Nationalists—thereby engaging the United States anew in the Chinese civil war. In October, ignoring warnings from Peking that its troops would intervene, Washington directed American units to cross the thirty-eighth parallel into North Korea. The result was a military collision between the United States and the Chinese Communists. The accumulation of these moves had profound political effects.

The most crucial of these, in Peking's view, was the American commitment to the Nationalists on Taiwan. Formerly controlled by Japan, the island had been returned to China at the end of World War II. But now it was occupied by the Nationalists, who relied for their survival on United States assistance. There were American troops on the island, and American warships patrolled its waters. The United States supplied Chiang Kai-shek with vast amounts of military aid, and all this support was given a legal rationale in a 1954 treaty pledging to protect the Nationalist regime against a Communist assault. Moreover, Washington backed Chiang Kai-shek's claim to speak for China at the United Nations, and exerted pressure on its allies to do the same. To the Communists, then, these actions represented intolerable interference in China's internal affairs, and the Taiwan question became the key obstacle to establishment of relations between the United States and the Chinese Communists.

Curiously, though, the sharp differences separating Washington and Peking did not prevent them from carrying on official, if irregular, diplomatic conversations. Formally termed Ambassadorial Talks, these conversations started in Geneva in 1955 and continued in Warsaw, and they produced one tangible achievement—an agreement by the Chinese to release a number of American military and civilian prisoners who had been held captive in China.[39] But the meetings also served as a kind of "hot line" between the United States and the Chinese Communists that was occasionally effective. When the Communists feared an invasion by Chiang Kai-shek in the spring of 1962, for example, President Kennedy used the Warsaw channel to allay their apprehensions. During the Vietnam war, the Warsaw conversations again helped to avoid a miscalculation that might have pushed the United States and China into a conflict that neither wanted.

Over the years, however, the United States and the Chinese Communists were unable to reach a real modus vivendi, often because of ill-timed or uncoordinated shifts in their respective foreign policies. In the mid-1950s, shelving the knotty Taiwan problem temporarily, Chou En-lai offered to permit American newsmen to visit China and proposed other measures designed to ease tensions with the United States. But his overtures were rejected by Secretary of State John Foster Dulles, who decried them as "propaganda" maneuvers. Dulles's hostility toward the Communists was such, in fact, that he refused to shake hands with Chou when the two men met at the 1954 Geneva Conference on Indochina. Beginning in the early 1960s, the United States contrastingly undertook gradual steps aimed at breaking down the barriers with Peking. But the Chinese, now striving to demonstrate their revolutionary purity to the Soviet Union, adamantly rebuffed any *détente* with Washington so long as the Taiwan question had not been resolved on their terms.

To a large extent, the rigid American attitude toward Communist China during the 1950s stemmed from Senator Joseph McCarthy's purge of the State Department. McCarthy had compelled the Truman and Eisenhower Administrations to dismiss or transfer a number of American officials with valuable experience in China, alleging that they had contributed to the Communists' victory there. Among those fired were John Stewart Service, John Carter Vincent, and John Paton Davies, whose purported "crimes" as foreign-service officers in China during World War II had been to report objectively on the ineptitude of the Chiang Kai-shek regime. Other victims of the McCarthy era included Robert Barnett, who was born in China and had served there as an adviser to General Claire Chennault. Slated to become Director of Chinese Affairs in the State Department, Barnett's name appeared on one of McCarthy's "lists" in 1951 and, though there was no evidence against him, he was "advised" to accept a post in Europe. The departure of these and other specialists like them deprived Washington of men with imaginative ideas on China and created an atmosphere of "knee-jerk anti-Communism" that discouraged any innovations that might relax tensions between the United States and Peking.[40]

The evangelical anti-Communism personified by Senator McCarthy persisted after his death in the spirit infused into the State Department by Secretary of State Dulles, who considered initiatives toward Peking to be heretical. In December 1961, however, President Kennedy appointed W. Averell Harriman as Assistant Secretary of State for Far East Affairs. Though Harriman's principal assignment was to reach a peace settlement in Laos, then threatened by war, he brought back some of the China specialists who had been eclipsed earlier and commissioned them to chart a new American policy toward Peking. They outlined a series of steps that included the revision of the total United States embargo on trade with China that had been decreed at the outset of the Korean War, a modification of the ban on travel to China by Americans, and, among other things, a proposal to invite Peking to join in disarmament talks. These specialists were not optimistic at that stage that Peking would reply to their initiatives, provided they were actually taken. Underlying their strategy, instead, was the idea that a fresh "climate" might, over the long term, evoke a Chinese Communist response. It was this strategy, under different circumstances, that later proved successful for President Nixon.

The trend set by Harriman was continued and amplified by his successor, Roger Hilsman. He broadened his staff to include such younger China experts as Lindsey Grant, Allen S. Whiting, and James C. Thomson, Jr., and they promoted the first official public United States overture to Peking. Speaking in San Francisco on December 13, 1963, Hilsman expressed the hope that "evolutionary forces" inside Communist China might eventually contribute to a Sino-American *rapprochement*, adding that Washington intended to "keep the door open" to the possibility of a negotiated settlement of its differences with Peking.[41]

Mild as it looked in retrospect, that overture was daring for its time. Indeed, members of Hilsman's staff were doubtful, as they drafted his speech, that it would gain prior acceptance from the Secretary of State, Dean Rusk, who regarded attempts at a thaw with Peking to be detrimental to United States interests. Preparing to depart for a conference abroad, Rusk hastily approved the Hilsman statement, but soon afteward, apparently regretting his decision, he countered Hilsman's initiative with a tough address of his own. Speaking in Tokyo on January 28, 1964, he asserted that the Chinese Communists scorned peace and warned that "free nations must not reward the militancy of Peking."[42] Predictably, the

Communists denounced Hilsman, calling his hope of "peaceful evolution" in China a case of "self-delusion." [43] Judging from the evidence that emerged during the Cultural Revolution, however, the American overture may have left an impression on some Chinese minds.

The legacy of the McCarthy era was still so strong in Washington in the mid-1960s that State Department officials were reluctant to consort with China specialists who had been criticized by the Senator. On one occasion, when Hilsman and his staff invited the eminent Harvard expert John Fairbank to address a group of government employees concerned with China, they held their meeting at the Washington home of John D. Rockefeller IV rather than at the State Department building. As one of the organizers recalled later: "We figured that they couldn't accuse Rockefeller of being a Communist." [44]

With the Johnson Administration immersed in the Vietnam war, there were no significant gestures made toward China until December 1965. At that time, acting at the behest of the celebrated heart specialist Dr. Paul Dudley White and others, President Johnson amended travel restrictions to allow American doctors and health experts to visit China. Soon after that, he also eased the limitations on travel to China for teachers, athletes, businessmen, and, among others, members of Congress. In speeches, too, Johnson defined "reconciliation" with Peking as an ultimate American policy goal.[45] Against that background, then, President Nixon's dramatic move in July 1971 was less a "turning of the tide" than the logical continuation of a trend that had begun a decade earlier.

In Peking, meanwhile, the conduct of foreign policy had been paralyzed by the Cultural Revolution throughout most of 1967. All of China's forty-six ambassadors abroad except Huang Hua, the envoy to Cairo, had been recalled home for "re-education." On more than one occasion, radicals had physically occupied the Foreign Ministry, destroyed documents, manhandled officials, and harassed Foreign Minister Ch'en Yi. Ch'en was said to have lost twenty-seven pounds during his ordeals and Mao, deploring his mistreatment, reportedly commented: "I cannot show him to foreign guests in this condition."

But as the Army accelerated its drive to impose order in China during early 1968, there were indications that Chou En-lai and his moderate colleagues were edging toward the resumption of normal diplomatic activity. They signed a trade agreement with Ceylon, played host to Nepalese dignitaries, apologized for their earlier troubles with Cambodia, started to repair their damaged ties with Burma, and, in July 1968, granted exit visas to several British diplomats who had been refused permission to return home.[46] Counterpointing these signs of flexibility, however, prominent Peking radicals like Ch'en Po-ta and Chiang Ch'ing sought to subvert the movement toward moderation in China's foreign affairs. They seemed particularly eager to block efforts aimed at reaching a *détente* with the United States, and their obstruction would make contacts between Peking and Washington extremely difficult at times.

Two major developments in 1968 evidently convinced Chou En-lai and his associates that some kind of *rapprochement* with the United States might be in China's interest. The first of these was the widespread domestic revulsion in the United States against the Vienam war. This suggested to the Peking leaders that American forces would sooner or later be withdrawn from Southeast Asia; China could play a role in a peace settlement covering the region. Even more significant to the Chinese was the Soviet invasion of Czechoslovakia and the enunciation of the "Brezhnev doctrine," which asserted Moscow's right to intervene in Communist countries whose policies deviated from Kremlin standards. The Soviet action persuaded the Peking leaders that the Russians were quite capable of attacking China. The Chinese apparently calculated, therefore, that their defenses could be reinforced by a closer diplomatic relationship with the United States.

In the Chinese view, the Americans had sustained a decisive setback in Vietnam by the middle of 1968. Peking perceived evidence of this defeat in the antiwar demonstrations then occurring with increasing frequency in the United States, in the popularity of such "doves" as Senators Robert Kennedy and Eugene McCarthy, and in the announcement by President Johnson on March 31 that he would not run for re-election. They were also impressed by Johnson's decision to call a total halt to American air raids north of the seventeenth parallel, an event Peking noted without its usual adverse comment.[47] The American writer Edgar Snow, who visited China somewhat later, reported being told by a senior Peking official: "Nixon is getting out of Vietnam." [48]

The same estimate of American policy was indirectly expressed in an authoritative Chinese assessment of the current situation in the Far East. Reviewing the history of the previous two decades, a Peking analysis accused the United States of having repeatedly tried to "strangle" the Chinese Communist regime. But now, the analysis concluded, the "heavy defeat" suffered by the United States in Vietnam had "seriously upset its deployments for a war of aggression against China and Asia." [49] In short, the Peking statement implied, the American threat had receded. Now, it was clear, the Russians represented the new danger.

Mao himself was reported to have put his personal imprimatur on the shift in Peking's foreign policy at a plenary session of the Chinese Communist Party Central Committee held in October 1969. Declaring that the Soviet Union had become China's "greatest enemy," he proposed that Peking seek to establish relations with Western nations that agreed to recognize the Communist claim to sovereignty over Taiwan.[50] As usual, however, Mao's public pronouncement merely served to endorse a strategy that Chou En-lai and his civilian and military colleagues had already been pursuing for nearly a year.

By 1969, the Soviet build-up along the Chinese frontier had reached huge proportions. Roughly two hundred thousand Soviet troops were deployed in the area facing Manchuria, and an equal number had been transferred to the region adjacent to Sinkiang. Beginning in early 1966, the Kremlin also moved nearly a hundred thousand men into the People's Republic of Mongolia.[51] Outfitted with the latest tanks, aircraft, and nuclear-tipped missiles, the Soviet units were superior in firepower to anything the Chinese could muster. Peking's forces, stretched from Manchuria through Sinkiang, numbered more than a million men. But in contrast to the Russians, whose contingency plans probably called for strikes against China's nuclear installations and industrial cities, the Chinese were relying on a "defense-in-depth." In the event of war, they hoped to take advantage of their large population to drown an invader in an "ocean of people." Or, as their statements said, making a virtue of necessity: "The outcome of war is decided by the people, not by one or two new types of weapons." [52]

Matching their troop deployments, the Russians escalated their propaganda campaigns against Peking. Authoritative Soviet commentaries vilified Mao as a "nationalistic anti-Marxist" who had come to dominate China "through the use of violence and unbridled demagogy." [53] A series of Moscow broadcasts beamed to China and manifestly designed to demoralize the Chinese Army stressed the superiority of Soviet weaponry, asserting that "a powerful modern arsenal" rather than Maoist doctrine was the "crucial criteria for victory." [54] The Kremlin also instructed its operatives abroad to contact Chinese Nationalist diplomats and journalists. One Soviet agent, the colorful journalist Victor Louis, even visited Taiwan, where he talked with high Nationalist officials and later wrote accounts of his trip for the American press.[55]

At the same time, the Russians accelerated an ambitious program to strengthen their influence from Japan through the states of Southeast Asia to India and Pakistan. They sent cultural delegations to the Philippines, signed trade accords with Singapore and Malaysia, reinforced their naval fleet in the Pacific and Indian Oceans, and not long afterward, the Soviet Communist Party Secretary General, Leonid Brezhnev, proposed an Asian "collective security" system that, Moscow spokesmen indicated, would be designed to "contain" Communist China's "hegemonistic pretensions." [56] That proposal, redolent of Dulles's geopolitical pacts, appeared to have been primarily contrived to create pyschological havoc in Peking. For it failed to go far beyond the rhetorical stage.

But the Chinese leaders did register a visible jolt on August 20, 1968, when Soviet and Warsaw Pact troops invaded Czechoslovakia. Until then, the confrontation between Moscow and the Dubcek regime had been a real dilemma for the Chinese. They were inclined to sympathize with Dubcek as a victim of Soviet "big-power chauvinism," but their fierce hostility to "revisionism" prevented them from openly supporting the Czechoslovak reformers. As a result, they adopted the rather tortuous expedient of assailing the Kremlin for having encouraged the Prague liberals to deviate from orthodox Marxism.[57] Now, however, Moscow's invasion of Czechoslovakia simplified the issue. The Kremlin's "naked armed intervention" highlighted the "grisly fascist features" of the Soviet "renegade clique," Peking publicists asserted as they compared the Russian action to Hitler's occupation of the Czechoslovak Sudetenland prior to World War II and the American "aggression" in Vietnam.[58]

This response by the Chinese partly reflected their consistent view of themselves as the defenders of small nations against the "super-powers." More profound, though, was Peking's new fear that the Russians were not above invading China as they had Czechoslovakia. Chou En-lai openly voiced this fear in a speech on September 30, when he claimed that the Kremlin was "stepping up armed provocations against China while intensifying its aggression and threats against Eastern Europe." He accused the Russians of stationing "massive" troop concentrations in Mongolia and along the border, and added that their aircraft were violating Chinese airspace with increasing frequency.[59] Peking backed up Chou's accusation with statistics alleging that Soviet military aircraft flew twenty-nine sorties for purposes of "reconnaissance, harassment, and provocation" over Heilungkiang during a period of twenty-one days in August, and that the Russians had violated the Chinese border more than a hundred times during the previous seven months. Linking these alleged forays to the Soviet thrust into Czechoslovakia, Peking asserted that these intrusions had been "in no way accidental." [60] Flatly denying the charges, Moscow described them as Peking's "feeble contribution to the anti-Soviet hysteria unleashed in the imperialist reaction to the events in Czechoslovakia." [61]

In the face of this growing Soviet threat, the Chinese made a move that was to be the start of a wholly new direction in their foreign policy. On November 26, they issued a formal Foreign Ministry statement proposing that the Sino-American Ambassadorial Talks in Warsaw, which had been repeatedly postponed over the past year, be resumed on February 20, 1969—at a time when the newly elected President, Richard Nixon, "will have been in office for a month" and his Administration had been "able to make up its mind" about China.[62]

The Chinese Foreign Ministry statement was extraordinarily subdued in style and substance compared to the fiery utterances of the Cultural Revolution. At a Warsaw meeting in September 1966, for example, the Chinese spokesman had demanded that the United States "get out of Asia" and dismissed American desires for "peaceful cooperation" with China as "high-sounding words" that were "not worth a penny." [63] Now, in contrast, Peking recommended soberly that the United States and China could improve their ties by adhering to the "five principles of peaceful coexistence." [64] Similarly, Liu Shao-ch'i had been denounced in October 1967 for "advocating national egoism and betraying proletarian internationalism" by suggesting that China could "develop friendly relations" with the United States once American troops were out of Taiwan.[65] Now Peking put forth that very line, declaring that the United States and China could reach an agreement if Washington merely withdrew its military and naval forces from Taiwan and the Taiwan Strait.[66] Underscoring this policy switch, the Peking press publicized a 1949 Mao essay which had hailed the value of negotiations and emphasized the advantages of making "temporary concessions" to enemies in order to "win them over to our side or neutralize them politically." [67]

Peking's policy shift predictably nettled the Kremlin, and Russian commentators were quick to claim that China was "colluding" with the United States against the Soviet Union. Indeed, many of these indictments were minor versions of China's anti-Soviet propaganda. One Moscow broadcast, for example, contended that the "Maoist clique" was "kowtowing to the imperialists and sabotaging national liberation movements" around the world.[68] And others accused the Chinese of servicing American warships in Hong Kong or selling military equipment to the United States for use in Vietnam.[69] Particularly galling to the Kremlin was Peking's decision to inaugurate contacts with a president whose career had been built on his anti-communism. But Nixon's record may have been precisely what appealed to the Chinese at that point in time.

As they looked back on their own experience, Chinese Communists perceived that they had fared better with Republicans than with Democrats. After all, they had gone to war in Korea against the Truman Administration, but had signed a truce with President

Eisenhower. Kennedy and Johnson had escalated the Vietnam conflict, while Nixon was basing his electoral campaign on a pledge to wind down the war. Ideology also colored the Chinese analysis of the American political dynamic. Republicans, they believed, were closer to "monopoly capital," the real source of power in the United States, and they were convinced that Nixon, as a representative of the capitalist "ruling class," could operate with an authority that the Democrats lacked. Finally, the Chinese were perhaps gratified to see Nixon's past hostility to the Soviet Union. From their viewpoint, there was a certain reality in the old adage that "the enemy of my enemy is my friend"—or at least an expedient ally.

During his election campaign, Nixon had shown signs of a new attitude toward Peking. In August 1968, at the Republican National Convention in Miami, he voiced the view that the United States must eventually negotiate with China, which he described as "the next super-power" [70] and expressed the hope that he might visit Peking "if they would give me a visa." Soon after assuming office, he made it known that breaking the twenty-year deadlock in Sino-American relations was one of his priorities. In the course of a discussion with a group of American specialists on China at the White House, a conservative scholar warned Nixon against any switch in United States policy. The President replied: "I used to share your opinion, but I've changed." [71]

The shaping of a new foreign policy was as intricate, difficult, and perilous a process for Nixon as it was for Chou En-lai. Both had to take into account their domestic opposition as well as the potential reactions of their allies. Nixon, for example, could not afford to incur the wrath of the conservative American politicans who had contributed to his election. He was also wary of alienating the Chinese Nationalist, South Vietnamese, South Korean, Thai, and other Asian regimes that had committed themselves to America's anti-Communist strategy in the past. Similarly, Chou En-lai and his colleagues faced the resistance of the prominent radicals in the Party regime, and they were sensitive to pressures coming from the North Vietnamese, North Korean, and other Communist movements whose positions would be weakened by a Sino-American *rapprochement*. Above all, Nixon and Chou had to overcome the deep mutual hostility and mistrust that had characterized relations between the United States and China for decades. Thus they proceeded slowly, cautiously, and with extreme secrecy. And neither could run the risk of being rebuffed by the other.

Nixon was particularly anxious to avoid any advances that might provoke a rejection from Peking. In effect, his design was based on the judgment that the pragmatic Chinese leaders would respond on their own initiative to his overtures if he could create a climate that encouraged them to realize that a *détente* with the United States served their own vital interests. Only twelve days after his inauguration, then, Nixon took the first step in the long march that would, he hoped, ultimately bring him to Peking.

On February 1, 1969, he instructed Dr. Henry Kissinger, his chief foreign-policy adviser, to begin exploring avenues that might open the way to Peking. Kissinger thereupon initiated two related tactics. On one hand, he signaled the President's general plan to French, East European, and other diplomats with contacts in the Chinese capital in the expectation that they would pass on the word to the Communist leadership. At the same time, he ordered his own staff to review America's China policy and to offer recommendations that might induce a nod from the Communists.[72] Within three months, hints from Washington indicated that the Nixon plan was in operation.

In a speech on April 22, for instance, Secretary of State William Rogers referred to China for the first time as the "People's Republic." [73] Soon afterward, in the first of a series of gestures aimed at revising the United States embargo on trade with Peking, the President authorized Americans to purchase a hundred dollars' worth of Communist merchandise. Meanwhile, Nixon sought the assistance of key European leaders who might help to clear the path to Peking. On a visit to Paris in March 1969, he discussed the China question with Charles de Gaulle, apparently obtaining the French President's pledge to help his effort.[74] Five months later, Nixon traveled to Rumania and there enlisted the even more important cooperation of President Nicolae Ceausescu, whose independence from Moscow had given him unusual leverage with the Chinese.[75] Nixon's visit to Bucharest came at the end of a round-the-world trip during which he enunciated the so-called "Guam Doctrine," his policy for a "lower profile" in Asia.

A measure of Peking's receptivity to the Nixon overtures was reflected in several esoteric and often negative ways. Chinese propagandists greeted the President's modification of the trade embargo with significant silence, and they conspicuously refrained from denouncing Secretary of State Rogers when he visited Hong Kong during the summer of 1969. At the same time, however, evidence suggested that the radicals in Peking could still muster enough influence to hinder moves designed to break the deadlock with the United States. When a minor Chinese diplomat in the Netherlands defected to Washington in February, for example, the radicals apparently seized on the incident to compel the Peking moderates to cancel the session of the Sino-American Ambassadorial Talks to be held in Warsaw that month.[76] But these problems merely delayed rather than stopped the trend toward reconciliation between the United States and China. For Peking was still confronted by the overwhelming challenge of the Soviet Union, which made its need for a *détente* with the United States imperative. The Russian challenge in fact turned into an urgent threat when an actual battle between Chinese and Soviet troops erupted.

The scene of the clash was an uninhabited island—called Damansky by the Russians and Chenpao by the Chinese—situated in the frozen Ussuri River separating Manchuria from the Soviet Union's easternmost Maritime Provinces. Only Soviet sources have given a detailed account of the event, gleaned from survivors and from a special investigation team. As they told the story on the morning of March 2, 1969, about three hundred Chinese troops dressed in white camouflage crossed the ice to the island the night before, dug foxholes, and laid telephone wire back to their command post in an apparent plan to provoke an incident. At about eleven o'clock the next morning, the Russians observed twenty or thirty armed Chinese moving toward the island, shouting Maoist slogans as they approached. A Soviet platoon drove out in military vehicles to warn them to halt. According to the Kremlin's version, the Russians dismounted and locked arms in an attempt to block the Chinese. At that point, the advancing Chinese scattered to the side, exposing a second line of Chinese troops who opened fire with submachine guns, killing seven Russians outright. Simultaneously, the Soviet account claimed, the entrenched Chinese also opened fire with mortars, machine guns, and antitank artillery. The Chinese then charged the remaining Russians, and the skirmish ended two hours later with thirty-one Soviet soldiers dead. The number of Chinese casualties was never reported by Peking.[77]

In an exchange of angry protests, the Chinese and Russians immediately accused each other of having triggered the incident. But even though the local Chinese commander probably took the initiative, as the evidence appeared to indicate, a clash along the volatile frontier was almost certain to have occurred sooner or later.

After studying most of the available documents, one American scholar [78] has concluded that the Peking leaders had decided on a "tough" line toward the Soviet Union. According to his theory, Chou En-lai and the Chinese Army commanders may have sought a diversion from the domestic tensions then arising from their efforts to curb the Cultural Revolution, and needed a war scare to justify their calls for national unity. Consistent with this approach, they may also have felt compelled to discourage the increasingly menacing Soviet build-up along the border and ordered Chinese patrols to intensify their activities, even to the point of countering the Russians with force if necessary. As a result, the Chinese commander in the vicinity of the disputed Ussuri River island could well have sparked the incident in the belief that he was obeying Peking's directives—or simply from an excess of zeal.

Another theory has been advanced suggesting that Lin Piao personally gave the order to provoke the attack in the belief that the clash would reinforce his authority in Peking. The Soviet civilian and military leaders, meanwhile, appeared to be pushing as well for a showdown with China, and they had undoubtedly instructed Russian officers in the frontier region to check Chinese provocations. Thus it was likely that the Soviet unit involved in the March 2 incident would have shot first had it not been pre-empted by the Chinese.

On March 15, indeed, the Russians evidently did strike the first blow. This time, there was no element of surprise. Both sides were prepared for a second round, and the engagement resembled a set-piece battle. According to a plausible reconstruction of the event, the Chinese and Russians began exchanging mortar and artillery fire at about ten o'clock in the morning. Soon afterward, a regiment of some two thousand Chinese charged across the ice to gain possession of part of the island. Outnumbered, the Russians retreated and, adopting the tactic employed by American troops during the Korean War, allowed the Chinese "human wave" to advance. Then they counterattacked with large numbers of tanks, armored cars, and infantry in armored personnel carriers, covering their action with a fierce artillery barrage of Chinese positions as far inland as four miles. The battle ended after nine hours. The Russians lost about sixty men, while Chinese casualties were said to have run as high as eight hundred killed and wounded.[79] Following the battle, the Soviet forces systematically defoliated large tracts of forest on their side of the Ussuri River in order to open a clear field to the Chinese border. Fearful of being trapped in a bigger engagement yet to come, thousands of Russian civilians who had been resettled in the frontier zone abandoned their farms and fled back to the European parts of the Soviet Union.[80]

The Soviet initiative in the second Ussuri River battle had apparently been prompted by three principal motives. First, the Russians simply wanted to wreak revenge on the Chinese for the first attack. Second, they had evidently calculated that a failure on their part to react forcefully would have marked them as weaklings and hence damaged their prestige. And finally, they seemed to believe that military pressure would persuade Peking to concede to a boundary settlement on their terms. The Russians pursued this tough strategy throughout the spring and summer.

In mid-June, focusing on a sparsely populated and ill-defended sector of the Chinese frontier, they thrust into Sinkiang province.[81] Following that raid, Soviet forces reportedly constructed fortifications inside the Chinese area in order to secure their own communications in the frontier zone.[82] Sinkiang inevitably erupted in another clash in August, with the Russians deploying tanks, aircraft, and other sophisticated equipment in a brief but large-scale battle.[83] Meanwhile, Moscow continued to strengthen its forces along the Ussuri River sector, where Khabarovsk and Vladivostok were particularly vulnerable to a Chinese assault. Matching these actions, the Kremlin offered Peking the chance to resolve the disputed border question—on Soviet conditions.

On March 29, two weeks after the second Ussuri River clash,

the Russians proposed that boundary negotiations begin "in the nearest future." They made it clear, however, that they could not accept Peking's demand that the past border treaties be acknowledged as "unequal." The boundaries were not only "natural" but, the Soviet note insisted, they had been given "legal status" in the nineteenth-century accords signed by the Tsarist regime and the Ch'ing dynasty administration. The Chinese were warned to expect further blows if the dispute dragged on. The statement pointedly recalled that "the Japanese aggressors [in the 1930s] were administered a crushing rebuff." [84]

The Chinese predictably rejected the Soviet proposal, reasserting that talks would be fruitless unless Moscow agreed in advance to recognize the nineteenth-century boundary treaties as "unequal." [85] By now, the question of the "unequal treaties" had become more crucial to the Chinese than the boundary itself. They had made it plain time and again that they were not calling for the return of all the territory lost by China throughout history. Yet they could not retreat from the principle they had enunciated, for several reasons. In part, their national pride was at stake. Nor could they capitulate on the border issue without jeopardizing their claims to Hong Kong, Macao, sectors of their contested frontier with India, and other areas, the most important of which was, of course, Taiwan. If they dropped their demand that Moscow acknowledge the invalidity of the old treaties, the Peking leaders felt, their claim to sovereignty over Taiwan would collapse and their crusade to unseat the rival Chiang Kai-shek regime be subverted.

Somewhat comparable considerations prompted Soviet intransigence. The Russians could not recognize the illegitimacy of their boundaries with China without courting the risk of inciting Poland, Rumania, Turkey, and other states adjacent to the Soviet Union to dun them with territorial claims. Nor could the Kremlin plausibly accept the principle of "unequal treaties" without facing the potential danger of protests from the Lithuanians, Latvians, Estonians, Ukrainians, Kazakhs, and other nationalities inside the Soviet Union, many of whom resented Moscow's domination. Distrusting Peking as they did, the Russians also feared that even a theoretical concession on their part would provide the Chinese with a pretext to overrun areas of Siberia that, as a Kremlin statement put it, had been acquired "by the Soviet people only at the price of immense efforts and sacrifices." [86] Thus Russian attitudes were governed by a chauvinistic emotion at least equal to the nationalism of the Chinese.

Atavistic Russian passions were vividly personified in Yevgeny Yevtushenko, the liberal Soviet poet. After the first border clash in March, he composed a poem entitled "On the Red Snows of the Ussuri," warning that the Russians were prepared to crush the Chinese just as the knights of old Muscovy had defeated the Mongol hordes at the battle of Kulikovo in 1380.

> Vladimir and Kiev, observe in the murky dusk
> The bombs in the new Mongol quivers.
> But warning bells will peal should they come,
> And there will be enough warrior knights
> For many more Kulikovos.[87]

Chinese nationalist sentiment was expressed in a succession of rallies around the country attended, according to Peking statistics, by more than 400 million people. Terming them "new Tsars," speakers at these rallies denounced the Kremlin leaders for striving to "turn the Soviet Union into a larger Russian Empire" than that controlled by the old Moscow rulers.[88] This theme was obviously contrived to unify the population, and its effectiveness could be discerned in Chinese communities outside China. In Hong Kong, for example, the anti-Communist newspaper *Daily Light* was stirred to a pitch of patriotic fervor. Despite the "many changes" wrought by the Communists, it said in a front-page editorial, "the national spirit of the Chinese people still flourishes." [89] Hong Kong Chinese, many of them refugees from communism, also displayed their patriotism by crowding into local cinemas to see "Anti-China Atrocities of the New Tsars," a propaganda film produced in Peking. Documenting China's case against Moscow, the film portrayed Chinese troops finally overcoming the Russians as the narrator warned that the Soviet "revisionists" would be "wiped out thoroughly, wholly, and completely" if they "dare to continue their intrusions into the sacred territory of our great motherland." [90] This rhetoric was paralleled, meanwhile, by urgent and extensive Soviet and Chinese defense efforts to the frontier areas.

In addition to accelerating troop deployments in the region, the

Russians initiated measures aimed at mobilizing the populations near the border. A campaign to sharpen military preparedness was begun in the Central Asian republics of Kazakhstan, Tadzhikistan, and Kirgiz with a program to train youths as artillerymen, tank drivers, radio operators, and border guards. On March 10, a similar program was inaugurated under military auspices in the Maritime Province adjacent to Manchuria.[91] The Kremlin also attempted to encourage the movement of settlers from western parts of the Soviet Union to the border zones from which thousands of frightened Russian farmers had fled during the first frontier clashes. Moscow offered land grants and attractive loans to volunteers, but the migration scheme failed to generate much enthusiasm.[92] The Soviet defense effort was thus primarily a military deployment of troops and equipment.

The Peking defense plan, on the other hand, was essentially predicated on the mobilization of people—and the program was designed to serve economic, social, and political as well as military purposes. It afforded Peking the chance to decentralize the economy by transferring industries that were formerly concentrated in coastal cities and vulnerable regions like Manchuria. It was also a device to shift fractious Red Guards and other youths to the countryside. And it provided local Army commanders and government officials with the opportunity to restore and in some cases stiffen the controls that had broken down during the Cultural Revolution.

Following the border battles in March, the Peking authorities issued a series of directives aimed at increasing the country's grain reserves, for both economic and military reasons. Peasants in Kwangtung province were reportedly compelled to contribute 10 per cent of their monthly rice ration to collective granaries.[93] In the Shanghai area, told that China might face a protracted war, farm families were instructed to store a six months' supply of food.[94] State agents in several other regions also used the defense drive to extract larger percentages of rice, wheat, and other cereals from peasants than were required by procurement quotas. According to official accounts published in August, about 20 per cent of China's production brigades had overfulfilled their annual grain procurement targets ahead of schedule. At the same time, some provincial regimes curbed private cultivation and marketing by peasants. In late July, for instance, the Canton Revolutionary Committee put the city's "free" markets under State control and ordered peasants to sell their private produce only to government purchasing depots at fixed prices.[95]

Peking also accelerated a campaign to disperse urban factories and workshops throughout the hinterlands. *Red Flag* called this a "strategic redeployment" destined to create "reliable industrial bases" around the country and thus increase China's "maneuverability" in the event of an enemy attack. "Each locality could conduct the war autonomously, wipe out the enemy, and win the conflict."[96]

This ambitious decentralization program probably began in the fall of 1968. A sampling of published evidence disclosed that a boiler factory and a welding rod plant were transferred from Canton to towns deeper in Kwangtung province, and a shipyard situated on the Pearl River east of the city was relocated farther into the interior. The Shanghai authorities moved a large textile mill into the suburbs, advising its employees that the installation would now be safe from "possible air raids." In line with this "strategic redeployment," communes were also exhorted to develop small nitrogenous-fertilizer plants, electric power stations, iron and steel works, tool factories, and other small enterprises that could be constructed with little investment.[97] To a significant degree, then, the Chinese leaders seemed to be taking advantage of the war scare to promote projects similar to those pushed during the Great Leap Forward.

During the summer, as the danger of war appeared to be growing, a vast drive was initiated to build air-raid shelters in China's major cities. In Canton, a tremendous tunnel complex was laid out, with underground passages leading from the center of the city to White Cloud Hill, near the airport. Striving to keep the city's residents alert, the Canton military garrison conducted frequent air-raid drills, often with Chinese aircraft flying overhead in simulated attacks.[98] Ships entering Shanghai and other Chinese ports, meanwhile, were being given instructions on harbor positions to adopt in the event of air raids.[99] And even Peking was digging bomb shelters in what a Hungarian correspondent there described as a "frenzy of activity."[100]

Loyal to their conviction that an invader would be "drowned in an ocean of people," Chinese strategists mounted a rigorous program of military training for civilians rather than intensive troop deployments. A key feature of this program was the reactivation of the People's Militia, whose estimated 7 million recruits consisted mainly of peasants and students who had been transferred to the countryside.[101] Thousands of members of the militia were reportedly incorporated into a paramilitary organization known as the Production and Construction Corps. The corps had originally been formed by the Army to serve as a labor force in Sinkiang province. Now, however, similar contigents were being established throughout the country. They were also being moved into areas close to the border with the Soviet Union, apparently to bear the brunt of an initial enemy assault while regular Army troops stood at distances of about two hundred miles from the frontier in counterattacking formations.[102] Confronted by the enormity of Soviet military power, many professional Chinese officers must have taken a skeptical view of the militia's ability to stop the Russian juggernaut. An attempt to dispel this skepticism was mirrored in an official rationale of the militia's role:

> Is the Militia now outdated? No, absolutely not! It is true that modern arms have some impact on war, but no modern weapon changes the objective laws of war nor the great truth that "the Army and the people are the foundation of victory." On the contrary, the larger the scale of war and the more complicated the war situation, the more necessary it is to bring the masses into full play and to turn the whole nation into soldiers.[103]

Doubts about the efficacy of the militia was only one of the problems facing the Peking leaders as they tried to mobilize for war. In several places, troops and civilian officials questioned the reality of the Soviet threat, claiming that the Russians "would not dare to invade." [104] Members of the militia were blamed for "taking the enemy lightly" or arguing that a war, if it came, would only affect the border areas.[105] Apathy even extended into regions adjacent to the Soviet Union. A Heilungkiang province broadcast complained of "the lethargy of people who have little or no awareness" of the danger of war.[106] And, as it had in 1965, when the threat of an American attack loomed large, the possibility of war again revived the long-standing strategic debate that divided professional Chinese officers and Maoist ideologues—with the ideologues repeating that the Army required more political indoctrination, and the professionals emphasizing the need for "practical training." Against the ideologues' insistence on continual political meetings and indoctrination sessions, the *Liberation Army Daily* stated: "It will not do to rely solely on lectures. More time must be given to training." [107]

By the middle of the summer, reports from China revealed that special teams were advising Army officers and government officials throughout the country to expect an "inevitable" Soviet assault against such targets as the Chinese gaseous-diffusion plant at Lanchow, in the northern province of Kansu, and the atomic test site at Lop Nor, in Sinkiang. One document distributed at these briefings was a new Peking directive authorizing troops to intensify their suppression of "anarchists," "counterrevolutionaries," and "subversive elements" who might "obstruct war preparedness." [108] And a Communist spokesman in Hong Kong took pains to tell a Western journalist that the war preparations were "not just a gimmick to rally a disunited people behind the Mao regime" but were being made "in deadly earnest because of the continued danger of a Soviet attack." [109]

The Kremlin's increasingly belligerent rhetoric was largely responsible for these Chinese fears. In one statement, Soviet Deputy Defense Minister Matvey V. Zakharov bluntly warned Peking that the Russians had the capability to launch a "blitzkrieg" against China.[110] Even more threatening was an article by Victor Louis, the Soviet publicist. Plainly calculated to shock Peking, his article disclosed that Soviet missiles were already zeroed in on Chinese nuclear installations and other targets, adding that the Kremlin would not hesitate to act against China as it did against Czechoslovakia. Louis pointed out that China's most vulnerable region was Sinkiang, and suggested that Muslim dissidents in that area might well form a cohesive movement that would call on the Soviet Union for "fraternal help." Implicit in the Louis scenario, then, was the possibility that the Russians might stir up a Muslim revolt as they did in 1962—but use it this time as a pretext to invade Sinkiang in much the same way that they intervened in Czechoslovakia.

The Soviet Union is adhering to the doctrine that socialist countries have the right to interfere in each other's affairs in their own interests or those of others who are threatened. The fact that China is many times larger than Czechoslovakia and might offer active resistance is, according to Marxist theoreticians, no reason for not applying this doctrine.[111]

At the same time, changes in Soviet military personnel in the areas bordering China indicated that there was a reality to Russian rhetoric. The Kremlin promoted several younger officers to command posts in the region and, significantly, they placed a missile expert, General Vladimir F. Tolubko, in charge of the frontier zone adjacent to Manchuria.[112] The Russians had earlier set up missile sites at two places in Mongolia, both within easy range of Peking and Manchuria's industrial cities.[113]

In line with their carrot-and-stick strategy, the Kremlin leaders continued to parallel their menacing gestures with offers to negotiate with the Chinese. An opportunity for Sino-Soviet talks finally emerged with the death of Ho Chi Minh in early September. The North Vietnamese President's funeral presented an occasion for prominent Communists from around the world to assemble in Hanoi and, while there, the most autonomous among them maneuvered to mediate the dispute. Rumanian Premier Ion Gheorghe Maurer, for example, reportedly urged Chou En-lai to open discussions with Soviet Premier Kosygin.[114] And Kosygin, who arrived in Hanoi after Chou's departure, asked the North Vietnamese to help arrange a meeting with the Chinese.[115]

The North Vietnamese were desperately anxious to avert a war between Moscow and Peking. A conflict, they realized, would force them to choose sides and deprive them of their profitably neutral position, and it would totally cut them off from Russian military supplies that traversed China. Thus they stressed the necessity for "solidarity within the socialist camp" and, following Ho Chi Minh's death, publicized a document quoting him as deploring "the dissensions that are dividing the fraternal parties" and calling for "the restoration of unity." [116] In addition, the North Vietnamese leaders actively pressed the Chinese to accept the Soviet invitation to discuss the border issue. The result, on September 11, was a brief yet decisive encounter between Chou and Kosygin in Peking that at least took the Chinese and Russians off their collision course.

A terse Chinese report revealed rather casually that the encounter took place as Kosygin "was passing through Peking on his way home." [117] Actually, the Soviet Premier's journey was far more complicated. After requesting a meeting with Chou En-lai, he had left Hanoi without a reply. He then stopped at Calcutta and proceeded to Dyushambe, the capital of Soviet Tadzhikistan in Central Asia. Chou's affirmative answer probably reached him somewhere en route, and he doubled back to Peking, where his reception was frosty. The Chinese refused to permit him to enter the city, insisting instead that their meeting be held in an airport lounge. Though infuriated by this lack of courtesy, Kosygin nevertheless did most of the talking during the four-hour encounter and his statements essentially reflected the Kremlin's sweet-and-sour strategy.

He reminded Chou En-lai that the Soviet Union had the military muscle to bomb China back to the Han dynasty, and further warned him that a war between the two Communist giants would be a world conflict. He therefore proposed that the two countries seek to avoid such a catastrophe by opening negotiations to resolve their specific boundary problems and also to discuss the resumption of trade. In that way, Moscow and Peking could at least return to normal diplomatic relations even if their ideological schism remained unhealed.[118] Chou, however, asserted that an over-all boundary accord was not possible until Moscow acknowledged that Tsarist Russia had illegally seized Chinese territory. He agreed to Kosygin's proposal to open talks—but he recommended that both sides pull back their troops from the frontier in order to "avert armed conflicts" that might impede even a limited settlement.[119]

Quite plainly, then, the Russians had frightened Peking into conceding to some kind of modus vivendi, and the Chinese virtually admitted that they had been driven by fear to negotiate. Alleging that there were "a handful of war maniacs" in the Kremlin who would "dare to raid China's strategic sites," they declared: "There is no reason whatsoever for China and the Soviet Union to fight a war over the boundary questions." [120]

On October 19, a thirty-man Soviet delegation arrived in Peking to begin the border negotiations. The Russian group was headed by First Deputy Foreign Minister Vasili V. Kuznetsov, a former Soviet Ambassador to China who had, in his youth, worked in a Pittsburgh steel mill. Representing the Chinese was Deputy Foreign Minister Ch'iao Kuan-hua, an experienced and sophisticated official who had the rare distinction of having obtained a doctorate in philosophy in Germany.

The talks between the two delegations were to drag on for more than a year, their only visible result being that they arrested what appeared to be a slide toward war in late 1969. But they did nothing to halt the exchanges of vitriolic propaganda between Peking and Moscow. Nor did they discourage either the Chinese or the Russians from continuing to reinforce their respective frontier zones. In 1971, the Kremlin was still building up its troop strength in Siberia and Central Asia while the Chinese were stiffening their air defenses with new radar networks, surface-to-air missiles, and other modern equipment.[121]

But the persistent Soviet threat indirectly stimulated Peking's increased diplomatic flexibility and, as the decade of the 1970s opened, the Chinese were engaged in an assortment of different maneuvers designed to win recognition abroad. Diluting their pretensions to ideological purity, they made overtures to "revisionist" Yugoslavia. They repaired their frayed ties with Burma and began wooing such anti-Communist Asian states as the Philippines and Malaysia, and they supported Pakistan's military regime despite its slaughter of thousands of East Pakistan peasants whose struggle for independence would, under different circumstances, have been hailed by Peking as a "national liberation movement." Their rice-for-rubber trade accord with Ceylon also prompted the Chinese to ignore a revolutionary peasant revolt in that country.[122]

A striking example of Peking's new pragmatism was its agreement on October 13, 1970, to establish diplomatic relations with Canada. Twenty months earlier, when the negotiations on this issue began, the Chinese had stubbornly demanded that the Canadians recognize the Communist regime as the "sole legal Government" for all China, including Taiwan. The Canadians refused, asserting that they would neither endorse nor oppose Peking's position on the status of the island. After repeated delays, the Chinese finally yielded to a compromise formula that acquiesced to Canada's decision merely to "note" their claim to sovereignty over Taiwan.[123] That major concession, dramatizing as it did Peking's desire to play a role in world politics, had an immediate impact. On November 20, for the first time in twenty years, a majority of General Assembly members voted to seat the Communists in the United Nations as the representative of China. Peking was barred from actual representation by a two-thirds majority rule that had been contrived by the United States.[124] A year later, however, the Nixon Administration agreed to scrap that rule and support Peking's claim to United Nations representation—on condition that the Chiang Kai-shek regime retained a place in the General Assembly.[125]

The change in relations between the United States and the Chinese Communists began to become perceptible toward the end of 1969. In a significant address aimed at reassuring the Peking leadership, a member of President Nixon's cabinet declared that the United States "did not seek to exploit" the Sino-Soviet dispute for its own advantages, and would refrain from associating "with either side against the other." [126] At the same time, Nixon also continued his gradual efforts to reach an accommodation with the Communists. His speeches stressed that "no stable and enduring international order is conceivable" without China's "contribution." [127] And he carried on his program of revising discriminatory American trade and travel restrictions toward China. In early 1970, by way of a reply, the Chinese resumed the formal diplomatic talks in Warsaw after a two-year suspension.

The first outright indication that the Communists were actually embarking on a new policy toward the United States was visible in Peking on October 1, 1970, the twenty-first anniversary of the founding of the People's Republic of China. On that day, Mao invited his old American biographer Edgar Snow to stand beside him on the rostrum of the Tienanmen Gate. When their photograph was published in the *People's Daily* nearly three months later, it was accompanied by one of Mao's quotations stating that "peoples of the world, including the American people, are all our friends." [128] That esoteric signal, hardly noticed at the time, augured a fresh Chinese approach to the United States called "people's diplomacy."

Peking's next step in that direction came on April 7, 1971, when a Chinese table-tennis team in Japan officially invited a group of fifteen American ping-pong players to tour China.[129] Accompanied by the representatives of four American news media, the athletes created a sensation in China and around the world. Soon afterward, Edgar Snow was authorized by the Chinese to publish an article revealing that Mao had told him that Nixon would be welcomed in Peking "either as a tourist or as President" because "at present the problems between the United States and China would have to be solved" with him.[130]

Until April, the President had been in secret contact with the Chinese through various intermediaries, the most prominent among them Pakistani President Yahya Khan and Rumanian President Nicolae Ceaucescu. So by the time Edgar Snow published Mao's invitation Nixon already knew that the Chinese had endorsed the idea of his visiting Peking. But to put an affirmative response on the record, the President went out of his way in a speech on April 29 to say that he expected to visit China "in some capacity." [131]

The next step was to begin making practical arrangements for the trip. On July 9, concocting a story that he was ill with stomach trouble en route home from Vietnam, Kissinger flew from Pakistan to Peking for two days of conversations with Chou En-lai. He returned to Peking in October, and preparations for the President's visit were completed by late 1971.

Speaking to a group of Cairo newsmen in Peking in November, Vice-Premier Li Hsien-nien sardonically pointed out that "a visit by the chief of a state that regards itself as one of the two superpowers" required vast planning—while, in contrast, visits between "friends" like the Chinese and Egyptians could be organized "in ten minutes." [132] But despite that comment, the Chinese authorities were amazingly cooperative in the huge operation that the President's trip entailed. One indication was their willingness to permit American television networks, which function with an enormous superstructure of technicians and electronic paraphernalia, to install themselves in Peking for the duration of Nixon's visit.

The President's week-long trip to China, which began on February 21, 1972, was a spectacular event. Nixon, his wife, the White House party, and the newsmen accompanying them were feted in lavish style, and some members of the United States group were almost speechless when, after years of Sino-American distrust and hostility, a Chinese military orchestra played "Turkey in the Straw" at a banquet in Peking. The President was received by Mao, and the edition of the *People's Daily* featuring a front-page photograph of the two men shaking hands was sold out on the streets of Peking within three hours of its appearance.

Nixon and Chou En-lai also discussed bilateral questions, such as the establishment of scientific, cultural, sports, journalistic, and trade exchanges between the United States and China. They talked at great length as well about problems ranging from Vietnam and Japan to Korea, the Soviet Union, and the conflict between India and Pakistan. Perhaps the most consequential result of the meeting, evidently reached after hard bargaining, was a pledge by the President that the United States would "progressively" withdraw its forces and military installations from Taiwan "as the tension in the area diminishes." That pledge, combined with an acknowledgment that Taiwan is a province of China, was designed to set in motion a political process that would encourage the Communists and the Nationalists to resolve their differences without outside interference. This essentially conformed to the demands that the Peking regime had set forth since its foundation in 1949.

Though the issues dividing the United States and China were not easily resolved—and would not be for some time to come—the summit meeting had inaugurated a new dialogue between the two nations, and that was significant in itself. For the United States, it spelled the end of more than twenty years of striving to "contain" the Chinese Communists, a policy that had proved to be as costly as it was fruitless. For the Peking regime, it meant the attainment of big-power status.

Peking's position as a big power had been given international recognition in the autumn, when the People's Republic of China won the right to occupy the Chinese seat at the United Nations and Chiang Kai-shek's Nationalists were expelled from the world organization. Though the Nixon Administration seemingly had made an attempt to prevent that result, it was really unruffled by the outcome of the United Nations vote. For in President Nixon's view, the main priority was the establishment of a relationship between the United States and Peking. He was ready to pay a price for that achievement.

The initial contact between the United States and Communist China appeared at first to play in Peking's favor. Even though

Nixon sought to reassure them that his "new relationship" with the Communists would "not be made at the expense of old friends," Chiang Kai-shek's Nationalists were immediately demoralized by the loss of the American support they had enjoyed for two decades. The Japanese, whom Nixon had circumvented in pursuing his overtures to Peking, also felt that they had been outmaneuvered. And the Kremlin reacted with predictable hostility, asserting that "those who advocate a United States *rapprochement* with China are rabid haters of the Soviet Union." [133]

At the same time, however, the new Russian attitude toward the United States was bound to create difficulties for the Chinese Communists. In particular, they would be confronted by the disappointment of the North Vietnamese, whose long struggle against the United States, they now perceived, might now be subverted by a diplomatic deal between Washington and Peking. Sensing North Vietnam's apprehensions, the Russians moved quickly in the fall of 1971 to fortify their influence in Hanoi. The Chinese Communists also had reason to fear that a *détente* between themselves and the United States might prompt Japan to rearm—a possibility that alarmed them. They had cause to be concerned, too, that the Japanese might seek an alignment with the Soviet Union.

But whatever evolved from a reconciliation between the United States and Communist China, a new balance of forces in Asia had surely been set in motion. The bipolarity of the 1950s was finished. The triangular rivalry involving Moscow, Peking, and Washington, which had characterized the latter half of the 1960s, had also come to an end. And the 1970s promised to feature an array of multipolar relationships that would make the pursuit of peace and stability in the Far East complicated, hazardous, and yet hopeful.

It would be years before the impact of a *rapprochement* with the United States on internal China could be measured. But there was a certain irony, so soon after the cataclysmic Cultural Revolution, in the potentiality of a reconciliation between the world's foremost "imperialists" and the world's "purest" revolutionaries. Thus, if the meeting between Mao and Nixon augured far-reaching international consequences, it also underlined a new stage in China's domestic development.

CHAPTER 22

A Postscript to Revolution

We can still say that what we gained was
far, far more than we lost.
— CHOU EN-LAI, November 1970

We must still wage a protracted struggle to
fulfill the task of further consolidating the
dictatorship of the proletariat politically,
ideologically, economically, and organiza-
tionally.

— Red Flag, July 1971

MAO TSE-TUNG, obsessed by his lifetime ambition to politicize
the Chinese "masses," had consistently extolled the virtues
of instability. As he portrayed himself in a poetic parable, he was the
legendary Golden Monkey wrathfully wielding the "massive cudgel" of "class struggle" in recurrent efforts to perpetuate revolution.[1]
Thus he had interrupted the orderly progress of the first years of the
Communist regime with episodes like the Hundred Flowers campaign and the Great Leap Forward. And thus, above all, he instigated the Cultural Revolution in order to prevent the restoration of
bureaucratic rule by what he regarded to be a new class of latter-day
mandarins.

As the 1970s opened, Mao's devastating campaign was over,
and seemed to be a distant echo. No longer were rebellion and disorder exalted. The Red Guards had disappeared and their mentors,
like K'ang Sheng and Ch'en Po-ta, had been eclipsed or even purged.
Foreign observers as well as the official Chinese press now depicted
China as a responsible nation of diligent, disciplined citizens ener-

getically engaged in shaping a new kind of society. The world also seemed to accept the new portrait of China as an emerging power that would soon play a decisive role in international affairs.

Was this image a faithful reflection of reality? Had genuine harmony returned to China—or was this stable interlude destined to be disrupted by fresh turbulence? To what extent had the Cultural Revolution transformed the "souls" of the Chinese people? And how would the ferment of the late 1960s affect China in the future?

Mao himself candidly acknowledged in a conversation with Edgar Snow that China had been immersed in "great chaos" during the Cultural Revolution.[2] But certain sectors had been carefully shielded from the tumult and, as a consequence, they registered remarkable achievements despite the disorder that shook the country.

The first artificial satellite launched by Peking, in April 1970, for example, revealed that the Chinese had managed to manufacture sophisticated electronic equipment, without which the space shot would have been impossible. In the opinion of scientific experts, this equipment probably included a computer equal to any Western model of its caliber. Other components in the satellite testified to highly advanced techniques in China's metallurgical, chemical, and machinery industries. The space shot suggested as well that Peking was moving quickly toward the construction of an impressive arsenal of medium-range and intercontinental ballistic missiles. The intercontinental missiles were expected to be able to carry three-megaton thermonuclear devices, which the Chinese had tested in experimental detonations during the late 1960s. Nor had the Cultural Revolution seriously impaired China's capacity to produce superior fighter and bomber aircraft and, according to some sources, Peking was building nuclear-powered submarines.[3]

With their characteristic resilience, the Chinese also succeeded in putting industrial and agricultural production back on an even keel after the Cultural Revolution. According to Chou En-lai, China's output of cotton cloth in 1970 was the largest in the world. Peking also had attained self-sufficiency in oil. Steel production, which had been set back by troubles in industrial areas, was recovering. The output of chemical fertilizer, long neglected, was rising and would be adequate for China's needs by 1975. And grain production, the index of agricultural conditions, had been more than 240 million tons in 1970—an increase of 25 per cent over 1957, generally regarded as the last peak year. Through rationing, rigorous procurement efforts, and wheat imports from Canada, Australia, and other countries, the Chinese had accumulated about 40 million tons in grain reserves by the beginning of 1971.[4]

Other innovations too seemed to be working in favor of a better balanced society. Public hygiene, promoted through the campaign of the "barefoot doctors," was improving in the rural areas. This campaign was partly aimed at disseminating birth-control information and techniques among peasants in an effort to curb the growth of China's huge population, calculated to reach a billion by the end of the century. The forced or voluntary migration of urban young people, cadres, workers, and unemployed city dwellers to the countryside, though fraught with difficulties, also promised to contribute to a breakdown of the barriers that had traditionally separated China's cities from its rural regions. The trend toward decentralization was further encouraged by the drive to transfer or open modest factories and workshops in small towns and villages. Partly motivated by defense strategy, this effort was also designed to help to mechanize agriculture.

In contrast to the heady days of the Cultural Revolution, when ideology was in command, Peking publicists now stressed the importance of technological specialization. While ritualistically criticizing "bourgeois intellectuals," for example, a *Red Flag* editorial warned against "rejecting the experts" or "denying or neglecting the role of specialists." [5] Primary and secondary schools, again functioning as educational institutions, had returned to curricula as conventional as they had featured before the Cultural Revolution. A visitor to a Peking secondary school in the spring of 1971 found students taking courses in mathematics, physics, chemistry, history, geography, and other routine subjects—even though instruction was heavily flavored with moralistic references to the works of Mao. A French class, for example, was heard to be reciting, "*Unissons-nous pour remporter des victoires encores plus grandes!*" while an English class declaimed its equivalent: "Let us unite to achieve even greater victories!" Students also combined studies with such jobs as carpentry and gardening. Many teachers were those who had served before the Cultural Revolution, and they were now protected against student criticism by soldiers stationed inside the school. But educational periods had been shortened, and classes now included a larger proportion of workers and peasants, whose lack of preparation was creating problems.[6]

These and other changes were attributed by Peking publicists to the "victory" of the Cultural Revolution. In many ways, however, present policies seemed to be similar to those pursued during periods when Liu Shao-ch'i and Mao's other adversaries in the former Party apparatus had been pre-eminent. The process of political and economic decentralization, for instance, was essentially a continuation of a program that had begun as far back as 1956 with the creation of regional Party bureaus and the delgation of increased fiscal authority to local officials. The switch in focus from heavy industry to agriculture had also been encouraged by the old Party machine in the early 1960s as an urgent measure aimed at preventing famine during the disastrous aftermath of the Great Leap Forward. Much of the current emphasis on technological expertise had been stressed as well by Mao's opponents prior to the Cultural Revolution. Nor was there, in the early 1970s, any substantial shift away from reliance on material incentives of the kind instituted by the former Party leaders. To a significant extent, therefore, the restoration of stability following the Cultural Revolution represented a return to many of the policies and practices that Mao had sought to eradicate in his ambitious effort to promote permanent revolution. The rhetoric of his campaign still reverberated throughout China. Yet its basic realities seemed to have evaporated.

At the same time, though, the Cultural Revolution had left a variety of problems that would not be resolved without enormous difficulty. The collective leadership put in place to succeed Mao consisted of old men whose future was limited. As the purge of Lin Piao and his comrades in late 1971 demonstrated, they were not deeply united. Thus their group was likely to be beset by further rivalries and tensions as they faced a future without Mao, the emblem of their cohesion. And the prospect of renewed dissension in China was complicated by two important elements.

The Army had taken over the country's principal administrative positions, though functioning for the most part as a civilian rather than strictly military force. But its guns were within easy reach, and, in the event of revived disorder, there was no reason to expect that it would refrain from intervening even more vigorously than it had in 1967 and 1968. Concern about the Army's role was reflected in constant exhortations to troops to obey the new Party apparatus. The possibility of fresh turbulence existed, meanwhile, in the millions of Red Guards and other young activists who had been uncorked by Mao in the Cultural Revolution and afterward suppressed, often brutally. Like the rebellious *Sheng-wu-lien* in Hunan province, which denounced Chou En-lai as a "red capitalist" and even assailed Mao, many of these people were disenchanted and embittered by what they considered to be a betrayal of the promise of power they had been given. And Peking's awareness of this danger was reflected in increasingly intensive attempts by the Chinese leaders to clamp down on the "ultraleftist" May 16th Detachment, which by mid-1971 seemed to have become a generic term to embrace a wide assortment of radicals who refused to conform to new trends.

Perhaps most important—and least visible to an outside observer—was the impact of the Cultural Revolution on the social fabric of China. As Lucian Pye has pointed out, Chinese political culture tends to operate on a basis of domination and submission, leaving little room for reconciliation between enemies. This phenomenon has long been apparent in the unusually high degree of sensitivity among Chinese to real or imagined slights and insults, epitomized in the traditional concept of "face." [7] It has also been manifest in the extent to which clan feuds and "blood debts" have persisted among them from generation to generation. Just as the clashes, public humiliations, and other forms of degradation imposed by rival factions on one another during the Cultural Revolution were often expressions of long-standing local vendettas, so this hostility was almost certain to persist into the future, challenging any real restoration of social unity. The Chairman of the Peking Revolutionary Committee, Hsieh Fu-chih, perceived this problem when he urged Red Guards to curb their savagery, warning them that the families of their victims would live solely for vengeance.

The only predictable feature of China under the Communists has been its unpredictability. Despite the enormous flow of information that came out of China during the Cultural Revolution, too little is known about the country's inner workings to assure the reliability of forecasts. And the task of "China-watching" is bound to become more complex as the present leadership group is replaced by younger figures who have lived in the shadow of Mao's generation. At the beginning of the 1970s, however, authority in China appeared to be reverting to a routinized bureaucracy of the kind that Mao desperately tried to crush—while the Chinese people, for all their enterprise and diligence, seemed to accommodate uneasily to conditions as their rulers grope for a system capable of governing one-quarter of mankind. In short, China was still in the throes of experimentation.

By welcoming the Communist regime into the international community, the world could aid China with capital and technological assistance, and help the Chinese to regain the dignity their centuries-old struggles for survival have earned them. But the solutions to China's immense problems would be found by the Chinese themselves. More than any individual in modern times, Mao led them to the rediscovery of their grandeur by inculcating them with a spirit of national identity, a sense of purpose, and a dedication to self-reliance. But in his success lay the seeds of his chief failing. Unwilling to adjust to the prose of stable administration, he sought to sustain the poetry of revolution. Yet if his visionary goals were unrealistic, their partial attainment at least gave China a stature it had not enjoyed for centuries. A lesser man would have died satisfied with his accomplishment. The depth of his disappointment, then, reflected the dimensions of his unfulfilled dream.

REFERENCE NOTES

INDEX

REFERENCE NOTES

In these notes the *Joint Publications Research Service* is regularly abbreviated *JPRS*; the *Selections from China Mainland Magazines*, SCMM; the *Selections from China Mainland Magazines (Supplement)*, SCMM (*Supp.*); the *Survey of China Mainland Press*, SCMP; and the *Survey of China Mainland Press (Supplement)*, SCMP (*Supp.*).

Chapter 1. The Vision and the Challenge

1. Mao Tse-tung, "Speech at the Chengtu Conference," March 22, 1958, *JPRS*, No. 90 (February 12, 1970), p. 49; "Talk at the Hangchow Conference," December 21, 1965, *ibid.*, p. 3.
2. Mao Tse-tung, "Speech at a Central Committee Work Conference," October 25, 1966, *ibid.*, pp. 58–59.
3. New China News Agency, April 27, 1969.
4. See *JPRS*, No. 90, p. 57.
5. Mao Tse-tung, "The Foolish Old Man Who Removed the Mountains," June 11, 1945, *Selected Works* (Peking, 1965), III, 322.
6. See Richard Lowenthal, "Unreason and Revolution," Irving Howe, ed., *Beyond the New Left* (New York, 1970), pp. 55–84; Benjamin I. Schwartz, "China and the West in the 'Thought of Mao Tse-tung,'" Ping-ti Ho and Tang Tsou, eds., *China in Crisis* (Chicago, 1968), pp. 365–79.
7. Charles B. McLane, *Soviet Strategies in Southeast Asia* (Princeton, N.J., 1966), pp. 4–5.
8. See Ping-ti Ho, "Salient Aspects of China's Heritage," *China in Crisis*, pp. 15ff.
9. *Ibid.*, pp. 30ff.

10. Mao Tse-tung, "Rectify the Party's Style of Work," February 1, 1942, *Selected Works*, III, 50.
11. André Malraux, *Anti-Memoirs* (London, 1968), pp. 392–94.

Chapter 2. The Ailing Giant

1. See Ping-ti Ho, "Salient Aspects of China's Heritage," and Kwang-ching Liu, "Nineteenth Century China," Ping-ti Ho and Tang Tsou, eds., *China in Crisis* (Chicago, 1968), pp. 19ff, 95ff; also John Fairbank, Edwin O. Reischauer, and Albert M. Craig, *East Asia, The Modern Transformation* (Boston, 1965), p. 89.
2. See Fairbank *et al.*, *op. cit.*, pp. 99ff.
3. See Ping-ti Ho, *The Ladder of Success in Imperial China: Aspects of Social Mobility, 1368–1911* (New York, 1962), pp. 48–49.
4. See Stuart Schram, "Mao Tse-tung and Secret Societies," *China Quarterly*, No. 27 (July–September 1966), pp. 1ff.
5. See Harold Isaacs, *The Tragedy of the Chinese Revolution* (Stanford, Calif., 1961), p. 175.
6. Cited in Robert Payne, *Mao Tse-tung* (New York, 1969), p. 7.
7. Cited *ibid.*, p. 12.
8. Kwang-ching Liu, *op. cit.*; Fairbank *et al.*, *op. cit.*
9. Mao Tse-tung, "On Tactics Against Japanese Imperialism," *Selected Works* (Peking, 1965), I, 178.
10. Quoted in Franz Schurmann and Orville Schell, *Imperial China* (New York, 1967), pp. 108, 109. The translation is by Harley Farnsworth MacNair.
11. Cited in Fairbank *et al.*, *op. cit.*, p. 177.
12. Cited *ibid.*, p. 382.
13. *Ibid.*, p. 320.
14. Cited *ibid.*, p. 392.
15. Ch'i Pen-yu, "Patriotism or National Betrayal?" *Peking Review*, April 7, 1967, pp. 10–12.

Chapter 3. The Moving of a Rebel

1. Quoted in Jerome Ch'en, *Mao* (Englewood Cliffs, N.J., 1969), p. 2.
2. Edgar Snow, *Red Star Over China* (New York, 1961), p. 125.
3. *Ibid.*, p. 126.
4. Jerome Ch'en, *Mao and the Chinese Revolution* (London, 1965), p. 19.
5. Snow, *op. cit.*, p. 130.
6. *Loc. cit.*
7. *Loc. cit.*
8. *Ibid.*, p. 131.
9. See Stuart Schram, *Mao Tse-tung* (London, 1966), p. 25.
10. Cited *ibid.*, p. 41.

Reference Notes

11. Snow, *op. cit.*, p. 138.
12. Schram, *op. cit.*, p. 43.
13. "A Conversation between Mao Tse-tung and his Niece, Wang Hai-jung," Peking wall poster, February 1967.
14. Mao Tse-tung, "Talk at the Hangchow Conference," December 21, 1965, *JPRS*, No. 90 (February 12, 1970), p. 3.
15. Mao Tse-tung, speech delivered at the School for Military Affairs, February 20, 1967, quoted in wall poster of the 5th Middle School, Peking, February 21, 1967.
16. Mao Tse-tung, conversation with Comrades Ch'en Po-ta and K'ang Sheng (1965), in *JPRS*, No. 90, p. 26.
17. Ch'en, *Mao and the Chinese Revolution*, pp. 63ff.
18. Snow, *op. cit.*, pp. 155ff.
19. Mao Tse-tung, "The Immortals" (trans. Michael Bullock and Jerome Ch'en), in Ch'en, *Mao and the Chinese Revolution*, p. 347.
20. See Schram, *op. cit.*, p. 56.
21. Cited in Benjamin I. Schwartz, *Chinese Communism and the Rise of Mao* (Cambridge, Mass., 1951), p. 37.
22. Cited in John Fairbank, Edwin O. Reischauer, and Albert M. Craig, *East Asia, The Modern Transformation* (Boston, 1965), p. 678.
23. Mao Tse-tung, "Report on an Investigation of the Peasant Movement in Hunan," *Selected Works* (Peking, 1965), I, 23ff.
24. Robert Payne, *Mao Tse-tung* (New York, 1969), p. 145.
25. Snow, *op. cit.*, pp. 72ff; Agnes Smedley, *Battle Hymn of China* (New York, 1943), pp. 168–69.
26. Mao Tse-tung, "Recruit Large Numbers of Intellectuals," *Selected Works*, II, 302.
27. Cited in Schram, *op. cit.*, pp. 220–21.
28. Benjamin I. Schwartz, "The Evolution of the Chinese Communist Party and Its Impact on Chinese Communist Policy since 1949," speech delivered at University of Michigan, March 1958.
29. See Ch'en, *Mao*, p. 22.
30. *Chingkangshan News*, Tsinghua University, Peking, March 15, 1967, translated by Union Research Institute, Hong Kong, April 14, 1967.
31. Liu Shao-chi, "On the Party," *Collected Works 1945–57* (Hong Kong, 1969), pp. 29–30.
32. See Edgar Snow, *Random Notes on Red China* (Cambridge, Mass., 1968), p. 3.
33. See Chalmers Johnson, *Peasant Nationalism and Communist Power* (Stanford, Calif., 1962), p. 73.
34. Mao Tse-tung, conversation with French delegation at Hangchow, September 1964, unpublished.
35. Ch'en, *Mao and the Chinese Revolution*, p. 240.
36. Theodore H. White and Annalee Jacoby, *Thunder Out of China* (New York, 1946), p. 132.
37. Evans Carlson, *Twin Stars of China* (New York, 1940), p. 80.

38. William Whitson, "The Concept of Military Generation: The Chinese Communist Case," unpublished manuscript, July 1968, p. 8.
39. Ch'en, *Mao and the Chinese Revolution*, p. 374.
40. Mao Tse-tung, "The Momentous Change in China's Military Situation," *Selected Works*, IV, 288.
41. John Gittings, *The Role of the Chinese Army* (London, 1967), pp. 3ff; Ch'en, *Mao and the Chinese Revolution*, pp. 281ff.
42. Schram, *op. cit.*, p. 244.

Chapter 4. Cracks in the Monolith

1. I am indebted to Edward Behr of *Newsweek*, who was present at the evening with Mao, for providing me with a description of the encounter. Details of the conversation are contained in an unpublished record made available by informed sources.
2. Edgar Snow, "Interview with Mao," *The New Republic*, February 27, 1965, p. 23.
3. André Malraux, *Anti-Memoirs* (London, 1968), pp. 383–84.
4. Mao Tse-tung, "Reply to Comrade Kuo Mo-jo," reprinted in *China Pictorial*, April 1967, p. 49 (inset).
5. William Whitson, "The Concept of Military Generation: The Chinese Communist Case," unpublished manuscript, July 1968.
6. *Ibid.*
7. Hsu Kai-yu, *Chou En-lai: China's Gray Eminence* (New York, 1968), p. 109; see also Whitson, *op. cit.*
8. Mao Tse-tung, "Problems of War and Strategy," November 6, 1938, *Selected Works* (Peking, 1965), II, 224.
9. Mao Tse-tung, "On Coalition Government," April 24, 1945, *Selected Works*, III, 296.
10. See Stuart Schram, "The Party in Chinese Communist Ideology," *China Quarterly*, No. 38 (April–June 1969), pp. 2–3.
11. Quoted *ibid.*, p. 3.
12. Variations of this anecdote have been related by many refugees interviewed in Hong Kong. One form of the anecdote is contained in Mao's speech at the Eighth Plenary Session of the Communist Party Eighth Central Committee, July 1959, reprinted in *The Case of P'eng Teh-huai* (Hong Kong, 1968), p. 21.
13. Malraux, *op. cit.*, p. 394.
14. Chang Kuo-t'ao, Introduction to *Collected Works of Liu Shao-chi* (Hong Kong, 1969), p. i.
15. *Ibid.*, pp. vi–vii.
16. Quoted in Schram, *op. cit.*, p. 6.
17. Liu Shao-ch'i, "On Self-Cultivation of Communists," *Collected Works*, p. 162.
18. Liu Shao-ch'i, "On Inner-Party Struggle," *ibid.*, p. 343.

Reference Notes

19. Liu Shao-ch'i, "Liquidate the Menshevik Ideology," *ibid.*, p. 446.
20. Liu Shao-ch'i, "On the Party," *ibid.*, pp. 29–30.
21. Liu Shao-ch'i, "Concluding Report at the National Land Conference," July 13, 1947, SCMM, No. 651, April 22, 1969, p. 20.
22. Tibor Mende, *China and Her Shadow* (New York, 1962).
23. See William Whitson, "The Field Army in Chinese Communist Military Politics," *China Quarterly*, No. 37 (January–March 1969), p. 11. I am also indebted, for much of this material, to Whitson's "The Concept of Military Generation."
24. John Gittings, *The Role of the Chinese Army* (London, 1967), pp. 294–99.
25. Alexander L. George, *The Chinese Communist Army in Action* (New York, 1967), p. 170.
26. Frank E. Armbruster, "China's Conventional Military Capability," Ping-ti Ho and Tang Tsou, eds., *China in Crisis* (Chicago, 1968), p. 171.
27. Gittings, *op. cit.*, p. 126.
28. Quoted in Ellis Joffe, *Party and Army: Professionalism and Political Control in the Chinese .Officer Corps, 1949–64* (Cambridge, Mass., 1967), p. 2.
29. For material and quotations in this and the following paragraphs, I am indebted to Joffe's *Party and Army*; see esp. pp. 30, 39–42, 49.
30. Mao Tse-tung, "Speech at Symposium of Group Leaders of the Enlarged Meeting of the Military Commission," June 28, 1958, SCMM (*Supp.*), No. 21 (April 2, 1968), p. 6.
31. Quoted in Gittings, *op. cit.*, p. 162.
32. Lo Jung-huan, "Continue to Promote the Glorious Tradition of the Chinese People's Liberation Army," *People's Daily* (Peking), August 1, 1955, cited in Joffe, *op. cit.*, p. 74.
33. Tung Ching, "An Evaluation of the Passé Concept," *Liberation Army Daily* (Peking), August 29, 1958, cited *ibid.*, p. 79.
34. Cited in Gittings, *op. ct.*, p. 173.
35. Cited in Joffe, *op. cit.*, p. 82.
36. "Opinions of Non-Military Comrades on the Army," *Liberation Army Daily* (Peking), May 23, 1957, cited *ibid.*, p. 82.
37. On this and the next paragraphs, see *ibid.*, pp. 87–89.
38. Cited in Alice Langley Hsieh, *Communist China's Strategy in the Nuclear Era* (Englewood Cliffs, N.J., 1962), p. 1.
39. Su Yü, "Strengthen National Defense, Consolidate the Fruits of Victory of the Revolution!" *People's Daily* (Peking), August 1, 1957, cited *ibid.*, p. 67.
40. Cited in John Gittings, *Survey of the Sino-Soviet Dispute* (London, 1968), p. 83.
41. John Foster Dulles, "Report from Asia," *The Department of State Bulletin*, XXXII, No. 821 (March 21, 1955), 459–60.

42. Schram, *op. cit.*, p. 12.
43. Mao Tse-tung, "Socialist Upsurge in China's Countryside," cited in Stuart Schram, *Mao Tse-tung* (London, 1966), p. 281.
44. Cheng Chu-yuan, *Scientific and Engineering Manpower in Communist China, 1949–1963* (Washington, D.C., 1965), p. 237.
45. Liu Shao-ch'i, "Speech at the 1951 National Propaganda Work Conference," and "Speech to Forum of Chinese People's Political Consultative Conference," May 13, 1951, *SCMM*, No. 652 (April 21, 1969), pp. 1, 11.
46. Liu Shao-ch'i, "Work Directive for Tientsin," April 24, 1949, *ibid.*, p. 12.
47. *Ibid.*, p. 11.
48. Mao Tse-tung, "On the People's Democratic Dictatorship," *Selected Works*, IV, 421.
49. Mao Tse-tung, "Instruction Given at the Spring Festival Conference Concerning Educational Work," February 14, 1964, *Current Background*, No. 891 (October 8, 1969), p. 42.
50. Mao Tse-tung, "Speech at the Chinese Communist Party's National Conference on Propaganda Work" (Peking, 1966), p. 26.
51. Liu Shao-ch'i, "Political Report of the Central Committee of the Communist Party of China to the Eighth National Congress of the Party," September 15, 1956, *Eighth National Congress of the Communist Party of China* (Peking), I, 37.
52. *Ibid.*, p. 74.
53. Teng Hsiao-p'ing, "Report on the Revision of the Constitution of the Communist Party of China," September 16, 1956, *ibid.*, pp. 213–14.
54. Lu Ting-yi, "Let a Hundred Flowers Bloom, a Hundred Schools of Thought Contend," quoted in Richard H. Solomon, "One Party and One Hundred Schools: Leadership, Lethargy, or *Luan*," *Current Scene*, October 1, 1969, p. 10.
55. Kenneth R. Walker, "Collectivization in Retrospect: The Socialist High Tide of August 1955–Spring 1956," *China Quarterly*, No. 26 (April–June 1966), pp. 22–25.
56. Quoted *ibid.*, p. 22n.
57. *Ibid.*, pp. 7ff.
58. Mao Tse-tung, "The Question of Agricultural Cooperatives," July 31, 1955, *Communist China, 1955–1959: Policy Documents with Analysis*, with a Foreword by Robert R. Bowie and John K. Fairbank (Cambridge, Mass., 1962), p. 94.
59. Liu Shao-ch'i, "Speech at the 1951 National Propaganda Work Conference," *SCMM*, No. 652, p. 3.
60. Liu Shao-ch'i, "Political Report . . . to the Eighth National Congress," pp. 19, 20.
61. Mao Tse-tung, "Socialist Upsurge in China's Countryside," *Communist China, 1955–1959: Policy Documents*, p. 118.

62. Li Choh-ming, "Economic Development," *China Quarterly*, No. 1 (January–March 1960), p. 42.
63. In *Communist China, 1955–1959: Policy Documents*, p. 7.
64. *Ibid.*, pp. 7–8.
65. Mao Tse-tung, "Speech to the Central Work Conference," October 1966, *JPRS*, No. 90; see also *Yomiuri* (Tokyo), January 7, 1967.
66. Liu Shao-ch'i, "Political Report . . . to the Eighth National Congress," pp. 19–20, 65, 96, 103.
67. Teng Hsiao-p'ing, "Report on the Revision of the Constitution of the Communist Party of China," *Eighth National Congress of the Communist Party of China*, I, 200.
68. "The Criminal History of the Big Conspirator, Big Ambitionist, Big Warlord P'eng Teh-huai," published by Peking Red Guard Congress, Tsinghua University, Chingkangshan Corps, August 1967, *The Case of P'eng Teh-Huai* (Hong Kong, 1968), p. 201.
69. *The New York Times*, October 26, 1970.
70. Richard H. Solomon, "One Party and 'One Hundred Schools,'" *Current Scene*, October 1, 1969, pp. 36–37.
71. "More on the Historical Experience of the Dictatorship of the Proletariat," December 29, 1956, *Communist China, 1955–1959: Policy Documents*, pp. 257ff.
72. Mao Tse-tung, "On the Correct Handling of Contradictions Among the People," *ibid.*, p. 273.
73. See Roderick MacFarquhar, *The Hundred Flowers* (London, 1960), pp. 45, 51.
74. Cited in *ibid.*, pp. 87–88.
75. *Ibid.*, p. 52.
76. Mao Tse-tung, "Twenty Manifestations of Bureaucracy," January 1967, *JPRS*, No. 90, pp. 40–43.
77. Cited in MacFarquhar, *op. cit.*, p. 261.
78. Cited in Solomon, *op. cit.*, pp. 32–33.
79. See Frederick C. Teiwes, "The Purge of Provincial Leaders 1957–1958," *China Quarterly*, No. 27 (July–September 1966), p. 14.

Chapter 5. The Leap That Failed

1. "Resolution of the Central Committee of the Chinese Communist Party on the Establishment of People's Communes in Rural Areas," August 29, 1958, *Communist China, 1955–1959: Policy Documents with Analysis*, with a Foreword by Robert R. Bowie and John K. Fairbank (Cambridge, Mass., 1962), p. 456.
2. "Hold High the Red Flag of People's Communes and March On," *People's Daily* (Peking), September 3, 1958, *ibid.*, p. 460.
3. Stuart Schram, "Mao Tse-tung and Secret Societies," *China Quarterly*, No. 27 (July–September, 1966), p. 16.

Reference Notes

4. Mao Tse-tung, "Speech at the Supreme State Conference," January 28, 1958, SCMM (Supp.), No. 21 (April 2, 1968), pp. 2–5.
5. Quoted in Richard Hughes, *The Chinese People's Communes* (London, 1960), p. 38.
6. Quoted in Li Choh-ming, "Economic Development," *China Quarterly*, No. 1 (January–March, 1960), p. 46.
7. Tibor Mende, *China and Her Shadow* (New York, 1962), p. 71.
8. Li, *op. cit.*, p. 44.
9. Liu Shao-ch'i, "Report on the Work of the Central Committee of the Communist Party of China to the Second Session of the Eighth National Congress," *Collected Works* (Hong Kong, 1969), p. 10.
10. Quoted in Schram, *Mao Tse-tung* (London, 1966), p. 271.
11. New China News Agency, August 12, 1958.
12. "Peking Scientists Plan Higher Goals," New China News Agency, June 6, 1958, *Communist China, 1955–1959: Policy Documents*, p. 17.
13. The following material is based on extensive interviews by the author with Albert Belhomme in Hong Kong in 1963. Portions of the interview appeared in Stanley Karnow, "The G.I. Who Chose Communism," *Saturday Evening Post*, November 16, 1963.
14. Mao Tse-tung, "Speech at the Supreme State Conference," p. 2.
15. Based on an interview in Hong Kong by the author.
16. "Letter of the Chinese Communist Party to the Communist Party of the Soviet Union," February 29, 1964, in John Gittings, *Survey of the Sino-Soviet Dispute* (London, 1968), p. 139.
17. Chou En-lai, "Report on Adjusting the Major Targets of China's 1959 National Plan," August 26, 1959, *Communist China, 1955–1959: Policy Documents*, pp. 540ff.
18. Lord Montgomery, *The Sunday Times* (London).
19. Conversation between Ch'en Yi and Walton A. Cole, general manager of Reuters News Agency, January 18, 1960.
20. Interview by author with Hong Kong government officials, 1961.
21. Communicated to author by Bernard Ullmann, Agence France-Presse.
22. Stanley Karnow, "Why They Fled: Refugee Accounts," *Current Scene*, October 15, 1963, p. 3.
23. Interview with a refugee by author.
24. Karnow, "Why They Fled," p. 12.
25. See C. S. Chen and Charles P. Ridley, eds., *Rural People's Communes in Lien Chiang* (Stanford, Calif., 1969).
26. *Ibid.*, pp. 101, 102.
27. *Ibid.*, pp. 109, 140.
28. These documents, obtained by the Central Intelligence Agency, can be consulted in J. Chester Cheng, ed., *The Politics of the Chinese Red Army* (Stanford, Calif., 1964). See pp. 279–80.
29. *Ibid.*, p. 284.
30. *Ibid.*, pp. 284, 584, 281.

31. *Ibid.*, p. 43.
32. *Ibid.*, p. 287.

Chapter 6. The Marshal vs. Mao

1. Mao Tse-tung, "A Letter to Production Team Leaders," November 29, 1959, *Current Background*, No. 891 (October 8, 1969), pp. 34–35.
2. Lord Montgomery, *The Sunday Times* (London).
3. *People's Daily* (Peking), November 4 and May 13, 1958.
4. James T. Myers, "The Fall of Chairman Mao," *Current Scene*, June 15, 1968, p. 3.
5. "Resolution on Some Questions Concerning the People's Communes," December 10, 1958, *Communist China, 1955–1959: Policy Documents with Analysis*, with Foreword by Robert R. Bowie and John K. Fairbank (Cambridge, Mass., 1962), pp. 492–95.
6. "Decisions Approving Comrade Mao Tse-tung's Proposal That He Will Not Stand as Candidate for Chairman of the People's Republic of China for the Next Term of Office," December 10, 1958, *ibid.*, pp. 487–88.
7. Red Guard wall posters, quoted in *Mainichi Shimbun* (Tokyo), January 5, 1967.
8. "Decision Approving Comrade Mao Tse-tung's Proposal That He Will Not Stand . . . ," *Communist China, 1955–1959: Policy Documents with Analysis*, pp. 487–88.
9. General Kung Chu, Introduction, *The Case of P'eng Teh-Huai* (Hong Kong, 1968), pp. i–iii; also private notes of Chang Kuo-t'ao.
10. Quoted in Kung, *op. cit.*, p. xiii.
11. "P'eng Teh-huai's Crimes in the 'Resist-U.S. and Aid-Korea War,'" published by *Mass Criticism and Repudiation Bulletin* (Canton), October 5, 1967, cited *ibid.*, p. 153.
12. "The Criminal History of the Big Conspirator, Big Ambitionist, Big Warlord P'eng Teh-huai," published in August 1967 by Peking Red Guard Congress, Tsinghua University, Chingkangshan Corps, cited *ibid.*, p. 201.
13. "Principal Crimes of P'eng Teh-huai, Big Ambitionist and Schemer," in *Chingkang Mountains* (Canton), September 5, 1967, cited *ibid.*, p. 176.
14. Mao Tse-tung, "Speech at a Meeting," October 24, 1966, *JPRS*, No. 90 (February 12, 1970), p. 10.
15. Soviet government statement, September 21, 1963, quoted in John Gittings, *Survey of the Sino-Soviet Dispute* (London, 1968), p. 98.
16. *Life*, June 12, 1959.
17. "Statement by the Spokesman of the Chinese Government," August 15, 1963, in Gittings, *op. cit.*, p. 105.
18. *People's Daily* (Peking), November 2, 1957.

19. David A. Charles, "The Dismissal of Marshal P'eng Teh-huai," *China Quarterly*, No. 8 (October–December 1961), pp. 63–76.
20. "Letter of the Chinese Communist Party Central Committee to the Central Committee of the Communist Party of the Soviet Union," February 27, 1964, *People's Daily* (Peking), May 9, 1964.
21. Mao Tse-tung, "Speech at the Enlarged Meeting of the Military Commission of the Chinese Communist Party Central Committee . . . ," September 11, 1959, SCMM (*Supp.*), No. 21 (April 2, 1968), p. 37.
22. Cited in Stuart Schram, *Mao Tse-tung* (London, 1966), pp. 276–77.
23. Private source.
24. P'eng Teh-huai, "Excerpts from Talks at the Meeting of the Northwest Group of the Lushan Meeting," July 3–10, 1959, *The Case of P'eng Teh-huai*, pp. 1–5.
25. P'eng Teh-huai, "Letter of Opinion," *ibid.*, pp. 7–13.
26. Mao Tse-tung, "Comment on the Article 'How Should the Revolutionary Mass Movement be Handled by Marxists,' " August 15, 1959, SCMM (*Supp.*), No. 21, p. 31.
27. Mao Tse-tung "Talk on July 10," *ibid.*, p. 10.
28. Mao Tse-tung "Speech at the Eighth Plenary Session of the Chinese Communist Party Eighth Central Committee," July 23, 1959, *ibid.*, pp. 11–18; see also *The Case of P'eng Teh-huai*, pp. 15–26. The various versions of this speech differ only slightly in wording. I have therefore taken the liberty of using those parts of different versions which best seemed to convey Mao's intentions.
29. Charles, *op. cit.*, p. 68.
30. "The Criminal History of . . . P'eng Teh-huai," *The Case of P'eng Teh-huai*, p. 205.
31. Mao Tse-tung, "Letter to Chang Wen-t'ien," August 2, 1959, SCMM (*Supp.*), No. 21, p. 24.
32. Mao Tse-tung, "Comment on a Letter," July 26, 1959, *ibid.*, p. 19.
33. Mao Tse-tung, "The Origin of Machine Guns and Trench Mortars and Other Things," August 16, 1959, *ibid.*, p. 33.
34. Mao Tse-tung, "Speech at the Enlarged Meeting of the Military Commission," September 11, 1959, *ibid.*, p. 35.
35. Mao Tse-tung, "Talk at the Eighth Plenary Session of the Chinese Communist Party Eighth Central Committee," August 2, 1959, *The Case of P'eng Teh-huai*, pp. 27–30.
36. P'eng Teh-huai, "Speech at the Eighth Plenary Session of the Eighth Central Committee," August 1959, *ibid.*, pp. 31–38.
37. "Resolution of the Eighth Plenary Session of the Eighth Central Committee Concerning the Anti-Party Clique Headed by P'eng Teh-huai," August 16, 1959, *ibid.*, pp. 34–44.
38. P'eng Teh-huai, "Letter to Mao Tse-tung," September 9, 1959, *ibid.*, pp. 45–46.
39. Order of the Chairman of the People's Republic of China, September 17, 1959, *ibid.*, p. 47

40. P'eng Teh-huai, Record of Interrogation, December 28, 1966–January 5, 1967, *ibid.*, pp. 119–22.

Chapter 7. *The Party Takes Command*

1. "Comment on Liu Shao-chi's 1961 Visit to Hunan," *SCMM* (*Supp.*), No. 26 (June 27, 1968), pp. 1–18.
2. "The Whole Party and the Whole People Go In for Agriculture in a Big Way," *Red Flag*, No. 17, reprinted in *Peking Review*, September 14, 1960, pp. 32–36.
3. Liu Shao-ch'i, "Speech at Party Work Conference," 1962, and "Speech at Meeting of Office of Finance and Trade," October 1960, cited in "Forty Instances of the Reactionary Statements of the Top Party Person in Authority," *The Rural Youth* (Shanghai), May 10, 1967.
4. "Struggle in China's Countryside Between Two Roads," *People's Daily* (Peking), November 23, 1967.
5. Quoted in *Current Background*, No. 878 (April 28, 1969), p. 8.
6. *Ibid.*, pp. 7, 13.
7. *Ibid.*
8. "Stand Firm on the Policy of Letting a Hundred Flowers Bloom and a Hundred Schools of Thought Contend in Academic Research," *Red Flag*, No. 5 (February 28, 1961), *SCMP*, No. 2451 (March 8, 1961), p. 2.
9. *China Youth*, September 2, 1961, *SCMP*, No. 2581 (September 19, 1961), pp. 1–7.
10. Sven Lindquist, *China in Crisis* (London, 1963), pp. 44–48.
11. Liu Shao-ch'i, "Speech Made on January 27, 1962," *Current Background*, No. 652, p. 30.
12. See Merle Goldman, "The Unique 'Blooming and Contending' of 1961–62," *China Quarterly*, No. 37 (January–March 1969).
13. *Ibid.*, pp. 70–73.
14. Liu Mein-chin (pseudo. Wu Han), "Hai Jui Upbraids the Emperor," *People's Daily* (Peking), June 16, 1959, quoted in James R. Pusey, *Wu Han: Attacking the Present Through the Past* (Cambridge, Mass., 1969), pp. 15–16.
15. *People's Daily* (Peking), May 29, 1967, p. 3.
16. See Goldman, *op. cit.*, pp. 76–83.
17. Charles Neuhauser, "The Chinese Communist Party in the 1960's: Prelude to the Cultural Revolution," *China Quarterly*, No. 32 (October–December 1967), pp. 14–16.
18. *Kwangming Daily* (Peking), August 9, 1967, quoted in *South China Morning Post* (Hong Kong), October 6, 1967.
19. Liu Shao-chi, "How to Be a Good Communist," *Collected Works* (Hong Kong, 1969), pp. 219ff.
20. See Stanley Karnow, "Sinkiang: Soviet Rustlers in China's Wild West," *The Reporter*, June 18, 1964.

Reference Notes

21. Interviews with Chang Kuo-t'ao by the author.
22. Quoted in Philip Bridgham, "Mao's Cultural Revolution: Origin and Development," *China Quarterly*, No. 90 (January–March 1967), p. 4.
23. New China News Agency, March 6, 1954.
24. "The Whole Country Must Learn from the PLA," *People's Daily* (Peking), February 1, 1964.
25. See Richard H. Solomon, "One Party and 'One Hundred Schools': Leadership, Lethargy of *Luan*," *Current Scene*, October 1, 1969.
26. *Ibid.*
27. Quoted in Ellis Joffe, "The Chinese Army on the Eve of the Cultural Revolution," a paper prepared for the Conference on Government in China, August 18–23, 1969.
28. Stanley Karnow, *The Washington Post*, September 17, 1967; also interviews in Hong Kong.
29. Fred L. Karpin, *The Washington Post*, April 29, 1967.
30. Bridgham, *op. cit.*, pp. 8–9.
31. New China News Agency, June 6, 1966.
32. *People's Daily* (Peking), July 14, 1964.
33. "Draft Resolution of the Central Committee of the Chinese Communist Party on Some Problems in Current Rural Work," May 20, 1963, cited in Richard Baum and Frederick C. Tiewes, *Szu-Ching: The Socialist Education Campaign of 1962–66* (Berkeley, Calif., 1968), pp. 60–61.
34. *Ibid.*
35. See Ting Wang, "Profile of Wang Kuang-mei," *Far Eastern Economic Review*, June 22, 1967, p. 654.
36. Quoted in Baum and Tiewes, *op. cit.*, p. 120.
37. Liu Shao-chi, "Self-Criticism," *Collected Works* (Hong Kong), p. 362.
38. *Liberation Daily*, Peking Domestic Service, November 13, 1964.
39. "Resolutely Boycott Bourgeois Thoughts and Modes of Living," *Liberation Daily* (Shanghai), October 11, 1964.
40. Shanghai *Evening Post*, December 15, 1964.
41. "The Basic Difference Between Us and Comrade Feng Ting," *People's Liberation Army Journal*, December 1964.
42. Interview in Hong Kong by author.
43. Mao Tse-tung, "Spring Festival Day in Education," February 13, 1964; "Talk with the Nepalese Delegation on Education Problems, 1964," *Current Background*, No. 891, p. 46.
44. Edgar Snow, "Interview with Mao," *The New Republic*, February 27, 1965, p. 23.
45. Mao Tse-tung, "On Khrushchev's Phoney Communism and Its Historical Lessons for the World," *Red Flag*, July 14, 1964, cited in A. Doak Barnett, *China After Mao* (Princeton, N.J., 1967), pp. 148–49, 183.
46. *Ibid.*, pp. 178, 183–192 *passim*.
47. *Ibid.*, p. 192.

48. Danish News Agency, May 24, 1966, quoted in John Gittings, *Survey of the Sino-Soviet Dispute* (London, 1968), p. 160.
49. Snow, *op. cit.*, pp. 22–23.
50. Quoted in Uri Ra'anan, "Peking's Foreign Policy Debate 1965–1966," Ping-ti Ho and Tang Tsou, eds., *China in Crisis* (Chicago, 1968), pp. 36–37.
51. *People's Daily* (Peking), February 9, 1965.
52. Li Tso-p'eng "Strategically Pitting One Against Ten, Tactically Pitting Ten Against One," *Red Flag*, December 22, 1964.
53. Quoted in Ra'anan, *op. cit.*, p. 44.
54. Quoted *ibid.*, p. 44.
55. Quoted *ibid.*, p. 45.
56. Quoted *ibid.*, p. 53.
57. Snow, *op. cit.*, p. 18.
58. *Peking Review*, September 3, 1965.
59. Lin Piao, "Long Live the Victory of People's War," September 3, 1965, quoted in Ra'anan, *op. cit.*, pp. 54ff.
60. Quoted in Donald Zagoria, "The Strategic Debate in Peking," *China in Crisis*, p. 267.
61. "Manifold Crimes of the Counter-Revolutionary Revisionist Element Lo Jui-ch'ing," *Struggle* (Peking), January 30, 1967.

Chapter 8. The Opening Salvos

1. Mao Tse-tung, "A Talk to Foreign Visitors," August 31, 1967, *SCMP*, No. 4200 (June 18, 1968), p. 2.
2. See Neale Hunter, *Shanghai Journal* (New York, 1969), p. 5.
3. See Philip Bridgham, "Mao's Cultural Revolution: Origin and Development," *China Quarterly*, No. 29 (January–March, 1967), p. 16.
4. *Peking Review*, October 1, 1965, pp. 8–12.
5. Quoted in Richard H. Solomon, "One Party and 'One Hundred Schools': Leadership, Lethargy, or *Luan*," *Current Scene*, October 1, 1969.
6. See Joan Robinson, *The Cultural Revolution in China* (London, 1969), p. 51.
7. Cited in Hunter, *op. cit.*, p. 20.
8. Yao Wen-yuan, "On the New Historical Play *Dismissal of Hai Jui*," *People's Daily* (Peking), November 30, 1965.
9. Quoted in Hunter, *op. cit.*, p. 18.
10. P'eng Chen, "Talk at the Festival of Peking Opera on Contemporary Themes," July 1, 1964, in *Red Flag*, No. 14, July 14, 1964.
11. P'eng Chen, "Speech at China's National Day Celebration in Peking," New China News Agency, October 1, 1965.
12. *People's Daily* (Peking), November 30, 1965.
13. Wu Han, "Self-Criticism on *Dismissal of Hai Jui*," *People's Daily*, (Peking), December 30, 1965.

14. Bridgham, *op. cit.*, p. 19.
15. Solomon, *op. cit.*
16. "The February Outline Report," *Peking Chingkangshan*, May 27, 1967.
17. *Ibid.*
18. *Peking Review*, June 2, 1967, pp. 10–16.
19. *People's Daily* (Peking), June 19, 1966.
20. *Peking Chingkangshan*, May 27, 1967.
21. *Ibid.*
22. *Red Flag*, No. 9, July 3, 1966, quoted in Bridgham, *op. cit.*, p. 22.
23. "Circular of the Central Committee of the Communist Party of China, May 16, 1966," New China News Agency, May 16, 1967.
24. Kuo Mo-jo, "Learn from the Masses of Workers, Peasants, and Soldiers and Serve Them," *Kwangming Daily* (Peking), April 28, 1966.
25. Yao Wen-yuan, "Destroy the 'Gangster Inn' Run by Teng T'o, Wu Han, and Liao Mo-sha," Shanghai *Wen Hui Pao*, May 10, 1966.
26. "Chronology of Important Events in the Struggle Between the Two Lines in the Field of Higher Education," *SCMM* (*Supp.*), No. 18 (February 26, 1968), p. 30.
27. Roderick MacFarquhar, *The Hundred Flowers* (London, 1960), p. 264.
28. See Victor Nee, *The Cultural Revolution at Peking University* (New York, 1969), pp. 28–29.
29. New China News Agency, June 1, 1967.
30. See Nee, *op. cit.*, pp. 53–56.
31. See *People's Daily* (Peking), June 2, 1966.
32. Mao Tse-tung, "Talks to Central Committee Leaders," July 21, 1966, *Current Background*, No. 891 (October 8, 1969), p. 58.
33. See V. I. Lenin, *Writings on the Commune* (New York, 1968), pp. 91, 116–17.
34. *People's Daily* (Peking), June 2, 1966.
35. *The New York Times*, June 6, 1966.
36. New China News Agency, June 5, 1966.
37. Nee, *op. cit.*, p. 60.
38. Stanley Karnow, *The Washington Post*, July 18, 1966.
39. Cited in Louis Barcata, *China in the Throes of the Cultural Revolution* (New York, 1968), p. 53.
40. *People's Daily* (Peking), June 1, 1966.
41. Jack Gray and Patrick Cavendish, *Chinese Communism in Crisis* (New York, 1968), pp. 118–19.
42. See Nee, *op. cit.*, pp. 42–43.
43. Mao Tse-tung, "On Khrushchev's Phoney Communism and Its Historical Lessons for the World," July 14, 1964, in A. Doak Barnett, *China After Mao* (Princeton, N.J., 1967), p. 193.
44. See Solomon, *op. cit.*
45. Mao Tse-tung, "Talks to Central Committee Leaders," July 21, 1966, *Current Background*, No. 891, pp. 58–59.

46. *Ibid.*
47. Liu Shao-ch'i, "Self Criticism," October 23, 1966, *Collected Works* (Hong Kong, 1969), p. 358.
48. Liu Shao-ch'i, "Self-Examination," July 9, 1967, *Collected Works*, pp. 372–73.
49. Nee, *op. cit.*, pp. 61–62.
50. *Ibid.*, pp. 62–63.
51. *Ibid.*, p. 64.
52. *People's Daily* (Peking), December 20, 1966.
53. Chu-Yuan Cheng, *Scientific and Engineering Manpower in Communist China, 1949–1953* (Washington, D.C., 1965), pp. 45–47.
54. New China News Agency, March 31, 1967.
55. Ting Wang, "Profile of Wang Kuang-mei," *Far Eastern Economic Review*, June 22, 1967, p. 654; "Dossiers of Wang Kuang-mei, *Supplement to Worker-Peasant-Soldier*, September 1967, *Current Background* (supplement), No. 27 (June 8, 1968), pp. 6off.
56. New China News Agency, March 31, 1967; Jean Esmein, *La Révolution Culturelle* (Paris, 1970), p. 11.
57. K'uai Ta-fu, "A Big-Character Poster Entitled 'Let's Think,' " June 21, 1966, *Current Background* (supplement), No. 20 (March 18, 1968), p. 6.
58. K'uai Ta-fu, "Speeches at the June 27th Debate," *ibid.*, p. 25.
59. K'uai Ta-fu, "Statement Concerning the June 27th Meeting," *ibid.*, p. 16.
60. K'uai Ta-fu, "Two Letters to Comrade Yeh Lin," *ibid.*, pp. 46–47.
61. K'uai Ta-fu, "To Admit and Examine Mistakes in the Presence of the Party and All Revolutionary Teachers and Students of the University," *ibid.*, pp. 53–55.
62. K'uai Ta-fu, "An Open Letter to the Premier," *ibid.*, pp. 57–58.
63. See Stanley Karnow, *The Washington Post*, December 28, 1966.
64. See Andrew Watson, "Revolution in Sian," *Far Eastern Economic Review*, April 20, 1967.
65. Using the pseudonym Dai, the young Chinese recounted his experiences to two American scholars in Hong Kong. See Gordon A. Bennett and Ronald N. Montaperto, *Red Guard* (New York, 1971), pp. 33–49.
66. Hunter, *op. cit.*, pp. 29–30.
67. *Ibid.*, pp. 39–40.
68. *Ibid.*, pp. 39–40.
69. *Ibid.*, pp. 44, 48.
70. *Ibid.*, pp. 58–60.
71. New China News Agency, July 25, 1966.
72. Mao Tse-tung, "Swimming," quoted *ibid.*
73. *Ibid.*
74. Mao Tse-tung, "Speech at a Certain Conference, July 21, 1966," *Current Background*, No. 892, pp. 35–37.

Chapter 9. The Children's Revolt

1. *Red Flag*, August 6, 1967.
2. Mao Tse-tung, "A Letter to the Red Guards of the Middle School Attached to Tsinghua University," August 1, 1966, *Current Background*, No. 981 (October 8, 1969), p. 63.
3. Mao Tse-tung, "Bombard the Headquarters—My First Big-Character Poster," August 5, 1966, *ibid.*, p. 63.
4. Liu Shao-chi, "Talk at a Debate at the Peking College of Construction Engineering," August 2, 1966, *Collected Works* (Hong Kong, 1969), pp. 331–33.
5. Liu Shao-chi, "Talk to the Great Proletarian Cultural Revolution Corps," August 3, 1966, *ibid.*, p. 351.
6. Liu Shao-chi, "Talk to the Work Team of the Peking College of Construction Engineering," August 4, 1966, *ibid.*, p. 351.
7. Mao Tse-tung, "Talk to Foreign Visitors," August 31, 1967, SCMP, No. 4200, p. 2.
8. Lin Piao, "Speech at the Eleventh Plenary Session of the Eighth Central Committee of the Chinese Communist Party," SCMP (*Supp.*), No. 159 (December 16, 1966), pp. 38–40.
9. Lee Pat-po, "Unleashing the Youth," *Far Eastern Economic Review*, August 17, 1967, p. 327.
10. Thomas Robinson, "Chou En-lai and the Cultural Revolution in China," unpublished manuscript, the Rand Corporation (Santa Monica, Calif.).
11. "Decision of the Chinese Communist Party Central Committee Concerning the Great Proletarian Cultural Revolution," New China News Agency, August 8, 1966.
12. Ch'en Po-ta, "Speech at Peking University," July 23, 1966, JPRS, No. 394 (May 10, 1967), p. 2.
13. K'ang Sheng, "Speech at Peking Normal University," July 1966[?], JPRS, No. 398 (June 8, 1967), p. 5.
14. Ch'en Po-ta, *op. cit.*
15. Lin Piao, "Speech at Peking's Mass Rally Celebrating the Great Proletarian Cultural Revolution," *Peking Review*, No. 35 (August 26, 1966), pp. 8–9.
16. From an official film of the August 18, 1966, rally shown in Hong Kong.
17. Peking Radio, August 23, 1966.
18. "The Factions in Canton," a privately prepared study obtained in Hong Kong.
19. From an interview conducted by the author in Hong Kong.
20. Neale Hunter, *Shanghai Journal* (New York, 1969), p. 65.
21. *Ibid.*, p. 68.

Reference Notes

22. Gordon A. Bennett and Ronald N. Montaperto, *Red Guard* (New York, 1971).
23. New China News Agency, August 23, 1966.
24. *Yang-chen Wan-pao* (Canton), August 24, 1966.
25. "Hundred Rules for Destroying the Old and Establishing the New," Red Guards of the Peking Municipal No. 26 Middle School, September 1, 1966. Pamphlet obtained by author in Hong Kong.
26. From a interview by the author with Branko Bogunivic, Tanjug correspondent in Peking.
27. See Bennett and Montaperto, *op. cit.*, for the following material from Dai's account.
28. *Asahi* (Tokyo), January 8, 1967.
29. *Yomiuri* (Tokyo), January 8, 1967.
30. Reuters, August 26, 1966.
31. *Hong Kong Standard*, September 1, 1966.
32. Private sources and interviews in Hong Kong.
33. *China News Summary* (Hong Kong), July 24, 1967.
34. Chou En-lai, "Speech to Red Guard Representatives," September 1, 1966, *Current Background*, No. 819 (March 10, 1967), p. 19.
35. Stanley Karnow, *The Washington Post*, September 25, 1966.
36. Robert Tung, "The Sins of the Capitalists," *Far Eastern Economic Review*, September 8, 1966, pp. 441ff.
37. Private sources in Hong Kong.
38. *Peking Review*, No. 37 (September 23, 1966), p. 10.
39. *Peking Review*, No. 39 (September 23, 1966), p. 10.
40. Changchun Radio, September 2, 1966.
41. Honan Radio, September 21, 1966.
42. Chengtu Radio, November 11, 1967.
43. Stanley Karnow, *The Washington Post*, August 6, 1967.
44. Chengtu Radio, November 11, 1967.
45. *Ibid.*, September 13, 1966.
46. Kweishow Radio, June 23, 1967.
47. See *China News Summary* (Hong Kong), September 22, 1966.
48. *Current Background*, No. 855, June 17, 1968.
49. *People's Daily* (Peking), September 11, 1966.
50. Bennett and Montaperto, *op. cit.*, pp. 91–111.
51. From an interview conducted in Hong Kong by the author.
52. Bennett and Montaperto, *op. cit.*
53. See Stanley Karnow, *The Washington Post*, May 21, 1970.
54. Chou En-lai, "Speech on September 25, 1966," in *Collection of Leaders' Speeches* published by Tsinghua University Defend-the-East Corps, November 1966, cited in Robinson, *op. cit.*
55. See Robinson, *op. cit.*
56. Chou En-lai, "Speech to Red Guard Representatives," pp. 16–17.
57. Chou En-lai, "Speech on September 25, 1966."

58. *Ibid.*
59. Chou En-lai, "Speech to Red Guard Representatives," p. 19.
60. Chou En-lai, "Speech on September 25, 1966."
61. Chou En-lai, "Speech at Altar of Agriculture Park on September 13, 1966," *Current Background*, No. 819 (March 10, 1967), p. 41.
62. Chou En-lai, "Speech on September 9, 1961," *JPRS*, No. 394 (May 10, 1967), p. 1.
63. Chou En-lai, "Urgent Instructions by Telephone," October 24, 1966, *SCMM (Supp.)*, No. 15 (May 8, 1967), pp. 22–23.
64. Chou En-lai, "Speech on September 25, 1966," and "Speech to Red Guard Representatives," p. 18.
65. Ch'en Yi, "To Red Guards on Welcoming Foreign Guests and Overseas Chinese," *Collection of Materials Pertaining to the Great Proletarian Cultural Revolution* (Canton), October 28, 1966.
66. "Regulations of the Chinese Communist Party Central Committee and the State Council Concerning the Protection of the Security of Party and State Secrets during the Great Cultural Revolution Movement," September 8, 1966. Document obtained by author in Hong Kong.
67. New China News Agency, September 19, 1966.
68. New China News Agency, September 23, 1966.
69. *Red Guard Daily* (Canton), No. 15 (December 22, 1966), *JPRS*, No. 383 (March 13, 1967), p. 1.
70. See his remarks in "Speech on September 25, 1966."
71. *Yomiuri Shimbun* (Tokyo), September 26, 1966, cited in Robinson, *op. cit.*
72. *Ibid.*
73. See Mao Tse-tung, "Speeches at Central Committee Work Conference," October 24–25, 1966, *Current Background*, No. 891 (October 8, 1969), pp. 70–75; see also *JPRS*, No. 90 (February 12, 1970), pp. 8–16.
74. Liu Shao-chi, "Self-Criticism," *Collected Works*, pp. 375ff.
75. Cited in *Nihon Keizai* (Tokyo), January 5, 1967; *Yomiuri* (Tokyo), January 10, 1967.
76. Ch'en Po-ta, "Speech on October 25, 1966 at Central Committee Conference," obtained from private sources.
77. New China News Agency, October 31, 1966.
78. Stanley Karnow, *The Washington Post*, November 12, 1966.
79. New China News Agency, December 3, 1966; see also *Peking Review*, November 9, 1966, p. 5.
80. New China News Agency, November 3, 1966.
81. Hunter, *op. cit.*, pp. 138–40.
82. From an interview conducted by the author in Hong Kong.
83. Bennett and Montaperto, *op. cit.*
84. See *Far Eastern Economic Review*, December 1, 1966, p. 477.
85. "Tao Chu Is the Khrushchev of Central-South China," in publication of the Revolutionary Rebel Liaison Center of Red Guards of Metro-

politan Universities and Colleges, February 22, 1967, *Current Background*, No. 824 (April 27, 1967), p. 2.

86. From private sources in Peking.
87. "Remove the Mask of Tao Chu as a 'Proletarian Revolutionary,' " *Peking Chingkangshan*, January 11, 1967, *Current Background*, No. 824 (April 27, 1967), p. 26.
88. *South China Morning Post* (Hong Kong), January 6, 1967.
89. *Yomiuri* (Tokyo), December 29, 1966.
90. *People's Daily* (Peking), December 25, 1966.
91. *Yomiuri* (Tokyo), January 4, 1967.
92. *Red Flag*, December 31, 1966.

Chapter 10. *The January Tempest*

1. Mao Tse-tung, "Talk to Foreign Visitors," August 31, 1967, *SCMP*, No. 4200 (June 18, 1968), p. 3.
2. Wall poster, March 4, 1967, *China Topics* (Hong Kong), March 10, 1967.
3. This and the following quotations from Mao Tse-tung, "Talk to Foreign Visitors," *op. cit.*, pp. 2–4.
4. New China News Agency, December 31, 1966.
5. Tanjug News Agency, December 7, 1966; *Izvestia* (Moscow), December 11, 1966.
6. "Comment of the Chinese Communist Party Central Committee on the Transmission of the Report of the Work Group Concerning the Problem of Lo Jui-ch'ing's Mistakes," May 16, 1966, *Chinese Communist Party Documents of the Great Proletarian Cultural Revolution* (Hong Kong, 1968), pp. 31–32.
7. "Struggle Meeting Against P'eng Chen *et al.*," January 5, 1967, *SCMP* (*Supp.*), No. 165 (March 10, 1967), pp. 1–5.
8. Chou En-lai, speech to a Red Guard conference, reported in *Tokyo Shimbun*, January 11, 1967; quoted in Thomas Robinson, "Chou En-lai and the Cultural Revolution in China," unpublished manuscript, the Rand Corporation (Santa Monica, Calif.), August 1971.
9. See *Current Scene*, May 31, 1967, pp. 11–12.
10. *Sankei* (Tokyo), January 9, 1967.
11. For the details of this incident, see *Current Scene*, May 31, 1967, pp. 7–11.
12. *Sankei* (Tokyo), January 16, 1967.
13. Agence France-Presse, March 28, 1968.
14. Neale Hunter, *Shanghai Journal* (New York, 1969), pp. 141ff.
15. *Ibid.*, pp. 153ff.
16. *Wen Hui Pao* (Shanghai), January 11, 1967.
17. Hunter, *op. cit.*, p. 213.
18. "Message of Greetings from Chinese Communist Party Central Committee, the State Council, the Military Commission and the Cultural

Reference Notes

Revolution Group to the Revolutionary Rebel Organizations in Shanghai," January 11, 1967, *Current Background*, No. 852 (May 6, 1968), p. 38.

19. Mao Tse-tung, "Speech at a Meeting of the Cultural Revolution Group," January 9, 1967, *Current Background*, No. 892 (October 21, 1969), p. 47.
20. *People's Daily* (Peking), January 22, 1967.
21. *Sankei* (Tokyo), January 21, 1967.
22. New China News Agency, February 1, 1967.
23. *China News Summary* (Hong Kong), January 19, 1967.
24. See Andrew Watson, "Showdown in Sian," *Far Eastern Economic Review*, May 18, 1967, pp. 404–406.
25. *Asahi* (Tokyo), January 24, 1967; also *The Washington Post*, January 23, 1967.
26. *Asahi* (Tokyo) and *Tokyo Shimbun*, January 8, 1967.
27. Urumchi Radio, September 14 and 16, 1966.
28. *Ibid.*, November 30, 1966.
29. Donald W. Klein and Anne B. Clark, *Biographic Dictionary of Chinese Communism 1921–1965* (Cambridge, Mass., 1971), p. 904.
30. William Whitson, "The Concept of Military Generation: The Chinese Communist Case," unpublished manuscript, July 1968.
31. "The January 26 Counter-Revolutionary Sanguinary Incident at Shih-ho-tzu Sinkiang," mimeographed handbill by Sinkiang rebel groups, January 20, 1967, *SCMP* (*Supp.*), No. 185 (May 27, 1967), pp. 1–4.
32. *Nihon Keizai* (Tokyo), January 26, 1967; *Mainichi* (Tokyo), January 28, 1967.
33. "Accusation by a Comrade-in-Arms Saved from the Mouth of a Tiger," *Tienshan Beacon Fire*, January 15, 1968, *Current Background*, No. 855 (June 17, 1968), pp. 5–8.
34. *Mainichi* (Tokyo), January 29, 1967.
35. *China Topics*, February 20, 1969; *Nihon Keizai* (Tokyo), February 1, 1967.
36. "Regulations of the Chinese Communist Party Central Committee, the State Council and the Military Commission of the Central Committee," February 11, 1967, *Current Background*, No. 852 (May 6, 1968), pp. 68–71.
37. Gordon A. Bennett and Ronald N. Montaperto, *Red Guard* (New York, 1971), p. 153.
38. Canton Radio, January 11, 1967.
39. *South China Morning Post* (Hong Kong), January 14, 1967.
40. Bennett and Montaperto, *op. cit.*, p. 154.
41. "Some Views on Present Situation of the Great Proletarian Cultural Revolution in the Canton Area," Kwangtung *Red Guard*, February 10, 1967, *SCMP*, No. 3929 (May 1, 1967), p. 3.
42. "Facts of the January 22 Seizure of Power," *ibid.*, p. 8.
43. "Message from the Chinese Communist Party Kwangtung Provincial

Committee to all Party Members, Cadres, and the People of the Province," *ibid.*, p. 12.

44. "Facts of the January 22 Seizure of Power," *ibid.*, p. 7.
45. New China News Agency, January 28, 1967.
46. "News in Brief," *Red Banner* (Peking), January 30, 1967, *SCMP* (*Supp.*), No. 176 (April 14, 1967), p. 28.
47. "Drag Out the Handful of Counter-Revolutionaries in the 'Hui Nationality Rebel Regiment' to Face the Public," *Pei-ching Jih-pao* (Peking), February 12, 1967, *SCMP* (*Supp.*), No. 177 (April 19, 1967), pp. 29–32.
48. *Asahi* (Tokyo), January 10, 1967.
49. These and following quotations from Chiang Ch'ing, "Revolutionary Rebels Should Form a Great Alliance and Seize Power after the Pattern of the Paris Commune," *New Peking University*, January 28, 1967, *SCMP* (*Supp.*), No. 174 (April 10, 1967), p. 14.
50. Chiang Ch'ing, "Speech on January 17, 1967," *Railway Red Banner*, January 20, 1967, *SCMP* (*Supp.*), No. 171 (March 30, 1967), p. 11.
51. *Nihon Keizai* (Tokyo), January 7, 1967.
52. "News in Brief," *Red Banner* (Peking), January 30, 1967.
53. *Red Banner News*, published by the South China Technical College, September 10, 1967.
54. "Whom Are Such Schools Meant For?" *Criticism and Reform in Middle Schools* (Peking), June 19, 1967, *SCMP* (*Supp.*), No. 200 (August 31, 1967), p. 33.
55. *Ibid.*, p. 30.
56. Bennett and Montaperto, *op. cit.*, pp. 137–41.
57. *Sankei* (Tokyo), October 7, 1967.
58. "See What Kind of Goods the 'United Action Committee' Is," *Chingkangshan* (Peking), January 23, 1967, *SCMP*, No. 3905 (March 23, 1967), p. 16.
59. *Sankei* (Tokyo), October 7, 1967.
60. "What the Commotion of the 'United Action Committee' Has Explained," *Peking Middle School Cultural Revolution Paper*, February 10, 1967, *SCMP* (*Supp.*), No. 183 (May 16, 1967), pp. 18–19.
61. *Life*, April 30, 1971.
62. See Philip Bridgham, "Mao's Cultural Revolution in 1967: The Struggle to Seize Power," *China Quarterly*, No. 34 (April–June 2968), p. 10.
63. "Ch'en Po-ta and Chiang Ch'ing Talk to Students," January 26, 1967, *The East Is Red* (Peking), February 4, 1967.

Chapter 11. The Revolt of the Proletariat

1. *Red Flag*, January 12, 1967.
2. *Current Scene*, VI, No. 5 (March 15, 1968), p. 18.
3. "Three Years of Blood and Tears," *Canton Aid-Agriculture Red Flag*

(Canton), No. 7, (January 1968), *China Topics* (Hong Kong), May 27, 1968.

4. *Revolutionary Youth* (Canton), November 10, 1967.
5. See *Current Scene*, VI, No. 5, p. 21.
6. *Ibid.*, pp. 4–6.
7. See Philip Bridgham, "Mao's Cultural Revolution in 1967: The Struggle to Seize Power," in *China Quarterly*, No. 34 (April–June 1968), pp. 8–9.
8. See Neale Hunter, "Port in a Storm," *Far Eastern Economic Review*, June 22, 1967, pp. 663–67.
9. See *ibid.*
10. *Mainichi* (Tokyo), February 28, 1967.
11. *China News Analysis* (Hong Kong), No. 65 (March 10, 1967), p. 5.
12. New China News Agency, January 11, 1967.
13. *Current Scene*, V, No. 8 (May 19, 1967), p. 3.
14. *People's Daily* (Peking), January 20, 1967.
15. *Current Scene*, V, No. 8, p. 4.
16. *Asahi* (Tokyo), February 11, 1967.
17. "News for Reference," *Revolutionary Workers' Paper* (Peking), January 20, 1967, *SCMP* (*Supp.*), No. 169 (March 20, 1967), p. 10.
18. New China News Agency, March 3, 1967.
19. *Asahi* (Tokyo), January 12, 1967.
20. *Kwangming Daily* (Peking), January 20, 1967.
21. *Nihon Keizai* (Tokyo), January 16, 1967.
22. *Current Scene*, V, No. 8, p. 13.
23. "News for Reference," p. 10.
24. Li Hsin, "Denounce Hsiao Wang-tung's Crimes of Practicing Economism," *Marching Journal* (Peking), January 28, 1967, *SCMP* (*Supp.*), No. 174 (April 10, 1967), pp. 10–11.
25. "Smash Anti-Revolutionary Economism," in *ibid.*, pp. 8–9.
26. *Nihon Keizai* (Tokyo), January 12, 1967.
27. Mainichi (Tokyo), February 18, 1967.
28. *Sankei* (Tokyo), January 19, 1967.
29. *Yomiuri* (Tokyo), February 4, 1967.
30. Kiangsi Radio, January 30, January 23, 1967; Kiangsu Radio, January 24, 1967; Canton Radio, January 17, 1967; New China News Agency, January 15, 1967; *Wen Hui Pao* (Shanghai), January 20, 1967; Fukien Radio, January 24, 1967; *People's Daily* (Peking), January 23, 1967; New China News Agency, January 26, 1967.
31. "An Appeal to All Revolutionary Commune Members and Poor, Middle and Lower Peasants," Shanghai wall poster, January 14, 1967.
32. *Wen Hui Pao* (Shanghai), February 12, 1967.
33. *Liberation Daily* (Shanghai), February 16, 1967; see also *Current Scene*, V, No. 16 (October 2, 1967), p. 7.
34. *Wen Hui Pao* (Shanghai), January 5, 1967.

35. *Ibid.* January 9, 1967.
36. See Neale Hunter. *Shanghai Journal* (New York, 1969), p. 215.
37. *Ibid.*
38. *Ibid.*, p. 218.
39. "Document of the Chinese Communist Party Central Committee, the State Council and the Military Commission," January 11, 1967, *Current Background*, No. 852 (May 6, 1968), p. 39.
40. *Yomiuri* (Tokyo), January 19, 1967.
41. "Notification by the Chinese Communist Party Central Committee on Opposition to Economism," January 11, 1967, *Current Background*, No. 852, pp. 40–41.
42. "Notification by the Chinese Communist Party Central Committee Concerning Broadcasting Stations," January 11, 1967, *ibid.*, p. 43.
43. *People's Daily* (Peking), January 30, 1967.
44. Hunter, *Shanghai Journal*, p. 220.
45. Chou En-lai, speech of January 17, 1967, in *Railway Red Banner*, SCMP (*Supp.*), No. 171 (March 30, 1967), p. 12.
46. *Asahi* (Tokyo), January 12, 1967.
47. Chou En-lai, "Directive to the Proletarian Revolutionary Rebels," *Red Staff Members and Workers* (Peking), January 29, 1967, *JPRS*, No. 396 (May 22, 1967), p. 4.

Chapter 12. Out of the Barrel of a Gun

1. "Decision of the Chinese Communist Party Central Committee, the State Council, the Military Commission of the Central Committee and the Cultural Revolution Group on Resolute Support for the Revolutionary Masses of the Left," January 23, 1967, *Current Background*, No. 852 (May 6, 1968), p. 49.
2. Mao Tse-tung, "A Talk to Foreign Visitors," August 31, 1967, *SCMP*, No. 4200 (June 18, 1968), p. 3.
3. Mao Tse-tung, "Speech at the Enlarged Meeting of the Military Commission" (as relayed by Premier Chou En-lai on January 27, 1967), *Current Background*, No. 892 (October 21, 1969), p. 49.
4. *Peking Review*, October 14, 1966, p. 3.
5. William W. Whitson, *The Political Dynamics of the Chinese Communist Military Elite* (privately printed, Hong Kong, 1969), p. 15.
6. "Urgent Directive of the Military Commission and the General Political Department on the Great Proletarian Cultural Revolution in Military Academies and Schools," October 5, 1966, *Current Background*, No. 852, pp. 19–20.
7. Whitson, *op. cit.*, p. 14.
8. Ho Lung, "Speech at Meeting of Revolutionary Teachers, Students and Staffs of Various Military Colleges and Schools of the Whole People's Liberation Army Who Have Come to Establish Revolutionary Experi-

ences in Peking," November 13, 1966, *SCMM* (*Supp.*), No. 16 (June 5, 1967), pp. 34–35.

9. Yeh Chien-ying, "Speech at the Cultural Revolution Rally of All Army Academies," October 5, 1966, *Current Background*, No. 819 (March 10, 1967), pp. 63–64.

10. Hsu Hsiang-ch'en, "Speech at Meeting of Revolutionary Teachers, Students and Staffs . . . in Peking," November 13, 1966, *SCMM* (*Supp.*), No. 16 (June 5, 1967), pp. 34–35.

11. *Liberation Army Daily* (Peking), January 14, 1967.

12. "Down with Ho Lung, Conspirator Seeking to Usurp Power in the Party, the Government and the Army," *New Peking University*, January 20, 1967; "Down with Ho Lung," pamphlet compiled by the Chingkang Mountain Corps, Tsinghua University, November 1967, *Current Background*, No. 859 (August 8, 1968), pp. 2, 15, 24–25.

13. "Black Line of Ho Lung's Clique," *Physical Culture Combat Bulletin*, November 14, 1967, cited in *Current Background*, No. 859, p. 27.

14. *Asahi* (Tokyo), May 8, 1967.

15. *Sankei* (Tokyo), May 9, 1967.

16. *Mainichi* (Tokyo), February 7, 1967.

17. "Down with the Old Swine Chu Teh," *The East Is Red* (Peking), February 11, 1967, *SCMP* (*Supp.*), No. 172 (April 3, 1967), p. 21.

18. *Ashai* (Tokyo), January 24, 1967; Whitson, *op. cit.*, p. 18.

19. *Sankei* (Tokyo), February 2, 1967.

20. *China Topics* (Hong Kong), January 19, 1967.

21. "Directive of the Military Commission of the Central Committee Reiterating the Implementation of the Cultural Revolution Stage by Stage and Group by Group in Military Regions," January 28, 1967, *Current Background*, No. 852 (May 18, 1968), p. 56.

22. "Instruction to the People's Liberation Army" (as relayed by Vice-Chairman Yeh Chien-ying on January 27, 1967), *Current Background*, No. 892 (October 21, 1969), p. 50.

23. "Order of the Military Commission of the Central Committee," January 28, 1967, *Current Background*, No. 852, p. 54.

24. "Notification by the Chinese Communist Party Central Committee and the State Council Concerning the Question of Exchange of Revolutionary Experiences on Foot by Revolutionary Teachers, Students and Red Guards," February 3, 1967, *ibid.*, p. 59.

25. "Supplementary Notice of the Chinese Communist Party Central Committee Concerning the Question of Broadcasting Stations," January 23, 1967; "Order of the State Council and the Military Commission of the Central Committee Concerning the Takeover of the Civil Aviation System by the Army," January 26, 1967, in *ibid.*, pp. 51, 53.

26. Thomas W. Robinson, "Chou En-lai and the Cultural Revolution in China" (unpublished manuscript), p. 80.

27. Lin Piao, "Speech on March 30, 1967," obtained from a private source.

28. "Document of the Chinese Communist Party Central Committee, the

State Council and the Military Commission," January 11, 1967, *Current Background*, No. 852, p. 39.

29. "Document of the Chinese Communist Party Central Committee," January 19, 1967, *ibid.*, p. 48.
30. "Notification by the Chinese Communist Party Central Committee Ordering That the Spearhead of Struggle May Not Be Directed Against the Armed Forces," January 14, 1967, *ibid.*, p. 46.
31. *Mainichi* (Tokyo), January 25, 1967.
32. *Yomiuri* (Tokyo), January 24, 1967.
33. Neale Hunter, *Shanghai Journal* (New York, 1969), pp. 244ff.
34. *Wen Hui Pao* (Shanghai), February 6, 1967.
35. Mao Tse-tung, "Speech at His Third Meeting with Chang Ch'un-ch'iao and Yao Wen-yuan," February 1967, *JPRS*, No. 90 (February 12, 1970), p. 44; wall poster, March 4, 1967, *China Topics* (Hong Kong), March 10, 1967.
36. Ellis Joffe, "The Chinese Army in the Cultural Revolution: The Politics of Intervention," *Current Scene*, VIII, No. 8 (December 7, 1970), pp. 10–11.
37. New China News Agency, January 24, 1967.
38. Private source in Hong Kong.
39. New China News Agency, January 24, 1967.
40. *Kwangming Daily* (Peking), March 23, 1967.
41. *Red Flag*, No. 4, cited on Peking Radio, February 27, 1967.
42. *Red Flag*, February 1967, *SCMM*, No. 566 (March 6), 1967, p. 1.
43. Donald W. Klein and Anne B. Clark, *Biographic Dictionary of Chinese Communism 1921–1965* (Cambridge, Mass., 1971), pp. 708–10; and Parris H. Chang, "The Revolutionary Committee in China," *Current Scene*, VI, No. 9 (June 1, 1968), p. 8.
44. Chang, *op. cit.*, p. 4; *People's Daily* (Peking), March 21, 1967.
45. Peking Domestic Service, February 9, 1967.
46. New China News Agency, February 1, 1967.
47. *People's Daily* (Peking), February 2, 1967.
48. *Red Flag*, No. 5 (March 1967), *SCMM*, No. 572 (April 17, 1967), p. 11.
49. "The People's Liberation Army Takeover of the Municipal Public Security Bureau Is Very Fine," and "The People's Liberation Army Takes Over Control of the Municipal Public Security Bureau," *Peiching Jih-pao* (Peking), February 12, 1967, *SCMP (Supp.)*, No. 174 (April 10, 1967), pp. 1–3.
50. *China News Summary* (Hong Kong), March 15, 1967.
51. "Documents of the Chinese Communist Party Central Committee," *Current Background*, No. 852, p. 96.
52. "Chinese Communist Party Central Committee's Letter to Poor and Lower-Middle Peasants and Cadres at All Levels in Rural People's Communes Throughout the Country," *ibid.*, p. 90.
53. New China News Agency, March 22, 1967.

54. This and the following data from an interview conducted by the author in Hong Kong.
55. Chou En-lai, "Talk to Revolutionary Rebels of Industrial and Communications Departments," February 1, 1967, *Red Staff Members and Workers*, March 2, 1967, *SCMP* (*Supp.*), No. 178 (April 24, 1967), p. 21ff.
56. See *The Washington Post*, February 25, 1967.
57. *Asahi* (Tokyo), February 18, 1967.
58. Philip Bridgham, "Mao's Cultural Revolution in 1967: The Struggle to Seize Power," *The China Quarterly*, No. 34 (April–June, 1968), p. 13.
59. *Mainichi* (Tokyo), February 25, 1967.
60. New China News Agency, February 3, 1967.
61. *South China Morning Post* (Hong Kong), February 27, 1967.
62. New China News Agency, March 2, 1967.
63. *Ibid.*
64. *Red Flag*, February 23, 1967.
65. *People's Daily* (Peking), February 15, 1967.
66. Kweichow Radio, March 8, 1967.
67. *People's Daily* (Peking), February 26, 1967.
68. New China News Agency, February 27, 1967.
69. *Red Flag*, March 1967.

Chapter 13. The Army Attempts to Rule

1. Peking Radio, January 30, 1967.
2. *China Topics* (Hong Kong), April 25, 1967.
3. Lin Piao, "Speech on March 30, 1967," from a private source.
4. *China News Summary* (Hong Kong), March 27, 1969.
5. *People's Daily* (Peking), February 24, 1967.
6. Ellis Joffe, "The Chinese Army in the Cultural Revolution: The Politics of Intervention," *Current Scene*, VIII, No. 8 (December 7, 1970), pp. 13–14.
7. See Stanley Karnow, *The Washington Post*, May 25, 1967.
8. Lin Piao, "Report to the Ninth National Congress of the Communist Party of China," April 14, 1969, in *Current Background*, No. 880 (May 9, 1969), p. 30.
9. Lin Piao, "Speech on March 30, 1967."
10. See Victor C. Falkenheim, "The Cultural Revolution in Kwangsi, Yunnan, and Fukien," *Asian Survey*, IX, No. 8 (August 1969), pp. 582–84.
11. *Ibid.*, pp. 587–88.
12. See "Yunnan Provincial Revolutionary Committee Born in the Midst of Armed Clashes," *Facts and Features* (Taipei), I, No. 24 (September 18, 1968), pp. 11–13.
13. Falkenheim, *op. cit.*, pp. 591–93; New China News Agency (Foochow), February 16, 1967.

14. "Regulations of the Chinese Communist Party Central Committee, the State Council and the Military Commission of the Central Committee," February 11, 1967, *Current Background*, No. 852 (May 18, 1968), pp. 68–70.
15. Urumchi Radio, February 11, 1967.
16. Tashkent Radio, February 18 and 23, 1967.
17. From a private source in Alma Ata.
18. Paul Hayer and William Heaton, "The Cultural Revolution in Inner Mongolia," *The China Quarterly*, No. 36 (October–December 1968), pp. 116–18.
19. *Ibid.*, p. 119.
20. Agence France-Presse (Peking), January 26, 1967.
21. Hayer and Heaton, *op. cit.*, pp. 122ff.
22. See Stanley Karnow, *The Washington Post*, May 25, 1971.
23. "Chronology of the Cultural Revolution in the Tibet Region," *Red Rebel Paper* (Lhasa), August 6, 1967, *SCMP* (*Supp.*), No. 216 (January 26, 1968), pp. 30–31.
24. *China Topics* (Hong Kong), August 30, 1968.
25. *Hindustan Times* (New Delhi), October 24, 1967.
26. *China Topics* (Hong Kong), August 30, 1968.
27. *Ibid.*
28. Agence France-Presse (Gangtok, Sikkim), February 16, 1967.
29. "Please See How Cruelly the Handful of Persons in the Military Region Party Committee Persecuted the Rebels," a Lhasa handbill, February 10, 1967, *SCMP* (*Supp.*), No. 179 (April 26, 1967), p. 113.
30. "Chronology of Cultural Revolution in Tibet," p. 39.
31. *China Topics* (Hong Kong), August 30, 1968.
32. "Chronology of Cultural Revolution in Tibet," p. 40.
33. *Ibid.*, p. 41.
34. "Stalemate in Szechwan," *Current Scene*, VI, No. 11 (July 1, 1968), p. 6.
35. Cited in Thomas Jay Matthews, "The Cultural Revolution in Szechwan" (unpublished manuscript), June 1971.
36. See *ibid.*
37. "Stalemate in Szechwan," p. 6.
38. *Ibid.*, pp. 6–7.
39. "A Bloodstained Scrap of Paper," *Combat Corps News* (Peking), May 30, 1967, in *SCMP* (*Supp.*), No. 191 (July 14, 1967), p. 11.
40. New China News Agency, February 24, 1967.
41. *China Topics* (Hong Kong), August 18, 1967.
42. Kweichow Radio, July 13, 1967.
43. "A Bloodstained Scrap of Paper," p. 11; "Important Speeches of Central Leaders on March 15, 1968," *SCMP*, No. 4181 (May 20, 1968), p. 2.
44. Parris H. Chang, "The Revolutionary Committee in China," *Current Scene*, VI, No. 9 (June 1, 1968), p. 10.

45. "A Short Talk with Revolutionary People in the Capital on the Great Proletarian Cultural Revolution in Honan," *Honan Revolutionary Rebel General Command Post*, March 8, 1967, SCMP (*Supp.*), No. 185 (June 22, 1967), p. 6.
46. *Ibid.*, pp. 11–12.
47. *Ibid.*
48. Premier Chou En-lai, Directive of February 17, 1967, SCMP (*Supp.*), No. 177 (April 19, 1967), p. 23.
49. Chang, *op. cit.*, p. 11.
50. "Order of the Military Commission of the Party Central Committee," February 8, 1967, SCMP, No. 3900 (March 16, 1967), p. 1.
51. Gordon A. Bennett and Ronald N. Montaperto, *Red Guard* (New York, 1971).
52. See Donald W. Klein and Anne B. Clark, *Biographic Dictionary of Chinese Communism 1921–65* (Cambridge, Mass., 1971), pp. 405–406.
53. "Who Led the Doctrine Guards Astray?" *Red Banner News* (Canton), September 10, 1967.
54. See Ezra Vogel, *Canton Under Communism* (Cambridge, Mass., 1969), pp. 329–30.
55. Bennett and Montaperto, *op. cit.*
56. *Ibid.*
57. *Ibid.*
58. "The Crimes of Wu Chuan-pin, a Counter-Revolutionary Bug," *Sun Yat-sen University Combat Bulletin* (Canton), August 4, 1968, SCMP, No. 4257 (November 13, 1968), pp. 1–5.
59. "Supreme Directive of the Kwangtung Military District," March 1, 1967, SCMP, No. 3905 (March 23, 1967), pp. 1–6.
60. "Report on an Investigation into the Facts of Persecution of the August First Combat Corps," *Steel August First* (Canton), October 15, 1967, SCMP, No. 4096 (January 10, 1968), pp. 1–8.
61. "Kwangtung Provincial Military District Command's Self-Criticism," *ibid.*, pp. 9–12.
62. Bennett and Montaperto, *op. cit.*

Chapter 14. The Radical Resurgence

1. *Asahi* (Tokyo), March 16, 1967.
2. Chou En-lai, "Speech to Representatives of Different Parties and Different Departments of the State Council," April 30, 1967, from a private source.
3. *Asahi* (Tokyo), March 16, 1967.
4. *Ibid.*
5. K'uai Ta-fu, "Analysis of the Present Situation," *Red Worker* (Nanking), March 24, 1967, SCMP (*Supp.*), No. 188 (June 22, 1967), pp. 1–3.

6. *Red Flag*, March 9 and 22, 1967.
7. Lin Chieh, "Courageously Forging Ahead in the Teeth of Great Storms of Class Struggle," *Red Flag*, April 3, 1967.
8. Mao Tse-tung, "Conversation with Premier Chou En-lai on Power Struggle," Jerome Ch'en, *Mao Papers* (New York, 1970), pp. 48–49.
9. From interviews conducted by the author in Hong Kong.
10. See *South China Morning Post* (Hong Kong), April 14, 1967.
11. See *Tokyo Shimbun*, January 11, 1967.
12. See *Yomiuri* (Tokyo), April 10, 1967.
13. See *Asahi* (Tokyo), March 27, 1967.
14. *The Washington Post*, April 3, 1967.
15. Ch'i Pen-yu, "Patriotism or National Betrayal?" *Red Flag*, April 1, 1967.
16. Liu Shao-ch'i, "Confession," Summer 1967, *Collected Works* (Hong Kong, 1969), pp. 365–68.
17. *People's Daily* (Peking), April 8, 1967.
18. Liu Shao-ch'i, "How to Be a Good Communist," *Collected Works*, pp. 162–63.
19. "Down with Liu Shao-ch'i," pamphlet published by the Chingkangshan Fighting Corps of the Fourth Hospital, Peking, May 1967, *Current Background*, No. 834 (August 17, 1967).
20. This quotation and the following material from "Three Trials of Pickpocket Wang Kuang-mei," pamphlet compiled by the South Sea Great Wall Fighting Detachment of the Chingkangshan Corps, Tsinghua University, *Current Background*, No. 848 (February 27, 1968), pp. 1–39; also *Current Scene*, VI, No. 6 (April 15, 1968).
21. Wang Kuang-mei, "Letter of April 20, 1967," and "Self-Examination of June 28, 1967," *Current Background*, No. 848, pp. 40–41.
22. *Asahi* (Tokyo), April 6, 1967.
23. Robinson, *op. cit.*
24. From a private source in Peking.
25. "What Ch'en Yi Did in Yunnan," January 23, 1967, based on information supplied to Huang Feng-lin, Director of the Public Relations Department of Yunnan, *SCMM*, No. 635 (December 2, 1968), p. 6.
26. Melvin Gurtov, *The Foreign Ministry and Foreign Affairs in China's Revolution*, a Rand Corporation memorandum (Santa Monica, Calif., March, 1969), p. 5.
27. "Ch'en Yi Is an Active Vanguard in Blowing Up the December Dark Wind," *Red Banner*, April 6, 1967, *SCMP (Supp.)*, No. 183 (May 16, 1967).
28. "Ch'en Yi's Self-Examination," January 24, 1967, pamphlet published by the Red Guards of the Second Foreign Languages Institute, *SCMM*, No. 636 (December 9, 1968), pp. 5–6.
29. "Speeches by Ch'en Po-ta and Chou En-lai," January 24, 1967, *ibid.*, p. 7.
30. *Red Guard Combat Paper* (Canton), April 8, 1967.

31. Ch'en Yi, "Speech of February 12, 1967," *SCMM*, No. 636 (December 9, 1968), p. 25.
32. Stanley Karnow, *The Washington Post*, May 9, 1967.
33. Gurtov, *op. cit.*, pp. 27–28; Reuters (Peking), May 15, 1967.
34. Gurtov, *op. cit.*, p. 30.
35. New China News Agency, April 30 and May 1, 1967.
36. See "Drag Out Yao Teng-shan, Big Political Pickpocket," *Red Guard Paper* (Peking), September 15, 1967, *SCMP (Supp.)*, No. 213 (December 13, 1967), pp. 4–5.
37. "T'an Chen-lin's Black Words," *Red Guard News*, April 5, 1967, *SCMP (Supp.)*, No. 238 (November 8, 1968), p. 8.
38. "T'an Chen-lin in the 'February Adverse Current,' " *Sun Yat-sen University Red Flag* (Canton), April 4, 1968, *SCMP*, No. 4169 (May 2, 1968), p. 7.
39. "Manifestations of the 'February Adverse Current' in the Ministry of Agriculture," *Red Guard News*, April 5, 1967, *SCMP (Supp.)*, No. 238 (November 8, 1968), p. 12.
40. "T'an Chen-lin in the 'February Adverse Current,' " p. 9.
41. "Manifestations of the 'February Adverse Current' in the Ministry of Agriculture," p. 12.
42. "Look at T'an Chen-lin, Filial Scion of the Landlord Class," *New Agriculture,* p. 12.

Chapter 15. The Troubled Spring

1. "Decision of the Chinese Communist Party Central Committee on the Question of Anhwei," March 27, 1967; "Decision of the Chinese Communist Party Central Committee on the Handling of the Inner Mongolia Question," April 13, 1967; and "Decision of the Chinese Communist Party Central Committee, the State Council, the Military Commission of the Central Committee, and the Cultural Revolution Group Concerning the Question of Tsinghai," March 24, 1967, *Current Background*, No. 852 (May 6, 1968), pp. 109–19 *passim*.
2. "Document of the Chinese Communist Party Central Committee," April 1, 1967, *ibid.*, pp. 111–12.
3. "Order of the Military Commission of the Chinese Communist Party Central Committee," *ibid.*, pp. 115–16.
4. See William W. Whitson, *The Political Dynamics of the Chinese Communist Military Elite* (privately printed, Hong Kong, 1969), p. 33.
5. *Yomiuri* (Tokyo), May 27, 1967.
6. See Philip Bridgham, "Mao's Cultural Revolution in 1967: The Struggle to Seize Power," *China Quarterly*, No. 34 (April–June 1968), p. 20.
7. *Liberation Army Daily* (Peking), April 20, 1967.
8. *Red Flag*, May 12, 1967.
9. See Bridgham, *loc. cit.*

10. "Report to the Revolutionary Masses on the Public Examination of Mistakes Made in the Work of Supporting the Left," submitted by the Shantung Provincial Revolutionary Committee and Tsinan Military District to the Cultural Revolution Group, May 31, 1967, reprinted in *Canton Medical College Red Flag*, July 10, 1967, *SCMP*, No. 4061 (November 16, 1967), pp. 11–12; "Document of the Chinese Communist Party Central Committee," *Current Background*, No. 852, p. 13.

11. *Nihon Keizai* (Tokyo), April 7, 1967.

12. Chiang Ch'ing, "Do New Services for the People," April 13, 1967, *The East Is Red* (Peking), June 3, 1967, *SCMP* (*Supp.*), No. 192, July 17, 1967, pp. 7–15.

13. *Wen Hui Pao* (Shanghai), April 28, 1967.

14. *People's Daily* (Peking), May 21, 1967.

15. Hsieh Fu-chih, "Speech to Peking University Red Guards," May 7, 1967, from a private source in Peking.

16. Bridgham, *op. cit.*, p. 20.

17. Hsieh Fu-chih, "Speech to Peking University Red Guards," May 7, 1967.

18. *Tokyo Shimbun*, May 5, 1967.

19. *Sankei* (Tokyo), May 31, 1967.

20. From a private source in Peking.

21. See *Asahi* (Tokyo), May 1, 1967.

22. *Ibid.*, April 27, 1967.

23. *Yomiuri* (Tokyo), May 20, 1967.

24. "The Strongest Protest," Shihchiachuang wall posters, June 13, 1967, *SCMP* (*Supp.*), No. 195 (July 31, 1967), pp. 18–19; *Sankei* (Tokyo), June 9, 1967.

25. *Mainichi* (Tokyo), May 31, 1967.

26. "Appalling Bloody Incident of June 6," Selected Big-Character Posters (Changsha), June 11, 1967, *SCMP* (*Supp.*), No. 193 (July 21, 1967), pp. 3–6.

27. *Asahi* (Tokyo), June 9, 1967; *Mainichi* (Tokyo), June 10, 1967.

28. "A Cruel Scene," Selected Big-Character Posters (Changsha), June 11, 1967, *SCMP* (*Supp.*), No. 193, p. 9.

29. "Letter of Accusation to the People of the Whole Country," untitled Red Guard newspaper, July 3, 1967, *SCMP*, No. 197 (August 14, 1967), pp. 31–35.

30. "Whither China?" January 6, 1968, *Printing System Red Flag*, March 1968, Union Research Service (Hong Kong), Vol. 51, Nos. 19 & 20, June 7, 1968. See also John Gittings, "Student Power in China," *Far Eastern Economic Review*, June 27, 1968, pp. 648–50.

31. Cited in *February Seven News* (Honan), June 5, 1967.

32. "Ho Yun-hung's Underground Twelve Black Articles," handbill distributed in Chengchow, April 12, 1967.

33. *February Seven News* (Honan), June 5, 1967.

34. Parris H. Chang, "The Revolutionary Committee in China," *Current Scene*, VI, No. 9 (June 1, 1968), p. 12.
35. Chengchow Radio, May 25, 1967.
36. "Long Premeditated Counter-Revolutionary Incident," *The East Is Red* (Peking), June 7, 1967, *SCMP* (*Supp.*), No. 192, (July 17, 1967), pp. 16–17.
37. "Fragrant Plants Thrive in Blood-Bathed Honan," *February Seven News* (Honan), June 5, 1967, in *ibid.*, pp. 22–23.
38. Chengchow Radio, May 26, 1967.
39. *Tokyo Shimbun*, June 2, 1967.
40. "The Hearts of Revolutionary Rebels Are Linked Together," *The East Is Red* (Peking), June 7, 1967, *SCMP* (*Supp.*), No. 192, pp. 19–21.
41. *Mainichi* (Tokyo), June 2, 1967.
42. Chengchow Radio, May 30, 1967.
43. *Ibid.*, June 1, 1967.
44. "Cudgels Cannot Strike Down Heroes Nor Can Spears Pierce the 'West Honan Group,'" *West Honan Combat Bulletin* (June 30, 1967), *SCMP* (*Supp.*), No. 197 (August 14, 1967), pp. 6–7.
45. "Heroic and Tenacious Are the Young Revolutionary Fighters of the 'August Sixteen' Corps" *ibid.*, p. 15.
46. See *The Washington Post*, June 3, 1967.
47. Chang, *op. cit.*, p. 18.
48. "Important Speeches of Central Leaders on March 15, 1968," *SCMP*, No. 4181 (May 20, 1968), p. 2; *China Topics* (Hong Kong), August 11, 1967.
49. Thomas J. Matthews, "The Cultural Revolution in Szechwan," (unpublished ms.) June 1971.
50. "Speeches at the Meeting for Reading the Chinese Communist Party Central Committee's Decision on the Handling of the Szechwan Question," *August 26 Gunfire* (Peking), May 12, 1967, *SCMP* (*Supp.*), No. 190 (July 6, 1967), p. 31.
51. "Chinese Communist Party Central Committee's Notice on the Rehabilitation of Comrade Lin Chieh-ting of Ipin District Party Committee, Szechwan Province," April 4, 1967, *Special Issue of Reference Material* (Canton), May 1968, *SCMP*, No. 4196 (June 12, 1968), p. 5.
52. *Asahi* (Tokyo), May 1, 1967.
53. Kyoto News Agency (Tokyo), May 8, 1967.
54. *Sankei* (Tokyo), May 18, 1967.
55. "Red Blood, Heroic Epic," *Red Flag News* (Peking), May 22, 1967, *SCMP* (*Supp.*), No. 189 (June 30, 1967), pp. 11–16.
56. "Only Sacrifice Can Show Your Strong Determination," *Red Flag News* (Peking), May 22, 1967, *ibid.*, pp. 1–10; "Greet the New High Tide in the Cultural Revolution in Szechwan," *August 26 Gunfire* (Peking), May 12, 1967, *SCMP* (*Supp.*), No. 190, pp. 23–26.

57. "Decision of the Chinese Communist Party Central Committee on the Handling of the Szechwan Question," May 7, 1967, *August 26 Gunfire* (Peking), May 12, 1967, *SCMP (Supp).*, No. 190, pp. 20–23.
58. "Speeches at the Meeting . . . on the Handling of the Szechwan Question," *ibid.*, p. 27.
59. *Ibid.*, pp. 29–30.
60. *Ibid.*, pp. 31–34.
61. *Ibid.*, p. 28.
62. "Important Speeches of Central Leaders on March 15, 1968," *SCMP*, No. 4181, pp. 1–10.
63. *Ibid.*, p. 5.
64. *Yomiuri* (Tokyo), May 9, 1967.
65. *Sankei* (Tokyo), May 23, 1967.
66. *Nihon Keizai* (Tokyo), May 23, 1967; "News from Chengtu," *Corps Combat News* (Peking), May 30, 1967, *SCMP (Supp.)*, No. 191, (July 14, 1967), p. 6.
67. "Statement of Congress of Red Guards on Surrendering of Arms and Ammunition, *ibid.*, pp. 13–14.
68. Matthews, *op. cit.*
69. Stanley Karnow, *The Washington Post*, August 6, 1967.
70. "News in Brief," *Storm Over Chungking*, June 14, 1967, *SCMP (Supp.)*, No. 192 (July 17, 1967), p. 2.
71. Matthews, *op. cit.*
72. *The New York Times*, June 16, 1967.
73. *Sankei* (Tokyo), June 23, 1967.
74. *Yomiuri* (Tokyo), June 8, 1967.
75. *The Washington Post*, May 25, 1967.
76. *South China Morning Post* (Hong Kong), June 15, 1967.
77. From an interview with Wu Shu-ting, former director of Chunghua Book Company, a Communist firm, following his defection to Taiwan, August 22, 1967.
78. Anthony Dicks, "The Hong Kong Situation," an Institute of Current World Affairs Study, September 5, 1967.
79. *South China Morning Post* (Hong Kong), May 1, 8, and 28, 1967.
80. Stanley Karnow, *The Washington Post*, May 19, 1967.
81. *Ibid.*, July 9, 1967.
82. *Ibid.*, July 10, 1967.
83. *Tiger Standard* (Hong Kong), August 21, 1967.
84. *South China Morning Post* (Hong Kong), August 25, 1967.
85. Yang Kwong, "Welcome to Greater Victory," speech delivered in Hong Kong, September 30, 1967, from a private source.
86. "Why Is *Hung-wei-chun* Said to Be an Illegal Organization," *Revolutionary Tower* (Shanghai), March 10, 1967, *SCMP (Supp.)*, No. 184 (May 24, 1967), pp. 21–22.
87. Shanghai Radio, June 9, 1967.

88. *Asahi* (Tokyo), July 23, 1967.
89. *Ibid.*, July 13, 1967.
90. "Circular Order of the Chinese Communist Party Central Committee, the State Council, the Central Military Commission, and the Cultural Revolution Group Concerning the Strict Prohibition of Armed Struggle, Illegal Arrest, and Looting and Sabotage," June 6, 1967, *Chinese Communist Party Documents of the Great Proletarian Revolution, op. cit.*, pp. 463–64.
91. Bridgham, *op. cit.*, p. 22.
92. *Ibid.*, p. 23; Joffe, *op. cit.*, p. 16.

Chapter 16. Explosion on the Yangtze

1. Kunming Radio, July 3, 1967.
2. Roderick MacFarquhar, *The Hundred Flowers* (London, 1960), pp. 130ff.
3. Thomas W. Robinson, *The Wuhan Incident: Local Strife and Provincial Rebellion During the Cultural Revolution* (The Rand Corporation, Santa Monica, Calif., December 1970), pp. 11–12.
4. William Whitson, "The Field Army in Chinese Communist Military Politics," *China Quarterly*, No. 37 (January–March 1969), pp. 1–30.
5. From an interview conducted by the author with William Whitson.
6. Deborah S. Davis, "The Cultural Revolution in Wuhan," unpublished manuscript; *Who's Who in Communist China* (Hong Kong, 1969), p. 399; "Truth of Persecution of Comrade Li Ta by T'ao Chu and Wang Jen-chung," *Outcry Combat Bulletin* (Canton), January 1968, *SCMP*, No. 4141 (March 19, 1968), pp. 1–13.
7. Davis, *op. cit.*
8. Wuhan Radio, September 16, 1966.
9. *Ibid.*, January 9, 1967.
10. *Ibid.*, February 3, 1967.
11. "A Brief Introduction to the Various Organizations in the Wuhan Area," *Second Steel Headquarters Thunderstorm*, July 27, 1967, *SCMP* (*Supp.*), No. 202 (September 11, 1967), pp. 9–11.
12. *Ibid.*, pp. 9–11; see also Robinson, *op. cit.*, p. 11.
13. "Speeches by Central Leaders at Reception of Tseng Ssu-yü, Liu Feng, and other Comrades of the Wuhan Military District," June 12–13, 1968, *Hung-ssu Tung-hsin* (Canton), July 12, 1968.
14. Wuhan Radio, February 18, 1967.
15. *Mainichi* (Tokyo), May 22, 1967.
16. *Yomiuri* (Tokyo), June 16, 1967.
17. "Wuhan Is in Critical Danger," *Red Rebel Headquarters* (Canton), July 15, 1967; "Some Iron-clad Proof of Ch'en Tsai-tao's Engineering of Counter-Revolutionary Rioting," combined edition of *Kang-erh-szu*

and *Wei Tung* (Wuhan), July 25, 1967; both in *SCMP* (*Supp.*), No. 202 (September 11, 1967), pp. 17–18.

18. "Most Solemn Declaration on the Wuhan Situation," a Peking wall poster, June 25, 1967.
19. "Some Iron-clad Proof of Ch'en Tsai-tao's Engineering of Counter-Revolutionary Rioting," pp. 18–19.
20. *Sankei* (Tokyo), September 29, 1967.
21. *Ibid.*
22. "Notes on Chairman Mao's Two Visits to Wuhan," *Cultural Revolution Bulletin* (Canton), April 1968, SCMP, No. 4172 (May 7, 1968), pp. 11–14.
23. *Sankei* (Tokyo), September 29, 1967; Robinson, *op. cit.*, p. 16; "The Wuhan Storm—An Account of the July 20 Incident," *Red Flag of the Peking Aeronautical Institute*, July 29, 1967.
24. "Important Talks of the Central Committee Leaders," *Chingkangshan* (Peking), July 26, 1967, *SCMP* (*Supp.*), No. 199 (August 24, 1967), p. 29.
25. Robinson, *op. cit.*, p. 17.
26. "The Wuhan Storm . . ."
27. Robinson, *op. cit.*, p. 19; "Important Talks of the Central Committee Leaders," p. 29.
28. Robinson, *loc. cit.*
29. *Sankei* (Tokyo), September 29, 1967; Robinson, *loc. cit.*
30. Stanley Karnow, *The Washington Post*, July 26, 1967.
31. "How Did Comrade Wang Li Escape from Danger?" Red Guard tabloid of the Wuhan New China Technical College, Kaiping edition, September 16, 1967, published by Union Research Service (Hong Kong), Vol. 48, No. 23 (September 19, 1967).
32. "The Wuhan Storm . . ."
33. *Sankei* (Tokyo), September 29, 1967; quoted in Robinson, *op. cit.*, p. 20.
34. *Ibid.*
35. New China News Agency, July 28, 1967; *People's Daily* (Peking), July 29, 1967.
36. Robinson, *op. cit.*, p. 24.
37. New China News Agency, July 29, 1967.
38. Stanley Karnow, *The Washington Post*, August 1, 1967.
39. Canton Radio, August 4, 1967; see also Robinson, *op. cit.*, p. 26.
40. *Nihon Keizai* (Tokyo), October 15, 1967.
41. *Sankei* (Tokyo), September 29, 1967.
42. See "An Account of the Struggle Against the Counter-Revolutionary Element Ch'en Tsai-tao," *Third Headquarters Combat Bulletin* (Canton), November 3, 1967, Union Research Service (Hong Kong), Vol. 49, No. 13 (November 14, 1967).
43. *Journalistic Soldiers* (Canton), November 9, 1967.

44. "Speeches by Central Leaders at Reception of Tseng Ssu-yü, Liu Feng, and other Comrades of the Wuhan Military District."
45. "Attack by Reasoning, Defend by Force," undated leaflet, Lhasa, *SCMP* (*Supp.*), No. 220 (March 8, 1968), p. 18.
46. See *ibid.*; *Sankei* (Tokyo), August 22, 1967; *Tokyo Shimbun*, August 31, 1967.
47. New China News Agency July 25, 1967.
48. *People's Daily* (Peking), July 30, 1967.
49. *Red Flag*, July 30, 1967; *People's Daily* (Peking), *Liberation Army Daily* (Peking), July 31, 1967.
50. *China News Summary* (Hong Kong), July 27, 1967.
51. Chien Yu-shen, *China's Fading Revolution* (Hong Kong, 1969), pp. 68–72.

Chapter 17. The Guns of August

1. A Peking wall poster, August 14, 1967.
2. See *Tokyo Shimbun*, August 31, 1967.
3. *Ibid.*, and *Sankei* (Tokyo), August 22, 1967.
4. Tsinan Radio, July 31, 1967; Stanley Karnow, *The Washington Post*, August 3, 1967.
5. Tsingtao Radio, August 12, 1967; Tsinan Radio, August 11, 1967.
6. "Important Talks of the Central Committee Leaders," *Chingnangshan* (Peking), July 26, 1967, *SCMP* (*Supp.*), No. 199, August 24, 1967, p. 24.
7. Ceteka News Agency (Prague), August 4, 1967.
8. Thomas J. Matthews, "The Cultural Revolution in Szechwan," unpublished manuscript.
9. Agence France-Presse, August 30, 1967.
10. Chien Yu-shen, *China's Fading Revolution* (Hong Kong, 1969), p. 27.
11. "Important Talks of Central Committee Leaders," *SCMP* (*Supp.*), No. 199, p. 24.
12. New China News Agency, August 20, 1967.
13. "Stalemate in Szechwan," *Current Scene*, VI, No. 11 (July 1, 1968), p. 10.
14. Matthews, *op. cit.*
15. "Speech by Comrade Chang Ku-hua at Meeting Inaugurating and Celebrating the Szechwan Provincial Revolutionary Committee," *Szechwan Daily*, June 2, 1968, *SCMP* (*Supp.*), August 19, 1968, p. 14.
16. Gordon A. Bennett and Ronald N. Montaperto, *Red Guard* (New York, 1971), p. 184.
17. "Canton Urgently Calls," *New South Uprooting Revisionism* (Canton), July 28, 1967, *SCMP* (*Supp.*), No. 199 (August 24, 1967), p. 7.
18. "An Eyewitness Account of the Tragic Case of Bloodshed on July 23," *The East Is Red* (Canton), August 2, 1967, *SCMP* (*Supp.*), No. 201, (September 5, 1967), pp. 1ff.

19. Bennett and Montaperto, *op. cit.*, p. 200.
20. "Premier Chou En-lai Receives Representatives of Canton Revolutionary Rebel Groups in Peking," *No. Three Headquarters Combat Bulletin,* August 24, 1967, SCMP, No. 4041 (October 13, 1967), pp. 11–13.
21. Bennett and Montaperto, *op. cit.*, p. 197.
22. *Sankei* (Tokyo), August 13, 1967; *South China Morning Post* (Hong Kong), August 14, 1967.
23. *Asahi* (Tokyo), August 23, 1967; *Sankei* (Tokyo), September 28, 1967.
24. Stanley Karnow, *The Washington Post,* August 18, 1967.
25. Bennett and Montaperto, *op. cit.*, pp. 201–202.
26. *China Topics* (Hong Kong), January 1968.
27. Liu Shao-ch'i, "Self-Examination," July 9, 1967, *Collected Works* (Hong Kong, 1969), pp. 369–77.
28. *Tokyo Shimbun,* August 3, 1967; *Sankei* (Tokyo), September 26, 1967.
29. *Asahi* (Tokyo), August 4, 1967.
30. See *Sankei* (Tokyo), and *Tokyo Shimbun,* August 16, 1967.
31. Stanley Karnow, *The Washington Post,* August 25, 1967.
32. *Sankei* (Tokyo), August 16, 1967.
33. I am indebted to Warren Unna for this information.
34. "Speech of Comrade Sydney Rittenberg, an American Friend, at an Oath-taking Rally for the Thorough Destruction of the Sinister Headquarters of Liu and Teng," *Corps Combat News* (Canton), May 8, 1967.
35. "A Mysterious American," *Cultural Revolution Bulletin,* March 1968, SCMP, No. 4165 (April 26, 1968), pp. 1–3.
36. "Bring to Public Notice Wang Li's August 7 Speech," *Red Guard Paper* (Peking), October 18, 1967, SCMP (*Supp.*), No. 214 (December 27, 1967), pp. 6–9.
37. Melvin Gurtov, *The Foreign Ministry and Foreign Affairs in China's Revolution,* a Rand Corporation memorandum (Santa Monica, Calif., March 1969), p. 54.
38. Stanley Karnow, *The Washington Post,* August 24, 1967.
39. Gurtov, *op. cit.*, pp. 58–61.
40. Stanley Karnow, *The Washington Post,* August 24, 1967.
41. Agence France-Presse, August 22, 1967; *Hong Kong Standard,* August 23, 1967; *Sankei* (Tokyo), October 3, 1967.
42. See Seymour Topping, *The New York Times,* June 21, 1971.
43. See William W. Whitson, *The Political Dynamics of the Chinese Communist Military Elite* (privately printed, Hong Kong, 1969), p. 35.
44. "Deputy Supreme Commander Lin's Important Directive," August 9, 1967, *Chu-ying Tung-fang-hung* (Canton), SCMP, No. 4036.
45. *Ibid.*, p. 3.
46. *Ibid.*, pp. 5–6.
47. Whitson, *op. cit.*, p. 37.
48. *Journalistic Soldiers* (Canton), November 6, 1967.
49. New China News Agency, September 2, 1967.

50. Chien, *op. cit.*, p. 70.
51. *Sankei* (Tokyo), August 12, 1967.
52. Chien Yu-shen, *loc. cit.*
53. "Drag Out Yao Teng-shan, Big Political Pickpocket," *Red Guard Paper* (Peking), September 15, 1967, SCMP (*Supp.*), No. 213 (December 13, 1967), pp. 4–5.
54. Seymour Topping, *The New York Times*, June 21, 1971.
55. "Order Issued by the Chinese Communist Party Central Committee, the State Council, Central Military Affairs Committee, the Central Cultural Revolution Group Forbidding Seizure of Arms, Equipment and Other Military Supplies from the People's Liberation Army," September 5, 1967, SCMP, No. 4026, September 22, 1967, pp. 1–2.
56. This and the following quotations from "Speech by Chiang Ch'ing on September 5 When the Central Leaders Received Anhwei Representatives for the Third Time," *Chingkang Mountains* (Peking), September 20, 1967, SCMP (*Supp.*), No. 209 (November 3, 1967), pp. 1–5; see also *China Topics* (Hong Kong), September 1967, and Stanley Karnow, *The Washington Post*, September 24, 1967.
57. *China Topics* (Hong Kong), September 1967.
58. Parris H. Chang, "The Fallen Idols," *Far Eastern Economic Review*, August 22, 1968, p. 352.
59. From a private source in Peking.

Chapter 18. Dialectics in Action

1. Lin Piao, "Report to the Ninth National Congress of the Communist Party of China," April 14, 1969, New China News Agency, April 27, 1969.
2. K'ang Sheng, "Summaries of Speeches by Members of the Central Cultural Revolution Group at an Enlarged Meeting of the Peking Revolutionary Committee," September 1, 1967, *China Topics* (Hong Kong), September 1967 (appendix).
3. "Great Supreme Commander Inspects Kiangsi Province," *Politics and Law Red Flag* (Canton), October 17, 1967, SCMP, No. 4070 (November 30, 1967), p. 6.
4. "Chairman Mao's Latest Supreme Instructions During His Inspection Tour in Central and Southern Parts of China," *ibid.*, p. 3.
5. *Rural Youth* (Shanghai), October 25, 1967, in Union Research Service (Hong Kong), Vol. 49, p. 138.
6. "Chairman Mao's Latest Instructions," *Cultural Revolution Bulletin* (Canton), October 9, 1967, in SCMP, No. 4060 (November 15, 1967), pp. 1–2; "Chairman Mao's Latest Supreme Instructions During His Inspection Tour . . ." SCMP, No. 4070, p. 3.
7. "Chairman Mao's Latest Instructions," SCMP, No. 4060, pp. 1–2.
8. New China News Agency, September 26, 1967.

9. *People's Daily* (Peking), September 9, 1967.
10. "Important Speeches of Central Leaders," September 17, 1967 (Canton: Pearl River Movie Studio, October 1, 1967), Union Research Service (Hong Kong), Vol. 49, 91–94.
11. "Premier Chou's Speech to the Representatives of the Mass Organizations of the Canton Area," September 27, 1967, *Red Rebel Paper* (Lhasa), October 12, 1967, *SCMP (Supp.)*, No. 215 (January 19, 1968), pp. 1–12.
12. See *China Topics* (Hong Kong), October 26, 1967.
13. Chenkiang Radio, September 17, 1967.
14. Peking Radio, September 19, 1967.
15. Hunan Radio, October 13 and 20, 1967.
16. New China News Agency, September 12, 1967.
17. *China News Summary* (Hong Kong), October 5, 1967.
18. "Important Speeches of Central Leaders," September 17, 1967, Union Research Service, Vol. 49, p. 92.
19. Jack Chen, "Treason at the Top," *Far Eastern Economic Review*, July 17, 1971, pp. 21–23.
20. *China Topics* (Hong Kong), September 1967.
21. *China News Summary* (Hong Kong), September 20, 1967.
22. See Stanley Karnow, *The Washington Post*, October 30, 1967.
23. *China News Summary* (Hong Kong), December 14, 1967; January 4, 1968.
24. Stanley Karnow, *The Washington Post*, January 11, 1968.
25. Philip Bridgham, "Mao's Cultural Revolution: The Struggle to Seize Power," *China Quarterly*, No. 41 (January–March 1970), p. 5.
26. "Speeches by Leaders of Central Committee," Canton pamphlet, October 1967, quoted in *ibid.*, p. 6.
27. "Chairman Mao's Latest Supreme Instructions . . ." *SCMP*, No. 4070, p. 3.
28. "Vice-Premier Hsieh Fu-chih's Important Speech on Questions of 'Ninth Party Congress' and 'Party Organization,'" October 26, 1967, *Cultural Revolution Bulletin* (Canton), December 11, 1967, *SCMP*, No. 4097 (January 11, 1968), pp. 1–2.
29. Jurgen Domes, "The Role of the Military in the Formation of Revolutionary Committees," *China Quarterly*, No. 44 (October–December 1970), pp. 122–23.
30. *Ibid.*, pp. 126–131.
31. Private sources in Hong Kong.
32. New China News Agency, October 20, 1967.
33. Shanghai Radio, February 12, 1968.
34. Honan Radio, February 14, 1968.
35. Anhwei Radio, January 16, 1968.
36. Inner Mongolia Radio, January 20, 1968.
37. *China Topics* (Hong Kong), May 21, 1968.

38. "Premier Chou's Talk at a Reception for Revolutionary Masses of X X Industrial Systems," *Cultural Revolution Storm* (Canton), February 1968, *SCMP*, No. 4148 (March 28, 1968), pp. 3–9.
39. *Wen Hui Pao* (Shanghai), September 16, 1967.
40. Anhwei Radio, January 19, 1968.
41. *Wei Hui Pao* (Shanghai), January 11, 1968.
42. Honan Radio, February 24, 1968.
43. William Whitson, "The Political Dynamics of the Chinese Communist Military Elite," unpublished manuscript, p. 45.
44. John Gittings, "Student Power in China," *Far Eastern Economic Review*, June 27, 1968, p. 648.
45. "Whither China?" January 6, 1968, *Printing Red Flag* (Canton), March 1968, *SCMP*, No. 4190 (June 4, 1968), pp. 1–18.
46. Quoted in Gittings, *op. cit.*, p. 650.
47. Whitson, *op. cit.*, p. 39.
48. *Wen Hui Pao* (Shanghai), December 31, 1967.
49. *Ibid.*, March 29, 1968.
50. Anhwei Radio, April 26, 1968.
51. Shanghai Radio, June 11, 1968.
52. "Nine-Point Instructions Given by Vice Supreme Commander Lin During His Reception of All Comrades of the Party Committee of the Air Force," *Cultural Revolution Bulletin* (Canton), March 1968, *SCMP*, No. 4164 (April 25, 1968), p. 6.
53. *Wen Hui Pao* (Shanghai), June 6, 1968.
54. "Important Speeches by Central Leaders on March 15," publisher and date unknown, *SCMP*, No. 4181 (May 20, 1968), p. 8; "Important Speeches by Central Leaders on March 18," *Red Rebel Corps*, Yingte Middle School, Kwangtung, *SCMP*, No. 4182 (May 21, 1968), p. 8.
55. "Speeches by Communist Leaders," *East Is Red* (Canton), April 1968, *SCMP*, No. 4168 (May 1, 1968), p. 4.
56. "Important Speeches by Central Leaders at 100,000-Man Rally in Peking on March 27," *Pearl River Film Studio East Is Red* (Canton), April 1968, *SCMP*, No. 4172, May 7, 1968, p. 2.
57. "Yang Cheng-wu's Eight Major Crimes," unnamed tabloid, May 1968, *SCMP*, No. 4168, May 27, 1968, pp. 1–5.
58. "An Important Speech by Vice-Chairman Lin at Reception of Army Cadres on March 25," *Kung-lien* (Canton), April 1968, *SCMP*, No. 4173 (May 8, 1968), pp. 2–4.
59. Whitson, *op. cit.*, p. 44.
60. "If Nieh Jung-chen Does Not Surrender, He Will Be Exterminated," *September 16 Bulletin* (Peking), August 1968, *SCMP*, No. 4240 (August 16, 1968), p. 3.
61. New China News Agency, July 31, 1967.
62. Ellis Joffe, "The Chinese Army in the Cultural Revolution: The Politics of Intervention," *Current Scene*, VIII, No. 8 (December 7, 1970), pp. 20–21.

hai), August 25, 1968, *SCMP* (*Supp.*), No. 235 (September 23, 1968), pp. 1–4.

8. "No Mischievous Acts Will Be Allowed!," *Red Guard Combat Bulletin* (Shanghai), August 15, 1968, *ibid.*, p. 14.

9. Chengtu Radio, September 4, 1968.

10. Shensi Radio, August 8, 1968.

11. Private source in Hong Kong.

12. Chekiang Radio, August 13, 1968.

13. Chekiang Radio, August 31 and September 11, 1968.

14. Stanley Karnow, *The Washington Post*, February 21, 1969.

15. Private source in Hong Kong.

16. New China News Agency, December 23, 1968.

17. *China Reporting Service* (Hong Kong), February 6, 1969; New China News Agency, December 22, 1969.

18. New China News Agency, January 21, 1969.

19. *Ibid.*, January 22, 1969.

20. Stanley Karnow, *The Washington Post*, December 10, 1969.

21. "Chairman Mao Sends His Son to Participate in Agricultural Production," *Red Guard Combat News* (Shanghai), December 30, 1968.

22. *China Topics* (Hong Kong), August 27, 1970; *The New York Times*, September 24, 1970.

23. I am indebted to John Pattison of Melbourne, Australia, for this report.

24. Stanley Karnow, *The Washington Post*, April 13, 1969.

25. Based on interviews in Hong Kong.

26. *People's Daily* (Peking), January 19, 1969.

27. Private sources in Hong Kong.

28. Stanley Karnow, *The Washington Post*, May 7, 1969.

29. Stanley Karnow, *The Washington Post*, June 3, 1970.

30. New China News Agency, October 10, 1969.

31. Colina MacDougall, "The Cultural Revolution in the Countryside: Back to 1958?" *Current Scene*, Vol. VII, No. 7 (April 11, 1969), pp. 7–10; Philip Bridgham, "Mao's Cultural Revolution in 1967: The Struggle to Seize Power," *China Quarterly*, No. 34 (April–June 1968), pp. 9–10.

32. *Red Flag*, August 25, 1968.

33. Bridgham, *op. cit.*, p. 10.

34. New China News Agency, November 24, 1968.

35. *Ibid.*, August 25, 1968.

36. Stanley Karnow, *The Washington Post*, October 19, 1968.

37. "Vice-Premier Hsieh Fu-chih's Important Speech on Questions of 'Ninth Party Congress' and 'Party Organization'," October 26, 1967, *Cultural Revolution Bulletin* (Canton), December 11, 1967, *SCMP*, No. 4097 (January 11, 1968), p. 2.

38. Honan Radio, November 19, 1968.

39. *Ibid.*, December 5, 1968.

63. "An Important Speech by Vice-Chairman Lin Piao at a Reception . . ," p. 2.

64. *Ibid.*, p. 9.

65. Domes, *op. cit.*, pp. 143–45.

Chapter 19. *The Storm Before the Calm*

1. *Wen Hui Pao* (Shanghai), March 26, 1968.

2. Agence France-Presse, January 31, 1968.

3. *China News Summary* (Hong Kong), January 31, 1968.

4. "Niu Hui-lin and His Like, Who Stirred Up Armed Struggle to Undermine Chairman Mao's Great Strategic Plan, Deserve a Myriad Deaths," *New Peking University* (Peking), March 30, 1968, *SCMP* (*Supp.*), No. 224 (May 6, 1968), pp. 23–27.

5. Agence France-Presse, April 28, 1968.

6. Hsieh Fu-chih, "Speech to 13th Plenum of the Peking Municipal Revolutionary Committee," May 15, 1968, *Cultural Revolution Bulletin* (Canton), July 1968, in *China News Summary* (Hong Kong), July 8, 1968.

7. "Important Speeches by Central Leaders on March 15," publisher and date unknown, *SCMP*, No. 4181 (May 20, 1968), p. 2.

8. "Premier Chou's Speech to Representatives of the Mass Organizations of Canton Area," September 27, 1967, *Red Rebel Paper* (Lhasa), October 12, 1967, *SCMP* (*Supp.*), No. 215 (January 19, 1968), p. 3.

9. "Summary of Second Meeting of Representatives of All Mass Organizations of Canton Area Who Have Returned to Canton from Peking," publisher and date unknown, *SCMP*, No. 4106 (January 24, 1968), pp. 1–4.

10. "Flag Faction Thugs, Abominable Deeds in No. 3 Middle School," *Red Flag Revolutionary Rebel Headquarters of Chiangmen Municipal No. 3 Middle School*, December 15, 1967, *SCMP*, No. 4108 (January 26, 1968), pp. 4–5.

11. "Record of Joint Examination of Chen Kuo-hsung," December 19, 1967, *ibid.*, p. 7.

12. "A Political Conspiracy to Sabotage the Establishment of Provincial and Municipal Revolutionary Committees," *Committee of the Municipal Automobile Repair Workshop under the Workers Revolutionary Alliance*, February 28, 1968, *SCMP*, No. 4144 (March 22, 1968), pp. 1–3.

13. *Southern Daily* (Canton), February 23, 1968.

14. *South China Morning Post* (Hong Kong), February 23, 1968.

15. From interviews conducted by the author in Hong Kong.

16. Stanley Karnow, *The Washington Post*, June 30, 1968.

17. *China News Summary* (Hong Kong), June 20, 1968.

18. Reuters, June 17, 1968.

19. *South China Morning Post* (Hong Kong), June 27, 1968.

20. From Communist sources in Hong Kong.
21. Stanley Karnow, "Letter from Hong Kong," *Encounter*, April 1969, p. 89.
22. From private sources in Hong Kong.
23. "Crime of Wuchow Rebel Army in Violating the Ten-Point Agreement," *Voice of Proletarians* (Wuchow), December 30, 1967, SCMP, No. 4110 (February 2, 1968), p. 1.
24. "Decision Concerning the Question of Kwangsi," *Red Rebels*, Chiangmen (Kwangtung), December 4, 1967, SCMP, No. 4157 (April 11, 1968), pp. 1–3.
25. "Urgent Dispatch from Kweilin," *Voice of Proletarians* (Wuchow), December 30, 1967, SCMP, No. 4113 (February 7, 1968), p. 4.
26. *Ibid.*, p. 5.
27. Joint Investigation Group of the December 6 Incident, December 9, 1967, Union Research Service (Hong Kong), Vol. 29, No. 26 (December 29, 1967).
28. "True Story of Counter-revolutionary Incident in Jungan County, Kwangsi," *April 22 Bulletin* (Liuchow), May 29, 1968, SCMP, No. 4202 (June 20, 1968), pp. 1–3.
29. "In Various Parts of Kwangsi," *Angry Waves of the West River* (Canton), June 1968, SCMP, No. 4223 (June 22, 1968), pp. 16–18.
30. "A General Mobilization Order for Counter-revolutionary Massacre," *Angry Waves of the West River* (Canton), June 1968, SCMP, No. 4215 (July 11, 1968), p. 1.
31. "Message to the People of the Whole Country," *Grand Army Bulletin* (Canton), July 1968, SCMP, No. 4235 (August 9, 1968), pp. 5–7.
32. "Liuchow Revolutionary Rebel Grand Army Proposes Ten Measures for Stopping Armed Struggle," *Grand Army Bulletin* (Canton), July 1968, SCMP, No. 4234 (August 8, 1968), pp. 7–8.
33. "Message to the People of the Country," *Angry Waves of the West River* (Canton), June 1968, SCMP, No. 4220 (July 18, 1968), pp. 7–13.
34. See Karnow, "Letter from Hong Kong," p. 86.
35. See Stanley Karnow, *The Washington Post*, August 30, 1968.
36. *Sing Tao Daily* (Hong Kong), August 13, 1968.
37. "Dispatch from Kwangsi," *Political Department of Kwangsi Alliance Command*, July 3, 1968, SCMP, No. 4224 (July 24, 1968), pp. 1–2.
38. Stanley Karnow, *The Washington Post*, July 3, 1968.
39. "Chinese Communist Party Central Committee's New Directive on the Kwangsi Problem," *Revolutionary Rebel Forces* (Liuchow), July 12, 1968, SCMP, No. 4226 (July 26, 1968), pp. 1–2.
40. "Important Instructions by Leaders of the Chinese Communist Party Central Committee, and Central Cultural Revolution Group at Reception of Comrades from Mass Organizations and Army Cadres from Kwangsi," July 1968, *Kwangsi Branch Office of Mao Tse-tung Thought*

Study Class, July 26, 1968, Union Research Service (Hong Kong), Vol. 53, No. 9 (October 29, 1968).
41. "Chinese Communist Party Central Committee's New Directive on Kwangsi Problem," p. 3.
42. "Notice of the Chinese Communist Party Central Committee, State Council, Military Commission and Central Cultural Revolution Group," *Middle School Red Guards* (Canton), July 1968, SCMP, No. 4232 (August 6, 1968), pp. 1–3.
43. "Important Instructions by Leaders . . . at a Reception of Comrades from Kwangsi."
44. "Notice by Chinese Communist Party Central Committee, State Council, Military Affairs Commission, and Central Cultural Revolution Group," *East Wind Workers* (Canton), August 1, 1968, SCMP, No. 4258 (September 16, 1968), pp. 1–3.
45. "Important Instructions by Leaders . . . at a Reception of Comrades from Kwangsi."
46. Stanley Karnow, *The Washington Post*, August 28, 1968.
47. John Gittings, "Kwangtung: Anatomy of a Clamp-Down," *Far Eastern Economic Review*, September 5, 1968, pp. 464–65.
48. Gordon A. Bennett and Ronald N. Montaperto, *Red Guard* (New York, 1971), p. 183.
49. "Chou En-lai Refutes Wu Chuan-pin," *Sun Yat-sen University Combat News* (Canton), August 7, 1968.
50. "Minutes of a Meeting Held by the Provincial Revolutionary Committee on the Afternoon of July 31," *Workers Commentaries* (Canton), August 1968, SCMP, No. 4265, September 25, 1968, pp. 1–10.
51. *Ming Pao* (Hong Kong), September 2, 1968.
52. Kirin Radio, July 23, 1968.
53. Stanley Karnow, *The Washington Post*, August 13, 1968.

Chapter 20. The Road to Recovery

1. New China News Agency, August 6 and 8, 1968; Stanley Karnow, *The Washington Post*, August 10, 1968.
2. New China News Agency, August 14, 1968.
3. Jurgen Domes, "The Role of the Military in the Formation of Revolutionary Committees," *China Quarterly*, No. 44 (October–December 1970), pp. 137–42.
4. New China News Agency, July 31, 1968.
5. New China News Agency, August 1, 1968.
6. "Vice-Premier Hsieh's Seven-Point Directive to the Mao Thought Propaganda Team at Tsinghua University," private source in Peking.
7. "Clear Away Obstacles to Greet the Workers' Army Marching into the Institutes of Higher Learning," *Red Guard Combat Bulletin* (Shang-

40. *Wen Hui Pao* (Shanghai), October 18, 1968.
41. *Ibid.*, October 19, 1968.
42. *Ibid.*, October 8, 1968.
43. *Ibid.*, October 18, 1968.
44. *Ibid.*
45. *People's Daily* (Peking), September 30, 1968.
46. Shanghai Radio, February 6, 1969.
47. *People's Daily* (Peking), February 20, 1969.
48. *Ibid.*, May 3, 1969.
49. John Gittings, "Lin Piao's Gospel," *Far Eastern Economic Review*, May 8, 1969, p. 335.
50. New China News Agency, April 27, 1969; Gittings, *op. cit.*, pp. 336–37; *China Topics* (Hong Kong), May 19, 1969.
51. *Tokyo Shimbun*, October 27, 1969.
52. New China News Agency, April 28, 1968; *China Topics* (Hong Kong), January 22, 1968.
53. New China News Agency, April 28, 1968.
54. Donald W. Klein and Lois B. Hager, "The Ninth Central Committee," *China Quarterly*, No. 45 (January–March 1971), pp. 41–42.
55. *China Topics* (Hong Kong), November 18, 1969.
56. Stanley Karnow, *The Washington Post*, August 29, 1969.
57. *Ibid.*, see also *The New York Times*, September 3, 1969.
58. Moscow Radio, March 27, 1970; *Hong Kong Standard*, March 25, 1970.
59. Stanley Karnow, *The Washington Post*, June 4, 1970.
60. *Ibid.*, May 21, 1970.
61. New China News Agency, October 1, 1969.
62. *Ibid.*, September 30, 1969; *China News Summary* (Hong Kong), September 25, 1969, and October 2, 1969.
63. *People's Daily* (Peking), November 5, 1969.
64. Stanley Karnow, *The Washington Post*, November 11, 1969.
65. *Ibid.*
66. *China News Summary* (Hong Kong), September 25, 1969.
67. Lee Lescaze, *The Washington Post*, December 16, 1970.
68. New China News Agency, December 16, 1969.
69. *China News Summary* (Hong Kong), November 21, 1969.
70. Kwangtung Radio, November 23, 1969.
71. *Red Flag*, January 5, 1970.
72. Lee Lescaze, *The Washington Post*, February 18, 1971; *The New York Times*, August 26, 1971.
73. Private source.
74. *The New York Times*, August 8, 1971.
75. *Peking Review*, July 2, 1971, p. 20.
76. Chiang Ch'ing, "Do New Services for the People," April 13, 1967, *The East Is Red* (Peking), June 3, 1967, SCMP (*Supp.*), No. 192 (July 17, 1967), p. 8.

77. See Stanley Karnow, *The Washington Post*, November 10 and 27, 1971.
78. *The New York Times*, October 8, 1971.
79. Private sources in Washington.
80. Peking Radio, October 20, 1971.
81. Ninghsia Radio, November 5, 1971.
82. *People's Daily* (Peking), November 2, 1971.
83. I am indebted to Colonel William Whitson for this analysis.
84. *Peking Review*, No. 50, December 10, 1971, p. 5.

Chapter 21. Rejoining the World

1. *The New York Times*, July 16, 1971.
2. *Red Flag*, August 16, 1971.
3. See John K. Fairbank, "China's Foreign Policy in Historical Perspective," *Foreign Affairs*, April 1969, pp. 451–53.
4. *Asahi Shimbun* (Tokyo), August 1, 1964; *Sekai Shuho* (Tokyo), August 11, 1964.
5. *People's Daily* (Peking), May 9, 1964.
6. Stanley Karnow, *The Washington Post*, March 12, 1969.
7. Cited *ibid.*, October 13, 1968.
8. V. M. Khvostov, "The Chinese 'Account' and Historical Truth," *Mezhdunarodnaya Zhizn*, October 1964, quoted in John Gittings, *Survey of Sino-Soviet Dispute* (London, 1968), pp. 165–66.
9. "Soviet Government Statement," September 21, 1963, in *ibid.*, p. 162.
10. *People's Daily* (Peking), September 6, 1963.
11. Stanley Karnow, *The Washington Post*, March 12, 1968.
12. Vladimir Dedijer, *Tito* (New York, 1953), p. 322; see also *Mainichi* (Tokyo), March 9, 1967; *Red Flag*, January 5, 1964.
13. *Mainichi* (Tokyo), March 9, 1967.
14. Gittings, *op. cit.*, p. 14.
15. New China News Agency, October 26, 1954; Gittings, *op. cit.*, p. 19.
16. *People's Daily* (Peking), September 1, 1963.
17. *Pravda* (Moscow), September 21, 1963.
18. Quoted in Gittings, *op. cit.*, p. 331.
19. *Red Flag*, January 5, 1960.
20. *People's Daily* (Peking), December 4, 1963.
21. Gittings, *op. cit.*, pp. 175–76.
22. *People's Daily* (Peking), August 15, 1963.
23. See Donald Zagoria, *Vietnam Triangle* (New York, 1967), pp. 105–111.
24. Quoted *ibid.*, p. 111.
25. *People's Daily* (Peking), November 11, 1965.
26. Stanley Karnow, *The Washington Post*, September 10, 1969.
27. "Letter of the Chinese Communist Party Central Committee to the Central Committe of the Communist Party of the Soviet Union," July 14, 1965, Gittings, *op. cit.*, p. 263.

28. Allen Whiting, "How We Almost Went to War With China," *Look*, April 29, 1969.
29. Private sources.
30. Lin Piao, "Long Live the Victory of People's War," quoted in Uri Ra'anan, "Peking's Foreign Policy Debate 1965–1966," Ping Ti-ho and T'ang Tsou, eds. *China in Crisis* (Chicago, 1968), pp. 54ff.
31. Stanley Karnow, *The Washington Post*, August 22, 1967.
32. *The Washington Post*, October 13, 1967.
33. *Hoc Tap* (Hanoi), May 1967.
34. Stanley Karnow, *The Washington Post*, October 2, 1968.
35. A. Doak Barnett, *A New U.S. Policy Toward China* (Washington, D. C., 1971), p. 5.
36. *Ibid.*, pp. 7–8.
37. *The China White Paper*, August 1969 (Stanford, Calif.), p. xvi.
38. Allen Whiting, *China Crosses the Yalu* (New York, 1960), pp. 34–46.
39. Kenneth T. Young, *Diplomacy and Power in Washington-Peking Dealings, 1953–1967* (Chicago, 1967), p. 12.
40. Stanley Karnow, *The Washington Post*, July 25, 1971.
41. *The New York Times*, December 14, 1963.
42. *Ibid.*, January 29, 1964.
43. *People's Daily* (Peking), February 19, 1964.
44. Stanley Karnow, *The Washington Post*, July 25, 1971.
45. *Ibid.*; Barnett, *op. cit.*, p. 16.
46. Melvin Gurtov, *The Foreign Ministry and Foreign Affairs in China's Revolution*, a Rand Corporation memorandum (Santa Monica, Calif., March 1969), pp. 66–68.
47. *People's Daily* (Peking), November 3, 1968.
48. Edgar Snow, "A Conversation with Mao Tse-tung," *Life*, April 20, 1971.
49. Stanley Karnow, *The Washington Post*, September 30, 1969.
50. Private sources in Peking.
51. *The New York Times*, May 24, 1969.
52. Inner Mongolia Radio, November 11, 1969.
53. *Kommunist*, Moscow, June 26, 1968.
54. Moscow Radio, December 31, 1967; Moscow Radio, May 26, 1968.
55. See Stanley Karnow, *The Washington Post*, December 2, 1968; Associated Press, February 3, 1969.
56. *The New York Times*, June 14, 1969.
57. Stanley Karnow, *The Washington Post*, August 3, 1968.
58. New China News Agency, August 22, 1968; *People's Daily* (Peking), August 23, 1968.
59. New China News Agency, September 30, 1968.
60. New China News Agency, September 16, 1968.
61. *Izvestia* (Moscow), November 2, 1968.
62. New China News Agency, November 26, 1968.

63. *South China Morning Post* (Hong Kong), December 1, 1968.
64. New China News Agency, November 26, 1968.
65. *People's Daily* (Peking), October 16, 1967.
66. New China News Agency, November 26, 1968.
67. Stanley Karnow, *The Washington Post*, November 26, 1968.
68. Moscow Radio, November 29, 1968.
69. Moscow Radio, December 13, 1968.
70. Associated Press, August 6, 1968.
71. Stanley Karnow, *The Washington Post*, July 16, 1971.
72. Don Oberdorfer, *The Washington Post*, April 23, 1971; John Osborne, "Signals to Mao," *The New Republic*, May 1, 1971; Stanley Karnow, "The Meaning of Nixon's China Coup," *The Progressive*, September 1971.
73. Associated Press, April 22, 1969.
74. Edith Lenart, "U.S.–China: The Matchmakers," *Far Eastern Economic Review*, August 21, 1971, pp. 14–15.
75. Edith Lenart, "Backdoor to China," *Far Eastern Economic Review*, August 21, 1969.
76. Stanley Karnow, *The Washington Post*, February 20, 1969.
77. Moscow Radio, March 8, 1969; *New Times* (Moscow), May 18, 1969.
78. See Thomas W. Robinson, *The Sino-Soviet Border Dispute: Background, Development and the March 1969 Clash* (Rand Corporation Study, Santa Monica, Calif., August 1970), pp. 41–71.
79. *Ibid.*, pp. 38–40.
80. From interviews conducted by the author in Khabarovsk.
81. *The New York Times*, June 12, 1969.
82. Stanley Karnow, *The Washington Post*, August 20, 1969.
83. *The New York Times*, August 14, 1969.
84. Tass, March 30, 1969.
85. New China News Agency, May 24, 1969.
86. Tass, March 30, 1969.
87. Reuters, March 19, 1969.
88. Stanley Karnow, *The Washington Post*, March 6, 1969.
89. *Ming Pao* (Hong Kong), March 5, 1969.
90. Stanley Karnow, *The Washington Post*, May 16, 1969.
91. *The New York Times*, March 11, 1969.
92. *South China Morning Post* (Hong Kong), April 22, 1969.
93. Private source in Hong Kong.
94. *Sing Tao* (Hong Kong), September 12, 1969.
95. *China News Summary* (Hong Kong), August 15, 1969.
96. Stanley Karnow, *The Washington Post*, October 15, 1969.
97. *Ibid.*
98. *The New York Times*, November 21, 1969.
99. Private sources in Hong Kong.

Reference Notes

100. Hungarian News Agency MTI, Budapest, January 16, 1970.
101. Stanley Karnow, *The Washington Post*, December 4, 1969.
102. Private sources in Hong Kong.
103. *Liberation Army Daily* (Peking), November 27, 1969.
104. Kiangsi Radio, July 31, 1969.
105. *China News Summary* (Hong Kong), July 1, 1969.
106. Heilungkiang Radio, July 7, 1969.
107. See Stanley Karnow, *The Washington Post*, December 19, 1969.
108. *Ibid.*, September 11, 1969; *China Topics* (Hong Kong), January 28, 1970.
109. Agence France-Presse, November 16, 1969.
110. Stanley Karnow, *The Washington Post*, October 9, 1969.
111. Victor Louis, "Will Russian Rockets Czech-mate China?" *Evening News* (London), September 16, 1969.
112. Reuters, December 6, 1969.
113. *The Sunday Times* (London), October 6, 1968.
114. *The New York Times*, September 12, 1969.
115. Sanzo Nosaka, Japanese Communist Party Chairman, *Kyodo* (Tokyo), September 12, 1969.
116. *Nhan Dan* (Hanoi), September 1, 1969; *The New York Times*, September 12, 1969.
117. New China News Agency, September 11, 1969.
118. *The New York Times*, September 25, 1969.
119. Stanley Karnow, *The Washington Post*, October 10, 1969.
120. Stanley Karnow, *The Washington Post*, October 8, 1969.
121. Private sources in Washington.
122. Lee Lescaze, *The Washington Post*, May 21, 1971.
123. *The New York Times*, October 14, 1970.
124. *Ibid.*, November 21, 1970.
125. *Ibid.*, September 17, 1971.
126. Associated Press, September 5, 1969.
127. Associated Press, February 19, 1970.
128. Edgar Snow, "Aftermath of the Cultural Revolution," *New Republic*, April 10, 1971, p. 18.
129. *The New York Times*, April 8, 1971.
130. Edgar Snow, "A Conversation with Mao Tse-tung," *Life*, April 30, 1971.
131. *The New York Times*, April 30, 1971.
132. *Al-Jumhuriyah*, Cairo, November 18, 1971.
133. Tass, August 10, 1971.

Chapter 22. A Postscript to Revolution

1. Mao Tse-tung, "Reply to Comrade Kuo Mo-jo," *Ten More Poems of Mao Tse-tung* (Hong Kong, 1967), p. 14.

Reference Notes

2. Edgar Snow, "A Conversation with Mao Tse-tung," *Life*, April 20, 1971.
3. Stanley Karnow, *The Washington Post*, July 6, 1970; *The New York Times*, May 31, 1971.
4. Edgar Snow, "The Open Door," *The New Republic*, March 27, 1971.
5. *Red Flag*, August 22, 1971.
6. *The New York Times*, May 7, 1971.
7. Lucian Pye, "Hostility and Authority in Chinese Politics," *Problems of Communism*, May–June 1968, pp. 10–22.

Index

Artillery, 384, 437–38

Association of Chinese Paleontologists, 97

Atrocities, 210, 259, 346, 434, 438. *See also* Cultural Revolution, brutality during

Attack By Reason Defend By Force Great Column, 429

August 1 Combat Corps, 314–15, 316

Australia, 333; wheat imports from, 128, 513

Autumn Harvest Uprising, 43

Aviation Institute, 383

"Backyard furnaces" program, 92, 101–102, 103, 118

Banditry, 15, 17, 18, 31, 43, 68, 69, 105, 300; Mao and, 121. *See also* Chiang Kai-shek, "bandit extermination campaign"

Bandung conference, 476

Banks, 160, 274, 285, 440

"Barbarians," 8, 21, 22, 473

"Barefoot doctors," 450–51, 513

Barnett, Robert, 485

Belgium, imports from, 128

Belhomme, Albert, 97–102, 103, 104, 105, 106–107

Bergson, Henri, 114

Birth control, 173, 451, 513; campaign halted by Mao, 92

Black market, 106–107, 129, 138, 272

Bolsheviks, 10, 36, 38, 58

Borodin, Michael, 40

Botanical Research Institute, Chinese Academy of Sciences, 105

Bourgeoisie, 80-82, 86, 122, 130; Chou on, 227; denunciations of, 177, 211, 215, 452–53; Mao on, 142, 145. *See also* Capitalism; Middle class

Boxer Rebellion, 17, 25–27; Cultural Revolution compared with, 324

Braun, Otto, 44, 59

Brezhnev, Leonid, 149, 255, 490

"Brezhnev doctrine," 488

Bridges, 368; blockading of, 372, 373, 376

Britain, 368, 473, 482, 488; attacks on headquarters, 360, 394; in Hong Kong disorders, 361–62; intervention by, 20-21, 39

Buddhism, 30; and secret societies, 16, 17; Taipings and, 18

Bureaucracy, 12, 14–15, 24; capitalist contacts, 216–17; efforts to topple, 139–40, 239, 248, 264–65, 310; hawkishness on Vietnam, 148–49, 152; in Hong Kong, 360; intransigence toward Mao, 158–61, 385; literary attacks on Mao, 131–32, 134, 139; Lin Piao and, 455; Mao and, 33, 46, 56, 62, 90, 93–94, 110, 119, 145, 147, 192, 516; Red Guards and, 194–95, 217–18, 225–226, 235, 253, 288; resistance to Cultural Revolution, 205, 336, 337; in Revolutionary Committees, 419; shattering of, 400, 420; students and, 172, 176–77, 248. *See also* Politburo

Burma, 32, 167, 183, 392, 393, 506

Burundi, defector in, 192

Cadres, 128–29, 200, 416–17; and Great Leap Forward, 100, 102, 122, 140; manipulation of peasants, 96, 97, 98; Mao and, 142, 408; misappropriations by, 108; tests of loyalty, 163–64, 178–79

Cairo, 487, 508

Calcutta, 505

California Institute of Technology, 344

Cambodia, 392, 394, 481, 488

Canada, 506; wheat imports from, 128, 513

Canals, 66

Canton, 8, 21, 22, 25, 27, 33, 39, 53, 140, 379; black market center, 107; Cultural Revolution in, 187–89, 203, 207–209, 212, 253–55, 312, 314–16; hospitals, 104; mass transfer of students from, 449–50; military moves to impose order, 292,